Readings in Contemporary Rhetoric

Karen A. Foss
Sonja K. Foss
Robert Trapp

WAVELAND

PRESS, INC.

Prospect Heights, Illinois

For information about this book, contact:
Waveland Press, Inc.
P.O. Box 400
Prospect Heights, Illinois 60070
(847) 634-0081
www.waveland.com

Printed in the United States of America

7 6 5 4 3 2 1

CONTENTS

PREFACE

This volume of readings and bibliography is designed as a supplement to *Contemporary Perspectives on Rhetoric*, which provides overviews of the works of 11 contemporary rhetorical theorists: I. A. Richards, Ernesto Grassi, Chaïm Perelman and Lucie Olbrechts-Tyteca, Stephen Toulmin, Richard Weaver, Kenneth Burke, Jürgen Habermas, bell hooks, Jean Baudrillard, and Michael Foucault. Our hope is that these readings provide a more in-depth understanding of the theorists summarized by offering greater development of ideas that could be addressed only in general terms in *Contemporary Perspectives on Rhetoric*. In addition, these readings provide an opportunity to engage the theorists' ideas in their own words, which also can provide a richer understanding of their ideas. In some cases, we offer one lengthy essay that captures core ideas of a theorist. In other instances, we provide several examples to capture the distinctly different styles and approaches of a theorist.

The bibliographies that follow the readings are provided to encourage further exploration of the ideas of these theorists as they have been examined, understood, interpreted, and critiqued by others. The bibliographies by no means include all of the works that have been written about each scholar. The amount of scholarship produced about each of these theorists is considerable, and locating all of it would be an almost impossible task. In addition, the availability of such sources on the Internet makes a comprehensive bibliography in this form less necessary than it once was. We hope, however, that these bibliographies offer a starting place for students who wish to pursue particular concepts or theories in greater detail.

1

THE PHILOSOPHY OF RHETORIC
LECTURE I

I. A. Richards

These lectures are an attempt to revive an old subject. I need spend no time, I think, in describing the present state of Rhetoric. Today it is the dreariest and least profitable part of the waste that the unfortunate travel through in Freshman English! So low has Rhetoric sunk that we would do better just to dismiss it to Limbo than to trouble ourselves with it—unless we can find reason for believing that it can become a study that will minister successfully to important needs.

As to the needs, there is little room for doubt about them. Rhetoric, I shall urge, should be a study of misunderstanding and its remedies. We struggle all our days with misunderstandings, and no apology is required for any study which can prevent or remove them. Of course, inevitably *at present,* we have no measure with which to calculate the extent and degree of our hourly losses in communication. One of the aims of these lectures will be to speculate about some of the measures we should require in attempting such estimates. "How much and in how many ways may good communication differ from bad?" That is too big and too complex a question to be answered as it stands, but we can at least try to work towards answering some parts of it; and these explanations would be the revived subject of Rhetoric.

From *The Philosophy of Rhetoric* (1936), pp. 3–20. Reprinted by permission of Oxford University Press.

Though we cannot measure our losses in communication we can guess at them. We even have professional guessers: teachers and examiners, whose business is to guess at and diagnose the mistakes other people have made in understanding what they have heard and read and to avoid illustrating these mistakes, if they can, themselves. Another man who is in a good position from which to estimate the current losses in communication is an author looking through a batch of reviews, especially an author who has been writing about some such subject as economics, social or political theory, or criticism. It is not very often that such an author must honestly admit that his reviewers—even when they profess to agree with him—have seen his point. That holds, you may say, only of bad writers who have written clumsily or obscurely. But bad writers are commoner than good and play a larger part in bandying notions about in the world.

The moral from this comes home rather heavily on a Lecturer addressing an audience on such a tangled subject as Rhetoric. It is little use appealing to the hearer as Berkeley did: "I do . . . once for all desire whoever shall think it worth his while to understand . . . that he would not stick in this or that phrase, or manner of expression, but candidly collect my meaning from the whole sum and tenor of my discourse, and laying aside the words as much as possible, consider the bare notions themselves . . ."

The trouble is that we *can* only "collect the whole sum and tenor of the discourse" from the words, we cannot "lay aside the words"; and as to considering "the bare notions themselves. . . ." Berkeley was fond of talking about these "bare notions," these "naked undisguised ideas," and about "separating from them all that dress and encumbrance of words." But an idea or a notion, when unencumbered and undisguised, is no easier to get hold of than one of those oiled and naked thieves who infest the railway carriages of India. Indeed an idea, or a notion, like the physicist's ultimate particles and rays, is only known by what it does. Apart from its dress or other signs it is not identifiable. Berkeley himself, of course, has his doubts: "laying aside the words as much as possible, consider . . ." That "as much as possible" is not very much; and is not nearly enough for the purposes for which Berkeley hoped to trust it.

We have instead to consider much more closely how words work in discourse. But before plunging into some of the less whelming divisions of this world-swallowing inquiry, let me glance back for a few minutes at the traditional treatment of the subject; much might be learnt from it that would help us. It begins, of course, with Aristotle, and may perhaps be said to end with Archbishop Whately, who wrote a treatise on Rhetoric for the *Encyclopædia Metropolitana* that Coleridge planned. I may remark, in passing, that Coleridge's own *Essay on Method*, the preface to that Encyclopædia, has itself more bearing on a possible future for Rhetoric than anything I know of in the official literature.

Whately was a prolific writer, but he is most often remembered now perhaps for an epigram. "Woman," he said, "is an irrational animal which pokes the fire from the top." I am not quoting this, here at Bryn Mawr, to prejudice you against the Archbishop: any man, when provoked, might venture such an unwarrantable and imperceptive generalization. But I do hope to prejudice you further against his modes of treating a subject in which he is, according to no less an authority than Jebb, the best modern writer. Whately has another epigram which touches the very heart of our problem, and may be found either comforting or full of wicked possibilities as you please: here it is. "Preachers nobly aim at nothing at all and hit it!" We may well wonder just what the Archbishop meant by that.

What we have to surmise is how Whately, following and summing up the whole history of the subject, can proceed as he did! He says quite truly that "Rhetoric is not one of those branches of study in which we can trace with interest a progressive improvement from age to age"; he goes on to discuss "whether Rhetoric be worth any diligent cultivation" and to decide, rather half-heartedly, that it is—provided it be taken not as *an* Art of discourse but as *the* Art—that is to say, as a philosophic discipline aiming at a mastery of the fundamental laws of the use of language, not just a set of dodges that will be found to work sometimes. That claim—that Rhetoric must go deep, must take a broad philosophical view of the principles of the Art—is the climax of his Introduction; and yet in the treatise that follows nothing of the sort is attempted, nor is it in any other treatise that I know of. What we are given by Whately instead is a very ably arranged and discussed collection of prudential Rules about the best sorts of things to say in various argumentative situations, the order in which to bring out your propositions and proofs and examples, at what point it will be most effective to disparage your opponent, how to recommend oneself to the audience, and like matters. As to all of which, it is fair to remark, no one ever learned about them from a treatise who did not know about them already; at the best, the treatise may be an occasion for realizing that there is skill to be developed in discourse, but it does not and cannot teach the skill. We can turn on the whole endeavour the words in which the Archbishop derides his arch-enemy Jeremy Bentham: "the proposed plan for the ready exposure of each argument resembles that by which children are deluded, of catching a bird by laying salt on its tail; the existing doubts and difficulties of debate being no greater than, on the proposed system, would be found in determining what Arguments were or were not to be classified" in which places in the system.

Why has this happened? It has happened all through the history of the subject, and I choose Whately because he represents an inherent tendency in its study. When he proceeds from these large-scale questions of the Ordonnance of arguments to the minute particulars of discourse—under the rubric of Style—the same thing happens. Instead of a philosophic inquiry into how words work in discourse, we get the usual postcard's-worth of crude common sense:— be clear, yet don't be dry; be vivacious, use metaphors when they will be understood not otherwise; respect usage; don't be longwinded, on the other hand don't be gaspy; avoid ambiguity; prefer the energetic to the elegant; preserve unity and coherence.... I need not go over to the other side of the postcard. We all know well enough the maxims that can be extracted by patient readers out of these agglomerations and how helpful we have all found them!

What is wrong with these too familiar attempts to discuss the working of words? How words work is a matter about which every user of language is, of necessity, avidly curious until these trivialities choke the flow of interest. Remembering Whately's recommendation of metaphor, I can put the mistake best perhaps by saying that all they do is to poke the fire from the top. Instead of tackling, in earnest, the problem of how language works at all, they assume that nothing relevant is to be learnt about it; and that the problem is merely one of disposing the given and unquestioned powers of words to the best advantage. Instead of ventilating by inquiry the sources of the whole action of words, they merely play with generalizations about their effects, generalizations that are uninstructive and unimproving unless we go more deeply and by another route into these grounds. Their conception of the study of language, in brief, is frustratingly distant or macroscopic and yields no return in understanding—either practical or theoretical—unless it is supplemented by an intimate or microscopic inquiry which endeavours to look into the structure of the meanings with which discourse is composed, not merely into the effects of various large-scale disposals of these meanings. In this Rhetoricians may remind us of the Alchemists' efforts to transmute common substances into precious metals, vain efforts because they were not able to take account of the internal structures of the so-called elements.

The comparison that I am using here is one which a modern writer on language can hardly avoid. To account for understanding and misunderstanding, to study the efficiency of language and its conditions, we have to renounce, for a while, the view that words just have their meanings and that what a discourse does is to be explained as a composition of these meanings—as a wall can be represented as a composition of its bricks. We have to shift the focus of our analysis and attempt a deeper and more minute grasp and try to take account of the structures of the smallest discussable units of meaning and the ways in which these vary as they are put with other units. Bricks, for all practical purposes, hardly mind what other things they are put with. Meanings mind intensely—more indeed than any other sorts of things. It is the peculiarity of meanings that they do so mind their company; that is in part what we mean by calling them meanings! In themselves they are nothing—figments, abstractions, unreal things that we invent, if you like—but we invent them for a purpose. They help us to avoid taking account of the peculiar way in which any part of a discourse, in the last resort, does what it does only because the other parts of the surrounding, uttered or unuttered discourse and its conditions are what they are. "In the last resort"—the last resort here is mercifully a long way off and very deep down. Short of it we are aware of certain stabilities which hide from us this universal relativity or, better, interdependence of meanings. Some words and sentences still more, do seem to mean what they mean absolutely and unconditionally. This is because the conditions governing their meanings are so constant that we can disregard them. So the weight of a cubic centimeter of water seems a fixed and absolute thing because of the constancy of its governing conditions. In weighing out a pound of tea we can forget about the mass of the earth. And with words which have constant conditions the common sense view that they have fixed proper meanings, which should be learned and observed, is justified. But these words are fewer than we suppose. Most words, as they pass from context to context, change their meanings; and in many different ways. It is their duty and their service to us to do so. Ordinary discourse would suffer anchylosis if they did not, and so far we have no ground for complaint. We are extraordinarily skilful in some fields with these shifts of sense—especially when they are of the kind we recognize officially as metaphor. But our skill fails; it is patchy and fluctuant; and, when it fails, misunderstanding of others and of ourselves comes in.

A chief cause of misunderstanding, I shall argue later, is the Proper Meaning Superstition. That is, the common belief—encouraged officially by what lingers on in the school manuals as Rhetoric—that a word has a meaning of its own (ideally, only one) independent of and controlling its use and the purpose for which it should be uttered. This superstition is a recognition of a certain kind of stability in the meanings of certain words. It is only a superstition when it forgets (as it commonly does) that the stability of the meaning of a word comes from the constancy of the contexts that give it its meaning. Stability in a word's meaning is not something to be assumed, but always something to be explained. And as we try out explanations, we discover, of course, that—as there are many sorts of constant contexts—there are many sorts of stabilities. The stability of the meaning of a word like *knife*, say, is different from the stability of a word like *mass* in its technical use, and then again both differ from the stabilities of such words, say, as *event, ingression, endurance, recurrence,* or *object,* in the paragraphs of a very distinguished predecessor in this Lectureship. It will have been noticed perhaps that the way I propose to treat meanings has its analogues with Mr. Whitehead's treatment of things. But indeed no one to whom Berkeley has mattered will be very confident as to which is which.

I have been suggesting—with my talk of macroscopic and microscopic inquiries—that the theory of language may have something to learn, not much but a little, from the ways in which the physicist envisages stabilities. But much closer analogies are possible with some of the patterns of Biology. The theory of interpretation is obviously a branch of biology—a branch that has not grown very far or very healthily yet. To remember this may help us to avoid some traditional mistakes—among them the use of bad analogies which tie us up if we take them too seriously. Some of these are notorious; for example, the opposition between form and content, and the almost equivalent opposition between matter and form. These are wretchedly inconvenient metaphors. So is that other which makes language a dress which thought puts on. We shall do better to think of a meaning as though it were a plant that has grown—not a can that has been filled or a lump of clay that has been moulded. These are obvious inadequacies; but, as the history of criticism shows, they have not been avoided, and the perennial efforts of the reflective to amend or surpass them—Croce is the extreme modern example—hardly help.

More insidious and more devastating are the over-simple mechanical analogies which have been brought in under the heading of Associationism in the hope of explaining how language works. And thought as well. The two problems are close together and similar and neither can be discussed profitably apart from the other. But, unless we drastically remake their definitions, and thereby dodge the main problems, Language and Thought are not—need I say?—one and the same. I suppose I must, since the Behaviorists have so loudly averred that Thought is sub-vocal talking. That however is a doctrine I prefer, in these lectures, to attack by implication. To discuss it explicitly would take time that can, I think, be spent more fruitfully. I will only say that I hold that any doctrine identifying Thought with *muscular* movement is a self-refutation of the observationalism that prompts it—heroic and fatal. And that an identification of Thought with an activity of the nervous system is to me an acceptable hypothesis, but too large to have interesting applications. It may be left until more is known about both; when possibly it may be developed to a point at which it might become useful. At present it is still Thought which is most accessible to study and accessible largely through Language. We can all detect a difference in our own minds between thinking of a dog and thinking of a cat. But no neurologist can. Even when no cats or dogs are about and we are doing nothing about them except thinking of them, the difference is plainly perceptible. We can also say "dog" and think "cat."

I must, though, discuss the doctrine of associations briefly, because when we ask ourselves about how words mean, some theory about trains of associated ideas or accompanying images is certain to occur to us as an answer. And until we see how little distance these theories take us they are frustrating. We all know the outline of these theories: we learn what the word "cat" means by seeing a cat at the same time that we hear the word "cat" and thus a link is formed between the sight and the sound. Next time we hear the word "cat" an image of a cat (a visual image, let us say) arises in the mind and that is how the word "cat" means a cat. The obvious objections that come from the differences between cats; from the fact that images of a grey persian asleep and of a tabby stalking are very different, and from some people saying they never have any imagery, must then be taken account of, and the theory grows very complex. Usually, images get relegated to a background and become mere supports to something hard to be precise about—an idea of a cat—which is supposed then to be associated with the word "cat" much as the image originally was supposed to be associated with it.

This classical theory of meaning has been under heavy fire from many sides for more than a century—from positions as different as those of Coleridge, of Bradley, of Pavlov and of the *gestalt* psychologists. In response it has elaborated itself, calling in the aid of the conditioned-reflex and submitting to the influence of Freud. I do not say that it is incapable, when amended, of supplying us with a workable theory of meaning. . . . [But] simple associationism does not go far enough and is an impediment unless we see this, I am merely reminding you that a clustering of associated images and ideas about a word in the mind does not answer our question: "How does a word mean?" It only hands it on to them, and the question becomes: "How does an idea (or an image) mean what it does?" To answer that we have to go outside the mind and inquire into its connections with what are not mental occurrences. Or (if you prefer, instead, to extend the sense of the word "mind") we have to inquire into connections between events which were left out by the traditional associationism. And in leaving them out they left out the problem.

For our purposes here the important points are two. First, that ordinary, current, undeveloped associationism is ruined by the crude inapposite physical metaphor of impressions stamped on the mind (the image of the cat stamped by the cat), impressions then linked and combined in clusters like atoms in molecules. That metaphor gives us no useful account either of perception or of reflection, and we shall not be able to think into or think out any of the interesting problems of Rhetoric unless we improve it.

Secondly the appeal to *imagery* as constituting the meaning of an utterance has, in fact, frustrated a large part of the great efforts that have been made by very able people ever since the 17th Century to put Rhetoric back into the important place it deserves among our studies. Let me give you an example. Here is Lord Kames—who, as a judge of the Court of Session in Scotland, was not without a reputation for shrewdness—being, I believe, really remarkably silly.

In *Henry V* (Act IV, scene I) Williams in a fume says this of what "a poor and private displeasure can do against a monarch": "You may as well go about to turn the sun to ice with fanning in his face with a peacock's feather." Lord Karnes comments, "The peacock's feather, not to mention the beauty of the object, completes the image: an accurate image cannot be formed of that fanciful operation without conceiving a particular feather; and one is at a loss when this is neglected in the description." (*Elements of Criticism*, p. 372.)

That shows, I think, what the imagery obsession can do to a reader. Who in the world, apart from a theory, would be "at a loss" unless the sort of feather we are to fan the sun's face with is specified? If we cared to be sillier than our author, we could pursue him on his theory, by asking whether it is to be a long or a short feather or whether the sun is at its height or setting? The whole theory that the point of Shakespeare's specification is to "complete the image," in Kames' sense, is utterly mistaken and misleading. What *peacock* does, in the context there, is obviously to bring in considerations that heighten the idleness, the vanity, in Williams' eyes, of "poor and private displeasures against a monarch." A peacock's feather is something one might flatter oneself with. Henry has said that if the King lets himself be ransomed he will never trust his word after. And Williams is saying, "You'll never trust his word after! What's that! Plume yourself upon it as much as you like, but what will that do to the king!"

Lord Kames in 1761, blandly enjoying the beauty and completeness of the lively and distinct and accurate image of the feather he has produced for himself, and thereby missing, it seems, the whole tenor of the passage, is a spectacle worth some attention. . . .

[Lord Kames's] theories about trains of ideas and images are typical 18th Century Associationism—the Associationism of which David Hartley is the great prophet—and the applications of these theories in the detail of Rhetoric are their own refutation. We have to go beyond these theories, but however mistaken they may be, or however absurd their outcome may sometimes seem, we must not forget that they are beginnings, first steps in a great and novel venture, the attempt to explain in detail how language works and with it to improve communication. As such, these attempts merit the most discerning and the most sympathetic eye that we can turn upon them. Indeed, it is impossible to read Hartley, for example, without deep sympathy if we realize what a task it was that he was attempting. Not only when he writes, in his conclusion, in words which speak the thoughts of every candid inquirer: "This is by no means a full or satisfactory Account of the Ideas which adhere to words by Association. For the Author perceives himself to be still a mere novice in these speculations; and it is difficult to explain Words to the Bottom by Words; perhaps impossible." (On Man, 277.) But still more when he says: "All that has been delivered by the Ancients and Moderns, concerning the power of Habit, Custom, Example, Education, Authority, Party-prejudice, the Manner of learning the manual and liberal Arts, Etc., goes upon this Doctrine as its foundation, and may be considered as the detail of it, in various circumstances. I hope here to begin with the simplest case, and shall proceed to more and more complex ones continually, till I have exhausted what has occurred to me on this Subject." (On Man, p. 67.)

The man who wrote that was not "poking the fire from the top." His way of ventilating the subject may not have been perfectly advised, but he saw what needed doing and it is no wonder that Coleridge for a while admired Hartley beyond all other men. For upon the formation and transformations of meanings—which we must study with and through words—all that Hartley mentions, and much more, goes as its foundation. For it is no exaggeration to say that the fabrics of all our various worlds are the fabrics of our meanings. I began, you recall, with Berkeley, with—to use Mr. Yeats' noble lines—

> God appointed Berkeley who proved all things a dream,
> That this preposterous pragmatical pig of a world, its farrow that so solid
>   seem,
> Must vanish on the instant did the mind but change its theme.

Whatever we may be studying we do so only through the growth of our meanings. To realize this turns some parts of this attempted direct study of the modes of growth and interaction between meanings, which might otherwise seem a niggling philosophic juggle with distinctions, into a business of great practical importance. For this study is theoretical only that it may become practical. Here is the paragraph in which Hobbes condenses what he had learnt from his master, Bacon:

> The end or scope of philosophy is, that we may make use to our benefit of effects formerly seen, or that, by the application of bodies to one another, we may produce the like effects of those we conceive in our mind, as far forth as matter, strength and industry, will permit, for the commodity of human life. For the inward glory and triumph of mind that a man may have for the mastery of some difficult and doubtful matter, or for the discovery of some hidden truth, is not worth so much pains as the study of Philosophy requires; nor need any man care much to teach another what he knows himself, if he think that will be the only benefit of his labour. The end of knowledge is power; and the use of theorems (which, among geometricians, serve for the finding out of properties) is for the construction of problems; and, lastly, the scope of all speculation is the performance of some action, or thing to be done.

2

THE SECRET OF "FEEDFORWARD"

I. A. Richards

It has all been like writing a book (and I have written many): As you come toward the end, you begin, you think, to see how you should have done it. This is an illusion, as with the book, because it becomes a different book in the writing, a different life. And it will be the same, I am sure, with this little essay. In spite of the generous limits allowed me, it will be impossible to do more than summarize my lessons, and, as I close it, I will realize that I have been trying to learn some of the more important of them over again.

Long ago, a banker friend, who had sat through many a big deliberative international meeting watching the doodling, told me that a doctor he knew had a custom of putting a number of little targets into his mazy web: bulls-eye, inner, outer, and off. After each contribution to the discussion, he would scan the deliberators, pencil poised, and mark on one of his targets where he thought the shot had gone. This impressed me, and for a time I tried it out. But not for long. I could not learn to feel sure enough beforehand about what was being aimed at. I found I had no such clear designs as those that the doctor must have entertained. But the attempt taught me this: how often I saw where I should be going only by setting out for somewhere else.

This situation is illustrated by a story a Catholic friend once told me. Whether he made it up or not I won't guess; it is a very Catholic story. It seems that Cervantes was calling on a painter in Toledo. On an easel were the

From *Saturday Review*, February 3, 1968, pp. 14–17.

beginnings of a picture. Cervantes asked what the picture was to be of. "Why, that depends," replied the painter, "on how it turns out. If it has a beard, it is St. John the Baptist. If it has not, it is the Immaculate Conception!"

Most ventures of mine—books and poems included—have been like this. They came along by fighting hard from the start to find out what they were. They were rarely set designs, fixed beforehand. When they tried to be so, they collapsed early or switched over to be something else. The typical venture for me is a poem which begins by setting itself a problem. It doesn't let me know what its problem is, and I suspect it usually doesn't know that itself. But I am sure it has one and that the solution will be the end—in both senses: goal and terminus—of the poem. Often, but not always, the first lines to be formed get pushed down to become the final phrases. In its end is the beginning.

The process by which any venture of this creative sort finds itself, and so pursues its end, is something I have learned, I hope, something about. Indeed, I am not sure I have learned anything else as important. Although I never learned to play the doctor's target game, I have been able to realize what a prime role what I have come to call "feedforward" has in all our doings. Feedforward, as I see it, is the reciprocal, the necessary condition of what the cybernetics and automation people call "feedback."

Whatever we may be doing, some sort of preparation for, some design arrangement for one sort of outcome rather than another is part of our activity. This may be conscious, as an expectancy—or unconscious, as a mere assumption. If we are walking downstairs, a readiness in the advanced leg (but indeed in our whole body) to meet something solid under its toe is needed if we are to continue. Usually, on the stairs, this feedforward is fulfilled. There is confirmatory feedback at the end of each step cycle—the foot finds the expected, the presupposed footing. Compare pitch-dark and broad daylight as to the degree of awareness we may have of our feedforward. If the feedback does not come, if it is falsifying and not verifying, we have to do something else and rather quickly. The point is that feedforward is a needed prescription or plan for a feedback, to which the actual feedback may or may not conform.

Evidently, feedforward is a product of former experience: a selective reflection of what has been relevant in similar activity in our past. It can be crude and it can be delicate. Much of it, for economy's sake, must be routine (as in walking downstairs) in order to deal appropriately with the exceptional. Watch good tennis players and you see how exquisitely, how variously, and how ramifyingly feedforward and feedback are playing their game for them. We may well wonder how there can be *time* between all that must be exactly noted and all that must be exactly done. Nothing could better show us to what a degree feedforward can be developed. If with tennis, why not with more essential human abilities? Any exhibition of superlative skill can make us marvel that, in teaching, say, or in statesmanship, we tolerate so many underdeveloped performers.

As most examples suggest, feedforward and feedback need not be—indeed, commonly are not—fully conscious. Modern conjectural models of brain-mind activity suppose almost unimaginably complex systems of minimal unit cycles organized in hierarchies: cycles of cycles, of activity, all from lowest to highest levels guided by feedback. Of most of this we are certainly not conscious.

Against such a background it is, we all know too well, by no means easy to say, or to conceive, what this invaluable little word "we" is talking about. The question is one we are usually discreet enough not to raise. So, too, with "conscious." We may be ready to allow that between what is conscious and what isn't there may be many degrees, but what any "I" may have to do with what it isn't at all conscious of is again something we hardly know how to go into. Linger on this and we may well find the trouble spreading. Who can be clear about what an "I" and its consciousness have to do with one another?

What I have thought I have learned through reflection on the interplay between feedforward and feedback is the wisdom of making close friends with such doubts and, indeed, of carefully cultivating their acquaintance. By shying away from them, by wanting more certainty than I could have, I never, as I recall, gained in security—rather the opposite. When I closeted myself with my confidences and thought so to be secure in any view, I found this was that grim old sense of "secure" used in Judges XVIII where the Danite spies exultantly inform the slaughterers: "Behold there is a people in Laish that dwell there quiet and secure, far from any allies"; adding as a whet: "And are ye still?"

The lesson was that in all kinds of ventures—in teaching of many varieties, in the design of instruction, in the exploration of remote cultures (Chinese, African, Indian), in composing as in trying to comprehend poems, in propounding theories of comprehension—things went best when I had least conviction of the rightness of the feedforward by which each step was being guided. Long ago, in 1919, C. K. Ogden and I, when writing the first draft of *The Meaning of Meaning*, used to joke about "finding too many convictions in a thinker's record" and to allude to archbishops and other leaders of the faiths as "notorious convicts." That was at a time when we were ourselves exuberantly convinced—particularly of the wrongheadedness of other people. Later, I became, I have hoped, more of an adept in uncertainty.

This is not a matter of large-scale external prognostications: how a book or an opinion would be received—the doctor's target game. In that sort of guessing I was always aware enough of inability. No, it was the necessary step-by-step feedforward: the witting or unwitting or midway surmises by which, say, a word tried out in writing a poem would open or close possibilities for the following phrases—it was in this sort of thing that I had to learn how to be duly tentative. And, too, to be prepared for the way feedback from the outcome of a step would interact with my feedforward. The next steps, I had to learn, would often be fed forward by some combination of the fresh feedback with former feedforward. And the less *convinced* that had been, the more open it was to modification in the further venture.

This held, I came to see, not only in the peculiar process of trying out alternates and submitting to outcomes by which a poem finds itself, but in other crafts, too. In the design of instruction—say, in literacy or in a second language—the actual outcome, the ease or difficulty (better, the discernment or trouble) with which a learner takes a step, is much more instructive to the designer if he has kept himself as little committed as he can be to the *detail* of what he is trying out. Meanwhile, however, constancy and attachment to the *principles* of the design (as opposed to the minutiae of its implementation) is required. For these principles have (or should have) governed the choice of the detail; it is these principles which are really under trial (not some one of a number of possible embodiments), and unless the principles stay constant, fertile interplay between what is looked for (feedforward) and what actually happens (feedback) is precluded. The experimentation will not lead to the strengthening or weakening or emendation of the principles, which should be its main purpose.

As I elaborate this, the reader may recognize it as the celebrated open-mindedness, the suspension of judgment, and the hypothetical procedure that figure in so many accounts of scientific inquiry. If so, it is—the resemblance to the process above sketched of the composition of a poem is, at least, suggestive. And so is the resemblance to the process of learning to read or to speak a second language encouraged by a self-critical theory of the design of instruction, where the student is invited to explore an intelligible sequence of oppositions and connections rather than to memorize what he hopes teacher would like to hear from him. Indeed, all species of mental activity deeply resemble one another.

I took to writing poems late in life, and, if I rightly recall, was prevented earlier by a mistaken notion that good lines and stanzas ought to present themselves to the poet without the labor of achieving compromises between frustrations. Remember, however, Coleridge's warning: "Let us not introduce an Act of Uniformity against poets." It may very well be that different sorts of poetry, in different sorts of poets, come into being in different ways. Abstract words easily hoodwink us. I have just been adding marginalia and a skeptical commentary on one of my books, long out of print, published in 1926, whose title was *Science and Poetry*. Its new title when it comes into life again in 1968 will be: *Poetries and Sciences*. The old book was youthfully dogmatic, and in its very title evoked some sort of dramatic confrontation between antagonists. The new title is relatively modest and pacific. In 1926 I had no useful experience in writing poems of any sort. I had also little or no useful experience in any sort of experimental inquiry. In those days, I think, I never asked myself whether the pages of *Science and Poetry* were either, or what, if neither, they could be. If the question occurred to me then, I must have been canny enough to put it aside. I was too much committed to my preclusions to be a kind host to such queries.

Feedforward is, as I see it, highly various. At one end of the scale, it can be a highly articulate examinable process, the sort of thing known as scientific hypothesis waiting to be OK'd or destroyed by evidence. At the other, it may be hardly cognized or embodied at all, even in the vaguest schematic image. It can be no more than a readiness to be surprised or disturbed by one kind of event rather than by another: greenlighted or redlighted by it. As suggested above, billions of hierarchically systematic cycles, through which we live and move and have our being, are guided in all they do for one another by concord or discord in their feedforward-feedback. And it is perhaps a reasonable suggestion that much in what we call ourselves and admit to be "us" includes these billions of concordant cycles. When our dinner agrees with us we seem to be digesting it. When it does not, we do not seem to be so much in charge. Or, as Tommy put it when his mother told him not to sneeze so: "I don't sneeze, Mummy, it sneezes me!"

However such matters may be, feedforward has come to seem for me a notion indispensable to an adequate theory of conduct and a necessary part of an account of feedback. I labeled it so in *Speculative Instruments*, a title I took from Coleridge. It was indeed one of the chief speculative instruments there discussed. Launching the label, I thought soon to meet some echo or comment. But no such feedback has come. This talk of it here is thus a rejoinder to that taciturnity. What matters, though, is how the quality of our conduct may depend on the character of our feedforward. And not only on its character as tentative, provisional, corrigible—so much stressed above—but on other characters to which these may be due.

Consider another and a peculiarly interesting example of feedforward: what you have it in mind to say *before* you have begun to put it into any sort of words. This feedforward can be very definite. It can unhesitatingly reject any and all of your efforts to say it. "No," you note, "that isn't it at all." Even when you have gone a long way toward finding a way to say it, your feedforward can still purse its lips: "Not quite, it should be better!" Note that here we do not have two fully developed ways of saying it before us to be compared. We have only a series of offered attempts being judged by reference to something else—this inevitably mysterious thing I am calling the feedforward. In relation to this, the ways of saying it that have occurred to you are feedback: reports of outcomes of your attempts at saying it. And we may note further that sometimes it is the other way about—as when your tennis ball or target shot is out. Or when you really drop a brick and have to ask yourself: "What *could* I have been thinking to have said that?" These considerations apply to all modes of would-be communication: enunciating national policies, composing poems, addressing juries, poor David Balfour's *gomeril* behaviors in wooing Catriona, etc.

This leads me into another feedforward problem about which, too, I do at least devoutly hope that I have managed to learn something—somehow or other and at long last. This is the recognition in our feedforward of diversities of "point of view." There is something known as tact, which some have and some haven't. It is widely esteemed, but in some matters despised. It can be unreservedly condemned by certain rather wooden-eyed types of moralists. What I am talking about is a swift, before-the-event recognition of how something will seem to people looking at it from angles other than our own.

This last has brought the *point of view* metaphor into sharper focus. It is so familiar that it can easily be supposed of no more consequence than the metaphor in the phrase "leg of the table." Look into it more closely, however, and it can seem to become momentous, nothing less than a set of hints toward a series of new concepts for the new education required for the current and the coming worlds.

Let us consider rather closely the literal sense, the original, visual situation from which this metaphor comes. Take some object—the Statue of Liberty, for instance—which can be gazed at from north, south, east, west and intermediate directions, from below and above, from far and near. No normal person above a certain age has any difficulty in allowing that such objects must look very different when seen from varying viewpoints and distances. And some people, after seeing a suitable object from one or more angles, can form a fairly good guess—a not too insecure feedforward—as to how it will appear from other angles. Those who can do this—or think they can—tend to say, "Surely this is something we all can do!" But not at all. When I was last working at experiments in depiction—at the Visual Arts Center, Harvard—this was one of the questions my seminar looked into. We found that for relatively simple, easily perceived objects—a twisted paper clip, a leaf, a key . . . seen from the north, say, at full leisure and under good conditions—comparatively few people were able at all clearly to imagine, describe, draw how the thing would look from east, west, or intermediate directions. And if the object were turned and then shown again, the estimates offered of how and how much it had been turned went often wildly astray. The participants, moreover, were design-school or fine-arts students with, it is to be supposed, more than average concern and ability with visual perception.

Among the aims of these experiments (which are not yet extensive enough to warrant more than speculative applications), two are especially relevant here: 1) to find out what educational techniques might be devised to help people in looking at things from all sides and in putting the views intelligibly together; 2) to explore further the educational opportunities in this metaphor from optical viewing and intellectual and moral viewing. Long leaps, no doubt, but there seems ground for a hunch that practice and comparison between one's own and others' performances can lead to improvement. And, for another, that increased interest in what *seeing* is like can, at the least, encourage the realization that to view a question from one side only is not enough. And, further yet, that to regard it fully and fairly even from one side only involves venturesome feedforward (verifiable and falsifiable) as to how it is likely to seem to others in other positions.

What I hope I have learned about this is to ask, more often and more searchingly, of utterances that claim some importance—political, poetical, practical—whether they seem to be guided and guarded by reasonable feedforward as to how people of very different prepossessions are likely to take them. And this leads to a gloomy impression. Far too many of the voices that make us glow or wince speak too often as though they had the thing itself—

the whole thing and nothing but the thing—presented to them. And not just, in fact, a view of it: a view formed under special circumstances which only a minority of the auditors can possibly share.

I seem to hear this disability-derived confidence loading the channels in almost all spheres: in criticism and in politics of all parties as much as in preaching. In none of them can failure to inquire into the dissident position (or to try to) be a worthy, rather than a comico-tragical, ground for a belief that one is right. "I just cannot understand anyone taking any other view on this" is a confession of a lack of competence. And I have at the end of this essay to be rather careful not to join these well filled ranks. But, alas, why people are not likely to approve the overall view of viewpoint dependence I have been trying to present is clear. The history of controversy as spiritual warfare—of religious and ideological and national, as well as factional conflicts—is there to explain it.

3

WHAT BASIC ENGLISH IS

I. A. Richards

Rudolph Hess, shortly before his flight to England, announced at a party conference that when the Nazis had won, English would become "a minor Germanic dialect of no world importance." We have glanced at some of the linguistic reasons why that would have been regrettable. His utterance contrasts well with Bismarck's view that the most significant event of the nineteenth century was the acceptance of English as the language of North America. We have now to see why English can be made easier for any learner than any other major language, how a streamlined English suited to the general affairs of the world has been produced, and what has been and may be done with this form of English.

Basic English is English made simple by limiting the number of its words to 850, and by cutting down the rules for using them to the smallest number necessary for the clear statement of ideas. And this is done without change in the normal order and behavior of these words in everyday English. This is the first point to make clear. Basic English, though it has only 850 words, is still normal English. It is limited in its words and its rules, but it keeps to the regular forms of English. And though it is designed to give the learner as little trouble as possible, it is no more strange to the eyes of my readers than these lines, which are in fact in Basic English. The reader to whom all this is new may get some amusement from attempting to see for himself, before I give a fuller account of the system, where I first went into Basic on this page.

The second point to make clear is that even with so small a word list and so simple a structure it is possible to say in Basic English anything needed

From *Basic English and Its Uses* (1943). New York: W. W. Norton, pp. 23–44.

for the general purposes of everyday existence—in business, trade, industry, science, medical work—in all the arts of living, in all the exchanges of knowledge, desires, beliefs, opinions, and news which are the chief work of a language. It is true that if we go outside the field of general interests and into special branches of the sciences, the arts or the trades, we will have to have other words, not listed among the 850. But the senses of these other words may be made clear in footnotes with the 850; or by teaching given through Basic English. Or they may be seen in the *General Basic English Dictionary*, which, using only the Basic words, gives the senses of twenty thousand other English words. In this way Basic becomes a framework in which words needed for special purposes take their place and from and through which they take their senses. A knowledge of the 850 and of the rules by which they are put together is enough, however, for talk and writing on all everyday general levels.

It would not be hard to put all this book has to say into Basic. It would be clear but not very bright reading. The same words—because there are only 850 of them—would keep coming back again and again. A reader who has the rest of the English language gets a little tired of Basic writing after a time. So I return (with this word *return*, which is not one of the Basic words) to a less confined medium. I have shown, I hope, in the last two paragraphs that Basic is normal English when properly written, and that it can say somewhat complicated things in a reasonably lucid and acceptable fashion.

But this last point no longer needs demonstration. Far too much has been written in Basic on too many subjects for doubt to linger, in the minds of any who have studied the literature, as to the scope and powers of this miniature English. Of course, there is bad Basic and good Basic—as there is bad English and good English. The fact that many people write English wretchedly is no evidence that English is a poor language. Basic, thanks to the care with which its specification was prepared, has been able to adopt as its ruling principle from the outset, "If it is bad English, it is bad Basic."

The third most important point about Basic is that it is not merely a list of words, governed by a minimum apparatus of essential English grammar, but a highly organized system designed throughout to be as easy as possible for a learner who is totally ignorant of English *or of any related language*. It is a language for all the world, not just for those who happen to have some related language as their mother tongue. It is easier for them, naturally enough. The ideas its words carry accord more readily with theirs, its constructions parallel theirs more closely. And, no doubt, by exploiting those parallels, it might have been possible to give them, in some slight degree, a privileged entrance to English. But that would have been at the cost of a radical injustice to speakers of languages remote from English. On the most neutral grounds, the Chinese have a very strong claim to consideration by framers of a world language. There are so many of them, and the part they should play in the world should be second to none. A simplified English, if put forward as a planetary language, must be made as accessible as possible to peoples other than those of Indo-European tongues—and it so happens, through the unique peculiarities of English, that this could be done without any measurable cost in added difficulty for cognate language groups. This third point about Basic is, then, that it is a simplification of English designed equally, so far as the structure of English permits, for users of all languages whatsoever.

The fourth main point is this. If a language is to be easy to learn we must not only cut its words down to a minimum and regularize its grammar; we must also study very carefully the meanings of every one of its words and decide upon the central, pivotal or key meaning of each one of them. Parallel to the reduction and ordering of its vocabulary, there must be a reduction and ordering of the meanings of the words it recommends. It should be obvious that the task of mastering a set of words will be immensely lightened if, for each one of them, the central meaning be presented first. This central meaning will be the meaning by reference to which its other meanings can be most easily understood. All this has been done with Basic, and yet of the many distinctive characteristics of Basic, this so far has received least attention. It may seem a refined point, but it is essential. Clarity upon it makes all the difference in the world to our conception of language learning. A set of meanings which, if presented in one order, is merely a burden upon the memory can become, if offered in another order, a pleasurable exercise of intelligence. Many examples will appear in what follows. Here I need only say that this selective ordering of the meanings of the Basic words was quite half the task which its originator, Mr. C. K. Ogden, undertook and carried through.

Here let me sketch the story of the discovery of Basic English. I say "discovery" rather than "invention," to stress the point that Basic English was a possibility inherent in the development of English, something needing to be disengaged from full English, not something made up. It had its origin, perhaps, in 1920 when Ogden and I were considering the analysis and control of the meanings of the word "meaning" and writing a book we called *The Meaning of Meaning*. But in a sense Basic English dates back earlier for Ogden was already deeply read in the history of attempts to frame a universal language and much concerned with the problem. He was then collecting materials on "word magic" for a major work on the influence of language on thought.

In our joint work we came to the theory and practice of definition. In comparing definitions—definitions of anything, from a sense quality to a force and from a rabbit to a concept—we were struck by the fact that whatever you are defining, certain words keep coming back into your definitions. Define them, and with them you could define anything. That suggests that there might be some limited set of words in terms of which the meanings of all other words might be stated. If so, then a very limited language—limited in its vocabulary but comprehensive in its scope—would be possible. This was by no means a new idea; it has haunted many analytic philosophers through the centuries, among whom Leibnitz and Bishop Wilkins are the best known; but it set Ogden on the track which later led to Basic English.

This initial idea had many discouraging aspects. Ogden has an abnormally developed capacity for verbal experimentation—a natural gift for rephrasing which he has systematically cultivated. Perhaps he is the first man to take a talent possessed by many of the best scholar-journalists and develop it deliberately into an instrument of experimental linguistic research. A little of this experimentation soon made two things dauntingly evident: that even if such a limited language could perhaps be worked out in some ten years, it would be too abstract and difficult for practical use. Furthermore, as it seemed then, in 1920, such a language would not be in the least like everyday English. It would be an academic curiosity, not a general instrument for the common purposes of the world.

Ogden found the way out of these difficulties in part through study of the nature of the verb—aided by some suggestive hints from Jeremy Bentham, whose writings on language he was to edit. But chiefly it was due to his extraordinarily persistent experimentation. Saying the same thing in other ways became more than a game for him; it became a passion—pursuing constantly a clear-cut goal, a minimum comprehensive English, streamlined at every point to offer the least possible resistance to a learner and yet render him at the earliest moment the maximum amount of service. Though Ogden was blessed with exceptionally able collaborators—among whom Miss L. W. Lockhart and the late Dr. F. G. Crookshank must be mentioned—Basic English is essentially the creation of a heightened gift of critical experimentation in a mind unusually well fortified by the relevant linguistic sciences and disciplines.

By 1927 it was clear that an English able to cover the necessary ground and limited to less than a thousand words was feasible. What remained was chiefly a statesman's problem: how best to reconcile all the rival claims— simplicity, economy, regularity, ease of learning, scope, clarity, naturalness, grace; how to balance this local advantage against that for the common good. These were points which could only be worked out through prolonged and very tedious trial and comparison. It is worth remarking that the final design for Basic English was fully tested as against possible alternative designs during this final period and before the first publications in 1929.

So much, for the present, as to how Basic came into being. That such a small number of words is able to take over the work—at certain levels and for certain purposes—of the rest of the language is a very surprising fact. In later pages I will be attempting to say how they do it. But first we have to be clear about the sorts of words there are in Basic. Only then will we see how they may be put together to do the work of other words.

The last *paragraph* was again in Basic. If I now *translate* (put) some of it back into fuller English, *italicizing* (putting in sloping print) the words that are not in Basic, that may *suggest* something (give some idea) of the process:

> So much, for the *moment*, as to how Basic *originated*. That so *few* words *can deputize*—at certain levels and for certain purposes—for the *remainder* of the language is *astonishing*. In a later *chapter* I shall *try* to *explain* how they do it. But first we have to be clear about the sorts of words

there are in Basic. Only then will we see how they may be *combined* to *convey* the meanings of other words.

On pages 23–26 will be seen the Basic Word List. Its 850 words are divided into three main classes. There are six hundred names of things, one hundred and fifty names of qualities (adjectives) and one hundred "operations," as Ogden calls them: words that put the others into significant relationship with one another. It is these one hundred operations or structure words which most need our attention here. Indeed they are in many ways the most important words in Basic: They are those that give the learner and the teacher of Basic the greater part of their trouble; they are those upon which the simplicity of Basic chiefly depends; they are those whose study gives most insight into the structure not only of Basic but of full English as well; and they are those from which we can learn most about the nature, the resources, and the limitations of language in general. A careful study of these one hundred words is a course in grammar, in linguistics, and in theory of meaning.[1] Here, however, we are concerned only with how the right choice of these one hundred words completely changes the prospects for English as a world language.

A glance down the operations column shows that the first eighteen words (from *come* to *will*) are what are usually called verbs. Ogden, for sound but not altogether simple reasons, prefers to call them "operators." The work they are capable of doing is unlike that of other English verbs in certain important respects which will be noted later. They may be divided into four sets. The first ten (*come* to *take*) are names of irreducibly simple acts. *Seem* somewhat resists this classification or indeed any description. It is easiest to think of it as complementary to *be*. (We *seem* wise and good perhaps; we *are* perhaps foolish and bad.) But the others name what we do, or what things do, and between them they cover our doings, and the doings of things, in a peculiarly comprehensive fashion. Into the meanings of other verbs comes some component able to be carried by one or more of these operators (as *enter*, for example, has the meaning of *come in*, and *meditate* has a meaning which may be carried by *give thought* or *take thought*). And this is what has been meant by the claim that Basic has "no verbs." Its use of these superverbs or operators allows it to dispense with the rest.

Next come *be, do,* and *have* which do such a lion's share of the work in English either as full verbs or as auxiliaries. Then come *say, see, send*. These are luxury conveniences in Basic and not strictly indispensable. We could cover their uses with other Basic words. When we *say* something, we *put* it into words; when we *see* something it *is* in view or we *have* it before our eyes; when we *send* someone we *make* him *go*, and so on. But these periphrases would be awkward, and these three words are of such general utility that it is better to have them on the list. Lastly come *may* and *will*, auxiliaries of possibility and permission, and of futurity.

All these words in Basic take all the inflections of full English. Thus *give* is a head word, under which might be listed in a full table *gives, gave, giving,* and *given*. This raises puzzling questions as to how words are to be counted. If we list all the inflections of a verb, just when do we stop? Do we list *kept* in "I kept it" and "It was kept" as two separate entries, though they are the same in form? We would probably list *put* in "I put it here now" and "I put it there yesterday" as two, if we listed *give* and *gave* separately. But then, since "I am," "You are," and "He is" use different forms, why not list *give* five times to correspond with *I, you, you* (plural), *we, they*—adding another two entries for the imperative and the infinitive? Similar quandaries arise in counting the pronouns. Ogden listed *I, he, you* and left it at that, knowing well that one-page list of head words would not be the place where an intelligent person would look for their plurals (*we, you, they*) or, for the neutral (*it*), the feminine (*she*), the accusatives, and the possessives (*him, her, it, his, her, its*, etc.). Similarly *who* covers *whom, whose, which*, and *what*. As with *more, most*, which go with *much*, and *less, least*, he saw that a table of related forms was what the learner needed for such things. The Word List is not a manual of Basic, but the briefest, compactest possible specification of the language. I mention all these trivia because hostile critics of Basic have been very willing to take time out to complain about such points instead of consulting one of the texts (*The Basic Words* or *The ABC of Basic English*) which would at once have answered all their questions, and relieved their professed bewilderment. My reader must forgive me for taking time out here to answer them. There is in fact an expanded model of the Basic Word List which includes all forms under the 850 head words, including plurals of all nouns and all recommended compound words (*undergo*, for example). But that is a comparatively unwieldy thing. It is hardly manageable by a printer and was in fact handmade in China, where all available copies remain. It is a good thing to hang on a classroom wall, but not so generally useful as Ogden's summary.

The reduction of the verbs to eighteen was the key to the discovery of Basic. It explains what otherwise would seem impossible: the vast covering power of such a mere handful of words. These "operators," in combination with other Basic words, translate adequately more than four thousand verbs of full English. And they do it sometimes with gain in force and clarity. We shall compare some examples later. The use of these words, in place of more learned-looking words, has for centuries been increasing for simple, colloquial, informal speech and writing. Students of the history of English knew, of course, that words like *make, take, put, get*, and *give* had been extending their spheres of influence in the language, but no one before Ogden's demonstration realized how vast a domain these unobtrusive little words had won. Willing, serviceable little workers, they were less impressive than the more literary verbs, but handier and safer. We shall see in connection with the teaching of Basic how this translation works out. Here a few examples will suffice. People *inserted* and *extracted* less and less, *put in* and *took out* more and more. Followers of Dr. Johnson at his most characteristic might be reluctant to give up words like *abandon, abdicate, abjure, cede, desert, desist, forgo, forsake . . . relinquish, renounce, resign, vacate, withdraw*, and *yield* in place of *give up*—their homely

Basic English Word List

Operations 100		Qualities		
		100 General		50 Opposites
come	some	able	material	awake
get	such	acid	medical	bad
give	that	angry	military	bent
go	this	automatic	natural	bitter
keep	I	beautiful	necessary	blue
let	he	black	new	certain
make	you	boiling	normal	cold
put	who	bright	open	complete
seem	and	broken	parallel	cruel
take	because	brown	past	dark
be	but	cheap	physical	dead
do	or	chemical	political	dear
have	if	chief	poor	delicate
say	though	clean	possible	different
see	while	clear	present	dirty
send	how	common	private	dry
may	when	complex	probable	false
will	where	conscious	quick	feeble
about	why	cut	quiet	female
across	again	deep	ready	foolish
after	ever	dependent	red	future
against	far	early	regular	green
among	forward	elastic	responsible	ill
at	here	electric	right	last
before	near	equal	round	late
between	now	fat	same	left
by	out	fertile	second	loose
down	still	first	separate	loud
from	then	fixed	serious	low
in	there	flat	sharp	mixed
off	together	free	smooth	narrow
on	well	frequent	sticky	old
over	almost	full	stiff	opposite
through	enough	general	straight	public
to	even	good	strong	rough
under	little	great	sudden	sad
up	much	grey	sweet	safe
with	not	hanging	tall	secret
as	only	happy	thick	short
for	quite	hard	tight	shut
of	so	healthy	tired	simple
till	very	high	true	slow
than	tomorrow	hollow	violent	small
a	yesterday	important	waiting	soft
the	north	kind	warm	solid
all	south	like	wet	special
any	east	living	wide	strange
every	west	long	wise	thin
no	please	male	yellow	white
other	yes	married	young	wrong

Things
400 General

account	company	end	impulse	mine
act	comparison	error	increase	minute
addition	competition	event	industry	mist
adjustment	condition	example	ink	money
advertisement	connection	exchange	insect	month
agreement	control	existence	instrument	morning
air	cook	expansion	insurance	mother
amount	copper	experience	interest	motion
amusement	copy	expert	invention	mountain
animal	cork	fact	iron	move
answer	cotton	fall	jelly	music
apparatus	cough	family	join	name
approval	country	father	journey	nation
argument	cover	fear	judge	need
art	crack	feeling	jump	news
attack	credit	fiction	kick	night
attempt	crime	field	kiss	noise
attention	crush	fight	knowledge	note
attraction	cry	fire	land	number
authority	current	flame	language	observation
back	curve	flight	laugh	offer
balance	damage	flower	law	oil
base	danger	fold	lead	operation
behavior	daughter	food	learning	opinion
belief	day	force	leather	order
birth	death	form	letter	organization
bit	debt	friend	level	ornament
bite	decision	front	lift	owner
blood	degree	fruit	light	page
blow	design	glass	limit	pain
body	desire	gold	linen	paint
brass	destruction	government	liquid	paper
bread	detail	grain	list	part
breath	development	grass	look	paste
brother	digestion	grip	loss	payment
building	direction	group	love	peace
burn	discovery	growth	machine	person
burst	discussion	guide	man	place
business	disease	harbor	manager	plant
butter	disgust	harmony	mark	play
canvas	distance	hate	market	pleasure
care	distribution	hearing	mass	point
cause	division	heat	meal	poison
chalk	doubt	help	measure	polish
chance	drink	history	meat	porter
change	driving	hole	meeting	position
cloth	dust	hope	memory	powder
coal	earth	hour	metal	power
color	edge	humor	middle	price
comfort	education	ice	milk	print
committee	effect	idea	mind	process

Things
400 General (cont'd)

produce	river	sky	structure	unit
profit	road	sleep	substance	use
property	roll	slip	sugar	value
prose	room	slope	suggestion	verse
protest	rub	smash	summer	vessel
pull	rule	smell	support	view
punishment	run	smile	surprise	voice
purpose	salt	smoke	swim	walk
push	sand	sneeze	system	war
quality	scale	snow	talk	wash
question	science	soap	taste	waste
rain	sea	society	tax	water
range	seat	son	teaching	wave
rate	secretary	song	tendency	wax
ray	selection	sort	test	way
reaction	self	sound	theory	weather
reading	sense	soup	thing	week
reason	servant	space	thought	weight
record	sex	stage	thunder	wind
regret	shade	start	time	wine
relation	shake	statement	tin	winter
religion	shame	steam	top	woman
representative	shock	steel	touch	wood
request	side	step	trade	wool
respect	sign	stitch	transport	word
rest	silk	stone	trick	work
reward	silver	stop	trouble	wound
rhythm	sister	story	turn	writing
rice	size	stretch	twist	year

200 Picturable

angle	boat	carriage	drain	garden
ant	bone	cat	drawer	girl
apple	book	chain	dress	glove
arch	boot	cheese	drop	goat
arm	bottle	chest	ear	gun
army	box	chin	egg	hair
baby	boy	church	engine	hammer
bag	brain	circle	eye	hand
ball	brake	clock	face	hat
band	branch	cloud	farm	head
basin	brick	coat	feather	heart
basket	bridge	collar	finger	hook
bath	brush	comb	fish	horn
bed	bucket	cord	flag	horse
bee	bulb	cow	floor	hospital
bell	button	cup	fly	house
berry	cake	curtain	foot	island
bird	camera	cushion	fork	jewel
blade	card	dog	fowl	kettle
board	cart	door	frame	key

Things
200 Picturable (cont'd)

knee	nose	rail	sock	thumb
knife	nut	rat	spade	ticket
knot	office	receipt	sponge	toe
leaf	orange	ring	spoon	tongue
leg	oven	rod	spring	tooth
library	parcel	roof	square	town
line	pen	root	stamp	train
lip	pencil	sail	star	tray
lock	picture	school	station	tree
map	pig	scissors	stem	trousers
match	pin	screw	stick	umbrella
monkey	pipe	seed	stocking	wall
moon	plane	sheep	stomach	watch
mouth	plate	shelf	store	wheel
muscle	plough	ship	street	whip
nail	pocket	shirt	sun	whistle
neck	pot	shoe	table	window
needle	potato	skin	tail	wing
nerve	prison	skirt	thread	wire
net	pump	snake	throat	worm

Summary of Rules
Plurals in "s."
Derivatives in "er," "ing," "ed" from 300 nouns.
Adverbs in "ly" from qualifiers.
Degree with "more" and "most."
Questions by inversion and "do."
Operators and pronouns conjugate in full.
Measurement, numerals, currency, calendar, and international terms in English form.

Basic rendering—but a public unblessed by and unprotected by a sound training in philology escaped multiple dangers. So did the language itself. Every language is under constant attack by the tongues of its less expert users. One has only to watch—in a Chinese university, for example—the degradation of such learned words, when used without awareness of their implications, to see that they need protection. Basic English, by providing invulnerable but adequate substitutes for these more delicate instruments, can serve our language as a fender. It can guard full English from those who will blur all its lines and blunt all its edges if they try to write and talk it before they have learned to read it.

Apart from the amazing power these words have to take over the work of other verbs, they are in themselves the most indispensable verbs of full English. They have to be learned and well learned anyhow by anyone learning English. By concentrating on them, Basic can teach them as no system that adds further verbs can.

Below the verbs in Column One come twenty words (*about* to *with*) whose peculiarity is that they handle positions and directions. Basic groups them together as "directives," separating them from the other preposition-adverbs for an interesting reason. All these much-used little words have, of course, a great variety of meanings in full English. In general the usefulness of a word and the variability of its uses go together, as we would expect. It is useful because it will do so many things. Naturally, the words best worth teaching will be the hardest to teach—unless you succeed in analyzing and arranging their uses so that as far as possible the links between the meanings become obvious. If you can do that, these words in a large measure teach themselves. This, it will be remembered, was my fourth point above. Ogden's analysis of the uses of these directives, and his separation of those that are intelligible (if taught in the right order) from those that are not, is perhaps the clearest example of this. As a contribution to the teaching of English (Basic or full) it is second only to his "break-down" of the verb.

In their central uses—those to be taught first—all these twenty words have to do with position or direction in *space*. In these uses they can all be illustrated in one diagram.

So presented this is obvious enough. But it is surprising how few teachers of English have used these physical senses in elucidating other uses of these words that are not physical. I suspect they have been daunted by the word "metaphor." And that is as though an engineer let himself be daunted by the word "stress." It is not suggested that teachers should explain the *theory* of metaphor to their classes. To teach that is no light undertaking. But if a series of examples is presented (leg of a man, leg of a dog, leg of a table) the connections between the uses of a word which metaphor has established become very easily apparent. The whole art of learning a language is in recognizing familiar features in new settings.

Of the other uses of these directive words, some are simple metaphors from these space senses, some are rather more complex metaphors going by steps, and some are irrational and incomprehensible accidents of the history of the language, and therefore cannot be understood and have to be just learned and remembered as brute facts. The important thing to do in teaching them is to separate and postpone these irrational "idioms" and give the others in the order that makes them most lucid and intelligible to the learner. Then he can see how and why the words do what they do in English.

Consider here the word *on*. "On the table," "on the wall," "on the earth," "on earth," "Monday," "on view," "on my mind," "on approval," "on a line," "on no account," "going on," "and so on." Try out the effects of substituting *in* for *on* in a large collection of such phrases. That brings out better than anything else what the problem of teaching the indispensable words of English in the most economical fashion is. . . . Here the point is that it is possible to choose a key sense for *on* and an order for the presentation of the other uses that makes all those that are intelligible relatively easy to master. In most pre-Basic teaching any and every use of *on* which happened to turn up has been given equal attention. Such hugger-mugger methods are wickedly wasteful of mental energy, the most valuable commodity in the world.

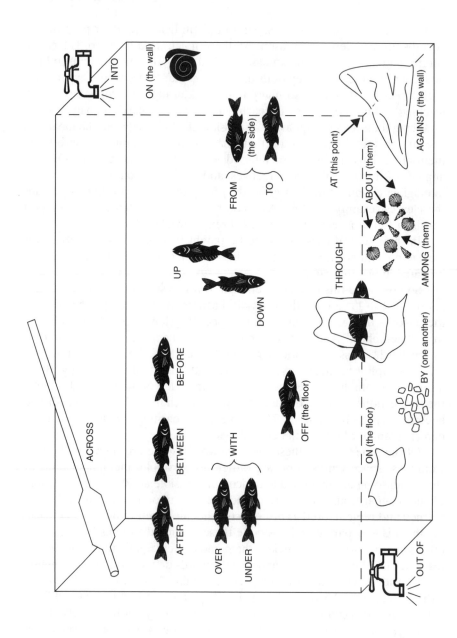

A similar selective ordering of their uses has been given in Basic, to all its words. The recommendations are recorded in *The Basic Words*. As a result, learning Basic, if these recommendations are followed, becomes a much lighter task than the learning of the same 850 words in the full range of their senses taken at random. But many who have thought they were studying Basic seem hardly to have looked into *The Basic Words* or to be aware as yet of the possibilities of economy that little book offers.

The rest of our tour of the Basic Word List can be made more swiftly. The same principles apply throughout. Why any one word appears on it depends on the absence of others. Occasional overlaps (*boot, shoe; sock, stocking* are the most conspicuous) are explained by trade of other special customs. It must not be forgotten that comprehensiveness is a prime aim, though no one pretends or has ever pretended that any small set of words can cover everything. What would the rest of the language be doing if it could! Nonetheless, the seeming omissions that for a while puzzle most English-speaking persons who take up Basic cease to be troublesome when the other words or phrases with which the gap can be filled have been noticed. *Can* for example is replaced through *possible, able to, let*, and *may*. Both *can* and *may* are tricky words for a beginner in English. It is altogether best to let him master *may* first. Then, if he is going on to the rest of English, *can* will be an easier problem for him; similarly with *must*, whose meanings are handled through *have to* and *necessary*. In general in judging these decisions we should try to see them with the eyes of a learner of English, rather than with a mind that has full English at its disposal.

Among the six hundred names of things are many that at first sight may be taken to be verbs: *act, attack, attempt, change, fall*, for example. In Basic they are nouns. The powers of the operators allow such words to be used in phrases that make a verb use of them unnecessary. Thus in Basic we do not *act* in any of the confusing senses of that verb, but we may *take* the part of Hamlet in the play. In general we *do* whatever it is. Again, in Basic we do not *attempt* something or *attack* someone, we *make* an attempt or an attack; we do not *change* things, we *make* changes in them; we do not *fall*, we *have* a fall, and so on. But these indications would be misleading unless I point out at once that Basic, through the rule summarized by "derivatives in -er, -ing, and -ed from three hundred nouns," has many other ways of handling these meanings. We may add *-er* to these words to give us the name of the agent— the actor, attacker, and so on. With three of these (*actor, creditor, sailor*) the spelling is *-or* and not *-er*. This one percent irregularity is not troublesome. To the same words we may add *-ing*, to give us nouns for the action and corresponding adjectives: "The acting was bad," "He is the acting manager," "He was acting in the manager's place." This is a far simpler way of teaching these uses than through the nomenclature of participles and gerunds—that bane of so many schoolchildren's days. Similarly, we may add *-ed* to give us another adjective. "The play was acted." This provides us with the past participles and the passives of our three hundred words, without bringing in the complexities of the full verb and the construing difficulties it occasions.

The application of this rule is in practice much simpler than may appear. The meanings of the nouns, as they are taught in Basic, really control the use of these endings when they are needed. The list of the three hundred and a full discussion will be found in *The ABC of Basic English*. As Ogden there notes (p. 82), there are other words in the Basic List that take some of these endings, and English speakers writing in Basic may use them with due care. Whether they will be clear to learners depends, of course, on the rest of the sentence and the occasion.

It is in connection with this rule that the charge has been made that Basic creates "wholly unnecessary difficulties . . . difficulties lacking in Standard English." This is wholly false. The alleged difficulties are troubles only to an ankylotic grammarian viewing Basic from the standpoint of a complete knowledge of English. They do not exist for the foreign learner. He does not look on his task from that standpoint. He has not yet learned full English. What the rule in fact does is to *postpone* difficulties until the learner is at a stage when they will be less of a threat to his progress.

This last point may be stressed. Rules such as this are formulated for the convenience of teachers and expositors. They are guides rather than drill sergeants. Unfortunately grammar is the subject that of all others arouses the most obstinate propensities in the human mind. It is not an accident that grammarians by tradition are furious and rage. The formulation of any rule is to them a professional challenge to argue hard cases regardless of whether the general advance of a learner is helped thereby or hindered. It is easy to forget what rules and system are for. Too many teachers fall into this oblivion likewise. Too often in language teaching it is as though we confused hairdressing with famine relief; our pupils are starving for means of expression, and we spend our time combing away at their unruly syntax or erratic phonemes.

The other summarized rules on the Basic List, except the last, explain themselves. We add *s* to most of the nouns to make their plurals, but follow normal English custom in all the exceptions. We add *-ly* to the adjectives to form adverbs (*kind, kindly*), but make all the normal adjustments of spelling (*able, ably*). We form comparatives with *more* and *most*, but also, with short words, use *-er* and *-est* (*smaller* and *the smallest*). *Good* and *bad* take *better, best* and *worse, worst*. Questions follow normal practice and, as we have seen, all the forms of the operators and pronouns are used.

Finally comes a formula that has been the occasion for a considerable amount of misunderstanding. It concerns a point of general policy. Ogden, looking realistically at the learner's actual situation, the real difficulties of language learning as opposed to vocabulary assimilation, and the means of communication already available, recognized that the numbers, for example, are not in the same position as most other English words. The learner has the figures to use; all he has to learn is how to spell and pronounce them. He has no subtleties or variations of meaning to deal with. Similarly, in a less degree, with the names of the days of the week and the months of the year. The calendar presents them better than any text that does not just reprint it. Again, the metric system is adopted by nineteen governments, current in other countries, and all but universal for science. Its English pronunciation is the only task that remains. The other measurement terms in English possess, also, scientific definiteness of meaning. But, alas, the actual measures employed vary distressingly from region to region, and from trade to trade. This was another reason for excluding them from a general-purposes list, a reason applying also to currency terms. The main argument, though, for making numerals and calendar, measurement and currency terms addenda to the Basic List is their specific notational character. In this they are like proper names or mathematical or chemical signs, rather than like the general run of the common nouns of the language. They belong essentially to the nomenclatures of the sciences.

In addition to these there are the international words mentioned in this rule. Basic at present recognizes fifty words as current in all parts of the world wherever there is some likelihood of anyone's needing them. Typical are *bar, piano, restaurant*, and *telephone*, the names of and some of the terms in the chief sciences, and titles such as *president*. They are used by Basic, but it would have been silly to include them as though they were a part of the language that has to be taught.

This brings me to a side of Basic which to many offers some of its most interesting possibilities: its use as a connecting framework through which the language of science could become international. This promise which Basic presents has always had a very important place in Ogden's design. It is obviously absurd that anything that is so much the common concern of mankind as the advance of science should be held up, continually, by language barriers, if there is any way of overcoming them. Anyone aware, even in one field, of the amount of relevant data and suggestion, which is hidden from him merely by his inability to read effectively in enough languages, will feel this. It is felt most acutely by natives of the linguistically isolated countries. A scientific worker in Australia, Brazil, or China, if he is to keep "abreast of his subject," must, as a rule, equip himself to read effectively in three foreign languages. In the near future he may well have to add Russian as a fourth. By the time he has so equipped himself he is years behind his fortunate rivals in more polyglot centers. There is little need to stress the point except by adding that *effective* reading (as opposed to the vague reading which is one of the most damaging ways of wasting our time) is harder to achieve, in view of the manner in which even very important papers are commonly written, than is currently assumed. If there is a way of avoiding these frustrations we should give it our best attention.

Ogden has recently published a report on the progress of Basic toward a solution of these difficulties in the volume *Basic for Science* which supersedes the earlier *Basic English Applied: Science* (1931). It is written in Basic, and for the scientifically minded would be the most suitable example of Basic writing to examine. It is documented with specimens of the use of Basic, ranging from popular expositions to abstracts of advanced research. It contains also a representative selection from the forthcoming *Basic Science Dictionary*, and the latest forms of the short lists of scientific terms which enable a proficient in Basic to write for students conversant with a science but limited in their English.

Clearly enough, such students do not require a full mastery even of Basic before being able to profit from such writings. The technical terms of their subject replace for them many everyday words which a novel in Basic, for example, is likely to employ. What they do need is familiarity and ease with the Basic constructions and with the words that are most useful, in explanations, in accounts of procedure, and in describing causal and other relations. They do not get this from ordinary courses in English until a very late stage. Basic, from the very fact that it economizes in its words and uses a defining description where a larger language would use some special word brought in for the purpose, gives training in this sort of language almost from the start.

We may therefore hope that the slow progress toward the internationalization of the nomenclatures of the sciences, halted by the wars, will gain fresh impetus as it is realized that Basic English supplies the framework through which the vast vocabularies of science and technology could operate supranationally. The transportation, as it were, is ready and waiting—all that has to be done is to regularize the verbal packings of the already standardized goods that have to be interchanged.

But Basic has done much more in this scientific field than "stand and wait." A Basic Science Library—"a program of science in Basic, designed for the general reader, the learner of English, and the teaching of science in schools"—has been assembled as a nucleus for further developments. The first of them, *A Basic Astronomy*, appeared in 1934, and a version of Faraday's *The Chemical History of a Candle*, two selections from the writings of J. B. S. Haldane, *Science and Well-Being* and *The Outlook of Science* made by William Empson, and *Living Things*, an introduction to biology by J. W. N. Sullivan, followed. More recent examples are H. S. Hatfield's *European Science, What Things Are Made of* and *Inventions and Their Uses in Science Today*, and A. P. Rossiter's *The Growth of Science*. The last two have reached a large public through becoming "Pelican Specials" issued by Penguin Books.

Those who know what an utter dearth of serious, intellectually mature reading matter in linguistically simple form is encountered by every student of English from China to Peru will best understand what even these beginnings can accomplish. They fit into the school and college programs of those who are learning English as an aid to their work in science, but they are by no means limited to that use. In China—to speak of the foreign conditions I know best—the main incentive behind the learning of English is interest in what is most distinctive about the West, its science. And a school program in English cannot begin to feed this curiosity with information and suggestions too early. In the teaching texts produced by the Orthological Institute of China, the elementary physiology of breathing and nutrition and the essentials of hygiene are taken up as early as the Second Book, before the students have got much more than halfway through the 850 words. That is what the selection of those words makes possible. Anyone who has some such special field in view can begin work on it without waiting for the whole Basic vocabulary to be assimilated, or even for the introduction of all the Basic constructions. The teaching of the remainder can well be combined with study of important subject matter. This is not the least of the enormous advantages, as to motivation, possessed by Basic.

This flexibility of Basic, which comes from the reduction of the verb and the separation of the structural operation words from the content vocabulary, is what I should finally stress in this chapter. Many critics who went not much further in their preliminary study than a glance over the Word List, and who supposed that anything that they did not immediately understand about the system must be a blunder, have complained of its rigidity. . . . Basic has, in fact, through its supplementary lists of words—lists for science, for economics, for the study of English poetry, for the Bible—arranged things so that special interests should be able to develop themselves at the earliest possible moment through Basic. One hundred and fifty extra nouns and adjectives permit a very dignified and faithful new translation of the Bible. In practice they take over the work of much the same number of words of less Biblical use. As aids to informed reading of it are *The Bible: What It Is and What Is in It* by E. Evans and T. H. Robinson, and *African Beliefs and Christian Faith* by Edwin W. Smith. Again, students who wish to get to Shakespeare's English as quickly as possible will find the text of his *Julius Caesar* printed opposite a version in Basic English, with elaborate glosses, information on his language and background materials in Basic in the footnotes.[2] There are also available in Basic the passages from Plutarch from which Shakespeare worked. In yet a third direction, students who wish to enlarge their English constructions beyond those of Basic, by passing gradually to the free use of verbs, will find the way prepared in my abridged version of Plato's *Republic*, where verbs parallel to nouns in Basic (*to change, to know*, etc.) are put to work. A version of Plato's *Meno*, made in strict Basic by J. Rantz, might be used as an introduction to the Platonic themes.

In these and other ways, Basic goes out to meet the needs of diverse people. It by no means stays cribbed and confined within its defensive stronghold of 850 proud words, as some ill-informed persons have alleged. It will be agreed, I think, that even the sketch I have given here shows evidence of the catholicity of Basic, its readiness to take due regard of different interests and purposes. With a main stress on science, it still gives the world its most universally readable Bible, and its experimental versions of other great books are from Shakespeare and Plato. The other items on its book list will confirm this impression. All these are first fruits. I think they show, to those who read them, that the tree was of good stock and well planted and that Basic has begun to put the materials and techniques for a common culture before the world.

I am making no attempt to sketch the history of the spread of Basic through its first ten years. The war interrupted too many promising starts—

in China, Japan, Czechoslovakia, Denmark, Greece, to mention only a few instances—and it has put too many obstacles in the way of communications with other countries, too many of the best workers have been diverted by war needs, and curtailments due to the war have interfered with too many developments for any adequate up-to-date presentation to be possible. This is no moment for a historical summary. Thanks in a large measure to support from the Rockefeller Foundation and the Payne Fund, more progress has been made than anyone with a realistic awareness of the difficulties such a radical innovation in language teaching must encounter can readily believe. Basic is not among the casualties of the war. As that supreme demonstration of our need for a wider general culture and for clearer exchanges of man's better ideas was spread over the planet, Basic enterprises suffered along with so many other attempts toward a more reasonable future. The frustration is temporary; essential work has continued—though not as it would have done in a peaceful world. When the time comes, the necessary materials and instrumentalities will be found ready.

Notes

[1] Such a course prepared for classroom use may be found in *Words at Work* by Miss Christine Gibson of the Harvard Commission on English Language Studies.

[2] For suggestions on uses of this text in the English classroom, see "On Teaching Shakespeare" by Christine Gibson, *The English Journal*, September, 1942.

4

METAPHOR AS AN ELEMENT OF ORIGINARY LANGUAGE

Ernesto Grassi

The Problem

The process of speaking rationally constitutes a legitimation of our statements, and all teaching based on the choice of such method consists in giving, clarifying, and explaining "reasons." In teaching, the teacher points them out. In so doing, however, all pedagogical activity is reduced to the transference of something known only to the instructor: it is a monologue, not a dialogue. Knowledge, which marks Western culture, has differed clearly, ever since its origins, from mere opinion (*dóxa*): what we have an opinion about can surely be true, but it is different from what we know, in so far as opinion is not backed by reasons.

In the *Meno*, Plato uses an interesting metaphor to explain this difference: He compares opinion to a slave who, if not chained, can always escape. The "chain" anchors assertions to reason.[1] Knowledge, understood as a rational process, implies the exclusion of all uncertainty about the subject matter to which we anchor our statements. The basis of knowledge acquires,

From *The Primordial Metaphor* (1994). Translated by Laura Pietropaola and Manuela Scarci. Binghamton, NY: Medieval & Renaissance Texts & Studies, pp. 3–14.

therefore, a normative, controlling character: only grounded knowledge can be considered valid. For this reason the Greeks called the principles on which knowledge is grounded the *archai* (in fact, *archein* means to rule, to be in charge, and the *archontes* were those who ruled, those who were in charge).

The *archai* we are referring to must be valid anywhere at any time, and the language which expresses this way of thinking must be logical and rational. Consequently, any kind of poetic, imaginative, rhetorical language, namely language limited to a specific time and place, must be excluded from the sphere of theoretical or scientific thought. In this sphere it cannot claim any rights. But we must not forget that modern analytic philosophy and logical positivism deny metaphysics the ability to create scientific thought. The validity of the rational process is limited to the sphere marked by the principles and axioms on which science has laid its foundations. In turn, such principles and axioms cannot, of themselves, be scientific, since, by definition, they cannot be proven: to justify them by resorting to some original evidence or intuition would open the door to arbitrariness. Consequently, any humanism that attempts to transcend formal thinking by taking into consideration the problems of life and man must be excluded, and with it must be rejected any "pathetic" elements inherent in poetic or rhetorical language. Rational and scientific language must necessarily leave out of its scope the passions[2] of man. Its ideal is a mathematical one and the link between the human world and rationality generates the terror of falling into subjectivism and arbitrariness.

The "E" at Delphi

How does classical antiquity view the problem of the indemonstrability of principles and, therefore, of their archaic character? In order to clarify the terms of the problem, I shall turn to Plutarch's treatise *On the "E" at Delphi*. The treatise tells of a sacred offer made to Apollo.[3] The Delphic coins carrying the image of the Emperor Hadrian (AD 117–138) show a frontal view of the great temple of Apollo at Delphi. Between two central columns, high on the coin, hangs the striking capital letter "E." What is its meaning? To understand the discussion about it recorded in the treatise we must keep in mind that in ancient writing, still adhered to in fifth-century inscriptions, the letter *epsilon* (e) can signify either the conjunction "if" or the verbal form "you are."

Long before Plutarch wrote his treatise in the form of a dialogue, the meaning of the symbol had become the object of several hypotheses. Plutarch reviews them all. The first hypothesis, proposed in the text by Plutarch's brother Lamprias, states that "E" is simply the fifth letter of the alphabet and that, as such, it is the graphic representation of the number 5. Placed on the pediment of the temple of Apollo, it signifies that the god is witness to the belief that the true original sages of Greece were five in number (Chilon, Thales, Solon, Bias and Pittacus). This thesis can be described as historical.

In the second interpretation, "E" is the second vowel of the Greek alphabet and, according to Plutarch's text, symbolizes the sun, the second planet, equivalent in essence to Apollo, the Lord of Delphi, the very light of Wisdom. This interpretation is astronomical in nature.

In the third interpretation, "E" stands for "if," as in "if only the heavens . . . ," namely, the beginning of the formulaic official prayer with which at Delphi one would address Apollo: "Oh, if only our god . . . etc." This is an essentially sacred interpretation.

The fourth interpretation is the one which calls our attention. Its advocate Theon states that "E" is the linguistic particle expressing the conditional function "if" which indicates the basis and point of departure of every rational judgement: if we posit a premise, we must draw from it a specific conclusion. The linguistic particle, therefore, takes on the connotations of a warning: whoever makes a pilgrimage to Delphi is committed to rational thinking and thus honors Apollo, god of rationality. This is a philosophical interpretation. The passage of interest to us is the following:

> And since philosophy is directed at truth, since the light of truth is proof, and sentence structure the origin of proof, it is understandably the word that creates and achieves this connection which wise men dedicate to the god who loves truth above all. The god is a seer, and the faculty of seeing is that faculty which points from the present or past into the future: nothing is created without a cause and nothing is seen without a reason. . . .[4]

Moreover, Plutarch states further on: "Therefore, though it may be risky to say this, I shall not omit to say that the tripod of truth is reason itself, which first draws the conclusion from the premiss, then proceeds to the existence of the thing, and thence to the completion of the proof."[5] This text contains the most radical rationalization, and the most radical demythologization not only of philosophical thought, but also of the faculty of foresight, originally attributed to divine beings. Here philosophy is identified solely with the rational ability of reaching conclusions, of providing proof and of "fore-seeing"; consequently, prophecy is the result of a purely rational process.

Plutarch's treatise deserves further consideration because the entire argument, despite its rational nature, is enveloped from the very beginning in the aura of the sacred, of the divine. The god helps his beseechers as the originary force which arouses and assists those who address questions to him. But how? Plutarch provides the following answer:

> Since . . . inquiry is the beginning of philosophy, and wonder and uncertainty the beginning of inquiry, it seems only natural that the greater part of what concerns the god should be concealed in riddles, and should call for some account of the wherefore and an explanation of its cause.[6]

The Problem of Wonder

Why is the sense of wonder, as the origin of inquiry, of primary importance to the essence of philosophy? Why is a sacred significance attributed to this sense of wonder?

Both Plato and Aristotle relate the phenomenon of wonder (*thaumazein*) to the origin of philosophy. In the *Theaetetus*, Socrates argues that philosophy originates from wonder and states that "he was a good genealogist who made Iris the daughter of Thaumas."[7] Aristotle describes the relation between wonder and the origin of philosophy and says that "it is owing to their wonder that men both now begin and at first began to philosophize."[8]

The grammarian and lexicographer Hesychius gives in his lexicon the following synonyms for *thauma*: *ekplexis* (shock); *xenisma* (estrangement); and for *thaumazein*: *theasthai* (to look) and *manthanein* (to learn, to understand).[9] A later etymological definition also derives *thaumazein* from *theasthai*.[10] The etymological connection established both in antiquity and in modern times between *thaumazo* and *theaomai* points to the area in which the interpretation of the term *thaumazein* is to be looked for: on the one hand in "seeing," and on the other in the domain of "immediacy," which establishes the relationship between "wonder" and "emerging vision," already present in the prephilosophical use of the term *thaumazein*.[11]

Perhaps the connection we have emphasized between seeing and wondering is best expressed in the genealogy of the goddess Iris, who is introduced in the passage I have already quoted from Plato's *Theaetetus* as the personification of the wonder of philosophy. In this genealogy we find the elements already contained in the etymological allusions: estrangement and the questions it engenders. Iris is the daughter of Thaumas, who, as the son of Gaea, creator of all things in heaven and on earth, is directly associated with the beginning of all existence, which, as the originary and non-deducible being, fills with wonder. Iris is the personification of the rainbow, which joins heaven and earth, above and below, everything visible. As the daughter of Thaumas, Iris presides over the relationships between gods and men and is the winged messenger and the giver of the word, according to the etymology of her name deriving from *erein*, "to say," "to speak." Moreover, according to Alcaeus, the union of Iris with the rain god Zephyrus produced Eros, the god of love, who answers every question and satisfies every impulse.[12]

The relation between wonder and the need to question emerges only if something presents itself to us as a problem: no one, in fact, will question what is unequivocal. It is rather what "concerns us," what awakens our interest, that becomes the object of a question. Questions arise only when something demands clarification, because uncertainty would be intolerable. In other words, we must find ourselves in the realm of an originary tension for our "at-tention" to be awakened. That is why the estrangement referred to by Hesychius in his lexicon is related to shock.

Philosophical *Pistis*

We must now ask ourselves the following question: Can we find in the Greek philosophical tradition a continuing presence of this issue which can provide us with the foundation for our thesis on the origin of metaphoric, historical language?

In his *Metaphysics* Aristotle makes a statement of capital importance:

> For those who wish to get clear of difficulties it is advantageous to state the difficulties well; for the subsequent free play of thought implies the solution of the previous difficulties, and it is not possible to untie a knot which one does not know [. . .]. Therefore one should have surveyed all the difficulties beforehand [. . .] because people who inquire without first stating the difficulties are like those who do not know where they have to go.[13]

In order to understand the significance of this passage, we must stress the pre-eminence of metaphoric language *vis-à-vis* logical language. First of all, Aristotle, in the cited passage, uses a metaphor: "it is not possible to untie a knot of which one does not know." This metaphor points out that the feeling of nonindifference before a problem is concretely experienced when one is "tied" in a "knot" to an objectivity from which he cannot free himself. Only by going back to it will he be able to recognize his ignorance, a fact which constitutes the first step towards knowledge as well as the way to dispel the state of uncertainty in which he finds himself.

The objectivity of the source, of that which is "originary," manifests itself concretely as the responsibility of taking on a task that must be accomplished. Such urgency appears primarily as a sense of wonder. It is immediate (un-mediated) and therefore it is indicative rather than demonstrative. Consequently, it awakens the need to ask questions so that we may unveil the meaning of phenomena by freeing an "originary vision" (*theasthai*) of them. Moreover, wonder has a pathetic nature: *pathos*, the emotion accompanying wonder, is the expression of our experience of being compelled to seek an explanation.

Since the phenomenon of wonder occurs within the realm of what is originary, of what is not deducible, the *thaumazein* is the expression of the experience of astonishment and estrangement. This is why the originary manifests itself only instantaneously and directly with all the characteristics of a compelling force and of an urgent need in the here and now of existence. It manifests itself in human history and is not logically deducible. It is exclusively in this realm that man experiences wonder as the origin of knowledge. It is also in this experience that we find the source of the meaning of the mysterious "e" at Delphi, and not in Plutarch's rational interpretation of it.

Now, where can we find legitimation for our interpretation of the origin of knowledge, as conceived by Aristotle—to whom we traditionally attribute the notion of the pre-eminence of rational thought and language? Aristotle's position with respect to the structure and the archaic status of principles must be included in our discussion of the problem of *arché*, of the manifestation of the meaning of individual beings and of the nonrational structure of language. Aristotle maintains that "not to know of what things one may demand demonstration, and of what one may not, argues simply want of education.[14] In his *Posterior Analytics*, he insists on this point using the term *pistis* (conviction, belief), a term of fundamental importance in the history of Western thought. He states:

> Hence if we know and are convinced because of the primitives, we both know and are convinced of them better, since it is because of them that we know and are convinced of what is posterior.[15]

The Christian tradition has attributed a religious significance to the word *pistis*. In the Aristotelian passage, however, the term is found in relation to the analysis of the structure of principles, of the *archai*. If scientific knowledge is born of the persuasion grounded in demonstration, it follows that he who has attained knowledge by virtue of such demonstration (persuasion) must necessarily possess an even firmer conviction (*pistis*) of the principles on which it is grounded.[16] What does *pistis* mean here? It cannot be understood as a renunciation of knowledge—a dogmatic faith—nor can it be reduced to opinion (*dóxa*). What constitutes then the structure of originary knowledge which governs the world of human knowledge?

To answer such a question we must go back to the founding principle of Aristotelian logic and see how it should be interpreted. The principle of non-contradiction is considered by Aristotle the basic principle of thinking and speaking: "The same attribute cannot at the same time belong and not belong to the same object and in the same respect."[17]

We can interpret correctly the Aristotelian statement only if we take into consideration the way in which Aristotle demonstrates his axiom. But by asking such a question, are we not risking contradiction, right from the start? It is obvious that the principle of a demonstration, given its *archaic* status, cannot be logically proven, because it is itself the very foundation of logic. Aristotle, in fact, does not offer a logical, rational proof but a proof he calls "elenctic." What is its structure?

The Greek verb *elegchein* means, among other things, "to tie to the pillory"; whoever is tied in such a manner is "exposed" to eventual derision. The elenctic demonstration is radically different from a rational one because it does not resort to reason for its own legitimation; it resorts rather to the indication of an undeniable connection. In fact, whoever denies the principle of contradiction, if he wishes to say something that has meaning, must necessarily make use of it. He must acknowledge its dominion.[18] To exist is to be "tied" to the need for the significant word.

Even if he were to have recourse to silence—so as not to be obliged to contradict himself—his silence would be a meaningful statement as well. Man is chained to the pillory of the word. He must speak: his very silence is a sign of this.

Is this our Promethean fate? In depicting the lament of Prometheus who, chained to the solitude of the rock, is exposed to the derision of the day and the darkness of the night, Aeschylus has him exclaim: "Under such suffering, speech and silence are alike beyond me."[19]

Pistis is neither opinion, nor rational knowledge. Nor is it a dogmatic conviction related to a religious revelation. The elenctic nature of the principle of contradiction compels us to acknowledge the presence of suffering, of endurance, which testifies to the impossibility of an escape from meaning. *Pistis* must be here understood as the result of a fundamental experience, of a task which implies at once the signal of a question and the need for an answer. In the context of such experience, the temporal and spatial significance of beings manifests itself each time in accordance with the urgency of the here and now. Thus man finds himself called upon to respond to his passionate need to speak and to question.

Since being is present in all statements relative to individual beings— i.e., participles or entities participating in being (in fact, we say that every being exists, is)—the original need to respond to its calling expresses itself in an appropriate verbal form. But what verbal form does it assume? It does not take on a logical, deductive form; it assumes, rather, an indicative metaphorical one, by virtue of which every expression *is itself* and, at the same time, is not itself since it is only the response to the call of being, which asserts itself in the here and now of existence. It is not an abstract word, dissociated from time and space; it is rather a historical, rhetorical word.

We can therefore draw a conclusion which is essential to the formulation of our problem: Rational thought no longer represents the originary approach to the understanding of the being of beings. In such a context being is enveloped in contradiction, in the abyss[20] of what is rationally undefinable. But, from a different perspective, the undefinable fills us with wonder. Wonder moves us and turns us away from a nonhistorical consideration of beings.

Metaphor as the Root of Knowledge: Coluccio Salutati

Is there a tradition which offers a foundation for a conception of knowledge rooted in the historicity of ontological experience? Does the humanist tradition offer us such a possibility? A correct understanding of Humanism has been hindered by the pre-eminence of German idealism, which denied it any philosophical value precisely because it is grounded on rhetorical and metaphorical thought; by Heidegger's antihumanistic thesis; and by the interpretation of Humanism as essentially a Christian reflection on Platonism.

With regard to the concept of knowledge, Western philosophy rejected, from the very beginning, the speculative function of rhetorical language for its being anchored to the here and now of existence; consequently, it expressed a negative judgement on metaphor, since metaphor transfers and transforms the meaning of a word and, in so doing, destroys its rational precision.

We would like to propose a different thesis: That which is—namely, individual beings, participants in and participles of being, for only as such do they exist—manifests itself in reality exclusively in a concrete historical situation, defined by the here and now of existence. All beings, in their openness to being, are expressions of a call, an appeal that must be answered in the urgency of every moment. The appeals, in whose realm we exist, are everchanging and new, and the meaning of beings is transformed according to the modality of our responses to the appeals.

We shall reformulate our question: Is there a tradition which allows us to identify a nonrational foundation of knowledge, by virtue of which metaphor and rhetorical language acquire a philosophical function? I have tried elsewhere[21] to reconstruct this tradition and here I shall summarize it with references to *De Laboribus Herculis* by Coluccio Salutati (1331–1406).[22]

Salutati states that *scientia* originates in a metaphorical activity which consists of the discovery, of the "invention" (from *inventio* meaning "to find") of *similitudines* which identify on each occasion the everchanging differing meaning of beings. In order to understand his thesis we must begin with the analysis of the arguments and of the terminology he used in this text, which differ immensely from those of traditional metaphysics. Salutati maintains that *scientia* has its origins in the Muses, not in just one of them, but in the common activity of all nine. Only the Muses make possible the search for knowledge, *scientiam quaerere*,[23] and the achievement of *doctrina perfecta*.[24] We shall limit our analysis to the interpretation of the first six Muses.

First of all, Salutati indicates the method and the point of departure for the scholar. Strikingly, this method (*meta odou*) does not constitute a rational, pedagogical set of directions, but is rather a response to three existential impulses. The scholar must heed the impulse to Glory; he must feel desperately and passionately the desire to attain knowledge. Salutati identifies this impulse with the first of the Muses, Clio: *Prima namque cogitationi discere cupientium primum occurrit fame celebritas que Gloria est.*[25] We are clearly nowhere near any rational presupposition as far as the method is concerned.

The second originary impulse we must respond to is the impulse to pleasure (*edoné*). Again it is a passion, it is the pleasure in learning personified by another muse, Euterpe: *Alteram vero ponit Euterpen, quod Latine dicit nihil aliud esse quam "bene delectans."*[26]

The third presupposition behind the quest for knowledge is represented by Melpomene: *Tertiam autem Melpomenem statuit, hoc est, inquit, "Meditationem faciens permancre."*[27] Perseverance in study is also necessary: it is not a passion, but an attitude (*exis*).

Therefore, the path to follow in our search for knowledge is characterized by a threefold commitment.

After having made these considerations on method, how does Salutati identify the other constitutive elements of knowledge? They are defined in relation to three nonrational activities. The first is sensory *perceptio*, the passion of the senses, the passionate experience of what manifests itself through the sensory organs and constitutes the premise of every search. This is the world of phenomena, of all that appears (*phainomenon, phaineshai*). This passion of the senses, again represented by a muse, is seen by Salutati as the faculty of perception which produces the germs of knowledge: *Sequentem autem Taliam locavit in ordine, quam "capacitatem" vult sive "germina ponentem."*[28]

Let us keep in mind that phenomena, all that appears, do not acquire meaning in an abstract manner, of themselves; their meaning is determined by that of which the senses, in so far as they are organs, are the instruments.

Organs of what, then? Certainly of a passion in every way originary, non-deducible, the passion of a Muse, as Salutati calls it. We are dealing with a passionate experience linked to an *originary reality*, which compellingly asserts itself in and through its instruments, the sensory organs. It is therefore an indicative, not a demonstrative passion, and as such it is nondeducible and must be recognized as a force arising from the mystery of the abyss. Consequently, Salutati defines it as the expression of a Muse, thus advancing a thesis essentially antithetical to traditional metaphysics, whose point of departure is the problem of individual beings and their logical definition. Salutati grounds his thesis on the passion of the appeal of the abyss within which the meaning of every being emerges.

Salutati, however, points out that mere perception—the submersion of oneself in the ocean of perceptible phenomena—is not sufficient to acquire knowledge, *doctrina, scientia*. Two other human faculties are necessary. The first is memory, because we need to remember the *perceptum*, that which has been revealed by the sensory organs: . . . *parum est didicisse nisi commemores iam percepta, quintam Polimiam enumerat quasi "multa memorantem."*[29] Memory is represented by Polyhymnia, the Muse whose name, according to Salutati, signifies the ability to remember many things. What is being proposed is a form of remembering as *ri-cor-dare*, that is to say a return to the heart of the matter, or to its being.

But as Salutati observes—we limit ourselves to perceiving and remembering the essence of that which is manifest, if we halt before the phenomena, all our efforts to acquire *scientia* are futile. In fact, he who does not make the effort to find similarity among things is not yet a learned man: *Verum adhuc doctus non est qui ex his que perceperit nescit in similium inventionem erumpere.*[30] Erato is the Muse who presides over the finding of similarities (*similia inveniens*), who presides over knowledge and allows for the passage from the similar to the similar (*de similibus in similia se trasferre*).[31] Therefore, for those who wish to discover the essence of *scientia*, Erato's activity, which follows perception and memory, is absolutely decisive.

What is the meaning of finding, of discovering the *similitudo*? It is to provide the premise for the transfer of meanings, to discern the origin of *metapherein*, the very essence of poetic language. Thus, knowledge is grounded on metaphoric language, which pertains to the realm of poetry.

Salutati repeatedly stresses the "fascinating" effect of poetry, which depends on the fact that poetic language is metaphorical or transferred. The language of the poets separates men from that which the senses make manifest (*adeo revocavit a sensibus*) so that they believe in something completely different from that which they have perceived through their eyes (*quod ipsos id fecerit opinari cuius contrarium visibiliter percepissent*).[32]

What exactly triggers for Salutati the perception of *similitudines*, the perception of what different beings have in common? It is *ingenium*. It is the poet who reveals the historicity of our world (*ingenii altitudine*).[33]

Incidentally, in Salutati's thesis we find expressed what Vico, three centuries later, would consider the essence of the humanist tradition.

At this point we must ask ourselves what does the stimulus to learn consist of and in the realm of what type of experience does knowledge disclose itself? On the basis of our discussion, we must point out that only in passionate experience can we find a sign of the appeal of being addressed to all that becomes manifest. *Scientia* originates in the urgency of compelling, concrete questions: problems originate from man's historicity, in the situation determined by them. In this sense, the humanist tradition must be lauded for having cultivated philology in view of the understanding of our historical tradition. Humanist education has provided the image of man developing and shaping himself through the study of the meaning of words forever changing in accordance with the historical perspective within which words must be experienced. Now, to return to our initial statement regarding an ideal for teaching, we can reaffirm that such an ideal does not consist in the knowledge imparted by the teacher, nor is it a mere mnemonic exercise on the part of the student. Teaching must be based on a sense of wonder, or the emotion awakened by the text to be studied. It is a wonder which is nurtured by experiencing the changes of the meaning of the words in the act of interpretation. Only in this way can we be filled with wonder before the ingenious, inventive activity of writers who try to respond in various historical situations, to the different appeals of originary reality. Each work becomes thus a metaphor of the urgent appeal of originary reality, which we can identify only through the passionate experience of the Muse, characteristic of an essentially humanist tradition, and not by virtue of the *ratio*.

Notes

[1] *Meno*, 97d–98a.

[2] The reader is warned that "passion" and its derivatives are always meant etymologically (from the Latin *pati*) as a form of suffering (translators' note).

[3] Text and English translation by F. C. Babbit in *Plutarch's Moralia*, vol. 5 (Cambridge, MA: Harvard Univ. Press, 1936), 193–253.

[4] 387 a–b.

[5] 387 c.

[6] 385 c.

[7] *Theaetetus*, 155 d. English translation by F. M. Cornford in Plato, *The Collected Dialogues*, ed. E. Hamilton and H. Cairns (Princeton, NJ: Princeton Univ. Press, 1961).

[8] *Metaphysics* 982 b 12. English translation by W. D. Ross in *The Complete Works of Aristotle*, the revised Oxford translation, ed. J. Barnes (Princeton, NJ: Princeton Univ. Press, 1984).

[9] *Hesychii Alexandrini Lexicon*, ed. K. Latle (Hauniae: Ejnar Munksgaard, 1966), 2:308.

[10] H. Frisk, *Griechisches etymologisches Wörterbuch*, ed. H. Frisk (Heidelberg: 1960), 1:656.

[11] Homer, *Iliad* 18, 467 ff.; *Odyssey* 3, 373; 7, 145; 10, 326.

[12] Alcaeus, fr. 13 in *Poetae Lyrici Graeci*, ed. T. Bergk (Leipzig: 1882), vol. 3; fr. 8 in *Anthologica Lyrica*, vol. 4, *Poetae Melici*, ed. H. Diehl (Leipzig: 1923).

[13] *Metaphysics* 995 a 27–37.

[14] *Metaphysics* 1006 a 5.

[15] *Analytica Posteriora* 72 a 30ff. English translation by J. Barnes in *The Complete Works of Aristotle*.

[16] *Analytica Posteriora* 72 a 35.

[17] *Metaphysics* 1005 b 19.

[18] *Metaphysics* 1006 a 20.

[19] Aeschylus, *Prometheus Bound*, 105–106. English translation by P. Vellacott (Penguin Books, 1961).

[20] The reader is warned that "abyss" is here the equivalent of the German *Abgrund* understood etymologically as *ab-Grund* (translators' note).

[21] E. Grassi, *Renaissance Humanism: Studies in Philosophy and Poetics,* Medieval and Renaissance Texts and Studies, vol. 51 (Binghamton, NY, 1988).

[22] Coluccio Salutati, *De Laboribus Herculis*, ed. B. L. Ullman (Zurich: Thesauri Mundi, 1951).

[23] Salutati, I, 9, 11.

[24] Salutati, I, 9, 14.

[25] Salutati, I, 9, 10.

[26] Salutati, I, 9, 11.

[27] Salutati, I, 9, 12.

[28] Ibid.

[29] Ibid.

[30] Ibid.

[31] Ibid.

[32] Salutati, I, 1, 18.

[33] Salutati, II, *prima editio. Liber primus*, 587.

5

FOLLY AS A
PHILOSOPHICAL PROBLEM

Ernesto Grassi
Maristella Lorch

The Demands of Life

Human existence stands in the permanent necessity of coping with and organizing its environment. This environment within which the living being lives is identified by means of the phenomena which reveal themselves through the senses in different situations. What is unveiled by their activity counts as the answer to a demand of life. In the realm of organic life, there is a continuous transition from one demand to another.

The demands of life are unequivocal, and they follow each other according to an established, rigid plan which is the warranty of reality.

The living being proceeds through different, transitory stages in confronting the necessity of coping with and organizing the environment in different situations: in seeking nutrition, in reproduction. It passes from an environment that is no longer valid to surroundings that have implications which are not yet open or clear to it. But it is precisely in this process that the living being forms and shapes its own structure. If the living being fails in this task, it becomes ill and perishes.

But with man the situation is different than with other living beings. He encounters objects through his senses as things to be defined through language,

From *Folly and Insanity in Renaissance Literature* (1986). Binghamton, NY: Medieval & Renaissance Texts & Studies, pp. 35–48.

through "naming." This naming of beings—language—accompanies the need for an understanding of beings. Without it, all words and the beings themselves would be meaningless. That which acts, urges us, and makes itself known in the beings that appear to us, can be understood only if it is revealed in the light of language, of semantic signs.

The naming of beings, that is, the act of speaking, arises to meet a claim or a demand. The "word" thereby receives and obtains a principal function of meaning.

Here "reality" receives a double meaning. Reality in the "everyday" sense applies to the beings with which we live and act and about which we talk and reflect, i.e., it covers all those beings which capture our attention in everyday life. This is the "region" in which we emerge completely by the traditional meaning of words and the language into which we have been born; it is the "region" of our worries, hopes and anxieties.

Beings which appear to us through the senses become manifest to us within the frame of verbal *is, was* or *will be*, i.e., as temporal modalities of what we understand under the name of "Being." Hence not only are we obliged to ask ourselves what we mean by "Being" and how this "Being"— which is the origin of our speaking about beings—is structured; but with this question we also enter into the realm of an original reality upon which our "everyday" understanding of being depends. Therefore, this problem has its primacy vis-à-vis all the worries, hopes and anxieties that we have about beings in our "everyday" life.

Rational Thought

Traditional Western thought beginning with Socrates took its departure from the question of the Being of beings by means of a process of rational inference, discussing this topic in the context of the relationship between beings and thought taken as the problem of logical truth about beings. Ever since Aristotle, it has been maintained in traditional Western metaphysics that the object of knowledge is only that which "is"—what is as what is (ὄυ ᾗ ὄν)— namely that Being which is eternal (ἀΐδιον) and unmoving (ἀκίνητον). Traditional metaphysics affirms that everything is either a principle (ἀρχή) or follows from it as what is first and what governs. According to such an interpretation, true reality is deduced by a rational process from what is "original" or "first," from "Being" conceived as the highest thing that is, as that which truly is.

I have pointed out elsewhere[1] that neither when Descartes calls upon the "cogito" as an original axiom for the definition of knowledge, nor when Kant deduces knowledge from original forms of experience and thought, nor when Hegel gives an a priori dialectical deduction of the real, do we ever leave this model of rational thought. The apriorism of German Idealism was the final metaphysical conclusion of such a conception. For this reason the only scientific kind of language is the language of logic; rhetorical, poetic language is excluded from the framework of science, which includes philosophy and metaphysics. Rational thought claims to have a "hold" on the essence (οὐσία) of phenomena by means of the concept (ὅρος) and the definitions by which it can "grasp" it.

All empirical variations that are not general are unessential. Mere "human language," i.e., our ordinary language, which makes use of images, metaphors and analogies cannot claim to be scientific. This is why poetry belongs to literature and rhetoric is considered only an art of persuasion.

We speak, therefore, of "scientific" thinking or acting whenever a person is proceeding in a "rational" manner. The well-justified desire for "reasonableness" arises from the need of proceeding from a solid, well-established ground. The Greeks considered this starting-point the essence of ἐπιστήμη.

On the other hand, in everyday language we find that thinking, speaking, or acting without well-grounded reasons is judged as opinion (δόξα), or faulty knowledge, or folly; we never decide, thereby, whether in a specific case such behavior is just influenced by the power of passion, by some fault of knowledge or by the irrationality of folly. But traditional metaphysics is opposed by the whole of contemporary thought in the form of analytic philosophy and pure logic. These observe the rule that logical, well-founded thinking is possible exclusively within the frame of a "formal" system. Within such a formal system, proof is to be carried out by recourse to reasons, but there is no way of founding original reasons and, in this way, arriving at metaphysical assertions. First reasons are unprovable because of their nondeducible character. Every reference to the obviousness of first reasons, to their being *given* as a matter of fact, only leaves the door open for subjectivity, arbitrariness and mysticism. The reasons providing the exclusive starting-points of a certain system cannot be proved within and by the system itself, since it is through these reasons that the activity of demonstration within the system is made possible at all.

The reasonable world into which analytic philosophy puts us today turns out to be a purely formal one, and only as such is it sound, unbroken, and firmly within the frame of quite special limits.

In this case we are obliged to pose the following question: Is not purely formal activity without an ultimate reason, i.e., the "formal thinking" of analytic philosophy, itself nothing but insanity?

The Insufficiency of Causal Thinking

In the tradition of Western thought, from Socrates onward, philosophizing, as a form of knowledge, is identified with rational, causal thought. Therefore, the problem of logical truth is preeminent: in order to reach the latter, we have to adduce reasons for our own affirmations: logical demonstration, clarification consists precisely in this. The traditional model of rational thought includes the causal explanation: every phenomenon has a cause, and we understand reality when we can identify this cause. The process of progressive clarification by giving causes in their sequence brings one to the first or primal cause which provides the ultimate "meaning" of phenomena and, by thus explaining them, leads to the truth.

As a consequence, all myths, all poetry, all fictions—in as much as they are pure affirmation, simple narration—lose "scientific" meaning and fall to the level of fable, of literary narrative which is unable to attain the commanding height of rational, scientific concept.

But let us consider the structure of traditional causal explanation of the "meaning" of phenomena. This matter was posed in an exemplary way by Aristotle in the *Physics*. Aristotle explains the "becoming" of beings, their signification, with his theory of the four causes and contends that this theory provides a rational explanation of the meaning of beings.

Let me summarize here this traditional conception. The *material cause* constitutes the substratum of the becoming of beings, the original substructure of all change, which is formless (a-morphous) and, as such, an obscure ὕλη, the "dark wood," the *selva*, as the Greek term indicates. The *formal cause* determines this undifferentiated matter and thus allows it to appear within precise limits or borders. It is the form which clarifies the obscurity of the primitive original "dark wood." In order for matter to make this appearance, an efficient cause is necessary, an operating cause, a ποιεῖν, that realizes the form chosen from multiple possibilities. The concretion of the form, in view of which something takes place, reveals itself thus in its realization as the final cause. Traditional interpretation illustrates the outline of this rising and disappearing of beings with the example of the artist who bestows a form on passive matter with the final aim of making manifest the *idea* εἶδος = form) which he has in mind and which in this manner becomes concrete and is brought into the open.

The multiple possibilities of matter constitute the obscurity, the dark wood (ὕλη) in which the artist, for example, finds himself before the creative act which gives birth to the work. The form, the concept, the *idea* actively dominates and illuminates the passivity of matter. The efficient cause makes the concept concrete, since the final aim of the act is the realization of the *idea* that the artist, i.e., the creator, has found or invented (in the sense of *invenire*) something in his own mind. Without the invention, the forming of the idea or form, we would have no process of becoming in the sense of beings.

The problem now is: Can we grasp the *idea* on the basis of a rational causal explanation? What does the causal description of becoming explain? The cause is the *not yet* of the effect and, at the same time, its *no longer* once it has been realized. Causal relations show us only the temporal sequence of the moments of becoming, but never their meaning, their *idea*, for that cannot be deduced from the temporal sequence.

A sound that we explain as the effect of a cause (percussion) may have the meaning of a call or a warning; it may be the expression of fear or of joy. The model of the causal process thus proves to be totally abstract in its structure. In the traditional example of the artist the causal process by which the work comes about does not explain the birth of the work as *this* work rather than another. This is determined by the "invention" of the *idea*, and this "invention" is not rationally deducible from causal, temporal becoming.

Erasmus' Praise of Folly and Moria

In the foregoing reflections we noted that the environment of life is identified by means of the phenomena which our senses reveal to us and that, in the biological realm, this revelation counts as the response to the demands of life. Man, however, encounters what his sense organs reveal to him as something that is not immediately determined but is to be determined through language. The naming of beings does not just meet the demands of life, it meets the demands of Being.

Why do we now suddenly speak of the demand of "Being" instead of the demand of "life?" Because that which acts and urges and the respectively appearing beings can be understood only in the light of an understanding of the meanings of Being which cannot—as we said—be explained causally. It is said of every stone, of every plant, of man: It (or he or she) *is, was* or *will be*, i.e., the "naming" of the beings—language—occurs to meet the demand for an understanding of the meaning of Being. Without it, all words and the beings themselves would be meaningless.

Comprehension of Being cannot be deduced through an abstraction from beings, because we must first know the meaning of Being in order to recognize beings. Furthermore, if the original horizon for revealing the meaning of beings is neither deducible nor comprehensible through rational, causal thinking, then we might recognize that the manifestation of beings—in the realm where we live, act and think—is rooted in an original area that is not rational.

The task of thought consists then in delimiting the area in which beings originally have their significance. Such a project entails seeing beings in regard to the power of the claim in the light of which our "being-in-the-world" is first revealed and realized.

This justifies two tasks: philosophy's essential claim can no longer be directed to "logical truth" but strictly to the "unconcealedness" of beings. Second, when the original form by which beings become manifest is not rational, not deducible, not causal, then such a manifestation of beings—in the realm where we live and act and think—corresponds to the German expression *Wahn* [*illusion* or *folly*]. Kluge's etymological dictionary refers us for the expression *Wahn* to the Middle High German "wān": hope, expectation. The Gothic word "wēns" (hope) indicates also the Germanic "wāēni," "wānō," (expectation). The root "uēn," to strive (for), is connected with "gewinnen" (to win), "gewöhnen" (to be accustomed), "Wonne" (delight) and "Wunsch" (wish, desire). Corresponding to these, Kluge stresses that this root has a parallel meaning in the non-Germanic languages for the words "wánati," "wanóti," "wünscht" in the Latin word "venus" which means love or charm. [2] "Wahn" is the expression of power of a claim under which man lives, and it is in this sense that the Greeks speak of "divine mania." Sophocles, full of awareness of such a cognition, writes: "All forebodings may take place when the god sends such a storm".[3]

Can we find in Western philosophy a thinker who treats the question we have hinted at, who allows us to comprehend more deeply the problem of "folly" in its philosophical significance? We can, in the humanist Erasmus' *Moriae Encomium*. Erasmus composed his work during his return from Rome to the North in the summer of 1509. The occasion for writing was really his desire to avoid the danger of being "overwhelmed" during his journey by unmusical and illiterate conversations, as he asserts in his introductory dedication to his friend Thomas More [ἀμούσοις et illiteratis fabulis].[4]

The occasion of this work, apparently, is unscientific or even playful from the traditional point of view. It was written as a jeu d'esprit, an "ingenii nostri lusum." He plays on the association deriving from the name of his friend Thomas More, to whom the work is dedicated, and the Greek term *μωρός*:

> admonuit me Mori cognomen tibi gentile, quod tam ad Moriae vocabulum accedit.[5]

The traditional interpretation tells us that this work is a satire on man and the society of the time. The Latin title *Stultitiae laus* seems to justify this interpretation, because the term "stultus" is an adjective which indicates a human attitude. In the view of such an interpretation, the work seems to have no fundamental philosophical content: it should be understood rather as an historical, critical writing on an epoch.

However, to understand the problem of this treatise, we are obliged to ask what the term *moria* originally meant and how this meaning changes historically.

The Greek word μωρός means *dull, stupid, thick*, and indicates a physical or mental defect in a person. The word is usually used psychologically and mentally in a deprecatory manner. It refers to a general inferiority in thinking and behaving. By *μωρία*, man falls under a ruling power which confuses his mind and induces him to "crazy" or "insane" actions.[6] In the Greek version of the Old Testament—especially in the Proverbs and in the Book of Wisdom—μωρός is used to designate the person who lacks φρόνησις, i.e., one who is ἄφρων. As a consequence, he does not come either to the intelligence of God or to any other reasonable knowledge. He is a person who does not see with his own seeing eyes and does not hear with his own hearing ears.[7]

In the New Testament, specifically in the writings of St. Paul, the term *μωρία* (and *stultitia* in Jerome's version) undergoes a deep-rooted change of meaning. A radical conversion occurs in First Corinthians. Worldly wisdom for St. Paul means *stultitia* before God[8] and at this point the term keeps its original, negative significance. The Christian faith, however, is ridiculed as stupidity by the philosophers in Athens—i.e., by the wisdom of this world. Against these philosophers Paul polemically identifies μωρία with true, original knowledge: it is precisely the Christians who, because of their faith, pass for *stulti* in the eyes of the world. What is rejected as *stultitia* in the opinion of the Greek scholars is raised by Paul to the sign of true knowledge.[9] The

Christian admonition, therefore, is: The one who tries to be "wise" will appear *stultus* in the eyes of his fellows in life and society.

"Moria" on the Stage of World History

The term *moria* acquires new meaning in the work of Erasmus. *Moria* for Erasmus has a fundamental meaning which holds *not only for the range of the human world*, as it would if we understood *stultitia* only as a human condition and the *Praise of Folly* only as a satirical critique of the society of his time. He affirms that *moria* is the deeper root of the *unveiling of all beings* and, by its undeducibility and nonrationatity, an abysmal folly which has nothing to do with a subjective insanity. *Through its power the world appears*.

Moria is explicitly identified by Erasmus with that divinity in whose claim *all beings* are revealed. It is a power which "extends so widely" and cannot be circumscribed "within the narrow limits of a definition, because "it enjoys the combined worship of all kinds of creatures" [. . . cuius numen tam late pateat . . . in cuius cultum omne rerum genus ita consentiat]. [10]

Under the banner of *Moria* "all degrees of life," and not only man, reveal themselves. Thus, Erasmus tells of and explicitly underlines—something his interpreters do not sufficiently understand—*brutorum ingenium stulticiamque*,[11] stressing especially that these beings are happy exactly because they comply with the original plan of life as it is designed by *Moria*. An interpretation of the *Praise of Folly* as merely a treatise on the folly of mankind does not correspond to Erasmus' own assertions about the text.

Moria—in whose sign things "clear up"—is born, according to her own testimony,

> in the Isles of the Blest, where everything grows without effort—*they plough not, nor do they sow*. In those isles there is no work, no age, no disease. [16]

> in ipsis insulis fortunatis, ubi ἄσπαρτα καὶ ἀνήροτα omnia proveniunt. In quibus neque labor, neque senium, neque morbus est ullus. [78]

Here is the power of eternal nature!

Moria appeals to its propitious activity and respective utility for man, and pretends for this reason to be a goddess. This is a function as described by Pliny[12] which must be attributed to the divine as one of the characteristics it should have. In such a manner *Moria* demonstrates its reality and claims for itself the corresponding recognition against those who are of the opinion that it does not deserve such an honor:

> Now, lest my claim to divinity should seem unsubstantiated, listen carefully and I will show you how many benefits I bestow on gods and men alike and how widely my divine power extends. . . . The essence of divinity is to give aid to mortals. [17]

> Nunc, ne cui sine causa videar mihi deae nomen usurpare, quantis commoditatibus deos simul et homines adficiam quamque late meum

pateat numen, arrectis auribus accipite. . . . Hoc demum esse deum, iuvare mortales. [80]

Erasmus polemically asserts that *Moria*, as the original force and guide governing the world and as the power in whose claim beings are revealed, does not need temples and worship; and this is an essential difference between the cult of Folly and all ancient and modern religions:

> Furthermore, why should I want a temple, since the *whole world*, unless I am badly mistaken, is a *splendid temple dedicated to me?* . . . I consider that I am being worshipped with the truest devotion when men everywhere do precisely what they now do: embrace me in their hearts, express me in their conduct, represent me in their lives [75; italics mine].

> Praeterea cur templum desiderem, cum *orbis hic universus templum mihi sit*, ni fallor, *pulcherrimum?* . . . Ego me tum religiosisissime coli puto, cum passim (ut faciunt omnes) animo complectuntur, moribus exprimunt, vita repraesentant [134; italics mine].

The recognition of *Moria* has its roots in the hearts of man:

> Why should I need a bit of incense or grain or a goat or a hog, when all mortals everywhere in the world worship me with the kind of homage that even the theologians rank highest of all? [75]

> Quid enim est cur tusculum aut molam aut hircum aut suem requiram, cum mihi mortales omnes ubique gentium eum cultum persolvant, qui vel a theologis maxime probari solet? [134]

The main concern of Erasmus' *Encomium* resides in this question: What becomes manifest in the claim of *Moria*? By the claim of *Moria* the "stage" opens up on which the scene of world history is set. This problem does not deal with the question of traditional metaphysics, i.e., with logical truth, in order to deduce the determination of beings from it. What Erasmus reveals is not discussed in the manner of a traditional, rational treatise, but rather in the form of a narration, a tale, and a rhetorical one at that, for this narrative is also an oration. It is a eulogy, which is one of the three forms of rhetorical speech; at the same time its irony is a form of metaphor. Is this form of speech merely *belles-lettres* or does it have a principal and clear theoretical significance? We will return to this problem later. But what is the difference between folly as we have interpreted it and insanity?

Insanity and Folly

In the traditional view folly is interpreted as schizophrenia, a species of insanity; it is interpreted in an absolutely different way than *moria* and the problem which we pointed out as the question of how and by what means beings appear. Insanity as schizophrenia is considered as the loss of vital contact with the reality that constitutes one's proper surroundings or environment, while other mental faculties, such as memory and intelligence, are neither changed nor lost.

This loss of contact with reality is said to be the loss of contact with the environment of the individual person. Without a relation to the specific environment, man is not capable of survival. E. Minkowski argues:

> The vital contact with reality concerns above all the ground or essence of the living person in its relation to the environment. . . . Events emerge from it like small islands and they convulse the most intimate sides of our person. And this, our person, in its turn, vibrates like a taut string in unison with them. Our person penetrates the environment and reacts to it in such a manner that it adds the elements of its inner life to the surroundings.[13]

What is here called the environment does not indicate an "external" space, objectively existing in itself, to which "inner life" is added. Rather, there is a very close relation between the subject and its environment: the two interact. In this close relation of environment to inner life something particular happens. There appears the stage of a "theater"—in the original sense of the Greek expression, θέατρου from θεάομαι as the space of "vision" in which we as actors live, act and reflect.

In his tragedy *Ajax*, Sophocles analyzes all the steps in such an insanity. After the conquest of Troy Ajax does not receive the arms of the dead Achilles as a sign of appreciation of his valor. Ajax's ambition, his desire for recognition, is deeply hurt; his victory in life, within his community and his kinship, is frustrated. Ajax plans to take revenge by killing Odysseus and Agamemnon. He starts out on his way from his tent by night to commit the murder. In order to protect Odysseus, however, Athena confuses the mind of Ajax, who sets upon a herd of cattle and in his insanity carries out a senseless massacre. By this insanity the goddess preserves Ajax from spilling blood by assassination; when he later regains his consciousness, Ajax feels cruelly dishonored. The price he pays for his insanity is suicide.

There is a double tragedy in the insanity of Ajax caused by a double suffering. The schizophrenic state overcomes him like a wave that completely changes and transforms reality, the environment. Suddenly, things lose their inter-relations. The interstices between things are suddenly void, and he stands at a place which he does not experience any longer as a "real" place. Time loses its existential tension, shrinking together in the slackness of a lack of expectations. Ajax feels abandoned and expects something hopeless; he finds himself at the brink of an abyss: death as the end, not as redemption. The environment to which he has been accustomed is slowly replaced by another which may be perceived in those signs that we attribute to insanity. This new environment extinguishes the preceding reality.

The experience of such a state is completed by the continuous, possessive comparison between the two environments, one's "own" and the "normal" one. This comparison is dominated by the negative, or even destructive, judgement about the supposedly "normal" environment. Therefore, the concern, if not urge, to come to grips exclusively with the beings that surround one in order to make an exception for oneself in the everyday world seems to be the effect of an unrealistic "folly." In this condition of insanity, the power of life as we normally experience it appears to be senseless.

Such an experience causes a double suffering. The first, hopeless suffering is that of being entangled in a world of beings, in a world whose meaning has disappeared. All attempts to assert oneself in this environment, which has become totally insecure, must fail, and fatigue is the consequence. The second suffering derives from the consciousness that this calamity does not strike from "outside" (possibly caused by an event that is happening to oneself), but arises from one's own "inner" world. Not only that: Such a person experiences and celebrates with horror in his own state of existence the "unmasking" of life which is felt to be the expression of an "empty" power, an "empty" claim.

Sophocles' *Ajax* has shown this double tragedy by the insanity of the hero and his awakening from it, his deeply hurt ambition due to his failure. This attempted self-assertion, the vehement attempt to prove his ability to assert his being, catapulted him into the wrong ways of frenzy. He loses his relation to his environment. He suffers from the loss of his own identity. Once awakened from insanity, he compares the two environments and does not know any longer where his place is, where he is. His honor is definitively lost, and the only solution to this experience for him is suicide. This is the meaning of Sophocles' verses:

> Ajax, so long as the mad fit was on him,
> Himself felt joy at all his wretchedness,
> Though we, his sane companions, grieved indeed.
> But now that he's recovered and breathes clear,
> His own anguish totally masters him,
> While we are no less wretched than before.
> Is not this a redoubling of our grief?[14]

* * * * *

We can now distinguish "insanity" from "folly" (*Wahn*). Insanity takes place whenever man is incapable of meeting that which we can name the claim of Being. This is always manifest for man in a concrete situation, urging him to the appropriate response so as to meet the claim made on him. The "situation" in which man respectively finds himself determines his "environment." Therefore, insanity is the incapacity of "getting down" to things, of arranging things in the right manner, having the ends meet with respect to the environment. It is an illness: the insanity of Ajax.

Folly as *insanity*, as a *sickness*, means that the individual moves exclusively in the circle of his subjectivity, and it is exactly this of which the "unearthly" consists, because man does not find himself any longer within the horizon which comprehends Being as his original "home." It is no longer the real that reveals itself to him, but the terrifying form of pure subjectivity as the incapacity to meet the claim of *moria*. The unity of the contingent beings with Being, which reveals itself in the concrete situation, opens up the immense "stage" of the world with all the unfolding of all its dramas, with all the actions contained in it.

Notes

[1] Ernesto Grassi, *Rhetoric as Philosophy: The Humanist Tradition* (University Park, Pa.: Pennsylvania State University Press, 1980); see also E. Grassi, "Humanism and Heidegger's Thesis of the End of Philosophy," *Philosophy and Rhetoric* 13, no. 2 (Spring 1980): 79–98.

[2] Friedrich Kluge, ed. *Etymologisches Wörterbuch der Deutschen Sprache* (Berlin, 1900; rpt. 1963), p. 833.

[3] *Oedipus Colonus*, 1504.

[4] Desiderius Erasmus, "Prefatory Letter to Thomas More" in *The Praise of Folly*, trans. Clarence H. Miller (New Haven: Yale Univ. Press, 1979), p. 1 [=*Folly*]. Citations (slightly normalized) to the Latin text are to the critical edition by Clarence H. Miller in *Opera omnia Desiderii Erasmi Roterodami* (Amsterdam: North Holland, 1979), vol. 4 [=*Moria*]: Citations are also given in the text.

[5] *Folly*, p. 2.

[6] See Sophocles, *Ajax*, 594; Euripides, *Hippolytus*, 964.

[7] Jeremiah 5:21.

[8] I Cor. 3:19, "Sapientia enim huius mundi, stultitia est apud Deum."

[9] "Verbum enim crucis pereuntibus quidem stultitia est. . . . Si quis videtur inter vos sapiens esse . . ., stultus fiat ut sit sapiens. . . . Nos stulti propter Christum." I Cor. 1:18; 3:18; 4:10. See also 2:14.

[10] *Folly*, p. 13; *Moria*, p. 74.

[11] *Moria*, p. 113.

[12] Pliny *Natural History*, transl. H. Rackham, Loeb Classical Library (London, 1938; rpt. 1944), 2.5.18.

[13] Eugene Minkowski, *La Schizophrénie* (Paris, 1937), p. 62.

[14] *Ajax*, trans. John Moore, in *The Complete Greek Tragedies*, ed. David Grene and Richmond Lattimore (Chicago, 1957; rpt. New York, 1967), 271–77.

6

THE NEW RHETORIC
A THEORY OF
PRACTICAL REASONING

Chaïm Perelman

The Loss of a Humanistic Tradition.—The last two years of secondary education in Belgium used to be called traditionally "Poetry" and "Rhetoric." I still remember that, over forty years ago, I had to study the "Elements of Rhetoric" for a final high-school examination, and I learned more or less by heart the contents of a small manual, the first part of which concerned the syllogism and the second the figures of style. Later, in the university, I took a course of logic which covered, among other things, the analysis of the syllogism. I then learned that logic is a formal discipline that studies the structure of hypothetico-deductive reasoning. Since then I have often wondered what link a professor of rhetoric could possibly discover between the syllogism and the figures of style with their exotic names that are so difficult to remember.

Lack of clarity concerning the idea of rhetoric is also apparent in the article on the subject in the *Encyclopædia Britannica*, where rhetoric is defined as "the use of language as an art based on a body of organized knowledge." But what does this mean? The technique or art of language in general, or only that of literary prose as distinct from poetry? Must rhetoric be conceived of as the art of oratory—that is, as the art of public speaking? The author of the article notes that for Aristotle rhetoric is the art of persuasion.

Reprinted with permission from *The Great Ideas Today* © 1970 by Encyclopædia Britannica, Inc.

We are further told that the orator's purpose, according to Cicero's definition, is to instruct, to move, and to please. Quintilian sums up this view in his lapidary style as *ars bene dicendi*, the art of speaking well. This phrase can refer either to the efficacy, or the morality, or the beauty of a speech, this ambiguity being both an advantage and a drawback.

For those of us who have been educated in a time when rhetoric has ceased to play an essential part in education, the idea of rhetoric has been definitely associated with the "flowers of rhetoric"—the name used for the figures of style with their learned and incomprehensible names. This tradition is represented by two French authors, César Chesneau, sieur Dumarsais, and Pierre Fontanier, who provided the basic texts for teaching what was taken for rhetoric in the eighteenth and nineteenth centuries. The work of Dumarsais, which first appeared in 1730 and enjoyed an enormous success, is entitled *Concerning tropes or the different ways in which one word can be taken in a language*.[1] Fontanier's book, reprinted in 1968 under the title *The figures of discourse*, unites in one volume two works, which appeared respectively in 1821 and 1827, under the titles *A classical manual for the study of tropes* and *Figures other than tropes*.[2]

These works are the outcome of what might be called the stylistic tradition of rhetoric, which was started by Omer Talon, the friend of Petrus Ramus, in his two books on rhetoric published in 1572. The extraordinary influence of Ramus hindered, and to a large extent actually destroyed, the tradition of classical rhetoric that had been developed over the course of twenty centuries and with which are associated the names of such writers as Aristotle, Cicero, Quintilian, and St. Augustine.

For the ancients, rhetoric was the theory of persuasive discourse and included five parts: *inventio, dispositio, elocutio, memoria,* and *actio.* The first part dealt with the art of finding the materials of discourse, especially arguments, by using common or specific *loci*—the *topoi* studied in works which, following Aristotle's example, were called *Topics*.[3] The second part gave advice on the purposive arrangement or order of discourse, the *method*, as the Renaissance humanists called it. The third part dealt mainly with style, the choice of terms and phrases; the fourth with the art of memorizing the speech; while the fifth concerned the art of delivering it.

Ramus also worked for the reform of logic and dialectic along the lines laid down by Rodolphus Agricola in his *De inventione dialectica* (1479) and by the humanists who followed him in seeking to break away from scholastic formalism by restoring the union of eloquence and philosophy advocated by Cicero. This reform consisted essentially in rejecting the classical opposition between science and opinion that had led Aristotle to draw a distinction between analytical and dialectical reasoning—the former dealing with necessary reasonings, the latter with probable ones. Analytical reasoning is the concern of Aristotle's *Analytics*,[4] dialectical reasoning that of the *Topics, On Sophistical Refutations*, and the *Rhetoric*.[5]

Against this distinction, this is what Ramus has to say in his *Dialectic*:

> Aristotle, or more precisely the exponents of Aristotle's theories, thought that there are two arts of discussion and reasoning, one applying to science and called Logic, the other dealing with opinion and called Dialectic. In this—with all due respect to such great masters—they were greatly mistaken. Indeed these two names, Dialectic and Logic, generally mean the very same thing, like the words *dialegesthai* and *logizesthai* from which they are derived and descended, that is, dispute or reason. . . . Furthermore, although things known are either necessary and scientific, or contingent and a matter of opinion, just as our sight can perceive all colors, both unchanging and changeable, in the same way the art of knowing, that is Dialectic or Logic, is one and the same doctrine of reasoning well about anything whatsoever. . . . [6]

As a result of this rejection, Ramus unites in his *Dialectic* what Aristotle had separated. He divides his work into two parts, one concerning invention, the other judgment. Further, he includes in dialectic parts that were formerly regarded as belonging to rhetoric: the theory of invention or *loci* and that of disposition, called *method*. Memory is considered as merely a reflection of these first two parts, and rhetoric—the "art of speaking well," of "eloquent and ornate language"—includes the study of tropes, of figures of style, and of oratorical delivery, all of which are considered as of lesser importance.

Thus was born the tradition of modern rhetoric, better called stylistic, as the study of techniques of unusual expression. For Fontanier, as we have seen, rhetoric is reduced to the study of figures of style, which he defines as "the more or less remarkable traits and forms, the phrases with a more or less happy turn, by which the expression of ideas, thoughts, and feelings removes the discourse more or less far away from what would have been its simple, common expression." [7]

Rhetoric, on this conception, is essentially an art of expression and, more especially, of literary conventionalized expression; it is an art of style. So it is still regarded by Jean Paulhan in his book *Les fleurs de Tarbes ou la terreur dans les lettres* (1941, but published first as articles in 1936).

The same view of rhetoric was taken in Italy during the Renaissance, despite the success of humanism. Inspired by the Ciceronian ideal of the union of philosophy with eloquence, humanists such as Lorenzo Valla sought to unite dialectic and rhetoric. But they gave definite primacy to rhetoric, thus expressing their revolt against scholastic formalism.

This humanistic tradition continued for over a century and finally produced in the *De principiis* by Mario Nizolio (1553) its most significant work from a philosophical point of view. Less than ten years later, however, in 1562, Francesco Patrizi published in his *Rhetoric* the most violent attack upon this discipline, to which he denied any philosophical interest whatsoever. Giambattista Vico's reaction came late and produced no immediate result. Rhetoric became a wholly formal discipline—any living ideas that it contained being included in Aesthetics.

Germany is one country where classical rhetoric has continued to be carefully studied, especially by scholars such as Friedrich Blass, Wilhelm

Kroll, and Friedrich Solmsen, who devoted most of their lives to this study. Yet, even so, rhetoric has been regarded only as the theory of literary prose. Heinrich Lausberg has produced a most remarkable work, which is the best tool in existence for the study of rhetorical terminology and the structure of discourse, and yet in the author's own eyes it is only a contribution to the study of literary language and tradition.[8]

The old tradition of rhetoric has been kept longest in Great Britain—it is still very much alive among Scots jurists—-thanks to the importance of psychology in the empiricism of Bacon, Locke, and Hume, and to the influence of the Scottish philosophy of common sense. This tradition, in which the theory of invention is reduced to a minimum and interest is focused on the persuasive aspect of discourse, is represented by such original works as George Campbell's *The Philosophy of Rhetoric* (1776) and Richard Whately's *Elements of Rhetoric* (1828). In this work, Whately, who was a logician, deals with argumentative composition in general and the art of establishing the truth of a proposition so as to convince others, rhetoric being reduced to "a purely managerial or supervisory science."[9] His disciple, the future Cardinal John Henry Newman, applied Whately's ideas to the problems of faith in his *Grammar of Assent* (1870). This outlook still consists in seeing in rhetoric only a theory of expression. It was the view adopted by Ivor Armstrong Richards in his *Principles of Literary Criticism* (published in 1924) and in his *Philosophy of Rhetoric* (1936).

While in Europe rhetoric has been reduced to stylistics and literary criticism, becoming merely a part of the study of literature insofar as it was taught at all, in the United States the appearance of a speech profession brought about a unique development.

Samuel Silas Curry, in a book entitled *The Province of Expression* (1891), was the first to emphasize spoken discourse and its delivery, rather than the composition of literary prose, and to claim autonomy for speech as opposed to written composition. "Expression," as he understood it, did not mean the way in which ideas and feelings are expressed in a literary form, but instead the manner in which they are communicated by means of an art of "delivery." Concern for this element, apparently one of lesser importance, clearly reveals a renewed interest in the audience, and this interest helped to promote the creation of a new "speech profession," separate from the teaching of English and of English literature. Under the influence of William James, James Albert Winans published a volume entitled *Public Speaking* (1915) that firmly established a union between professors of speech and those of psychology. With the cooperation of specialists in ancient and medieval rhetoric, such as Charles S. Baldwin, Harry Caplan, Lane Cooper, Everett Lee Hunt, and Richard McKeon, the whole tradition of classical rhetoric has been retraced. This study has been continued and further developed in the works of Wilbur Samuel Howell, Donald C. Bryant, Karl R. Wallace, Walter J. Ong, Lloyd F. Bitzer, Douglas Ehninger, and Marie K. Hochmuth. The work of these scholars—the titles of which can be found in the Bibliography that has been regularly published by the *Quarterly Journal of Speech* since 1915—constitutes a unique achievement which is as yet too little known outside the United States.[10]

An Ornamental or a Practical Art?

There is nothing of philosophical interest in a rhetoric that has turned into an art of expression, whether literary or verbal.[11] Hence it is not surprising that the term is missing entirely from both André Lalande's *Vocabulaire technique et critique de la philosophie* and the recent American *Encyclopedia of Philosophy* (1967). In the Western tradition, "Rhetoric" has frequently been identified with verbalism and an empty, unnatural, stilted mode of expression. Rhetoric then becomes the symbol of the most outdated elements in the education of the old regime, the elements that were the most formal, most useless, and most opposed to the needs of an equalitarian, progressive democracy.

This view of rhetoric as declamation—ostentatious and artificial discourse—is not a new one. The same view was taken of the rhetoric of the Roman Empire. Once serious matters, both political and judiciary, had been withdrawn from its influence, rhetoric became perforce limited to school exercises, to set speeches treating either a theme of the past or an imaginary situation, but, in any case, one without any real bearing. Serious people, especially the Stoics, made fun of it. Thus Epictetus declares: "But this facility of speaking and of ornamenting words, if there is indeed any such peculiar faculty, what else does it do, when there happens to be discourse about a thing, than to ornament the words and arrange them as hairdressers do the hair?"[12]

Aristotle would have disagreed with this conception of rhetoric as an ornamental art bearing the same relation to prose as poetics does to verse. For Aristotle, rhetoric is a practical discipline that aims, not at producing a work of art, but at exerting through speech a persuasive action on an audience. Unfortunately, however, those responsible for the confusion between the two have been able to appeal to Aristotle's own authority because of the misleading analysis he gave of the epideictic or ceremonial form of oratory.

In his *Rhetoric* Aristotle distinguishes three genres of oratory: deliberative, forensic, and ceremonial. "Political speaking," he writes, "urges us either to do or not to do something: one of these two courses is always taken by private counsellors, as well as by men who address public assemblies. Forensic speaking either attacks or defends somebody: one or other of these two things must always be done by the parties in a case. The ceremonial oratory of display either praises or censures somebody." But whereas the audience is supposed to act as a judge and make a decision concerning either the future (deliberative genre) or the past (forensic genre), in the case of an epideictic discourse the task of the audience consists in judging, not about the matter of discourse, but about the orator's skill.[13] In political and forensic discourse the subject of the discourse is itself under discussion, and the orator aims at persuading the audience to take part in deciding the matter, but

in epideictic discourse the subject—such as, for example, the praise of sol-
diers who have died for their country—is not at all a matter of debate. Such
set speeches were often delivered before large assemblies, as at the Olympic
Games, where competition between orators provided a welcome complement to the athletic contests. On such occasions, the only decision that the
audience was called upon to make concerned the talent of the orator, by
awarding the crown to the victor.

One might well ask how an oratorical genre can be defined by its literary
imitation. We know that Cicero, after having lost the suit, rewrote his *Pro
Milone* and published it as a literary work. He hoped that by artistically improving the speech, which had failed to convince Milo's judges, he might
gain the approbation of lovers of literature. Are those who read this speech
long after its practical bearing has disappeared any more than spectators? In
that case, all discourses automatically become literature once they cease to
exert a persuasive effect, and there is no particular reason to distinguish different genres of oratory. Yet it can be maintained, on the contrary, that the
epideictic genre is not only important but essential from an educational
point of view, since it too has an effective and distinctive part to play—that,
namely, of bringing about a consensus in the minds of the audience regarding the values that are celebrated in the speech.

The moralists rightly satirize the view of epideictic oratory as spectacle.
La Bruyère writes derisively of those who "are so deeply moved and touched
by Theodorus's sermon that they resolve in their hearts that it is even more
beautiful than the last one he preached." And Bossuet, fearful lest the real
point of a sermon be missed, exclaims: "You should now be convinced that
preachers of the Gospel do not ascend into pulpits to utter empty speeches
to be listened to for amusement."[14]

Bossuet here is following St. Augustine's precepts concerning sacred discourse as set forth in the fourth book of his work *On Christian Doctrine*. The
orator is not content if his listener merely accepts the truth of his words and
praises his eloquence, because he wants his full assent:

> If the truths taught are such that to believe or to know them is enough,
> to give one's assent implies nothing more than to confess that they are
> true. When, however, the truth taught is one that must be carried into
> practice, and that is taught for the very purpose of being practised, it is
> useless to be persuaded of the truth of what is said, it is useless to be
> pleased with the manner in which it is said, if it be not so learnt as to be
> practised. The eloquent divine, then, when he is urging a practical truth,
> must not only teach so as to give instruction, and please so as to keep up
> the attention, but he must also sway the mind so as to subdue the will.

The listener will be persuaded, Augustine also claims,

> if he be drawn by your promises, and awed by your threats; if he reject
> what you condemn, and embrace what you commend; if he grieve when
> you heap up objects for grief, and rejoice when you point out an object for

joy; if he pity those whom you present to him as objects of pity, and shrink from those whom you set before him as men to be feared and shunned.[15]

The orator's aim in the epideictic genre is not just to gain a passive adherence from his audience but to provoke the action wished for or, at least, to awaken a disposition so to act. This is achieved by forming a community of minds, which Kenneth Burke, who is well aware of the importance of this genre, calls *identification*. As he writes, rhetoric "is rooted in an essential function of language itself, a function that is wholly realistic and is continually born anew; the use of language as a symbolic means of inducing cooperation in beings that by nature respond to symbols."[16] In fact, any persuasive discourse seeks to have an effect on an audience, although the audience may consist of only one person and the discourse be an inward deliberation.

The distinction of the different genres of oratory is highly artificial, as the study of a speech shows. Mark Antony's famous speech in Shakespeare's *Julius Caesar*[17] opens with a funeral eulogy, a typical case of epideictic discourse, and ends by provoking a riot that is clearly political. Its goal is to intensify an adherence to values, to create a disposition to act, and finally to bring people to act. Seen in such perspective, rhetoric becomes a subject of great philosophical interest.

Thinking about Values

In 1945, when I published my first study of justice,[18] I was completely ignorant of the importance of rhetoric. This study, undertaken in the spirit of logical empiricism, succeeded in showing that *formal justice* is a principle of action, according to which beings of one and the same essential category must be treated in the same way.[19] The application of this principle to actual situations, however, requires criteria to indicate which categories are relevant and how their members should be treated, and such decisions involve a recourse to judgments of value. But on positivistic methods I could not see how such judgments could have any foundation or justification. Indeed, as I entirely accepted the principle that one cannot draw an "ought" from an "is"— a judgment of value from a judgment of fact—I was led inevitably to the conclusion that if justice consists in the systematic implementation of certain value judgments, it does not rest on any rational foundation: "As for the value that is the foundation of the normative system, we cannot subject it to any rational criterion: it is utterly arbitrary and logically indeterminate.... The idea of value is, in effect, incompatible both with formal necessity and with experiential universality. There is no value which is not logically arbitrary."[20]

I was deeply dissatisfied with this conclusion, however interesting the analysis, since the philosophical inquiry, carried on within the limits of logical empiricism, could not provide an ideal of practical reason, that is, the establishment of rules and models for reasonable action. By admitting the soundness of Hume's analysis, I found myself in a situation similar to Kant's.

If Hume is right in maintaining that empiricism cannot provide a basis for either science or morals, must we not then look to other than empirical methods to justify them? Similarly, if experience and calculation, combined according to the precepts of logical empiricism, leave no place for practical reason and do not enable us to justify our decisions and choices, must we not seek other techniques of reasoning for that purpose? In other words, is there a logic of value judgments that makes it possible for us to reason about values instead of making them depend solely on irrational choices, based on interest, passion, prejudice, and myth? Recent history has shown abundantly the sad excesses to which such an attitude can lead.

Critical investigation of the philosophical literature yielded no satisfactory results. The French logician Edmond Goblot, in his work *La logique des jugements de valeur*,[21] restricted his analysis to derived or instrumental value judgments, that is, to those judgments that use values as a means to already accepted ends, or as obstacles to their attainment. The ends themselves, however, could not be subjected to deliberation unless they were transformed into instrumental values, but such a transformation only pushes further back the problem of ultimate ends.

We thus seem to be faced with two extreme attitudes, neither of which is acceptable: subjectivism, which, as far as values are concerned, leads to skepticism for lack of an intersubjective criterion; or an absolutism founded on intuitionism. In the latter case, judgments of value are assimilated to judgments of a reality that is *sui generis*. In other words, must we choose between A. J. Ayer's view in *Language, Truth, and Logic* and G. E. Moore's view in *Principia Ethica*? Both seem to give a distorted notion of the actual process of deliberation that leads to decision making in practical fields such as politics, law, and morals.

Then too, I agreed with the criticisms made by various types of existentialism against both positivist empiricism and rationalistic idealism, but I could find no satisfaction in their justification of action by purely subjective projects or commitments.

I could see but one way to solve the dilemma to which most currents of contemporary philosophy had led. Instead of working out *a priori* possible structures for a logic of value judgments, might we not do better to follow the method adopted by the German logician Gottlob Frege, who, to cast new light on logic, decided to analyze the reasoning used by mathematicians? Could we not undertake, in the same way, an extensive inquiry into the manner in which the most diverse authors in all fields do in fact reason about values? By analyzing political discourse, the reasons given by judges, the reasoning of moralists, the daily discussions carried on in deliberating about making a choice or reaching a decision or nominating a person, we might be able to trace the actual logic of value judgments which seems continually to elude the grasp of specialists in the theory of knowledge.

For almost ten years Mme L. Olbrechts-Tyteca and I conducted such an inquiry and analysis. We obtained results that neither of us had ever expected. Without either knowing or wishing it, we had rediscovered a part of

Aristotelian logic that had been long forgotten or, at any rate, ignored and despised. It was the part dealing with dialectical reasoning, as distinguished from demonstrative reasoning—called by Aristotle *analytics*—which is analyzed at length in the *Rhetoric*, *Topics*, and *On Sophistical Refutations*. We called this new, or revived, branch of study, devoted to the analysis of informal reasoning, *The New Rhetoric*.[22]

Argumentation and Demonstration

The new rhetoric is a theory of argumentation. But the specific part that is played by argumentation could not be fully understood until the modern theory of demonstration—to which it is complementary—had been developed. In its contemporary form, demonstration is a calculation made in accordance with rules that have been laid down beforehand. No recourse is allowed to evidence or to any intuition other than that of the senses. The only requirement is the ability to distinguish signs and to perform operations according to rules. A demonstration is regarded as correct or incorrect according as it conforms, or fails to conform, to the rules. A conclusion is held to be demonstrated if it can be reached by means of a series of correct operations starting from premises accepted as axioms. Whether these axioms be considered as evident, necessary, true, or hypothetical, the relation between them and the demonstrated theorems remains unchanged. To pass from a correct inference to the truth or to the computable probability of the conclusion, one must admit both the truth of the premises and the coherence of the axiomatic system.

The acceptance of these assumptions compels us to abandon pure formalism and to accept certain conventions and to admit the reality of certain models or structures. According to the classical theory of demonstration, which is rejected by formalism, the validity of the deductive method was guaranteed by intuition or evidence—by the natural light of reason. But if we reject such a foundation, we are not compelled to accept formalism. It is still insufficient, since we need good reasons to accept the premises from which we start, and these reasons can be good only for a mind capable of judging them. However, once we have accepted the framework of a formal system and know that it is free from ambiguity, then the demonstrations that can be made within it are compelling and impersonal; in fact, their validity is capable of being controlled mechanically. It is this specific character of formal demonstration that distinguishes it from dialectical reasoning founded on opinion and concerned with contingent realities. Ramus failed to see this distinction and confused the two by using a faulty analogy with the sight of moving and unmoving colors.[23] It is sometimes possible, by resorting to prior arrangements and conventions, to transform an argument into a demonstration of a more or less probabilistic character. It remains true, nonetheless, that we must distinguish carefully between the two types of reasoning if we want to understand properly how they are related.

An argumentation is always addressed by a person called the orator—whether by speech or in writing—to an audience of listeners or readers. It aims at obtaining or reinforcing the adherence of the audience to some thesis, assent to which is hoped for. The new rhetoric, like the old, seeks to persuade or convince, to obtain an adherence which may be *theoretical* to start with, although it may eventually be manifested through a disposition to act, or *practical*, as provoking either immediate action, the making of a decision, or a commitment to act.

Thus argumentation, unlike demonstration, presupposes a meeting of minds: the will on the part of the orator to persuade and not to compel or command, and a disposition on the part of the audience to listen. Such mutual goodwill must not only be general but must also apply to the particular question at issue; it must not be forgotten that all argumentation aims somehow at modifying an existing state of affairs. This is why every society possesses institutions to further discussion between competent persons and to prevent others. Not everybody can start debating about anything whatever, no matter where. To be a man people listen to is a precious quality and is still more necessary as a preliminary condition for an efficacious argumentation.

In some cases there are detailed rules drawn up for establishing this contact before a question can be debated. The main purpose of procedure in civil and criminal law is to ensure a balanced unfolding of the judicial debate. Even in matters where there are no explicit rules for discussion, there are still customs and habits that cannot be disregarded without sufficient reason.

Argumentation also presupposes a means of communicating, a common language. The use of it in a given situation, however, may admit of variation according to the position of the interlocutors. Sometimes only certain persons are entitled to ask questions or to conduct the debate.

From these specifications it is apparent that the new rhetoric cannot tolerate the more or less conventional, and even arbitrary, limitations traditionally imposed upon classical rhetoric. For Aristotle, the similarity between rhetoric and dialectic was all-important.[24] According to him, they differ only in that dialectic provides us with techniques of discussion for a common search for truth, while rhetoric teaches how to conduct a debate in which various points of view are expressed and the decision is left up to the audience. This distinction shows why dialectic has been traditionally considered as a serious matter by philosophers, whereas rhetoric has been regarded with contempt. Truth, it was held, presided over a dialectical discussion, and the interlocutors had to reach agreement about it by themselves, whereas rhetoric taught only how to present a point of view—that is to say, a partial aspect of the question—and the decision of the issue was left up to a third person.[25]

It should be noted, however, that for Plato dialectic alone does not attain to metaphysical truth. The latter requires an intuition for which dialectic can only pave the way by eliminating untenable hypotheses.[26] However, truth is the keynote for dialectic, which seeks to get as close to the truth as possible through the discursive method. The rhetorician, on the other hand, is described as trying to outdo his rivals in debate, and, if his judges are gross and ignorant, the triumph of the orator who shows the greatest skill in flattery will by no means always be the victory of the best cause. Plato emphasizes this point strongly in the *Gorgias*, where he shows that the demagogue, to achieve victory, will not hesitate to use techniques unworthy of a philosopher. This criticism gains justification from Aristotle's observation, based evidently on Athenian practice, that it belongs to rhetoric "to deal with such matters as we deliberate upon without arts or systems to guide us, in the hearing of persons who cannot take in at a glance a complicated argument, or follow a long chain of reasoning.[27]

For the new rhetoric, however, argumentation has a wider scope as nonformal reasoning that aims at obtaining or reinforcing the adherence of an audience. It is manifest in discussion as well as in debate, and it matters not whether the aim be the search for truth or the triumph of a cause, and the audience may have any degree of competence. The reason that rhetoric has been deemed unworthy of the philosopher's efforts is not because dialectic employs a technique of questions and answers while rhetoric proceeds by speeches from opposing sides.[28] It is not this but rather the idea of the unicity of truth that has disqualified rhetoric in the Western philosophical tradition. Thus Descartes declares: "Whenever two men come to opposite decisions about the same matter one of them at least must certainly be in the wrong, and apparently there is not even one of them who knows; for if the reasoning of the second was sound and clear he would be able so to lay it before the other as finally to succeed in convincing *his* understanding also."[29] Both Descartes and Plato hold this idea because of their rejection of opinion, which is variable, and their adoption of an ideal of science based on the model of geometry and mathematical reasoning—the very model according to which the world was supposed to have been created. *Dum Deus calculat, fit mundus* [While God calculates, the world is created] is the conviction not only of Leibniz but of all rationalists.

Things are very different within a tradition that follows a juridical, rather than a mathematical, model. Thus in the tradition of the Talmud, for example, it is accepted that opposed positions can be equally reasonable; one of them does not have to be right. Indeed, "in the Talmud two schools of biblical interpretation are in constant opposition, the school of Hillel and that of Shammai. Rabbi Abba relates that, bothered by these contradictory interpretations of the sacred text, Rabbi Samuel addresses himself to heaven in order to know who speaks the truth. A voice from above answers him that these two theses both expressed the word of the Living God."[30]

So too, for Plato, the subject of discussion is always one for which men possess no techniques for reaching agreement immediately:

> Suppose for example that you and I, my good friend (Socrates remarks to Euthyphro), differ about a number; do differences of this sort make us enemies and set us at variance with one another? Do we not go at once to arithmetic, and put an end to them by a sum? . . . Or suppose that we differ about magnitudes, do we not quickly end the differences

by measuring? ... And we end a controversy about heavy and light by resorting to a weighing machine? ... But what differences are there which cannot be thus decided, and which therefore make us angry and set us at enmity with one another? I dare say the answer does not occur to you at the moment, and therefore I will suggest that these enmities arise when the matters of difference are the just and unjust, good and evil, honourable and dishonourable.[31]

When agreement can easily be reached by means of calculation, measuring, or weighing, when a result can be either demonstrated or verified, nobody would think of resorting to dialectical discussion. The latter concerns only that cannot be so decided and, especially, disagreements about values. In fact, in matters of opinion, it is often the case that neither rhetoric nor dialectic can reconcile all the positions that are taken.

Such is exactly how matters stand in philosophy. The philosopher's appeal to reason gives no guarantee whatever that everyone will agree with his point of view. Different philosophies present different points of view, and it is significant that a historian of pre-Socratic philosophy has been able to show that the different points of view can be regarded as antilogies or discourses on opposite sides, in that an antithesis is opposed in each case to a thesis.[32] One might even wonder with Alexandre Kojève, the late expert in Hegelian philosophy, whether Hegelian dialectic did not have its origin, not in Platonic dialectic, but rather in the development of philosophical systems that can be opposed as thesis to antithesis, followed by a synthesis of the two. The process is similar to a lawsuit in which the judge identifies the elements he regards as valid in the claims of the opposed parties. For Kant as well as for Hegel, opinions are supposed to be excluded from philosophy, which aims at rationality. But to explain the divergencies that are systematically encountered in the history of philosophy, we need only call these opinions the natural illusions of reason as submitted to the tribunal of critical reason (as in Kant) or successive moments in the progress of reason toward Absolute Spirit (as in Hegel).

To reconcile philosophic claims to rationality with the plurality of philosophic systems, we must recognize that the appeal to reason must be identified not as an appeal to a single truth but instead as an appeal for the adherence of an audience, which can be thought of, after the manner of Kant's categorical imperative, as encompassing all reasonable and competent men. The characteristic aspect of philosophical controversy and of the history of philosophy can only be understood if the appeal to reason is conceived as an appeal to an ideal audience—which I call the universal audience—whether embodied in God,[33] in all reasonable and competent men, in the man deliberating or in an elite.[34] Instead of identifying philosophy with a science, which, on the positivist ideal, could make only analytical judgments, both indisputable and empty, we would do better to abandon the ideal of an apodictic philosophy. We would then have to admit that in the discharge of his specific task, the philosopher has at his disposal only an argumentation that he can endeavor to make as reasonable and systematic as possible without ever being able to make it absolutely compelling or a demonstrative proof. Besides, it is highly unlikely that any reasoning from which we could draw reasons for acting could be conducted under the sign of truth, for these reasons must enable us to justify our actions and decisions. Thus, indirectly, the analysis of philosophical reasoning brings us back to views that are familiar in existentialism.

Audiences display an infinite variety in both extension and competence: in extent, from the audience consisting of a single subject engaged in inward deliberation up to the universal audience; and in competence, from those who know only *loci* up to the specialists who have acquired their knowledge only through a long and painstaking preparation. By thus generalizing the idea of the audience, we can ward off Plato's attack against the rhetoricians for showing greater concern for success than for the truth. To this criticism we can reply that the techniques suited for persuading a crowd in a public place would not be convincing to a better educated and more critical audience, and that the worth of an argumentation is not measured solely by its efficacy but also by the quality of the audience at which it is aimed. Consequently, the idea of a rational argumentation cannot be defined *in abstracto*, since it depends on the historically grounded conception of the universal audience.

The part played by the audience in rhetoric is crucially important, because all argumentation, in aiming to persuade, must be adapted to the audience and, hence, based on beliefs accepted by the audience with such conviction that the rest of the discourse can be securely based upon it. Where this is not the case, one must reinforce adherence to these starting points by means of all available rhetorical techniques before attempting to join the controverted points to them. Indeed, the orator who builds his discourse on premises not accepted by the audience commits a classical fallacy in argumentation—*a petitio principii*. This is not a mistake in formal logic, since formally any proposition implies itself, but it is a mistake in argumentation, because the orator begs the question by presupposing the existence of an adherence that does not exist and to the obtaining of which his efforts should be directed.

The Basis of Agreement

The objects of agreement on which the orator can build his argument are various. On the one hand, there are facts, truths, and presumptions; on the other, values, hierarchies, and *loci* of the preferable.[35]

Facts and truths can be characterized as objects that are already agreed to by the universal audience, and, hence, there is no need to increase the intensity of adherence to them. If we presuppose the coherence of reality and of our truths taken as a whole, there cannot be any conflict between facts or truths on which we would be called to make a decision. What happens when such a conflict seems to occur is that the incompatible element loses its status and becomes either an illusory fact or an apparent truth, unless we can eliminate the incompatibility by showing that the two apparently incompatible truths apply to different fields. We shall return to this argumentative method later when dealing with the dissociation of ideas.

Presumptions are opinions which need not be proved, although adherence to them can be either reinforced, if necessary, or suppressed by proving the opposite. Legal procedure makes abundant use of presumptions, for which it has worked out refined definitions and elaborate rules for their use.

Values are appealed to in order to influence our choices of action. They supply reasons for preferring one type of behavior to another, although not all would necessarily accept them as good reasons. Indeed, most values are particular in that they are accepted only by a particular group. The values that are called universal can be regarded in so many different ways that their universality is better considered as only an aspiration for agreement, since it disappears as soon as one tries to apply one such value to a concrete situation. For argumentation, it is useful to distinguish concrete values, such as one's country, from abstract values, such as justice and truth. It is characteristic of values that they can become the center of conflict without thereby ceasing to be values. This fact explains how real sacrifice is possible, the object renounced being by no means a mere appearance. For this reason, the effort to reinforce adherence to values is never superfluous. Such an effort is undertaken in epideictic discourse, and, in general, all education also endeavors to make certain values preferred to others.

After values, we find that accepted hierarchies play a part in argumentation. Such, for example, are the superiority of men over animals and of adults over children. We also find double hierarchies as in the case in which we rank behavior in accordance with an accepted ranking of the agents. For this reason, such a statement as "You are behaving like a beast" is pejorative, whereas an exhortation to "act like a man" calls for more laudable behavior.

Among all the *loci* studied by Aristotle in his *Topics*, we shall consider only those examined in the third book, which we shall call *loci of the preferable*. They are very general propositions, which can serve, at need, to justify values or hierarchies, but which also have as a special characteristic the ability to evaluate complementary aspects of reality. To *loci of quantity*, such as "That which is more lasting is worth more than that which is less so" or "A thing useful for a large number of persons is worth more than one useful for a smaller number," we can oppose *loci of quality*, which set value upon the unique, the irremediable, the opportune, the rare—that is, to what is exceptional instead of to what is normal. By the use of these *loci*, it is possible to describe the difference between the classical and the romantic spirit. [36]

While it establishes a framework for all nonformal reasoning, whatever its nature, its subject, or audience, the new rhetoric does not pretend to supply a list of all the *loci* and common opinions which can serve as starting points for argumentation. It is sufficient to stress that, in all cases, the orator must know the opinion of his audience on all the questions he intends to deal with, the type of arguments and reasons which seem relevant with regard to both subject and audience, what they are likely to consider as a strong or weak argument, and what might arouse them, as well as what would leave them indifferent.

Quintilian, in his *Institutes of Oratory*, points out the advantage of a public-school education for future orators: it puts them on a par and in fellowship with their audience. This advice is sound as regards argumentation on matters requiring no special knowledge. Otherwise, however, it is indispensable for holding an audience to have had a preliminary initiation into the body of ideas to be discussed.

In discussion with a single person or a small group, the establishment of a starting point is very different from before a large group. The particular opinions and convictions needed may have already been expressed previously, and the orator has no reason to believe that his interlocutors have changed their minds. Or he can use the technique of question and answer to set the premises of his argument on firm ground. Socrates proceeded in this way, taking the interlocutor's assent as a sign of the truth of the accepted thesis. Thus Socrates says to Callicles in the *Gorgias*:

> If you agree with me in an argument about any point, that point will have been sufficiently tested by us, and will not require to be submitted to any further test. For you could not have agreed with me, either from lack of knowledge or from superfluity of modesty, nor yet from a desire to deceive me, for you are my friend, as you tell me yourself. And therefore when you and I are agreed, the result will be the attainment of perfect truth.[37]

It is obvious that such a dialogue is out of the question when one is addressing a numerous assembly. In this case, the discourse must take as premises the presumptions that the orator has learned the audience will accept.[38]

Creating "Presence"

What an audience accepts forms a body of opinion, convictions, and commitments that is both vast and indeterminate. From this body the orator must select certain elements on which he focuses attention by endowing them, as it were, with a "presence." This does not mean that the elements left out are entirely ignored, but they are pushed into the background. Such a choice implicitly sets a value on some aspects of reality rather than others. Recall the lovely Chinese story told by Meng-Tseu: "A king sees an ox on its way to sacrifice. He is moved to pity for it and orders that a sheep be used in its place. He confesses he did so because he could see the ox, but not the sheep."[39]

Things present, things near to us in space and time, act directly on our sensibility. The orator's endeavors often consist, however, in bringing to mind things that are not immediately present. Bacon was well aware of this function of eloquence:

The affection beholdeth merely the present; reason beholdeth the future and sum of time. And therefore the present filling the imagination more, reason is commonly vanquished; but after that force of eloquence and persuasion hath made things future and remote appear as present, then upon the revolt of the imagination reason prevaileth.[40]

To make "things future and remote appear as present," that is, to create presence, calls for special efforts of presentation. For this purpose all kinds of literary techniques and a number of rhetorical figures have been developed. *Hypotyposis* or *demonstratio*, for example, is defined as a figure "which sets things out in such a way that the matter seems to unfold, and the thing to happen, before our very eyes."[41] Obviously, such a figure is highly important as a persuasive factor. In fact, if their argumentative role is disregarded, the study of figures is a useless pastime, a search for strange names for rather farfetched and affected turns of speech. Other figures, such as *repetition, anaphora, amplification, congerie, metabolè, pseudo direct discourse, enallage,* are all various means of increasing the feeling of presence in the audience. [42]

In his description of facts, truths, and values, the orator must employ language that takes into account the classifications and valuations implicit in the audience's acceptance of them. For placing his discourse at the level of generality that he considers best adapted to his purpose and his audience, he has at hand a whole arsenal of linguistic categories—substantives, adjectives, verbs, adverbs—and a vocabulary and phrasing that enable him, under the guise of a descriptive narrative, to stress the main elements and indicate which are merely secondary.

In the selection of data and the interpretation and presentation of them, the orator is subject to the accusation of partiality. Indeed, there is no proof that his presentation has not been distorted by a tendentious vision of things. Hence, in law, the legal counsel must reply to the attorney general, while the judge forms an opinion and renders his decision only after hearing both parties. Although his judgment may appear more balanced, it cannot achieve perfect objectivity—which can only be an ideal. Even with the elimination of tendentious views and of errors, one does not thereby reach a perfectly just decision. So too in scientific or technical discourse, where the orator's freedom of choice is less because he cannot depart, without special reason, from the accepted terminology, value judgments are implicit, and their justification resides in the theories, classifications, and methodology that gave birth to the technical terminology. The idea that science consists of nothing but a body of timeless, objective truths has been increasingly challenged in recent years. [43]

The Structure of Argument

Nonformal argument consists, not of a chain of ideas of which some are derived from others according to accepted rules of inference, but rather of a web formed from all the arguments and all the reasons that combine to achieve the desired result. The purpose of the discourse in general is to bring the audience to the conclusions offered by the orator, starting from premises that they already accept—which is the case unless the orator has been guilty of a *petitio principii*. The argumentative process consists in establishing a link by which acceptance, or adherence, is passed from one element to another, and this end can be reached either by leaving the various elements of the discourse unchanged and associated as they are or by making a dissociation of ideas.

We shall now consider the various types of association and of dissociation that the orator has at his command. To simplify classification, we have grouped the processes of association into three classes: quasi-logical arguments, arguments based upon the structure of the real, and arguments that start from particular cases that are then either generalized or transposed from one sphere of reality to another.[44]

Quasi-logical Arguments

These arguments are similar to the formal structures of logic and mathematics. In fact, men apparently first came to an understanding of purely formal proof by submitting quasi-logical arguments, such as many of the *loci* listed in Aristotle's *Topics*, to an analysis that yielded precision and formalization. There is a difference of paramount importance between an argument and a formal proof. Instead of using a natural language in which the same word can be used with different meanings, a logical calculus employs an artificial language so constructed that one sign can have only one meaning. In logic, the principle of identity designates a tautology, an indisputable but empty truth, whatever its formulation. But this is not the case in ordinary language. When I say "Business is business," or "Boys will be boys," or "War is war," those hearing the words give preference, not to the univocity of the statement, but to its significant character. They will never take the statements as tautologies, which would make them meaningless, but will look for different plausible interpretations of the same term that will render the whole statement both meaningful and acceptable. Similarly, when faced with a statement that is formally a contradiction—"When two persons do the same thing it is not the same thing," or "We step and we do not step into the same river,"—we look for an interpretation that eliminates the incoherence.

To understand an orator, we must make the effort required to render his discourse coherent and meaningful. This effort requires goodwill and respect for the person who speaks and for what he says. The techniques of formalization make calculation possible, and, as a result, the correctness of the reasoning is capable of mechanical control. This result is not obtained without a certain linguistic rigidity. The language of mathematics is not used for poetry any more than it is used for diplomacy.

Because of its adaptability, ordinary language can always avoid purely formal contradictions. Yet it is not free from incompatibilities, as, for instance, when two norms are recommended which cannot both apply to the same situation. Thus, telling a child not to lie and to obey his parents lays one open to ridicule if the child asks, "What must I do if my father orders me to lie?" When such an antinomy occurs, one seeks for qualifications or amendments—and recommends the primacy of one norm over the other or points out that there are exceptions to the rule. Theoretically, the most elegant way of eliminating an incompatibility is to have recourse to a dissociation of concepts—but of this, more later. Incompatibility is an important element in Socratic irony. By exposing the incompatibility of the answers given to his insidious questions, Socrates compels his interlocutor to abandon certain commonly accepted opinions.

Definitions play a very different role in argumentation from the one they have in a formal system. There they are mostly abbreviations. But in argumentation they determine the choice of one particular meaning over others—sometimes by establishing a relation between an old term and a new one. Definition is regarded as a rhetorical figure—the oratorical definition—when it aims, not at clarifying the meaning of an idea, but at stressing aspects that will produce the persuasive effect that is sought. It is a figure relating to choice: the selection of facts brought to the fore in the definition is unusual because the *definiens* is not serving the purpose of giving the meaning of a term.[45]

Analysis that aims at dividing a concept into all its parts and interpretation that aims at elucidating a text without bringing anything new to it are also quasi-logical arguments and call to mind the principle of identity. This method can give way to figures of speech called *aggregation* and *interpretation* when they serve some purpose other than clarification and tend to reinforce the feeling of presence.[46]

These few examples make it clear that expressions are called figures of style when they display a fixed structure that is easily recognizable and are used for a purpose different from their normal one—this new purpose being mainly one of persuasion. If the figure is so closely interwoven into the argumentation that it appears to be an expression suited to the occasion, it is regarded as an argumentative figure, and its unusual character will often escape notice.

Some reasoning processes—unlike definition or analysis, which aim at complete identification—are content with a partial reduction, that is, with an identification of the main elements. We have an example of this in the rule of justice that equals should be treated equally. If the agents and situations were identical, the application of the rule would take the form of an exact demonstration. As this is never the case, however, a decision will have to be taken about whether the differences are to be disregarded. This is why the recourse to precedent in legal matters is not a completely impersonal procedure but always requires the intervention of a judge.

Arguments of reciprocity are those that claim the same treatment for the antecedent as for the consequent of a relation—buyers-sellers, spectators-actors, etc. These arguments presuppose that the relation is symmetrical. Unseasonable use of them is apt to have comic results, such as the following story, known to have made Kant laugh:

At Surat an Englishman is pouring out a bottle of ale which is foaming freely. He asks an Indian who is amazed at the sight what it is that he finds so strange. "What bothers me," replies the native, "isn't what is coming out of the bottle, but how you got it in there in the first place."

Other quasi-logical arguments take the transitivity of a relation for granted, even though it is only probable: "My friends' friends are my friends." Still other arguments apply to all kinds of other relations such as that between part and whole or between parts, relations of division, comparison, probability. They are clearly distinct from exact demonstration, since, in each case, complementary, nonformal hypotheses are necessary to render the argument compelling.[47]

Appeal to the Real

Arguments based on the structure of reality can be divided into two groups according as they establish associations of succession or of co-existence.

Among relations of succession, that of causality plays an essential role. Thus we may be attempting to find the causes of an effect, the means to an end, the consequences of a fact, or to judge an action or a rule by the consequences that it has. This last process might be called the pragmatic argument, since it is typical of utilitarianism in morals and of pragmaticism in general.[48]

Arguments establishing relations of coexistence are based on the link that unites a person to his actions. When generalized, this argument establishes the relation between the essence and the act, a relation of paramount importance in the social sciences. From this model have come the classification of periods in history (Antiquity, the Middle Ages), all literary classifications (classicism, romanticism), styles (Gothic, baroque), economic or political systems (feudalism, capitalism, fascism), and institutions (marriage, the church).[49] Rhetoric, conceived as the theory of argumentation, provides a guidance for the understanding both of the manner in which these categories were constituted and of the reasons for doing so. It helps us grasp the advantages and the disadvantages of using them and provides an insight into the value judgments that were present, explicitly or implicitly, when they took shape. The specificity of the social sciences can be best understood by considering the methodological reasons justifying the constitution of their categories—Max Weber's *Idealtypus*.

Thanks to the relations of coexistence, we are also able to gain an understanding of the argument from authority in all its shapes as well as an appreciation of the persuasive role of *ethos* in argumentation, since the discourse can be regarded as an act on the orator's part.[50]

Establishing the Real

Arguments attempting to establish the structure of reality are first arguments by example, illustration, and model; second, arguments by analogy.

The example leads to the formulation of a rule through generalization from a particular case or through putting a new case on the same footing as an older one. Illustration aims at achieving presence for a rule by illustrating it with a concrete case. The argument from a model justifies an action by showing that it conforms to a model. One should also mention the argument from an antimodel; for example, the drunken Helot to whom the Spartans referred as a foil to show their sons how they should not behave.

In the various religions, God and all divine or quasi-divine persons are obviously preeminent models for their believers. Christian morality can be defined as the imitation of Christ, whereas Buddhist morality consists in imitating Buddha. The models that a culture proposes to its members for imitation provide a convenient way of characterizing it.[51]

The argument from analogy is extremely important in nonformal reasoning. Starting from a relation between two terms *A* and *B*, which we call the *theme* since it provides the proper subject matter of the discourse, we can by analogy present its structure or establish its value by relating it to the terms *C* and *D*, which constitute the *phoros* of the analogy, so that *A* is to *B* as *C* is to *D*. Analogy, which derives its name from the Greek word for proportion, is nevertheless different from mathematical proportion. In the latter the characteristic relation of equality is symmetrical, whereas the *phoros* called upon to clarify the structure or establish the value of the *theme* must, as a rule, be better known than the *theme*. When Heraclitus says that in the eyes of God man is as childish as a child is in the eyes of an adult, it is impossible to change the *phoros* for the *theme*, and vice versa, unless the audience is one that knows the relationship between God and man better than that between a child and an adult. It is also worth noting that when *man* is identified with *adult*, the analogy reduces to three terms, the middle one being repeated twice: *C* is to *B* as *B* is to *A*. This technique of argumentation is typical of Plato, Plotinus, and all those who establish hierarchies within reality.

Within the natural sciences the use of analogy is mainly heuristic, and the intent is ultimately to eliminate the analogy and replace it with a formula of a mathematical type. Things are different, however, in the social sciences and in philosophy, where the whole body of facts under study only offers reasons for or against a particular analogical vision of things.[52] This is one of the differences to which Wilhelm Dilthey refers when he claims that the natural sciences aim at explaining whereas the human sciences seek for understanding.

The metaphor is the figure of style corresponding to the argument from analogy. It consists of a condensed analogy in which one term of the *theme* is associated with one term of the *phoros*. Thus "the morning of life" is a metaphor that summarizes the analogy: Morning is to day what youth is to life. Of course, in the case of a good many metaphors, the reconstruction of the complete analogy is neither easy nor unambiguous. When Berkeley, in his *Dialogues*,[53] speaks of "an ocean of false learning," there are various ways to supply the missing terms of the analogy, each one of which stresses a different relation unexpressed in the metaphor.

The use of analogies and metaphors best reveals the creative and literary aspects of argumentation. For some audiences their use should be avoided as much as possible, whereas for others the lack of them may make the discourse appear too technical and too difficult to follow. Specialists tend to hold analogies in suspicion and use them only to initiate students into their discipline. Scientific popularization makes extensive use of analogy, and only from time to time will the audience be reminded of the danger of identification of *theme* and *phoros*.[54]

The Dissociation of Ideas

Besides argumentative associations, we must also make room for the dissociation of ideas, the study of which is too often neglected by the rhetorical tradition. Dissociation is the classical solution for incompatibilities that call for an alteration of conventional ways of thinking. Philosophers, by using dissociation, often depart from common sense and form a vision of reality that is free from the contradictions of opinion.[55] The whole of the great metaphysical tradition, from Parmenides to our own day, displays a succession of dissociations where, in each case, reality is opposed to appearance.

Normally, reality is perceived through appearances that are taken as signs referring to it. When, however, appearances are incompatible—an oar in water looks broken but feels straight to the touch—we must admit, if we are to have a coherent picture of reality, that some appearances are illusory and may lead us to error regarding the real. One is thus brought to the construction of a conception of reality that at the same time is capable of being used as a criterion for judging appearances. Whatever is conformable to it is given value, whereas whatever is opposed is denied value and is considered a mere appearance.

Any idea can be subjected to a similar dissociation. To real justice we can oppose apparent justice and with real democracy contrast apparent democracy, or formal or nominal democracy, or quasi democracy, or even "democracy" (in quotes). What is thus referred to as apparent is usually what the audience would normally call justice, democracy, etc. It only becomes apparent after the criterion of real justice or real democracy has been applied to it and reveals the error concealed under the name. The dissociation results in a depreciation of what had until then been an accepted value and in its replacement by another conception to which is accorded the original value. To effect such a depreciation, one will need a conception that can be shown to be valuable, relevant, as well as incompatible with the common use of the same notion.

We may call "philosophical pairs" all sets of notions that are formed on the model of the "appearance-reality" pair. The use of such pairs makes clear how philosophical ideas are developed and also shows how they cannot be dissociated from the process of giving or denying value that is typical of all ontologies. One thus comes to see the importance of argumentative devices in the development of thought, and especially of philosophy.[56]

Interaction of Arguments

An argumentation is ordinarily a spoken or written discourse, of variable length, that combines a great number of arguments with the aim of winning the adherence of an audience to one or more theses. These arguments interact within the minds of the audience, reinforcing or weakening each other. They also interact with the arguments of the opponents as well as with those that arise spontaneously in the minds of the audience. This situation gives rise to a number of theoretical questions.

Are there limits, for example, to the number of arguments that can be usefully accumulated? Does the choice of arguments and the scope of the argumentation raise special problems? What is a weak or an irrelevant argument? What is the effect of a weak argument on the whole argumentation? Are there any criteria for assessing the strength or relevance of an argument? Are such matters relative to the audience, or can they be determined objectively?

We have no general answer to such questions. The answer seems to depend on the field of study and on the philosophy that controls its organization. In any case, they are questions that have seldom been raised and that never have received a satisfactory answer. Before any satisfactory answer can be given, it will be necessary to make many detailed studies in the various disciplines, taking account of the most varied audiences.

Once our arguments have been formulated, does it make any difference what order they are presented in? Should one start, or finish, with strong arguments, or do both by putting the weaker arguments in the middle—the so-called Nestorian order? This way of presenting the problem implies that the force of an argument is independent of its place in the discourse. Yet, in fact, the opposite seems to be true, for what appears as a weak argument to one audience often appears as a strong argument to another, depending on whether the presuppositions rejected by one audience are accepted by the other. Should we present our arguments then in the order that lends them the greatest force? If so, there should be a special technique devoted to the organization of a discourse.

Such a technique would have to point out that an exordium is all-important in some cases, while in others it is entirely superfluous. Sometimes the objections of one's opponent ought to be anticipated beforehand and refuted, whereas in other cases it is better to let the objections arise spontaneously lest one appear to be tearing down straw men.[57]

In all such matters it seems unlikely that any hard-and-fast rules can be laid down, since one must take account of the particular character of the audience, of its evolution during the debate, and of the fact that habits and procedures that prove good in one sphere are no good in another. A general rhetoric cannot be fixed by precepts and rules laid down once for all. But it must be able to adapt itself to the most varied circumstances, matters, and audiences.

Reason and Rhetoric

The birth of a new period of culture is marked by an eruption of original ideas and a neglect of methodological concerns and of academic classifications and divisions. Ideas are used with various meanings that the future will distinguish and disentangle. The fundamental ideas of Greek philosophy offer a good example of this process. One of the richest and most confused of all is that expressed by the term *logos*, which means among other things: word, reason, discourse, reasoning, calculation, and all that was later to become the subject of logic and the expression of reason. Reason was opposed to desire and the passions, being regarded as the faculty that ought to govern human behavior in the name of truth and wisdom. The operation of *logos* takes effect either through long speeches or through questions and answers, thus giving rise to the distinction noted above between rhetoric and dialectic, even before logic was established as an autonomous discipline.

Aristotle's discovery of the syllogism and his development of the theory of demonstrative science raised the problem of the relation of syllogistic—the first formal logic—with dialectic and rhetoric. Can any and every form of reasoning be expressed syllogistically? Aristotle is often thought to have aimed at such a result, at least for deductive reasoning, since he was well aware that inductive reasoning and argument by example are entirely different from deduction. He knew too that the dialectical reasoning characteristic of discussion, and essentially critical in purpose, differed widely from demonstrative reasoning deducing from principles the conclusions of a science. Yet he was content to locate the difference in the kind of premises used in the two cases. In analytical, or demonstrative, reasoning, the premises, according to Aristotle, are true and ultimate, or else derived from such premises, whereas in dialectical reasoning the premises consist of generally accepted opinions. The nature of reasoning in both cases was held to be the same, consisting in drawing conclusions from propositions posited as premises.[58]

Rhetoric, on the other hand, was supposed to use syllogisms in a peculiar way, by leaving some premises unexpressed and so transforming them into enthymemes. The orator, as Aristotle saw, could not be said to use regular syllogisms; hence, his reasoning was said to consist of abbreviated syllogisms and of arguments from example, corresponding to induction.

What are we to think of this reduction to two forms of reasoning of all the wide variety of arguments that men use in their discussions and in pleading a cause or justifying an action? Yet, since the time of Aristotle, logic has confined its study to deductive and inductive reasoning, as though any argument differing from these was due to the variety of its content and not to its form. As a result, an argument that cannot be reduced to canonical form is regarded as logically valueless. What then about reasoning from analogy? What about the *a fortiori* argument? Must we, in using such arguments, always be able to introduce a fictive unexpressed major premise, so as to make them conform to the syllogism?

It can be shown that the practical reasoning involved in choice or decision making can always be expressed in the form of theoretical reasoning by introducing additional premises. But what is gained by such a move? The reasoning by which new premises are introduced is merely concealed, and resort to these premises appears entirely arbitrary, although in reality it too is the outcome of a decision that can be justified only in an argumentative, and not in a demonstrative manner.[59]

At first sight, it appears that the main difference between rhetoric and dialectic, according to Aristotle, is that the latter employs impersonal techniques of reasoning, whereas rhetoric relies on the orator's *ethos* (or character) and on the manner in which he appeals to the passions of his audience (or *pathos*).[60, 61] For Aristotle, however, the *logos* or use of reasoning is the main thing, and he criticizes those authors before him, who laid the emphasis upon oratorical devices designed to arouse the passions. Thus he writes:

> If the rules for trials which are now laid down in some states—especially in well-governed states—were applied everywhere, such people would have nothing to say. All men, no doubt, think that the laws should prescribe such rules, but some, as in the court of Areopagus, give practical effect to their thoughts and forbid talk about non-essentials. This is sound law and custom. It is not right to pervert the judge by moving him to anger or envy or pity—one might as well warp a carpenter's rule before using it.

For this reason, after a long discussion devoted to the role of passion in oratorical art, he concludes:

> As a matter of fact, it [rhetoric] is a branch of dialectic and similar to it, as we said at the outset.[62]

To sum up, it appears that Aristotle's conception, which is essentially empirical and based on the analysis of the material he had at his disposal, distinguishes dialectic from rhetoric only by the type of audience and, especially, by the nature of the questions examined in practice. His precepts are easy to understand when we keep in mind that he was thinking primarily of the debates held before assemblies of citizens gathered together either to deliberate on political or legal matters or to celebrate some public ceremony. There is no reason, however, why we should not also consider theoretical and, especially, philosophical questions expounded in unbroken discourse. In this case, the techniques Aristotle would have presumably recommended would be those he himself used in his own work, following the golden rule that he laid down in his *Nicomachean Ethics*, that the method used for the examination and exposition of each particular subject must be appropriate to the matter, whatever its manner of presentation.[63]

After Aristotle, dialectic became identified with logic as a technique of reasoning, due to the influence of the Stoics. As a result, rhetoric came to be regarded as concerned only with the irrational parts of our being, whether will, the passions, imagination, or the faculty for aesthetic pleasure. Those who, like Seneca and Epictetus, believed that the philosopher's role was to bring man to submit to reason were opposed to rhetoric, even when they used it, in the name of philosophy. Those like Cicero, on the other hand, who thought that in order to induce man to submit to reason one had to have recourse to rhetoric, recommended the union of philosophy and eloquence. The thinkers of the Renaissance followed suit, such as Valla, and Bacon too, who expected rhetoric to act on the imagination to secure the triumph of reason.

The more rationalist thinkers, like Ramus, as we have already noted, considered rhetoric as merely an ornament and insisted on a separation of form and content, the latter alone being thought worthy of a philosopher's attention. Descartes adopted the same conception and reinforced it. He regarded the geometrical method as the only method fit for the sciences as well as for philosophy and opposed rhetoric as exerting an action upon the will contrary to reason—thus adopting the position of the Stoics but with a different methodological justification. But to make room for eloquence within this scheme, we need only deny that reason possesses a monopoly of the approved way of influencing the will. Thus, Pascal, while professing a rationalism in a Cartesian manner, does not hesitate to declare that the truths that are most significant for him—that is, the truths of faith—have to be received by the heart before they can be accepted by reason:

> We all know that opinions are admitted into the soul through two entrances, which are its chief powers, understanding and will. The more natural entrance is the understanding, for we should never agree to anything but demonstrated truths, but the more usual entrance, although against nature, is the will; for all men whatsoever are almost always led into belief not because a thing is proved but because it is pleasing. This way is low, unworthy, and foreign to our nature. Therefore everybody disavows it. Each of us professes to give his belief and even his love only where he knows it is deserved.
>
> I am not speaking here of divine truths, which I am far from bringing under the art of persuasion, for they are infinitely above nature. God alone can put them into the soul, and in whatever way He pleases. I know He has willed they should enter into the mind from the heart and not into the heart from the mind, that He might make humble that proud power of reason. . . .[64]

To persuade about divine matters, grace is necessary; it will make us love that which religion orders us to love. Yet it is also Pascal's intention to conduce to this result by his eloquence, although he has to admit that he can lay down the precepts of this eloquence only in a very general way:

> It is apparent that, no matter what we wish to persuade of, we must consider the person concerned, whose mind and heart we must know, what principles he admits, what things he loves, and then observe in the thing in question what relations it has to these admitted principles or to these objects of delight. So that the art of persuasion consists as much in

knowing, how to please as in knowing how to convince, so much more do men follow caprice than reason.

Now of these two, the art of convincing and the art of pleasing, I shall confine myself here to the rules of the first, and to them only in the case where the principles have been granted and are held to unwaveringly; otherwise I do not know whether there would be an art for adjusting the proofs to the inconstancy of our caprices.

But the art of pleasing is incomparably more difficult, more subtle, more useful, and more wonderful, and therefore if I do not deal with it, it is because I am not able. Indeed I feel myself so unequal to its regulation that I believe it to be a thing impossible.

Not that I do not believe there are as certain rules for pleasing as for demonstrating, and that whoever should be able perfectly to know and to practise them would be as certain to succeed in making himself loved by kings and by every kind of person as in demonstrating the elements of geometry to those who have imagination enough to grasp the hypotheses. But I consider, and it is perhaps my weakness that leads me to think so, that it is impossible to lay hold of the rules.[65]

Pascal's reaction here with regard to formal rules of rhetoric already heralds romanticism with its reverence for the great orator's genius. But before romanticism held sway, associationist psychology developed in eighteenth-century England. According to the thinkers of this school, feeling, not reason, determines man's behavior, and books on rhetoric were written based on this psychology. The best known of these is Campbell's *The Philosophy of Rhetoric*, noted above.[66] Fifty years later, Whately, following Bacon's lead, defined the subject of logic and of rhetoric as follows:

I remarked in treating of that Science [Logic], that Reasoning may be considered as applicable to two purposes, which I ventured to designate respectively by the terms "Inferring" and "Proving," i.e., the ascertainment of the truth by investigation and the *establishment* of it to the satisfaction of another; and I there remarked that Bacon, in his *Organon*, has laid down rules for the conduct of the former of these processes, and that the latter belongs to the province of Rhetoric; and it was added, that to *infer*, is to be regarded as the proper office of the Philosopher, or the Judge;—to *prove*, of the Advocate.[67]

This conception, while stressing the social importance of rhetoric, makes it a negligible factor for the philosopher. This tendency increases under the influence of Kant and of the German idealists, who boasted of removing all matters of opinion from philosophy, for which only apodictic truths are of any importance.

The relation between the idea that we form of reason and the role assigned to rhetoric is of sufficient importance to deserve studies of all the great thinkers who have said anything about the matter—studies similar to those of Bacon by Prof. Karl Wallace and of Ramus by Prof. Walter J. Ong.[68] In what follows, I would like to sketch how the positivist climate of logical empiricism makes possible a new, or renovated, conception of rhetoric.

Within the perspective of neopositivism, the rational is restricted to what experience and formal logic enable us to verify and demonstrate. As a result, the vast sphere of all that is concerned with action—except for the choice of the most adequate means to reach a designated end—is turned over to the irrational. The very idea of a reasonable decision has no meaning and cannot even be defined satisfactorily with respect to the *whole* action in which it occurs. Logical empiricism has at its disposal no technique of justification except one founded on the theory of probability. But why should one prefer one action to another? Only because it is more efficacious? How can one choose between the various ends that one can aim at? If quantitative measures are the only ones that can be taken into account, the only reasonable decision would seem to be one that is in conformity with utilitarian calculations. If so, all ends would be reduced to a single one of pleasure or utility, and all conflicts of values would be dismissed as based on futile ideologies.

Now if one is not prepared to accept such a limitation to a monism of values in the world of action and would reject such a reduction on the ground that the irreducibility of many values is the basis of our freedom and of our spiritual life; if one considers how justification takes place in the most varied spheres—in politics, morals, law, the social sciences, and, above all, in philosophy—it seems obvious that our intellectual tools cannot all be reduced to formal logic, even when that is enlarged by a theory for the control of induction and the choice of the most efficacious techniques. In this situation, we are compelled to develop a theory of argumentation as an indispensable tool for practical reason.

In such a theory, as we have seen, argumentation is made relative to the adherence of minds, that is, to an audience, whether an individual deliberating or mankind as addressed by the philosopher in his appeal to reason. Whately's distinction between logic, as supplying rules of reasoning for the judge, and rhetoric, providing precepts for the counsel, falls to the ground as being without foundation. Indeed, the counsel's speech that aims at convincing the judge cannot rest on any different kind of reasoning than that which the judge uses himself. The judge, having heard both parties, will be better informed and able to compare the arguments on both sides, but his judgment will contain a justification in no way different in kind from that of the counsel's argumentation. Indeed, the ideal counsel's speech is precisely one that provides the judge with all the information that he needs to state the grounds for his decision.

If rhetoric is regarded as complementary to formal logic and argumentation as complementary to demonstrative proof, it becomes of paramount importance in philosophy, since no philosophic discourse can develop without resorting to it. This became clear when, under the influence of logical empiricism, all philosophy that could not be reduced to calculation was considered as nonsense and of no worth. Philosophy, as a consequence, lost its status in contemporary culture. This situation can be changed only by developing a philosophy and a methodology of the reasonable. For if the rational is restricted to the field of calculation, measuring, and weighing, the reasonable is left with the vast field of all that is not amenable to quantitative and formal techniques. This field, which Plato and Aristotle began to explore by means of dialectical and rhetorical devices, lies open for investigation by the new rhetoric.

Further Developments

I introduced the new rhetoric to the public for the first time over twenty years ago, in a lecture delivered in 1949 at the Institut des Hautes Etudes de Belgique.[69] In the course of the same year, the Centre National de Recherches de Logique was founded with the collaboration of the professors of logic in the Belgian universities. In 1953 this group organized an international colloquium on the theory of proof, in which the use and method of proof was studied in the deductive sciences, in the natural sciences, in law, and in philosophy—that is, in the fields where recourse to reasoning is essential.[70] On that occasion Prof. Gilbert Ryle presented his famous paper entitled "Proofs in Philosophy," which claims that there are no proofs in philosophy: "Philosophers do not provide proofs any more than tennis players score goals. Tennis players do not try in vain to score goals. Nor do philosophers try in vain to provide proofs; they are not inefficient or tentative provers. Goals do not belong to tennis, nor proofs to philosophy."[71]

What, then, is philosophical reasoning? What are "philosophical arguments"? According to Ryle, "they are operations not *with* premises and conclusions, but operations *upon* operations with premises and conclusions. In proving something, we are putting propositions through inference-hoops. In some philosophical arguments, we are matching the hoops through which certain batches of propositions will go against a worded recipe declaring what hoops they should go through. Proving is a one-level business; philosophical arguing is, anyhow sometimes, an interlevel business."[72]

If the notion of proof is restricted to the operation of drawing valid inferences, it is undeniable that philosophers and jurists only rarely prove what they assert. Their reasoning, however, does aim at justifying the points that they make, and such reasoning provides an example of the argumentation with which the new rhetoric is concerned.[73]

The part played by argumentation in philosophy has given rise to numerous discussions and to increasing interest, as is shown by the special issue of the *Revue Internationale de Philosophie* of 1961 devoted to the subject, by the colloquium on philosophical argumentation held in Mexico City in 1963,[74] by the collection of studies published by Maurice Natanson and Henry W. Johnstone, Jr., entitled *Philosophy, Rhetoric and Argumentation*,[75] and by the special number of *The Monist* in 1964 on the same subject.

Professor Johnstone has for many years been particularly interested in this topic and has published a book and many papers on it.[76] To further the study of the relation between philosophy and rhetoric, he organized with Prof. Robert T. Oliver, then head of the Speech Department at Pennsylvania

State University, a colloquium in which philosophers and members of the speech profession met in equal numbers to discuss the question. The interest aroused by this initiative led to the founding in 1968 of a journal called *Philosophy and Rhetoric*, edited jointly by Professor Johnstone and Prof. Carroll C. Arnold.

That so much attention should be focused on argumentation in philosophical thought cannot be understood unless one appreciates the paramount importance of practical reason—that is, of finding "good reasons" to justify a decision. In 1954 I drew attention to the role of decision in the theory of knowledge,[77] and Gidon Gottlieb further developed it, with particular attention to law, in his book *The Logic of Choice*.[78]

Argumentation concerning decision, choice, and action in general is closely connected with the idea of justification, which also is an important element in the idea of justice. I have attempted to show that the traditional view is mistaken in claiming that justification is like demonstration but based on normative principles.[79] In fact, justification never directly concerns a proposition but looks instead to an attitude, a decision, or an action. "Justifying a proposition" actually consists in justifying one's adherence to it, whether it is a statement capable of verification or an unverifiable norm. A question of justification ordinarily arises only in a situation that has given rise to criticism: no one is called upon to justify behavior that is beyond reproach. Such criticism, however, would be meaningless unless some accepted norm, end, or value had been infringed upon or violated. A decision or an action is criticized on the ground that it is immoral, illegal, unreasonable, or inefficient—that is, it fails to respect certain accepted rules or values. It always occurs within a social context; it is always "situated." Criticism and justification are two forms of argumentation that call for the giving of reasons for or against, and it is these reasons that ultimately enable us to call the action or decision reasonable or unreasonable.

In 1967 a colloquium was held on the subject of demonstration, verification, justification, organized jointly by the Institut International de Philosophie and the Centre National de Recherches de Logique.[80] At that meeting I emphasized the central role of justification in philosophy. Among other things, it enables us to understand the part played by the principle of induction in scientific methodology. Prof. A. J. Ayer claimed that the principle of induction cannot be based on probability theory;[81] yet it did seem possible to give good reasons for using induction as a heuristic principle.[82] But this is only a particular case of the use of justification in philosophy. It is essential wherever practical reason is involved.

In morals, for example, reasoning is neither deductive nor inductive, but justificative. Lucien Lévy-Bruhl, in his famous book *La Morale et la science des moeurs* (1903), criticized the deductive character of much traditional moral philosophy and proposed the conception of the science of morals that made it a sociological discipline, inductive in character. Yet in morals absolute preeminence cannot be given either to principles—which would make morals a deductive discipline—or to the particular case—which would make it an inductive discipline. Instead, judgments regarding particulars are compared with principles, and preference is given to one or the other according to a decision that is reached by resorting to the techniques of justification and argumentation.[83]

The idea of natural law is also misconceived when it is posed in ontological terms. Are there rules of natural law that can be known objectively? Or is positive law entirely arbitrary as embodying the lawmaker's sovereign will? A satisfactory positive answer cannot be given to either question. We know that it is imperative for a lawmaker not to make unreasonable laws; yet we know too that there is no one single manner, objectively given, for making just and reasonable laws. Natural law is better considered as a body of general principles or *loci*, consisting of ideas such as "the nature of things," "the rule of law," and of rules such as "No one is expected to perform impossibilities," "Both sides should be heard"—all of which are capable of being applied in different ways. It is the task of the legislator or judge to decide which of the not unreasonable solutions should become a rule of positive law. Such a view, according to Michel Villey, corresponds to the idea of natural law found in Aristotle and St. Thomas Aquinas—what he calls the classical natural law.[84]

For government to be considered legitimate, to have authority, there must be some way of justifying it. Without some reasonable argumentation for it, political power would be based solely on force. If it is to obtain respect, and not only obedience, and gain the citizens' acceptance, it must have some justification other than force. All political philosophy, in fact, aims at criticizing and justifying claims to the legitimate exercise of power.[85]

Argumentation establishes a link between political philosophy and law and shows that the legislator's activity is not merely an expression of unenlightened will. From lack of such a theory, Hume and Kelsen were right in making a sharp distinction between what is and what ought to be and claiming that no inference can be made from one to the other. Things take a different outlook, however, when one recognizes the importance of argumentation in supplying good reasons for establishing and interpreting norms. Kelsen's pure theory of the law then loses the main part of its logical justification.[86] The same befalls Alf Ross's realist theory of the law, as has been shown in the remarkable essay by Prof. Stig Jørgensen.[87]

The new rhetoric has also been used to throw new light upon the educator's task, on the analysis of political propaganda, on the process of literary creation, as well as on the reasoning of the historian.[88] But it is in the field of law that it has made the largest impact.[89] Recent studies and colloquia devoted to the logic of law testify to the keen interest that the subject has aroused, especially among French-speaking jurists.[90] The faculty of law at Brussels has just inaugurated a new series of lectures, entitled "Logic and Argumentation."[91]

Lawyers and philosophers working in collaboration have shown that the theory of argumentation can greatly illuminate the nature of legal reasoning.

The judge is obliged by law to pass sentence on a case that comes before him. Thus Article 4 of the Code Napoléon declares: "The judge who, under pretext of the silence, the obscurity, or the incompleteness of the law, refuses to pass sentence is liable to prosecution for the denial of justice." He may not limit himself to declaring that there is an antinomy or lacuna in the legal system that he has to apply. He cannot, like the mathematician or formal logician, point out that the system is incoherent or incomplete. He must himself solve the antinomy or fill in the lacuna. Ordinary logic by itself would suffice to show the existence of either an antinomy or a lacuna, but it cannot get him out of the resulting dilemma: only legal logic based on argumentation can accomplish that.

To conclude this general, but far from exhaustive, survey, it is necessary to stress again the import that the new rhetoric is having for philosophy and the study of its history. Twenty years ago, for example, the *Topics* and *Rhetoric* of Aristotle were completely ignored by philosophers, whereas today they are receiving much attention.[92] Renewed interest in this hitherto ignored side of Aristotle has thrown new light upon his entire metaphysics[93] and attached new importance to his notion of *phronesis* or prudence.[94] Renewed attention is being given to the classical rhetoric of Cicero,[95] and we are now gaining a better understanding of the historical development of rhetoric and logic during the Middle Ages and the Renaissance.[96]

It is possible too that the new rhetoric may provoke a reconsideration of the Hegelian conception of dialectic with its thesis and antithesis culminating in a synthesis, which might be compared to a reasonable judge who retains the valid part from antilogies. This new rhetorical perspective may also help us to a better understanding of the American pragmatists, especially of C. S. Peirce, who, in his approximation to Hegel's objective logic, aimed at developing a *rhetorica speculativa*.[97]

For these inquiries to be pursued, however, the theory of argumentation must awaken the interest of philosophers and not merely that of lawyers and members of the speech profession. In a synoptic study of the subject, Professor Johnstone deplores the fact that the theory of argumentation is still little known in the United States, although it is now well known in Europe.[98] Attention has been focused on the problems raised by the use of practical reason, and the field has been explored and mapped by theoreticians and practitioners of the law. There is much that philosophers could learn from this work if they would cease confining their methodological inquiries to what can be accomplished by formal logic and the analysis of language.[99] A more dynamic approach to the problems of language would also reveal the extent to which language, far from being only an instrument for communication, is also a tool for action and is well adapted to such a purpose.[100] It may even prove possible to achieve a synthesis of the different and seemingly opposed tendencies of contemporary philosophy, such as existentialism, pragmaticism, analytical philosophy, and perhaps even a new version of Hegelian and Marxist dialectic.[101]

Notes

Passages in *Great Books of the Western World* are referred to by the initials "*GBWW*," followed by volume, page number, and page section. Thus, "*GBWW*, Vol. 39, p. 210b" refers to page 210 in Adam Smith's *The Wealth of Nations*, which is Volume 39 in *Great Books of the Western World*. The small letter "b" indicates the page section. In books printed in single column, "a" and "b" refer to the upper and lower halves of the page. In books printed in double column, "a" and "b" refer to the upper and lower halves of the left column, "c" and "d" to the upper and lower halves of the right column. For example, "Vol. 53, p. 210b" refers to the lower half of page 210, since Volume 53, James's *Principles of Psychology*, is printed in single column. On the other hand, "Vol. 7, p. 210b" refers to the lower left quarter of the page, since Volume 7, Plato's *Dialogues*, is printed in double column.

[1] Dumarsais, *Des tropes ou des différents sens dans lesquels on peut prendre un même mot dans une même langue* (1818; reprint ed., Geneva: Slatkine Reprints, 1967).

[2] Pierre Fontanier, *Les figures du discours*, ed. Gérard Genette (Paris: Flammarion, 1968).

[3] *GBWW*, Vol. 8, pp. 139–223.

[4] *GBWW*, Vol. 8, pp. 37–137.

[5] *GBWW*, Vol. 8, pp. 139–253; Vol. 9, pp. 585–675.

[6] Petrus Ramus, *Dialectic*, 1576 edition, pp. 3–4; also in the critical edition of *Dialectique*, 1555, ed. Michel Dassonville (Geneva: Librairie Droz, 1964), p. 62. Cf. Walter J. Ong, *Ramus: Method, and the Decay of Dialogue* (Cambridge, Mass.: Harvard University Press, 1958).

[7] Fontanier, *Les figures du discours*, p. 64. *See also* J. Dubois, F. Edeline, J. M. Klinkenberg, P. Minguet, F. Pire, and H. Trinon, *Rhétorique générale* (Paris: Larousse, 1970).

[8] Heinrich Lausberg, *Handbuch der literarischen Rhetorik*, 2 vols. (Munich: M. Hueber, 1960).

[9] Douglas Ehninger, ed., *Whately's Elements of Rhetoric* (Carbondale: Southern Illinois University Press, 1963), p. xxvii.

[10] Robert T. Oliver and Marvin G. Bauer, eds., *Re-establishing the Speech Profession: The First Fifty Years* (New York: Speech Association of the Eastern States, 1959). *See also* Frederick W. Haberman and James W. Cleary, eds., *Rhetoric and Public Address: A Bibliography, 1947–1961* (Madison: University of Wisconsin Press, 1964). Prof. Carroll C. Arnold of Pennsylvania State University has graciously supplied me the following information: "The statement about the bibliography in *Quarterly Journal of Speech* is not quite correct. The 'Bibliography of Rhetoric and Public Address' first appeared in the *Quarterly Journal of Speech* in 1947 and was published there annually to 1951. From 1952 through 1969, the bibliography was annually published in *Speech Monographs*. As it happens, the bibliography will cease to be published in *Monographs* and, beginning with this year, 1970, will be published in a *Bibliographical Annual*, published by the Speech Association of America. As far as I know, this bibliography remains the only multilingual listing of works (admittedly incomplete) on rhetoric published in the United States."

[11] *See* Vasile Florescu, "Retorica si reabilitarea ei in filozofia contemporanea" [Rhetoric and its rehabilitation in contemporary philosophy] in *Studii de istorie a filozofiei universale*, published by the Institute of Philosophy of the Academy of the Socialist Republic of Rumania (Bucharest, 1969), pp. 9–82.

[12] *Discourses* II. 23; *GBWW*, Vol. 12, pp. 170–71.

[13] *Rhetoric* I. 1358b 1–13; *GBWW*, Vol. 9, p. 598.

[14] Ch. Perelman and L. Olbrechts-Tyteca, *The New Rhetoric*, trans. John Wilkinson and Purcell Weaver (Notre Dame, Ind. University of Notre Dame Press, 1969), p. 50. French edition: *La nouvelle rhétorique* (Paris: Presses universitaires de France, 1958).

[15] *On Christian Doctrine* IV. 13, 12; *GBWW*, Vol. 18, p. 684.

[16] Kenneth Burke, *A Rhetoric of Motives* (New York: Prentice-Hall, 1950), p. 43.

[17] Act III, scene ii; *GBWW*, Vol. 26, pp. 584c ff.

[18] Ch. Perelman, *The Idea of Justice and the Problem of Argument*, trans. John Petrie (New York: Humanities Press, 1963), pp. 1–60.

[19] Ibid., p. 16.

[20] Ibid., pp. 5–7.

[21] Edmond Goblot, *La logique des jugements de valeur* (Paris: Colin, 1927).

22 Perelman and Olbrechts-Tyteca, *The New Rhetoric*. *See also* Olbrechts-Tyteca, "Rencontre avec la rhétorique," in *La théorie de l'argumentation*, Centre Nationale de Recherches de Logique (Louvain: Editions Nauwelaerts, 1963), 1, pp. 3–18 (reproduces nos. 21–24 of *Logique et Analyse*).

23 This identification is faulty, as dialectical reasoning can no more than commonplaces (*topoi*) be reduced to formal calculation. Cf. Otto Bird, "The Tradition of the Logical Topics: Aristotle to Ockham," *Journal of the History of Ideas* 23 (1962): 307–23.

24 See *Rhetoric* I. 1354a 1–6, 1355a 35–37, 1355b 8–10, 1356a 30–35, 1356b 35, 1356b 37–38; *GBWW*, Vol. 9, pp. 593–96.

25 Plato, *Republic* I. 348a–b; *GBWW*, Vol. 7, p. 306.

26 *Republic* 511; *GBWW*, Vol. 7, p. 387. *Seventh Letter* 344b; *GBWW*, Vol. 7, p. 810.

27 *Rhetoric* I. 1357a 1–4; *GBWW*, Vol. 9, p. 596.

28 Plato, *Cratylus* 390c; *GBWW*, Vol. 7, pp. 88–89. *Theaetetus* 167d; *GBWW*, Vol. 7, p. 526.

29 *Rules for the Direction of the Mind; GBWW*, Vol. 31, p. 2.

30 *Babylonian Talmud, Seder Mo'ed* 2, 'Erubin 136 (ed. Epstein). Cf. Ch. Perelman, "What the Philosopher May Learn from the Study of Law," *Natural Law Forum* 11 (1966): 3–4; idem, "Désaccord et rationalité des décisions," in *Droit, morale et philosophie* (Paris: Librairie générale de droit et de jurisprudence, 1968), pp. 103–10.

31 *Euthyphro* 7; *GBWW*, Vol. 7, pp. 193–94.

32 *See* Clémence Ramnoux, "Le développement antilogique des écoles grecques avant Socrate," in *La dialectique* (Paris: Presses universitaires de France, 1969), pp. 40–47.

33 Plato, *Phaedrus* 273c; *GBWW*, Vol. 7, p. 138.

34 Perelman and Olbrechts-Tyteca, *The New Rhetoric*, §§ 6–9.

35 Ibid., §§ 15–27.

36 Ch. Perelman and L. Olbrechts-Tyteca, "Classicisme et Romantisme dans l'argumentation," *Revue Internationale de Philosophie*, 1958, pp. 47–57.

37 Plato, *Gorgias* 487 d–e; *GBWW*, Vol. 7, p. 273.

38 Perelman and Olbrechts-Tyteca, *The New Rhetoric*, p. 104.

39 Ibid., p. 116.

40 *Advancement of Learning*, Bk. II, xviii, 4; *GBWW*, Vol. 30, p. 67.

41 *Rhetorica ad Herennium* 4. 68.

42 Perelman and Olbrechts-Tyteca, *The New Rhetoric*, § 42.

43 To mention only a few works besides Thomas Kuhn's *The Structure of Scientific Revolutions* (Chicago, Ill.: University of Chicago Press, 1962), there is Michael Polanyi's fascinating work significantly entitled *Personal Knowledge* (London: Routledge & Kegan Paul, 1958). The social, persuasive, nay, the rhetorical aspect, of scientific methodology was stressed by the physicist John Ziman in his brilliant book *Public Knowledge* (London: Cambridge University Press, 1968). The latter is dedicated to the late Norwood Russell Hanson, whose *Patterns of Discovery* (London: Cambridge University Preis, 1958), and *The Concept of the Positron* (London: Cambridge University Press, 1963), gave much weight to the new ideas.

44 Perelman and Olbrechts-Tyteca, *The New Rhetoric*, §§ 45–88.

45 Ibid., pp. 172–73.

46 Ibid., p. 176.

47 Ibid., §§ 45–59.

48 *See* J. S. Mill, *Utilitarianism; GBWW*, Vol. 43, pp. 443 ff.

49 Ch. Perelman, ed., *Les catégories en histoire* (Brussels: Editions de l'Institut de Sociologie, 1969).

50 Perelman and Olbrechts-Tyteca, *The New Rhetoric*, §§ 60–74.

51 Ibid., §§ 78–81.

52 Ch. Perelman, "Analogie et métaphore en science, poésie, et philosophie," *Revue Internationale de Philosophie*, 1969, pp. 3–15; *see also* Hans Blumenberg, *Paradigmen zu einer Metaphorologie* (Bonn: H. Bouvier, 1960), and Enzo Melandri, *La linea e il circolo: Studio logico-filosofico sull'analogia* (Bologna: Il Mulino, 1968).

53 George Berkeley, *Works*, 2 vols. (London, 1843), 2:259.

54 Perelman and Olbrechts-Tyteca, *The New Rhetoric*, §§ 82–88.

55 Ch. Perelman, "Le réel commun et le réel philosophique," in *Etudes sur l'histoire de la philosophie, en hommage à Martial Guéroult* (Paris: Fischbacher, 1964), pp. 127–38.

56 Perelman and Olbrechts-Tyteca, *The New Rhetoric*, §§ 89–92.

57 Ibid., §§ 97–105.

58 *Topics* I. 100a 25–32; *GBWW*, Vol. 8, p. 143.

59 Ch. Perelman, "Le raisonnement pratique," in *Contemporary Philosophy*, ed. Raymond Klibansky (Florence: La Nuova Italia, 1968–), 1:168–76.

60 *Rhetoric* I. 1356a 5–18; *GBWW*, Vol. 9, p. 595.

61 *See* Paul I. Rosenthal, "The Concept of Ethos and the Structure of Persuasion," *Speech Monographs*, 1966, pp. 114–26.

62 *Rhetoric* I. 1354a 19–27, 1356a 30–31; *GBWW*, Vol. 9, pp. 593, 595–96.

63 *Ethics* I. 1094b 12–27; *GBWW*, Vol. 9, pp. 339–40.

64 *On Geometrical Demonstration*; *GBWW*, Vol. 33, p. 440.

65 Ibid., p. 441.

66 Cf. V. M. Bevilacqua, "Philosophical Origins of George Campbell's Philosophy of Rhetoric," *Speech Monographs*, 1965, pp. 1–12; and Lloyd F. Bitzer, "Hume's Philosophy in George Campbell's Philosophy of Rhetoric," *Philosophy and Rhetoric*, 1969, pp. 139–66.

67 Whately, *Elements of Rhetoric* (1828), pp. 6–7.

68 Karl Wallace, *Francis Bacon on Communication and Rhetoric* (Chapel Hill: University of North Carolina Press, 1943); and Ong, *Ramus: Method, and the Decay of Dialogue*.

69 It was published in 1950 in the *Revue Philosophique de la France et de l'Etranger* under the title "Logique et Rhétorique," 75th year, pp. 1–35, and reprinted in Ch. Perelman and L. Olbrechts-Tyteca, *Rhétorique et philosophie* (Paris: Presses universitaires de France, 1952), pp. 1–48.

70 The *Proceedings* appeared in the *Revue Internationale de Philosophie*, 1954, 27–28.

71 Gilbert Ryle, "Proofs in Philosophy," *Revue Internationale de Philosophie*, 1954, p. 150.

72 Ibid., p. 156.

73 *See* in this respect Perelman and Olbrechts-Tyteca, *Rhétorique et philosophie*, especially "La quête du rationnel," and "De la preuve en philosophie." The latter was published in English in the *Hibbert Journal* 52 (1954): 354–59. The same theme was dealt with more fully in the articles "Self-evidence and Proof," published in Perelman, *The Idea of Justice and the Problem of Argument*, pp. 109–24; and "Self-evidence in Metaphysics," *International Philosophical Quarterly*, 1964, pp. 1–19.

74 Reports published in the *Symposium Sobre la Argumentación Filosofica*, Mexico. 1963.

75 Maurice Natanson and Henry W. Johnstone, Jr., eds., *Philosophy, Rhetoric and Argumentation* (University Park: Pennsylvania State University Press, 1965). *See also* Stanislaw Kaminski, "Argumentacja filozoficzna w ujeciu analitykow" [The philosophic argumentation in the conception of the analysts] in *Rozprawy Filozoficzne* (Toruń, Poland: TNT, 1969), pp. 127–42.

76 Henry W. Johnstone, Jr., *Philosophy and Argument* (University Park: Pennsylvania State University Press, 1959); idem, "Philosophy and Argumentum ad Hominem," *Journal of Philosophy* 49 (1952): 489–98; idem, "The Methods of Philosophical Polemic," *Methodos* 5 (1953): 131–40; idem, "New Outlooks on Controversy," *Review of Metaphysics* 12 (1958): 57–67; idem, "Can Philosophical Arguments Be Valid," *Bucknell Review* 11 (1963): 89–98; idem, "Self -refutation and Validity," *The Monist*, 1964, pp. 467–85.

77 Perelman, *The Idea of Justice and the Problem of Argument*, pp. 88–97.

78 Gidon Gottlieb, *The Logic of Choice* (London: George Allen & Unwin, 1968).

79 *See* Ch. Perelman, "Jugements de valeur, justification et argumentation," *Revue Internationale de Philosophie*, 1961, 11, 327–35; reprinted in Perelman, *Justice et raison* (Brussels: Presses universitaires de Bruxelles, 1963). Also in Perelman, *Justice* (New York: Random House, 1967), chap. 4.

80 *Entretiens de Liège* (Louvain: Nauwelaerts, 1968).

81 A. J. Ayer, "Induction and the Calculus of Probabilities," in *Entretiens de Liège*, pp. 95–108.

82 Cf. Ch. Perelman, "Synthèse finale," in *Entretiens de Liège*, pp. 338–40.

83 *See* "Jugement moral et principes moraux," and "Scepticisme moral et philosophie morale," in Perelman, *Droit, morale et philosophie*.

[84] Michel Villey, *Leçons d'histoire de la philosophie du droit* (Paris: Dalloz, 1957), and, especially, "Questions de logique juridique dans l'histoire de la philosophie du droit," in *Etudes de Logique Juridique* 2, Centre National de Recherches de Logique (Brussels: Bruylant, 1967), pp. 3–22.

[85] Ch. Perelman, "Autorité, idéologie et violence," in *Annales de l'Institut de Philosophie de l'Université Libre de Bruxelles* (Brussels: Editions de l'Institut de Sociologie, 1969), pp. 9–20.

[86] Ch. Perelman, "La théorie pure du droit et l'argumentation," in *Law, State, and International Legal Order: Essays in Honor of Hans Kelsen*, ed. Salo Engel and Rudolf A. Métall (Knoxville: University of Tennessee Press, 1964), pp. 225–32.

[87] "Argumentation and Decision," in *Festkrift Alf Ross*, ed. Mogens Blegvad, Max Sørenson, and Isi Foighel (Copenhagen: Juristforbundets Förlaget, 1969), pp. 261–84 (with numerous bibliographical notes).

[88] Max Loreau, "Rhetoric as the Logic of the Behavioral Sciences," trans. Lloyd I. Watkins and Paul D. Brandes, *Quarterly Journal of Speech*, 1965, pp. 455–63; Otto Pöggeler, "Dialektik und Topik," in *Hermeneutik und Dialektik*, ed. J. C. B. Mohr (Tübingen, Germany, 1970), 2:273–310. Cf. "Education et rhétorique," in Perelman, *Justice et raison*, pp. 104–17; and B. Gillemain, "Raison et rhétorique, les techniques de l'argumentation et la pédagogie," *Revue de l'Enseignement Philosophique*, 1960, (3), 1961, (2); Paolo Facchi, ed., *La propaganda politica in Italia* (Bologna: Società editrice il Mulino, 1960). Also, Renato Barilli, *Poetica e retorica* (Milan, 1969); Ch. Perelman, ed., *Raisonnement et démarches de l'historien*, 2d ed. (Brussels: Editions de l'Institut de Sociologie, 1965); and Giulio Preti, *Retorica e logica* (Turin: G. Einaudi, 1968).

[89] Edgar Bodenheimer, "A Neglected Theory of Legal Reasoning," *Journal of Legal Education*, 1969, pp. 373–402.

A. H. Campbell, "On Forgetting One's Law," *The Journal of the Society of Public Teachers of Law*, London, 1963.

George G. Christie, "Objectivity in the Law," *Yale Law Journal*, 1963, pp. 1311–50.

Per Olaf Ekelöf, "Topik und jura," in *Universitetet och forskningen* [University and science], ed. Birger Lindskog (Uppsala, 1968), pp. 207–24. The author also refers to Stephen E. Toulmin's *The Uses of Argument* (London: Cambridge University Press, 1958), in which Toulmin develops a theory of topics without referring to rhetoric or even to the idea of an audience.

Alessandro Giuliani, *Il concetto di prova: Contributo alla logica giuridica* (Milan: A. Giuffrè, 1961); idem, "L'élément juridique dans la logique médiévale," in *La théorie de l'argumentation* (*see* note 22), pp. 540–90; idem, "Influence of Rhetoric on the Law of Evidence and Pleading," *The Juridical Review*, 1969; idem, "La logique juridique comme théorie de la controverse," *Archives de Philosophie du Droit*, 1966, pp. 87–113; idem, *La controversia, Contributo alla logica giuridica* (Pavia, Italy: Pubblicazioni della Università di Pavia, 1966).

Graham Hughes, "Rules, Policy and Decision-Making," in *Law, Reason, and Justice: Essays in Legal Philosophy*, ed. Graham Hughes (New York: New York University Press, 1969), pp. 101–35.

Luis Recaséns-Siches, *La lógica de los problemas humanos* (Mexico: Dianoia, 1964), pp. 3–34. "The Logic of the Reasonable as Differentiated from the Logic of the Rational," in *Essays in Jurisprudence in Honor of Roscoe Pound*, ed. Ralph A. Newman (Indianapolis, Ind. Bobbs-Merrill Co., 1962).

Julius Stone, *Legal System and Lawyers' Reasonings* (London: Stevens & Sons, 1964), pp. 325–37

Ilmar Tammelo, "The Law of Nations and the Rhetorical Tradition of Legal Reasoning," in *Indian Yearbook of International Affairs* (Madras: Diocesan Press, 1964), pp. 227–58.

Renato Treves, "Metaphysics and Methodology in the Philosophy of Law," in Hughes, *Law, Reason, and Justice*, pp. 235–54.

Theodor Viehweg, *Topik und Jurisprudenz* (Munich: Beck-Verlag, 1963), and his introduction to the German edition of my studies on justice, *Die Gerechtigkeit* (Munich: Beck-Verlag, 1967).

Franz Wieacker, "Zur praktischen Leistung der Rechtsdogmatik," in Mohr, *Hermeneutik und Dialektik*, 2:311–36.

George Wróblewski, "Legal Reasonings in Legal Interpretation," in *Etudes de Logique Juridique* 3 (Brussels: Bruylant, 1969), pp. 3–31.

[90] *See* the volume of the *Archives de Philosophie du Droit* of 1961 devoted to the logic of law; the colloquium of Toulouse on legal logic, *Annales de la Faculté de Droit de Toulouse*, 1967, fasc. I;

that of the *Instituts d'Etudes Judiciaires de Paris*, 1967, of which the Proceedings appeared under the title *La logique judiciaire* (Paris: Presses universitaires de France, 1969). The next Congress of the International Association for Legal Philosophy, which will be held in Brussels in 1971, will deal with the same theme.

[91] *See* Ch. Perelman, "Droit, logique et argumentation," *Revue de l'Université de Bruxelles*, 1968, pp. 387–98. The works produced by the legal section of the Centre National de Recherches de Logique have undeniably brought a remarkable contribution to a renewed outlook of the whole subject (*see* A. Bayart, "Le Centre National Belge de Recherches de Logique," *Archives de Philosophie du Droit*, 1968, pp. 171–80; and Paul Foriers, "L'état des recherches de logique juridique en Belgique," in *Etudes de Logique Juridique* 2, pp. 23–42). Besides numerous articles written by members and of which several appeared in the *Journal des Tribunaux*, Brussels, the Center has published, since 1961, three large volumes, respectively entitled *Le fait et le droit* (Brussels: Bruylant, 1961), *Les antinomies en droit* (Brussels: Bruylant, 1965), and *Le problème des lacunes en droit* (Brussels: Bruylant, 1968).

[92] We will mention, in this respect, W. A. de Pater's thesis *Les topiques d'Aristote et la dialectique platonicienne*, Etudes Thomistiques, vol. 10 (Fribourg: Editions St. Paul, 1965), as well as the fact that the 3rd Symposium Aristotelicum of Oxford has been entirely devoted to the *Topics* (G. E. L. Owen, ed., *Aristotle on Dialectic* [Oxford: Clarendon Press, 1968]).

[93] Pierre Aubenque, *Le problème de l'être chez Aristote* (Paris: Presses universitaires de France, 1962).

[94] Pierre Aubenque, *La prudence chez Aristote* (Paris: Presses universitaires de France, 1963).

[95] Alain Michel published, in 1960, an essay on the philosophical foundations of the art of persuasion entitled *Rhétorique et philosophie chez Cicéron* (Paris: Presses universitaires de France), while Renato Barilli devoted an important, lively chapter to Cicero in his *Poetica e retorica* (*see* note 88).

[96] We have already mentioned Alessandro Giuliani, whose works cover the period stretching from Aristotle to the Scottish philosophy, without neglecting medieval logic, and shed new light on the history of legal logic. Mention must also be made of G. Chevrier's suggestive study "Sur l'art de l'argumentation chez quelques romanistes médiévaux au XIIe et au XIIIe siècle," *Archives de Philosophie du Droit*, 1966, pp. 115–48. Finally let us recall the well-known works of Eugenio Garin and of his disciples, which have drawn attention again to the Italian philosophy of the Renaissance and to fifteenth- and sixteenth-century humanism, in which discussions concerning the relations between philosophy, dialectic, and rhetoric occupied a central place: Garin, *Medioevo e Rinascimento* (Bari, Italy: Laterza, 1961); and Garin, Paolo Rossi, and Cesare Vasoli, eds., *Testi umanistici su la retorica* (Rome: Fratelli Bocca, 1953). Besides Garin's own writings, we must mention those of Paolo Rossi: "La celebrazione della retorica e la polemica antimetafisica nel *De principiis* di Mario Nizolio," in *La crisi dell'uso dogmatico delle ragione*, ed. Antonio Banfi (Milan, 1953), pp. 99–221; and Cesare Vasoli, *La dialettica e la retorica dell'umanesimo* (Milan: Feltrinelli, 1968).

[97] C. S. Peirce, *Collected Papers*, 6 vols., ed. Charles Hartshorne and Paul Weiss (Cambridge, Mass.: Harvard University Press, 1931–35), 1:444.

[98] Klibansky, *Contemporary Philosophy* (*see* note 59), 1:177–84.

[99] *See* my article "What the Philosopher May Learn from the Study of Law," *Natural Law Forum* 11 (1966): 1–12, reproduced as an appendix to the volume *Justice*.

[100] Cf. Ch. Perelman and L. Olbrechts-Tyteca, "Les notions et l'argumentation," *Archivio di filosofia*, Rome, 1955, pp. 249–69; idem, "De la temporalité comme caractère de l'argumentation," *Archivio di Filosofia*, 1958, pp. 115–33. L. Olbrechts-Tyteca, "Les définitions des statisticiens," *Logique et Analyse* 3 (1960): 49–69. Ch. Perelman, "Avoir un sens et donner un sens," in *Thinking and Meaning*, Entretiens d'Oxford, in *Logique et Analyse*, 1962, pp. 235–39.

[101] Ch. Perelman, "The Dialectical Method and the Part Played by the Interlocutor in the Dialogue," in Perelman, *The Idea of Justice and the Problem of Argument*, pp. 161–67; idem, "Dialectique et Dialogue," in *Hermeneutik und Dialektik* (*see* note 88), 2:77–84.

7

THE TYRANNY
OF PRINCIPLES

Stephen Toulmin

If this were a sermon (and perhaps it is), its text would be the quotation attributed to H. L. Mencken that hangs in the staff lounge at The Hastings Center:

> For every human problem, there is a solution that is simple, neat, and wrong.[1]

Oversimplification is a temptation to which moral philosophers are not immune, despite all their admirable intellectual care and seriousness; and the abstract generalizations of theoretical ethics are, I shall argue, no substitute for a sound tradition in practical ethics.

These days, public debates about ethical issues oscillate between, on the one hand, a narrow dogmatism that confines itself to unqualified general assertions dressed up as "matters of principle" and, on the other, a shallow relativism that evades all firm stands by suggesting that we choose our "value systems" as freely as we choose our clothes. Both approaches suffer from the same excess of generality. The rise of anthropology and the other human sciences in the early twentieth century encouraged a healthy sense of social and cultural differences; but this was uncritically taken as implying an end to all objectivity in practical ethics. The subsequent reassertion of ethical objectivity

From *Hastings Center Report*, December 1981, pp. 31–39. Reproduced by permission. © The Hastings Center.

has led, in turn, to an insistence on the absoluteness of moral principles that is not balanced by a feeling for the complex problems of discrimination that arise when such principles are applied to particular real-life cases. So, the relativists have tended to overinterpret the need for discrimination in ethics, discretion in public administration, and equity in law, as a license for general personal subjectivity. The absolutists have responded by denying all real scope for personal judgment in ethics, insisting instead on strict construction in the law, on unfeeling consistency in public administration, and—above all—on the "inerrancy" of moral principles.

I propose to concentrate my attention on this last phenomenon—the revival of a tyrannical absolutism in recent discussions about social and personal ethics. I find it reflected in attitudes toward politics, public affairs, and the administration of justice, as much as toward questions of "ethics" in a narrower and more personal sense. My main purpose will be to ask: What is it about our present situation that inclines us to move in that direction? By way of reply, I shall argue that, in all large industrialized societies and cultures—regardless of their economic and political systems—ethics, law, and public administration have recently undergone similar historical transformations, so that all three fields are exposed to the same kinds of pressures, face common difficulties, and share in the same resulting public distrust. And I shall try to show what we can learn about those shared problems, and about the responses that they call for, by studying the common origins of our basic ethical, legal, and political ideas. All my central examples will be concerned with the same general topic: the nature, scope, and force of "rules" and "principles" in ethics and in law. Three personal experiences helped to bring these problems into focus for me.

Three Personal Experiences

Human Subjects Research

For several years in the mid-1970s, I worked as a staff member with the National Commission for the Protection of Human Subjects of Biomedical and Behavioral Research, which was established by the U.S. Congress, with the task of reporting and making recommendations about the ethics of using human subjects in medical and psychological research. Eleven commissioners—five of them scientists, the remaining six lawyers, theologians, and other nonscientists—were instructed to make recommendations about publicly financed human experimentation: in particular, to determine under what conditions subjects belonging to certain vulnerable groups (such as young children and prisoners) could participate in such research without moral objection.[2]

Before the Commission began work, many onlookers assumed that its discussions would degenerate into a Babel of rival opinions. One worldly commentator remarked in the *New England Journal of Medicine*, "Now (I suppose) we shall see matters of eternal principle decided by a six to five vote."[3] But things did not work out that way. In practice, the commissioners were never split along the line between scientists and nonscientists. In almost every case they came close to agreement even about quite detailed recommendations—at least for so long as their discussions proceeded taxonomically, taking one difficult class of cases at a time and comparing it in detail with other clearer and easier classes of cases.

Even when the Commission's recommendations were not unanimous, the discussions in no way resembled Babel: the commissioners were never in any doubt what it was that they were *not quite unanimous about*. Babel set in only afterwards. When the eleven individual commissioners asked themselves what "principles" underlay and supposedly justified their adhesion to the consensus, each of them answered in his or her own way: the Catholics appealed to Catholic principles, the humanists to humanist principles, and so on. They could agree; they could agree what they were agreeing about; but, apparently, they could not agree why they agreed about it.

This experience prompted me to wonder what this final "appeal to principles" really achieved. Certainly it did not add any weight or certitude to the commissioners' specific ethical recommendations, for example, about the kind of consent procedures required in biomedical research using five-year-old children. They were, quite evidently, surer about these shared, particular judgments than they were about the discordant general principles on which, in theory, their practical judgments were based. If anything, the appeal to principles undermined the recommendations by suggesting to onlookers that there was more disharmony than ever showed up in the commissioners' actual discussions. So, by the end of my tenure with the Commission I had begun to suspect that the point of "appealing to principles" was something quite else: not to give particular ethical judgments a more solid foundation, but rather to square the collective ethical conclusions of the Commission as a whole with each individual commissioner's other *non*ethical commitments. So (it seemed to me) the principles of Catholic ethics tell us more about Catholicism than they do about ethics, the principles of Jewish or humanist ethics more about Judaism or humanism than about ethics. Such principles serve less as foundations, adding intellectual strength or force to particular moral opinions, than they do as corridors or curtain walls linking the moral perceptions of all reflective human beings, with other, more general positions—theological, philosophical, ideological, or *Weltanschaulich*.

Abortion

The years of the National Commission's work were also years during which the morality of abortion became a matter of public controversy. In fact, the U.S. Congress established the Commission in the backwash of the Supreme Court's ruling on the legality of abortion, following a public dispute about research on the human fetus. And before long the public debate about abortion acquired some of the same puzzling features as the proceedings of the Commission itself. On the one hand, there were those who could discuss the morality of abortion temperately and with discrimination, acknowledging that here, as in other agonizing human situations, conflicting considerations are involved and that a just, if sometimes painful, balance has to be struck between different rights and claims, interests and responsibilities.[4] That temperate approach underlay traditional common law doctrines about abortion before the first statutory restrictions were enacted in the years around 1825. It was also the approach adopted by the U.S. Supreme Court in the classic case, *Roe* v. *Wade*; and, most important, it was the approach clearly spelled out by Thomas Aquinas, whose position was close to that of the common law and the Supreme Court. (He acknowledged that the balance of moral considerations necessarily tilts in different directions at different stages in a woman's pregnancy, with crucial changes beginning around the time of "quickening."[5]) On the other hand, much of the public rhetoric increasingly came to turn on "matters of principle." As a result, the abortion debate became less temperate, less discriminating, and above all less resolvable. Too often, in subsequent years, the issue has boiled down to pure head-butting: an embryo's unqualified "right to life" being pitted against a woman's equally unqualified "right to choose." Those who have insisted on dealing with the issue at the level of high theory thus guarantee that the only possible practical outcome is deadlock.

Social Welfare Benefits

My perplexities about the force and value of "rules" and "principles" were further sharpened as the result of a television news magazine program about a handicapped young woman who had difficulties with the local Social Security office. Her Social Security payments were not sufficient to cover her rent and food, so she started an answering service, which she operated through the telephone at her bedside. The income from this service—though itself less than a living wage—made all the difference to her. When the local Social Security office heard about this extra income, however, they reduced her benefits accordingly; in addition, they ordered her to repay some of the money she had been receiving. (Apparently, they regarded her as a case of "welfare fraud.") The television reporter added two final statements. Since the report had been filmed, he told us, the young woman, in despair, had taken her own life. To this he added his personal comment that "there should be a *rule* to prevent this kind of thing from happening."

Notice that the reporter did not say, "The local office should be given discretion to waive, or at least bend, the existing rules in hard cases." What he said was, "There should be an *additional* rule to prevent such inequities in the future." Justice, he evidently believed, can be ensured only by establishing an adequate system of rules, and injustice can be prevented only by adding more rules.

Hence, the questions that arise from these experiences: What force and function do rules or principles truly possess, either in law or in ethics? What social and historical circumstances make it most natural and appropriate to discuss legal and ethical issues in the language of "rules" and "principles"? Why are our own contemporary legal and ethical discussions so preoccupied with rules and principles? And to what extent would we do better to look for justice and morality in other directions?

Rules in Roman Law

Far from playing an indispensable part in either law or ethics, "rules" have only a limited and conditional role. The current vogue for rules and principles is the outcome of certain powerful factors in recent social history; but these factors have always been balanced against counterweights. Justice has always required both law and equity, while morality has always demanded both fairness and discrimination. When this essential duality is ignored, reliance on unchallengeable principles can generate, or become the instrument of, its own subtle kind of tyranny.

My reading soon led me back to Peter Stein's *Regulae Juris*, which traces the development of the concept of a "rule" in Roman law from its beginnings to the modern era.[6] His account of the earliest phases of Roman law was for me the most striking part. For the first three hundred years of Roman history, the legal system made no explicit use of the concept of rules. The College of Pontiffs acted as the city's judges, and individual pontiffs gave their adjudications on the cases submitted to them. But they were not required to cite any general rules as justifications for their decisions. Indeed, they were not required to give reasons at all. Their task was not to argue, but rather to pontificate.

How was this possible? How can any system of law operate in the absence of rules, reasons, and all the associated apparatus of binding force and precedent? Indeed, in such a situation can we say a true system of law exists at all? Those questions require us to consider the historical and anthropological circumstances of early Rome. Initially Rome was a small and relatively homogeneous community, whose members shared a correspondingly homogeneous tradition of ideas about justice and fairness, property and propriety, a tradition having more in common with Sir Henry Maine's ideas about traditional "customary law" than with the "positive law" of John Austin's *Province of Jurisprudence Determined*.[7] In any such community the functions of adjudication tend to be more arbitral than regulatory. Like labor arbitrators today, the judges will not be as sharply bound by precedent as contemporary high court judges. So the disputes that the pontiffs adjudicated were typically ones about which the traditional consensus was ambiguous; the balance of rights and obligations between the parties required the judgment call of a trusted and disinterested arbitrator. In these marginal cases all that the arbitrator may be able to say is, "Having taken all the circumstances into account, I find that on this particular occasion it would, all in all, be more reasonable to tilt the scale to A rather than to B." This ruling will rest, not on the application of general legal rules, but rather on the exercise of judicial discrimination in assessing the balance of particulars. Initially, "pontificating" did not mean laying down the law in a dogmatic manner. Rather, it meant resolving marginal disputes by an equitable arbitration, and the pontiffs had the trust of their fellow citizens in doing so.

This state of affairs did not last. Long before the first Imperial codification, Roman law began to develop the full apparatus of "rules" with which we ourselves are familiar. Stein suggests that five sets of factors contributed to this new reliance on *regulae*.[8] First, as the city grew, the case load increased beyond what the pontiffs themselves could manage. Junior judges, who did not possess the same implicit trust as the pontiffs, were brought in to resolve disputes; so the consistency of their rulings had to be "regularized." Second, with the rise of lawyering as a profession, law schools were set up and *regulae* were articulated for the purpose of teaching the law. Discretion, which had rested earlier on the personal characters of the pontiffs themselves and which is not so easy to teach, began to be displaced by formal rules and more teachable argumentative skills. Third, Rome acquired an empire, and foreign peoples came under the city's authority. Their systems of customary law had to be put into harmony with the Roman system, and this could be done only by establishing a concordance between the "rules" of different systems. Fourth, the empire itself developed a bureaucracy, which could not operate except on the basis of rules. Finally, the intellectual discussion of law was pursued in the context of Greek philosophy. Although Cicero, for example, was a practicing attorney, he was also a philosophical scholar with a professional interest in the Stoic doctrine of the *logos*, or "universal reason."

What followed the resulting proliferation of rules and laws is common knowledge. First, a functional differentiation grew up between two kinds of issues. On the one hand, there were issues that could be decided by applying *general* rules or laws, on the basis of the maxim that like cases should be treated alike. On the other hand, there were issues that called for discretion, with an eye to the *particular* features of each case, in accordance with the maxim that significantly different cases should be treated differently. This functional differentiation became the ancestor of our own distinction between legal and equitable jurisdiction. Second, the Emperor Constantine decided as a matter of imperial policy to bring equitable jurisdiction under his personal control by reserving the equitable function to his own personal court and chancellor. Out in the public arena, judges were given the menial task of applying general rules with only the minimum of discretion. Once legal proceedings were exhausted, the aggrieved citizen could appeal to the Emperor as *parens patriae* ("father of the fatherland") for the benevolent exercise of clemency or equity. Politically, this division of labor certainly did the Emperor no harm; but it also sowed the first seeds of public suspicion that the Law is one thing, Justice another.[9]

Carried over into the modern English-speaking world, the resulting division between courts of law and courts of equity is familiar to readers of Charles Dickens. And although during the twentieth century most Anglo-American jurisdictions have merged legal and equitable functions in the same courts,[10] it is still widely the case that equitable remedies can be sought only in cases where legal remedies are unavailable or unworkable—so that in this respect the dead hand of Constantine still rules us from the grave.

The Ethics of Strangers

Life in late-twentieth-century industrial societies clearly has more in common with life in Imperial Rome than it has with the Rome of Horatius at the Bridge or with Mrs. Gaskell's *Cranford*. Our cities are vast, our populations are mixed and fragmented, our public administration is bureaucratic, our jurisdictions (both domestic and foreign) are many and varied. As a result, the moral consensus and civic trust on which the pontificate of early Rome depended for its general respect and efficacy often appear to be no more than a beguiling dream. The way we live now, people have come to value uniformity above responsiveness, to focus on law at the expense of equity, and to confuse "the rule of law" with a law of rules. Yet the balance between law and equity still needs to be struck, even if new ways need to be found that answer our new needs. From this point on, I shall work my way toward the question: how, in our actual situation, can that balance best be redressed?

In law, in ethics, and in public administration alike, there is nowadays a similar preoccupation with general principles and a similar distrust of individual discretion. In the administration of social services, the demand for equality of treatment makes us unwilling to permit administrators to "temper the wind to the shorn lamb"—that strikes us as unfair, and therefore unjust.[11] (The equation of justice with fairness is thus a two-edged sword.) In the professions, a widespread fear that professionals are taking unfair advantage of their fiduciary positions has contributed to the recent wave of malpractice suits. In the courts, judges are given less and less room to exercise discretion, and many lawyers view juries as no more trustworthy than judges; the more they are both kept in line by clear rules, or so it seems, the better.[12] As for public discussions of ethics, the recognition of genuine moral complexities, conflicts, and tragedies, that can be dealt with only on a case-by-case basis, is simply unfashionable. Victory in public argument goes, rather, to the person with the more imposing principle. Above all, many people involved in the current debate seem to have forgotten what the term "equity" actually means. They assume that it is just a literary synonym for "equality."[13] So, a demand for the uniform application of public policies leads to a submerging of the discretionary by the rigorous, the equitable by the equal. Faced with judicial injustices, we react like the television reporter, declaring, "There ought to be a law against it," even where it would be more appropriate to say, "In this particular case, the law is making an ass of itself."

The same applies to the operation of our bureaucracies, and to the emphasis on principles in moral judgments.

In all three fields, we need to be reminded that equity requires not the imposition of uniformity or equality on all relevant cases, but rather reasonableness or responsiveness (*epieikeia*) in applying general rules to individual cases.[14] Equity means doing justice with discretion around, in the interstices of, and in areas of conflict between our laws, rules, principles, and other general formulas. It means being responsive to the limits of all such formulas, to the special circumstances in which one can properly make exceptions, and to the trade-offs required where different formulas conflict. The degree to which such marginal judgments can be regularized or routinized remains limited today, just as it was in early Rome. Faced with the task of balancing the equities of different parties, a judge today may well be guided by previous precedents; but these precedents only illuminate broad maxims, they do not invoke formal rules.[15] Likewise, professional practice may be described in cut-and-dried terms as a matter of "routine and accepted" procedures only in the artificial context of a malpractice suit. In the actual exercise of his profession, a surgeon, say, may sometimes simply have to use his or her own best judgment in deciding how to proceed conscientiously. Finally, in ethics, moral wisdom is exercised not by those who stick by a single principle come what may, absolutely and without exception, but rather by those who understand that, in the long run, no principle—however absolute—can avoid running up against another equally absolute principle; and by those who have the experience and discrimination needed to balance conflicting considerations in the most humane way.[16]

By looking at the effects of changing social conditions and modes of life on our ethical perceptions, I believe we can best hit on the clues that will permit us to unravel this whole tangle of problems. A century ago in *Anna Karenina* Leo Tolstoy expressed a view which, though in my opinion exaggerated, is none the less illuminating. During his lifetime Tolstoy lived to see the abolition of serfdom, the introduction of railways, the movement of population away from the country to the cities, and the consequent emergence of modern city life; and he continued to have deep reservations about the possibility of living a truly moral life in a modern city. As he saw matters, genuinely "moral" relations can exist only between people who live, work, and associate together: inside a family, between intimates and associates, within a neighborhood. The natural limit to any person's moral universe, for Tolstoy, is the distance he or she can walk, or at most ride. By taking the train, a moral agent leaves the sphere of truly moral actions for a world of strangers, toward whom he or she has few real obligations and with whom dealings can be only casual or commercial. Whenever the moral pressures and demands become too strong to bear, Tolstoy has Anna go down to the railway station and take a train somewhere, anywhere. The final irony of Tolstoy's own painful life was that he finally broke away from his home and family, only to die in the local stationmaster's office.[17] Matters of state policy and the like, in

Tolstoy's eyes, lay quite outside the realm of ethics. Through the figure of Constantin Levin, he made clear his skepticism about all attempts either to turn ethics into a matter of theory or to make political reform an instrument of virtue.[18]

What Tolstoy rightly emphasized is the sharp difference that exists between our moral relations with our families, intimates, and immediate neighbors or associates, and our moral relations with complete strangers. In dealing with our children, friends, and immediate colleagues, we both expect to—and are expected to—make allowances for their individual personalities and tastes, and we do our best to time our actions according to our perception of their current moods and plans. In dealing with the bus driver, the sales clerk in a department store, the hotel barber, and other such casual contacts, there may be no basis for making these allowances, and so no chance of doing so. In these transient encounters, our moral obligations are limited and chiefly negative—for example, to avoid acting offensively or violently. So, in the ethics of strangers, respect for rules is all, and the opportunities for discretion are few. In the ethics of intimacy, discretion is all, and the relevance of strict rules is minimal.[19] For Tolstoy, of course, only the ethics of intimacy was properly called "ethics" at all—that is why I described his view as exaggerated. But in this respect the ethics of John Rawls is equally exaggerated, though in the opposite direction. In our relations with casual acquaintances and unidentified fellow citizens, absolute impartiality may be a prime moral demand; but among intimates a certain discreet partiality is, surely, only equitable, and certainly not unethical. So a system of ethics that rests its principles on "the veil of ignorance" may well be "fair," but it will also be—essentially—an ethics for relations between strangers.[20]

The Stresses of Lawsuits

Seeing how Tolstoy felt about his own time, what would he have thought about the life we lead today? The effects of the railways, in blurring the boundary between the moral world of the immediate community and the neutral world beyond, have been only multiplied by the private car, which breaks that boundary down almost completely. Living in a high-rise apartment building, taking the car from its underground garage to the supermarket and back, the modern city dweller may sometimes wonder whether he has any neighbors at all. For many of us, the sphere of intimacy has shrunk to the nuclear family, and this has placed an immense strain on family relations. Living in a world of comparative strangers, we find ourselves short on civic trust and increasingly estranged from our professional advisors. We are less inclined to give judges and bureaucrats room to use their discretion, and more determined to obtain equal (if not always equitable) treatment. In a world of complete strangers, indeed, equality would be about the only virtue left.

Do not misunderstand my position. I am not taking a nostalgia trip back to the Good Old Days. The world of neighborliness and forced intimacy, of both geographical and social immobility, had its vices as well as its virtues. Jane Austen's caricature of Lady Catherine de Burgh in *Pride and Prejudice* reminds us that purchasing equity by submitting to gross condescension can make its price too dear:

> God bless the Squire and his relations,
> and keep us in our proper stations.

Any biography of Tolstoy reminds us that his world, too, had a darker side. Those who are seduced by his admiration for the moral wisdom of the newly emancipated peasantry will find an antidote in Frederick Douglass's memoirs of slave life on the Maryland shore. Nor am I deploring apartment buildings and private cars. People usually have reasons for living as they do, and attacking modernity in the name of the morality of an earlier time is an act of desperation, like building the Berlin Wall. No, my question is only: If we accept the modern world as it is—apartment buildings, private cars, and all—how can we strike the central balance between the ethics of intimates and the ethics of strangers, between uniformity of treatment and administrative discretion, and between equity and law, in ways that answer our contemporary needs?

To begin with the law: current public stereotypes focus on the shortcomings of the adversary process, but what first needs to be explained is just where the adversary system has gone astray, and in what fields of law we should be most concerned to replace it. That should not be hard to do. Given that we handle our moral relations with intimates and associates differently from our moral relations with strangers, is not some similar differentiation appropriate between our legal relations with strangers, on the one hand, and with intimates, associates, and close family members on the other?

Even in the United States, the homeland of the adversary system, at least two types of disputes—labor-management conflicts and the renegotiation of commercial contracts—are dealt with by using arbitration or conciliation rather than confrontation.[21] That is no accident. In a criminal prosecution or a routine civil damage suit arising out of a car collision, the parties are normally complete strangers before the proceedings and have no stake in one another's future, so no harm is done if they walk out of the court vowing never to set eyes on each other again. By contrast, the parties to a labor grievance will normally wish to continue working together after the adjudication, while the disputants in a commercial arbitration may well retain or resume business dealings with one another despite the present disagreement. In cases of these kinds, the psychological stresses of the adversary system can be quite destructive: by the time an enthusiastic litigating attorney has done his bit, further labor relations or commercial dealings may be psychologically impossible. So in appraising different kinds of court proceedings, we need to consider how particular types of judicial episodes fit into the larger life histories of the individuals who are parties to them, and what impact the form of proceedings can have on those life histories.

A lawsuit that pits the full power of the state against a criminal defendant is one thing: in that context, Monroe Freedman may be right to underline the merits of the adversary mode, and the positive obligations of zealous defense advocacy.[22] A civil suit that pits colleagues, next-door neighbors, or family members against each other is another thing: in that context resort to adversary proceedings may only make a bad situation worse. So, reasonably enough, the main locus of dissatisfaction with the adversary system is those areas of human life in which the psychological outcomes are most damaging: family law, for example. By the time that the father, mother, and children involved in a custody dispute have all been zealously represented in court, the bad feelings from which the suit originally sprang may well have become irremediable. It is just such areas as family law that other nations (such as West Germany) have chosen to handle by arbitration rather than litigation, in chambers rather than in open court, so providing much more room for discretion.

I am suggesting, then, that a system of law consisting wholly of rules would treat all the parties coming before it in the ways appropriate to strangers. By contrast, in legal issues that arise between parties who wish to continue as close associates on an intimate or familiar level, the demands of equality and rule conformity lose their central place. There, above all, the differences between the desires, personalities, hopes, capacities, and ambitions of the parties most need to be taken into account; and only an adjudicator with authority to interpret existing rules, precedents, and maxims in the light of, and in response to, those differences will be in a position to respect the equities of all the parties involved.

Reviving the Friendly Society

In public administration, especially in the field of social services, the crucial historical changes were more recent, yet they appear much harder to reverse. Two centuries ago most of what we now call the social services—then known, collectively, as "charity"—were still dispensed through the churches. Local ministers of religion were generally trusted to perform this duty equitably and conscientiously; and in deciding to give more to (say) Mrs. Smith than Mrs. Jones, they were not strictly answerable to any supervisor, still less bound by a book of rules. (As with the Squirearchy, of course, this arrangement had its own abuses: the Rev. Mr. Collins could be as overbearing in his own way as Lady Catherine de Burgh.) Even a hundred years ago many such charitable functions were still carried on by private organizations, like those in Britain which were charmingly known as "friendly societies." But by this time things were beginning to change. A friendly clergyman is one thing, but a friendly *society* is more of an anomaly: in due course irregularities in the administration of those organizations—like those in some trade union pension funds today—provoked government supervision, and a Registrar of Friendly Societies was appointed to keep an eye on them.

From that point on, the delivery of social services has become ever more routinized, centralized, and subject to bureaucratic routine. It should not take horror stories, like that of the handicapped young woman's answering service, to make us think again about the whole project of delivering human services through a bureaucracy: one only has to read Max Weber. The imperatives of bureaucratic administration require determinate procedures and full accountability; while a helping hand, whether known by the name of "charity" or "social services," can be truly equitable only if it is exercised with discretion, on the basis of substantive and informed judgments about need rather than formal rules of entitlement.

What might be done, then, to counter the rigors of bureaucracy in this field? Or should late-twentieth-century societies look for other ways of lending a collective hand to those in need? In an exemplary apologia for bureaucracy, Herbert Kaufman of the Brookings Institution has put his finger on many of the key points.[23] If we find public administration today complex, unresponsive, and procedure-bound, he argues that this is almost entirely our own fault. These defects are direct consequences of the demands that we ourselves have placed on our public servants in a situation increasingly marked by diversity, democracy, and distrust. Since we are unwilling to grant discretion to civil servants for fear that it will be abused, we leave ourselves with no measure for judging administrators' performance other than *equality*. As Kaufman remarks, "If people in one region discover that they are treated differently from people in other regions under the same program, they are apt to be resentful and uncooperative."[24]

Hence there arises a "general concern for uniform application of policy," which can be guaranteed only by making the rulebook even more inflexible. Yet is our demand for equality and uniformity really so unqualified that we are determined to purchase it at any price? If we were certain that our own insistence on absolute fairness made the social services dehumanizing and dehumanized, might we not consider opting for other, more *equitable* procedures even though their outcomes might be less *equal*?

Alternatively, perhaps we should reconsider the wholesale nationalization of charity that began in the early twentieth century. Plenty of uncorrupt private pension finds still operate alongside governmental retirement and old-age pension schemes, and a few communally based systems of welfare and charity remain trusted just because their accountability is to a particular community. Among the Ismailis, for instance, the world-wide branch of Islam of which the Aga Khan is the head, tithing is still the rule, and no promising high school graduate misses the chance of going to college merely because he comes from a poor family. Despite governmental programs, that is no longer true of the United States. So perhaps we have let ourselves become too skeptical too soon about the friendliness of "friendly societies," and we should take more seriously the possibility of reviving social instruments with local roots, which do not need to insist on rigidly rule-governed procedures. That is of course a large "perhaps." The social changes that led to the nationalization of charity are powerful and longstanding, and thus far they have shown little sign of weakening. Given a choice, people may prefer to continue putting up with bureaucratic forms and procedures that they can grumble at with impunity if in this way they can avoid putting themselves at the mercy of social or communal relationships that they may find onerous.

Frail Hopes and Slender Foundations

In the field of ethics, all these difficulties are magnified. There I have one firm intellectual conviction, and one somewhat frailer hope on the social level. In a 1932 poem Robert Frost wrote:

> Don't join too many gangs. Join few if any.
> Join the United States, and join the family.
> But not much in between, unless a college.[25]

Frost, in his curmudgeonly way, captures that hostility toward communal ties and restraints which, since Tolstoy's day, has continued to undermine our "intermediate institutions" or "mediating structures." Toward the nuclear family and the nation, people do indeed still feel some natural loyalty; "but not much in between, unless a college." During the last thirty years, even the nation-state has lost much of its mystique, leaving the family exposed to stresses that it can hardly support. It is my frail social hope that we may find some new ways of shaping other intermediate institutions toward which we can develop a fuller loyalty and commitment: associations larger than the nuclear family, but not so large that they defeat in advance the initial presumption that our fellow members are trustworthy. For it is only in that context, I suspect, that the ethics of discretion and intimacy can regain the ground it has lost to the ethics of rules and strangers.

Where might we look for the beginnings of such associations? Traditionally their loci were determined by religious and ethnic ties, and these are still sometimes used constructively to extend the range of people's moral sympathies beyond the immediate household. But we scarcely need to look as far as Ulster or Lebanon to see the other side of that particular coin. Membership in schools and colleges has some of the same power, as Frost grudgingly admits, though it is a power that tends to operate exclusively rather than generously. The great ethical hope of the Marxists was that "working-class solidarity" would, in effect, create a vast and cohesive extended family within which the dispossessed would find release from psychological as well as from political and economic oppression. But by now, alas, the evidence of history seems to show that awareness of shared injuries sets different groups against one another quite as often as it unites them. For some of us, the bonds of professional association are as powerful as any. The physicians of Tarrytown or the attorneys of Hyde Park probably have a close understanding of, feeling for, and even trust in one another; and despite all other reservations about my fellow academics, I do still have a certain implicit trust in their professional responsibility and integrity. So each year, without any serious anxiety, I vote for colleagues whom I have never even met to serve on the boards that manage my pension funds. If it were proved that those elected representatives had been milking the premiums and salting them away in a Swiss bank, that revelation would shake up my moral universe more radically than any dishonesty among public figures on the national level.

True, these are frail hopes and provide only slender foundations to build on. Yet, in the realm of ethics, frail hopes and slender foundations may be what we should learn to live with as much better than nothing. And that brings me to the intellectual point about which I am much more confident. If the cult of absolute principles is so attractive today, that is a sign that we still find it impossible to break with the "quest for certainty" that John Dewey tried so hard to discredit.[26] Not that we needed Dewey to point out the shortcomings of absolutism. Aristotle himself had insisted that there are no "essences" in the realm of ethics, and so no basis for any rigorous "theory" of ethics. Practical reasoning in ethics, as elsewhere, is a matter of judgment, of weighing different considerations against one another, never a matter of formal theoretical deduction from strict or self-evident axioms. It is a task less for the clever arguer than for the *anthropos megalopsychos*, the "large-spirited human being."[27]

It was not for nothing, then, that the members of the National Commission for the Protection of Human Subjects were able to agree about the ethical issues for just so long as they discussed those issues taxonomically. In doing so they were reviving the older, Aristotelian procedures of the casuists and rabbinical scholars, who understood all along that in ethics, as in law, the best we can achieve in practice is for good-hearted, clear-headed people to triangulate their way across the complex terrain of moral life and problems. So, starting from the paradigmatic cases that we do understand—what in the simplest situations harm is, and fairness, and cruelty, and generosity—we must simply work our way, one step at a time, to the more complex and perplexing cases in which extremely delicate balances may have to be struck. For example, we must decide on just what conditions, if any, it would be acceptable to inject a sample group of five-year-old children with an experimental vaccine from which countless other children should benefit even though the risks fall on those few individuals alone. Ethical argumentation thus makes most effective progress if we think of the "common morality" in the same way as we think about the common law:[28] if, for instance, we develop our perception of moral issues by the same kind of progressive triangulation that has extended common law doctrines of tort into the areas, first of negligence and later of strict liability.[29]

Meanwhile, we must remain on guard against the moral enthusiasts. In their determination to nail their principles to the mast, they succeed only in blinding themselves to the equities embodied in real-life situations and problems. Their willingness to legislate morality threatens to transform the most painful and intimate moral quandaries into adversarial confrontations between strangers. To take one example, by reintroducing uncompromising legal restraints to enjoin all procedures of abortion whatever, they are pitting a woman against her own newly implanted zygote in some ghastly parody of a landlord-tenant dispute. This harsh inflexibility sets the present day moral enthusiasts in sharp contrast to Aristotle's *anthropoi megalopsychoi,* and recalls Tolstoy's portrait of Alexei Karenin's associate, the Countess Ivanovna, who in theory was a supporter of all fashionable good causes but in practice was ready to act harshly and unforgivingly.

When Pascal attacked the Jesuit casuists for being too ready to make allowances in favor of penitents who were rich or highborn, he no doubt had a point.[30] But when he used this point as a reason for completely rejecting the case method in ethics, he set the bad example that is so often followed today: assuming that we must withdraw discretion entirely when it is abused and impose rigid rules in its place, instead of inquiring how we could adjust matters so that necessary discretion would continue to be exercised in an equitable and discriminating manner. I vote without hesitation against Pascal and for the Jesuits and the Talmudic scholars. We do not need to go as far as Tolstoy and claim that an ethics modeled on law rather than on equity is no ethics at all. But we do need to recognize that a morality based entirely on general rules and principles is tyrannical and disproportioned, and that only those who make equitable allowances for subtle individual differences have a proper feeling for the deeper demands of ethics. In practice the casuists may occasionally have been lax; but they grasped the essential, Aristotelian point about applied ethics: it cannot get along on a diet of general principles alone. It requires a detailed taxonomy of particular, detailed types of cases and situations. So, even in practice, the faults of the casuists—such as they were—were faults on the right side.

Notes

1 President Jimmy Carter used this quotation in a speech and attributed it to H. L. Mencken. However, the Humanities Section of the Enoch Pratt Library in Baltimore has been unable to locate it in Mencken's works.

2 The work of the U.S. National Commission for the Protection of Human Subjects of Biomedical and Behavioral Research will be discussed more fully in a paper to be published in a forthcoming Hastings Center volume on the "closure" of technical and scientific discussions.

3 So, at any rate, current legend reports. On the other hand, having worked through the files of the *Journal* for 1974–75 without finding any article or editorial on the subject, I am inclined to suspect that this may have been a casual remark by the late Dr. Franz Ingelfinger, the distinguished editor of the periodical.

4 Daniel Callahan, *Abortion: Law, Choice and Morality* (New York: Macmillan, 1970); John T. Noonan, Jr., ed., *The Morality of Abortion: Legal and Historical Perspectives* (Cambridge, Mass.: Harvard University Press, 1970).

5 Thomas Aquinas, *Commentarium Libro Tertio Sententiarum,* D.3, Q.5, A.2, Solutio.

6 Peter Stein, *Regulae Juris* (Edinburgh: Edinburgh University Press, 1966), pp. 4–10.

7 Lloyd A. Fallers, *Law without Precedent* (Chicago: University of Chicago Press, 1969): see also the classical discussion by Sir Henry Maine in *Lectures on the Early History of Institutions* (1914).

8   Stein, pp. 26ff, 80–82, 124–27.

9   For the subsequent influence of this division on the Anglo-American legal tradition, see (e.g.) John H. Baker, *An Introduction to English Legal History* (Toronto and London: Butterworths, 1979).

10 Politically speaking, of course, the decline of monarchical sovereignty made the formal division of law from equity less functional; so it is no surprise that the nineteenth century saw its abolition both in the constitutional monarchy of England and also in the republican United States.

11 John Rawls, *A Theory of Justice* (Cambridge, Mass.: Harvard University Press, 1971) is only the most recent systematic exposition of this position, which has become something of a philosophical commonplace, at any rate since Kant raised the issue of "universalizability" in the late eighteenth century.

12 See, e.g., Kenneth C. Davis, *Discretionary Justice* (Urbana, Ill.: Univ. of Illinois Press, 1969); Ralph A. Newman, *Equity and Law* (Dobbs Ferry, NY: Oceana, 1961); and particularly Ralph A. Newman, ed., *Equity in the World's Legal Systems* (Brussels: Bruylant, 1973).

13 This seems to be true even of so perceptive an author as Herbert Kaufman, in his ingenious tract, *Red Tape: its Origins, Uses and Abuses* (Washington, D.C.: Brookings Institution, 1977), pp. 76–77: "Quite apart from protective attitudes toward specific programs, general concern for uniform application of policy militates against wholesale devolution. Not that uniformity automatically assures equity or equality of treatment. . . ."

14 The *locus classicus* for the discussion of the notion of *epieikeia* (or "equity") is Aristotle's *Nicomachean Ethics*, esp. 1136b30–1137b32. See also Max Hamburger's useful discussion in *Morals and Law: the Growth of Aristotle's Legal Theory* (New Haven: Yale University Press, 1951).

15 Henry L. McClintock, *Handbook of the Principles of Equity*, 2nd ed. (St. Paul, Minn.: West, 1948) pp. 52–54; John N. Pomeroy, *A Treatise on Equity Jurisprudence* (San Francisco: Bancroft Whitney, 1918–19), secs 360–63.

16 Hence Aristotle's emphasis on the need for a person of sound ethical judgment to be an *anthropos megalopsychos*.

17 This image of the steam locomotive had a powerful hold on Tolstoy's imagination: it recurs, for example, in *War and Peace*, where he compares the ineluctable processes of history to the movements of the pistons and cranks of a railway engine, as a way of discrediting the assumption that "world historical figures" like Napoleon can exercise any effective freedom of action in the political realm.

18 This is the central theme of the closing book of *Anna*, in which Tolstoy documents his own disillusion with social and political ethics through the character of Constantin Levin.

19 Notice how Aristotle treats the notion of *philia* as complementary to that of "equity." As he sees, the nature of the moral claims that arise within any situation depend on how closely the parties are related: indeed, it might be better to translate *philia* by some such term as "relationship" instead of the customary translation, "friendship," since his argument is intended to be analytical rather than edifying.

20 Rawls, *Theory of Justice*.

21 In United States labor law practice, arbitrators are guided by the published decisions of previous arbitrations, but not bound by them, since their own decisions normally turn on an estimate of the exact personal and group relations between the workers and managers involved in the particular dispute. Indeed, in Switzerland—here, as elsewhere, an extreme case—the results of labor arbitrations are not even published, on the ground that they are a "purely private matter" as between the immediate parties.

22 Monroe Freedman, *Lawyers' Ethics in an Adversary System* (Indianapolis: Bobbs Merrill, 1975). In this connection, current Chinese attempts to turn criminal proceedings into a species of chummy conciliation between the defendant and his fellow citizens can too easily serve to conceal tyranny behind a mask of paternalistic goodwill.

23 Kaufman, *Red Tape*.

24 *Ibid.*, p. 77.

[25] Robert Frost, "Build Soil—a Political Pastoral," in *Complete Poems of Robert Frost* (New York: Holt, Rinehart & Winston, 1949), pp. 421–32, at p. 430.

[26] John Dewey, *The Quest for Certainty* (New York: Putnam, 1929).

[27] Aristotle's "large spirited person"—commonly but wrongly translated as "great souled man," ignoring the care with which the Greeks differentiated between *anthropoi* (human beings) and *andres* (men)—is the final hero of the *Nicomachean Ethics*: the key feature of such a person was, for him, the ability to act on behalf of a friend from an understanding of that friend's own needs, wishes, and interests.

[28] We are indebted to Alan Donagan for reintroducing the idea of the "common morality" into philosophical ethics, in his book, *The Theory of Morality* (Chicago: University of Chicago Press, 1977).

[29] Edward H. Levi, *Introduction to Legal Reasoning* (Chicago: University of Chicago Press, 1948).

[30] Pascal's *Lettres Provinciales* were originally published in 1656–57, during the trial of his friend Antoine Arnauld, whose Jansenist associations made him a target for the Jesuits. Pascal's journalistic success with these letters did a great deal, by itself, to bring the tradition of "case reasoning" in ethics into discredit: so much so that the art of casuistics has subsequently been known by the name of "casuistry"—a word which the *Oxford English Dictionary* first records as having been used by Alexander Pope in 1725, and whose very form, as the dictionary makes clear, is dyslogistic. (It belongs to the same family of English words as "popery," "wizardry" and "sophistry," all of which refer to the *disreputable* employment of the arts in question.)

8

THEORY AND PRACTICE

Albert R. Jonsen
Stephen Toulmin

In the public debate about moral issues such as racial equality and abortion, deeply felt convictions struggle against an ambiguity the locus of which is not hard to identify. We inherit two distinct ways of discussing ethical issues. One of these frames these issues in terms of principles, rules, and other general ideas; the other focuses on the specific features of particular kinds of moral cases. In the first way general ethical rules relate to specific moral cases in a *theoretical* manner, with universal rules serving as "axioms" from which particular moral judgments are deduced as theorems. In the second, this relation is frankly *practical*, with general moral rules serving as "maxims," which can be fully understood only in terms of the paradigmatic cases that define their meaning and force.

The modes of argument associated with each approach are familiar provided that we consider them one at a time. When we discuss specific cases of conscience in concrete detail and practical terms, aside from the abstract theoretical arguments of moral theology and philosophical ethics, we understand either mode of reasoning well enough. But if we ask how these two kinds of arguments relate together, we find ourselves at a loss.

> How far and in what respects do general ethical doctrines carry weight when we deal with specific moral problems in complex practical situations?
>
> Conversely, how far and in what respects can one rely on particular perceptions about specific situations when criticizing general doctrines in ethical theory?

From *The Abuse of Casuistry: A History of Moral Reasoning* (1988). Berkeley and Los Angeles: University of California Press, pp. 23–46.

Nowadays the received view is that particular moral decisions simply apply universal ethical rules to particular cases; while moral decisions are sound to the extent that they are validly deduced from such rules:

> In this situation, such an action would be murder;
> Murder is invariably and universally wrong;
> *So*, acting in that way would be inescapably wrong.

The least we can do to reply to this view is to argue, first, that it oversimplifies a far more complex practical relationship and, second, that the "applying" and "deducing" which moral reasoning is said to involve are quite mysterious, unless we show in detail *just how* appeals to "universal principles"—whether framed in religious, philosophical, or everyday terms—help to resolve moral quandaries in practice. Certainly the experience of the National Commission casts some doubt on this view. So long as the commissioners discussed specific cases, their consensus showed how far they shared moral perceptions in practice: the moment they turned to consider the theoretical principles that underlay those particular perceptions, they lacked a similar consensus. How, then, can it be said that the particular judgments about which they evidently *agreed* were, all alike, "deduced from" universal principles about which they openly and plainly *disagree*?

The Classical Account

The relevance of general matters of abstract theory to the specific problems of concrete practice may be obscure in ethics; but it has never been obscure *only* in ethics. So let us start by asking how this general relationship was originally analyzed in antiquity, and then see what light this classical account still throws on current issues.

The first explicit account was developed by the philosophers of classical Athens. Their prototype of "theoretical" reasoning was *geometry*. There the starting point was a few general statements the meaning of which was clear and the truth of which was beyond question: from these were derived, by formal deduction, conclusions that were neither obvious nor self-explanatory. Starting from elementary definitions and statements about lines and angles, surfaces and solids, for instance, one might prove the famous theorem of Pythagoras, that

> the area of a square constructed on the longest side of a right-angled triangle is equal to the sum of the areas of squares constructed on the two shorter sides;

or the far more surprising result attributed to Plato's student, Theaetetus, (who died tragically early) that

> only five ways exist of fitting together equilateral plane figures, e.g., triangles, squares or pentagons, so as to form regular convex solids.[1]

The rigor of geometry was so appealing, indeed, that for many Greek philosophers formal deduction became the ideal of *all* rational argument. On this view an opinion can be accepted as "knowledge," or an argument as truly solid, only if it is related deductively ("necessarily") to clear and obvious initial principles. So, it seemed, the whole of geometry might follow necessarily from an unquestioned set of definitions and general statements; and these were subsequently organized into canonical form, as the "axioms" of Euclidean geometry. In due course, too (the hope was), other sciences would find their own unquestioned general principles to serve as their starting points, in explaining, for example, the natures of animals, plants, and the other permanent features of the world.[2]

If this were only done, all true sciences would be able to argue with the same necessity as geometry. When the scientist (geometer, zoologist, or whatever) works with clear and self-evident theoretical principles, his certainty of their truth will outweigh all his opinions about the particular facts he uses to explain them. He will grasp the definitions of "equilateral plane figure" and "regular convex solid" with more certainty than he can ever have about Theaetetus' theory of the five regular convex solids. Indeed, all sciences with well-formulated principles share this feature: their general principles are better understood, and known with greater certainty, than any of the specific conclusions they are used to explain.

How far, on this classical account, does the scope of "theory" reach? Not all of our knowledge, Aristotle argued, is of this sort; nor do we have this theoretical kind of certainty in every field.[3] In *practical* fields we grasp particular facts of experience more clearly, and have more certainty of their truth, than we ever do about the general principles that we may use to account for them. As an illustration, he cites the everyday belief that chicken is good to eat (i.e., nourishing).[4] Knowing *that* chicken is good to eat, he argues, is one thing, but knowing *what makes it* good to eat is quite another. Practical experience assures us of the initial fact quite apart from any subsequent nutritional explanation. What makes chicken good to eat is perhaps the fact that it is a light meat: that being so, a scientific explanation will read,

> Chicken is a light meat; light meats are easy to digest; so chicken is easy to digest. That is why it is good to eat.

But the true explanation may be quite other, or even unknown. Still, however uncertain the explanation remains in theory, the gastronomic fact that chicken is good to eat is not, in practice, seriously in doubt. Direct human experience testifies to it in advance of any explanation.

How is it that in such cases we are surer of the facts to which experience testifies directly than we are of the general principles that explain them? Why is the relationship between principles and instances here apparently reversed? The reason (Aristotle adds) is that we have left the realm of Theory for that of Practice.[5] In the realm of Practice, certitude no longer requires a prior grasp of definitions, general principles, and axioms, as in the realm of Theory. Rather, it depends on accumulated experience of particular situations; and this practical experience gives one a kind of wisdom—*phronesis*—different from the abstract grasp of any theoretical science—*episteme*. On Aristotle's account this reversed relationship between principles and cases is typical of those fields of knowledge that are by nature "'practical" rather than "theoretical."[6]

The realm of the practical included, for Aristotle, the entire realm of *ethics*: in his eyes the subject matter of moral reflection lay within the sphere of practical wisdom rather than theoretical comprehension. . . . For the moment (one may remark), if Aristotle was right about this, the reversed locus of certitude in the deliberations of the National Commission should have been expected![7]

The classical account of Theory and Practice involved three further distinctions. In theoretical fields such as geometry, statements or arguments were *idealized*, *atemporal*, and *necessary*:

1. They were "idealized" in the following sense. Concrete physical objects, cut out of metal in the shapes of triangles or circles, can never be made with perfect precision, nor can the metal sheets from which they are cut stay perfectly flat, so that they exemplify the truths of geometry only approximately. The idealized "straight lines" and "circles" of geometry, by contrast, exemplify such truths with perfect exactness.

2. They were "atemporal" in the following sense. Any geometrical theorem that is true at one time or on one occasion will be true at any time and on any occasion. Pythagoras did not "prove" some temporal concrete fact that just happened to be true in his particular time but a permanent relationship that held good "universally." So there was no question of his theorem *ceasing* to be true at some later time.

3. Finally, theoretical arguments were "necessary" in a twofold sense. The arguments of Euclidean geometry depended for their validity both on the correctness of the initial axioms and definitions and on the inner consistency of the subsequent deductions. Granted Euclid's axioms, all of his later theorems were "necessary consequences" of those initial truths. If any of the theorems were questioned, conversely, this implied either that their starting point was incorrect or else that the steps taken in passing to the theorems were formally fallacious.

In all three respects, practical statements and arguments differed from theoretical ones by being *concrete, temporal,* and *presumptive*.

1. They were "concrete" in the following sense. Chickens are never idealized entities, and the things we say about cooking make no pretense to geometrical perfection. A particular chicken may be "exceptionally delicate," but it is never "only approximately [still less, ±0.05%] a chicken." Thus the truth of practical statements rests on direct experience: abstraction or idealization do not protect them from experiential challenges.

2. They were "temporal" in this sense. The same experience that teaches what is normally the case *at any time* also teaches what is the case *only sometimes*. (Chicken is edible all year round, but game birds are stringy if taken out of season.) Truths of practical experience thus do not hold

good "universally" or "at *any* time": rather, they hold "on occasion" or "at *this or that* moment"—that is, usually, often, at most always.

3. Finally, practical arguments were "presumptive" in this sense. Chicken is normally good to eat, so a particular chicken just brought from the store is "presumably" good to eat. In unusual cases that conclusion may be open to rebuttal: the chicken in question may have been left too long in summer heat and gone bad. The presumptive conclusion is, however, open to doubt "in point of fact": no one is denying the initial generalization, or questioning the formal validity of the presumptive inference. Still, if we depart far enough from the "normal" or "typical" cases, reasonable conclusions based on the soundest presumptive arguments may, in practice, be upset.

All three crucial features of the classical account were connected. Statements in geometry were atemporal, and its arguments necessary, just because they did not refer to familiar objects such as metal plates and chickens but to idealized entities such as *the circle* and *the triangle*. By contrast, practical statements were temporal and the corresponding arguments presumptive simply because they referred to actual events, agents, and objects, particular circumstances, and specific places and times. When telescoped together, these distinctions had another, unhelpful effect. They turned the original contrast of Theory with Practice into an outright divorce. So the "atemporal" world of intellectual reflection and certain knowledge was set apart from the "temporal" world of practical actions and corrigible opinions; and the timeless insights of intellectual theorists were esteemed above the workaday experience of the practical craftsman. Eventually the "atemporality" of Theory was even interpreted as implying that its subject matter was Immutable and its truths Eternal, and it became associated with the unchanging *celestial* world. Meanwhile the temporality of Practice was equated with Transitoriness and linked to the changeableness of *terrestrial* things. With this divorce the "immortal" world of universal theoretical principles was separated from the "mortal" world of particular practical skills and cases.[8] The ripples caused by this equation have been influencing Western thinking ever since.

The Classical Account and Its Modern Relevance

How far is this account of Theory and Practice still relevant today? Certainly skeptics can find reason to ignore it. Nobody today credits Euclidean geometry with the universal absolute truth it promised 2,500 years ago: the mathematical creation of non-Euclidean geometries brought to light an unlimited range of axiom systems, each of which generates a consistent sequence of theorems. Nor does anyone today suppose that the theories of natural science share the formal certainty of geometrical theorems, whether Euclidean or non-Euclidean; still less that they are as abstract as Greek geometry. Over the last two hundred years, in fact, scientists have given up trying to "prove" their theoretical principles self-evidently true; rather, they now take pride in being "empirical" philosophers. So at a time when science and technology are interacting so closely, we can no longer suppose that an unbridgeable intellectual gulf divides the theoretical insights of science from the practical procedures of the arts, crafts, or industry.

The divorce of Theory from Practice is thus a thing of the past, and no purpose is served by reviving it. As an analytic contrast, however, we cannot ignore the *distinction* between them, for two distinct reasons. First, the problem of matching principles (e.g., ethical principles) to cases (e.g., moral cases) affects all fields of human experience in which general rules are invoked to support practical decisions that require specific actions affecting the personal circumstances of individual human beings. In clinical medicine and civil engineering, economics and politics, quite as much as in ethics, the universality of general principles must still be squared with the particularity of specific decisions.

Issues of public administration, law, and medicine (as of ethics) thus become truly problematic just at the point at which rules, laws, and other theoretical generalizations apply ambiguously or marginally, or at which alternative rules or principles point in contrary directions and have to be arbitrated between. Three sample scenarios will illustrate the point:

> An elderly widow comes to the Social Security office, claiming that she has been wrongly deprived of her old-age pension payments. On investigation it turns out that the contributions her immigrant husband paid before his death were barely sufficient to qualify her for a pension at all.

> A patient comes to a physician's office with an unusual combination of fever and pallor, earache and bronchial congestion. The doctor is in doubt whether this is an unusually severe case of the current influenza or whether it indicates, rather, the far more dangerous onset of a more serious disease—for example, meningitis.

> A plaintiff testifies in civil court that she injured herself on a defective stairway, which her landlord negligently left unrepaired. Another tenant testifies, to the contrary, that the staircase was not badly maintained and alleges that the plaintiff was drunk at the time of the fall.

What is involved in dealing with such problems? All three issues involve matters of judgment, which arise out of initially ambiguous or marginal situations where no "universal principle" can settle the matter once and for all. In real life practical issues of these kinds are resolved by looking at the concrete details of particular cases. Are there, after all, weighty reasons of equity to allow the widow's claim to a pension, treat the sick patient on the basis of the less probable but more threatening diagnosis, or award the injured tenant damages in spite of her possible contributory drunkenness? At the end of the day we simply have to decide in which direction the strongest demands of administrative equity, the most pressing medical indications, or the testimony of the most credible witnesses finally point *in this case*.

Once this practical judgment is exercised, the resulting decisions will (no doubt) be "formally entailed by" the relevant generalizations, but that connection throws no light on the grounds by which the decisions are arrived at, or on the considerations that tilt the scale toward one general course of action rather than the other. What such decisions involve can be explained only in *substantive* and *circumstantial* terms. The demands of administrative equity, the significance of alternative diagnoses and therapeutic indications, or the probative weight of contrary witnesses: all of these raise questions of rational substance, not logical form, and particular decisions (say, to prescribe a treatment designed to deal with the likely influenza while guarding against a possible meningitis) call for substantive balancing of the foreseeable risks and prospective benefits of alternative actions, with an eye to the detailed circumstances of the actual situation.

The analytic contrast between Theory and Practice is important for a second reason: the classical account implied both that theoretical statements can make universal claims which hold good at any place or time *only* if they are as idealized as the axioms or theorems of Greek geometry, and that theoretical arguments lead to necessary conclusions *only* if they are cut off from concrete objects and practical experience. By our standards both implications are exaggerated; but each of the classical contrasts in itself can still throw light on the current practice of the sciences: notably, on the contrasted ways in which intellectual problems arise *within* theories (when general ideas are dealt with in their own terms) and *outside* them (when those general ideas are applied to specific cases, or in particular circumstances).

In scientific theory today general ideas are no longer divorced from actual objects, yet they are still "idealized" in a weaker sense: they refer directly only to preselected objects, which exemplify them precisely enough to be relevant to the theory. In practical professions such as medicine, by contrast, the procedures are "concrete" in a similarly weakened sense: they apply equally to every case that presents itself, and every instance is equally relevant for practical purposes. To physicists engaged in refining gravitation theory, the motions of planets and earth satellites are of direct interest, whereas the fluttering of a falling sheet of paper is not. Astronomical movements and falling papers both exemplify gravitation, but planets and satellites provide straightforward and unadulterated cases of gravitation in action, in a way that fluttering papers do not. Even if we recorded a sheet of paper's falling precisely, using a high-speed cinema camera, the gravitational aspects of that event cannot in practice be separated from the effects of air currents and other outside influences. Being directly interested in exact theoretical issues and general ideas, physical scientists thus learn from planetary movements in a way they cannot learn from falling sheets of paper: in a physicist's eyes (so to say) the fluttering papers "do not count." So the standing of the physical sciences as exact, idealized, and theoretical disciplines is purchased only at a price. They are "exact and idealized" because they are highly *selective*: they pay direct attention only to circumstances and cases that are "abstracted" (i.e., selected out) as being relevant to their central theoretical goals.

In the same weaker sense, practical fields such as law, medicine, and public administration deal with concrete actual cases, not with abstract idealized situations. They are directly concerned with immediate facts about specific situations and individuals: general ideas concern them only indirectly, as they bear on the problems of those particular individuals. Unlike natural scientists, who are free to decide in advance which types of situations, cases, or individuals they may (or need not) pay attention to, physicians, lawyers, and social service workers face myriad professional problems the moment any client walks through the door. They may end up by referring some of those clients to other, more appropriate professionals, but they cannot choose to ignore them or their problems. Where scientists study specific cases for any light they can throw on general theoretical ideas, members of the service professions, conversely, study general ideas for any help they can give in dealing with specific practical cases.

The intellectual claims of scientific theory today may no longer refer beyond the familiar changing world of temporal experience, but in their own way scientific principles are still "atemporal": covering *all* relevant cases, *anywhere*, at *any* time. Conversely, the practical goals of the service professions are still, in the corresponding sense, "temporal": focusing on *specific* cases and *particular* occasions. A physicist lecturing about high-energy particle theory may refer both to observations made last week at the Stanford Linear Accelerator Center and to events that supposedly took place long ago, soon after the cosmological Big Bang. Because his concerns are not specifically tied to particular times or places, there is nothing incongruous in his discussing both in the same terms. The fundamental question for him is, "What phenomena are shared at all times, in all contexts?" and the *universality* of theory makes all times and places equivalent. Conversely, what matters most to the practicing lawyer or physician is the *particularity* of the problems facing this individual client or patient here and now: his professional duty is to find out the unique features of the present client's particular problems.

This contrast, between the *atemporal* focus of scientific theory and the preoccupation of legal and medical practice with the *here and now*, is a crucial difference between "theory" and "practice" as those terms are now understood. Scientists study particular events occurring here and now primarily for the light they can throw on universal atemporal theories: practitioners appeal to universal atemporal theories chiefly for the help they may give in dealing with practical problems arising here and now. So, far from reflecting any opposition between Theory and Practice, the varied concerns of scientists and practitioners complement one another.

Another feature of the analytic contrast between Theory and Practice concerns the solidity of argument in each. Within scientific theories today arguments are no longer accepted on a priori grounds alone, but they are still "necessary" in a less ambitious sense. So long as any scientific conclusion follows from theoretical principles strictly, that inference is valid formally quite as much as substantively. Conversely, when practical arguments go beyond the scope of any formal theory their conclusions are "presumptive" in a similar sense. Their soundness depends not on formal validity alone but on the richness of the substantive support for any general ideas they use and the accuracy with which any particular case has been recognized and classified.

Clinical physicians and medical scientists, for instance, may have occasion to discuss the same bacterial infections in either of two ways. They may do so in *general theoretical terms*:

> When an acute bacterial infection is treated with a suitable antibiotic agent, the multiplication of the bacteria is checked and the body's immune system fights the infection off quickly; but when the infection is not so treated, the bacteria multiply unchecked and the immune system takes longer to overcome the infection. Administration of an appropriate antibiotic is thus an effective therapy for such infections.

Given that the index of an antibiotic's effectiveness is the speed with which it helps the body throw off infection, the relationships presented in this argument are indisputable and even "demonstrative." As it stands, however, this argument does not tell us how bacterial infections can be identified in practice, or what antibiotics are effective against which infections. Thus even in clinical contexts, theoretical arguments are detached from the details of actual experience.

Alternatively, a physician may report, as follows, on the *condition of an individual patient*:

> This patient displayed typical symptoms of a bacterial infection, and initial laboratory tests showed streptococci in the blood. After a week of anti-streptococcal antibiotics, however, there has been no significant improvement.
>
> Further tests are required, to determine if the first lab tests were incorrect or incomplete, and other bacteria were masked by the streptococci; or if we are here faced with a new strain of streptococci, which calls for the use of different antibiotics. While this is being checked out, the patient should continue to rest, take plenty of fluids, and give the existing treatment the best chance of working.

In this second case the solidity of the argument depends not on the formal validity of the inference but on ensuring that the present case is described as completely and accurately as practical purposes demand. As always, the presumption that the patient's condition would improve in a week or so is open to disappointment, but that failure casts no shadow on the general soundness of the corresponding argument. ("That is how things typically go," we may say, "but you meet the odd case that turns out differently.") So the original argument was either "off the point," as the infection was not what the lab results suggested, or else it was an occasion to identify a new strain of antibiotic-resistant streptococci. Either way, the issue is *substantive*: the relevance of our general ideas to the actual facts of this situation, and the failure of the initial presumption points the physicians toward fresh substantive discoveries.

Taken in its revised form, the classical contrast between Theory and Practice captures two points that are still important. To begin with, the word "arguments" has two functionally distinct senses, formal and substantial. Theoretical arguments are chains of proof, whereas practical arguments are methods for resolving problems. In the first, formal sense, an *argument* is a "chain of propositions, linked up so as to *guarantee* its conclusion. In the second, substantive sense, an *argument* is a network of considerations, presented so as to *resolve* a practical quandary. Taken in these two contrasted senses, "arguments" operate in quite different ways and have different kinds of intellectual merits. They conform to different patterns and must be analyzed in different terms.

Theoretical arguments are structured in ways that free them from any dependence on the circumstances of their presentation and ensure them a *validity* of a kind that is not affected by the practical context of use. In formal arguments particular conclusions are deduced from ("entailed by") the initial axioms or universal principles that are the apex of the argument. So the truth or certainty that attaches to those axioms *flows downward* to the specific instances to be "proved" (fig. 1).[9]

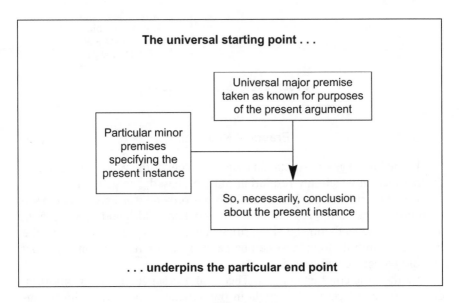

Fig. 1
Theoretical Argument

In the language of formal logic, the axioms are *major premises*, the facts that specify the present instance are *minor premises*, and the conclusion to be "proved" is deduced (follows *necessarily*) from the initial premises.

Practical arguments, by contrast, involve a wider range of factors than formal deductions and are read with an eye to their occasion of use. Instead of aiming at strict entailments, they draw on the outcomes of previous experience, carrying over the procedures used to resolve earlier problems and reapplying them in new problematic situations. Practical arguments depend for their power on how closely the *present* circumstances resemble those of the earlier *precedent* cases for which this particular type of argument was originally devised. So, in practical arguments, the truths and certitudes established in the precedent cases *pass sideways*, so as to provide "resolutions" of later problems (fig. 2).

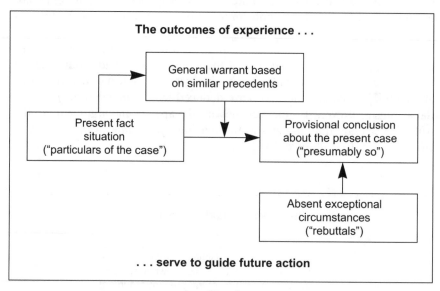

Fig. 2
Practical Reasoning

In the language of rational analysis, the facts of the present case define the *grounds* on which any resolution must be based; the general considerations that carried weight in similar situations provide *warrants* that help settle future cases. So the resolution of any problem holds good *presumptively*; its strength depends on the similarities between the present case and the precedents; and its soundness can be challenged (or *rebutted*) in situations that are recognized as *exceptional*.[10]

Further, the contrast between Theory and Practice, in its current form, departs from the classical formula in one crucial respect. It no longer involves an outright divorce, or professes to separate intellectual grasp of "unchanging entities" from technical know-how about "changeable objects."

Instead, it regards all the scientific and technological disciplines as ranged along a *spectrum*. Some of these come close to the theoretical extreme whereas others are basically practical; but all of them are in one or another respect both intellectual and technical, and each combines theoretical analysis and practical technique in its own distinctive way.

At one extreme, some branches of mathematics still aspire to the classical ideal of geometry. Their goal is full "axiomatization," by which theorems are linked into a single "deductive system," or piece of cohesive intellectual knitting. Moving along the spectrum, the branches of physics that have cosmological ambitions (e.g., particle physics or unified field theory) still refer in practice to concrete objects and situations and so are dependent on laboratory experiment and astronomical observation. The disciplines of biology lie further along the spectrum: biological theory does not aspire to the abstractness or universality of physical and chemical theory: rather, biologists select a specific "subject matter" and objects of study, using taxonomic keys and other identification techniques.[11]

Finally, toward the practical end of the spectrum are those activities the preeminent concern of which is to *change* the world rather than to *understand* it. Prime among these is clinical medicine: here we shall pay closest attention to the ways in which general physiological explanations, on the one hand, and clinical knowledge of particular cases, on the other, blend in the course of clinical practice. As we shall find, this provides a powerful model to use for analyzing the manner in which "theoretical" and "practical" considerations blend in the field of ethics as well.

Clinical Medicine as a Practical Enterprise

No professional enterprise today is closer to moral practice, or better exemplifies the special character of "practical" inquiries, than clinical medicine. Clinical practice, for a start, shares the emphasis on the certitude of direct experience that was for Aristotle a mark of the *practical*. Recall his appeal to the dietary virtues of chicken. We do not need a nutritional theory, he argues, in order to be sure that chicken is nourishing: on the contrary, it is only because we know from experience that chicken is in fact nourishing that the question, "What *makes* it that way?" arises at all. Clinical experience, likewise, gives physicians solid assurance of well-founded knowledge about health and disease, in advance of all explanations from biochemists and other scientists.[12] That practical knowledge, too, may be a point of departure for new scientific questions: for example, just because we already know that aspirin does in fact relieve headaches, we can go on to ask the scientific question, "*How* does it relieve them?"

Medicine blends theory and practice, intellectual grasp and technical skill, *episteme* and *phronesis*, in its own characteristic manner. It spans the spectrum of Theory and Practice, from the general theories of biomedical science at one extreme to the particular procedures of clinical practice at the other. In doing so it illustrates the complex and subtle ways in which theoretical and practical knowledge bear on each other. At one extreme, medicine overlaps into the natural sciences. Research in physiology and other biomedical fields aims to refine our general ideas (specifically, our general ideas about health and disease) quite as much as research in any other science. The central core of medicine, however, comprises practical procedures designed not to explain health and disease in theory but to treat illnesses and restore health, as a matter of practice. These procedures are the medical profession's collective property: though general in form, they comprise general practical skills (*technai*, in Aristotle's terms) rather than belonging to theoretical science (*episteme*). At the other extreme are the skills that are the individual physician's personal property. A doctor's skill in handling his patients' medical problems demands not only knowledge about the general practical techniques of diagnosis and therapy but also specific and particular kinds of clinical understanding. The central question for him is always, "Just what specific condition is affecting this particular patient, and just what should we do about it, *here and now?*"

In this last respect clinical knowledge requires what Aristotle calls "prudence" or *phronesis*: practical wisdom in dealing with particular individuals, specific problems, and the details of practical cases or actual situations. A working doctor does not rely only on a general understanding of diseases (nosology) and their treatment (therapeutics). A knowledge of medicine in general may be of no practical value in the absence of two more particular skills: the ability to recognize any particular patient's problems, as they present themselves here and now, and also to be able to treat them promptly and responsively, as they take their course.

Clinical medicine is thus *scientific* only in this sense: that the treatment of disease nowadays relies heavily on the generalized scientific knowledge developed by generations of research physicians and biologists. In other respects it is no more scientific today than it has ever been. The specificity of the ailments with which the working physician deals, and the individuality of the patients who suffer them, mark clinical medicine as falling squarely in the realm of practice, not theory. Often enough theory and practice intersect in clinical medicine today; yet with such different goals, they also at times conflict. A brief scenario will show how easily this can happen.

> An elderly woman is admitted to hospital suffering from half a dozen of the ailments common in old age. The admitting physician finds it hard to tell which of her signs, symptoms, and complaints are the effects of which ailment.

So far, so good: in such a situation the prudent physician concentrates on clinical management of the patient's immediate discomforts rather than making a heroic attempt to "cure" underlying conditions that do not lend themselves to full scientific understanding. But at this point a further complication arises:

> The attendant physician who takes the patient's history is not a primary
> care internist, ready to deal with all her problems as he finds them, but a
> research scientist in gerontology, who is professionally interested only in
> selected aspects of geriatric disease.

Now the contrast in goals and methods between scientific theory and clinical practice surfaces and may cause problems. From the standpoint of a research physician who views the patient's illness with theoretical eyes, her current medical condition may be of no scientific relevance. It may be so hard to sort out her multiple ailments and study them separately that for gerontological purposes her case has no more relevance than the falling of sheets of paper had for the purposes of gravitational research. The gerontologist faces a conflict of duties: as a clinical practitioner, his responsibility is to care for the patient in any way her condition requires, but as a scientist he has no direct interest in spending time on cases that do not promote his research. The usual division of labor in a research hospital may give him a way out of his conflict: he may refer the patient to a primary care internist who is concerned with her clinically, not scientifically, so freeing himself to look out for other patients whose medical conditions are more significant for science.

How, then, can we best characterize the relations between theory and practice in contemporary medicine? Is all clinical medicine—the reflective use of medical judgment in dealing with the specific conditions of particular patients—simply "applied biomedical science"? To answer that question either with a plain yes or with a flat no is equally misleading. Certainly major theoretical elements from the biomedical sciences lie behind modern clinical practice. But biology does not bear on clinical medicine in any simple or direct (let alone formal) way: their interrelations are substantive and subtle.

On the one hand, the rights or wrongs of any clinical procedure, as a way of treating a particular patient's current condition, is never simply or formally "deducible from the general principles of biological theory: no strict deductive links hold between them. Where the mechanisms of the disease that a particular patient presents are scientifically understood, the practitioner can properly draw on that understanding as intellectual background to his clinical decisions. But clinical knowledge does not automatically give out at the point where biology runs out of steam. If a case does not fall clearly within one or another of the classes of disease of which we have a full scientific grasp, the clinical tasks of diagnosis and treatment are less open to theoretical understanding, but they are no less typical elements of clinical practice. Just at this point modern medicine reverts to its earlier status, as an inherited craft or "mystery"; and as such, it is the current phase in a practical tradition the origins of which are much older than those of modern biological science. On the other hand, just because general biomedical theories and particular clinical decisions are not linked by a medical "geometry," there is no reason to despair of the substantive "rights and wrongs" of clinical decisions. Even without a rigorous theoretical basis, clinical judgments are not (as some would argue) the personal hunches or expressions of taste with which individual doctors respond to each practical situation in turn. The guarantees of medical objectivity do not, in practice, depend only on formal theoretical entailments: the strongest support for agreeing to a clinical diagnosis or a therapeutic proposal comes from substantive medical evidence. [13]

There is, of course, a germ of truth in the "personal" view. In a given case, when the doctor accepts a scientific theory or clinical procedure, his decision is not a mere hunch or matter of taste, but typically it does remain a matter of *personal judgment*. What is the subject matter of this judgment? When a doctor reviews a medical history and pattern of symptoms, what exactly does he "perceive"? We can define the object of clinical judgment more clearly if we think of this clinical perception as a kind of *pattern recognition*.

In clinical diagnosis the starting point is the current repertory of diseases, injuries, and disabilities for which descriptions exist in the medical literature. When instances of these conditions are encountered, on trauma ambulances or hospital wards, they are the teaching material required to help students or interns recognize the "presentation" of these conditions. Formally a medical condition is defined by the classical description, and this is a useful guide in identifying diseases that are met comparatively rarely. But a description is clinically fruitful only when it is based on perceptive study of actual cases, and it is practically effective only if paradigmatic cases exist to *show* in actual fact what can otherwise only be stated: namely, the actual onset, syndromes, and course typical of the condition. Given this *taxonomy* of known conditions and the paradigmatic cases that exemplify the various types, diagnosis then becomes a kind of perception, and the reasons justifying a diagnosis rest on appeals to analogy. As new cases present themselves for examination the physician collects details from each patient's history, his own immediate observations, and the results of laboratory tests and uses these facts to "place" a particular patient's condition in one or more of the recognized "types." Forced to choose among alternative diagnoses, he must decide how close (or analogous) the present case is to each of the possibilities. This diagnostic question may have only one answer: any diagnosis of a patient's diarrhea, say, may be ruled out, other than a *Salmonella* infection. But it is often necessary to take two or more possible diagnoses seriously; while on occasion physicians may be faced by complex combinations of distinct pathological conditions.

In marginal and ambiguous cases clinicians who are equally skilled and conscientious may share their information fully and have the best wills in the world; yet through J-"reading" the same history and symptoms differently, they may offer different diagnoses and treatment proposals for one and the same case. When this happens no conclusive evidence or arguments need be available to choose between their "readings"; but this does not mean that their judgments are subjective or uncheckable. Quite the contrary: as the patient's condition unfolds, the consequences of the rival views will show up in fact, making it clear just how "objectively" serious the differing implications of those judgments really were.

With or without an explicit scientific foundation, then, the heart of clinical practice and training comprises a taxonomy of medical conditions. Medical students and interns in training are shown cases that exemplify the constellations of symptoms, or "syndromes," typical of these varied conditions. In this way they learn what to look for as indicative of any specific condition and so how to recognize it if it turns up again on a later occasion. The key element in diagnosis is thus "syndrome recognition": a capacity to *re*-identify, in fresh cases, a disability, disease, or injury one has encountered (or read about) in earlier instances. In this respect clinical knowledge of particular cases is like the field botanist's mastery of botanical taxonomy, which permits him to identify a new specimen, first, say, as a monocotyledon, then as a member of the amaryllis family, finally as belonging to a South American genus, possibly *Alstroemeria*. Given the respective missions of botany and clinical medicine, the initial steps in both cases are to identify the samples at hand: for this purpose the indispensable tools are a rich enough taxonomy and experience in syndrome recognition.

Clinical medicine's central reliance on the taxonomy of illness also explains why the pattern of reasoning by which physicians link symptoms with diseases typically relies on *arguing from analogy*. The conclusions of diagnostic arguments usually embody three linked components.

1. A pattern of signs and symptoms (s_1, s_2, s_3 . . .) is cited which apparently includes enough of the distinctive elements of condition *a* rather than, say, *b* or *c* to warrant a presumptive diagnosis.
2. These similarities are judged close and distinctive enough to justify using treatment procedures appropriate to condition *a*.
3. The possibility of exceptions is guarded against by agreeing that the provisional diagnosis will be reconsidered in case further symptoms turn up (s_7, s_8, s_9 . . .) that are possible signs of the rarer conditions, *d*, *e*, or *f*.

The relations between a diagnostic conclusion and the evidence on which it is based (symptoms, onset, etc.) are precisely those typical of practical reasoning rather than theoretical proof. First, the conclusion is related to the evidence by *substantive* rather than formal connections. Second, the conclusion follows as a *rebuttable* presumption, not as a necessary entailment. Finally, the inference from the evidence to the conclusion is not timelessly valid, regardless of context, but thoroughly *circumstantial*: dependent on detailed facts about the circumstances and nature of the particular case. For this reason all diagnostic conclusions are tentative and open to reconsideration if certain crucial symptoms or circumstances have been overlooked or the later course of the illness brings important new evidence to light.

Casuistry and Diagnostics

Medicine is a useful model for the analysis of moral practice in several respects. Clinical medicine is prototypically "practical" both in Aristotle's sense of the term and also in contemporary usage; so the leading features of clinical practice help us to put flesh on Aristotle's schematic statements about the differences between "'practical wisdom" and "theoretical understanding." In moral as in medical practice, the resolution of practical problems draws on a central taxonomy of type cases, and the pattern of argument by paradigm and analogy is once again at work. Last but not least, when medicine is practiced conscientiously as well as skillfully, it becomes a prototypically *moral* enterprise. A doctor who diagnoses correctly and who prescribes successfully behaves meritoriously, not merely because his actions are *effective* but equally because, given his relationship to the patient, these kinds of actions are *appropriate*: that is, they fulfill his *duty* as a physician—so much so that one might even regard clinical practice as a "special case" of moral conduct generally.

It should not be surprising, therefore, if many features that mark off clinical medicine from more theoretical enterprises hold good for other kinds of moral conduct. So as we study the history of case morality—notably the "high casuistry" of late medieval and early modern Europe—we shall bear in mind the casuists' assumption that morality does indeed lie in the realm of practice, not theory, and remember what consequences this distinction implied for those who knew their Aristotle. Before we return to the question of how universal ethical principles relate to specific moral judgments in particular cases and embark on our account of the development of casuistry since antiquity, we should stop and pose the question, "How far do the patterns of practical reasoning employed in everyday moral life, and explicitly recognized in the casuistical tradition, share the crucial features of medical practice?"

Our examination of medicine brought the following key features of clinical practice to light:

1. The merits of clinical decisions are related to the theories of biomedical science, not by any strictly formal entailments but in more indirect, substantive ways.
2. The crucial points of clinical reference are the diseases, disabilities, and injuries contained in the current taxonomy of pathological conditions.
3. Diagnostic reasoning proceeds analogically, using medical taxonomy as a source of paradigm cases to which all comparisons refer back.
4. Clinical inferences and conclusions—being substantive and timely, not formal and atemporal—are presumptive, rebuttable, and open to revision in the light of fresh evidence.
5. Clinical arguments—being presumptive, not necessary—always leave room for conscientious physicians to reach different diagnostic opinions about marginal and ambiguous cases.

All these features of medical theory and clinical practice suggest parallel questions about ethical theory and moral practice.

To begin with the general relationship between theory and practice, our central problem about the relevance of universal ethical principles to particular moral decisions, is more easily resolved if we take the example of medicine seriously. The deadlock between ethical dogmatists, whose absolute principles admit of no exceptions, and moral relativists, who see no room for anything but local custom and individual taste, is inescapable only so long as we remain on the theoretical level; but in practical medicine this deadlock is easily resolved. The suggestion that particular clinical decisions are either necessary entailments of theoretical biology or else personal whims of individual physicians collapses the moment we recognize what indirect and lengthy chains of argument link clinical decisions back to, for example, biochemistry. As we shall now see, by taking a practical view of ethics we can again avoid the unpalatable choice between a strict "moral geometry" and the appeal to "personal preferences."

To begin with the relevance of *taxonomic* procedures to ethics, this was clear enough when the National Commission dealt with the ethics of human experimentation. One crucial factor in the commission's ability to agree on recommendations about specific types of cases was its reliance on a moral taxonomy by which kinds of human experimentation were first distinguished, then treated differently. Given that a taxonomic procedure is effective in this one moral situation, may it not be equally effective in resolving other kinds of moral problems? To what extent, for example, is research with children similar to research with the mentally infirm? The other parallels between practical reasoning in medical and moral contexts are no less apparent. If the practical analysis of moral issues means working with a taxonomy of moral cases and circumstances, it is also natural to use *analogical reasoning* to bring new and problematic types of cases into the classification system that summarizes the agreed resolutions of earlier, less problematic cases. So it need be no surprise that, like a modern clinician's diagnostic methods, the procedures that casuists have used to resolve moral problems appeal to understood and agreed *paradigms*, or *type cases*, from which they survey their way analogically to less understood, still disputed issues.

Judgments about moral issues, arrived at in the concrete circumstances of a practical case, can no more be abstracted from their detailed circumstances than can medical judgments about the present condition of individual patients. Clinical inferences and conclusions about particular cases are never necessary or contextless, always *presumptive* and *revisable* in the light of further experience, and there is no reason why matters should be any different in the moral realm. We may reasonably expect the same resistance to dogma, and the same kind of openness to experience, in practical case morality, as we rightly demand in case medicine or in case law.

One final parallel between morals and medicine deserves to be underlined. All detailed clinical inferences are presumptive; so clinical judgments about a patient's condition, and about the prognosis for his recovery, are never final. Honest and conscientious doctors may therefore read marginal or ambiguous cases differently, without being open to criticism. Surely the same is true more generally, of moral as well as medical judgments. If absolute agreement is too much to ask in the technical context of clinical medicine, must not the moral realm, too, leave room for honest and conscientious *differences of opinion*?

This question is neither idle nor empty; it has hidden subtleties to which we shall return. We may be prepared for differences of moral opinion between honest and conscientious individuals in *marginal and ambiguous* cases, for instance, but this in no way means that similar differences of opinion are admissible in *all kinds* of cases. Arguing from paradigm cases about preservation of life and telling the truth, the casuists, as we shall see, allowed no room for conscientious disagreement about cases of, say, willful cruelty to innocents or purely selfish deceit. In their eyes the locus of "conscience" was the class of cases over which the moral distinctions were still obscure, turned on marginal interpretations of the relevant considerations, or were so balanced between contraries that no accepted reading of the current taxonomy yielded a conclusive answer. So between the individual judgments required in ambiguous cases and the personal preferences of the moral relativists lie a million miles of distance. Like disagreements between careful physicians, again, serious differences of view among moral individuals may also lead to substantively different conclusions; and when this happens, these conclusions may teach us something about the "practical wisdom" of the individuals involved.

Yet when all these qualifications are taken into account, it is still true that moral arguments can no more lead to final and definitive conclusions than do the parallel arguments in clinical medicine. In both fields the best we can do is appraise the particular situation in which we find ourselves with the highest degree of clinical perceptiveness we can bring to the situation. But our judgments are always made at particular times, on the basis of the given facts and observations, and so are often "timely" and "context dependent." They remain, that is, *substantive* and *practical*, with all the fallibility and revisability that these terms imply.

Comparing practical morality with medicine, as we are doing here, is not original. St. Augustine, for instance, described morality as a discipline "which is a medicine of the mind."[14] Many thinkers in the European tradition of casuistry had an eye for the similarities between clinical and moral perception, and often drew explicit parallels between the tasks of moral advisers or confessors on the one hand and those of medical practitioners on the other. In the year 1215, for instance, the decrees of the Fourth Lateran Council, which required all Christians to confess their sins to a priest annually, compared these responsibilities:

> The confessor should be discreet and careful in the manner of experienced physicians . . . diligently inquiring about the circumstances of the sin and the sinner, whereby he can learn what sort of advice to offer and what remedies to employ, making diverse attempts to heal the ailing person.[15]

Nor is the basic pattern of reasoning by paradigm and analogy unfamiliar to those who know the tradition of casuistry at first hand. Writing about the methods of casuistry in his study, *Conscience and Its Problems*, Bishop Kenneth Kirk, the Anglican scholar and moralist from whom the title of this book is borrowed, acknowledges the role of taxonomy in case reasoning, whether in ethics or elsewhere. *Mutatis mutandis*, indeed—Bishop Kirk's statements about "casuistical method" might be read in a medical sense; and as such they sound very like an account of the steps required to identify and describe a new "clinical entity" in medicine. At any rate, his words may serve as a summary of the points about practical reasoning that we shall keep in mind as we explore the history and implications of the casuistical tradition:

> Casuistry is a process of applying old illustrations to new problems, to discover when the new corresponds to the old in its essential features, so that the same principle will cover both. The more we collect valid illustrations of each particular principle, the less room for doubt there will be about its applicability in normal circumstances; and the more hope there will be of reaching a definition so inclusive as to make further examination of instances superfluous. Then the law will be defined in relation to hitherto unforeseen areas in the map of conduct. Every such conquest of the hitherto undefined is in fact an achievement of casuistry.[16]

Notes

[1] Plato, *Timaeus* 53C–55C. On the role of the young Theaetetus in solving this Pythagorean problem, see A. E. Taylor, *A Commentary on Plato's Timaeus* (Oxford, 1928), 358–359. See *Theaetetus* 142A–148E.

[2] See Plato's *Republic* 524D–531C; Aristotle, *Posterior Analytics* I, xii–xiv, 77^a–79^b, and his books on specific scientific topics.

[3] Aristotle, *Eth. Nic. (Nicomachean Ethics)* VI, iii–vii.

[4] *Ibid.*, VI, vii, 1141^{b}19. The opinion that chicken is "good to eat," in the alternative sense of "tasty" is, of course, another matter.

[5] Ibid; VI, ii, 1139^{ab}.

[6] Ibid; VI, viii, 1142^a.

[7] See the *Prologue* to *The Abuse of Casuistry: A History of Moral Reasoning*.

[8] These notions became the basis of much later "Platonism," in its many and varied forms. Whether Plato himself is really committed to the view is less clear, but the starting points for this development can certainly be seen in, for example, the *Timaeus*, 90B–D.

[9] The idea of truth and certainty "flowing" in one or another direction within a network or system of propositions was developed by Imre Lakatos to distinguish between alternative doctrines in the philosophy of science: see, e.g., *Criticism and the Growth of Knowledge* (Cambridge, 1970).

[10] This pattern for analyzing practical arguments is presented in Stephen Toulmin, *The Uses of Argument* (Cambridge, Eng., 1958), and also in Stephen Toulmin, Richard Rieke, and Allan Janik, *An Introduction to Reasoning* (New York, 1983).

[11] In their turn, behavioral and social sciences blend theoretical and practical goals and methods in other (sometimes even inextricable) ways.

[12] The word *explanation* is used here for an account of underlying processes and mechanisms. In a weaker sense of the term, of course, one may still speak of clinical facts being "accounted for," and even "explained," when they are subjected to preliminary statistical analysis, even before their underlying mechanisms have been investigated.

[13] There have, of course, been historical periods during which physicians saw the relationship between theory and practice in more formal terms: consider the iatrochemical and iatromechanical schools of the seventeenth century, as discussed by Lester King, *The Philosophy of Medicine* (Cambridge, Mass., 1978), chaps. 4 and 5.

[14] Augustine, *Morals of the Catholic Church*, chap. 28.

[15] See Henry Denzinger and Adolf Schönmetzer, *Encheiridion Symbolorum Definitionum et Declarationum de Rebus Fidei et Morum*, edn. xxxiii (Rome, 1965), #2813: this standard manual is hereafter referred to as *D–S*.

[16] Kirk, *Conscience and Its Problems*, pp. 108–109.

9

THE *PHAEDRUS* AND THE NATURE OF RHETORIC

Richard Weaver

Our subject begins with the threshold difficulty of defining the question which Plato's *Phaedrus* was meant to answer. Students of this justly celebrated dialogue have felt uncertain of its unity of theme, and the tendency has been to designate it broadly as a discussion of the ethical and the beautiful. The explicit topics of the dialogue are, in order: love, the soul, speech-making, and the spoken and written word, or what is generally termed by us "composition." The development looks random, and some of the most interesting passages appear *jeux d'esprit*. The richness of the literary art diverts attention from the substance of the argument.

But a work of art which touches on many profound problems justifies more than one kind of reading. Our difficulty with the *Phaedrus* may be that our interpretation has been too literal and too topical. If we will bring to the reading of it even a portion of that imagination which Plato habitually exercised, we should perceive surely enough that it is consistently, and from beginning to end, about one thing, which is the nature of rhetoric.[1] Again, that point may have been misse d because most readers conceive rhetoric to be a system of artifice rather than an idea,[2] and the *Phaedrus*, for all its apparent divagation, keeps very close to a single idea. A study of its rhetorical structure, especially, may give us the insight which has been withheld, while making us feel anew that Plato possessed the deepest divining rod among the ancients.

From *The Ethics of Rhetoric* (1953). South Bend, IN: Regnery, pp. 3–26.

For the imaginative interpretation which we shall now undertake, we have both general and specific warrant. First, it scarcely needs pointing out that a Socratic dialogue is in itself an example of transcendence. Beginning with something simple and topical, it passes to more general levels of application; and not infrequently, it must make the leap into allegory for the final utterance. This means, of course, that a Socratic dialogue may be about its subject implicitly as well as explicitly. The implicit rendering is usually through some kind of figuration because it is the nature of this meaning to be ineffable in any other way. It is necessary, therefore, to be alert for what takes place through the analogical mode.

Second, it is a matter of curious interest that a warning against literal reading occurs at an early stage of the *Phaedrus*. Here in the opening pages, appearing as if to set the key of the theme, comes an allusion to the myth of Boreas and Oreithyia. On the very spot where the dialogue begins, Boreas is said to have carried off the maiden. Does Socrates believe that this tale is really true? Or is he in favor of a scientific explanation of what the myth alleges? Athens had scientific experts, and the scientific explanation was that the north wind had pushed her off some rocks where she was playing with a companion. In this way the poetical story is provided with a factual basis. The answer of Socrates is that many tales are open to this kind of rationalization, but that the result is tedious and actually irrelevant. It is irrelevant because our chief concern is with the nature of the man, and it is beside the point to probe into such matters while we are yet ignorant of ourselves. The scientific criticism of Greek mythology, which may be likened to the scientific criticism of the myths of the Bible in our own day, produces at best "a boorish sort of wisdom (ἀγροίκῳ τινὶ σοφίᾳ)." It is a limitation to suppose that the truth of the story lies in its historicity. The "boorish sort of wisdom" seeks to supplant poetic allegation with fact, just as an archaeologist might look for the foundations of the Garden of Eden. But while this sort of search goes on the truth flies off, on wings of imagination, and is not recoverable until the searcher attains a higher level of pursuit. Socrates is satisfied with the parable, and we infer from numerous other passages that he believed that some things are best told by parable and some perhaps discoverable only by parable. Real investigation goes forward with the help of analogy. "Freud without Sophocles is unthinkable," a modern writer has said.[3]

With these precepts in mind, we turn to that part of the *Phaedrus* which has proved most puzzling: why is so much said about the absurd relationship of the lover and the non-lover? Socrates encounters Phaedrus outside the city wall. The latter has just come from hearing a discourse by Lysias which enchanted him with its eloquence. He is prevailed upon to repeat this discourse, and the two seek out a shady spot on the banks of the Ilissus. Now the discourse is remarkable because although it was "in a way, a love speech," its argument was that people should grant favors to non-lovers rather than to lovers. "This is just the clever thing about it," Phaedrus remarks. People are in the habit of preferring their lovers, but it is much more intelligent, as the argument of Lysias runs, to prefer a non-lover. Accordingly, the first major topic of the dialogue is a eulogy of the non-lover. The speech provides good subject matter for jesting on the part of Socrates, and looks like another exhibition of the childlike ingeniousness which gives the Greeks their charm. Is it merely a piece of literary trifling? Rather, it is Plato's dramatistic presentation of a major thesis. Beneath the surface of repartee and mock seriousness, he is asking whether we ought to prefer a neuter form of speech to the kind which is ever getting us aroused over things and provoking an expense of spirit.

Sophistications of theory cannot obscure the truth that there are but three ways for language to affect us. It can move us toward what is good; it can move us toward what is evil; or it can, in hypothetical third place, fail to move us at all.[4] Of course there are numberless degrees of effect under the first two heads, and the third, as will be shown, is an approximate rather than an absolute zero of effect. But any utterance is a major assumption of responsibility, and the assumption that one can avoid that responsibility by doing something to language itself is one of the chief considerations of the *Phaedrus*, just as it is of contemporary semantic theory. What Plato has succeeded in doing in this dialogue, whether by a remarkably effaced design, or unconsciously through the formal pressure of his conception, is to give us embodiments of the three types of discourse. These are respectively the non-lover, the evil lover, and the noble lover. We shall take up these figures in their sequence and show their relevance to the problem of language.

The eulogy of the non-lover in the speech of Lysias, as we hear it repeated to Socrates, stresses the fact that the non-lover follows a policy of enlightened self-interest. First of all, the non-lover does not neglect his affairs or commit extreme acts under the influence of passion. Since he acts from calculation, he never has occasion for remorse. No one ever says of him that he is not in his right mind, because all of his acts are within prudential bounds. The first point is, in sum, that the non-lover never sacrifices himself and therefore never feels the vexation which overtakes lovers when they recover from their passion and try to balance their pains with their profit. And the non-lover is constant whereas the lover is inconstant. The first argument then is that the non-lover demonstrates his superiority through prudence and objectivity. The second point of superiority found in non-lovers is that there are many more of them. If one is limited in one's choice to one's lovers, the range is small; but as there are always more non-lovers than lovers, one has a better chance in choosing among many of finding something worthy of one's affection. A third point of superiority is that association with the non-lover does not excite public comment. If one is seen going about with the object of one's love, one is likely to provoke gossip; but when one is seen conversing with the non-lover, people merely realize that "everybody must converse with somebody." Therefore this kind of relationship does not affect one's public standing, and one is not disturbed by what the neighbors are saying. Finally, non-lovers are not jealous of one's associates. Accordingly they do not try to keep one from companions of intellect or wealth for fear that they may be outshone themselves. The lover, by contrast, tries to draw his beloved away from such companionship and so deprives him of improving associations. The argument is concluded with a generalization that one ought to grant favors not to the needy or the importunate, but to those who are able to repay. Such is the favorable account of the non-lover given by Lysias.

We must now observe how these points of superiority correspond to those of "semantically purified" speech. By "semantically purified speech" we mean the kind of speech approaching pure notation in the respect that it communicates abstract intelligence without impulsion. It is a simple instrumentality, showing no affection for the object of its symbolizing and incapable of inducing bias in the hearer. In its ideal conception, it would have less power to move than $2 + 2 = 4$, since it is generally admitted that mathematical equations may have the beauty of elegance, and hence are not above suspicion where beauty is suspect. But this neuter language will be an unqualified medium of transmission of meanings from mind to mind, and by virtue of its minds can remain in an unprejudiced relationship to the world and also to other minds.

Since the characteristic of this language is absence of anything like affection, it exhibits toward the thing being represented merely a sober fidelity, like that of the non-lover toward his companion. Instead of passion, it offers the serviceability of objectivity. Its "enlightened self-interest" takes the form of an unvarying accuracy and regularity in its symbolic references, most, if not all of which will be to verifiable data in the extramental world. Like a thrifty burgher, it has no romanticism about it; and it distrusts any departure from the literal and prosaic. The burgher has his feet on the ground; and similarly the language of pure notation has its point-by-point contact with objective reality. As Stuart Chase, one of its modern proponents, says in *The Tyranny of Words*: *"If we wish to understand the world and ourselves, it follows that we should use a language whose structure corresponds to physical structure"*[5] (italics his). So this language is married to the world, and its marital fidelity contrasts with the extravagances of other languages.

In second place, this language is far more "available." Whereas rhetorical language, or language which would persuade, must always be particularized to suit the occasion, drawing its effectiveness from many small nuances, a "utility" language is very general and one has no difficulty putting his meaning into it if he is satisfied with a paraphrase of that meaning. The 850 words recommended for Basic English, for example, are highly available in the sense that all native users of English have them instantly ready and learners of English can quickly acquire them. It soon becomes apparent, however, that the availability is a heavy tax upon all other qualities. Most of what we admire as energy and fullness tends to disappear when mere verbal counters are used. The conventional or public aspect of language can encroach upon the suggestive or symbolical aspect, until the naming is vague or blurred. In proportion as the medium is conventional in the widest sense and avoids all individualizing, personalizing, and heightening terms, it is common, and the commonness constitutes the negative virtue ascribed to the non-lover.

Finally, with reference to the third qualification of the non-lover, it is true that neuter language does not excite public opinion. This fact follows from its character outlined above. Rhetorical language on the other hand, for whatever purpose used, excites interest and with it either pleasure or alarm. People listen instinctively to the man whose speech betrays inclination. It does not matter what the inclination is toward, but we may say that the greater the degree of inclination, the greater the curiosity or response. Hence a "style" in speech always causes one to be a marked man, and the public may not be so much impressed—at least initially—by what the man is for or against as by the fact that he has a style. The way therefore to avoid public comment is to avoid the speech of affection and to use that of business, since, to echo the original proposition of Lysias, everybody knows that one must do business with others. From another standpoint, then, this is the language of prudence. These are the features which give neuter discourse an appeal to those who expect a scientific solution of human problems.

In summing up the trend of meaning, we note that Lysias has been praising a disinterested kind of relationship which avoids all excesses and irrationalities, all the dementia of love. It is a circumspect kind of relationship, which is preferred by all men who wish to do well in the world and avoid tempestuous courses. We have compared its detachment with the kind of abstraction to be found in scientific notation. But as an earnest of what is to come let us note, in taking leave of this part, that Phaedrus expresses admiration for the eloquence, especially of diction, with which the suit of the non-lover has been urged. This is our warning of the dilemma of the non-lover.

Now we turn to the second major speech of the dialogue, which is made by Socrates. Notwithstanding Phaedrus' enthusiastic praise, Socrates is dissatisfied with the speech of the non-lover. He remembers having heard wiser things on the subject and feels that he can make a speech on the same theme "different from this and quite as good." After some playful exchange, Socrates launches upon his own abuse of love, which centers on the point that the lover is an exploiter. Love ($\xi\rho\omega\varsigma$) is defined as the kind of desire which overcomes rational opinion and moves toward the enjoyment of personal or bodily beauty. The lover wishes to make the object of his passion as pleasing to himself as possible; but to those possessed by this frenzy, only that which is subject to their will is pleasant. Accordingly, everything which is opposed, or is equal or better, the lover views with hostility. He naturally therefore tries to make the beloved inferior to himself in every respect. He is pleased if the beloved has intellectual limitations because they have the effect of making him manageable. For a similar reason he tries to keep him away from all influences which might "make a man of him," and of course the greatest of these is divine philosophy. While he is working to keep him intellectually immature, he works also to keep him weak and effeminate, with such harmful result that the beloved is unable to play a man's part in crises. The lover is, moreover, jealous of the possession of property because this gives the beloved an independence which he does not wish him to have. Thus the lover in exercising an unremitting compulsion over the beloved deprives him of all praiseworthy qualities, and this is the price the beloved pays for accepting a lover who is "necessarily without reason." In brief, the lover is not motivated by benevolence toward the beloved, but by selfish appetite; and Socrates can aptly close with the quotation: "As wolves love lambs, so lovers love their loves." The speech is on the single theme of exploitation. It is important for us to keep in mind the object of love as here described, because another kind of love with a different object is later introduced into the dialogue, and we shall discuss the counterpart of each.

As we look now for the parallel in language, we find ourselves confronting the second of the three alternatives: speech which influences us in the direction of what is evil. This we shall call base rhetoric because its end is the exploitation which Socrates has been condemning. We find that base rhetoric hates that which is opposed, or is equal or better because all such things are impediments to its will, and in the last analysis it knows only its will. Truth is the stubborn, objective restraint which this will endeavors to overcome. Base rhetoric is therefore always trying to keep its objects from the support which personal courage, noble associations, and divine philosophy provide a man.

The base rhetorician, we may say, is a man who has yielded to the wrong aspects of existence. He has allowed himself to succumb to the sights and shows, to the physical pleasures which conspire against noble life. He knows that the only way he can get a following in his pursuits (and a following seems necessary to maximum enjoyment of the pursuits) is to work against the true understanding of his followers. Consequently the things which would elevate he keeps out of sight, and the things with which he surrounds his "beloved" are those which minister immediately to desire. The beloved is thus emasculated in understanding in order that the lover may have his way. Or as Socrates expresses it, the selfish lover contrives things so that the beloved will be "most agreeable to him and most harmful to himself."

Examples of this kind of contrivance occur on every hand in the impassioned language of journalism and political pleading. In the world of affairs which these seek to influence, the many are kept in a state of pupillage so that they will be most docile to their "lovers." The techniques of the base lover, especially as exemplified in modern journalism, would make a long catalogue, but in general it is accurate to say that he seeks to keep the understanding in a passive state by never permitting an honest examination of alternatives. Nothing is more feared by him than a true dialectic, for this not only endangers his favored alternative, but also gives the "beloved"—how clearly here are these the "lambs" of Socrates' figure—some training in intellectual independence. What he does therefore is dress up one alternative in all the cheap finery of immediate hopes and fears, knowing that if he can thus prevent a masculine exercise of imagination and will, he can have his way. By discussing only one side of an issue, by mentioning cause without consequence or consequence without cause, acts without agents or agents without agency,[6] he often successfully blocks definition and cause-and-effect reasoning. In this way his choices are arrayed in such meretricious images that one can quickly infer the juvenile mind which they would attract. Of course the base rhetorician today, with his vastly augmented power of propagation, has means of deluding which no ancient rhetor in forum or market place could have imagined.

Because Socrates has now made a speech against love, representing it as an evil, the non-lover seems to survive in estimation. We observe, however, that the non-lover, instead of being celebrated, is disposed of dialectically. "So, in a word, I say that the non-lover possesses all the advantages that are opposed to the disadvantages we found in the lover." This is not without bearing upon the subject matter of the important third speech, to which we now turn.

At this point in the dialogue, Socrates is warned by his monitory spirit that he has been engaging in a defamation of love despite the fact that love is a divinity. "If love is, as indeed he is, a god or something divine, he can be nothing evil; but the two speeches just now said that he was evil." These discourses were then an impiety—one representing non-love as admirable and the other attacking love as base. Socrates resolves to make amends, and the recantation which follows is one of the most elaborate developments in the Platonic system. The account of love which emerges from this new position may be summarized as follows.

Love is often censured as a form of madness, yet not all madness is evil. There is a madness which is simple degeneracy, but on the other hand there are kinds of madness which are really forms of inspiration, from which come the greatest gifts conferred on man. Prophecy is a kind of madness, and so too is poetry. "The poetry of the sane man vanishes into nothingness before that of the inspired madman." Mere sanity, which is of human origin, is inferior to that madness which is inspired by the gods and which is a condition for the highest kind of achievement. In this category goes the madness of the true lover. His is a generous state which confers blessings to the ignoring of self, whereas the conduct of the non-lover displays all the selfishness of business: "the affection of the non-lover, which is alloyed with mortal prudence and follows mortal and parsimonious rules of conduct, will beget in the beloved soul the narrowness which common folk praise as virtue; it will cause the soul to be a wanderer upon the earth for nine thousand years and a fool below the earth at last." It is the vulgar who do not realize that the madness of the noble lover is an inspired madness because he has his thoughts turned toward a beauty of divine origin.

Now the attitude of the noble lover toward the beloved is in direct contrast with that of the evil lover, who, as we have seen, strives to possess and victimize the object of his affections. For once the noble lover has mastered the conflict within his own soul by conquering appetite and fixing his attention upon the intelligible and the divine, he conceives an exalted attitude toward the beloved. The noble lover now "follows the beloved in reverence and awe." So those who are filled with this kind of love "exhibit no jealousy or meanness toward the loved one, but endeavor by every means in their power to lead him to the likeness of the god whom they honor." Such is the conversion by which love turns from the exploitative to the creative.

Here it becomes necessary to bring our concepts together and to think of all speech having persuasive power as a kind of "love."[7] Thus, rhetorical speech is madness to the extent that it departs from the line which mere sanity lays down. There is always in its statement a kind of excess or deficiency which is immediately discernible when the test of simple realism is applied. Simple realism operates on a principle of equation or correspondence; one thing must match another, or, representation must tally with thing represented, like items in a tradesman's account. Any excess or deficiency on the part of the representation invokes the existence of the world of symbolism, which simple realism must deny. This explains why there is an immortal feud between men of business and the users of metaphor and metonymy, the poets and the rhetoricians.[8] The man of business, the narrow and parsimonious soul in the allusion of Socrates, desires a world which is a reliable materiality. But this the poet and rhetorician will never let him have, for each, with his own purpose, is trying to advance the borders of the imaginative world. A primrose by the river's brim will not remain that in the poet's account, but is promptly turned into something very much larger and something highly implicative. He who is accustomed to record the world with an abacus cannot follow these transfigurations; and indeed the very occurrence of them subtly undermines the premise of his business. It is the historic tendency of the tradesman, therefore, to confine passion to quite narrow channels so that it will not upset the decent business arrangements of the world. But if the poet, as the chief transformer of our picture of the world, is the peculiar enemy of this mentality, the rhetorician is also hostile when practicing the kind of love proper to him. The "passion" in his speech is revolutionary, and it has a practical end.

We have now indicated the significance of the three types of lovers; but the remainder of the *Phaedrus* has much more to say about the nature of rhetoric, and we must return to one or more points to place our subject in a wider context. The problem of rhetoric which occupied Plato persistently, not only in the *Phaedrus* but also in other dialogues where this art is reviewed, may be best stated as a question: if truth alone is not sufficient to persuade men, what else remains that can be legitimately added? In one of the exchanges with Phaedrus, Socrates puts the question in the mouth of a personified Rhetoric. "I do not compel anyone to learn to speak without knowing the truth, but if my advice is of any value, he learns that first and then acquires me. So what I claim is this, that without my help the knowledge of the truth does not give the art of persuasion."

Now rhetoric as we have discussed it in relation to the lovers consists of truth plus its artful presentation, and for this reason it becomes necessary to say something more about the natural order of dialectic and rhetoric. In any general characterization rhetoric will include dialectic,[9] but for the study of method it is necessary to separate the two. Dialectic is a method of investigation whose object is the establishment of truth about doubtful propositions. Aristotle in the *Topics* gives a concise statement of its nature. "A dialectical problem is a subject of inquiry that contributes either to choice or avoidance, or to truth and knowledge, and that either by itself, or as a help to the solution of some other such problem. It must, moreover, be something on which either people hold no opinion either way, or the masses hold a contrary opinion to the philosophers, or the philosophers to the masses, or each of them among themselves."[10] Plato is not perfectly clear about the distinction between positive and dialectical terms. In one passage[11] he contrasts the "positive" terms "iron" and "silver" with the "dialectical" terms "justice" and "goodness"; yet in other passages his "dialectical" terms seem to include categorizations of the external world. Thus Socrates indicates that distinguishing the horse from the ass is a dialectical operation;[12] and he tells us later that a good dialectician is able to divide things by classes "where the natural joints are" and will avoid breaking any part "after the manner of a bad carver."[13] Such, perhaps, is Aristotle's dialectic which contributes to truth and knowledge.

But there is a branch of dialectic which contributes to "choice or avoidance," and it is with this that rhetoric is regularly found joined. Generally speaking, this is a rhetoric involving questions of policy, and the dialectic which precedes it will determine not the application of positive terms but that of terms which are subject to the contingency of evaluation. Here dialectical inquiry will concern itself not with what is "iron" but with what is "good." It seeks to establish what belongs in the category of the "just" rather than what belongs in the genus *Canis*. As a general rule, simple object words such as "iron" and "house" have no connotations of policy, although it is frequently possible to give them these through speech situations in which there is added to their referential function a kind of impulse. We should have to interpret in this way "Fire!" or "Gold!" because these terms acquire something through intonation and relationship which places them in the class of evaluative expressions.

Any piece of persuasion, therefore, will contain as its first process a dialectic establishing terms which have to do with policy. Now a term of Policy is essentially a term of motion, and here begins the congruence of rhetoric with the soul which underlies the speculation of the *Phaedrus*. In his myth of the charioteer, Socrates declares that every soul is immortal because "that which is ever moving is immortal." Motion, it would appear from this definition, is part of the soul's essence. And just because the soul is ever tending, positive or indifferent terms cannot partake of this congruence. But terms of tendency—goodness, justice, divinity, and the like—are terms of motion and

therefore may be said to comport with the soul's essence. The Soul's perception of goodness, justice, and divinity will depend upon its proper tendency,
while at the same time contacts with these in discourse confirm and direct
that tendency. The education of the soul is not a process of bringing it into
correspondence with a physical structure like the external world, but rather a
process of rightly affecting its motion. By this conception, a soul which is
rightly affected calls that good which is good; but a soul which is wrongly
turned calls that good which is evil. What Plato has prepared us to see is that
the virtuous rhetorician, who is a lover of truth, has a soul of such movement
that its dialectical perceptions are consonant with those of a divine mind. Or,
in the language of more technical philosophy, this soul is aware of axiological systems which have ontic status. The good soul, consequently, will not
urge a perversion of justice as justice in order to impose upon the common-
wealth. Insofar as the soul has its impulse in the right direction, its definitions will agree with the true nature of intelligible things.

There is, then, no true rhetoric without dialectic, for the dialectic provides that basis of "high speculation about nature" without which rhetoric in
the narrower sense has nothing to work upon. Yet, when the disputed terms
have been established, we are at the limit of dialectic. How does the noble
rhetorician proceed from this point on? That the clearest demonstration in
terms of logical inclusion and exclusion often fails to win assent we hardly
need state; therefore, to what does the rhetorician resort at this critical passage? It is the stage at which he passes from the logical to the analogical, or
it is where figuration comes into rhetoric.

To look at this for a moment through a practical illustration, let us suppose that a speaker has convinced his listeners that his position is "true" as
far as dialectical inquiry may be pushed. Now he sets about moving the listeners toward that position, but there is no way to move them except through
the operation of analogy. The analogy proceeds by showing that the position
being urged resembles or partakes of something greater and finer. It will be
represented, in sum, as one of the steps leading toward ultimate good. Let us
further suppose our speaker to be arguing for the payment of a just debt.
The payment of the just debt is not itself justice, but the payment of this particular debt is one of the many things which would have to be done before
this could be a completely just world. It is just, then, because it partakes of
the ideal justice, or it is a small analogue of all justice (in practice it will be
found that the rhetorician makes extensive use of synecdoche, whereby the
small part is used as a vivid suggestion of the grandeur of the whole). It is by
bringing out these resemblances that the good rhetorician leads those who
listen in the direction of what is good. In effect, he performs a cure of souls
by giving impulse, chiefly through figuration, toward an ideal good.

We now see the true rhetorician as a noble lover of the good, who
works through dialectic and through poetic or analogical association. However he is compelled to modulate by the peculiar features of an occasion,
this is his method.

It may not be superfluous to draw attention to the fact that what we have here outlined is the method of the *Phaedrus* itself. The dialectic appears in the dispute about love. The current thesis that love is praiseworthy is countered by the antithesis that love is blameworthy. This position is fully developed in the speech of Lysias and in the first speech of Socrates. But this position is countered by a new thesis that after all love is praiseworthy because it is a divine thing. Of course, this is love on a higher level, or love re-defined. This is the regular process of transcendence which we have noted before. Now, having rescued love from the imputation of evil by excluding certain things from its definition, what does Socrates do? Quite in accordance with our analysis, he turns rhetorician. He tries to make this love as attractive as possible by bringing in the splendid figure of the charioteer.[14] In the narrower conception of this art, the allegory is the rhetoric, for it excites and fills us with desire for this kind of love, depicted with many terms having tendency toward the good. But in the broader conception the art must include also the dialectic, which succeeded in placing love in the category of divine things before filling our imaginations with attributes of divinity.[15] It is so regularly the method of Plato to follow a subtle analysis with a striking myth that it is not unreasonable to call him the master rhetorician. This goes far to explain why those who reject his philosophy sometimes remark his literary art with mingled admiration and annoyance.

The objection sometimes made that rhetoric cannot be used by a lover of truth because it indulges in "exaggerations" can be answered as follows. There is an exaggeration which is mere wantonness, and with this the true rhetorician has nothing to do. Such exaggeration is purely impressionistic in aim. Like caricature, whose only object is to amuse, it seizes upon any trait or aspect which could produce titillation and exploits this without conscience. If all rhetoric were like this, we should have to grant that rhetoricians are persons of very low responsibility and their art a disreputable one. But the rhetorician we have now defined is not interested in sensationalism.

The exaggeration which this rhetorician employs is not caricature but prophecy; and it would be a fair formulation to say that true rhetoric is concerned with the potency of things. The literalist, like the anti-poet described earlier, is troubled by its failure to conform to a present reality. What he fails to appreciate is that potentiality is a mode of existence, and that all prophecy is about the tendency of things. The discourse of the noble rhetorician, accordingly, will be about real potentiality or possible actuality, whereas that of the mere exaggerator is about unreal potentiality. Naturally this distinction rests upon a supposal that the rhetorician has insight, and we could not defend him in the absence of that condition. But given insight, he has the duty to represent to us the as yet unactualized future. It would be, for example, a misrepresentation of current facts but not of potential ones to talk about the joys of peace in a time of war. During the Second World War, at the depth of Britain's political and military disaster, Winston Churchill likened the future of Europe to "broad sunlit uplands." Now if one had regard only for the hour, this was a piece of mendacity such as the worst charlatans are found committing; but if one took Churchill's premises and then considered the potentiality, the picture was within bounds of actualization. His "exaggeration" was that the defeat of the enemy would place Europe in a position for long and peaceful progress. At the time the surface trends ran the other way; the actuality was a valley of humiliation. Yet the hope which transfigured this to "broad sunlit uplands" was not irresponsible, and we conclude by saying that the rhetorician talks about both what exists simply and what exists by favor of human imagination and effort.[16]

This interest in actualization is a further distinction between pure dialectic and rhetoric. With its forecast of the actual possibility, rhetoric passes from mere scientific demonstration of an idea to its relation to prudential conduct. A dialectic must take place *in vacuo*, and the fact alone that it contains contraries leaves it an intellectual thing. Rhetoric, on the other hand, always espouses one of the contraries. This espousal is followed by some attempt at impingement upon actuality. That is why rhetoric, with its passion for the actual, is more complete than mere dialectic with its dry understanding. It is more complete on the premise than man is a creature of passion who must live out that passion in the world. Pure contemplation does not suffice for this end. As Jacques Maritain has expressed it; "love . . . is not directed at possibilities or pure essences; it is directed at what exists; one does not love possibilities, one loves that which exists or is destined to exist."[17] The complete man, then, is the "lover" added to the scientist; the rhetorician to the dialectician. Understanding followed by actualization seems to be the order of creation, and there is no need for the role of rhetoric to be misconceived.

The pure dialectician is left in the theoretical position of the non-lover, who can attain understanding but who cannot add impulse to truth. We are compelled to say "theoretical position" because it is by no means certain that in the world of actual speech the non-lover has more than a putative existence. We have seen previously that his speech would consist of strictly referential words which would serve only as designata. Now the question arises: at what point is motive to come into such language? Kenneth Burke in *A Grammar of Motives* has pointed to "the pattern of embarrassment behind the contemporary ideal of a language that will best promote good action by entirely eliminating the element of exhortation or command. Insofar as such a project succeeded, its terms would involve a narrowing of circumference to a point where the principle of personal action is eliminated from language, so that an act would follow from it only as a nonsequitur, a kind of humanitarian after-thought."[18]

The fault of this conception of language is that scientific intention turns out to be enclosed in artistic intention and not *vice versa*. Let us test this by taking as an example one of those "fact-finding committees" so favored by modern representative governments. A language in which all else is suppressed in favor of nuclear meanings would be an ideal instrumentality for the report of such a committee. But this committee, if it lived up to the ideal of its conception, would have to be followed by an "attitude-finding committee" to tell us what its explorations really mean. In real practice the fact-finding committee understands well enough that it is also an attitude-finding committee, and where it cannot show inclination through language of tendency, it usually manages to do so through selection and arrangement of the otherwise inarticulate facts. To recur here to the original situation in the dialogue, we recall that the eloquent Lysias, posing as a non-lover, had concealed designs upon Phaedrus, so that his fine speech was really a sheep's clothing. Socrates discerned in him a "peculiar craftiness." One must suspect the same today of many who ask us to place our faith in the neutrality of their discourse. We cannot deny that there are degrees of objectivity in the reference of speech. But this is not the same as an assurance that a vocabulary of reduced meanings will solve the problems of mankind. Many of those problems will have to be handled, as Socrates well knew, by the student of souls, who must primarily make use of the language of tendency. The soul is impulse, not simply cognition; and finally one's interest in rhetoric depends on how much poignancy one senses in existence. [19]

Rhetoric moves the soul with a movement which cannot finally be justified logically. It can only be valued analogically with reference to some supreme image. Therefore when the rhetorician encounters some soul "sinking beneath the double load of forgetfulness and vice" he seeks to re-animate it by holding up to its sight the order of presumptive goods. This order is necessarily a hierarchy leading up to the ultimate good. All of the terms in a rhetorical vocabulary are like links in a chain stretching up to some master link which transmits its influence down through the linkages. It is impossible to talk about rhetoric as effective expression without having as a term giving intelligibility to the whole discourse, the Good. Of course, inferior concepts of the Good may be and often are placed in this ultimate position; and there is nothing to keep a base lover from inverting the proper order and saying, "Evil, be thou my good." Yet the fact remains that in any piece of rhetorical discourse, one rhetorical term overcomes another rhetorical term only by being nearer to the term which stands ultimate. There is some ground for calling a rhetorical education necessarily an aristocratic education in that the rhetorician has to deal with an aristocracy of notions, to say nothing of supplementing his logical and pathetic proofs with an ethical proof.

All things considered, rhetoric, noble or base, is a great power in the world; and we note accordingly that at the center of the public life of every people there is a fierce struggle over who shall control the means of rhetorical propagation. Today we set up "offices of information," which like the sly lover in the dialogue, pose as non-lovers while pushing their suits. But there is no reason to despair over the fact that men will never give up seeking to influence one another. We would not desire it to be otherwise; neuter discourse is a false idol, to worship which is to commit the very offense for which Socrates made expiation in his second speech.

Since we want not emancipation from impulse but clarification of impulse, the duty of rhetoric is to bring together action and understanding into a whole that is greater than scientific perception.[20] The realization that just as no action is really indifferent, so no utterance is without its responsibility introduces, it is true, a certain strenuousity into life, produced by a consciousness that "nothing is lost." Yet this is preferable to that desolation which proceeds from an infinite dispersion or feeling of unaccountability. Even so, the choice between them is hardly ours to make; we did not create the order of things, but being accountable for our impulses, we wish these to be just.

Thus when we finally divest rhetoric of all the notions of artifice which have grown up around it, we are left with something very much like Spinoza's "intellectual love of God." This is its essence and the *fons et origo* of its power. It is "intellectual" because, as we have previously seen, there is no honest rhetoric without a preceding dialectic. The kind of rhetoric which is justly condemned is utterance in support of a position before that position has been adjudicated with reference to the whole universe of discourse[21]— and of such the world always produces more than enough. It is "love" because it is something in addition to bare theoretical truth. That element in addition is a desire to bring truth into a kind of existence, or to give it an actuality to which theory is indifferent. Now what is to be said about our last expression, "of God"? Echoes of theological warfare will cause many to desire a substitute for this, and we should not object. As long as we have in ultimate place the highest good man can intuit, the relationship is made perfect. We shall be content with "intellectual love of the Good." It is still the intellectual love of good which causes the noble lover to desire not to devour his beloved but to shape him according to the gods as far as mortal power allows. So rhetoric at its truest seeks to perfect men by showing them better versions of themselves, links in that chain extending up toward the ideal, which only the intellect can apprehend and only the soul have affection for. This is the justified affection of which no one can be ashamed, and he who feels no influence of it is truly outside the communion of minds. Rhetoric appears, finally, as a means by which the impulse of the soul to be ever moving is redeemed.

It may be granted that in this essay we have gone some distance from the banks of the Ilissus. What began as a simple account of passion becomes by transcendence an allegory of all speech. No one would think of suggesting that Plato had in mind every application which has here been made, but that need not arise as an issue. The structure of the dialogue, the way in which the judgments about speech concentre, and especially the close association of the true, the beautiful, and the good, constitute a unity of implication. The central idea is that all speech, which is the means the gods have given man to express his soul, is a form of eros, in the proper interpretation of the word. With that truth the rhetorician will always be brought face to face as soon as he ventures beyond the consideration of mere artifice and device.

Notes

1. Cf. A. E. Taylor, *Plato: the Man and his Work* (New York, 1936), p. 300.
2. Cf. P. Albert Duhamel, "The Concept of Rhetoric as Effective Expression," *Journal of the History of Ideas*, X, No. 3 (June, 1949), 344–56 *passim*.
3. James Blish, "Rituals on Ezra Pound," *Sewanee Review*, LVIII (Spring, 1950), 223.
4. The various aesthetic approaches to language offer refinements of perception, but all of them can be finally subsumed under the first head above.
5. *The Tyranny of Words* (New York, 1938), p. 80. T. H. Huxley in *Lay Sermons* (New York, 1883), p. 112, outlined a noticeably similar ideal of scientific communication: "Therefore, the great business of the scientific teacher is, to imprint the fundamental, irrefragable facts of his science, not only by words upon the mind, but by sensible impressions upon the eye, and ear, and touch of the student in so complete a manner, that every term used, or law enunciated should afterwards call up vivid images of the particular structural, or other, facts which furnished the demonstration of the law, or illustration of the term."
6. That is, by mentioning only parts of the total situation.
7. It is worth recalling that in the Christian New Testament, with its heavy Platonic influence, God is identified both with *logos*, "word, speech" (*John* 1:1); and with *agape*, "love" (2 *John* 4:8).
8. The users of metaphor and metonymy who are in the hire of businessmen of course constitute a special case.
9. Cf. 277 b: "A man must know the truth about all the particular things of which he speaks or writes, and must be able to define everything separately; then when he has defined them, he must know how to divide them by classes until further division is impossible; and in the same way he must understand the nature of the soul, must find out the class of speech adapted to each nature, and must arrange and adorn his discourse accordingly, offering to the complex soul elaborate and harmonious discourses, and simple talks to the simple soul."
10. 104 b.
11. 263 a.
12. 260 b.
13. 265 a.
14. In the passage extending from 246 a to 256 d.
15. Cf. 263 d ff.
16. Indeed, in this particular rhetorical duel we see the two types of lovers opposed as clearly as illustration could desire. More than this, we see the third type, the non-lover, committing his ignominious failure. Britain and France had come to prefer as leaders the rhetoricless businessman type. And while they had thus emasculated themselves, there appeared an evil lover to whom Europe all but succumbed before the mistake was seen and rectified. For while the world must move, evil rhetoric is of more force than no rhetoric at all; and Herr Hitler, employing images which rested on no true dialectic, had persuaded multitudes that his order was the "new order," *i.e.*, the true potentiality. Britain was losing and could only lose until, reaching back in her traditional past, she found a voice which could match his accents with a truer grasp of the potentiality of things. Thus two men conspicuous for passion fought a contest for souls, which the nobler won. But the contest could have been lost by default.
17. "Action: the Perfection of Human Life," *Sewanee Review*, LVI (Winter, 1948), 3.
18. *A Grammar of Motives* (New York, 1945), p. 90.
19. Without rhetoric there seems no possibility of tragedy, and in turn, without the sense of tragedy, no possibility of taking an elevated view of life. The role of tragedy is to keep the human lot from being rendered as history. The cultivation of tragedy and a deep interest in the value-conferring power of language always occur together. The *Phaedrus*, the *Gorgias*, and the *Cratylus*, not to mention the works of many teachers of rhetoric, appear at the close of the great age of Greek tragedy. The Elizabethan age teemed with treatises on the use of language. The essentially tragic Christian view of life begins the long tradition of homiletics.

Tragedy and the practice of rhetoric seem to find common sustenance in preoccupation with value, and then rhetoric follows as an analyzed art.

20   Cf. Maritain, *op. cit.*, pp. 3–4: "The truth of practical intellect is understood not as conformity to an extramental being but as conformity to a right desire; the end is no longer to know what is, but to bring into existence that which is not yet; further, the act of moral choice is so individualized, both by the singularity of the person from which it proceeds and the context of the contingent circumstances in which it takes place, that the practical judgment in which it is expressed and by which I declare to myself: this is what I must do, can be right only if, *hic et nunc*, the dynamism of my will is right, and tends towards the true goods of human life.

That is why practical wisdom, *prudentia*, is a virtue indivisibly moral and intellectual at the same time, and why, like the judgment of the conscience itself, it cannot be replaced by any sort of theoretical knowledge or science."

21   Socrates' criticism of the speech of Lysias (263 d ff.) is that the latter defended a position without having submitted it to the discipline of dialectic.

10

A RESPONSIBLE RHETORIC

Richard M. Weaver

Our discourse this morning is not so much about great issues as it is about how to think and talk about great issues. And if that title seems a little presumptuous I can only hope that what I have to say will bring it down to earth and show that there are issues also in the way in which we choose to talk about issues. Most Americans today accept the axiomatic truths that we live in a free society. I often wonder, however, how many of us realize that a free society is by definition a pluralistic society. The pluralistic society is one in which there are many different centers of authority, influence, and opinion competing with one another, arguing with one another, trying by various means to expand their spheres of influence and producing a great variety of richness and animation. In such a society there is no single voice, governmental, cultural, religious, or social. There are many voices, each speaking from its point of view and striving to maintain itself in the general competition of belief and support. In dire contrast stands the monistic ideal society, experienced by many millions of persons in other lands, which do have only one voice and which work by many means toward effecting a unanimity of opinion, belief, and settlement on all of the issues of this life. That system bears the name totalitarian, and it is by now an obvious fact that these two are engaged in a gigantic rivalry to capture the imagination of the world.

Having described and outlined this situation, I now wonder the second time of the Americans who realize that a free society means a pluralistic society: how many realize the special demands which a pluralistic society imposes on its members? I am not referring to paying taxes which you do without

From *Intercollegiate Review* (Winter 1967–77), pp. 81–87.

thinking. I am referring to just this: The pluralistic society by its very nature tolerates propaganda of all kinds of individual groups, organizations, institutions, and practically anything that is capable of articulation. And it does this on the strength of two suppositions: (1) There are many subjects in regard to which we do not think that we have arrived at the finite in truth. These subjects are still under study and investigation. Not all of the evidence is in, not all of the opinions have been expressed, and therefore, debate must go on. Hence the activity of our newspapers, public meetings, legislative assemblies, (barber shops, street corners,) etc. We accept the fact frankly that most issues, including some of vital relation to our welfare, are still in the realm of deliberative forensics. Then the second supposition. This is that there exists among our people enough good sense, education, and reflective intelligence to insure us that in this deliberative process we will come up with the right answer. Not always at once, not always without friction and expense, but in the long run it is felt that we will arrive at more sound conclusions than would, say, a council commisar or some other group delegating exclusive authority to think and to decide. In brief, it is the principle of our society that we can listen to propaganda from all the special interests including that of an incompetent administration and do a pretty fair job of sifting the true claims from the false.

I begin, then, with these preliminary considerations: that a free society is a pluralistic society, that a pluralistic society is one with countless propaganda from many sources, and that coping with propaganda requires a wide-spread critical intelligence which is largely the product of education. It is the last of these points that I wish to deal with directly. Does our educational system prepare people to deal with the vast amount of opinion, argumentation, and special pleading addressed to them today through all the channels provided by modern technology? I am inclined to think that it is not preparing them because we have largely ceased to teach rhetoric. If democracy means anything it means that everyone is an advocate of policy, he must listen to many arguments, and he must make arguments in refutation. He cannot make his honest-held views acceptable to others and he cannot disarm an opponent of an argument unless he has some understanding of the probative value of statements. What I propose to talk about in the next few minutes I want to refer to as responsible rhetoric.

Responsible rhetoric, as I conceive it, is a rhetoric responsible primarily to the truth. It measures the degree of validity in a statement, and it is aware of the sources of controlling that it employs. As such it is distinct from propaganda, which is the distortion of the truth for selfish purposes. In this connection I always like to think of Francis Bacon's statement "Rhetoric no more teaches man to support bad causes than logic teaches them to reason fallaciously."

Now the concepts that are involved in this have their foundation in philosophy and as we open this subject with our students at Chicago we say simply that there are four basic ways in which you can talk meaningfully about the world. This is the same as saying that there are four basic ways of thinking about reality or four basic ways of interpreting experience and they are in the language of philosophy: being, cause, relationship, and the fourth, which has a different kind of basis, authority. You can say that a thing is of such and such a kind or that it is the cause of a certain effect or that it has a significant resemblance to something else or that its truth is vouched by somebody that we ought to respect.

The first argument is based on definition. The second is based on cause and effect, the third is based on resemblance or comparison, the fourth is based on the prestige of some authority. Now, what I have just stated in rather abstract language is actually very common and recognizable by every-one, for these are the ways you can talk about things in ordinary discourse. If we say all good citizens are voters we make a statement of the first class. If we say war is the cause of inflation we make one of the second. If we say life is like a voyage we make one of the third group, and if we say the Bible says that the greatest of gifts is charity we make logic of the fourth. You will rec-ognize that assertions like these are the staple of ordinary expression. When-ever we set out to prove anything to anybody we find ourselves affirming that a certain thing exists as a member of a class or that it is known to be con-nected with a certain cause and effect or that it has points of significant re-semblance with something that is already well known or that it is stated by some authority and everybody who is anybody is supposed to respect. This is nothing more than an analysis of our actual modes of argument.

Now, I should like to spend more time on the theory of this, but owing to my limited time, I feel I'd never turn to concrete examples and show how these various techniques of persuasion have been employed in arguing posi-tions on the great questions of our history. They are the basic means of per-suasion, and you may expect to find one or more of them whenever men are pleading for a cause or a course of action. And to place this in a realistic con-text I should like to follow an historical order and take up certain issues ac-cording to their appearance in the development of our nation.

If this seems permissible let me go back to 1776 and the Declaration of Independence. The Declaration of Independence is essentially an argument. Jefferson was presenting to a candid world a taste for the independence of the American colonies. The argument is in that logical form known as the syllogism but we are here interested in its content. Where did Jefferson go for his matter, for the kind of thing that would supply the rhetorical push? And it shows very clearly that he went to the second item on our list, namely consequences or effects. The great bulk of this document was made out of a detailing of these consequences. He lifted a large number of particulars in which the commoners had suffered by the policy of the King of Great Brit-ain. Most of you recall the tenor if not the substance. He proposed the laws most necessary for the public good. These constitute the celebrated long train of abuses and all of them are, as you will instantly perceive, conse-quences. Now the argument for consequences rests upon this theory, a grave effect implies a grave cause and consequently, a grave cause implies a grave effect. Jefferson was pointing to these facts as grave events. The grave cause as he saw it was a desire to reduce the colonies under an absolute discipline and this cause was regarded as reason enough to justify a separation of the colonies from the mother country. It is announced, of course, at the end of the Declaration. If Jefferson could prove the cause he could prove the right to American independence.

For my next example I go forward about two generations to the period 1838. It was during this period that a tremendous division raged in the city over the nature of union. It was a time of exceptional friction in which great issues depending upon how the Constitution was to be construed, and the focal point of the debate was whether or not the Constitution was a contract. It was this question that drew forth those famous speeches of Webster, Calhoun, and Haynes which, taken with the *Federalist Papers*, proudly represent the highest levels of American thinking politically. I scarcely need point out that this was an argument involving definition, the first argument on our list. If it was possible to define the American constitution as a contract, certain things would necessarily flow from that definition. It was an important and of course different result for the contending party. If it was possible to define it not as a contract but as something binding, another set of results would ensue. Those oratorical giants and their successors wrestled for three decades to decide whether the constitution was this or that genus, in the genus compacts or outside that in some other genus. And you will find Abraham Lincoln presuming this argument in his First Inaugural Address.

I pass on now about 50 years to a period before our involvement in the first World War. This was the period of mounting national armaments accompanied by growing anxieties. There was also a growing resentment against war as a means of settling international differences. One of the most vehement spokesmen against war and specifically against competitive armaments was William Jennings Bryan, three times Democratic candidate for the presidency and Secretary of State under Wilson. In one of his speeches against competitive armament Bryan made use of the following illustration. Two neighbors have gotten into a disagreement and have become angry at one another. One of the neighbors goes out and buys a shotgun for defense. Word of this is soon conveyed to the other neighbor who goes out and buys a better shotgun. News of this along with much talk about his neighbor's hostile intention is soon conveyed to the first neighbor who decides to add still more to his defensive equipment and to be on the lookout for menacing acts. This series of actions goes on and on until one of the neighbors shoots the other in self defense. In this analogy the neighbors are any two nations in the world, the shotguns are armies and navies and those reports sent back and forth are the rumors and statements that create international tensions. It would be needless for me to point out how closely this analogy is to the relationship today between the West and the Soviet Union. But our interest in it lies in the content as an argument. It lies in the fact that it derives its force from the comparison of two instances. If the two instances resemble in all important respects and if the first instance proves to armed conflict then it is probable that the second instance will produce an armed prospect. It is a principle of logic that arguments based on comparison never yield anything more than probability. Probability is a matter of degree. The probability in our case today is a good many degrees short of certain.

Now, if we came down to the present time for an example of the last source of argument, which is authority, one of the great controversial questions of our time has been whether the United States should become involved with other nations in treaties and alliances supporting this and that policy. Those persons who are sometimes called isolationists have frequently evoked the name of George Washington in support of their position that we should not become so involved. Often they quote the sentence from the Farewell Address, "Why, by interweaving our destiny with that of a part of Europe, entangle our peace and prosperity in the toil of European ambition, rivalship, interest or caprice?" You will recognize at once that this is an appeal relying for its source upon authority. Now the appeal to authority, and we all make appeals of this type, is neither necessarily good [n]or necessarily bad. It all depends on the authority. Those who think this is a weak argument say that Washington did very well in his time but that was a century and a half ago. He had no conception of America as an imperial world power and no knowledge of the forces operating in this world. He is, in their eyes, a poor authority on this subject. The other side regards Washington as the father of this country, a farsighted statesman, and a man who because he was present at the birth of this nation had a deep insight into its essential character and its real mission in the world. Washington, they would say, believed that this nation would serve mankind best by rejecting the devious methods of power politics and by setting an upright example for the rest of the world. In their eyes, therefore, he is a good authority.

By now the question may be posed in your mind, what have these things to do with responsible rhetoric? Granting that they are useful for a man to know when he is embarked upon an argument, in what way do they make you more responsible? Well, he will of course never be responsible unless he is willing to be intellectually honest. But granted that, I would say that there are means of showing him the relationship of what he is saying to the truth. Or, expressed in another way, they are means of estimating the real truth value of any assertion or argument. And I think the best way to see this is to turn things around for a moment and look at matters from the other side, to look at some of the tricks that are employed by propagandists. As I said near the beginning, the chief reason people today are baffled by propagandists is that they have such poor understanding of the arts of persuasion. For the tricks of propaganda are nothing more than perversions of the devices of rhetoric. The propagandist is a rhetorician, but a base one, because he is using an accepted machinery of persuasion to seize and not to enlighten and edify.

Let's inspect a few examples. One of the commonest tricks of the propagandist in any age is name-calling. If he desires us to accept something, he applies a good name to it; if he desires us to reject it, applies an evil one. Name-calling is nothing more on earth but the arguments of damnation because the name is employed to define the thing. Or to put it in a class, if the name applied is a true one, then the argument must be viewed as honest, but the propagandist applies a name which is speciously good. That is to say, it looks good to the uncritical but actually it is not. To cite one example, such an abuse occurs today, (I am expressing a personal opinion here) with the Taft-Hartley Act being called a slave labor law. This is a name, you see, supposed to put it in a class. Is there any legitimate sense in which those who work under the provisions of that act can be called slaves? I cannot see it and apparently the sober sense of the country has rejected it. The propagandist here is taking over the law and trying to fit it into a category where it does not belong. His process is called a false name. This is, then, a perversion of the argument based on definition.

For the next example, I shall go not to political controversy but to advertisement, a great field, I regret to say, for the abuse of rhetoric. A year or so ago there appeared in magazines eye-catching full-page ads by the manufacturer of a certain metal and the burden of these advertisements was that this metal had won the war. The argument went about as follows. Without the metal which the company produces it is impossible to make steel of a certain hardness, and without steel of a requisite hardness it is impossible to make airplane motors and without airplane motors it would have been impossible to win the war. Therefore, this company, or at least its product, won the war. What we have here, ostensibly, is a piece of cause and effect reasoning. But as soon as we analyze it we see that it is a distortion because what it actually does is confuse cause and effect relationships by insisting that there is one cause when in fact multiple causes exist. Granting that this metal was one of the causes of the effect in history, still there were many many others and no honest inquiry into the causes of the phenomenon would make it appear the one. Short circuiting cause and effect reasoning is one of the easiest ways to deceive people. We must always be on our guard when great effects are claimed for a certain cause or when a certain effect is ascribed to a single cause as in ascribing the great depression altogether to Herbert Hoover. Causal reasoning is difficult even under the best circumstances and when a propagandist begins to tinker with it strange things may appear. Another type of abuse occurs when people are led along by false analogies.

These are arguments based on seeming rather than real similarities. Now as soon as you begin to examine the points of correspondence you find that the differences are more numerous or more important than the likenesses. Therefore, the two things being compared are different in a more fundamental way than they are alike. And different things ought to be done with respect to them. Again, I am expressing a personal opinion on this issue but to my mind one of the most misleading analogies today is the one that usually turns up for giving the vote to 18-year-olds. This argument asserts that 18-year-olds, being old enough to fight, are old enough to vote. True, only if you believe that fighting and voting are the same kind of thing, which I, for one, do not. Fighting requires strength, muscular coordination and, in a modern army, instant and automatic response to orders. Voting requires knowledge of men, history, reasoning power; it is essentially a deliberative activity. Army mules and police dogs are used to fight: nobody is interested in giving them the right to vote. This argument rests on a false analogy. People may be misled by analogy when they are not sufficiently critical. I come now to the fourth example in this series.

People may be misled by arguments based on authority when they are not sufficiently critical of the authority being used. But they can be misled in a more subtle way when an argument is expressed in language that distinctly echoes some famous or dear document, say the Declaration of Independence or the Gettysburg Address or the Bible. The language then sounds right; it reminds us vaguely of something we have been taught to respect. There is a type of subconscious urge in us to go along because that is the thing. The politicians or advertisers, as you are well aware, are trying to get people on their side by borrowing phrases and other stylistic elements too from famous or authoritative documents. The ethical questions here involved are whether the audience realizes the kind of pressure that is being brought to bear upon them. Thus, as I see it, an elementary understanding of these principles of rhetoric is not only helpful in the making of an argument, it is also most helpful in the criticizing of one and, beyond this, it is a surprisingly effective means of reading the character and intentions of the man behind the argument. As a man thinketh in his heart, so is he morally and intellectually. Once this truth is appreciated you find that you can judge a man not wholly by the specific thing he asks for but also by the way he asks for it. And the latter insight is sometimes very revealing.

There is one final question lurking in the background of this discussion which I would like to dodge though I recognize that ultimately it cannot be evaded. This is the question of whether any of these sources of argument, definition, cause, etc., is better than another one or whether it is possible to arrange them in some rational scale and say this is best, this is next best, etc. Personally, I think it is possible to rank them and say that one is better than another, but the reason that I dodge the question is that it leads straight to one's metaphysics and that, of course, would be a very long argument. Instead of pronouncing upon that question, therefore, I am going to make a suggestion which may start you reflecting upon the matter yourselves.

Follow utterances of some public figure, past or present, in whom you have a strong interest and know what he seems to prefer as the basis of his appeal when he is trying to persuade his audiences. Does he like to define things and argue deductively, does he like to dwell on results, is he fond of analogies, or does he prefer to fall back on authority and argue from the prestige of some great name? You will find that this examination will be both instructive and entertaining, and it may give you an understanding of the figure, the kind of understanding of the figure that you did not have before. It will show you what term he considered most persuasive when he talked about great issues. I am now at the end of my prepared discourse and am now ready to answer questions.

11

LIFE WITHOUT PREJUDICE

Richard Weaver

When one sets out to discover how "prejudice" became a fighting word, some interesting political history comes to light. Everybody is aware that this term is no longer used in its innocent sense of "prejudgment." It is used, instead, as a flail to beat enemies. Today the air resounds with charges of "prejudice," and the shrill note given it by the "liberals" and radicals suggests a considerable reservoir of feeling and purpose behind its invocation. This appears all the more striking when one recalls that in the controversial literature of a hundred years ago—or even of a couple of generations ago—you do not encounter the sort of waving of the bloody shirt of prejudice that greets you on all sides now. Men did not profess such indignation that other men had differing convictions and viewpoints. They rather expected to encounter these, and to argue with them as best they could. You do not find the tricky maneuvers and the air of what might be called ultraism that we are familiar with today.

What has changed the atmosphere? I would point to the worldwide revolutionary movement which has manifested itself in almost every land. The indictment for prejudice has been one of the most potent weapons in the armory of its agents. There is need to realize what this indictment masks and how it operates, both politically and logically.

It is getting to be a bore to bring communism into every article that deals with a topic of public concern, but here the connection is so close that one finds no option. For the doctrines of Moscow are the *fons et origo* of the great pressure to eradicate "prejudice." A prime object of militant communism is to produce a general social skepticism. Not that the Communists are skeptics themselves. They are the world's leading dogmatists and authoritarians. But in order to bring about their dogmatic reconstruction of the world they need to produce this skepticism among the traditional believers. They need to make people question the supports of whatever social order they enjoy, to encourage a growing dissatisfaction and a feeling that they have inherited a bad article. The more subtle of them realize, no doubt, that people can be made to forget how well a system is working right under their noses if they can be allured and distracted with "pie in the sky." The communist version of pie in the sky shall be dealt with in a moment, when the logical method is considered. Just now I emphasize this unfixing of faith as one of the steps in a large-scale and—it must be confessed—cunning plan. This worldwide revolutionary movement, openly conducted in some countries, operating from hiding in others, wants first of all to clear the ground.

To this end, what it knows that it must overcome is the binding element, or the cohesive force that holds a society together. For as long as this integrative power remains strong, the radical attack stands refuted and hopeless. This will explain the peculiar virulence with which Communists attack those transcendental unifiers like religion, patriotism, familial relationship, and the like. It will also explain, if one penetrates the matter shrewdly, why they are so insistent upon their own programs of conformity, leveling, and de-individualization.

However paradoxical it may appear at first sight, we find when we examine actual cases that communities create a shared sentiment, a oneness, and a loyalty through selective differentiation of the persons who make them up. A society is a structure with many levels, offices, and roles, and the reason we feel grateful to the idea of society is that one man's filling his role makes it possible for another to fill his role, and so on. Because the policeman is doing his policeman's job, the owner of the bakery can sleep well at night. Because plumbers and electricians are performing their functions, doctors and lawyers are free to perform theirs, and the reverse. This is a truistic observation, no doubt, but too little attention is given to the fact that society exists in and through its variegation and multiplicity, and when we speak of a society's "breaking down," we mean exactly a confusing of these roles, a loss of differentiation, and a consequent waning of the feeling of loyalty. Society makes possible the idea of vocation, which is the primary source of distinctions. The ceaseless campaign of the Communists to make every people a mass has as its object the erasing of those distinctions which are the expression of this idea. In the communist Utopia Comrade Jones would work in the mines, and Comrade Smith would write political articles for the party organ, or perhaps he would be assigned the task of proving the non-existence of metaphysics. Their "comradeship" would be of far greater importance than their vocations, but to what end? The answer to this lies in some Messianic idea derived from the prophecies of Marx, Lenin, and Stalin.

The point is that their hostility to distinctions of all kinds as we know them in our society conceals a desire to dissolve that society altogether. And we see that practically all traditional distinctions, whether economic, moral, social, or aesthetic, are today under assault as founded on a prejudice. This shows itself in everything from the more absurd theorems of "democratic action" to the ideal of "non-competitive education," by which teachers who ought to be on the dunce's stool themselves have been led half the distance to Moscow.

Although the aim is this general social skepticism, the Communists and their helpers are sufficiently experienced in ideological warfare to know that it is often bad policy to attack everything at once. To do this may cast doubt upon your own motives and cause people to suspect that something is wrong with you. Often the best tactic is to single out some special object and concentrate your force upon this, while feigning a benevolent attitude toward the rest of the order. This enables you to appear a critic and a patriot at the same time. It is a guiltless-looking role because most of us object to and would like to reform one or more of our country's institutions, even though we have profound attachment to it as a whole.

The difference with the Communist is that this is part of a plan to discredit and do away with the whole. And this is why it is important to note the political method by which he proceeds.

He knows that if you can weaken one after another of the supporting pillars, the structure must eventually collapse. He works, then, like a termite, except that he selects and directs his effort. First things first and one thing at a time. He chooses some feature of an order where there is a potential of resentment, or he may choose some feature about which people are simply soft-headed—that is to say, confused or uncertain. It may be the existence of rich men; it may be the right to acquire and use property privately; it may be the idea of discipline and reward in education; it may be some system of preferential advancement which produces envy in the less successful. His most common maneuver, as previously suggested, is to vilify this as founded upon "prejudice." The burden of his argument usually is that since these do not have perfectly rationalized bases, they have no right to exist. You will find especially that he pours his scorn—and this seems a most important clue to his mentality—upon those things for which people have a natural (and in his sense irrational) affection. The modern Communist, looking upon this world with its interesting distinctions and its prolific rewards and pleasures, may be compared to Satan peering into the Garden. Milton tells us that the arch-fiend

"Saw undelighted all delight."

The more he sees people attached to their theoretically impossible happiness, the more determined he is to bring on the fall.

Just as the marshals of the communist movement have worked politically with more cleverness than many people give them credit for, so they have often been better logicians than those in the opposite camp. The fact will partly explain the sense of frustration felt by defenders of our traditional structural Western society. In their polemic use of the term "prejudice," however, they have been better logicians in the shyster's way: they have confused the other side with a boldly maintained fallacy.

The fallacy contained in the charge "prejudice," as it is usually employed to impeach somebody's judgment, has long been familiar to logicians, by whom it was given the name *argumentum ad ignorantiam*. This signifies an argument addressed to ignorance. The reason for the appellation will appear in an analysis of how the fallacy operates. Those who are guilty of the *argumentum ad ignorantiam* profess belief in something because its opposite cannot be proved, or they assert the existence of something because the something possibly may exist. It is possible that life exists on Mars; therefore life does exist on Mars. In the realm where "prejudice" is now most an issue, it normally takes a form like this: you cannot prove—by the method of statistics and quantitative measurement—that men are not equal. Therefore men are equal. You cannot prove that human beings are naturally wicked. Therefore they are naturally good, and the contrary opinion is a prejudice. You cannot prove—again by the methods of science—that one culture is higher than another. Therefore the culture of the Digger Indians is just as good as that of Muncie, Indiana, or thirteenth-century France.

Generally speaking, this type of fallacious reasoning seeks to take advantage of an opponent by confusing what is abstractly possible with what is really possible or what really exists. Expressed in another way, it would substitute what is possible in theory for that which we have some grounds, even though not decisive ones, for believing. It is possible in some abstract sense that all men are equal. But according to the Bible, Aristotle, and most considerate observers, men are not equal in natural capacity, aptitude for learning, moral education, and so on. If you can get the first belief substituted for the second, on the claim that the second cannot be proved, you have removed a "prejudice." And along with it, you have removed such perception as you have of reality.

The "pie in the sky" appeal of the Communists consequently comes in this guise: you cannot prove the unworkability of the communist or statist Utopia; therefore it is workable. I say "cannot prove," although there are multitudinous evidences that it has never worked along the lines and with the motivations that are always suggested in its favor. One might indeed borrow a famous apothegm and say that all theory is for it and all experience is against it. However, since the appeal is to the dislocated, the resentful, the restless, and the malcontented, it has won its followers. We have seen how they charge the rest of us with being prejudiced in favor of the present order, or whatever feature of it they have singled out for attack. Often they manage to conceal the fallacy underlying their position by a vocabulary and a tone which intimidate the conservative into feeling ignorant.

A critical examination of their logic therefore deserves priority. But after we have seen the worst that can be said against the type of ideas which they condemn as prejudices, we ought to inquire whether such ideas are capable of positive good.

A number of years ago John Grier Hibben, a professor of logic at Princeton and later president of that university, wrote a temperate essay entitled "A Defense of Prejudice." Professor Hibben demonstrated in some detail why it is a mistake to classify all those notions which people denominate prejudices as illogical. A prejudice may be an unreasoned judgment, he pointed out, but an unreasoned judgment is not necessarily an illogical judgment. He went on to list three types of beliefs for which we cannot furnish immediate logical proof, but which may nevertheless be quite in line with truth.

First, there are those judgments whose verification has simply dropped out of memory. At one time they were reached in the same way as our "logical" conclusions, but the details of the process have simply been forgotten. It is necessary to the "economy of thought" that we retire from consciousness many of the facts that were once used to support our judgments. The judgments themselves remain as a kind of deposit of thought. They are not without foundation, though the foundation is no longer present to the mind with any particularity; and the very fact that we employ these judgments successfully from day to day is fair evidence that proof would be available if needed. The judgments are part of the learning we have assimilated in the process of developing a mind.

The second type of unreasoned judgments we hold is the opinions we adopt from others—our betters in some field of learning or experience. There is no need to labor the truth that we all appropriate such opinions on a considerable scale, and if we could not do so, books and institutions of learning would lose their utility. No man in a civilized society proves more than a small percentage of the judgments he operates on, and the more advanced or complex civilization grows, the smaller this proportion must become. If every man found it necessary to verify each judgment he proceeds on, we would all be virtual paupers in knowledge. It is well for every one to know something concerning the *methods* of verification, but this indeed differs from having to verify all over again the hard-won and accumulated wisdom of our society. Happily there *is* such a thing as authority.

The third class of judgments in Professor Hibben's list comprises those which have subconscious origin. The material that furnishes their support does not reach the focal point of consciousness, but psychology insists upon its existence. The intuitions, innuendoes, and shadowy suggestions which combine to form our opinion about, say, a character, could never be made public and formal in any convincing way. Yet only the most absurd doctrinaire would hold that they are therefore founded upon error. In some situations the mind uses a sort of oracular touchstone for testing what cannot be tested in any other way. My judgment that Mr. Blank, though a well-spoken and plausible gentleman, will one day betray his office is a conclusion I cannot afford to put aside, even though at the present moment I have no publicly verifiable facts from the space-time continuum which would prove it to another. It may be true that only those minds which are habituated to think logically can safely trust their intuitive conclusions, on the theory that the subconscious level will do its kind of work as faithfully as the conscious does its kind. This still leaves room for what may be termed paralogical inference.

When one thinks about these well-accepted and perfectly utilitarian forms of "prejudice," the objections of the rationalists seem narrow and intolerant.

There is, indeed, a good deal of empirical evidence for saying that rationalistic men are more intolerant than "prejudiced" men. The former take the position that their judgments are reasoned conclusions, and why should one swerve or deflect from what can be proved to all reasonable men? Such are often the authors of persecutions, massacres, and liquidations. The man who frankly confesses to his prejudices is usually more human and more humane. He adjusts amicably to the idea of his limitations. A limitation once admitted is a kind of monition not to try acting like something superhuman. The person who admits his prejudices, which is to say, his unreasoned judgments, has a perspective on himself.

Let me instance two cases in support of this point. When H. L. Mencken wrote his brilliant series of essays on men, life, and letters, he gave them a title as illuminating as it was honest—*Prejudices*. What he meant, if such a dull addition as a gloss may be permitted with Mencken, was that these were views based on such part of experience as had passed under his observation. There was no apology because some figures were praised and others were roundly damned, and there was no canting claim to "objectivity." Mencken knew that life and action turn largely on convictions which rest upon imperfect inductions, or samplings of evidence, and he knew that feeling is often a positive factor. The result was a tonic criticism unrivaled in its time. Did his "unfairness" leave him unread and without influence? He castigates religion in many ways, and I have known churchmen who admire him and quote him. He thought nothing sillier than the vaporizing of most of our radicals, yet numbers of these looked to him as a mentor in writing and as a leader in every libertarian crusade. In brief, they found in him a *man*, whose prejudices had more of reality than the slogans and catchwords on political banners.

The same lesson, it seems to me, can be read in the career of Dr. Samuel Johnson. Johnson lives in considerable measure through the vitality of his prejudices. When he says to an interlocutor, "Sir, I perceive you are a vile Whig," you know that he is speaking from a context of reality. It is not necessary that you "agree" with him. How many people do we ever "agree" with in any unreserved sense? That he hated Whigs, Scotsmen, and Americans we accept as a sign of character; it is a kind of signature. The heartiness of his likes and dislikes constitutes an ethical proof of all he puts forward. And so it is with any formed personality. A hundred popinjays can be found to discuss brilliantly; but you will not find on every corner a man whose opinions bear a kind of witness to the man himself.

Mencken, like Johnson, is, in his more abstract political thinking, a Tory. But both men—and this is a continuation of the story—proved kind in their personal relations, and both of them were essentially modest. Upon one occasion when Boswell confessed to Johnson that he feared some things he was entering in his journal were too small, the latter advised him that nothing is too small for so small a creature as man. This is good evidence that Johnson had achieved what I referred to as perspective, which carries with it a necessary humility. And while some may be startled to hear Mencken called a modest man, I can infer nothing but a real candor and humility from those bombastic and ironical allusions to himself which comprise much of the humor of his writings. The tone he adopted was a rhetorical instrument; he had faced his limitations.

I have given some space to these examples because I feel they show that the man of frank and strong prejudices, far from being a political and social menace and an obstacle in the path of progress, is often a benign character and a helpful citizen. The chance is far greater, furthermore, that he will be more creative than the man who can never come to more than a few gingerly held conclusions, or who thinks that all ideas should be received with equal hospitality. There is such a thing as being so broad you are flat.

Life without prejudice, were it ever to be tried, would soon reveal itself to be a life without principle. For prejudices, as we have seen earlier, are often built-in principles. They are the extract which the mind has made of experience. Try to imagine a man setting out for the day without a single prejudice. Let us suppose that he has "confessed" his prejudices in the manner of confessing sins and has decided to start next morning with a fresh mind as the sinner would start with a new soul. The analogy is false. Inevitably he would be in a state of paralysis. He could not get up in the morning, or choose his necktie, or make his way to the office, or conduct his business affairs, or, to come right down to the essence of the thing, even maintain his identity. What he does in actuality is arise at his arbitrary 7:15, select the necktie which he is prejudiced in favor of, set off relatively happy with his head full of unreasoned judgments, conduct a successful day's business and return home the same man he was, with perhaps a mite or two added to his store of wisdom.

When Mark Twain wrote, "I know that I am prejudiced in this matter, but I would be ashamed of myself if I were not," he was giving a therapeutic insight into the phenomenon of prejudice. There is a kind of willful narrowness which should be called presumption and rebuked. But prejudice in the sense I have tried to outline here is often necessary to our personal rectitude, to our loyalty to our whole vision. It is time, then for the whole matter of prejudice in relation to society and conduct to be reexamined and revalued. When this is done, it will be seen that the cry of "prejudice" which has been used to frighten so many people in recent years is often no more than caterwauling. It has a scary sound, and it has been employed by the illiberal to terrify the liberal. And since the "liberal," or the man who has not made up his mind about much of anything, is today perhaps the majority type, it has added a great deal to the world's trepidation and confusion. The conservative realizes that many orthodox positions, once abandoned in panic because they were thought to be indefensible, are quite defensible if only one gives a little thought to basic issues. Surely one of these positions is the right of an individual or a society to hold a belief which, though unreasoned, is uncontradicted. When that position is secured, we shall be in better shape to fight the battle against the forces of planned disintegration.

12

DRAMATISM

Kenneth Burke

Dramatism is a method of analysis and a corresponding critique of terminology designed to show that the most direct route to the study of human relations and human motives is via a methodical inquiry into cycles or clusters of terms and their functions.

The dramatistic approach is implicit in the key term "act." "Act" is thus a terministic center from which many related considerations can be shown to "radiate," as though it were a "god-term" from which a whole universe of terms is derived. The dramatistic study of language comes to a focus in a philosophy of language (and of "symbolicity" in general); the latter provides the basis for a general conception of man and of human relations. The present article will consider primarily the dramatistic concern with the resources, limitations, and paradoxes of terminology, particularly in connection with the imputing of motives.

The Dramatistic Approach to Action

Dramatism centers in observations of this sort: for there to be an *act*, there must be an *agent*. Similarly, there must be a *scene* in which the agent acts. To act in a scene, the agent must employ some means, or *agency*. And it can be called an act in the full sense of the term only if it involves a *purpose* (that is, if a support happens to give way and one falls, such motion on the agent's part is not an act, but an accident). These five terms (act, scene, agent, agency, purpose) have been labeled the dramatistic pentad; the aim of calling attention to

From *International Encyclopedia of the Social Sciences*, edited by David Sills (volume 7), The Macmillan Company & The Free Press, 1968, pp. 445–452. Reprinted by permission of The Gale Group.

them in this way is to show how the functions which they designate operate in the imputing of motives (Burke [1945–1950] 1962, Introduction). The pattern is incipiently a hexad when viewed in connection with the different but complementary analysis of *attitude* (as an ambiguous term for *incipient* action) undertaken by George Herbert Mead (1938) and by I. A. Richards (1959).

Later we shall consider the question whether the key terms of dramatism are literal or metaphorical. In the meantime, other important things about the terms themselves should be noted.

Obviously, for instance, the concept of scene can be widened or narrowed (conceived of in terms of varying "scope" or circumference). Thus, an agent's behavior ("act") might be thought of as taking place against a polytheistic background; or the over-all scene may be thought of as grounded in one god; or the circumference of the situation can be narrowed to naturalistic limits, as in Darwinism; or it can be localized in such terms as "Western civilization," "Elizabethanism," "capitalism," "D day," "10 Downing Street," "on this train ride," and so on, endlessly. Any change of the circumference in terms of which an act is viewed implies a corresponding change in one's view of the quality of the act's motivation. Such a loose yet compelling correspondence between act and scene is called a "scene–act ratio" (Burke [1945–1950] 1962, pp. 1–7).

All the terms are capable of similar relationships. A "purpose–agency ratio," for instance, would concern the logic of "means selecting," the relation of means to ends (as the Supreme Court might decide that an emergency measure is constitutional because it was taken in an emergency situation). An "agent–act ratio" would reflect the correspondence between a man's character and the character of his behavior (as, in a drama, the principles of formal consistency require that each member of the dramatis personae act in character, though such correspondences in art can have a perfection not often found in life). In actual practice, such ratios are used sometimes to explain an act and sometimes to *justify* it (*ibid.*, pp. 15–20). Such correlations are not strict, but analogical. Thus, by "scene–act ratio" is meant a proposition such as: Though agent and act are necessarily different in many of their attributes, some notable element of one is implicitly or analogously present in the other.

David Hume's *An Inquiry Concerning Human Understanding* (first published in 1748) throws a serviceable light upon the dramatistic "ratios." His treatise begins with the observation that "moral philosophy, or the science of human nature, may be treated after two different manners." One of these "considers man chiefly as born for action." The other would "consider man in the light of a reasonable rather than an active being, and endeavor to form his understanding more than cultivate his manners" ([1748] 1952, p. 451). Here, in essence, is the distinction between a dramatistic approach in terms of *action* and an approach in terms of *knowledge*. For, as a "reasonable being," Hume says, man "receives from science his proper food and nourishment. But man "is a sociable, no less than a reasonable being. . . . Man is also an active being; and from that disposition, as well as from the various necessities of human life, must submit to business and occupation" (*ibid.*, p. 452).

Insofar as men's actions are to be interpreted in terms of the circumstances in which they are acting, their behavior would fall under the heading of a "scene–act ratio." But insofar as their acts reveal their different characters, their behavior would fall under the heading of an "agent–act ratio." For instance, in a time of great crisis, such as a shipwreck, the conduct of all persons involved in that crisis could be expected to manifest in some way the motivating influence of the crisis. Yet, within such a "scene–act ratio" there would be a range of "agent–act ratios," insofar as one man was "proved" to be cowardly, another bold, another resourceful, and so on.

Talcott Parsons, in one of his earlier works, has analytically unfolded, for sociological purposes, much the same set of terministic functions that is here being called dramatistic (owing to their nature as implied in the idea of an "act"). Thus, in dealing with "the unit of action systems," Parsons writes:

> An "act" involves logically the following: (1) It implies an agent, an "actor." (2) For purposes of definition the act must have an "end," a future state of affairs toward which the process of action is oriented. (3) It must be initiated in a "situation" of which the trends of development differ in one or more important respects from the state of affairs to which the action is oriented, the end. This situation is in turn analyzable into two elements: those over which the actor has no control, that is which he cannot alter, or prevent from being altered, in conformity with his end, and those over which he has such control. The former may be termed the "conditions" of action, the latter the "means." Finally (4) there is inherent in the conception of this unit, in its analytical uses, a certain mode of relationship between these elements. That is, in the choice of alternative means to the end, in so far as the situation allows alternatives, there is a "normative orientation" of actions. (1937, p. 44)

Aristotle, from whom Aquinas got his definition of God as "pure act," gives us much the same lineup when enumerating the circumstances about which we may be ignorant, with corresponding inability to act voluntarily:

> A man may be ignorant, then, of who he is, what he is doing, what or whom he is acting on, and sometimes also what (e.g. what instrument) he is doing it with, and to what end (e.g. he may think his act will conduce to some one's safety), and how he is doing it (e.g. whether gently or violently). (*Nichomachean Ethics* 1111a5)

This pattern became fixed in the medieval questions: *quis* (agent), *quid* (act), *ubi* (scene defined as place), *quibus auxiliis* (agency), *cur* (purpose), *quo modo* (manner, "attitude"), *quando* (scene defined temporally).

The Nature of Symbolic Action

Within the practically limitless range of scenes (or motivating situations) in terms of which human action can be defined and studied, there is one over-all dramatistic distinction as regards the widening or narrowing of circumference.

This is the distinction between "action" and "sheer motion." "Action," is a term for the kind of behavior possible to a typically symbol-using animal (such as man) in contrast with the extrasymbolic or nonsymbolic operations of nature.

Whatever terministic paradoxes we may encounter en route (and the dramatistic view of terminology leads one to expect them on the grounds that language is primarily a species of action, or expression of attitudes, rather than an instrument of definition), there is the self-evident distinction between symbol and *symbolized* (in the sense that the *word* "tree" is categorically distinguishable from the *thing* tree). Whatever may be the ultimate confusions that result from man's intrinsic involvement with "symbolicity" as a necessary part of his nature, one can at least *begin* with this sufficiently clear distinction between a "thing" and its name.

The distinction is generalized in dramatism as one between "sheer motion" and "action." It involves an empirical shift of circumference in the sense that although man's ability to speak depends upon the existence of speechless nature, the existence of speechless nature does not depend upon man's ability to speak. The relation between these two distinct terministic realms can be summed up in three propositions:

(1) There can be no action without motion—that is, even the "symbolic action" of pure thought requires corresponding motions of the brain.

(2) There can be motion without action. (For instance, the motions of the tides, of sunlight, of growth and decay.)

(3) Action is not reducible to terms of motion. For instance, the "essence" or "meaning" of a sentence is not reducible to its sheer physical existence as sounds in the air or marks on the page, although material motions of some sort are necessary for the production, transmission, and reception of the sentence. As has been said by Talcott Parsons:

> Certainly the situation of action includes parts of what is called in common-sense terms the physical environment and the biological organism . . . these elements of the situation of action are capable of analysis in terms of the physical and biological sciences, and the phenomena in question are subject to analysis in terms of the units in use in those sciences. Thus a bridge may, with perfect truth, be said to consist of atoms of iron, a small amount of carbon, etc., and their constituent electrons, protons, neutrons and the like. Must the student of action, then, become a physicist, chemist, biologist in order to understand his subject? In a sense this is true, but for purposes of the theory of action it is not necessary or desirable to carry such analyses as far as science in general is capable of doing. A limit is set by the frame of reference with which the student of action is working. That is, he is interested in phenomena with an aspect not reducible to action terms only in so far as they impinge on the schema of action in a relevant way—in the role of conditions or means. . . . For the purposes of the theory of action the smallest conceivable concrete unit is the unit act, and while it is in turn analyzable into the elements to which reference has been made—end, means, conditions and guiding norms—further analysis of the phenomena of which

these are in turn aspects is relevant to the theory of action only in so far as the units arrived at can be referred to as constituting such elements of a unit act or a system of them. (1937, pp. 47–48)

Is Dramatism Merely Metaphorical?

Although such prototypically dramatistic usages as "all the world's a stage" are clearly metaphors, the situation looks quite otherwise when approached from another point of view. For instance, a physical scientist's relation to the materials involved in the study of motion differs in quality from his relation to his colleagues. He would never think of "petitioning" the objects of his experiment or "arguing with them," as he would with persons whom he asks to collaborate with him or to judge the results of his experiment. Implicit in these two relations is the distinction between the sheer motion of things and the actions of persons.

In this sense, man is defined literally as an animal characterized by his special aptitude for "symbolic action," which is itself a literal term. And from there on, drama is employed, not as a metaphor but as a fixed form that helps us discover what the implications of the terms "act" and "person" *really are*. Once we choose a generalized term for what people do, it is certainly as literal to say that "people act" as it is to say that they "but move like mere things."

Dramatism and the Social System

Strictly speaking, then, dramatism is a theory of terminology. In this respect a nomenclature could be called dramatistic only if it were specifically designed to talk, at one remove, about the cycle of terms implicit in the idea of an act. But in a wider sense any study of human relations in terms of "action" could to that extent be called dramatistic. A major difficulty in delimiting the field of reference derives from the fact that common-sense vocabularies of motives are spontaneously personalistic, hence innately given to drama-laden terms. And the turn from the naive to the speculative is marked by such "action words" as *tao*, *karma*, *dike*, *hodos*, *islâm* (to designate a submissive *attitude*), all of which are clearly dramatistic when contrasted with the terminological ideals proper to the natural sciences (Burke [1945–1950] 1962, p. 15).

The dramatistic nature of the Bible is proclaimed in the verb (*bara*) of the opening sentence that designates God's creative act; and the series of fiats that follows identifies such action with the principle of symbolicity ("the Word"). Both Plato's philosophy of the Good as ultimate motive and Aristotle's potentiality–actuality pair would obviously belong here, as would the strategic accountancy of active and passive in Spinoza's *Ethics* (Burke [1945–1950] 1962, pp. 146–152). The modern sociological concern with "values" as motives does not differ in principle from Aristotle's list of persuasive "topics" in his *Rhetoric*. One need not look very closely at Lucretius' atomism to discern the personality in those willful particles. Contemporary theories of role-taking would obviously fall within this looser usage, as indicated on its face by the term itself. Rhetorical studies of political exhortation meet the same test, as do typical news reports of people's actions, predicaments, and expressions. Most historiography would be similarly classed, insofar as its modes of systematization and generalization can be called a scientifically documented species of storytelling. And humanistic criticism (of either ethical or aesthetic sorts) usually embodies, in the broad sense, a dramatistic attitude toward questions of personality. Shifts in the locus and scope of a terminology's circumference allow for countless subdivisions, ranging from words like "transaction," "exchange," "competition," and "cooperation," or the maneuvers studied in the obviously dramalike situations of game theories, down to the endless individual verbs designed to narrate specifically what some one person did, or said, or thought at some one time. Thus Duncan (1962) has explicitly applied a dramatistic nomenclature to hierarchy and the sociology of comedy. Similarly, Goffman (1956) has characterized his study of "impression management" as "dramaturgical."

Does Dramatism Have a Scientific Use?

If the dramatistic nature of terms for human motives is made obvious in Burke's pentad (act, scene, agent, agency, purpose), is this element radically eliminated if we but introduce a *synonym* for each of those terms? Have we, for instance, effectively dodged the dramatistic "logic" if instead of "act" we say "response," instead of "scene" we say "situation" or "stimulus," instead of "agent" we say "subject" or "the specimen under observation in this case," instead of "agency" we say "implementation," and instead of "purpose" we use some term like "target"? Or to what extent has reduction *wholly* taken place when the dramatistic grammar of "active," "passive," and "reflexive" gets for its analogues, in the realm of sheer motion, "effectors," "receptors" (output, input), and "feedback," respectively? Might we have here but a *truncated* terminology of action, rather than a terminology intrinsically non-dramatistic? Such issues are not resolved by a dramatistic perspective; but they are systematically brought up for consideration.

A dramatistic analysis of nomenclature can make clear the paradoxical ways in which even systematically generated "theories of action" can culminate in kinds of observation best described by analogy with mechanistic models. The resultant of many disparate acts cannot itself be considered an act in the same purposive sense that characterizes each one of such acts (just as the movement of the stock market in its totality is not "personal" in the sense of the myriad decisions made by each of the variously minded traders). Thus, a systematic analysis of interactions among a society of agents whose individual acts variously reinforce and counter one another may best be carried out in terms of concepts of "equilibrium" and "disequilibrium" borrowed from the terminology of mechanics.

In this regard it should also be noted that although equilibrium theories are usually interpreted as intrinsically adapted only to an upholding of the *status quo*, according to the dramatistic perspective this need not be the case. A work such as Albert Mathiez's *The French Revolution* (1922–1927) could be viewed as the expression of an *anima naturaliter dramatistica* in that it traces step by step an ironic development whereby a succession of unintentionally wrong moves led to unwanted results. If one viewed this whole disorderly sequence as itself a species of order, then each of the stages in its advance could be interpreted as if "designed" to stabilize, in constantly changing circumstances, the underlying pattern of conditions favorable to the eventual outcome (namely, the kind of equilibrium that could be maintained only by a series of progressive developments leading into, through, and beyond the Terror).

Though a drama is a mode of symbolic action so designed that an audience might be induced to "act symbolically" in sympathy with it, insofar as the drama serves this function it may be studied as a "perfect mechanism" composed of parts moving in mutual adjustment to one another like clockwork. The paradox is not unlike that which happened in metaphysics when a mystical view of the world as a manifestation of God's purposes prepared the way for mechanistic views, since the perfect representation of such a "design" seemed to be a machine in perfect order.

This brings up the further consideration that mechanical models might best be analyzed, not as downright antidramatistic, but as fragments of the dramatistic. For whatever humanist critics might say about the "dehumanizing" effects of the machine, it is a characteristically *human* invention, conceived by the perfecting of some human aptitudes and the elimination of others (thus in effect being not inhuman, but man's powerful "caricature" of himself—a kind of mighty homunculus).

If, on the other hand, it is held that a dramatistic nomenclature is to be avoided in any form as categorically inappropriate to a science of social relations, then a systematic study of symbolic action could at least be of use in helping to reveal any hitherto undetected traces of dramatistic thinking that might still survive. For otherwise the old Adam of human symbolicity, whereby man still persists in thinking of himself as a *personal agent capable of acting,* may lurk in a symbol system undetected (a tendency revealed in the fact that the distinction between "action" and "sheer motion" so readily gets lost, as with a term like *kinesis* in Aristotle or the shift between the mechanistic connotations of "equilibrium" and the histrionic connotations of "equilibrist"). Similarly, since pragmatist terminologies lay great stress upon "agencies" (means) and since all machines have a kind of built-in purpose, any nomenclature conceived along the lines of pragmatist instrumentalism offers a halfway house between teleology and sheer aimless motion.

At one point dramatism as a critique of terminology is necessarily at odds with dramatism as applied for specifically scientific purposes. This has been made clear in an article by Wrong (1961), who charges that although "modern sociology after all originated as a protest against the partial views of man contained in such doctrines as utilitarianism, classical economics, social

Darwinism, and vulgar Marxism," it risks contributing to "the creation of yet another reified abstraction in socialized man, the status-seeker of our contemporary sociologists" (p. 190). He grants that "such an image of man is . . . valuable for limited purposes," but only "so long as it is not taken for the whole truth" (p. 190). He offers various corrections, among them a stress upon "role-playing," and upon "forces in man that are resistant to socialization," such as certain "biological" and "psychological" factors—even though some sociologists might promptly see "the specter of 'biological determinism'" (p. 191) and others might complain that already there is "too much 'psychologism' in contemporary sociology" (p. 192).

Viewed from the standpoint of dramatism as a critique of terminology, Wrong's article suggests two notable problems. Insofar as any science has a nomenclature especially adapted to its particular field of study, the extension of its *special* terms to provide a definition of man *in general* would necessarily oversociologize, overbiologize, overpsychologize, or overphysicize, etc., its subject; or the definition would have to be corrected by the addition of elements from other specialized nomenclatures (thereby producing a kind of amalgam that would lie outside the strict methodic confines of any specialized scientific discipline). A dramatistic view of this situation suggests that an over-all definition of man would be not strictly "scientific," but philosophical.

Similarly, the dramatistic concept of a scene–act ratio aims to admonish against an overly positivistic view of descriptive terms, or "empirical data," as regards an account of the conditions that men are thought to confront at a given time in history. For insofar as such a grammatical function does figure in our thoughts about motives and purpose, in the choice and scope of the terms that are used for characterizing a given situation dramatism would discern implicit corresponding attitudes and programs of action. If the principle of the scene–act ratio always figures in some form, it follows that one could not possibly select descriptive terms in which policies of some sort are not more or less clearly inherent. In the selection of terms for describing a scene, one automatically prescribes the range of acts that will seem reasonable, implicit, or necessary in that situation.

Dramatistic Analyses of Order

Following a lead from Bergson (1907, especially chapter 4), dramatism is devoted to a stress upon the all-importance of the negative as a specifically linguistic invention. But whereas Bergson's fertile chapter on "the idea of nothing" centers in the propositional negative ("It is not"), the dramatistic emphasis focuses attention upon the "moralistic" or "hortatory" negative ("Thou shalt not"). Burke (1961, pp. 183–196) has applied this principle of negativity to a cycle of terms implicit in the idea of "order," in keeping with the fact that "order," being a polar term, implies a corresponding idea of "disorder," while these terms in turn involve ideas of "obedience" or "disobedience" to the "authority" implicit in "order" (with further terministic radiations, such as the attitude of "humility" that leads to the act of obedience or the attitude of "pride" that leads to the act of disobedience, these in turn involving ideas of guidance or temptation, reward or punishment, and so on).

On the side of order, or control, there are the variants of faith and reason (faith to the extent that one accepts a given command, proscription, or statement as authoritative; reason to the extent that one's acceptance is contingent upon such proofs as are established by a methodic weighing of doubts and rebuttals). On the side of disorder there are the temptations of the senses and the imagination. The senses can function as temptations to the extent that the prescribed order does not wholly gratify our impulses (whether they are natural or a by-product of the very order that requires their control). Similarly, the imagination falls on the side of disorder insofar as it encourages interests inimical to the given order, though it is serviceable to order if used as a deterrent by picturing the risks of disorder—or, in other words, if it is kept "under the control of reason."

Midway between the two slopes of order and disorder (technically the realm where one can say yes or no to a thou-shalt-not) there is an area of indeterminacy often called the will. Ontologically, action is treated as a function of the will. But logologically the situation is reversed: the idea of the will is viewed as derivable from the idea of an act.

From ideas of the will there follow in turn ideas of grace, or an intrinsic ability to make proper choices (though such an aptitude can be impaired by various factors), and sacrifice (insofar as any choices involve the "mortification" of some desires). The dramatistic perspective thus rounds out the pattern in accordance with the notion that insofar as a given order involves sacrifices of some sort, the sacrificial principle is intrinsic to the nature of order. Hence, since substitution is a prime resource available to symbol systems, the sacrificial principle comes to ultimate fulfillment in vicarious sacrifice, which is variously rationalized, and can be viewed accordingly as a way to some kind of ultimate rewards.

By tracing and analyzing such terms, a dramatistic analysis shows how the negativistic principle of guilt implicit in the nature of order combines with the principles of thoroughness (or "perfection") and substitution that are characteristic of symbol systems in such a way that the sacrificial principle of victimage (the "scapegoat") is intrinsic to human congregation. The intricate line of exposition might be summed up thus: If order, then guilt; if guilt, then need for redemption; but any such "payment" is victimage. Or: If action, then drama; if drama, then conflict; if conflict, then victimage.

Adapting theology ("words about God") to secular, empirical purposes ("words about words"), dramatistic analysis stresses the perennial vitality of the scapegoat principle, explaining why it fits so disastrously well into the "logologic" of man's symbolic resources. It aims to show why, just as the two primary and sometimes conflicting functions of religion (solace and control) worked together in the doctrines of Christianity, we should expect to find their analogues in any society. Dramatism, as so conceived, asks not how the sacrificial motives revealed in the institutions of magic and religion might be eliminated in a scientific culture, but what new forms they take (Burke [1945–1950] 1962, pp. 406–408).

This view of vicarious victimage extends the range of those manifestations far beyond the areas ordinarily so labeled. Besides extreme instances like Hitlerite genocide, or the symbolic "cleansings" sought in wars, uprisings, and heated political campaigns, victimage would include psychogenic illness, social exclusiveness (the malaise of the "hierarchal psychosis"), "beatnik" art, rabid partisanship in sports, the excessive pollution of air and streams, the "bulldozer mentality" that rips into natural conditions without qualms, the many enterprises that keep men busy destroying in the name of progress or profit the ecological balance on which, in the last analysis, our eventual well-being depends, and so on.

The strongly terministic, or logological, emphasis of dramatism would view the scapegoat principle not primarily as a survival from earlier eras, but as a device natural to language here and now. Aristotle, in the third book of his *Rhetoric* (chapter 10), particularly stresses the stylistic importance of antithesis as a means of persuasion (as when a policy is recommended in terms of what it is *against*). In this spirit dramatism would look upon the scapegoat (or the principle of vicarious victimage) as but a special case of antithesis, combined with another major resource of symbol systems, namely, substitution.

In the polemics of politics, the use of the scapegoat to establish identification in terms of an enemy shared in common is also said to have the notable rhetorical advantage that the candidate who presents himself as a spokesman for "us" can prod his audience to consider local ills primarily in terms of alien figures viewed as the outstanding causes of those ills. In accord with this emphasis, when analyzing the rhetorical tactics of *Mein Kampf*, Burke (1922–1961) lays particular stress upon Hitler's use of such deflections to provide a "noneconomic interpretation of economic ills."

While recognizing the amenities of property and holding that "mine-ownness" or "our-ownness" in some form or other is an inevitable aspect of human congregation, dramatistic analysis also contends that property in any form sets the conditions for conflict (and hence culminates in some sort of victimage). It is pointed out that the recent great advances in the development of technological power require a corresponding extension in the realm of negativity (the "thou-shalt-nots" of control). Thus, the strikingly "positive" nature of such resources (as described in terms of "sheer motion") is viewed dramatistically as deceptive; for they may seem too simply like "promises," whereas in being *powers* they are *properties*, and all properties are *problems*, since powers are bones of contention (Burke 1960).

A dramatistic view of human motives thus culminates in the ironic admonition that perversions of the sacrificial principle (purgation by scapegoat, congregation by segregation) are the constant temptation of human societies, whose orders are built by a kind of animal exceptionally adept in the ways of symbolic action (Burke [1941] 1957, pp. 87–113).

Bibliography

Benne, Kenneth D. 1964 From Polarization to Paradox. Pages 216–247 in Leland P. Bradford, Jack R. Gibb, and Kenneth D. Benne (editors), *T-Group Theory and Laboratory Method: Innovation in Re-education*. New York: Wiley.

Bergson, Henri (1907) 1944 *Creative Evolution*. New York: Modern Library. First published in French.

Burke, Kenneth (1922–1961) 1964 *Perspectives by Incongruity and Terms for Order*. Edited by Stanley Edgar Hyman. Bloomington: Indiana Univ. Press. Two representative collections of readings from Burke's works. Each collection is also available separately in paperback from the same publisher.

Burke, Kenneth (1937) 1959 *Attitudes Toward History*. 2d ed., rev. Los Altos, CA: Hermes.

Burke, Kenneth (1941) 1957 *The Philosophy of Literary Form: Studies in Symbolic Action*. Rev. ed., abridged by the author. New York: Vintage. The Louisiana State University Press reprinted the unabridged edition in 1967.

Burke, Kenneth (1945–1950) 1962 *A Grammar of Motives* and *A Rhetoric of Motives*. Cleveland: World.

Burke, Kenneth 1955 Linguistic Approach to Problems of Education. Pages 259–303 in National Society for the Study of Education, Committee on Modern Philosophies and Education, *Modern Philosophies and Education*. Edited by Nelson B. Henry. National Society for the Study of Education Yearbook 54, Part 1. Univ. of Chicago Press.

Burke, Kenneth 1960 Motion, Action, Words. *Teachers College Record* 62:244–249.

Burke, Kenneth 1961 *The Rhetoric of Religion: Studies in Logology*. Boston: Beacon.

Burke, Kenneth 1966 *Language as Symbolic Action: Essays on Life, Literature, and Method*. Berkeley: Univ. of California Press.

Duncan, Hugh D. 1962 *Communication and Social Order*. Totowa, NJ; Bedminster Press.

Goffman, Erving (1956) 1959 *The Presentation of Self in Everyday Life*. Garden City, NY: Doubleday.

Hume, David (1748) 1952 An Inquiry Concerning Human Understanding. Pages 451–509 in *Great Books of the Western World*. Volume 35: Locke, Berkeley, Hume. Chicago: Benton.

Mathiez, Albert (1922–1927) 1962 *The French Revolution*. New York: Russell. First published in French in three volumes. A paperback edition was published in 1964 by Grosset and Dunlap.

Mead, George Herbert 1938 *The Philosophy of the Act*. Univ. of Chicago Press. Consists almost entirely of unpublished papers which Mead left at his death in 1931.

Parsons, Talcott 1937 *The Structure of Social Action: A Study in Social Theory With Special Reference to a Group of Recent European Writers*. New York: McGraw-Hill.

Richards, Ivor A. (1959) 1961 *Principles of Literary Criticism*. New York: Harcourt.

Rueckert, William H. 1963 *Kenneth Burke and the Drama of Human Relations*. Minneapolis: Univ. of Minnesota Press.

Wrong, Dennis H. 1961 The Oversocialized Conception of Man in Modern Sociology. *American Sociological Review* 26:183–193.

13

EPILOGUE
PROLOGUE IN HEAVEN

Kenneth Burke

Enter, IMPRESARIO, *his upper half in formal attire, with ragged pants and worn-out shoes. Addresses the audience:*

Ladies and Gentlemen: Try to imagine a single flash of thought in which, simultaneously with an inner uttering of the word "geometry," you also conceived in detail all the definitions, axioms, propositions, demonstrations, corollaries, scholia, lemmas and special cases that go with that discipline.

Or imagine every event of universal history, made accessible to contemplation in one momentary panorama that comprises all time and space, in every act, attitude, and relationship (a distillate both perfectly simple and infinitely complex, of what has unfolded, is unfolding and is yet to unfold throughout the endless aeons of universal development).

Further, imagine a discourse that is not expressed in words at all, but rather is like the sheer awareness that goes with the speaking or the hearing of words.

And, finally, imagine such intuitive expression as a dialogue between two persons that are somehow fused with each other in a communicative bond whereby each question is its own answer, or is answered even without being asked.

Such is the formal paradox underlying this discourse between The Lord and Satan.

Since, in the original Heavenly situation there is neither time nor space, the nearest we can come to suggesting the scene's intimacies and immensities

From *The Rhetoric of Religion: Studies in Logology* (1970). Berkeley and Los Angeles: University of California Press, pp. 273–316.

is to say that they are like a relation between contradictory ideas whereby things farthest apart are also closest together. Or like an infinite sphere, every point of which is both center and circumference, part and whole. Another way to imagine the setting dialogue is to think of a cathedral so vast that its interior is as horizonless as the sea in a fog, yet all is brilliantly clear—and this mighty architectural pile would be made not of materials but of the principles which an architect necessarily embodies in the act of drafting his plans.

I thank you. (*Exit—then returns.*)

No! Ladies and Gentlemen, my apologies, I should make a few more preparatory observations. First, the author of the heavenly dialogue which you are about to witness has asked me to point out that his account is *purely imaginary*: It involves a theory of purpose based on the definition of man as the "symbol-using animal."

(*Takes out a paper and reads.*)

Insofar as men are animals, they derive purposes from their physical nature. For instance, bodily hunger is enough to move them in search of food. Also, they can invent machines with "built-in" purposes, for instance missiles that will pursue a moving target with the persistence of a maniac, and that are responsible to no other kinds of signal.

But machines are given such purposes by men, since languages make it impossible for men to be content with sheer *bodily* purpose. And insofar as men "cannot live by bread alone," they are moved by doctrine, which is to say, they derive purposes from language, which tells them what they "ought" to want to do, tells them how to do it, and in the telling goads them with great threats and promises, even unto the gates of heaven and hell.

With language, a whole new realm of purpose arises, endless in scope, as contrasted with the few rudimentary purposes we derive from our bodies, the needs of food, drink, shelter and sex in their physical simplicity.

Language can even build purpose out of the ability to comment on the nature of purpose. However, the purposes that arise through the tangles made possible by language are not merely the old bodily appetites in a new form. They are appetites differing not just in degree but in kind. And the two kinds differ so greatly that, as tested by the wishes of the body, the purposes supplied by language (by doctrine) can amount even to a kind of built-in *frustration*. Simplest example: What hungry belly could be quieted by a poem in praise of food? Yet, as we have said, language will not let men be satisfied with sheer bodily purposes either, as other animals presumably are.

In any case, obviously, the talking animals' way of life in a civilization *invents* purposes. Rationalized by money (which is a language, a kind of purpose-in-the-absolute, a universal wishing well) empires arise. Such networks of production and distribution, made *possible* by language, become *necessary*. So, they raise problems—and many purposes are but attempts to solve those problems, plus the vexing fact that each "solution" raises further problems. (Confidentially, that's "the dialectic.")

But the very resources of language to which such quandaries owe their rise also goad men to further questioning. For language makes questioning easy. Given language, you can never be sure where quest ends and question begins. Hence, the search for some Grand Over-All Purpose, as with philosophers, metaphysicians, theologians.

Along these lines, the "Prologue in Heaven" which you are about to witness is a Parable of Purpose. . . . I thank you.

(*Exit. Faint drum roll in distance. Curtain rises—on what? Possibly on two chairs, in center of stage, under strong spotlight, turned half facing each other, half facing audience. All the rest of the stage in darkness, wholly indeterminate. Two voices off stage, approaching. Spotlight moves to where* SATAN *and* THE LORD *are entering, from left rear.* SATAN *first, hurriedly, but looking back as he proceeds. Then* THE LORD, *so deliberately that* SATAN *seems like a dog scouting ahead of his master.* THE LORD *is a Blakean bearded patriarch.* SATAN *is an agile youth, wears fool's cap with devil's horns, and a harlequin costume of two colors, dividing him down the middle. The speakers are obviously on quite friendly terms. As things develop, it will become apparent that* THE LORD *is affectionately amused by his young companion, while* SATAN, *over-hasty, mercurial, is an intense admirer of the older man. They come forward and take seats, with* SATAN *at* THE LORD's *right hand.*)

TL. Yes, I've definitively decided to do it. Or, rather, it will necessarily come about, unless I deliberately interfere with the processes of unfolding that began when I created time. In the first chaotic swirl, the eventual emergence of the Word-Using Animal was implicit. And I shall not interfere with those natural processes that, having led to beautiful gardens, can now, as it were, people the loveliest of them with this cantankerous animal.

S. What, then, in sum, is your decree, milord?

TL. It amounts to this: On planet Earth I will place a species of creature, describable by an enemy as vermin and endowed with the power of speaking, hence the powers of mechanical invention and political governance.

S. Since I know, milord, that you are nothing if not Design, I pray: Tell me why this design.

TL. It will round things out, with the symmetry of the circle.

S. I understand the symmetry of the circle. But I don't quite understand how the principle figures here.

TL. (*encouragingly*). Of course you do!

S. Of course I do! Necessarily, when you so envision me. It's this way: If nature gives birth to an animal that can talk, then by the same token nature becomes able to comment on itself. (*Smiles admiringly at* THE LORD.)

TL. And thus nature can circle back on itself. Yes, I'll go ahead with it. And in any case, the project as a whole is so much more inclusive, by comparison that stretch of symbol-using will not be as long as one flicker in all eternity. A protracted evolutionary process leads up to the point where the language-using animal emerges. And then there will be an infinitely long time of wordlessness again, as regards their kind of words, after the evolutionary process has moved on, in developments that leave this troublous species far behind.

S. (*pondering, half to himself*). But that odd kind of word they will use ... with syllables and sentences and whole speeches stretched out through time, like one of their corpses on a mortuary slab ... that's so different from our single, eternal, Unitive Word that creatively sums up all, in your exceptional Self, combining your Power, your Wisdom and your Love in the perfect simplicity of infinitely complex harmony.

TL. (*laughing*). Come, my lad, now you're talking like one of their theologians!

S. I should fear that you were deriding me, did I not know that there is no derision in you.

TL. Always, that morbid modesty of yours! Don't be so defensive. It's more complicated than that.

S. Necessarily your command is my obedience.

TL. I can't be all-powerful without being all-powerful. So, in the last analysis, *you* are but a function of *my* will.

S. You know I'm not complaining, milord. But I've heard tell among us that it's to be different with these new Word-Using Animals, the Earth-People. Is it true that in these new creatures you shall have solved a basic logical contradiction, in making it possible for them to disobey your all-powerful authority?

TL. It's more complicated than that. But you can take this much for granted: I have resolved no basic logical contradiction. No one can get around a contradiction in terms; for instance, I can't make a four-sided triangle. True, some of their metaphysicians will offer talk about "nothing" that has "being." But *I* must begin and end with the proposition that something is what it is.

S. Then their temporal kind of word will be like our eternal kind?

TL. It's more complicated than that. It will all center in their way of using the negative. With us, there is only the distinction between *is* and *is not*. But with them, the first negative will be of a different sort: It will involve the distinction between *shall* and *shall not*.

S. But we, too, have the distinction between *shall* and *shall not*. I feel your will as a command.

TL. But owing to the nature of our eternal simultaneity (what they will call the *nunc stans*), the command and the obedience are one. As you yourself have put it: My command is your obedience. But once the idea of *logical* contradiction is modified by the possibility of *temporal* contradiction, the command can be at one time, the obeying at another. And once there is the possibility of a breach between them, here are the makings of a contradiction, different from that of sheer logic.

S. If not a logical contradiction, then ... what kind, please?

TL. A whole cluster of their words could be used: above all, it might be called "moral" or "dramatic," because it has to do with action. And their words for morality, drama and action will all imply one another. But once the successiveness of time (and its similarly divisible partner, space) introduces the possibility of an interval between the command and the obedience, by the same token there is the possibility of disobedience.

S. I am glad to hear you say so. I myself have felt that there is a kind of "fall" implicit in your creating of a time-world (however praiseworthy, I hasten to add, this grand opus is in itself).

TL. True, one can't make divisions without having recourse to divisiveness—and divisiveness is in itself a "fall." Similarly, one can't create time without creating death; for the birth of each new moment is the death of the moment that preceded it. A further problem arises from the fact that the introduction of time (with its kind of succession so different from that of the syllogism) must introduce a notable tangle with regard to the negative, at the very start. For the earthy Word-Animal will encounter its first negatives (and don't forget the formative nature of such firsts) in terms of sheerly extra-logical contradiction. Precisely when emerging from its pre-verbal state, the human infant will learn "thou shalt not" quite some time before the grasp of words is strong enough to comprehend "it is not." The infant must learn the negative, first of all, as an aspect of action (of command, with a temporal breach that allows for both obedience and disobedience).

S. The infant will learn the logical "it *is* not" by first emerging out of sheerly infantile relations to parental "thou shalt not's"?

TL. Yes. And from then on, the complications will be unending. Above all (and here is an irony that should amuse you, since you are so confirmed an ironist): repeatedly, when meditating on human relations, their philosophers will begin where they should end, with the "is" and "is not."

S. (*exultantly*). I see it! I see it! And implicit in their supposedly objective versions of what is and is not, they will have concealed a set of shall's and shall-not's, which they will then proceed methodically to "discover"! What better comedy!

TL. You'll enjoy them, my lad. You will enjoy them greatly. Though made in my image, the Earth-People will necessarily incline towards that part of me which you would be, were our realm to be, like theirs, divisible.

S. But I am still unclear: In this breach between the command and the obedience, will they or will they not have freedom? We are free, in necessarily being indivisible parts of your freedom, which you possess in being constrained by nothing but your own self-willed principles of identity. But with these temporal verbalizers, is there to be a *deviant* kind of "freedom"?

TL. You *would* ask that, my lad! I see why I love you so greatly. If *my* negative ever broke loose from me, I'd know where to look for it.

S. Milord, I blush!

(*Pause.*)

TL. (*resuming*). Here's the soundest way to get at the problem: If this culminating creature I contemplate is to be a symbol-using animal, then by definition everything about it should be deducible from either its animality or its symbolicity. So let's treat of everything to do with it in terms of one or the other, either the genus (animality) or the differentia (symbolicity), or, naturally, the combination (or composite) of the two.

S. Then all else would follow by definition, as with us?

TL. It's more complicated than that. But let's start from there. That's a good first. Thus, note first of all, that purely by definition, the Word-Men, by being endowed with their particular kind of language (as the other animals are not) will have the power of answering questions or responding to commands.

S. That is, you are now to stress not their genus (animality) but their differentia (symbolicity)?

TL. And in this sense, they will have "responsibility." For what is responsibility but the ability to respond?

S. But everything "responds." If an Earth-Man kicks one of his pebbles, it will "respond" to the impetus of his blow.

TL. The pebble will not say a word.

S. *Touché!* "Response" in the full sense of the term involves "symbolicity."

TL. Good! Now let's take another step, this time towards *perfection.* You shall hear a lot more about "perfection" before this inquiry is ended. For the moment, consider our problem thus: So far as the *pure formality* of a question is concerned, the perfect answer would be Yes or No. Thus, even if a man gave the answer that he was predestined to give at the very crack of Creation, there would nonetheless be this *purely formal* sense in which every question permits of choice.

S. O miracles of form! No truth, no beauty, no goodness, even no expediency, without form!

TL. And men will know, too, that there is no purer act than pure form. And a pure act is by definition pure freedom. Further, inasmuch as they can give names to one another, they will be able to conceive of themselves as *Persons*. And a Person is, by definition, a being that can *act*. ("Things," by definition, can merely move, or be moved. They cannot "act.")

S. In the purely formal sense, then, a person is an entity that can answer yes or no to a command (which in turn implies the distinction between the yes of obedience and the no of disobedience).

TL. Exactly. And by the same token, such "persons" can lay claim to "freedom." For if an act weren't "free," it wouldn't be an "act."

TL and S (*in unison*). It would be sheer motion.

S. So it must be free, since it is by definition an act, and acts are by definition free.

TL. And by the same token, you get drama, since drama is based on action (with its grammatical partner, passion). That will be particularly important because of the large part that the arts of comedy and tragedy will play in their outlook, extending even to their ideas of ultimate salvation.

S. *O maraviglia!* I see by what a tightly bound logological cycle of terms the Wordy Animal must arrive necessarily at the idea of freedom.

TL. You are my favorite pupil.

S. I am most grateful for praise from so eminent a source. But am I to infer that their freedom is but an illusion?

TL. They will certainly confront sheer necessity in the sense that, as one of their philosophers might put it, each person will necessarily make his decisions in the particular situations into which he is "thrown" (and each of these situations will involve a series of motives not of his own choosing).

S. Then it *is* a sheer necessity! And the rest *is* but an illusion?

TL. It's more complicated than that. When I introduce their kind of words into my Creation, I shall really have let something loose. In dealing with ideas one at a time (or, as they will put it, "discursively") they can do many things which can't be done when, like us, all ideas are seen at once, and thus necessarily corrected by one another.

S. I see it! I see the paradox! Splendid! By their symbolicity, they *will* be able to deviate! A pebble can't make a mistake; it merely exemplifies the laws of motion and position; but an Earth-Man can give a *wrong* answer. At least in their *mistakes*, then, they will be "creative"; and to that extent they will be really free.

TL. Yes, and all sorts of new routes can be found, when you start putting things together piecemeal, rather than having everything there in its proper place, all at once, before you begin. Discursive terminologies will allow for a constant succession of permutations and combinations.

S. In sum, human freedom will reside in the ability to err, to deviate?

TL. Not quite that. The ability to be wrong within limits will also argue the ability to be right within limits. And insofar as these creatures are right, they will share in that higher freedom which we equate with necessity, an identity's inevitable necessity of being, in all its parts, the simple self-consistency that it must be, in order to be precisely what it is.

S. You have shown me how by the dramatistic nature of their terminology, they are in a sense "forced to be freed," since they will think of themselves as persons, and the idea of personality implies the idea of action, and the ideas of both freedom and necessity are intrinsic to the idea of an act. Could I ask, next: Is there some generative principle in their kind of language, some formal first from which its entire logic might be derived?

TL. Indeed there is. We've already considered it somewhat. It's the principle that you would use as your particular sign, were you to be in theory prescinded from the sum total of our identity.

S. Milord, the negative! Then that which most distinguishes the Word-People from other animals on Earth is also that which most distinguishes me: the one principle that might divide me from my Lord!

TL. That's it, my lad. And there is a sense in which there are the makings of division even here among us. For even pure identity implies the negation of non-identity. So you're always lurking there, my lad, implicitly a No without its Yes, even though (as seen from another angle) the two imply each other.

S. Milord, pray do not chide me! Yet, for all my love of negativity, I grant that the negative cannot exist. Anything that exists must, by the same token, be positively what it is.

TL. That will apply to *their* negative as well. It will be but a device of language, an *ens rationis*.

S. Why then would you make the negative so all-important?

TL. First, there is a sheer *principle* of negativity involved in their ability to use language at all. They must know that the word "tree" is *not* a tree, and so on.

S. They will be able to keep this distinction clear?

TL. By no means! Again and again, just because they have a word for something, and a feeling for the contexts in which the use of that word seems proper, they'll assume that there really is something to which the work is referring. Elaborate systems will be erected atop this error, doctrinal structures that are quite ingenious. But there will be enough rudimentary correspondence between words and things, with enough rudimentary awareness of the difference between the symbol and the symbolized, for them to find their way around, and multiply. Another kind of implicit negative will figure in the growth of their vocabularies. For instance, if they use a word *metaphorically*, they must know implicitly that they are *not* using it *literally*. For instance, if they say, "Ship the goods by rail," they must know that the "goods" are *not* the opposite of moral evils, and that the "shipping" does *not* have anything to do with ships. By making such allowances, they can greatly extend the usefulness of symbolicity. The ultimate along those lines will fit your leanings. I refer to irony, the way in which, for instance, they might say, "How intelligent he is!" while ironically implying the opposite, that the man is exceptionally stupid.

S. I do love it. And I grant that it starts in something as simple as that, though eventually it becomes quite complex. But what of the negative explicitly?

TL. It begins and ends in the two forms we have already considered: *shall not* and *is not*. The Yes-or-No of *shall not* get its quasi-positive in the idea of the "will," the hypothetical watershed that slopes off into either obedience or disobedience. In brief, recapitulating (and all true thought is but recapitulation): If acts involve persons, and personality involves decision, then inasmuch as decisions are "perfectly" conceived as the choice between Yes and No, it follows that implicit in the idea of action is the idea of the negative.

S. (*smiling ironically*). So the idea of action, which is to say the idea of morality, which is to say the idea of freedom, implies the principle of negativity, which is the hallmark of Satan! Imagine me soaring above it all, with bat-wings. What, milord, would I see?

TL. With the help of language, men will necessarily come upon the distinction between "mine" and "thine," along with sexually imagined ways of overriding this distinction. The principle of negativity will enable men to build up empires, all based on this distinction, which says in effect: "Thou shalt not take these things of mine, nor I of thine." Myriads of myriads of laws, deeds, contracts, precepts, prison sentences, educational policies, businesses, revolutions, religions, etc., etc., will be erected atop these simple beginnings: things that in themselves are positive, but that, in becoming labeled "mine" and "thine," take on the secret sacred sign of negativity. For in their essence, "mine" and "thine" are implicitly modes of negative command, ways of saying in effect: "No trespassing." The negative, so ingrained through the conscience, will build up a sense of guilt equally as vast as this bundle of negatively protected properties.

And from this sense of guilt there will arise the yearning for a new and all-inclusive positive, the demand for a supernal sacrifice literally existing and somehow serving by his suffering both to cancel off this guilt and to sanction the perpetuating of the conditions out of which the guilt arises.

S. And who—

TL. But I anticipate. We shall treat further of this ultimate step after you have been better prepared.

S. I tremble, milord. I have a sense of being on the verge of something. Please let us hurry back to our sheerly dialectical meditations.

TL. By all means. Sheerly logologically, we confront a manipulation of this sort: Inasmuch as words have contexts, if one of the Earthy thinkers sums up "everything" as the "determinate," then using the only resource he has left, he finds that the only possible context for the "determinate" is the "indeterminate," which thereby becomes the "ground" of the determinate and amounts to making "nothing" the ground of "everything." Or, if he starts with "time," he arrives at the "timeless," to which negative he can then give a positive look by calling it the "eternal."

S. Milord, haven't we also got to my realm by another route? Aren't we now in the realm of comedy?

TL. Yes, comedy—even Divine Comedy.

S. You have spoken of "everything," of "eternity," and of "nothing." If the Earth-People make an assertion about "everything," can they persuade themselves that they really are talking about "everything"?

TL. That's a delicate problem.

S. And when they talk about "nothing," are they talking about nothing or something? Or can they think that in using words for "the eternal," they are really talking about the eternal? Can they persuade themselves that it's as easy as that?

TL. I get your drift. But let's try a slightly different approach. They have another way of making the negative look positive. For instance, instead of saying "the unnatural," they can say "the preternatural" or "the supernatural." Let's try it from there. Suppose you asked me: If they talk about "the supernatural," are they really talking about the supernatural?

S. That approach does help. Obviously, by sheer definition, insofar as they are *natural* animals, they *can't* know anything about the supernatural. For if anything of the supernatural crossed over into the natural, then by sheer definition it would be part of the natural. How can they get around that purely formal problem?

TL. Your argument is irrefutable, and its underlying logic will plague them. But it isn't the proper "first" for the study of their languages. First comes their use of language as a means of getting along in their everyday affairs. It will help them guide their behavior, as their legs will help them to walk. In the course of such uses, they will learn the arts of petition, exhortation (persuasion and dissuasion). For language, as an instrument of guidance, is especially suited to persuade the language-using animal. Which means that they will use language to rule over one another—for persuasion implies governance. But governance in turn involves the need of *sanctions*.

S. "Sanctions"?

TL. In the course of governance, many kinds of inequality will develop. For instance, some of the Earth-People will be able to accumulate more property than they could intelligently use in a myriad lifetimes, short as their life span is to be. And many others will starve. In brief, there'll be much injustice.

S. It's revolting!

TL. Hence all the more need for "Sanctions." In the course of "proving" that such inequities are "right," sanctions will pile up like bat dung in a cave. (And bat dung, by the way, will be quite fertile.)

S. Then "sanctions" are just symbol-systems that justify injustice?

TL. No, my, lad. It's much more complicated than that. The range of language being what it is, the very propounding and treasuring of such sanctions will lead in turn to the equally persuasive *questioning* of them. And all these matters will come to metaphysics, political theory and the like, in short the higher criticism that grows out of such venerable piles.

S. But what's the use, if it all starts from the fact that their wordage in its wider ranges would talk of things which it is not equipped to discuss at all?

TL. True, by definition their speech will not be able to express the ineffable, any more than their eyes will be equipped to see the invisible. Even so, this persistent creature can reasonably assert: "Here's what you could say about the ineffable if it could be talked about. Here's what eternity would look like if it did have visibility. Here's what its music would be like, if it weren't inaudible. Here's how it would feel to the touch, if it weren't intangible. In brief, here's how the indeterminate should be discussed in terms of terms."

S. But isn't that wholly meaningless? Aren't your symbol-using creatures all set to be a breed that attains its "perfection" in sheer nonsense?

TL. You could make out a good positivistic argument along those lines, if you think of their words only as we in our transcendent wordlessness use words. That is, if you think of words as being relevant only when they are *about* something.

S. Did you not already imply that any other kind of language is but falsehood? Milord, you said that their way of using language will be like using legs. If they persist in using their languages to talk about our realm, wouldn't they be as accurate if they tried to walk through eternity on mortal legs?

TL. Some will try precisely that. And with admirable results, so far as worldly concepts of beauty are concerned. Indeed, always beneath the dance of words there will be the dance of bodies, the mimetic symbol-system that all these animals will come close to having in common, though their sedentary ways of living will cause them to forget it, like persons who, moving into a different part of the world when they were still quite young, come in time to forget the language of their childhood, the language most profoundly persuasive of all. But talk of the dance, and its body-language, brings us to exactly the next step in our unfolding.

S. And that is, milord? ...

TL. The nature of language as petition, exhortation, persuasion and dissuasion implies that, first of all, their words will be modes of posture, act, attitude, gesture. If one of their creatures strikes an attitude, such as kneeling in obeisance, that's real enough—and the same kind of reality can be carried into any words that go with it. Often these creatures will be swelling with pride and mutual self-congratulation at the very moment when they are unknowingly about to be caught in a cataclysm. Or they may lament at the very moment when they are unknowingly about to enter upon an era of exceptional delight. But in any case, *whether in error or not, the attitude will be wholly real while it prevails*.

S. Their task in ranging linguistically, then, will be to round out their sheer attitudinizings as thoroughly as possible?

TL. Yes, and some quite grandiosely architectonic enterprises will emerge in the process. And because *some* of the earth-creatures will be able to *range far* in such activity, *all* of them will be able to *range somewhat*.

S. Their most comprehensive symbol-systems, then, will be but a constant striking of attitudes?

TL. Yes—and thus, ultimately, a striking of attitudes towards the Great What-Is-It.

S. And, after all, that's us!

TL. Indeed it is!

(*Pause.*)

S. Milord, you know of my great admiration, for your workmanship. I fully realize the immense power, and scope, and subtlety of the Primal Act by which the world of time arises in principle. But in view of the perfect intuitive understanding by which we communicate, without the need of temporally stretched-out discourse, could you not somewhat contain the errors of the Word-Animal? Could you not permit him only the *virtues* of his symbolicity? I know you would make the best possible of worlds, but I do not see why their kind of words would be the best possible of worldly discourse.

TL. Discourse can be truly discourse only by having the power to be fully itself. Such a formal obligation applies always. For instance, don't you grant that you couldn't be truly yourself if you could be but half yourself, or the fragment of yourself which the Earth-People will take you to be?

S. Granted. But I could be something else. If you had made me but half myself, I could be wholly that. If you make a five rather than a ten, can't that five be wholly at one with itself in its five-ness?

TL. Your example really disproves your point. I couldn't make the time-world's number system without so making it that ten is just as necessarily implied in it as five. One can divide numbers, but one can't divide the principle of division. Arithmetic could be arithmetic at all only by having the possibility of fully being arithmetic. And so with the language of human discourse: implicit in its ability to be, there is its ability to range; and implicit in its ability to range, there is its ability to range far, even too far.

S. In asking that you show me the full range, I should be asking that you share your divine providence with me. As you know, I am saved from asking for such enlightenment on two scores: first, I could not encompass it; second, I would not, even if I could. For I already realize, from what you have said of the errors in earthly discourse, that in knowing everything you must pay attention to a staggering amount of trivialities worked out by the Earth-People. Being but an angel, that is, a messenger entrusted with but fragments of communication, I am necessarily but willingly humbled at the thought of your encyclopedic insomniac burdens. Or, more accurately, such infinite attentiveness would be overwhelmingly burdensome to the likes of *me*.

TL. Fortunately, we don't have to deal here with universal prescience. We need but consider the matter formally, in principle. First of all, for instance, there's that obvious range of the negative. The Earth-Men will become moral by obeying moral laws, all of which are either explicitly or implicitly negative, a set of thou-shalt-nots. But by the same token, people can in principle carry the negative a step further, and say no to any thou-shalt-nots. Thus the negative, in giving them the power to be moral, by the same token gives them the power to be immoral.

S. How greatly different my negativity is from theirs!

TL. Yes, but they won't know it. And in their failure to make the proper distinction, they'll dispraise you avidly.

S. If they're ingenious enough about it, I won't mind.

TL. Oh, they'll be plenty ingenious. Language makes great plotters, and they'll think of you as the very soul of conspiracy.

S. But inasmuch as your positives and my negatives mutually imply each other in perfect dialectic oneness, what could there be for me to conspire about?

TL. I already told you: "Everything." Though they'll be vague as to what their word "everything" refers to, they'll be clear enough in their conviction that the range of possible conspiracy ultimately involves "everything."

S. But isn't that too vague to keep them interested? After all, being animals, they will necessarily live by this particular thing and that particular thing. Far less than "everything" would be enough to choke them.

TL. No, they won't have to gag at "everything." For their very symbolicity will enable them to invent a particularized form of "everything," the most ingenious symbol-system of all: money. Money is intrinsically universalistic, since everything can have its monetary equivalent, its counterpart in terms of "price."

S. I see the pattern! What perfection! Money becomes a kind of generalized wishing. They won't directly reach for everything. They could even sincerely deny that they want everything. Yet they'll get there roundabout, by wanting the universal medium into terms of which everything is convertible!

TL. Yes, once they arrive at money, they will have arrived at desire in the absolute. Their love of money is the nearest they will ever come to symbolistically transcending their animal nature. A man can even starve to death hoarding the symbols that would buy him more than he could eat in many lifetimes. And men will kill themselves trying to amass more and more of the monetary symbols that represent good living.

S. How will they distinguish their devotion to this particular universalistic motive from their devotion to your kind of universalism?

TL. The attempt to answer that would get us back into the problem of the encyclopedic, though in reverse: for in general the history of the Word-Animal will be the history of the firm refusal to make such a distinction. In brief, they'll put *my* name on their *money*, and call it an act of piety.

S. How revolting!

TL. Now, my lad, reign in that winsome impetuosity of yours.

S. But, milord!

TL. It's a quite complicated situation. For you should also reflect that the quasi-divine universalism of money is reinforced by related attributes. For instance, in its nature as a medium of exchange, it is essentially communicative, hence it is a technical counterpart of love. Its nature as a power will similarly endow it, as monetary power can serve as a surrogate for sexual potency. Yet, whereas it is a prime symbol of contact (in acts of charity), it can establish such contact at a distance (as with the coin tossed to a leper)—and thereby paradoxically it allows for depersonalization, a quasi-divine transcending of excessive personal involvement. In reducing all things to terms of itself, it exemplifies perfectly the scientific law of parsimony (the perfect mode of rationalization required of a symbol-user's god). As I have noted elsewhere, in its nature as generalized wish it represents a kind of absolute purpose. Its relation to "freedom" is obvious, since it can purchase both mobility and security.

S. Will all the human tribes possess it?

TL. Only in the sense that it will be *implicit* in all economies. As a rule, however, it will attain its full grandeur only in large empires marked by an especially high development of religion. But the reference to religion reminds us that money will also tie in with connotations of the purgative, owing to the imagistic relation between "power" and "filth" (associations to which the human animal will be particularly prone owing to its codes of propriety in connection with the feces).

S. I see how perfectly it burlesques the godhead. Out of its simplicity there emerges a great complexity.

TL. Exactly. But now I'd like to ask you a question, as a test of your ingenuity. Imagine a situation of this sort: The outposts of an empire want the simple natives of a barter economy to work in plantations which the imperialists would introduce into the area. The natives already possess a simple non-monetary economy with which they are content. And the imperialists, in accordance with their principles of monetary "liberalism," are loath to impose outright conditions of enslavement. How could you solve that problem?

S. Splendid! Splendid! I see it! I could introduce some simple monetary tax, such as a hut tax or a tax on salt, the important point being that *it could not be paid in kind, but would have to be paid in money*. Then their non-monetary economy would no longer suffice, and they would have to work in the plantations, so as to earn the money needed to pay their taxes! This requirement alone would in effect "emancipate" them from their non-monetary economy. To use an expression employed in another connection, they would be "forced to be free"! What devilish possibilities!

TL. Right. But don't oversimplify, my lad. The simplicity, yes. But don't let it break away from the complexity, or, as the Earth-People will say, "All Hell breaks loose."

S. I am beneficently admonished. Pray, teach me further, milord, of the complexity that qualifies the simplicity. In particular, as regards these two occasions on which I have used the expression, "forced to be free," I can't just see how *they* will contrive to put determinism and free will together.

TL. You would if you were confined to their kind of terms. Don't forget that, on Earth, a sojourner will be able to wind up at the same place by going in opposite directions, if he but keeps going long enough. And insofar as Earth's languages will be developed in sympathy with nature, they also incorporate nature's humble paradoxes. Further, as regards the sheer formality of the situation, recall that, though terms in their formality come to a kind of crisis in the "free" choice between Yes and No, there is also the technical fact that terms are by definition "de-terministic."

S. Milord, I swoon!

TL. Hold up, young one. And having seen already how their words will provide freedom in principle, by allowing for either the affirmation of negation, or the negation of affirmation, or the negation of negation, note further this sheer design, how it follows *of necessity* from the nature of the Word-Animal's symbolicity: that out of the negative, *guilt* will arise. For the negative makes the law; and in the possibility of saying no to the law, there is guilt.

S. And if guilt, then punishment?

TL. It's more complicated than that. For money introduces the principle of *redemption*. That is, money will give them the idea of redemption by payment, which is to say, by *substitution*. For it would be a matter of substitution, if a man paid off an obligation by money whereas otherwise he might have been required to suffer actual physical torment.

S. Isn't there a principle of substitution in language itself, too?

TL. Yes, every synonym is a substitute. Every paraphrase is a substitute. And substitution by monetary symbolism is but a special case of symbolic substitution in general.

S. But why do you make this point about substitution?

TL. It's most important to their theologians. For if you carry this principle through to its completion, it implies that one person can suffer for another, as "payment" for the other's guilt.

S. Wouldn't that be unjust?

TL. Not insofar as it would be merciful. Mercy is a kind of friendly injustice, in not requiring of a given debtor the full amount of his debt.

S. Their theologians, then, will assume that you will not right the balance?

TL. On the contrary! And here enters the principle of perfection. The Earth-People win consider themselves so guilt-laden, that only a perfect sacrifice would be great enough to pay off the debt.

S. The morbid devils! Then they will think of themselves as permanently lost?

TL. No, they will conceive of a sacrifice so perfect that it could cancel off all their guilt, however mighty that guilt might be.

S. But only a god would be perfect enough for that!

TL. Quite right.

S. I tremble! You mean . . .

TL. Yes. And finally a cult will arise which holds that I, in my infinite mercy, will send my only begotten Son as the perfect sacrifice for the Earth-People's redemption.

S. Send your Son, to redeem such vermin! What pride they have! What haughtiness! How perfectly revolting!

TL. Easy, my lad. This issue can't be solved by a hothead. You must realize that this issue involves not only a principle of *theological* perfection, but also a principle of *logological* perfection. I told you that we should be hearing much about "perfection" before we were through.

S. I beg forgiveness if, in the heat of my indignation, I called The Lord's creatures "vermin." Insofar as they are examples of your workmanship, they are of course essentially good. I referred only to the ways in which the resources of their language bewitched them into becoming stormers of heaven itself. I don't resent them for their bungling ways of conceiving my negativity in terms of theirs. And I don't resent them for conceiving my ingenuity in terms of their conspiracies. But the thought that you would sacrifice your Son for them . . . faugh!

TL. Now you're talking like the very devil. Come out of it!

S. In your command is my obedience. Consider me restored.

TL. Good! Then let us complete the study of The Creation in principle.

S. Milord, do I understand you to mean that their symbolicity, for all its imperfection, contains in itself a principle of perfection by which the symbol-using animals are always being driven, or rather, towards which they are always striving, as with a lost man trying to answer a call in a stormy night?

TL. Now you are your better self again!

S. Milord, not by way of heckling, but in order to advance our meditations another necessary step, could I ask you this: Is it not true that the language-using animals will use many different languages, and that differences will cause them to think differently?

TL. Exactly.

S. Yet they will all think alike, insofar as they are language-using animals, and thus will have their modes of thought moulded generically by the nature of discourse?

TL. Exactly.

S. But is not this a contradiction in terms? They will all think alike, and they will all think differently!

TL. Your love of paradox is tricking you, even in the midst of your resolve to be contrite. Languages will differ, and in that sense each will have its own way of looking at things. But there are some important properties that all languages have in common. Thus, no human animal can live on the sheer *words* for food; no language can be without some such principles of order and transformation as will go by the name of grammar and syntax; all languages must have words that put things together and words that take things apart; all tribal idioms will have ways of naming and exhorting. Such elements, common to all languages, coupled with the conditions common to all bodies, will make for a common underlying logic. And this logic will all be headed in the same direction, aiming at the same ultimate perfection.

S. But are not *you* the only conceivable ultimate perfection?

TL. Exactly.

S. Then their idea of you is but a function of *language?*

TL. All orderly thought will be a function of their symbol-systems.

S. I refer not merely to the fact that they must conceive of things in terms of terms. I am asking more specifically whether the principle of perfection upon which they rely in their idea of you is reducible purely and simply to terms of the form underlying all language. Or otherwise put: Is there in all language a principle of perfection which makes all human thought behave as though it had begun in "the one true philosophy," which is still lying about in fragments, and which the Word-Animals are constantly striving, with partial success, to reconstruct in its entirety?

TL. How exacting do you want their idea of God to be? I am sure you would not be satisfied to let them conceive of God in terms of sheerly natural power (suggested to them by their experience as animals). We have already agreed that their confusing of God and money is regrettable. Later in our discussion we shall consider the objections to the conceiving of God in terms of human personality. And now you would deny them the right to conceive of God in terms of a perfection which is identical with an underlying principle of language. Are not such strictures as haughty in their way as the Earth-People will accuse you of being? Are you not in effect rebelling against them as absolutely as they will accuse you of rebelling against me? Would you not, in effect, be denying them the resources of their own minds, in effect be demanding that they think without thought?

S. I pray, milord, don't ask me; tell me.

TL. First, you should bear in mind that the principle of perfection takes many forms. Even the most misguided of absolutism is perfectionist, for instance. And the principle of perfection will be at work in all reductionism, and in all exaggeration, thus in both euphemism and its opposite; for the two most perfect functions of symbolism are total praise and total dispraise.

S. Then flattery would be perfectionist?

TL. Yes, but to an infinitesimal degree.

S. And liars will be lovers of perfection?

TL. They are so perfectionist, they would even revise the truth. You in particular will be conceived by men in accordance with the logic of perfection. As regards the many temptations with which they plague themselves and one another, you will represent the compleat tempter, the perfect principle of evil.

S. But omitting for the moment the consideration of your perfection, is not the principle of perfection itself perfectly reducible to logological terms?

TL. Symbolism is unthinkable without it. To call something by its right name, as judged by the given symbol-system in terms of which it is being named, is the very essence of perfectionism. But let us continue, for there are still some steps to be taken: We must first watch the logic of perfection gradually unfold, under the guidance of terministic symmetry. And in any case, you will agree that, even if their ideas of divine perfection were reducible to little more than a language-using animal's ultimate perception of its own linguistic forms, this could be a true inkling of the divine insofar as language itself happened to be made in the image of divinity.

S. If, that is, implicit in the principle of words *qua* words there really is The Word?

TL. Yes; if it were shining there all the time, like a light hid under a bushel.

S. But might I, without seeming disrespectful, ask a question about method, milord? Insofar as the Earth-People might seek to explain their motives in purely empirical, naturalistic terms, what then would properly happen to the "logic of perfection"?

TL. Before discussing what "would properly happen," let me tell you what *will* happen. In the name of empirical, scientific observation, the search for motives (men's theorizing on the nature of purpose) will lead to a constant procession of solemn, humorless caricatures that will greatly entrance you in your character as prankster. In the search for academic preferment or for quick sales in the book mart, their teachers and writers will slap together various oversimplified schemes that reduce human motives to a few drives or urges or itches involving food, sex, power, prestige and the like (schemes concocted in keeping with the logic of "firsts," but without the proper criticism of such procedures).

S. Such naive efforts at perfection sound amusing, particularly inasmuch as you indicate that both the pundits and the public will incline to take such parodies seriously. But is there no alternative: Must men choose flatly between such unintentional burlesques and an outright religious terminology of motives? Let us assume, for the sake of the argument, that there is nothing behind or beyond the linguistic forms but the non-religious kind of "supernatural" character they have in themselves (in the sense that the principles of grammar and syntax are not reducible to terms of material things like earth and water). In that case would there be no other choice but to shop around among the various *caricatures* of motivation?

TL. Even on a purely empirical basis, even if we assumed that theology is sheer fiction, and that there is no such motive as divine perfection influencing human life, the paradigms of theology and of its coy counterpart, metaphysics, would be no less cogent. The close connection between the form of words and the form of The Word (between theology and logology) would still be enough to justify the word-using animal in approaching its motivational problems through an architectonic that made full allowance for the nature of both human animality and human symbolicity. And such an architectonic is to be found, not in the solemn caricatures that reduce the problem of motives to a few absurdly simple themes, but in the full (or, if you will, fulsome) terminologies that can be developed in connection with the "logic of perfection." (A bright Greek will treat of it in terms of what he will call the "entelechy.")

S. But would not this make theology otiose? For would it not amount to saying that there is an adequate logological explanation for every theological tenet?

TL. Not necessarily. Above all, logology fails to offer grounds for the *perfection* of promises and threats that theology allows for. And there are incentives in both animality and symbolicity that will keep men always asking about *ultimate principles* of reward and punishment, in their attempts to scare the devil out of one another. Being creatures that necessarily think in terms of time, they will incline to conceive of such a culminative logical design in terms of sheerly *temporal* firsts and lasts. Hence, there is the goad towards theological translation into terms of a final destiny in an afterlife. A sheerly logological explanation must leave such doctrinally stimulated hunger unappeased.

S. Milord, may I ask how, in sum, this position would operate, if theology were to be studied from a strictly logological point of view?

TL. Yes, that's our central question. Besides relying upon the authority of their sacred texts, priests will argue for the correctness of many theological tenets by showing how these same principles apply in the sheerly empirical realm of nature. Non-believers will treat such lines of argument as further proof for their contention that theology is but a translation of the empirical realm into terms of a fictitiously transcendent realm. But in either case, all doctrine is by its very nature a system of words, or symbols—and so, there is always the wise possibility of using such theological nomenclatures for purely logological purposes.

S. And how would things line up, were theology to be used thus, as a parable for the guidance of logology?

TL. Thereby allowance would be made for a wholly ample dialectic, with each moment of a man's life being seen (or glimpsed) in terms of the entire conglomerate complexity (with its various strands of simplicity). Each fragment of experience is then interpreted as being somehow modified by a largely indefinite whole to which it more or less definitely refers. Things thereby transcend their nature as sheer things. They are found to move men not just by what they are in their blunt physicality, but also by what they *stand for* in the farthest reaches of symbolicity. Whatever their non-symbolic nature as sheer motion and position, they are seen to participate in the symbolic realm of action and rest. And the human agents will be seen similarly. "Perfectionist" theologies will never lose sight of this consideration. The quasi-scientific reductionist theories, with their caricatures of perfection, will not only never see it in the first place, but will be so constructed that they never even miss the loss.

S. But, when you treat of metaphysics as coy theology, and of symbolicity as transcending animality, I see another possibility here.

TL. Ever the schemer, my lad! I know what you mean—but go on and say it anyhow, just for the record.

S. Good! Think, then, of an idealistic metaphysics that was, by the same token, chock-full of logological usability. Then think of a revisionist who, in the name of materialism, supposedly threw out its theology. What then?

TL. You ingenious fellow! How fortunate it is that the nature of the dialectic makes it impossible for you to break loose! What a stormer of heaven you would be! There *will* be a doctrine such as you have tentatively formulated through sheer speculative enterprise. It will grow out of a metaphysics that yields beautifully to logological analysis. You will love, above all, its pronouncements on the principle of *Negativität*, and how it saturates the world of time.

S. But if it threw out theology bodily? What then?

TL. You can't get the principle of perfection out of a system as easily as that.

S. You mean: this self-styled anti-theology will be but theology under another name?

TL. Necessarily, my lad! Technically, logologically, it will be in essence a theology, since it retains in essence the principle of perfectionism. No matter how reductionist it tries to make its materialism be, it won't revise its origins to the point where this principle drops out. On the contrary, this principle will be there, uppermost, and flailing away. Mark my words: as regards our present logological considerations, this perfectionist promise, whether true or false, will be the most remarkable of its marks.

S. But will it allow for strictly logological analysis of itself?

TL. Unfortunately, no. In that regard, it will be like all sects when they have a sufficient majority to be in sure control.

S. Would you sanction it, milord?

TL. Empirically, I sanction dialectic, which giveth and taketh away. For such is time, and The Development. And the dialectic, in its fullness, is never without such a principle of transcendence, an Upward Way that, when reversed, interprets all incidental things in terms of the over-all fulfillment towards which the entire development is said to be striving. So far, so good. But where the Earth-People are concerned, any terminology is suspect to the extent that it does not allow for the progressive criticism of itself.

S. There should be no criticism to end all criticism?

TL. Not where the Earth-People are concerned. But the resources of the negative being what they are, authorities will continually arise which would say No definitively to any further questioning.

S. As here in heaven, milord?

TL. Yes, but without the perfect formal justification that we have for such absolutism. In fact, the very lack of justification will usually be the motive that prods men towards the propounding of worldly absolutes.

S. "Worldly absolutes." Is that not a contradiction in terms?

TL. Strictly speaking, yes. There can be no absolute authority but here in heaven. Just as, strictly speaking, there can be no perfection but here in heaven. Even the most powerful of worldly rulers must make allowance for countless conditions that will prevail independently of his decrees. Thus, on earth the "logic of perfection," however insistent, can prevail but relatively.

S. Where does that leave things with relation to worldly government? Would the most nearly perfect State be as absolutist as is humanly possible? Or would it seek as perfectly as possible to be relativistic?

TL. Different situations will favor different kinds of government, though the perfectionist tendency of theorists will be to plead for some one scheme as better than all others.

S. With you supplying the sanctions, and me the interferences?

TL. Insofar as the theories are theologically thorough, there will be terms for those roles. And all secular schemes will have equivalents, offered as grounding for the yeses and noes of choice. But theology presents the most perfect paradigms of such motivational schemes.

S. In effect, then, theology will serve men merely as a rhetoric for the sanctioning of their government, with its particular set of privileges?

TL. It's more complicated than that. In fact, it involves the one remaining major way in which the idea of supernatural God is built out of human components. We have considered views of God as the perfect exemplar of natural powers, as the ultimate of verbal perfection, and as the pure principle of such rationality and universality as come to a head in material production and distribution guided by the norms of monetary accountancy (a special case of verbal perfection). We have but to consider what is involved in the idea of God as the perfected projection of human personality.

S. A connection that would make it hard to draw the line between God and man.

TL. In one respect, they can draw the line by obscuring it, as when they conceive of a god incarnate, a supernatural entity translated into terms of nature, the timeless made temporal. Such an intermediate term, by formally uniting in one locus the opposite, mutually exclusive terms, "perfectly" represents the difference in the very act of bridging it.

S. But does this principle of personality have a range of implications as great as the other analogies we have considered?

TL. Decidedly! For one thing, out of this principle there will emerge one of man's two most imperious ideas: Love. (The other is Justice, or Duty; Love is to Duty as asking is to paying.) In sum: Purpose will have its origins in bodily desires, most notably the appetites of food and sex. In this respect, it will be grounded in man's animality. But it will attain an immaterial counterpart in the principle of communication. Hence, purpose will have a secondary grounding in man's symbolicity. Add, next, the ways of empire that develop among the various societies of symbol-using animals, and the conditions are set for their imagining of *love*, whether sacred or profane.

S. And, I assume, titillating mixtures of the two?

TL. There will be many opportunities for satanic enterprise along those lines.

S. Yet the diplomatic protocol of empire will be necessary for the imagining of either sacred or profane love?

TL. In principle, yes. Ideas of "personality" will draw heavily on the idea of a leader who, because he is in a position to represent all his people, is assumed by both them and himself to somehow be the intrinsic repository of their powers.

S. And none will be immune?

TL. The pattern will make itself felt also among those who, on the surface, seem most immune to it. Though even in its fullness it cannot be satisfying, its ubiquitous logological inevitability will continually threaten to make men dissatisfied with less. It will have its greatest sway among empires, but will operate also in simpler times to the extent that all times will contain the seeds of empire.

S. Why can it not be satisfying even in its fullness?

TL. Because the parts do not fit. By the tests of sheer animality, the "deathless essences" of sheer symbolicity will be a mockery. Yet, by their own tests, they really will transcend the sheerly material realm of corruption and death. The fall of all the trees in the world will not bring down the meaning of the word "tree." By the sheer act of utterance as such, there is a sense in which time will be transcended. Even the cry of a sailor perishing alone in mid-ocean must go on having-been-uttered eternally. It will have this perfection, this finishedness. In this sense the speech that teaches them to despair will be able, by its sheer nature as definition, to be as though enduring. For each utterance, like each person who does the uttering, will have a character. And a character, as such, is both what it will be (if its existent counterpart hasn't yet been born) and what it has been (if its existent counterpart has already died). In this technical sense, meanings really do transcend time. Yet, once you have said as much, the fact remains that, once the beings who understand a given language cease to be, the sweetest poem written in those words is dead. In a sense, the situation could be called regrettable. But if I was to create an animal capable of consecutive discourse (in contrast with our way of condensing all development into a perfect moment), then implicit in my act was the creation of time, and thus, corruption and death. And as one clear proof that, in its way, it's to be the best possible of worlds, we need but bear in mind what a solace death can be, when the ravages of time make men ready to leave life. It's a solace to know that one is not condemned to *have* to live for ever. In the implications of the irreversible flow of time there is also a promise of freedom. And, given the nature of an act, freedom in any form has its rewards. Yet, undeniably, a *composite* of animality and symbolicity is also analyzable as a kind of discord. Thus for instance, the idea of a beautiful woman, conceived after the analogy of queenliness and the fine arts, suggests inexorably a harsh rejoinder in sheerly physicalist terms.

S. In that sense, let me try my hand at a "fitting" definition: By a "beautiful" woman, they will mean a seductive surface which perversely and reconditely alludes to the possibilities of motherhood, while underneath there lies a dying assemblage of bones, ooze, drip, slime and potential stench.

TL. Your definition is perfectionist in a devilishly *re*-ductive sense. But at least, it serves to point up the problem, the contrast between temporally clinical factuality and transcendence through the symbol-saturated mysteries of empire.

S. "Mysteries of empire"? Please, milord, initiate me into those, the "mysteries of empire."

TL. (*laughing*). Were any of my Earth creatures to hear you say that, they would gape with incredulity. For when conceiving of us in terms of human governance, they will place you as the spirit of *revolt against* governance (though with one special twist; for often their given system of governance will itself be founded on revolt against some previous regime, and for this particular turn they will invoke *my* sanction rather than yours).

S. Their oversimplifications will be a constant rebuke to me, as regards the dialectical tendency of my negatives to seem averse, like viewing "near" and "far" as opposites, rather than noting that both are implicit in the idea of distance. But please, milord, more on mystery . . .

TL. Mystery in itself will not be without its usefulness in worldly governance. For, once a believer is brought to accept mysteries, he will be better minded to take orders without question from those persons whom he considers authoritative. In brief, mysteries are a good grounding for obedience, insofar as the acceptance of mystery involves a person in the abnegation of his own personal judgment. For in Earthy symbolicity, "reason" will be closely associated with *rule*. So, if a man, in accepting a mystery, accepts someone else's judgment in place of his own, by that same token he becomes subject willingly. That is, subjection is implicit in his act of belief.

S. That would explain the *use* of mystery as an instrument of governance. But what of its *origin*?

TL. An excellent question, my lad! Mystery will arise by a quite different route. Mystery is inescapable, insofar as temporal, factual knowledge is necessarily fragmentary, and symbol-systems are necessarily inadequate for the *ab intra* description of the non-symbolic.

S. That is, the makings of "mystery" are to be found in any lack of knowledge?

TL. Yes, by sheer definition, tautologically.

S. I have heard that your plans for the differentiation necessary to the symbol-using animal include a sexual dichotomy. Is that so?

TL. Yes, inasmuch as the first principle of distinction is dichotomization, and in the symbol-using animals' terminologies any such plus-or-minus distinction can be stated in sexual terms, either literally or metaphorically.

S. You mean, the human sexes will be related as Yes is to No?

TL. No, it's more complicated than that. First of all, they'll be related like question and answer (or, in the simpler communicative terminologies, like stimulus and response).

S. As regards these questions and answers, or stimuli and responses (and I take it for granted that either side can be on either side), will they be "mysteries" to each other?

TL. Yes, and particularly insofar as the seeds of empire will be implicit in even the simplest of tribes. Often, in primitive groups, the two kinds of symbol-using bodies that physically cooperate to the ends of tribal multiplication will separately congregate on the basis of their physical differences, as symbolically accentuated.

S. Then, this quasi-logical dichotomizing will prevail in more complex orders, too?

TL. Mysteries will arise socially, from different modes of life. The king will be a mystery to the peasant, and vice versa.

S. That will be "imperious" mystery?

TL. Yes, the "mysteries of empire" that you asked about.

S. But if mysteries arise from such differences, and if mysteries are also cherished, and if the cult of mystery encourages obedience, then insofar as empires have inequalities (like that between the king and the peasant) would it not be true that mystery can simultaneously both reflect inequality and perpetuate it?

TL. The problems of control will be so difficult (along with religion as a means of social or political control), I hesitate to let your statement stand.

S. Then consider me smacked down, milord. But I beg to ask just one more question. You have named two origins of mystery: one, its origin in the peculiar range of intelligent ignorance affecting all temporally bound symbol-using animals; two, a closely related point, its origin in such different modes of being and living as rightly or wrongly are felt to imply different modes of thought. And you have suggested a major incentive to foment such differences, owing to the nature of empire. Will there be any other source of mystery?

TL. Indeed, there will be. And to understand it, we must revert to our discussion of the relation between polytheism and monotheism. As the symbol-using tribe shifts from its understanding of motives in terms of many gods (or motivational sources!) to one god, arrangements that seemed quite rational in polytheistic terms become a mystery in terms of monotheism.

S. Milord, I tremble. Please explain.

TL. In terms of polytheism, it is readily explainable in "rational" terms why even a god might sacrifice some great treasure, for the redemption of mankind, in case he loved mankind and mankind was in captivity and thus in need of ransom.

S. That is, there was a rival power, a kind of pirate; he captured the loved person or persons; and the problem was to send a fitting substitute as ransom?

TL. Exactly.

S. But where is the mystery?

TL. It enters once you turn from polytheism to monotheism. For, from then on, *why is the ransom necessary?*

S. Please, milord, don't ask me; tell me.

TL. That's not the point!

S. Yes, you have made your point! And so, milord, our Perfect Principle of Summation, I pray, then, that you sum up your teachings as regards this mystery-ridden subject of personality.

TL. Good! First, note that it is itself intermediate, insofar as the human person will be compounded of animality and symbolicity (the natural and the verbal). Next, note well that such personality will not be just an individual identity, but will take its form with relation to the socio-political conditions into which the given "person" is "thrown" by the circumstances of birth and the like. Thus, there is a sense in which the principle of personality does sum up, or implicitly contain, the kind of social and political order in which it participates. We could even say, without straining a point, that *every* member of a given order in his way "represents" that order. And, finally, there is the perfectionist device whereby the "person" will conceive of his actual condition not purely and simply in itself, but in terms of some *idealized* role. And this last consideration is in effect like the dialectics of theology whereby, having conceived of godhead as a superperson by analogy with human personality, the theologian next conceives of human personality as "derived" from this divine principle or First.

S. In effect men will impute a role to God, as though God himself had a calling?

TL. Yes, and similarly they will impute to their gods various personal attitudes, emotions, and involvements in human affairs.

S. You refer to "gods." Would you say more on the relation between polytheism and monotheism?

TL. It's a complicated matter. (I'd rather not be so complicated in our discussion, since I am in essence simple. But I must be equal to all the tangles people will get themselves into.) Religion will be monistic in the sense that, no matter how large a pantheon the various tribes imagine, all their gods can be subsumed under the general head of "the divine." In this sense, there is a monistic principle underlying all polytheism. On the other hand, all religion will be polytheistic in the sense that, even in societies nominally monistic, there will be many ideas of the "one god," not only as religion evolves through time, but also in any given era. For not only will there be vast differences among sects professing belief in the same god; but also persons who hold to the same doctrine will understand it variously, according to the variety of their personalities and personal experiences. The rich man's god is likely to differ greatly from the poor man's, though both men attend the identical church. Also, monotheism will often have a gallery of "patron saints" that in effect divide up the general idea of divine protection into a variety of specialized roles.

S. The "logic of perfection" will apply equally to either theologies nominally monistic or those nominally polytheistic?

TL. It will be found in both. A sufficient reason for this would be the fact that kindred logological principles are implicit in all thoroughgoing human terminologies of motives.

S. Yet the various doctrines will be variously at odds?

TL. Necessarily. And even to such an extent that they will accuse one another of being . . . well, to use their way of putting it . . . the works of the devil.

S. That is, the other half of the monotheistic principle!

TL. No, it's more complicated than that. When they get to the point where god and devil are pitted against each other, as rival powers, they have not yet quite got to monotheism. In pure monotheism, the devil can be a power only through sufferance of the sole universal monarch.

S. You mean: they will think that you deliberately *allow me* to do all the vicious things they ascribe to me? How revolting!

TL. No, it's more complicated than that. The "logic of perfection" is introduced in another way at that point, as they will apply their dialectical prowess to avow that all evil designs of the devil are used by God as means of betterment.

S. Betterment for all men?

TL. Yes, except that many will be said to be predestinated to eternal torment in hell.

S. Do such views on hell also embody the "logic of perfection"?

TL. Don't be ironical, my lad. The idea of hell is the idea of a really perfect ending. Just as the saints will be said to hate with a perfect hate, so the idea of eternal hell is the perfection, or completion, of the idea of suffering, which in turn is the perfection of the idea of punishment, which in turn (along with the idea of eternal reward) is the perfection of the idea of the hortatory resources available to governmental authority in the act of enforcing its decrees, all of which comes to a head formally in the principle of the negative, for which hell is imagined its the corresponding place.

S. The idea of hell is derived basically, then, from man's personal relations to problems of worldly governance?

TL. Yes, but the problems of government can lead to a different but equally "perfect" ultimate design. Societies that believe in the transmigration of souls will be able to think of worldly status as itself the evidence of rewards and punishments for deeds done in a previous existence. In such a scheme, the perfect irrevocability of eternal hell is replaced by the notion that men can better or worsen their lot in later existences by their ways of acting beforehand. Since people are thus thought to be born into favorable or unfavorable social status on the basis of their previous conduct, such a design is both imagined after the analogy of the given social structure and also serves as a sanction for that structure. This design, too, has its peculiar kind of perfection, and is equally related to the personality of governance. But such perfection does not fit with the idea of a single life on earth, a kind of irrevocability that requires, for its corresponding perfection, the idea of equally irrevocable rewards or punishments. And there arises a corresponding rhetorical need, on the part of the theologians, to so perfect men's imaginations that they will be deterred from evil by imagining with suffi-cient vividness the awesome torments of eternal hell.

S. But if one man can deter another from evil by sufficiently appealing to his imagination, would it not follow that no man would be damned, if you, milord, but endowed all men with enough imagination to thoroughly realize the horror of such irrevocable suffering?

TL. But what of free will? If I made all men as imaginative as that, would they not all be necessarily saved?

S. I fear, milord, you are now discussing these matters logologically rather than theologically.

TL. We are discussing the motivational speculations of the symbol-us-ing animal. For us to speculate about theology in Heaven would be like an earth-person, on a sunny day, wondering what a sunny day would be like.

S. But at least couldn't you, without interfering with men's wills, im-prove the quality of their ideas on hell?

TL. From the theory of predestination it follows that I shall greatly alter men's knowledge of such matters—for their views will be found to change over the centuries. But you are putting the emphasis in the wrong place. You are overlooking the perfection of the grand design. Incidental problems nec-essarily arise, since the issue in its totality is too immense for any partial view to encompass. However, you can appreciate the general principles in their grand design. And, in contemplating them, you will understand the logologi-cal symmetry that infuses theological symmetry.

S. Would you, then, milord, kindly review these main principles, in sum?

TL. For sheerly logological perfection, few religions will be able to rival the religion (with its close variants) that names itself after my Son. Consid-ered even as sheer form it will be quite miraculous. Its merger of monothe-ism with the circumambient rites of pagan polytheism will be a major dialectical triumph, beginning with the way in which its early theorists will account for its borrowings from the earlier pagan traditions. The early fa-thers will explain that, long before the new doctrine emerged, the devil saw how things were shaping up. Accordingly, since he knew what the Christian rites would be like, he scattered similar practices among the pagan cults out of which the new religion would develop. In this way the devil could parody the true faith even before it had taken form. And thereby he could all the more successfully spread confusion among the faithful and the propagan-dized, since the emergent true faith would look deceptively much like the heathen parodies that had preceded it.

S. They will find ingenious ways of making me seem ingenious! And such a literary solution! Bookish, even.

TL. There'll be a book, too, a Book of Books, a very good book, excep-tionally well written and well translated.

S. I'll quote from it!

TL. But, to the quick summation, and the perfect symmetry: in their so-cieties, they will seek order. If order, then a need to repress the tendencies to disorder. If repression, then responsibility for imposing, accepting, or resisting the repression. If responsibility, then guilt. If guilt, then the need for redemption, which involves sacrifice, which in turn allows for substitution. At this point, the logic of perfection enters. Man can be viewed as perfectly depraved by a formative "first" offense against the foremost authority, an offense in which one man sinned for all. The cycle of life and death intrinsic to the nature of time can now be seen in terms that treat natural death as the result of this "original" sin. And the principle of perfection can be matched on the hopeful side by the idea of a perfect victim. The symmetry can be logologically rounded out by the idea of this victim as also the creative Word by which time was caused to be, the intermediary Word binding time with eternity, and the end towards which all words of the true doctrine are directed. As one of their saints will put it: "The way to heaven must be heaven, for He said: I am the way."

(TL *rises*. S *also rises immediately after*.)

TL. (*continuing*). The way to heaven (the means to the end, the agency for the attainment of purpose) must be heaven (scene), for He (agent) said (act as words): I am the way (act as The Word). Here is the ultimate of logological symmetry!

S. Formally, it is perfect. It is perfectly beautiful!

TL. It is truly culminative!

S. Words could do no more!

(*Pause*.)

S. (*pensively*). In some ways they will be dismal, in some ways they will have a feeling for the grandeurs of form. But when these Word-People are gone, won't the life of words be gone?

TL. Unfortunately, yes.

S. Then, what of us, the two voices in this dialogue? When words go, won't we, too, be gone?

TL. Unfortunately, yes.

S. Then of this there will be nothing?

TL. Yes . . . nothing . . . but it's more complica—

Sudden blackness, with loud, abrupt roll on two kettle drums in A and A-flat, gradually diminishing in volume and stretching out, into clearly distinguishable intervals . . . and so, finally, four deliberately spaced thumps [A . . . A-flat . . . A . . . A-flat], then one culminating blastlike thump on both A and A-flat simultaneously. During this time, the absolute darkness has gradually become transformed into a deep dim purple, spread uniformly across the general formlessness. Slow curtain.

Or, for a comparatively "happy" ending, include a further step, thus: Out of the deep purple twilight are heard remote fragments of hymn-like song, mostly meditative humming, but with an occasional distinguishable word such as pro nobis, miserere *and* gratia. *Slow curtain, as these sounds fade into silence.*

14

Flowerishes

Flowerishes

From *Collected Poems 1915–1968* (1968). Berkeley and Los Angeles: University of California Press, p. 297.

15

A PHILOSOPHICO-POLITICAL PROFILE

Jürgen Habermas

Could you tell us something of the sequence of the principal intellectual influences on your work? You are often represented as an heir of the Frankfurt School who gave its legacy a "linguistic turn," with a move from a philosophy of consciousness to one of language. Is this an accurate image—or did your interest in, at least, the American pragmatism of Dewey and Peirce actually predate your encounter with the work of Adorno and Horkheimer? In what period did you start to reflect on the ideas of Wittgenstein or Austin? Similarly, in the social sciences, was your concern with Weber or Parsons subsequent to an earlier, primarily Marxist, orientation—or did these coexist from the outset? What were the seasons of your engagement with the phenomenological tradition of Schütz, or the genetic psychology of Piaget and Kohlberg?

Apart from the summer semester in Zurich, I studied in Göttingen and Bonn between 1949 and 1954. As far as my areas of study were concerned, there was an almost unbroken continuity of subject matter and personnel stretching back through the Nazi period to the Weimar Republic. It is not at all the case that the German universities were opened up to outside influences immediately after the War. Thus, from the academic standpoint, I grew up in a provincial German context, in the world of German philosophy, in the form of a declining Neo-Kantianism, of the German Historical School,

From *Autonomy and Solidarity: Interviews* (1986). Edited and introduced by Peter Dews. London: Verso, pp. 149–177.

of phenomenology, and also philosophical anthropology. The most powerful systematic impulse came from the early Heidegger. As students we were familiar with Sartre and French existentialism, perhaps also a few works of American cultural anthropology. While working on my dissertation on Schelling I naturally read the young Marx. Löwith's *From Hegel to Nietzsche* encouraged me to read the young Hegelians; Lukács's *History and Class Consciousness* also made a strong impression on me. These first intrusions of "left-wing literature" did have the result that I rounded out my dissertation, which was strongly influenced by Heidegger, with an introduction setting late German Idealism in relation to Marx. Directly after my studies I became familiar with industrial sociology. I was then given a grant to do work on the concept of ideology—this gave me the chance to penetrate somewhat deeper into Hegelian Marxism and the sociology of knowledge, and I also read Adorno's *Prisms* and the *Dialectic of Enlightenment*. In Frankfurt, from 1956 in other words, Bloch and Benjamin were added, along with a few articles from the *Zeitschrift für Sozialforschung*, Marcuse's books, and a discussion—which was very lively at the time—around the so-called philosophical and anthropological Marx. A little later I tackled *Das Kapital* seriously, and in this connection I also read Dobb, Sweezy and Baran. I also learned sociology in these early Frankfurt years; above all I read empirical things on mass communications, political socialization, political sociology. At this point I first came into contact with Durkheim, Weber, and very cautiously with Parsons. More important than this were the Freud Lectures in 1956—since hearing the international elite, from Alexander and Spitz to Erikson and Binswanger, I have considered psychoanalysis, despite all the dire predictions, as something to be taken seriously.

During these years as Adorno's assistant, between 1956 and 1959, there evolved what later crystallized in the empirical investigations of *Student und Politik*, and in my first two books (*Strukturwandel der Öffentlichkeit* and *Theory and Practice*)—the attempt to continue the Hegelian and Weberian Marxism of the 1920s with other means. All this remained within the context of a very German tradition, or at least of one rooted in Germany—even though at the time, through my contact with Adorno and Horkhelmer, and later with Abendroth and Mitscherlich, I lived with a sense of having grown into different, decisively broader horizons of experience, of having been freed from provincial narrowness and a naively idealistic world.

In Heidelberg, from 1961 on, Gadamer's *Truth and Method* helped me to find my way back into academic philosophy. Hermeneutics interested me, on the one hand, in connection with questions of the logic of the social sciences, and on the other in comparison with the later philosophy of Wittgenstein. This was the period, therefore, of my first more intensive involvement with linguistic philosophy and analytical philosophy of science. Encouraged by my friend Apel, I also studied Peirce, as well as Mead and Dewey. From the outset I viewed American pragmatism as the third productive reply to Hegel, after Marx and Kierkegaard, as the radical-democratic branch of Young

Hegelianism, so to speak. Ever since, I have relied on this American version of the philosophy of praxis when the problem arises of compensating for the weaknesses of Marxism with respect to democratic theory. This inclination was also the basis of my later friendship with Dick Bernstein. In any event, when I returned to Frankfurt to take up Horkheimer's chair in 1964, I had a firm enough footing in Anglo-Saxon discussions to be able to distance myself from an overstrained concept of theory derived from Hegel.

In the mid-1960s Cicourel and ethnomethodology led me back to Schütz. At that time I viewed social phenomenology as a protosociology, carried out in the form of analyses of the life-world. This idea connected up with influences from another direction: I was fascinated both by Chomsky's programme for a general theory of grammar, and by Austinian speech-act theory, as systematized by Searle. All this suggested the idea of a universal pragmatics, with the aid of which I wanted above all to deal with the awkward fact that the normative foundations of the critical theory of society were entirely unclarified. Having rejected the orthodoxy of the philosophy of history, I had no wish to lapse back either into ethical socialism, or into scientism, or indeed into both at once. This explains why I hardly read Althusser. In the second half of the sixties, thanks to collaboration with accomplished coworkers like Offe and Oevermann, I worked my way into specific areas of sociology, primarily socialization and family research on the one hand, political sociology on the other. In the process I got to know Parsons better. I was already reading Piaget and Kohlberg, but it was only at our Starnberg Institute, that is, after 1971, that I became an adherent of genetic structuralism. It was also here that I first began a more intensive study of Weber.

So you can see that from the outset my theoretical interests have been consistently determined by those philosophical and sociotheoretical problems which arise out of the movement of thought from Kant through to Marx. My intentions and fundamental convictions were given their stamp by Western Marxism in the mid-1950s through a coming-to-terms with Lukács, Korsch and Bloch, Sartre and Merleau-Ponty, and of course with Horkheimer, Adorno and Marcuse. Everything else which I have made my own has only acquired its significance in connection with the project of a renewal of the theory of society grounded in this tradition.

In the twenty-five years since Strukturwandel der Öffentlichkeit, *you have produced a very large body of work, of increasing complexity and range, with impressive continuity of direction. At the same time, your thought has obviously also undergone certain alterations of substantive emphasis or conviction during this period. What do you regard as the most important such changes?*

The books which I published at the beginning of the 1960s implicitly express the conviction that the things I wanted to do could be accommodated more or less within the inherited theoretical framework—in this respect I felt a special affinity with the existentialist, i.e. the Marcusean variant of Critical Theory. What is more, Herbert Marcuse, with whom I became friends in the nineteen sixties, felt the same way. I still remember the day when he dedicated a copy of *One Dimensional Man* to me with a flattering quote from Benjamin—"to the hope of those without hope." However, the engagement with analytical philosophy, and also the positivist dispute, then reinforced my doubts about whether concepts of totality, of truth, and of theory derived from Hegel did not represent too heavy a mortgage for a theory of society which should also satisfy empirical claims. At that time, in Heidelberg and then back in Frankfurt, I believed that this problem was an epistemological one. I wanted to do away with it through a methodological clarification of the status of a doubly reflexive theory (reflexive with respect to its context of emergence and of application). The result was *Knowledge and Human Interests*, which was written between 1964 and 1968. I still consider the outlines of the argument developed in the book to be correct. But I no longer believe in epistemology as the *via regia*. The critical theory of society does not need to prove its credentials in the first instance in methodological terms; it needs a substantive foundation, which will lead out of the bottlenecks produced by the conceptual framework of the philosophy of consciousness, and overcome the paradigm of production, without abandoning the intentions of Western Marxism in the process. The result is *The Theory of Communicative Action*. In a brilliant article soon to be published in Britain,[1] Dick Bernstein expounds the particular problems which have forced me immanently to make repeated changes of position—away from "knowledge and human interests" to "society and communicative rationality."

What is your sense of the current intellectual conjuncture in the West? In "Does Philosophy Still Have a Purpose?" you suggested that Germanic philosophical intensity and originality were migrating to the United States, while Europe relapsed into a placid "Swissification."[2] Would you still hold to this judgement? More generally, most of your references in recent years have been along a German-American axis of comparison—as lately in your criticism of the different forms of neo-conservatism in the two countries. Is this due to biographical reasons, or does it express an underlying judgement about the predominance and relevance of these two cultures for the West as a whole in the late twentieth century? Would one be right in thinking that France and England, for example—central poles of reference in your treatment of bourgeois civilization in the eighteenth and nineteenth centuries in Strukturwandel—*have lost salience in your subsequent work?*

The reasons for this orientation towards developments in the USA are undoubtedly trivial—it is typical for the post-war generation of German philosophers and sociologists in general. Of course, there is also a background in power politics: the Federal Republic has come so close to being the 51st State of the Union that the only thing we still don't have is the right to vote. This total dependence has never before appeared so undisguisedly as it did in autumn 1983, with the stationing of missiles that was forced upon us. Nevertheless, I do in fact prefer a political culture which, like the American, dates from the eighteenth century. I marvel at the intellectual openness and readiness for discussion, this mixture of impartiality and engagement, that I find in American students more than here in Europe. For a German of my age and outlook there may also be the fact that in American universities we could follow very readily in the footsteps of German emigrants who had acquired a considerable reputation. In addition, the Institute for Social Research, where I have worked, eventually returned from the USA. And those members of the Institute who did not return—Marcuse, Löwenthal, Kirchheimer, Neumann and others—have made a big contribution to the dense web of personal and academic ties between here and over there. Today this web is in fact extending to a third generation of younger scholars.

Speaking of the younger people, it is evident that the influence of the French has been growing steadily for the last ten years or so. In questions of social theory, the most inventive impulses are coming from Paris—from people like Bourdieu, Castoriadis, Foucault, Gorz, Touraine and so on.

Finally, so far as England is concerned, you yourselves admit that I have been influenced by analytical philosophy. However, I would not wish to deny that there is a certain difference of climate between England and the Continent. There are no deep elective affinities between the spirit of empiricism, which is still dominant in your country, and German Idealism. A fermenting agent is lacking in the philosophical metabolism, which could mediate between the two mentalities—as pragmatism does, for example, in America. I believe I can detect this estrangement in basic philosophical convictions. For example, I observe a certain incomprehension in the way in which distinguished colleagues like Quentin Skinner or W. G. Runciman, even my friend Steven Lukes, write about my concerns. In their case the ontology of empiricism has become second nature. Of course there are also counter-examples such as Tony Giddens.

Recently you have argued that Horkheimer and Adorno can only find resistance to a totalized purposive rationality in the irrational mimetic powers of art and love, or in the "impotent rage of nature in revolt."[3] Although these strictures do pinpoint a certain tendency of classical Critical Theory, it is not clear that they can be applied without qualification to the thought of Adorno, who always remained conscious of the danger of appeals to an unmediated nature. Is it possible that in your desire to distance yourself from an unremitting negativism, and to rehabilitate the collaborative and constructive conception of Critical Theory current during the 1930s, you have been led into polemical exaggerations, and have underplayed the extent to which Adorno remained fundamentally committed to the ideals of autonomy and enlightenment, even at his most desperate?

I agree with you: at no point does Adorno and Horkheimer's critique of reason darken to a renunciation of what the great philosophical tradition, and in particular the Enlightenment, once intended, however vainly, by the concept of reason. Like Nietzsche, they both radicalize the critique of reason to the point of self-referentiality, in other words until this critique begins to undermine even its own foundations. But Adorno differs from the followers of Nietzsche, from Heidegger on the one hand and Foucault on the other, precisely in the fact that he no longer wishes to break out of the paradoxes of this critique of reason, which has now become as if subjectless—he wishes to endure in the performative contradiction of a negative dialectics, which directs the unavoidable medium of identifying and objectifying thought against itself. Through the exercise of endurance he believes himself to be remaining most nearly faithful to a lost, non-instrumental reason. This forgotten reason, belonging to prehistory, finds an echo only in the powers of a wordless mimesis. The mimetic can be circled around by negative dialectics, but it cannot—as Heidegger suggests—be revealed. The mimetic does allow one to sense what it is performing the role of stand-in for, but it permits no knowledge of a structure which could be characterized as rational. To this extent, Adorno cannot appeal to any structure heterogeneous to instrumental reason, against which the force of totalized purposive rationality must collide. In the passage that you mention I am in the process of pinning down such a resistant structure, namely the structure of a rationality which is immanent in everyday communicative practice, and which brings the stubbornness of life-forms into play against the functional demands of autonomized economic and administrative systems.

Can Adorno, in his evocations of reconciliation, justly be accused of surreptitiously employing categories of intersubjectivity from which he abstains philosophically, and can what he terms "love towards things" be simply reformulated in terms of undistorted communication? One might consider, for example, the following passage from Aesthetic Theory, *where Adorno seeks to evoke a reciprocal relation between nature and human technology, without in any way suggesting that nature could be legitimately viewed as a subject: "After the abolition of scarcity, the expansion of the productive forces could occur in a dimension which is different from the quantitative increase of production. There are intimations of this in functional buildings that have been adapted to forms and lines in the surrounding landscape; or in old architecture where the raw materials for buildings were taken from the surrounding area, and fitted in with it, as is the case with many castles and châteaux. What is called "culture landscape" in German is beautiful as the schema of this possibility. A rationality which took up such motifs could help to close the wounds of rationality."*[4] *In the light of such passages, would it not be plausible to suggest that there is a relation of complementarity—rather than of substitution—between Adorno's explorations of the subject-object relation, and your own theory of communication?*

If I may say so, I find your suggestion, that Adorno's *Aesthetic Theory* and my theory of communication should be viewed simply as supplementing each other, a little too innocuous. On the other hand, neither can one theory simply replace the other, if for no other reason than that I have said very little about aesthetic matters.

Albrecht Wellmer, who has a far more thorough understanding of these questions, has shown, in an outstanding discussion of "Truth, Illusion and

Reconciliation,"[5] how Adorno's aesthetic utopia "turns sour," so to speak, once its connection with the philosophy of history of the *Dialectic Enlightenment* is dissolved. If this is done, Adorno's aesthetic insights become independent of the metaphysical thesis that, with every new advance of subjectification, humanity becomes ever more deeply entangled in reification. To this negative view belongs the perspective, extended into a positive, of a reconciliation of human productivity with nature, which you recall in your quotation. Adorno's appeal to *"die Liebe zu den Dingen"* is not without irony, and yet in earnest. This love is a utopian counterimage to the despairing belief that subjectivity "works towards its own extinction by the force of its own logic." A theory of communication which breaks with the conceptual framework of the philosophy of subjectivity undermines this "logic," this apparently indissoluble internal relation between emancipation and subjugation. More specifically, it discovers that there is already a mimetic moment in everyday practices of communication, and not merely in art. Allow me to put this in Wellmer's words: "This must remain hidden to a philosophy which, like Adorno's, understands the function of concepts in terms of the polarity of subject and object; it cannot recognize, behind objectifying functions of language, communicative performances which are the condition of its own possibility. For this reason, it can only understand mimesis as the other of rationality . . . In order for the prior unity of the mimetic and the rational moment in the foundations of language to be recognized, a paradigm-shift is required. . . . For if intersubjectivity of "understanding, communicative action are no less constitutive of the sphere of mind than the objectification of reality in contexts of instrumental action, then the utopian perspective which Adorno seeks to elucidate with the concept of an unforced synthesis derived from the philosophy of consciousness, migrates into the sphere of discursive reason itself: undamaged intersubjectivity, the unforced togetherness of many, which would make possible a simultaneous nearness and distance, identity and difference of individuals, indicate a utopian projection whose elements discursive reason derives from the conditions of its own linguisticality."[6]

In a number of recent essays you have passed sharp judgements on post-structuralism, suggesting that the French post-structuralists must be seen as "Young Conservatives" who "on the basis of modernistic attitudes . . . justify an irreconcilable anti-modernism."[7] Could you expand on this assessment, if necessary drawing distinctions between different post-structuralist thinkers? And could you explain the discrepancy between your condemnation of post-structuralism, and your comparatively friendly reception of the work of Richard Rorty, which provides parallels to, and has in some cases been directly influenced by, post-structuralist themes?

As you will see from my lectures on the philosophical discourse of modernity, which are due to appear shortly, "condemnation" is not the appropriate word for my attitude towards post-structuralism. There are, of course, many similarities between negative dialectics and the procedures of

deconstruction on the one hand, between the critique of instrumental reason and the analysis of formations of discourse and power on the other. The
playful-subversive element of a critique of reason which is conscious of its
own paradoxical self-referentiality, and the exploitation of experiential possibilities which were first revealed by the aesthetic avant-garde—these two
things characterize a Nietzschean style of thought and presentation, which
founds the spiritual kinship of Adorno with Derrida on the one hand, and
with Foucault on the other. What separates him from these two figures, as
from Nietzsche himself—and this seems to me to be politically decisive—is
simply this: Adorno does not merely bale out of the *counter*-discourse which
has inhabited modernity ever since the beginning; rather, in his desperate
adherence to the procedure of determinate negation, he remains true to the
idea that there is no cure for the wounds of Enlightenment other than the
radicalized Enlightenment itself. Unlike Nietzsche and his disciples, Adorno
has no illusions about the genuinely modern origins of aesthetic experience,
in whose name modernity falls victim to a levelling, undialectical critique.

As far as Richard Rorty is concerned, I am no less critical of his contex-
tualist position. But at least he does not climb aboard the "antihumanist"
bandwagon, whose trail leads back in Germany to figures as politically unambiguous as Heidegger and Gehlen. Rorty retains from the pragmatist inheritance, which in many, though not all, respects he unjustly claims for
himself, an intuition which links us together—the conviction that a humane
collective life depends on the vulnerable forms of innovation-bearing, reciprocal and unforcedly egalitarian everyday communication. This intuition is
even more alien to Derrida and Foucault than to Adorno (who also remained a romantic of course, and not just as a composer).

*The question of post-structuralism has an obvious importance at the
present time, given the increasing penetration of this style of thought into the
Federal Republic. What do you consider to be the reasons for this success, and
what are your feelings about the repatriation of the thought of Nietzsche and
Heidegger in post-structuralist form?*

The influence of post-structuralism on the German universities is undoubtedly also connected with the situation in the academic job-market. The
horizon of expectations of the younger intellectuals has become so gloomy
that a negativistic mood has become widespread, which in part even flips
over into apocalyptic anticipations of revival. Social reality is doing something further: it is not miserly in the creation of ever new dangers which,
even on calmer consideration, appear as side-effects of purposive-rational
action, thus as dangers which we have brought upon ourselves. For this reason theories which grasp the whole as the untrue, and offer the affirmation
of the impossibility of escape as the only affirmation possible, not only match
the mood of the critique of civilization—they also have an increasing real-
ity-content. After all, how ought one to respond to the spectacle of the last
American election, in which all levels of reality triumphantly intermingled:

in which a play-actor president reveals to an enraptured public that, despite all asseverations of leadership and he-manship, he is merely playing at being president, and is promptly returned to office? To that kind of thing one can only reply with the cynical antics of the deconstructionists.

The situation is a little different with Heidegger, who still tends to inspire a holy terror in this country. The latest return of a felicitously de-Nazified Heidegger is, of course, based on the ahistorical reception of Heidegger in France and America—where he stepped on stage after the War, like a phoenix from the ashes, as the author of the "Letter on Humanism."

The suspicion of system in philosophy is characteristic of many currents in twentieth century thought. Scepticism about the possibility of philosophy as an ordered body of truths is characteristic of thinkers as diverse as Wittgenstein, Merleau-Ponty and Adorno. How would you defend the need for, and possibility of, systematic philosophy against these deeply rooted objections?

Since Hegel's death philosophical systems are no longer to be had with good conscience. Any thinker who, in the twentieth century, has asserted and practised the death, the supersession, the end, or the disbanding of philosophy, has therefore simply been belatedly carrying out a decree which was issued by the first generation of Young Hegelians. Ever since then philosophical thought has sought to step over into another medium. In this respect we have all remained contemporaries of the Young Hegelians—all post-modern ambitions notwithstanding. "After Philosophy"—the title of a collection of essays which Tom McCarthy is planning—characterizes a situation which, for me, has become so self-evident that I consider the grand gestures of the anti-systematists to be pretty superfluous. Any philosophical work implicitly renounces thinking in systems which weaves itself into the ramified network of the human and social sciences, without fundamentalist claims and with a fallibilistic consciousness, in order to contribute something of use whenever the problem of the presumptively universal features of knowledge, speech and action arises.

One of the most obvious general developments in your work has been the increasing prominence of the arguments and procedures of analytical philosophy. Could you explain the reasons for this transformation? What resources are offered by analytical philosophy which cannot be provided by other traditions, including the major German traditions?

In general, the example of analytical philosophy has been a salutary force in post-war German philosophy for no other reason than that it demanded a higher level of explicitness. I have learned most from Wittgenstein, Austin and Searle—as you know, I find instruments in their work for the investigation of general pragmatic presuppositions of the use of propositions in utterances.

One of the most prominent developments in English-speaking philosophy over the last ten years or so has been the emergence of new substantive works of

political philosophy (Rawls, Nozick, Dworkin, Walzer) and of a widespread de-
bate around them. How significant do you consider this development? And do
you feel that it would be appropriate for you to make a more direct intervention
into this debate than you have so far, given that the concerns of these thinkers in
many respects overlap with your own?

Besides speech-act theory, I could also have mentioned moral philosophy, at least the line of thought (from Baier and Singer to Rawls) in which
the substance of Kantian ethics is retrieved in a certain way in terms of linguistic philosophy. More recently, I myself have explained the discourse ethics approach, which Apel and I favour, more thoroughly.[8] This approach is
an attempt to reconstruct Kantian ethics with the help of the theory of communication. The suggestions which I have reworked in this process derive
above all from Rawls and Kohlberg. When I initiated a discussion of civil disobedience last year, in response to contemporary events, the work of Rawls
and Dworkin provided the most important points of reference. If you are under the impression that I have not been sufficiently engaged on this front,
this may be the result of my somewhat restricted understanding of the task
of philosophical ethics.

According to my conception, the philosopher ought to explain the
moral point of view, and—as far as possible—justify the claim to universality
of this explanation, showing why it does not merely reflect the moral intuitions of the average, male, middle-class member of a modern Western society. Anything further than that is a matter for moral discourse between
participants. Insofar as the philosopher would like to justify specific principles of a normative theory of morality and politics, he should consider this
as a proposal for the discourse between citizens. In other words: the moral
philosopher must leave the substantive questions which go beyond a fundamental critique of value-scepticism and value-relativism to the participants
in moral discourse, or tailor the cognitive claims of normative theory from
the outset to the role of a participant. In this way we gain a larger space for
the contribution of social theory to the diagnosis of the present. Admittedly,
ethical considerations are frequently of great methodological value in the
construction of such theories. I have discussed this question in *Legitimation
Crisis*, in connection with the problem of distinguishing particular from universal interests.

In your own recent writing stylistic considerations appear to have retreated in
favour of a more functional mode of expression, a shift which seems to be corre-
lated with the increasing importance of analytical philosophy in your work. Given
your remarks, in "Does Philosophy Still Have a Purpose?", about the end of
"great philosophy," the transformation of philosophy into a branch of "research,"
and the demise of the "style of philosophical thinking tied to individual scholar-
ship and personal representation",[9] would you consider a concern with style in
the work of a contemporary philosopher to be a diversion or a regression? Is what
is of value in a philosophical position always susceptible to direct statement?

The type of text changes in accordance with purpose, addressee, place and time—according to whether I am dealing with the theme of the *Berufsverbot*, or of civil disobedience in the public-political sphere, or whether I am giving a speech in honour of Gadamer, polemicizing against Gehlen, writing an obituary for Scholem, or whether I am attempting to justify a moral principle or to classify speech-acts. The rhetorical constituents vary in relation to these different purposes. We are now well aware, since Mary Hesse at the latest, that even the language of the sciences is shot through with metaphors; this is plainly true of the language of philosophy, which can never of course be entirely absorbed into its role as a stand-in for scientific theories with strong universal claims. But one cannot, like Derrida, conclude from the unavoidably rhetorical character of *every* kind of language, including philosophical language, that it is all one and the same—that the categories of everyday life and literature, science and fiction, poetry and philosophy, collapse into each other. For Derrida all cats are grey in the night of "writing." I would not wish to draw this conclusion. The use of language in the practices of everyday life stands under different restrictions from the language used in theory or in art, which is specialized for the solving of problems, or for an innovative disclosure of the world.

How would you summarize your present conceptions of truth? If any adequate approach to truth should include a theory of evidence and a theory of argument, would it be fair to say that your work so far has given much more attention to the latter than the former? Today, would you still maintain the categorical separation between "objectivity" and "truth,"[10] the experiential and the veridical, of the postscript to Knowledge and Human Interests?

The core of the discourse theory of truth can be formulated by means of three basic concepts: *conditions of validity* (which are fulfilled when an utterance holds good), *validity-claims* (which speakers raise with their utterances, for their validity), and *redemption* of a validity-claim (in the framework of a discourse which is sufficiently close to the conditions of an ideal speech situation for the consensus aimed at by the participants to be brought about solely through the force of the better argument, and in this sense to be "rationally motivated"). The basic intuition, then, is simply this. Validity-claims are explicitly thematized only in non-trivial cases, but it is precisely in these cases that there are no rules of verification available which would make it possible to decide directly whether certain conditions of validity are fulfilled or not. When claims to truth or justice become really obstinately problematic, there are no neat deductions or decisive pieces of evidence which could *enforce* an immediate decision for or against. Rather a play of argumentation is required, in which motivating reasons take the place of the unavailable knock-down arguments. If one accepts this description, it becomes clear that the following difficulty arises in the attempt to explain what it means to say that an utterance is valid. An utterance is valid when its conditions of validity are fulfilled. According to our description the fulfillment or non-fulfillment of conditions of validity, in problematic cases, can only be ascertained by means of the argumentative redemption of the corresponding validity-claims. The discourse theory of truth, then, explains what it means to redeem a validity-claim by an analysis of the general pragmatic presuppositions of the attainment of a rationally-motivated consensus. This theory of truth provides only an explication of meaning, it does not provide a criterion; in the end, however, it undermines the clear distinction between meaning and criterion.

To what extent is the notion of an ideal speech situation as a regulative principle of truth a circular one? If truth is defined as the consensus that would be reached by the speakers in an ideal speech situation, how could the existence of such a situation itself ever be truthfully ascertained? In other words, isn't the idea susceptible to the same kind of critique that Hegel made of Kant's theory of knowledge, and you of Hegel's, in Knowledge and Human Interests—*the "aporia of knowing before knowledge"?[11] Perhaps one could reformulate such a criticism another way. How could any speech situation be ideal, save in terms of the symmetry and sincerity of its speakers? But even at their most perfect, these conditions could normally only yield agreement rather than truth—that is, in abstraction from evidence, the opportunities for which can themselves never be ideal, since they always depend in some measure on historically changing techniques. Even the most flawlessly democratic and equal community of classical Greeks could not have discovered the laws of thermodynamics in the absence of modern optics. Isn't this one of the limits of any consensus theory of truth?*

The discourse theory of truth only claims to reconstruct an intuitive knowledge of the meaning of universal validity-claims which every competent speaker has at his or her disposal. "Ideal speech situation" is somewhat too concrete a term for the set of general and unavoidable communicative presuppositions which a subject capable of speech and action must make every time he or she wishes to participate seriously in argumentation. In answering your previous question I wanted to recall the fact that this intuitive knowledge of universal presuppositions of argumentation is linked with the preunderstanding of propositional truth and moral truth (or rightness). Of course, we know from philosophy and from the history of science that these ideas can be operationalized in very different ways; what counts at any given time as a good reason, as a proof, as an explanation, obviously depends on historically-changing background convictions, and also, as you suggest, on the associated techniques for controlling and observing nature; in short, on changing paradigms. But the paradigm-dependence of theories can be more readily harmonized with a discourse theory of truth than with a realist theory. The discourse theory is only incompatible with a Feyerabend-style paradigm-*relativism* because it sticks to the idea that paradigm-dependent ideas of truth and rightness nevertheless point towards a universal core of meaning.

How do you conceive the relation between philosophical and scientific truth-claims? Are philosophical truth-claims cognitive claims, and would a rational consensus ultimately guarantee the truth of the consensus theory of truth itself?

This is an interesting question, on which I have been working for a good while, although so far I do not have a conclusive answer to hand.

What is your attitude to psychoanalysis today? In Knowledge and Human Interests *you eloquently present it as the paradigm of a critical science serving an emancipatory interest. At the same time, you remark that Freud's metapsychology was a misunderstanding of his own project, whose instinct theory has never yielded "a single statement that has ever been tested experimentally."*[12] *But how far does this stricture apply to the main body of analytic theory itself? Even if the evidential weaknesses—widely aired—of psychoanalysis are set aside, doesn't the theory in fact present peculiar difficulties for a consensus theory of truth, insofar as the transactions between analyst and analysand are inherently confidential—i.e. non-extendable to others? In the gap between the "clinical" and the "ideal speech" situations, isn't there a temptation in your original account to fall back on essentially a pragmatic justification of Freud's theory— whose test becomes a change in the conduct of the patient, a "continuation of the self-formative process" indeterminable in direction or duration? This could seem close to the kind of Deweyan instrumentalism that you reject in the postscript. But the success rate even in these terms is not very high. In sum: isn't there much more question about the scientificity of many of Freud's claims, scrutinized in a large literature, than you allowed in the late sixties?*

My friend Mitscherlich once summed up his experience as a psychoanalyst in the following terms: therapy often achieves "no more than the transformation of illness into suffering, but into a suffering which enhances the status of *homo sapiens*, because it does not extinguish his freedom." I would like to make use of this statement to express my scepticism about criteria based on statistics of so-called success.

It certainly seems to be the case today that psychoanalytic research has come to a standstill, not only in Germany but on an international scale, and that intelligent young people prefer to go into other disciplines. But how definitive is this? Many disciplines have survived similar periods of stagnation. Even sociology is going through thin times at the moment. I have not done any work myself on Freud's metapsychology since the end of the sixties. But I find the attempts to bring Freud and Piaget together, which have been undertaken in various contexts, both exciting and fruitful. Beyond that, my interpretation of Freud in terms of communication theory still seems to me to be plausible. I cannot entirely accept your objection. I have never understood the therapeutic discourse as discourse or argumentation in the strict sense, because of the asymmetries between doctor and patient which are built into it. Of course it is inhabited, so to speak, by the *telos* of working to remove those asymmetries. For these reasons the patient also acquires in the end, at least in the ideal case, a freedom to say "yes" and "no" which immunizes him or her against the suggestive obtrusion of functional interpretations, which are, in a superficial sense, "life-assisting." What should be involved is, of course, the continuation, made possible *through reflexive insight*, of an interrupted, neurotically-inhibited process of formation of the self.

The Theory of Communicative Action *contains a fascinating reconstruction and critique of Weber's account of "rationalization" as a world-historical process. In it, you tax Weber with abandoning his own starting-point—the advent of substantive reasoning with the major religions—in his final focus on formal rationality alone, as the necessary matrix of modern capitalism; and you also point to significant lacunae in his regional theory of the origins of capitalism—his omission of the rise of modern science, and more generally, its bearers during the Renaissance. These are compelling demonstrations. What is not so clear, on the other hand, is whether you accept the main thrust of his thesis concerning the importance of the Protestant Ethic itself, as the engine of a rationalized life-world and so motor of early capitalism. Many historians have been highly sceptical of Weber's claims for Calvinism—one need only think of a critical survey of the evidence like Kurt Samuelson's* Religion and Economic Action, *or Trevor-Roper's essays on Erasmianism. Did you feel that these doubts fell outside the province of your treatment of Weber?*

I did indeed neglect the wide-ranging discussion around the question of whether and to what extent Weber's analysis of capitalism has proved correct. There were, above all, practical reasons for that—it would have required, if not another book, at the very least an additional chapter. It is also for these reasons—to reduce the burden of work—that I planned *The Theory of Communicative Action* as an intertwining of history of theory with systematic investigations. In Weber's case this had the additional advantage of illustrating a favourite idea of mine. Weber perceives with great acuity the narrowness of the Calvinistic doctrine of grace, and the repressive traits of the forms of life which bore the stamp of this doctrine; but Weber refuses to see this protestant ethic as a *one-sided* exploitation of a potential which was built into the universalist ethics of brotherhood. In fact, it is the selective model of capitalist rationalization as a whole which is mirrored in the protestant ethic.

Of course, such interests attached to the form of presentation should not be allowed to get the upper hand; otherwise one would become cynical about questions of truth. Insofar as I am familiar with the literature, I believe that Weber's thesis must be expanded and revised with regard to *other* social strata who were bearers of early capitalism. However, I doubt whether such revision would be forced to tamper with the general correlation of an ethics of conviction, worldly asceticism, and economic behaviour.

More generally, what is your view of the position and contribution of history as a discipline within the social sciences? You have always argued that "history as such is not capable of theory," because it is always a retrospective narrative—"whereas theoretical statements allow the derivation of conditional predictions of events that will occur in the future."[13] You contrast this incapacity for theory and prediction with the competence in these respects of sociology or evolutionary discourses. This distinction seems quite close to the neo-Kantian dichotomy between ideographic and nomothetic sciences. But is it warranted? It is difficult to see why historians like Taylor or Hobsbawm should be unable to make forecasts at least as reliable—to put it no higher—as those of sociologists like Bell or Dahrendorf, whom you cite as valid diagnosticians of the time. Don't warnings of the increasing dangers of nuclear war, for example, have a special weight when they come from a historian of the authority of Edward Thompson? Once such a sharp division is made between "history" and "theory," aren't the effects on historical materialism itself necessarily paradoxical—in the sense that to reconstruct it as theory, it has to be drastically reduced as history, in the evolutionary version presented in Communication and the Evolution of Society? *It would appear prima facie more plausible to imagine that Marxist (and other) historians would have more to contribute to the enterprise of reconstructing historical materialism than child psychologists. Couldn't one cite your* Strukturwandel *against yourself here, as a memorable example of a work at once and indivisibly historical and theoretical, and diagnostic to boot?*

The prognostic capacity of social theories was and is very limited—that could hardly be otherwise, given the high level of abstraction at which these statements concerning complex states of affairs are formulated. Nor do I doubt that a shrewd and politically-seasoned historian, with his or her experience-steeped intuitions, often judges contemporary developmental tendencies with an astonishing sureness of touch. It is for methodological reasons that I have insisted on a distinction—but not a distinction of rank—between historiography and social-scientific theory. If one introduces the viewpoint of social evolution into history without mediation, it is easy to fall victim to patterns of thought familiar from the philosophy of history, above all the danger of thinking in terms of historical teleology, which Marxists in particular have often enough succumbed to. The reflections which you refer to belonged in the context of the critique of historical objectivism, and of its unfortunate consequences for the political practice of so-called vanguard parties. I am not in any sense opposed to the necessity of theoretically-guided historical research. Theories, especially those of Marxist inspiration, ultimately only prove their worth by making a contribution to the explanation of concrete historical processes. I myself find it unfortunate that for the last two decades (if one disregards some shorter political writings) my interest has been taken up exclusively with problems which can be characterized in a broad sense as problems of theory construction. I must accept the criticism which, most recently, Tom Bottomore has directed at me in this respect.

What are the methodological grounds for the homologies you postulate between individual growth and social evolution? In The Theory of Communicative Action, *you remark that most adults in* all *societies can achieve the higher levels of moral and cognitive competence as described by Piaget and Kohlberg.*[14] *If this is so, how can the maturational sequence they posit help to explain the huge differences between such societies, when arrayed along a scale of rationalization of the world-views they exhibit?*

Empirical investigations come out strongly against the idea that all adult members of a society, even of modern Western societies, have acquired the capacity for formal-operational thought (in Piaget's sense) or for post-conventional judgements (in the sense of Kohlberg's theory of moral development). I maintain only (for example, with reference to tribal societies) that individuals can develop structures of consciousness which belong to a higher stage than those which are already embodied in the institutions of their society. It is primarily subjects who learn, while societies can take a step forward in the evolutionary learning-process only in a metaphorical sense. New forms of social integration, and new productive forces, are due to the institutionalization and exploitation of forms of knowledge which are individually acquired, but culturally stored and capable of transmission and so, in the long term, accessible to the collective. However, the process of social implementation only takes place as a consequence of political struggles and social movements, of the outrider-role of innovative marginal groups, and so on. Thus I start from the trivial assumption that subjects capable of speech and action cannot help but learn, and use this to support the assumption that ontogenetic learning processes acquire pacemaker functions. However, this thesis is contested by Klaus Eder in his *Habilitationsschrift* on the development of German constitutional law since the eighteenth century. He traces the innovative impulses back directly to *social* learning processes in the framework of new forms of association, namely to new experiences of egalitarian social relations, initially in the Masonic lodges, secret societies and readers' unions, later in the early socialist workingmen's associations.

Can a theory of emancipation avoid the idea of progress? You stress in The Theory of Communicative Action *that we cannot judge the worth of societies by the degree to which their life-worlds are rationalized, even in the sense of an "encompassing" rationality that is not only formal but substantive; suggesting that at best we can speak perhaps of the relative "health" or "sickness" of a given social order.[15] Earlier, however, in* Legitimation Crisis, *you criticized the use of such terms, drawn from biology, as fundamentally inapplicable to society.[16] Have you definitely changed your views here, or is this still a relatively unresolved issue for you? The difficulty seems to be to resist historical triumphalism—an Enlightenment complacency that devalues all anterior or alien social forms—without falling into political agnosticism. For if all epochs and societies are equally close to God, in Ranke's sense, why fight for a better one? A consistent cultural relativism must be conservative. In what direction do you think a solution to these dilemmas is to be looked for?*

I have not revised my conception in this respect, but continue to think that statements concerning the level of development of a society can only relate to *single* dimensions and to *universal* structures: to the reflexivity and complexity of social systems on the one hand, and to the social forces of production and forms of social integration on the other. One society may be superior to another with reference to the level of differentiation of its economic or administrative system, or with reference to technologies and legal institutions. But it does not follow that we are entitled to value this society more highly *as a whole*, as a concrete totality, as a form of life. You know that, in relation to objectifying knowledge and moral insight, the position I represent is one of cautious universalism. We observe tendencies towards a "progressive" rationalization of the lifeworld—not as a law, of course, but as a historical fact. Again and again those tendencies have been confirmed which distinguish modern societies from traditional ones—the increasing reflexivity of the cultural tradition, the universalization of values and norms, the freeing of communicative action from tightly circumscribed normative contexts, the diffusion of models of socialization which promote processes of individuation and the formation of abstract ego-identities, and so on. But all these "advances" concern the universal structures of life-worlds in general; they say nothing about the value of a concrete way of life. This value must be measured by other things, of the kind which we look for in clinical judgements: whether people in such and such circumstances have a "hard" life, whether they are alienated from themselves. For the intuition of an unspoiled life we apply yardsticks which are valid in the first instance in the context of our culture or plausible in the context of our tradition, which in any event cannot be generalized in the same way as the standards which we use in judging processes that involve learning—knowledge of nature or moral and legal ideas, which despite their paradigm-dependence, are not *entirely* incommensurable. So far I have no idea how the universal core of those merely clinical intuitions—if indeed they have one at all—can be theoretically grasped.

Can a morality of enlightenment skirt a commitment to happiness? If not, what is the bearing of a "discursive ethics" on it? In your essay on Benjamin, you evoke the possibility of a society at once freed of domination and devoid of meaning—rationality without felicity. Doesn't such a prospect undermine the argument that every truthful statement is "an anticipation of the good life"?[17] *Another way of putting the question would be this: you have argued on a number of occasions that ethics is a "reconstructive science"—while elsewhere you define such sciences as those, in contradistinction to critical theories, which are without practical effects on the conduct of agents.*[18] *But isn't the idea of a post facto ethic, an anodyne codification of existing practices, virtually a contradiction in terms?*

Let me start with a couple of general propositions. Morality has certainly to do with justice and also with the wellbeing of others, even with the promotion of the general welfare. But happiness cannot be brought about intentionally, and can only be promoted very indirectly. I prefer a relatively narrow concept of morality. Morality refers to practical questions which can be decided with reasons—to conflicts of action which can be resolved through consensus. Only those questions are moral in a strict sense which can be answered in a meaningful way from the Kantian standpoint of universalization—of what *all* could wish for. At the same time, I prefer a weak concept of moral theory. We have already touched on this: it should explain and justify the moral point of view, and nothing more. Deontic, cognitive and universal moral theories in the Kantian tradition are theories of justice, which must leave the question of the good life unanswered. They are typically restricted to the question of the *justification* of norms and actions. They have no answer to the question of how justified norms can be *applied* to specific situations and how moral insights can be *realized*. In short, one should not place excessive demands on moral theory, but leave something over for social theory, and the major part for the participants themselves—whether it be their moral discourses or their good sense. This merely advocatory role sets narrow limits to theory: whoever takes a risk upon him or herself, must be allowed to make his or her *own* decision. But now to your questions.

Moral theory proceeds reconstructively, in other words after the event. Aristotle was right in his opinion that the moral intuitions which theory clarifies must have been acquired elsewhere, in more or less successful socialization processes. However, I would also expect a critical theory to perform the task of making possible enlightening interpretations of situations, which affect our self-understanding and orientate us in action. Even social theory would overstep its competence, however, if it undertook to project desirable forms of life into the future, instead of criticizing existing forms of life. In so doing, it can refer to historically superfluous repressions, and to that untapped potential for rationality which can be read off from the state of the productive forces, the level of legal and moral ideas, the degree of individuation, and so on. For this reason Marxist theory cannot cash out the expression "socialism" in terms of a *concrete* form of life; at most it can indicate necessary conditions under which emancipated forms of life would be possible today.

How far is the realm of "inner nature" a source of potential values for you? You've written of a necessary "fluidification" of this nature in any post-conventional morality or society, and have suggested that art has a particularly significant role to play in such redispositions.[19] Could you give some examples of the kind of process you have in mind?

Our needs are only ever accessible to us in an interpreted form. In other words, language is constitutive for needs, in the light of which situations—which are always affectively tinged—are disclosed to us. Up till now the transformation of evaluative, need-interpreting languages has taken place in a nature-like manner; the changing of this vocabulary has taken place as part of the changing of linguistic world-pictures. To the extent that art and literature have become differentiated into a sphere with a logic of its own, and in this sense have become autonomous, a tradition of literary and art criticism has been established which labours to reintegrate the innovative aesthetic experiences, at first "mute," into ordinary language, and thus into the communicative practice of everyday life. In the medium of this criticism the formerly sluggish, nature-like process of revaluation of our evaluative vocabulary, our world-disclosing and need-interpreting language in general, becomes more and more reflexive; the whole process becomes, as it were, discursively fluidified. Central concepts such as the happiness, dignity, integrity of the person are now changing as if before our very eyes. Diffuse experiences, which crystallize out under transformed life-circumstances produced by changes in social structure, find their illuminating, suggestive, visible expression through cultural productivity. This is what Castoriadis means by "imagination." Benjamin, for example, investigated through Baudelaire those experiences of a mobilized, concentrated, metropolitan life-world which surfaced like a new continent in nineteenth-century Paris, the "capital of the nineteenth century," as he called it. Kafka and Musil can be seen as literary exemplifications of the experiential space of the collapsing Austrian Imperial and Royal Monarchy, Celan and Beckett of a world transformed by Auschwitz. Our moral-practical reflections and discourses are affected by this productivity, precisely to the extent that it is only in the light of such innovations that we can say what we *really* want, and above all: what we *cannot* want. Only in this light do we find a precise expression for our interests.

In recent years you have polemicized against theories of post-modernity, associating them with concepts of post-history and with the neo-conservative implications of post-structuralism. It is not entirely clear, however, whether you intend to deny that there are any developments to which the concept of post-modernism corresponds, or whether you are merely contesting the appropriateness of the designation. Would you deny, for example, that the shift away from the esotericism of high modern art to fusions of high and mass culture is a development to which the term "post-modernism" could be applied? In The Theory of Communicative Action *you hint at the emergence of a "post-avant-garde art" which would be "characterized by the simultaneity of realistic and engaged tendencies with the authentic continuation of that classical modernity which separated out the distinctive meaning of the aesthetic."[20] What examples would you give of works of art which are moving in this direction? And, given your refusal to deny all progressive potential to mass culture, would fusions of high and mass culture be one aspect of such a "post-avant-garde art"?*

Peter Bürger sees post-avant-garde art, art after the failure of the surrealist revolt, the contemporary scene in general, as being characterized by the juxtaposition of styles, which draw either on the formalist languages of the avant-garde, or on the inheritance of realistic or political-didactic styles and literatures. You can find examples in the museum of any large city. This juxtaposition also includes the by now ritualized forms of the "*Aufhebung*" of esoteric art. I would not interpret the contemporary scene in the sense of so-called post-modernism as a sign of the exhaustion or the "end" of modernism in art and architecture. Our situation testifies, rather, to the fact that the aesthetic experiences revealed by the twentieth century's avant-gardes find no access to a onesidedly rationalized everyday practice, but circle around restlessly before its portals in split-off specialist cultures. I share Adorno's reservations about mass culture, against Benjamin's overhasty hopes for its "profane illuminations," only to the extent that the fusion of high and trivial culture has, up till now, fallen short of its programmatic goal. Desublimated mass-art does not penetrate in a transforming, illuminating and liberating way into life-forms reified by capitalism, and deformed and distorted by consumerism and bureaucracy, but rather helps to advance these tendencies. It was not the hopes of the surrealists which were false, but their path—the *Aufhebung* of aesthetic illusion—was counter-productive.

One of the significant developments in your work over the last decade has been the progressive attenuation of the claims made for the "ideal speech situation." In The Theory of Communicative Action *you admit the utopian nature of the project of an ideal speech community, and you have also emphasized that the procedural rationality of argumentative grounding cannot provide the substance of a form of life as such. Even after having made the concessions, however, there might still be a tension between the telos of universal consensus and the human (and epistemological) value of conflict and diversity. It is this kind of tension to which Mill, whose conception of truth in some ways resembles your own, reveals himself to be sensitive when he writes, in* On Liberty: *"The loss of so important an aid to the intelligent and living apprehension of truth as is afforded by the necessity of explaining it to, or defending it against, opponents, though not sufficient to outweigh, is no trifling drawback from the benefit of its universal recognition." In* Strukturwandel *you suggest that Mill disguised his "resignation before the rational insolubility of competing interests in the public sphere" by means of a "perspectivist theory of knowledge."[21] However, as the above quotation makes clear, this is not entirely accurate. Mill does not doubt that truth ultimately entails consensus, but nevertheless perceives unanimity as purchased at the cost of other human values. Are you at all susceptible to this kind of consideration?*

I think I am—after all, my Marxist friends are not entirely unjustified in accusing me of being a radical liberal. I can only repeat what I have already stressed elsewhere. "Nothing makes me more nervous than the imputation that because the theory of communicative action focuses attention on the social facticity of recognized validity-claims, it proposes, or at least suggests, a rationalistic utopian society. I do *not* regard the fully transparent—let me add in this context: or indeed a homogenized and unified—society as an ideal, nor do I wish to suggest any other ideal—Marx was not the only one frightened by the vestiges of utopian socialism."[22] The ideal speech situation is, as I have said, a description of the conditions under which claims to truth and rightness can be discursively redeemed. In communicative action these validity-claims remain for the most part implicit and unproblematic, since the intersubjectively shared lifeworld holds in reserve a solid background of culturally self-evident truths, taken-for-granted assumptions. The action-coordinating role of processes of reaching understanding, which proceed by means of the criticism of validity-claims, does not conflict therefore with the pluralism of life-forms and interest. The fact that modern societies are differentiated in terms of life-forms and interest-positions, and are becoming increasingly differentiated, is a fact which does not put action orientated to reaching understanding out of service; of course, the need for understanding, which increases in step with this process, must be satisfied at higher and higher levels of abstraction. For this reason the consensual norms and principles become ever more in general.

There is also another way of meeting a need for understanding which goes beyond the available possibilities of reaching consensus; this need in fact disappears entirely as soon as socially-integrated domains of action are switched over to system-integration. That is precisely what happened to many areas of life in the wake of capitalist modernization. Money and power—more concretely, markets and administrations—take over the integrative functions which were formerly fulfilled by consensual values and norms, or even by processes of reaching understanding. Of course my thesis, which I develop in the second volume of *The Theory of Communicative Action* through a discussion of Parsons' theory of media, is this: that those domains of action which are specialized for the transmission of culture, social integration or the socialization of the young, rely on the medium of communicative action and cannot be integrated through money or power. A commercialization or bureaucratization must therefore generate—this is the thesis—disturbances, pathological side-effects in these domains. But here I am straying from your question about the rights of pluralism.

In your discussion of the structures of domination typical of capitalism, you stress the way in which these act to occlude and suppress "generalizable interests" as opposed to "particular interests" which they themselves covertly represent. You argue that difference between these two kinds of interest can in principle be established by a species of thought-experiment you call "simulated discourse."[23] Could you give an illustration of how this might work? One of the problems the distinction seems to raise is the status of interests that are not generalizable but are nevertheless perfectly valid—in other words, the question of the "natural" heterogeneity of interests, even in socialist society, in which different agents or groups will have a plurality of specific needs or exigencies, all in their own terms quite legitimate—regional, occupational, generational, and so on. How would your proposed model of "discursive will-formation," which appears to put a premium on consensus around generalizable interests, arbitrate conflicting demands of this sort?

The model of repressed generalizable interests is of course only a proposal for a way of criticizing interests which unjustly pass themselves off as general interests. This goal is also pursued by Marx in his critique of bourgeois legal forms, or in his critique of the doctrines of Smith and Ricardo. The model which I propose is designed to demonstrate the non-generalizability of interests which are presumed to be general. For example, an argument which arouses this suspicion today often crops up in social-democratic pronouncements: such and such a stimulus must be given to investment "in order to secure jobs."

Your objection is directed against an assumption which I do not in any way make. In no sense do I begin from the basis that in all, or even in the majority of political decisions, legal or administrative regulations, a general interest is at stake. Modern societies are not like that. Often, maybe in the majority of cases, the social matters which are nowadays regulated through state intervention concern only particular interest-groups. In such cases moral discourse could only have the aim of withdrawing legitimacy from the privileging of one side, which falsely claims to represent a general interest. When only particular interests are at stake, conflicts of action cannot be settled, even in ideal cases, through argumentation, but only through bargaining and compromise. Of course, the *procedures* of reaching compromise must for their part be judged from a normative standpoint. A fair compromise is not to be expected when— for instance—the parties involved do not have at their disposal the same positions of power or capacity to make threats. To give an example: when the complicated question arises of the effects of constitutional rights on third parties, one is entitled to expect that the ruling of the court will be supported by arguments; when it is a matter of the straightforward, but politically delicate question of the location of a nuclear power station, the most that can be expected is that a fair compromise will be arrived at. Compromises are not only widespread as a matter of fact, but also, from the normative standpoint, occupy a position which is not in any way to be despised. This is why I do not have any difficulties with the pluralism of interests. After all, we anticipate that the pluralism of life-forms and the individualism of life-styles would increase at an exponential rate in a society which deserves the name socialist.

One of the novelties of your work as a whole, viewed against the background of classical forms of Marxism, is a shift from "production" to "communication," both as an analytic focus and as a source of value. At the same time, you have always emphasized that you regard yourself as a materialist. Could you specify the terms of the materialism you defend?

Right from my earliest publications I understood "materialism" in the Marxist sense, as a theoretical approach which does not simply affirm the dependence of the superstructure on the base, the life-world on the imperatives of the accumulation process, as an ontological constant, so to speak, but which simultaneously explains and *denounces* this dependence as the latent function of a particular, historically transitory social formation. The transition from a production to a communication paradigm, which I advocate, does of course mean that the critical theory of society must no longer rely on the normative contents of the expressivist model of alienation and reappropriation of essential powers. The young Marx borrowed this model from the production aesthetics of Kant, Schiller and Hegel. The paradigm-shift from purposive activity to communicative action does not mean, however, that I am willing or bound to abandon the material reproduction of the life-world as the privileged point of reference for analysis. I continue to explain the selective model of capitalist modernization, and the corresponding pathologies of a one-sidedly rationalized life-world, in terms of a capitalist accumulation process which is largely disconnected from orientations towards use-value.

How far does the emergence of ecology, as a theory and a movement, qualify your earlier view that there is "only one theoretically fruitful attitude towards nature"—that informed by an interest in technical control?

The awareness of ecological cycles, of biotopes, of human-environment systems has certainly brought forward new themes, new questions, perhaps even new disciplines. As far as I can tell, however, from the methodological point of view these ecologically inspired investigations move entirely within the inherited framework. So far nothing seems to suggest that alternative natural sciences can be developed in a non-objectifying attitude, for example in the performative attitude of a partner in communication—theories in the tradition of the romantic or alchemistic philosophies of nature.

Notes

[1] "Introduction," in R. J. Bernstein, ed., *Habermas and Modernity*, Oxford 1985, pp. 1–32.
[2] *Philosophical-Political Profiles*, London 1983, p. 8.
[3] *Theorie des Kommunikativen Handelns*, II, Frankfurt 1981, p. 491.
[4] *AestheticTheory.* London 1984, pp. 69–70 (translation modified).
[5] L. v. Friedeburg, J. Habermas, eds., *Adorno-Konferenz 1983*, Frankfurt 1983, pp. 138 ff.
[6] Ibid., p. 150.
[7] "Modernity versus Post-Modernity," *New German Critique* No. 22, Winter 1981, p. 13. Reprinted as "Modernity—an Incomplete Project," in Hal Foster, ed., *Postmodern Culture*, London 1985, p. 14.
[8] "Diskursethik—Notizen zu cinem Begründungsprogramm," in *Moralbewusstsein und kommunikatives Handeln*, Frankfurt 1983, pp. 53–125.
[9] *Philosophical-Political Profiles*, pp. 1–2.
[10] *Knowledge and Human Interests*, London 1978, pp. 360–366.
[11] *Knowledge and Human Interests*, p. 21.
[12] *Knowledge and Human Interests*, p. 253.
[13] *Zur Rekonstruktion des historischen Materialismus*, Frankfurt 1976, pp. 204, 207.
[14] *The Theory of Communicative Action*, I, London 1984, p. 44.
[15] *The Theory of Communicative Action*, I, p. 73.
[16] *Legitimation Crisis*, London 1976, pp. 175–177.
[17] *Philosophical-Political Profiles*, pp. 115–158; *Knowledge and Human Interests*, p. 314.
[18] *Knowledge and Human Interests*, p. 378; *Theory and Practice*, London 1974, p. 23.
[19] *Communication and the Evolution of Society*, London 1979, p. 93.
[20] *Theorie des kommunikativen Handelns*, 11, p. 586.
[21] *On Liberty*, Harmondsworth 1982, p. 106; *Strukturwandel der Öffentlichkeit*, Neuwied 1962, p. 150.
[22] "A Reply to My Critics," in J. Thompson and D. Held, eds., *Habermas—Critical Debates*, London 1982, p. 235.
[23] *Legitimation Crisis*, p. 117.

16

LANGUAGE
TEACHING NEW WORLDS/
NEW WORDS

bell hooks

Like desire, language disrupts, refuses to be contained within boundaries. It speaks itself against our will, in words and thoughts that intrude, even violate the most private spaces of mind and body. It was in my first year of college that I read Adrienne Rich's poem, "The Burning of Paper Instead of Children." That poem, speaking against domination, against racism and class oppression, attempts to illustrate graphically that stopping the political persecution and torture of living beings is a more vital issue than censorship, than burning books. One line of this poem that moved and disturbed something within me: "This is the oppressor's language yet I need it to talk to you." I've never forgotten it. Perhaps I could not have forgotten it even if I tried to erase it from memory. Words impose themselves, take root in our memory against our will. The words of this poem begat a life in my memory that I could not abort or change.

When I find myself thinking about language now, these words are there, as if they were always waiting to challenge and assist me. I find myself silently speaking them over and over again with the intensity of a chant. They startle me, shaking me into an awareness of the link between languages and domination. Initially, I resist the idea of the "oppressor's language," certain that this construct has the potential to disempower those of us who are just learning to speak, who are just learning to claim language as a place where we make ourselves subject. *"This is the oppressor's language yet I need it to talk to you."* Adrienne Rich's words. Then, when I first read these words, and now, they make me think of standard English, of learning to speak against black vernacular, against the ruptured and broken speech of a dispossessed and displaced people. Standard English is not the speech of exile. It is the language of conquest and domination; in the United States, it is the mask which hides the loss of so many tongues, all those sounds of diverse, native communities we will never hear, the speech of the Gullah, Yiddish, and so many other unremembered tongues.

Reflecting on Adrienne Rich's words, I know that it is not the English language that hurts me, but what the oppressors do with it, how they shape it to become a territory that limits and defines, how they make it a weapon that can shame, humiliate, colo7nize. Gloria Anzaldúa reminds us of this pain in *Borderlands/La Frontera* when she asserts, "So, if you want to really hurt me, talk badly about my language." We have so little knowledge of how displaced, enslaved, or free Africans who came or were brought against their will to the United States felt about the loss of language, about learning English. Only as a woman did I begin to think about these black people in relation to language, to think about their trauma as they were compelled to witness their language rendered meaningless with a colonizing European culture, where voices deemed foreign could not be spoken, were outlawed tongues, renegade speech. When I realize how long it has taken for white Americans to acknowledge diverse languages of Native Americans, to accept that the speech their ancestral colonizers declared was merely grunts or gibberish was indeed *language*, it is difficult not to hear in standard English always the sound of slaughter and conquest. I think now of the grief of displaced "homeless" Africans, forced to inhabit a world where they saw folks like themselves, inhabiting the same skin, the same condition, but who had no shared language to talk with one another, who needed "the oppressor's language." *"This is the oppressor's language yet I need it to talk to you."* When I imagine the terror of Africans on board slave ships, on auction blocks, inhabiting the unfamiliar architecture of plantations, I consider that this terror extended beyond fear of punishment, that it resided also in the anguish of hearing a language they could not comprehend. The very sound of English had to terrify. I think of black people meeting one another in a space away from the diverse cultures and languages that distinguished them from one another, compelled by circumstance to find ways to speak with one another in a "new world" where blackness or the darkness of one's skin and not language would become the space of bonding. How to remember, to re-invoke this terror. How to describe what it must have been like for Africans whose deepest bonds were historically forged in the place of shared speech to be transported abruptly to a world where the very sound of one's mother tongue had no meaning.

I imagine them hearing spoken English as the oppressor's language, yet I imagine them also realizing that this language would need to be possessed, taken, claimed as a space of resistance. I imagine that the moment they realized the oppressor's language, seized and spoken by the tongues of the colonized, could be a space of bonding was joyous. For in that recognition was the understanding that intimacy could be restored, that a culture of resistance could be formed that would make recovery from the trauma of enslavement possible. I imagine, then, Africans first hearing English as "the oppressor's language" and then re-hearing it as a potential site of resistance. Learning English, learning to speak the alien tongue, was one way enslaved Africans began to reclaim their personal power within a context of domination. Possessing a shared language, black folks could find again a way to make community, and a means to create the political solidarity necessary to resist.

Needing the oppressor's language to speak with one another they nevertheless also reinvented, remade that language so that it would speak beyond the boundaries of conquest and domination. In the mouths of black Africans in the so-called "New World," English was altered, transformed, and became a different speech. Enslaved black people took broken bits of English and made of them a counter-language. They put together their words in such a way that the colonizer had to rethink the meaning of English language. Though it has become common in contemporary culture to talk about the messages of resistance that emerged in the music created by slaves, particularly spirituals, less is said about the grammatical construction of sentences in these songs. Often, the English used in the song reflected the broken, ruptured world of the slave. When the slaves sang "nobody knows de trouble I see—" their use of the word "nobody" adds a richer meaning than if they had used the phrase "no one," for it was the slave's *body* that was the concrete site of suffering. And even as emancipated black people sang spirituals, they did not change the language, the sentence structure, of our ancestors. For in the incorrect usage of words, in the incorrect placement of words, was a spirit of rebellion that claimed language as a site of resistance. Using English in a way that ruptured standard usage and meaning, so that white folks could often not understand black speech, made English into more than the oppressor's language.

An unbroken connection exists between the broken English of the displaced, enslaved African and the diverse black vernacular speech black folks use today. In both cases, the rupture of standard English enabled and enables rebellion and resistance. By transforming the oppressor's language, making a culture of resistance, black people created an intimate speech that could say far more than was permissible within the boundaries of standard English. The power of this speech is not simply that it enables resistance to white supremacy, but that it also forges a space for alternative cultural production and alternative epistemologies—different ways of thinking and knowing that were crucial to creating a counter-hegemonic worldview. It is absolutely essential that the revolutionary power of black vernacular speech not be lost in contemporary culture. That power resides in the capacity of black vernacular to intervene on the boundaries and limitations of standard English.

In contemporary black popular culture, rap music has become one of the spaces where black vernacular speech is used in a manner that invites dominant mainstream culture to listen—to hear—and, to some extent, be transformed. However, one of the risks of this attempt at cultural translation is that it will trivialize black vernacular speech. When young white kids imitate this speech in ways that suggest it is the speech of those who are stupid or who are only interested in entertaining or being funny, then the subversive power of this speech is undermined. In academic circles, both in the sphere of teaching and that of writing, there has been little effort made to utilize black vernacular—or, for that matter, any language other than standard English. When I asked an ethnically diverse group of students in a course I was teaching on black women writers why we only heard standard English spoken in the classroom, they were momentarily rendered speechless. Though many of them were individuals for whom standard English was a second or third language, it had simply never occurred to them that it was possible to say something in another language, in another way. No wonder, then, that we continue to think, "This is the oppressor's language yet I need it to talk to you."

I have realized that I was in danger of losing my relationship to black vernacular speech because I too rarely use it in the predominantly white settings that I am most often in, both professionally and socially. And so I have begun to work at integrating into a variety of settings the particular Southern black vernacular speech I grew up hearing and speaking. It has been hardest to integrate black vernacular in writing, particularly for academic journals. When I first began to incorporate black vernacular in critical essays, editors would send the work back to me in standard English. Using the vernacular means that translation into standard English may be needed if one wishes to reach a more inclusive audience. In the classroom setting, I encourage students to use their first language and translate it so they do not feel that seeking higher education will necessarily estrange them from that language and culture they know most intimately. Not surprisingly, when students in my Black Women Writers class began to speak using diverse language and speech, white students often complained. This seemed to be particularly the case with black vernacular. It was particularly disturbing to the white students because they could hear the words that were said but could not comprehend their meaning. Pedagogically, I encouraged them to think of the moment of not understanding what someone says as a space to learn. Such a space provides not only the opportunity to listen without "mastery," without owning or possessing speech through interpretation, but also the experience of hearing non-English words. These lessons seem particularly crucial in a multicultural society that remains white supremacist, that uses standard English as a weapon to silence and censor. June Jordan reminds us of this in *On Call* when she declares:

I am talking about majority problems of language in a democratic state, problems of a currency that someone has stolen and hidden away and then homogenized into an official "English" language that can only express nonevents involving nobody responsible, or lies. If we lived in a democratic state our language would have to hurtle, fly, curse, and sing, in all the common American names, all the undeniable and representative participating voices of everybody here. We would not tolerate the language of the powerful and, thereby, lose all respect for words, per se. We would make our language conform to the truth of our many selves and we would make our language lead us into the equality of power that a democratic state must represent.

That the students in the course on black women writers were repressing all longing to speak in tongues other than standard English without seeing this repression as political was an indication of the way we act unconsciously, in complicity with a culture of domination.

Recent discussions of diversity and multiculturalism tend to downplay or ignore the question of language. Critical feminist writings focused on issues of difference and voice have made important theoretical interventions, calling for a recognition of the primacy of voices that are often silenced, censored, or marginalized. This call for the acknowledgment and celebration of diverse voices, and consequently of diverse language and speech, necessarily disrupts the primacy of standard English. When advocates of feminism first spoke about the desire for diverse participation in women's movement, there was no discussion of language. It was simply assumed that standard English would remain the primary vehicle for the transmission of feminist thought. Now that the audience for feminist writing and speaking has become more diverse, it is evident that we must change conventional ways of thinking about language, creating spaces where diverse voices can speak in words other than English or in broken, vernacular speech. This means that at a lecture or even in a written work there will be fragments of speech that may or may not be accessible to every individual. Shifting how we think about language and how we use it necessarily alters how we know what we know. At a lecture where I might use Southern black vernacular, the particular patois of my region, or where I might use very abstract thought in conjunction with plain speech, responding to a diverse audience, I suggest that we do not necessarily need to hear and know what is stated in its entirety, that we do not need to "master" or conquer the narrative as a whole, that we may know in fragments. I suggest that we may learn from spaces of silence as well as spaces of speech, that in the patient act of listening to another tongue we may subvert that culture of capitalist frenzy and consumption that demands all desire must be satisfied immediately, or we may disrupt that cultural imperialism that suggests one is worthy of being heard only if one speaks in standard English.

Adrienne Rich concludes her poem with this statement:

I am composing on the typewriter late at night, thinking of today. How well we all spoke. A language is a map of our failures. Frederick Douglass wrote an English purer than Milton's. People suffer highly in poverty. There are methods but we do not use them. Joan, who could not read, spoke some peasant form of French. Some of the suffering are: it is hard to tell the truth; this is America; I cannot touch you now. In America we have only the present tense. I am in danger. You are in danger. The burning of a book arouses no sensation in me. I know it hurts to burn. There are flames of napalm in Cantonsville, Maryland. I know it hurts to burn. The typewriter is overheated, my mouth is burning, I cannot touch you and this is the oppressor's language.

To recognize that we touch one another in language seems particularly difficult in a society that would have us believe that there is no dignity in the experience of passion, that to feel deeply is to be inferior, for within the dualism of Western metaphysical thought, ideas are always more important than language. To heal the splitting of mind and body, we marginalized and oppressed people attempt to recover ourselves and our experiences in language. We seek to make a place for intimacy. Unable to find such a place in standard English, we create the ruptured, broken, unruly speech of the vernacular. When I need to say words that do more than simply mirror or address the dominant reality, I speak black vernacular. There, in that location, we make English do what we want it to do. We take the oppressor's language and turn it against itself. We make our words a counter-hegemonic speech, liberating ourselves in language.

17

REFLECTIONS ON
RACE AND SEX

bell hooks

Race and sex have always been overlapping discourses in the United States. That discourse began in slavery. The talk then was not about black men wanting to be free so that they would have access to the bodies of white women—that would come later. Then, black women's bodies were the discursive terrain, the playing fields where racism and sexuality converged. Rape as both right and rite of the white male dominating group was a cultural norm. Rape was also an apt metaphor for European imperialist colonization of Africa and North America.

Sexuality has always provided gendered metaphors for colonization. Free countries equated with free men, domination with castration, the loss of manhood, and rape—the terrorist act re-enacting the drama of conquest, as men of the dominating group sexually violate the bodies of women who are among the dominated. The intent of this act was to continually remind dominated men of their loss of power; rape was a gesture of symbolic castration. Dominated men are made powerless (i.e., impotent) over and over again as the women they would have had the right to possess, to control, to assert power over, to dominate, to fuck, are fucked and fucked over by the dominating victorious male group.

There is no psychosexual history of slavery that explores the meaning of white male sexual exploitation of black women or the politics of sexuality, no

From *Yearning: Race, Gender, and Cultural Politics* (1990). Boston: South End Press, pp. 57–64.

work that lays out all the available information. There is no discussion of sexual sado-masochism, of the master who forced his wife to sleep on the floor as he nightly raped a black woman in bed. There is no discussion of sexual voyeurism. And what were the sexual lives of white men like who were legally declared "insane" because they wanted to marry black slave women with whom they were sexually and romantically involved? Under what conditions did sexuality serve as a force subverting and disrupting power relations, unsettling the oppressor/oppressed paradigm? No one seems to know how to tell this story, where to begin. As historical narrative it was long ago supplanted by the creation of another story (pornographic sexual project, fantasy, fear, the origin has yet to be traced). That story, invented by white men, is about the overwhelming desperate longing black men have to sexually violate the bodies of white women. The central character in this story is the black male rapist. Black men are constructed, as Michael Dyson puts it, as "peripatetic phalluses with unrequited desire for their denied object—white women." As the story goes, this desire is not based on longing for sexual pleasure. It is a story of revenge, rape as the weapon by which black men, the dominated, reverse their circumstance, regain power over white men.

Oppressed black men and women have rarely challenged the use of gendered metaphors to describe the impact of racist domination and/or black liberation struggle. The discourse of black resistance has almost always equated freedom with manhood, the economic and material domination of black men with castration, emasculation. Accepting these sexual metaphors forged a bond between oppressed black men and their white male oppressors. They shared the patriarchal belief that revolutionary struggle was really about the erect phallus, the ability of men to establish political dominance that could correspond to sexual dominance. Careful critical examination of black power literature in the sixties and early seventies exposes the extent to which black women and men were using sexualized metaphors to talk about the effort to resist racist domination. Many of us have never forgotten that moment in *Soul on Ice* when Eldridge Cleaver, writing about the need to "redeem my conquered manhood," described raping black women as practice for the eventual rape of white women. Remember that readers were not shocked or horrified by this glamorization of rape as a weapon of terrorism men might use to express rage about other forms of domination, about their struggle for power with other men. Given the sexist context of the culture, it made sense. Cleaver was able to deflect attention away from the misogynist sexism of his assertions by poignantly justifying these acts as a "natural" response to racial domination. He wanted to force readers to confront the agony and suffering black men experience in a white supremacist society. Again, freedom from racial domination was expressed in terms of redeeming black masculinity. And gaining the right to assert one's manhood was always about sexuality.

During slavery, there was perhaps a white male who created his own version of *Soul on Ice*, one who confessed how good it felt to assert racial dominance

over black people, and particularly black men, by raping black women with impunity, or how sexually stimulating it was to use the sexual exploitation of black
women to humiliate and degrade white women, to assert phallocentric domination in one's household. Sexism has always been a political stance mediating racial domination, enabling white men and black men to share a common
sensibility about sex roles and the importance of male domination. Clearly both
groups have equated freedom with manhood, and manhood with the right of
men to have indiscriminate access to the bodies of women. Both groups have
been socialized to condone patriarchal affirmation of rape as an acceptable way
to maintain male domination. It is this merging of sexuality with male domination within patriarchy that informs the construction of masculinity for men of all
races and classes. Robin Morgan's book, *The Demon Lover: On The Sexuality of
Terrorism*, begins with rape. She analyses the way men are bonded across class,
race, and nationalities through shared notions of manhood which make masculinity synonymous with the ability to assert power-over through acts of violence
and terrorism. Since terrorist acts are most often committed by men, Morgan
sees the terrorist as "the logical incarnation of patriarchal politics in a technological world." She is not concerned with the overlapping discourses of race and
sex, with the interconnectedness of racism and sexism. Like many radical feminists, she believes that male commitment to maintaining patriarchy and male
domination diminishes or erases difference.

Much of my work within feminist theory has stressed the importance of
understanding difference, of the ways race and class status determine the degree to which one can assert male domination and privilege and most impor-
tantly the ways racism and sexism are interlocking systems of domination
which uphold and sustain one another. Many feminists continue to see them
as completely separate issues, believing that sexism can be abolished while
racism remains intact, or that women who work to resist racism are not supporting feminist movement. Since black liberation struggle is so often framed
in terms that affirm and support sexism, it is not surprising that white women
are uncertain about whether women's rights struggle will be diminished if
there is too much focus on resisting racism, or that many black women continue to fear that they will be betraying black men if they support feminist
movement. Both these fears are responses to the equation of black liberation
with manhood. This continues to be a central way black people frame our efforts to resist racist domination; it must be critiqued. We must reject the sexualization of black liberation in ways that support and perpetuate sexism,
phallocentrism, and male domination. Even though Michele Wallace tried to
expose the fallacy of equating black liberation with the assertion of oppressive
manhood in *Black Macho and the Myth of the Superwoman*, few black people
got the message. Continuing this critique in *Ain't I A Woman: Black Women
and Feminism*, I found that more and more black women were rejecting this
paradigm. It has yet to be rejected by most black men, and especially black
male political figures. As long as black people hold on to the idea that the
trauma of racist domination is really the loss of black manhood, then we invest

in the racist narratives that perpetuate the idea that all black men are rapists, eager to use sexual terrorism to express their rage about racial domination.

Currently we are witnessing a resurgence of such narratives. They are re-surfacing at a historical moment when black people are bearing the brunt of more overt and blatant racist assaults, when black men and especially young black men are increasingly disenfranchised by society. Mainstream white su-premacist media make it appear that a black menace to societal safety is at large, that control, repression, and violent domination are the only effective ways to address the problem. Witness the use of the Willie Horton case to discredit Dukakis in the 1988 Presidential election. Susan Estrich in her post-campaign articles has done a useful job of showing how racist stereo-types were evoked to turn voters against Dukakis, and how Bush in no way denounced this strategy. In all her articles she recounts the experience of be-ing raped by a black man fifteen years ago, describing the way racism deter-mined how the police responded to the crime, and her response. Though her intent is to urge societal commitment to anti-racist struggle, every article I have read has carried captions in bold print emphasizing the rape. The sub-versive content of her work is undermined and the stereotype that all black men are rapists is re-inscribed and reinforced. Most people in this society do not realize that the vast majority of rapes are not inter-racial, that all groups of men are more likely to rape women who are the same race as themselves.

Within popular culture, Madonna's video "Like a Prayer" also makes use of imagery which links black men with rape, reinforcing this representa-tion in the minds of millions of viewers—even though she has said that her intention is to be anti-racist, and certainly the video suggests that not all black men who are accused of raping white women are guilty. Once again, however, this subversive message is undermined by the overall focus on sex-ually charged imagery of white female sexuality and black male lust. The most subversive message in the video has nothing to do with anti-racism; it has to do with the construction of white females as desiring subjects who can freely assert sexual agency. Of course the taboo expression of that agency is choosing to be sexual with black men. Unfortunately this is a continuation of the notion that ending racist domination is really about issues of interracial sexual access, a myth that must be critiqued so that this society can confront the actual material, economic, and moral consequences of perpetuating white supremacy and its traumatic genocidal impact on black people.

Images of black men as rapists, as dangerous menaces to society, have been sensational cultural currency for some time. The obsessive media focus on these representations is political. The role it plays in the maintenance of racist domination is to convince the public that black men are a dangerous threat who must be controlled by any means necessary, including annihila-tion. This is the cultural backdrop shaping media response to the Central Park rape case, and the media has played a major role in shaping public re-sponse. Many people are using this case to perpetuate racial stereotypes and racism. Ironically, the very people who claim to be shocked by the brutality of this case have no qualms about suggesting that the suspects should be castrated or killed. They see no link between this support of violence as a means of social control and the suspects' use of violence to exercise control. Public response to this case highlights the lack of understanding about the interconnectedness of racism and sexism.

Many black people, especially black men, using the sexist paradigm that suggests rape of white women by black men is a reaction to racist domination, view the Central Park case as an indictment of the racist system. They do not see sexism as informing the nature of the crime, the choice of victim. Many white women have responded to the case by focusing solely on the brutal assault as an act of gender domination, of male violence against women. A piece in the *Village Voice* written by white female Andrea Kannapell carried captions in bold print which began with the statement in all capitals for greater emphasis, "THE CRIME WAS MORE SEXIST THAN RACIST. . . " Black women responding to the same issue all focused on the sexist nature of the crime, often giving examples of black male sexism. Given the work black women have done within feminist writing to call attention to the reality of black male sexism, work that often receives little or no attention or is accused of attacking black men, it is ironic that the brutal rape of a white woman by a group of young black males serves as the catalyst for admission that sexism is a serious problem in black communities. Lisa Kennedy's piece, "Body Double: The Anatomy of a Crime," also published in the *Village Voice*, acknowledges the convergence of racism and sexism as politics of domination that inform this assault. Kennedy writes:

> If I accept the premise of the coverage, that this rape is more heartbreaking than all the rapes that happen to women of color, then what happens to the value of my body? What happens to the quality of my blackness?

These questions remain unanswered, though she closes with "a call for a sophisticated feminist offensive." Such an offensive should begin with cultivating critical awareness of the way racism and sexism are interlocking systems of domination.

Public response to the Central Park case reveals the extent to which the culture invests in the kind of dualistic thinking that helps reinforce and maintain all forms of domination. Why must people decide whether this crime is more sexist than racist, as if these are competing oppressions? Why do white people, and especially feminist white women, feel better when black people, especially black women, disassociate themselves from the plight of black men in white supremacist capitalist patriarchy to emphasize opposition to black male sexism? Cannot black women remain seriously concerned about the brutal effect of racist domination on black men and also denounce black male sexism? And why is black male sexism evoked as though it is a special brand of this social disorder, more dangerous, more abhorrent and life-threatening than the sexism that pervades the culture as a whole, or the sexism that informs white male domination of women? These questions call attention to the either/or ways of thinking that are the philosophical underpinning of systems of domination. Progressive folks must then insist, wherever we engage in discussions of this crime or of issues of race and gender, on the complexity of our experience in a racist sexist society.

The Central Park crime involves aspects of sexism, male domination, misogyny, and the use of rape as an instrument of terror. It also involves race and racism; it is unlikely that young black males growing up in this society, attacking a white woman, would see her as "just a woman"—her race would be foremost in their consciousness as well as her sex, in the same way that masses of people hearing about this crime were concerned with identifying first her race. In a white supremacist sexist society all women's bodies are devalued, but white women's bodies are more valued than those of women of color. Given the context of white supremacy, the historical narratives about black male rapists, the racial identities of both victim and victimizers enable this tragedy to be sensationalized.

To fully understand the multiple meanings of this incident, it must be approached from an analytical standpoint that considers the impact of sexism and racism. Beginning there enables many of us to empathize with both the victim and the victimizers. If one reads *The Demon Lover* and thinks again about this crime, one can see it as part of a continuum of male violence against women, of rape and terror as weapons of male domination—yet another horrific and brutal expression of patriarchal socialization. And if one considers this case by combining a feminist analysis of race and masculinity, one sees that since male power within patriarchy is relative, men from poorer groups and men of color are not able to reap the material and social rewards for their participation in patriarchy. In fact they often suffer from blindly and passively acting out a myth of masculinity that is life-threatening. Sexist thinking blinds them to this reality. They become victims of the patriarchy. No one can truly believe that the young black males involved in the Central Park incident were not engaged in a suicidal ritual enactment of a dangerous masculinity that will ultimately threaten their lives, their well-being.

If one reads again Michael Dyson's piece "The Plight of Black Men," focusing especially on the part where he describes the reason many young black men form gangs—"the sense of absolute belonging and unsurpassed love"—it is easy to understand why young black males are despairing and nihilistic. And it is rather naive to think that if they do not value their own lives, they will value the lives of others. Is it really so difficult for folks to see the connection between the constant pornographic glorification of male violence against women that is represented, enacted, and condoned daily in the culture and the Central Park crime? Does racism create and maintain this blindspot or does it allow black people and particularly black men to become the scapegoats, embodying society's evils?

If we are to live in a less violent and more just society, then we must engage in anti-sexist and anti-racist work. We desperately need to explore and understand the connections between racism and sexism. And we need to teach everyone about those connections so that they can be critically aware and socially active. Much education for critical consciousness can take place in everyday conversations. Black women and men must participate in the construction of feminist thinking, creating models for feminist struggle that address the particular circumstances of black people. Still, the most visionary task of all remains that of re-conceptualizing masculinity so that alternative, transformative models are there in the culture, in our daily lives, to help boys and men who are working to construct a self, to build new identities. Black liberation struggle must be re-visioned so that it is no longer equated with maleness. We need a revolutionary vision of black liberation, one that emerges from a feminist standpoint and addresses the collective plight of black people.

Any individual committed to resisting politics of domination, to eradicating sexism and racism, understands the importance of not promoting an either/or competition between the oppressive systems. We can empathize with the victim and the victimizers in the Central Park case, allowing that feeling to serve as a catalyst for renewed commitment to anti-sexist and anti-racist work. Yesterday I heard this story. A black woman friend called to say that she had been attacked on the street by a black man. He took her purse, her house keys, her car keys. She lives in one of the poorest cities in the United States. We talked about poverty, sexism, and racial domination to place what had happened in a perspective that will enable both individual healing and political understanding of this crime. Today I heard this story. A white woman friend called to say that she had been attacked in her doorway by a black man. She screamed and he ran away. Neighbors coming to her aid invoked racism. She refused to engage in this discussion even though she was shocked by the intensity and degree of racism expressed. Even in the midst of her own fear and pain, she remained politically aware, so as not to be complicit in perpetuating the white supremacy that is the root of so much suffering. Both of these women feel rage at their victimizers; they do not absolve them even as they seek to understand and to respond in ways that will enrich the struggle to end domination—so that sexism, sexist violence, racism, and racist violence will cease to be an everyday happening.

18

CHOOSING THE MARGIN AS A SPACE OF RADICAL OPENNESS

bell hooks

As a radical standpoint, perspective, position, "the politics of location" necessarily calls those of us who would participate in the formation of counter-hegemonic cultural practice to identify the spaces where we begin the process of re-vision. When asked, "What does it mean to enjoy reading *Beloved*, admire *Schooldaze*, and have a theoretical interest in post-structuralist theory?" (one of the "wild" questions posed by the Third World Cinema Focus Forum), I located my answer concretely in the realm of oppositional political struggle. Such diverse pleasures can be experienced, enjoyed even, because one transgresses, moves "out of one's place." For many of us, that movement requires pushing against oppressive boundaries set by race, sex, and class domination. Initially, then, it is a defiant political gesture. Moving, we confront the realities of choice and location. Within complex and ever shifting realms of power relations, do we position ourselves on the side of colonizing mentality? Or do we continue to stand in political resistance with the oppressed, ready to offer our ways of seeing and theorizing, of making culture, towards that revolutionary effort which seeks to create space where there is unlimited access to the pleasure and power of

From *Yearning: Race, Gender, and Cultural Politics* (1990). Boston: South End Press, pp. 145–153.

knowing, where transformation is possible? This choice is crucial. It shapes and determines our response to existing cultural practice and our capacity to envision new, alternative, oppositional aesthetic acts. It informs the way we speak about these issues, the language we choose. Language is also a place of struggle.

To me, the effort to speak about issues of "space and location" evoked pain. The questions raised compelled difficult explorations of "silences"—unaddressed places within my personal political and artistic evolution. Before I could consider answers, I had to face ways these issues were intimately connected to intense personal emotional upheaval regarding place, identity, desire. In an intense all-night-long conversation with Eddie George (member of Black Audio Film Collective) talking about the struggle of oppressed people to come to voice, he made the very "down" comment that "ours is a broken voice." My response was simply that when you hear the broken voice you also hear the pain contained within that brokenness—a speech of suffering; often it's that sound nobody wants to hear. Stuart Hall talks about the need for a "politics of articulation." He and Eddie have engaged in dialogue with me in a deeply soulful way, hearing my struggle for words. It is this dialogue between comrades that is a gesture of love; I am grateful.

I have been working to change the way I speak and write, to incorporate in the manner of telling a sense of place, of not just who I am in the present but where I am coming from, the multiple voices within me. I have confronted silence, inarticulateness. When I say, then, that these words emerge from suffering, I refer to that personal struggle to name that location from which I come to voice—that space of my theorizing.

Often when the radical voice speaks about domination we are speaking to those who dominate. Their presence changes the nature and direction of our words. Language is also a place of struggle. I was just a girl coming slowly into womanhood when I read Adrienne Rich's words, "This is the oppressor's language, yet I need it to talk to you." This language that enabled me to attend graduate school, to write a dissertation, to speak at job interviews, carries the scent of oppression. Language is also a place of struggle. The Australian aborigines say "that smell of the white man is killing us." I remember the smells of my childhood, hot water corn bread, turnip greens, fried pies. I remember the way we talked to one another, our words thickly accented black Southern speech. Language is also a place of struggle. We are wedded in language, have our being in words. Language is also a place of struggle. Dare I speak to oppressed and oppressor in the same voice? Dare I speak to you in a language that will move beyond the boundaries of domination—a language that will not bind you, fence you in, or hold you? Language is also a place of struggle. The oppressed struggle in language to recover ourselves, to reconcile, to reunite, to renew. Our words are not without meaning, they are an action, a resistance. Language is also a place of struggle.

It is no easy task to find ways to include our multiple voices within the various texts we create—in film, poetry, feminist theory. Those are sounds and images that mainstream consumers find difficult to understand. Sounds and scenes which cannot be appropriated are often that sign everyone questions, wants to erase, to "wipe out." I feel it even now, writing this piece when I gave it talking and reading, talking spontaneously, using familiar academic speech now and then, "talking the talk"—using black vernacular speech, the intimate sounds and gestures I normally save for family and loved ones. Private speech in public discourse, intimate intervention, making another text, a space that enables me to recover all that I am in language, I find so many gaps, absences in this written text. To cite them at least is to let the reader know something has been missed, or remains there hinted at by words—there in the deep structure.

Throughout *Freedom Charter*, a work which traces aspects of the movement against racial apartheid in South Africa, this statement is constantly repeated: *our struggle is also a struggle of memory against forgetting*. In much new, exciting cultural practice, cultural texts—in film, black literature, critical theory—there is an effort to remember that is expressive of the need to create spaces where one is able to redeem and reclaim the past, legacies of pain, suffering, and triumph in ways that transform present reality. Fragments of memory are not simply represented as flat documentary but constructed to give a "new take" on the old, constructed to move us into a different mode of articulation. We see this in films like *Dreaming Rivers* and *Illusions*, and in books like *Mama Day* by Gloria Naylor. Thinking again about space and location, I heard the statement "our struggle is also a struggle of memory against forgetting"; a politicization of memory that distinguishes nostalgia, that longing for something to be as once it was, a kind of useless act, from that remembering that serves to illuminate and transform the present.

I have needed to remember, as part of a self-critical process where one pauses to reconsider choices and location, tracing my journey from small town Southern black life, from folk traditions, and church experience to cities, to the university, to neighborhoods that are not racially segregated, to places where I see for the first time independent cinema, where I read critical theory, where I write theory. Along that trajectory, I vividly recall efforts to silence my coming to voice. In my public presentation I was able to tell stories, to share memories. Here again I only hint at them. The opening essay in my book, *Talking Back*, describes my effort to emerge as critical thinker, artist, and writer in a context of repression. I talk about punishment, about mama and daddy aggressively silencing me, about the censorship of black communities. I had no choice. I had to struggle and resist to emerge from that context and then from other locations with mind intact, with an open heart. I had to leave that space I called home to move beyond boundaries, yet I needed also to return there. We sing a song in the black church tradition that says, "I'm going up the rough side of the mountain on my way home." Indeed the very meaning of "home" changes with experience of decolonization, of radicalization. At times, home is nowhere. At times, one knows only extreme estrangement and alienation. Then home is no longer just one place. It is locations. Home is that place which enables and promotes varied and everchanging perspectives, a place where one discovers new ways of seeing reality, frontiers of difference. One confronts and accepts dispersal and fragmentation as part of the construction of a new world order that reveals more fully where we are, who we can become, an order that does not demand forgetting. "Our struggle is also a struggle of memory against forgetting."

This experience of space and location is not the same for black folks who have always been privileged, or for black folks who desire only to move from underclass status to points of privilege; not the same for those of us from poor backgrounds who have had to continually engage in actual political struggle both within and outside black communities to assert an aesthetic and critical presence. Black folks coming from poor, underclass communities, who enter universities or privileged cultural settings unwilling to surrender every vestige of who we were before we were there, all "sign" of our class and cultural "difference," who are unwilling to play the role of "exotic Other," must create spaces within that culture of domination if we are to survive whole, our souls intact. Our very presence is a disruption. We are often as much an "Other," a threat to black people from privileged class backgrounds who do not understand or share our perspectives, as we are to uninformed white folks. Everywhere we go there is pressure to silence our voices, to co-opt and undermine them. Mostly, of course, we are not there. We never "arrive" or "can't stay." Back in those spaces where we come from, we kill ourselves in despair, drowning in nihilism, caught in poverty, in addiction, in every postmodern mode of dying that can be named. Yet when we few remain in that "other" space, we are often too isolated, too alone. We die there, too. Those of us who live, who "make it," passionately holding on to aspects of that "downhome" life we do not intend to lose while simultaneously seeking new knowledge and experience, invent spaces of radical openness. Without such spaces we would not survive. Our living depends on our ability to conceptualize alternatives, often improvised. Theorizing about this experience aesthetically, critically is an agenda for radical cultural practice.

For me this space of radical openness is a margin—a profound edge. Locating oneself there is difficult yet necessary. It is not a "safe" place. One is always at risk. One needs a community of resistance.

In the preface to *Feminist Theory: From Margin to Center*, I expressed these thoughts on marginality:

> To be in the margin is to be part of the whole but outside the main body. As black Americans living in a small Kentucky town, the railroad tracks were a daily reminder of our marginality. Across those tracks were paved streets, stores we could not enter, restaurants we could not eat in, and people we could not look directly in the face. Across those tracks was a world we could work in as maids, as janitors, as prostitutes, as long as it was in a service capacity. We could enter that world but we could

not live there. We had always to return to the margin, to cross the tracks to shacks and abandoned houses on the edge of town.

There were laws to ensure our return. Not to return was to risk being punished. Living as we did—on the edge—we developed a particular way of seeing reality. We looked both from the outside in and from the inside out. We focused our attention on the center as well as on the margin. We understood both. This mode of seeing reminded us of the existence of a whole universe, a main body made up of both margin and center. Our survival depended on an ongoing public awareness of the separation between margin and center and an ongoing private acknowledgement that we were a necessary, vital part of that whole.

This sense of wholeness, impressed upon our consciousness by the structure of our daily lives, provided us with an oppositional world-view—a mode of seeing unknown to most of our oppressors, that sustained us, aided us in our struggle to transcend poverty and despair, strengthened our sense of self and our solidarity.

Though incomplete, these statements identify marginality as much more than a site of deprivation; in fact I was saying just the opposite, that it is also the site of radical possibility, a space of resistance. It was this marginality that I was naming as a central location for the production of a counter-hegemonic discourse that is not just found in words but in habits of being and the way one lives. As such, I was not speaking of a marginality one wishes to lose—to give up or surrender as part of moving into the center—but rather of a site one stays in, clings to even, because it nourishes one's capacity to resist. It offers to one the possibility of radical perspective from which to see and create, to imagine alternatives, new worlds.

This is not a mythic notion of marginality. It comes from lived experience. Yet I want to talk about what it means to struggle to maintain that marginality even as one works, produces, lives, if you will, at the center. I no longer live in that segregated world across the tracks. Central to life in that world was the ongoing awareness of the necessity of opposition. When Bob Marley sings, "We refuse to be what you want us to be, we are what we are, and that's the way it's going to be," that space of refusal, where one can say no to the colonizer, no to the downpressor, is located in the margins. And one can only say no, speak the voice of resistance, because there exists a counter-language. While it may resemble the colonizer's tongue, it has undergone a transformation, it has been irrevocably changed. When I left that concrete space in the margins, I kept alive in my heart ways of knowing reality which affirm continually not only the primacy of resistance but the necessity of a resistance that is sustained by remembrance of the past, which includes recollections of broken tongues giving us ways to speak that decolonize our minds, our very beings. Once mama said to me as I was about to go again to the predominantly white university, "You can take what the white people have to offer, but you do not have to love them." Now understanding her cultural codes, I know that she was not saying to me not to love people of other races. She was speaking about colonization and the reality of what it means to be taught in a culture of domination by those who dominate. She was insisting on my power to be able to separate useful knowledge that I might get from the dominating group from participation in ways of knowing that would lead to estrangement, alienation, and worse—assimilation and co-optation. She was saying that it is not necessary to give yourself over to them to learn. Not having been in those institutions, she knew that I might be faced again and again with situations where I would be "tried," made to feel as though a central requirement of my being accepted would mean participation in this system of exchange to ensure my success, my "making it." She was reminding me of the necessity of opposition and simultaneously encouraging me not to lose that radical perspective shaped and formed by marginality.

Understanding marginality as position and place of resistance is crucial for oppressed, exploited, colonized people. If we only view the margin as sign marking the despair, a deep nihilism penetrates in a destructive way the very ground of our being. It is there in that space of collective despair that one's creativity, one's imagination is at risk, there that one's mind is fully colonized, there that the freedom one longs for is lost. Truly the mind that resists colonization struggles for freedom of expression. The struggle may not even begin with the colonizer; it may begin within one's segregated, colonized community and family. So I want to note that I am not trying to romantically re-inscribe the notion of that space of marginality where the oppressed live apart from their oppressors as "pure." I want to say that these margins have been both sites of repression and sites of resistance. And since we are well able to name the nature of that repression we know better the margin as site of deprivation. We are more silent when it comes to speaking of the margin as site of resistance. We are more often silenced when it comes to speaking of the margin as site of resistance.

Silenced. During my graduate years I heard myself speaking often in the voice of resistance. I cannot say that my speech was welcomed. I cannot say that my speech was heard in such a way that it altered relations between colonizer and colonized. Yet what I have noticed is that those scholars, most especially those who name themselves radical critical thinkers, feminist thinkers, now fully participate in the construction of a discourse about the "Other." I was made "Other" there in that space with them. In that space in the margins, that lived-in segregated world of my past and present. They did not meet me there in that space. They met me at the center. They greeted me as colonizers. I am waiting to learn from them the path of their resistance, of how it came to be that they were able to surrender the power to act as colonizers. I am waiting for them to bear witness, to give testimony. They say that the discourse on marginality, on difference has moved beyond a discussion of "us and them." They do not speak of how this movement has taken place. This is a response from the radical space of my marginality. It is a space of resistance. It is a space I choose.

I am waiting for them to stop talking about the "Other," to stop even describing how important it is to be able to speak about difference. It is not just important what we speak about, but how and why we speak. Often this speech about the "Other" is also a mask, an oppressive talk hiding gaps, absences, that space where our words would be if we were speaking, if there were silence, if we were there. This "we" is that "us" in the margins, that "we" who inhabit marginal space that is not a site of domination but a place of resistance. Enter that space. Often this speech about the "Other" annihilates, erases: "No need to hear your voice when I can talk about you better than you can speak about yourself. No need to hear your voice. Only tell me about your pain. I want to know your story. And then I will tell it back to you in a new way. Tell it back to you in such a way that it has become mine, my own. Re-writing you, I write myself anew. I am still author, authority. I am still the colonizer, the speaking subject, and you are now at the center of my talk." Stop. We greet you as liberators. This "we" is that "us" in the margins, that "we" who inhabit marginal space that is not a site of domination but a place of resistance. Enter that space. This is an intervention. I am writing to you. I am speaking from a place in the margins where I am different, where I see things differently. I am talking about what I see.

Speaking from margins. Speaking in resistance. I open a book. There are words on the back cover, *Never in the Shadows Again*. A book which suggests the possibility of speaking as liberators. Only who is speaking and who is silent. Only who stands in the shadows—the shadow in a doorway, the space where images of black women are represented voiceless, the space where our words are invoked to serve and support, the space of our absence. Only small echoes of protest. We are re-written. We are "Other." We are the margin. Who is speaking and to whom. Where do we locate ourselves and comrades.

Silenced. We fear those who speak about us, who do not speak to us and with us. We know what it is like to be silenced. We know that the forces that silence us, because they never want us to speak, differ from the forces that say speak, tell me your story. Only do not speak in a voice of resistance. Only speak from that space in the margin that is a sign of deprivation, a wound, an unfulfilled longing. Only speak your pain.

This is an intervention. A message from that space in the margin that is a site of creativity and power, that inclusive space where we recover ourselves, where we move in solidarity to erase the category colonized/colonizer. Marginality as site of resistance. Enter that space. Let us meet there. Enter that space. We greet you as liberators.

Spaces can be real and imagined. Spaces can tell stories and unfold histories. Spaces can be interrupted, appropriated, and transformed through artistic and literary practice.

As Pratibha Parma notes, "The appropriation and use of space are political acts."

To speak about that location from which work emerges, I choose familiar politicized language, old codes, words like "struggle, marginality, resistance." I choose these words knowing that they are no longer popular or "cool"—

hold onto them and the political legacies they evoke and affirm, even as I work to change what they say, to give them renewed and different meaning.

I am located in the margin. I make a definite distinction between that marginality which is imposed by oppressive structures and that marginality one chooses as site of resistance—as location of radical openness and possibility. This site of resistance is continually formed in that segregated culture of opposition that is our critical response to domination. We come to this space through suffering and pain, through struggle. We know struggle to be that which pleasures, delights, and fulfills desire. We are transformed, individually, collectively, as we make radical creative space which affirms and sustains our subjectivity, which gives us a new location from which to articulate our sense of the world.

19

TEACHING RESISTANCE
THE RACIAL POLITICS
OF MASS MEDIA

bell hooks

When I began the process of education for critical consciousness to radicalize my thinking and action, I relied on the writings and life practices of Malcolm X, Paulo Freire, Albert Memmi, Frantz Fanon, Amical Cabral, Walter Rodney, and a host of other thinkers. The work of these teachers and political mentors led me to think about the absence of a discourse on colonialism in the United States. When thinking about the kind of language commonly evoked to talk about black experience in white supremacist capitalist patriarchal North America, I was often struck by the pervasive use of euphemisms, words like "Jim Crow," "Uncle Tom," "Miss Ann," etc. These colorful terms obscured the underlying structures of domination that kept white supremacy in place. By socializing white and black citizens in the United States to think of racism in personal terms, individuals could think of it as having more to do with inherent prejudicial feelings than with a consciously mapped-out strategy of domination that was systematically maintained. Even though African Americans in the United States had no country, whites took over and colonized; as a structure of domination that is defined as the conquest and ownership of a people by another, colonialism aptly describes the process by which blacks were and continue to be subordinated by white supremacy.

In the beginning black folks were most effectively colonized via a structure of ownership. Once slavery ended, white supremacy could be effectively maintained by the institutionalization of social apartheid and by creating a philosophy of racial inferiority that would be taught to everyone. This strategy of colonialism needed no country, for the space it sought to own and conquer was the minds of whites and blacks. As long as a harsh brutal system of racial apartheid was in place, separating blacks from whites by laws, coercive structures of punishment, and economic disenfranchisement, many black people seemed to intuitively understand that our ability to resist racist domination was nurtured by a refusal of the colonizing mindset. Segregation enabled black folks to maintain oppositional worldviews and standpoints to counter the effects of racism and to nurture resistance. The effectiveness of those survival strategies was made evident by both civil rights movements and the militant resistance that followed in their wake. This resistance to colonialism was so fierce, a new strategy was required to maintain and perpetuate white supremacy. Racial integration was that strategy. It was the setting for the emergence of neo-colonial white supremacy.

Placed in positions of authority in educational structures and on the job, white people could oversee and eradicate organized resistance. The new neo-colonial environment gave white folks even greater access and control over the African-American mind. Integrated educational structures were the locations where whites could best colonize the minds and imaginations of black folks. Television and mass media were the other great neo-colonial weapons. Contemporary African Americans often ponder how it is possible for the spirit of resistance to be so diminished today even though the structures of our lives continue to be shaped and informed by the dictates of white supremacy. The spirit of resistance that remained strong from slavery to the militant sixties was displaced when whites made it seem as though they were truly ready to grant black folks social equality, that there were indeed enough resources to go around, that the imperialist wealth of this country could be equitably shared. These assumptions were easy to believe given the success of sixties black militant struggle. By the time the bubble burst, collectively black folks had let our guard down and a more insidious colonization of our minds began to take place. While the Eurocentric biases taught to blacks in the educational system were meant to socialize us to believe in our inherent inferiority, it was ultimately the longing to have access to material rewards granted whites (the luxury and comfort represented in advertising and television) that was the greatest seduction. Aping whites, assimilating their values (i.e., white supremacist attitudes and assumptions) was clearly the way to achieve material success. And white supremacist values were projected into our living rooms, into the most intimate spaces of our lives by mass media. Gone was any separate space apart from whites where organized militant resistance could emerge. Even though most black communities were and remain segregated, mass media bring white supremacy into our lives, constantly reminding us of our marginalized status.

With the television on, whites were and are always with us, their voices, values, and beliefs echoing in our brains. It is this constant presence of the colonizing mindset passively consumed that undermines our capacity to resist white supremacy by cultivating oppositional worldviews. Even though most African Americans do not identify with the experiences of whites in real life or have intimate relationships with them, these boundaries are crossed when we sit facing the television. When television was first invented and many black folks could not afford TVs or did not have the luxury of time to consume representations of whiteness all day long, a barrier still existed between the value system of the dominant white culture and the values of most black folks. That barrier was torn down when televisions entered every living room. Movies function in a similar way. Not surprising, when black Americans were denied easy access to white movies, black cinema thrived. Once the images of whiteness were available to everyone there was no black movie-going audience starving for black images. The hunger to see black folks on the screen had been replaced by the desire to be close to the Hollywood image, to whiteness. No studies have been done that I know of which look at the role mass media have played since 1960 in perpetuating and maintaining the values of white supremacy. Constantly and passively consuming white supremacist values both in educational systems and via prolonged engagement with mass media, contemporary black folks, and everyone else in this society, are vulnerable to a process of overt colonization that goes easily undetected. Acts of blatant racism are rarely represented in mass-media images. Most television shows suggest via the liberal dialogues that occur between white characters, or racially integrated casts, that racism no longer serves as a barrier. Even though there are very few black judges in the United States, television courtroom dramas cast black characters in these roles in ways so disproportionate to the reality that it is almost ludicrous. Yet the message sent to the American public and folks all over the world watching American TV is that our legal system has triumphed over racial discrimination, that not only is there social equality but that black folks are often the ones in power. I know of no studies that have examined the role television has played in teaching white viewers that racism no longer exists. Many white folks who never have intimate contact with black folks now feel that they know what we are like because television has brought us into their homes. Whites may well believe that our presence on the screen and in their intimate living spaces means that the racial apartheid that keeps neighborhoods and schools segregated is the false reflection and that what we see on television represents the real.

Currently black folks are often depicted on television in situations where they charge racist victimization and then the viewer is bombarded with evidence that shows this to be a trumped-up charge, that whites are indeed far more caring and able to be social equals than "misguided" blacks realize. The message that television sends then is that the problem of racism lies with black people—that it exists in our minds and imaginations. On a recent episode of

Law and Order a white lawyer directs anger at a black woman and tells her, "If you want to see the cause of racism, look in the mirror." Television does not hold white people responsible for white supremacy; it socializes them to believe that subjugation and subordination of black people by any means necessary is essential for the maintenance of law and order. Such thinking informed the vision of white folks who looked at the tape showing the brutal beating of Rodney King by a group of white men and saw a scenario where he was threatening white lives and they were merely keeping the peace.

Movies also offer us the vision of a world where white folks are liberal, eager to be social equals with blacks. The message of films like *Grand Canyon, Lethal Weapon, The Bodyguard*, and a host of other Hollywood films is that whites and blacks live together in harmony. Contemporary Hollywood films that show strife between races situate the tension around criminal behavior where black characters may exist as good or bad guys in the traditional racist cowboy scenario but where most whites, particularly heroic ones, are presented as capable of transcending the limitations of race.

For the most part television and movies depict a world where blacks and whites coexist in harmony although the subtext is clear; this harmony is maintained because no one really moves from the location white supremacy allocates to them on the race-sex hierarchy. Denzel Washington and Julia Roberts may play opposite one another in *The Pelican Brief* but there will not be a romance. True love in television and movies is almost always an occurrence between those who share the same race. When love happens across boundaries as in *The Bodyguard, Zebrahead*, or *A Bronx Tale*, it is doomed for no apparent reason and/or has tragic consequences. White and black people learning lessons from mass media about racial bonding are taught that curiosity about those who are racially different can be expressed as long as boundaries are not actually crossed and no genuine intimacy emerges. Many television viewers of all races and ethnicities were enchanted by a series called *I'll Fly Away* which highlighted a liberal white family's struggle in the South and the perspective of the black woman who works as a servant in their home. Even though the series is often centered on the maid, her status is never changed or challenged. Indeed she is one of the "stars" of the show. It does not disturb most viewers that at this moment in history black women continue to be represented in movies and on television as the servants of whites. The fact that a black woman can be cast in a dramatically compelling leading role as a servant does not intervene on racist/sexist stereotypes, it reinscribes them. Hollywood awarded its first Oscar to a black person in 1939 when Hattie McDaniel won as Best Supporting Actress in *Gone With the Wind*. She played the maid. Contemporary films like *Fried Green Tomatoes* and *Passion Fish*, which offer viewers progressive visions of white females, still image black women in the same way—as servants. Even though the black female "servant" in *Passion Fish* comes from a middle-class background, drug addiction has led to her drop in status. And the film suggests that working secluded as the caretaker of a sick white woman redeems the black woman. It was twenty-four years after McDaniel won her Oscar that the only black man to ever receive this award won Best Actor. Sidney Poitier won for his role in the 1960s film *Lilies of the Field*. In this film he is also symbolically a "mammy" figure, playing an itinerant worker who caretakes a group of white nuns. Mass media consistently depict black folks either as servants or in subordinate roles, a placement which still suggests that we exist to bolster and caretake the needs of whites. Two examples that come to mind are the role of the black female FBI agent in *The Silence of the Lambs*, whose sole purpose is to bolster the ego of the white female lead played by Jodie Foster. And certainly in all the *Lethal Weapon* movies Danny Glover's character is there to be the buddy who because he is black and therefore subordinate can never eclipse the white male star. Black folks confront media that include us and subordinate our representation to that of whites, thereby reinscribing white supremacy.

While superficially appearing to present a portrait of racial social equality, mass media actually work to reinforce assumptions that black folks should always be cast in supporting roles in relation to white characters. That subordination is made to appear "natural" because most black characters are consistently portrayed as always a little less ethical and moral than whites, not given to rational reasonable action. It is not surprising that it is those black characters represented as didactic figures upholding the status quo who are portrayed as possessing positive characteristics. They are rational, ethical, moral peacemakers who help maintain law and order.

Significantly, the neo-colonial messages about the nature of race that are brought to us by mass media do not just shape whites' minds and imaginations. They socialize black and other non-white minds as well. Understanding the power of representations, black people have in both the past and present challenged how we are presented in mass media, especially if the images are perceived to be "negative," but we have not sufficiently challenged representations of blackness that are not obviously negative even though they act to reinforce white supremacy. Concurrently, we do not challenge the representations of whites. We were not outside movie theaters protesting when the white male lead character in *Paris Trout* brutally slaughters a little black girl (even though I can think of no other image of a child being brutally slaughtered in a mainstream film) or when the lead character in *A Perfect World* played by Kevin Costner terrorizes a black family who gives him shelter. Even though he is a murderer and an escaped convict, his character is portrayed sympathetically whereas the black male father is brutally tortured presumably because he is an unloving, abusive parent. In *A Perfect World* both the adult white male lead and the little white boy who stops him from killing the black man are shown to be ethically and morally superior to black people.

Films that present cinematic narratives that seek to intervene in and challenge white supremacist assumption, whether they are made by black or white folks, tend to receive negative attention or none at all. John Sayles's film *The Brother from Another Planet* successfully presented a black male character in a lead role whose representation was oppositional. Rather than portraying a black male as a sidekick of a more powerful white male, or as a brute and sex fiend, he offered us the image of a gentle, healing, angelic black male spirit. John Waters's film *Hairspray* was able to reach a larger audience. In this movie, white people choose to be antiracist, to critique white privilege. Jim Jarmusch's film *Mystery Train* is incredibly deconstructive of racist assumptions. When the movie begins we witness a young Japanese couple arriving at the bus station in Memphis who begin to speak Japanese with a black man who superficially appears to be indigent. Racist stereotypes and class assumptions are challenged at this moment and throughout the film. White privilege and lack of understanding of the politics of racial difference are exposed. Yet most viewers did not like this film and it did not receive much attention. Julie Dash's film *Daughters of the Dust* portrayed black folks in ways that were radically different from Hollywood conventions. Many white viewers and even some black viewers had difficulty relating to these images. Radical representations of race in television and movies demand that we be resisting viewers and break our attachment to conventional representations. These films, and others like them, demonstrate that film and mass media in general can challenge neo-colonial representations that reinscribe racist stereotypes and perpetuate white supremacy. If more attention were given these films, it would show that aware viewers long for mass media that act to challenge and change racist domination and white supremacy.

Until all Americans demand that mass media no longer serve as the biggest propaganda machine for white supremacy, the socialization of everyone to subliminally absorb white supremacist attitudes and values will continue. Even though many white Americans do not overtly express racist thinking, it does not mean that their underlying belief structures have not been saturated with an ideology of difference that says white is always, in every way, superior to that which is black. Yet so far no complex public discourse exists that explains the difference between that racism which led whites to enjoy lynching and murdering black people and that wherein a white person may have a black friend or lover yet still believe black folks are intellectually and morally inferior to whites.

Mainstream media's endorsement of *The Bell Curve* by Richard J. Herrnstein and Charles Murray reflects the American public's willingness to support racist doctrine that represents black people as genetically inferior. Anti-racist white male thinker and activist Edward Herman reminds us of the danger of such acceptance in his essay "The New Racist Onslaught":

> Built on black slavery, with segregation and poverty helping reinforce stereotypes after 1865, racism has deep and persistent roots in this country. Today, racist Bob Grant has a radio audience of 680,000 in New York City, and racist Rush Limbaugh has a supportive audience of millions (extending to Supreme Court justice Clarence Thomas). Reagan with his repeated imagery of black welfare mothers exploiting the taxpayer, Bush

with Willie Horton and the menace of "quotas," and a slew of code words bandied about by politicians, show that polarizing racist language and political strategies are acceptable and even integral parts of mainstream culture today.

When black psyches are daily bombarded by mass media representations that encourage us to see white people as more caring, intelligent, liberal, etc., it makes sense that many of us begin to internalize racist thinking.

Without an organized resistance movement that focuses on the role of mass media in the perpetuation and maintenance of white supremacy, nothing will change. Boycotts remain one of the most effective ways to call attention to this issue. Picketing outside theaters, turning off the television set, writing letters of protest are all low-risk small acts that can become major interventions. Mass media are neither neutral nor innocent when it comes to spreading the message of white supremacy. It is not far-fetched for us to assume that many more white Americans would be anti-racist if they were not socialized daily to embrace racist assumptions. Challenging mass media to divest of white supremacy should be the starting point of a renewed movement for racial justice.

20

NEO-COLONIAL FANTASIES OF CONQUEST
HOOP DREAMS

bell hooks

Entering a movie theater packed tight with the bodies of white folks waiting to see *Hoop Dreams* I wanted to leave when it seemed that we (the two black folks I had come with—one of my five sisters and my ex-boyfriend) would not be able to sit together. Somehow I felt that I could not watch this film in a sea of whiteness without there being some body of blackness to anchor me—to see with me—to be a witness to the way black life was portrayed. Now, I have no problems with white filmmakers making films that focus on black life: the issue is only one of vision—perspective. Living in white supremacist culture no matter who is making a film about people of color, the politics of location matters. In the United States, white folks wanting to see and "enjoy" images of black folks on the screen is often in no way related to a desire to know real black people.

Sitting together in the packed crowd, every seat in the house taken, we joked about the atmosphere in the theater. It was charged with a sense of excitement, tension, and anticipation usually present at sports events. The focus on basketball playing may have allowed the audience to loosen up some but without knowing much about the content and direction of the film (whether it was serious or not) folks were clearly there to have fun. As the film began, a voyeuristic pleasure at being able to observe from a distance the lives of two black boys from working class and poor inner city backgrounds overcame the crowd. This lurid fascination with "watching" a documentary about two African-American teenagers striving to become NBA players was itself profound documentation of the extent to which blackness has become commodified in this society—the degree to which black life, particularly the lives of poor and underclass black people, can become cheap entertainment even if that is not what the filmmakers intended.

Filmmakers Peter Gilbert, Fred Marx, and Steve James make it clear in interviews that they want audiences to see the exploitative aspects of the sports systems in America even as they also want to show the positives. Gilbert declares: "We would like to see these families going through some very rough times, overcoming a lot of obstacles, and rising above some of the typical media stereotypes that people have about inner-city families." Note the way in which Gilbert does not identify the race of this family. Yet it is precisely the fact of blackness that gives this documentary popular cultural appeal. The lure of *Hoop Dreams* is that it affirms that those on the bottom can rise in this society, even as it is critical of the manner in which they rise. This film tells the world that the American dream works. As the exploitative white coach at St. Joseph's high school puts it as he is verbally whipping these black boys into shape: "This is America. You can make something of your life."

Contrary to the rave reviews *Hoop Dreams* has received, making it the first documentary film to be deemed by critics and moviegoers alike as worthy of an academy award for best motion picture, there is nothing spectacular or technically outstanding about this film. It is not an inventive piece of work. Indeed, it must take its place within the continuum of traditional anthropological and/or ethnographic documentary works that show us the "dark other" from the standpoint of whiteness. Inner city poor black communities seen as "jungles" by many Americans become in this film the boundary white filmmakers cross to document over a period of five years their subjects. To many progressive viewers, myself included, this film is moving because it acknowledges the positive aspects of black life that make survival possible. Even as I encouraged my family and everyone to see the film, I also encouraged us to look at it critically.

Contextualizing *Hoop Dreams* and evaluating it from a cinematic standpoint, is crucial to any understanding of its phenomenal success. The fact is it's not a great documentary. It is a compelling and moving real-life drama. Indeed, its appeal is a testimony to the culture's obsession with real life stories. In many ways the style of the film has much in common with those short documentary stories reported on the five o'clock news or on the more sensational programs like *Hard Copy*. In the United States, reviewers of the film, an overwhelming majority of whom are white, praised the work. Unlike many other films that examine the experience of black Americans (documentaries on Malcolm X, *Eyes on the Prize*, etc.), films that have overtly political content, that speak directly about issues of racism, the focus of this film was seen by many folks as more welcoming. It highlights an issue Americans of all races, but particularly white Americans, can easily identify with—the longing of young black males to become great basketball players. No doubt it is this standpoint that leads reviewers like David Denby in *New York* magazine to proclaim that *Hoop Dreams* is "an extraordinarily detailed and emotionally satisfying piece of work about American inner-city life, American hopes, American defeat." Such a comment seems highly ironic given the reality that it is precisely the way in which institutionalized racism and white supremacist attitudes in everyday American life actively prohibit black male participation in diverse cultural arenas and spheres of employment while presenting sports as the "one" location where recognition, success, and material reward can be attained. The desperate fear of not making it in American culture is the catalyst that drives the two young black males, Arthur Agee and William Gates, to dream of making a career as professional ballplayers. They, their family and friends, never imagine that they can be successful in any other way. Black and poor, they have no belief that they can attain wealth and power on any other playing field other than sports. Yet this spirit of defeat and hopelessness that informs their options in life and their life choices is not stressed in the film. Their longing to succeed as ballplayers is presented as though it is simply a positive American dream. The film suggests that it is only their potential to be exploited by adults who hope to benefit from their success (coaches, parents, siblings, lovers) that makes this dream a potential nightmare.

The most powerful moments in this film are those that subversively document the way in which these young black male bodies are callously objectified and dehumanized by the white male-dominated world of sports administration in America. *Hoop Dreams* shows audiences the way coaches and scouts searching to find the best ball players for their high school and college teams conduct themselves using an "auction block" mentality that to any aware viewer has to call to mind the history of slavery and the plantation economy that was built on the exploitation of young strong black male bodies. Just as the bodies of African-American slaves were expendable, the bodies of black male ballplayers cease to matter if they are not able to deliver the described product. Shrewdly, the filmmakers expose the ruthless agendas of grown-ups, particularly those paternalistic patriarchal white and black males, who are overinvested, whether emotionally or materially, in the two teenagers.

While the trials and tribulations Agee and Gates encounter on the playing field give *Hoop Dreams* momentum, it is their engagement with family and friends as well as their longing to be great ballplayers that provide the emotional pathos in this film. In particular, *Hoop Dreams* offers a different and rather unique portrayal of black mothers. Contrary to popular myths about matriarchal "hard" black women controlling their sons and emasculating them, the two mothers in this film offer their children necessary support and care. Clearly, it is Agee's mother Sheila who is exemplary in her efforts to be a loving parent, providing necessary discipline, support, and affirmation. Less charismatic, indeed she often appears to be trapped in a passive depressive stoicism. Gates' mother is kept in the background by the filmmakers. She is a single mother raising her children. The film does not show us how she provides economically.

Both Sheila and Arthur, Agee's mother and father, are articulate outspoken intelligent black folks. While the representation of their intelligence counters the stereotypes, the fact that they are not able to work together to keep the family healthy and free of major dysfunction reinforces other stereotypes. While the portrait of Sheila is positive, she is represented in the film as always more concerned with keeping the family together than the father. This is a traditional and often stereotypical way black women are represented in mass media, conveying the underlying racist and sexist assumption that they are somehow "better" than black men, more responsible, less lazy. Unfortunately, the news story reportorial style of the film precludes any complex investigation of Agee's father's drug addiction or the breakdown in their relationship. In keeping with stereotypical mass media portraits about poor black families, *Hoop Dreams* merely shows the failure of black male parents to sustain meaningful ties with their children. It does not critically interrogate the circumstances and conditions of that failure.

Even though one of the saddest moments in this film occurs as we witness Agee's loss of faith in his father, his mounting hostility and rage, he is never interrogated about the significance of this loss in the way he is questioned by the filmmakers about his attitudes towards basketball, education, etc. Concurrently, there is even less exploration of Gates' problematic relationship to his dad. Without any critical examination, these images of black father and son dynamics simply confirm negative stereotypes, compounding them by suggesting that even when black fathers are present in their children's lives they are such losers that they have no positive impact. In this way, the standpoint of the filmmakers creates a cinematic portrait that in no way illuminates the emotional complexity of black male life. Indeed, via a process of oversimplification the film makes it appear that the longing to play ball is the all-consuming desire in the lives of these young black men. That other longings they may have go unacknowledged and unfulfilled is not addressed by the filmmakers. Hence, there is no way to see how these states of deprivation and dissatisfaction intensify the obsession with succeeding in sports. Audiences are surprised when we suddenly see Gates with a pregnant girlfriend since until this scene appears the film has created a narrative that suggests basketball consumes all his energies.

This was obviously a strategic decision on the part of the filmmakers. For much of the dramatic momentum of *Hoop Dreams* is rooted in its evocation of competition dramatically evoked by the documentary footage of basketball games where audiences can cheer on the stars of the film, empathetically identifying their success or failure, or via the competition the film constructs between Agee and Gates. Even though we see glimpses of camaraderie between the two black males, by constantly comparing and contrasting their fate, the film creates a symbolic competition. The forces that oppose one another are the logic of racial assimilation which suggests that those black folks will be most successful who assume the values and attitudes of privileged whites and the logic of narrow nationalism which suggests that staying within one's own group is better because that is the only place where you can be safe, where you can survive. It is this latter vision that "wins" in the film. And it is perfectly in sync with the xenophobic nationalism that is gaining momentum among all groups in American culture.

Ultimately, *Hoop Dreams* offers a conservative vision of the conditions for "making it" in the United States. The context where one can make it is clearly within a nuclear family that prays together, that works hard, that completely and uncritically believes in the American dream. An almost religious belief in the power of competition to bring success permeates American life. The ethic of competition is passionately upheld and valued in Agee's family, so much so that it intensifies the schism between him and his dad. William Gates, who learns to critique the ethic of competition that he has been socialized to passively accept in white supremacist capitalist patriarchy, is portrayed as a victim. His longing to be a good parent, to not be obsessive with basketball, is not represented as a positive shift in thinking. After his health deteriorates, he is most often represented in the film as hopeless and defeated.

The triumphant individual in the film is Arthur Agee, who remains obsessed with the game. He continues to believe that he can win, that he can make it to the top. In her book *Memoir of a Race Traitor* the feminist writer Mab Segrest suggests that the ethic of competition undergirds the structure of racism and sexism in the United States, that to be "American" is to be seduced by the lure of domination, by conquest, by winning: "As a child of Europeans, a woman whose families have spent many generations on these shores, some of them in relative material privilege, my culture raised me to compete for grades, for jobs, for money, for self-esteem. As my lungs breathed in competition, they breathed out the stale air of individualism, delivering the toxic message; You are on your own." To be always in constant competition, hounded by the fear of failure, is the nature of the game in a culture of domination. A terrible loneliness shrouds Agee throughout *Hoop Dreams*. There is no escape. He has to keep playing the game. To escape is to fail. The subversive content of this film, its tragic messages, messages similar to those conveyed in other hot movies on the American scene *(Interview with a Vampire, Pulp Fiction, Natural Born Killers)*, are subsumed by the spectacle of playing the game—by the thrill of victory. Deposit the costs, the American dream of conquest prevails, and nothing changes.

21

AMERICA

Jean Baudrillard

I went in search of *astral* America,[1] not social and cultural America, but the America of the empty, absolute freedom of the freeways, not the deep America of mores and mentalities, but the America of desert speed, of motels and mineral surfaces. I looked for it in the speed of the screenplay, in the indifferent reflex of television, in the film of days and nights projected across an empty space, in the marvellously affectless succession of signs, images, faces, and ritual acts on the road; looked for what was nearest to the nuclear and enucleated universe, a universe which is virtually our own, right down to its European cottages.

I sought the finished form of the future catastrophe of the social in geology, in that upturning of depth that can be seen in the striated spaces, the reliefs of salt and stone, the canyons where the fossil river flows down, the immemorial abyss of slowness that shows itself in erosion and geology. I even looked for it in the verticality of the great cities.

I knew all about this nuclear form, this future catastrophe when I was still in Paris, of course. But to understand it, you have to take to the road, to that travelling which achieves what Virilio calls the aesthetics of disappearance.

For the mental desert form expands before your very eyes, and this is the purified form of social desertification. Disaffection finds its pure form in the barrenness of speed. All that is cold and dead in desertification or social enucleation rediscovers its contemplative form here in the heat of the desert. Here in the transversality of the desert and the irony of geology, the transpolitical finds its generic, mental space. The inhumanity of our ulterior, asocial,

From *America* (1988). Translated by Chris Turner. London: Verso, pp. 5–9.

superficial world immediately finds its aesthetic form here, its ecstatic form. For the desert is simply that: an ecstatic critique of culture, an ecstatic form of disappearance.

The grandeur of deserts derives from their being, in their aridity, the negative of the earth's surface and of our civilized humours. They are places where humours and fluids become rarefied, where the air is so pure that the influence of the stars descends direct from the constellations. And, with the extermination of the desert Indians, an even earlier stage than that of anthropology became visible: a mineralogy, a geology, a sidereality, an inhuman facticity, an aridity that drives out the artificial scruples of culture, a silence that exists nowhere else.

The silence of the desert is a visual thing, too. A product of the gaze that stares out and finds nothing to reflect it. There can be no silence up in the mountains, since their very contours roar. And for there to be silence, time itself has to attain a sort of horizontality; there has to be no echo of time in the future, but simply a sliding of geological strata one upon the other giving out nothing more than a fossil murmur.

Desert: luminous, fossilized network of an inhuman intelligence, of a radical indifference—the indifference not merely of the sky, but of the geological undulations, where the metaphysical passions of space and time alone crystallize. Here the terms of desire are turned upside down each day, and night annihilates them. But wait for the dawn to rise, with the awakening of the fossil sounds, the animal silence.

Speed creates pure objects. It is itself a pure object, since it cancels out the ground and territorial reference-points, since it runs ahead of time to annul time itself, since it moves more quickly than its own cause and obliterates that cause by outstripping it. Speed is the triumph of effect over cause, the triumph of instantaneity over time as depth, the triumph of the surface and pure objectality over the profundity of desire. Speed creates a space of initiation, which may be lethal; its only rule is to leave no trace behind. Triumph of forgetting over memory, an uncultivated, amnesic intoxication. The superficiality and reversibility of a pure object in the pure geometry of the desert. Driving like this produces a kind of invisibility, transparency, or transversality in things, simply by emptying them out. It is a sort of slow-motion suicide, death by an extenuation of forms—the delectable form of their disappearance. Speed is not a vegetal thing. It is nearer to the mineral, to refraction through a crystal, and it is already the site of a catastrophe, of a squandering of time. Perhaps, though, its fascination is simply that of the void. There is no seduction here, for seduction requires a secret. Speed is simply the rite that initiates us into emptiness: a nostalgic desire for forms to revert to immobility, concealed beneath the very intensification of their mobility. Akin to the nostalgia for living forms that haunts geometry.

Still, there is a violent contrast here, in this country, between the growing abstractness of a nuclear universe and a primary, visceral, unbounded vitality, springing not from rootedness, but from the lack of roots, a metabolic vitality, in sex and bodies, as well as in work and in buying and selling. Deep down, the US, with its space, its technological refinement, its bluff good conscience, even in those spaces which it opens up for simulation, is the *only remaining primitive society*. The fascinating thing is to travel through it as though it were the primitive society of the future, a society of complexity, hybridity, and the greatest intermingling, of a ritualism that is ferocious but whose superficial diversity lends it beauty, a society inhabited by a total metasocial fact with unforeseeable consequences, whose immanence is breathtaking, yet lacking a past through which to reflect on this, and therefore fundamentally primitive. . . . Its primitivism has passed into the hyperbolic, inhuman character of a universe that is beyond us, that far outstrips its own moral, social, or ecological rationale.

Only Puritans could have invented and developed this ecological and biological morality based on preservation—and therefore on discrimination—which is profoundly racial in nature. Everything becomes an overprotected nature reserve, so protected indeed that there is talk today of denaturalizing Yosemite to give it back to Nature, as has happened with the Tasaday in the Philippines. A Puritan obsession with origins in the very place where the ground itself has already gone. An obsession with finding a niche, a contact, precisely at the point where everything unfolds in an astral indifference.

There is a sort of miracle in the insipidity of *artificial paradises*, so long as they achieve the greatness of an entire (un)culture. In America, space lends a sense of grandeur even to the insipidity of the suburbs and "funky towns." The desert is everywhere, preserving insignificance. A desert where the miracle of the car, of ice and whisky is daily re-enacted: a marvel of easy living mixed with the fatality of the desert. A miracle of obscenity that is genuinely American: a miracle of total availability, of the transparency of all functions in space, though this latter nonetheless remains unfathomable in its vastness and can only be exorcised by speed.

The Italian miracle: that of stage and scene.

The American miracle: that of the obscene.

The profusion of sense, as against the deserts of meaninglessness.

It is metamorphic forms that are magical. Not the sylvan, vegetal forest, but the petrified, mineralized forest. The salt desert, whiter than snow, flatter than the sea. The effect of monumentality, geometry, and architecture where nothing has been designed or planned. Canyonsland, Split Mountain. Or the opposite: the amorphous reliefless relief of Mud Hills, the voluptuous, fossilized, monotonously undulating lunar relief of ancient lake beds. The white swell of White Sands . . . It takes this surreality of the elements to eliminate nature's picturesque qualities, just as it takes the metaphysics of speed to eliminate the natural picturesqueness of travel.

In fact the conception of a trip without any objective and which is, as a result, endless, only develops gradually for me. I reject the picturesque tourist round, the sights, even the landscapes (only their abstraction remains, in the prism of the scorching heat). Nothing is further from pure travelling than tourism or holiday travel. That is why it is best done in the extensive banality of deserts, or in the equally desert-like banality of a metropolis—not at any stage regarded as places of pleasure or culture, but seen televisually as scenery, as scenarios. That is why it is best done in extreme heat, the orgasmic form of bodily deterritorialization. The acceleration of molecules in the heat contributes to a barely perceptible evaporation of meaning.

It is not the discovery of local customs that counts, but discovering the immorality of the space you have to travel through, and this is on a quite different plane. It is this, together with the sheer distance, and the deliverance from the social, that count. Here in the most moral society there is, space is truly immoral. Here in the most conformist society, the dimensions are immoral. It is this immorality that makes distance light and the journey infinite, that cleanses the muscles of their tiredness.

Note

[1] "l'Amerique sidérale": this term and its variant forms have been rendered throughout by "astral" or the less familiar "sidereal," according to context. [Tr]

22

A MARGINAL SYSTEM
COLLECTING

Jean Baudrillard

Littré's dictionary defines "*objet*" in one of its meanings as "anything which is the cause or subject of a passion; figuratively—and par excellence—the loved object."

Let us grant that our everyday objects are in fact objects of a passion—the passion for private property, emotional investment in which is every bit as intense as investment in the "human" passions. Indeed, the everyday passion for private property is often stronger than all the others, and sometimes even reigns supreme, all other passions being absent. It is a measured, diffuse, regulating passion whose fundamental role in the vital equilibrium of the subject or the group—in the very decision to live—we tend not to gauge very well. Apart from the uses to which we put them at any particular moment, objects in this sense have another aspect which is intimately bound up with the subject: no longer simply material bodies offering a certain resistance, they become mental precincts over which I hold sway, they become things of which I am the meaning, they become my property and my passion.

The Object Abstracted from Its Function

If I use a refrigerator to refrigerate, it is a practical mediation: it is not an object but a refrigerator. And in that sense I do not possess it. A *utensil* is

From *The System of Objects* (1996). Translated by James Benedict. London: Verso, pp 85–106.

never possessed, because a utensil refers one to the world; what is possessed is always an object *abstracted from its function and thus brought into relationship with the subject.* In this context all owned objects partake of the same *abstractness*, and refer to one another only inasmuch as they refer solely to the subject. Such objects together make up the system through which the subject strives to construct a world, a private totality.

Every object thus has two functions—to be put to use and to be possessed. The first involves the field of the world's practical totalization by the subject, the second an abstract totalization of the subject undertaken by the subject himself outside the world. These two functions stand in inverse ratio to each other. At one extreme, the strictly practical object acquires a social status: this is the case with the machine. At the opposite extreme, the pure object, devoid of any function or completely abstracted from its use, takes on a strictly subjective status: it becomes part of a collection. It ceases to be a carpet, a table, a compass or a knick-knack and becomes an object in the sense in which a collector will say "a beautiful object" rather than specifying it, for example, as "a beautiful statuette." An object no longer specified by its function is defined by the subject, but in the passionate abstractness of possession all objects are equivalent. And just one object no longer suffices: the fulfillment of the project of possession always means a succession or even a complete series of objects. This is why owning absolutely any object is always so satisfying and so disappointing at the same time: a whole series lies behind any single object, and makes it into a source of anxiety. Things are not so different on the sexual plane: whereas the love relationship has as its aim a unique being, the need to possess the love object can be satisfied only by a succession of objects, by repetition, or, alternatively, by making the assumption that all possible objects are somehow present. Only a more or less complex organization of objects, each of which refers to all the others, can endow each with an abstractness such that the subject will be able to grasp it in that lived abstractness which is the experience of possession.

Collecting is precisely that kind of organization. Our ordinary environment is always ambiguous: functionality is forever collapsing into subjectivity, and possession is continually getting entangled with utility, as part of the ever-disappointed effort to achieve a total integration. Collecting, however, offers a model here: through collecting, the passionate pursuit of possession finds fulfillment and the everyday prose of objects is transformed into poetry, into a triumphant unconscious discourse.

The Object as Passion

"The taste for collection," says Maurice Rheims, "is a kind of passionate game."[1] For children, collecting is a rudimentary way of mastering the outside world, of arranging, classifying and manipulating. The most active time for childhood collecting is apparently between the ages of seven and twelve, during the latency period between early childhood and puberty. The urge to collect tends to wane with the onset of puberty, only to re-emerge as soon as that stage has passed. In later life, it is men over forty who most frequently fall victim to this passion. In short, there is in all cases a manifest connection between collecting and sexuality and this activity appears to provide a powerful compensation during critical stages of sexual development. This tendency clearly runs counter to active genital sexuality, although it is not simply a substitute for it. Rather, as compared with genitality, it constitutes a regression to the anal stage, which is characterized by accumulation, orderliness, aggressive retention, and so on. The activity of collecting is not in any sense equivalent to a sexual practice, for it is not designed to procure instinctual satisfaction (as in fetishism, for example); it may nevertheless produce intense satisfaction as a reaction. The object here takes on the full significance of a loved object: "Passion for the object leads to its being looked upon as a thing made by God. A collector of porcelain eggs is liable to believe that God never created a form more beautiful or more singular, and indeed that He devised this form solely for the greater delight of collectors."[2] Collectors are forever saying that they are "crazy about" this or that object, and they all without exception—even where the perversion of fetishism plays no part—cloak their collection in an atmosphere of clandestineness and concealment, of secrecy and sequestration, which in every way suggests a feeling of guilt. It is this passionate involvement which lends a touch of the sublime to the regressive activity of collecting; it is also the basis of the view that anyone who does not collect something is "nothing but a moron, a pathetic human wreck."[3]

The collector's sublimity, then, derives not from the nature of the objects he collects (which will vary according to his age, profession and social milieu) but from his fanaticism. And this fanaticism is identical whether it characterizes a rich connoisseur of Persian miniatures or a collector of matchboxes. The distinction that may legitimately be drawn here, to the effect that the collector loves his objects on the basis of their membership in a series, whereas the connoisseur loves his on account of their varied and unique charm, is not a decisive one. In both cases gratification flows from the fact that possession depends, on the one hand, on the absolute singularity of each item, a singularity which puts that item on a par with an animate being—indeed, fundamentally on a par with the subject himself—and, on the other hand, on the possibility of a series, and hence of an infinite play of substitutions. Collecting is thus qualitative in its essence and quantitative in its practice. If the feeling of possession is based on a confusion of the senses (of hand and eye) and an intimacy with the privileged object, it is also based just as much on searching, ordering, playing and assembling. In short, there is something of the harem about collecting, for the whole attraction may be summed up as that of an intimate series (one term of which is at any given time the favourite) combined with a serial intimacy.

Man never comes so close to being the master of a secret seraglio as when he is surrounded by his objects. Human relationships, home of uniqueness and conflict, never permit any such fusion of absolute singularity with infinite seriality—which is why they are such a continual source of anxiety. By contrast, the sphere of objects, consisting of successive and homologous terms, reassures. True, such reassurance is founded on an illusion, a trick, a process of abstraction and regression, but no matter. In the words of Maurice Rheims: "For man, the object is a sort of insentient dog which accepts his blandishments and returns them after its own fashion, or rather which returns them like a mirror faithful not to real images but to images that are desired." [4]

The Finest of Domestic Animals

Rheims's dog image is the right one, for pets are indeed an intermediate category between human beings and objects. The pathos-laden presence of a dog, a cat, a tortoise or a canary is a testimonial to a failure of the interhuman relationship and an attendant recourse to a narcissistic domestic universe where subjectivity finds fulfillment in the most quietistic way. Note, by the way, that these animals are not sexed (indeed, they are often neutered for their role as household pets); they are every bit as devoid of sex, even though they are alive, as objects are. This is the price to be paid if they are to provide emotional security: only their actual or symbolic castration makes it possible for them to serve as mitigators of their owners' castration anxiety. This is a part that all the objects that surround us also play to perfection. The object is in fact the finest of domestic animals—the only "being" whose qualities exalt rather than limit my person. In the plural, objects are the only entities in existence that can genuinely coexist, because the differences between them do not set them against one another, as happens in the case of living beings: instead they all converge submissively upon me and accumulate with the greatest of ease in my consciousness. Nothing can be both "personalized" and quantified so easily as objects. Moreover, this subjective quantifiability is not restricted: everything can be possessed, cathected or (in the activity of collecting) organized, classified and assigned a place. The object is thus in the strict sense of the word a mirror, for the images it reflects can only follow upon one another without ever contradicting one another. And indeed, as a mirror the object is perfect, precisely because it sends back not real images, but desired ones. In a word, it is a dog of which nothing remains but faithfulness. What is more, you can look at an object without it looking back at you. *That is why everything that cannot be invested in human relationships is invested in objects.* That is why regression of this kind is so easy, why people so readily practise this form of "retreat." But we must not allow ourselves to be taken in by this, nor by the vast literature that sentimentalizes inanimate objects. The "retreat" involved here really is a regression, and the passion mobilized is a passion for flight. Objects undoubtedly serve in a regulatory capacity with regard to everyday life, dissipating many neuroses and providing an outlet for all kinds of tensions and for energies that are in mourning. This is what gives them their "soul," what makes them "ours"—but it is also what turns them into the décor of a tenacious mythology, the ideal décor for an equilibrium that is itself neurotic.

A Serial Game

Yet this mediation would seem to be a poor one. How can consciousness let itself be fooled in this way? Such is the cunning of subjectivity: an object that is possessed can never be a poor mediation. It is always absolutely singular. Not in reality, of course: the possession of a "rare" or "unique" object is obviously the ideal aim of its appropriation, but for one thing the proof that a given object is unique can never be supplied in a real world, and, for another, consciousness gets along just fine without proof. The particular value of the object, its exchange value, is a function of cultural and social determinants. Its absolute singularity, on the other hand, arises from the fact of being possessed by me—and this allows me, in turn, to recognize myself in the object as an absolutely singular being. This is a grandiose tautology, but one that gives the relationship to objects all its density—its absurd facility, and the illusory but intense gratification it supplies.[5] What is more, while this closed circuit may also govern human relationships (albeit less easily), the relationship with objects has one characteristic that can never be found in the intersubjective realm: no object ever opposes the extension of the process of narcissistic projection to an unlimited number of other objects; on the contrary, the object imposes that very tendency, thereby contributing to the creation of a total environment, to that totalization of images of the self that is the basis of the miracle of collecting. For what you really collect is always yourself.

This makes it easier to understand the structure of the system of possession: any collection comprises a succession of items, but the last in the set is the person of the collector. Reciprocally, the person of the collector is constituted as such only if it replaces each item in the collection in turn. An analogous structure on the sociological level is to be found in the system of model and series: both the series and the collection serve to institute possession of the object—that is, they facilitate the mutual integration of object and person.[6]

From Quantity to Quality: The Unique Object

It may well be objected here that any exclusive passion for a single object on the part of an art lover suffices to demolish our hypothesis. It is quite clear, however, that the unique object is in fact simply the final term, the one which sums up all the others, that it is the supreme component of an entire paradigm (albeit a virtual, invisible or implicit one)—that it is, in short, the emblem of the series.

In the portraits in which he illustrates the passion of curiosity, La Bruyère puts the following words into the mouth of a collector of fine prints: "I suffer from a grave affliction which will surely oblige me to abandon all thought of prints till the end of my days: I have all of Callot except for one— and one which, to be frank, is not among his best works. Indeed, it is one of his worst, yet it would round out Callot for me. I have searched high and low for this print for twenty years, and I now despair of ever finding it." The equivalence experienced here between the whole series minus one and the final term missing from the series is conveyed with arithmetical certainty.[7] The absent final term is a symbolic distillation of that series without which it would not exist; consequently it acquires a strange quality, a quality which is the quintessence of the whole quantitative calibration of the series. This term is the unique object, defined by its final position and hence creating the illusion that it embodies a particular goal or end. This is all well and good, but it shows us how it is quantity that impels towards quality, and how the value thus concentrated on this simple signifier is in fact indistinguishable from the value that infuses the whole chain of intermediate signifiers of the paradigm. This is what might be called the symbolism of the object, in the etymological sense (cf. Greek *sumballein*, to put together), in accordance with which a chain of signifiers may be summed up in just one of its terms. The object is the symbol not of some external agency or value but first and foremost of the whole series of objects of which it is the (final) term. (This in addition to symbolizing the person whose object it is.)

La Bruyère's example illustrates another rule, too: that the object attains exceptional value only by virtue of its absence. This is not simply a matter of covetousness. *One cannot but wonder whether collections are in fact meant to be completed*, whether lack does not play an essential part here—a positive one, moreover, as the means whereby the subject reapprehends his own objectivity. If so, the *presence* of the final object of the collection would basically signify the death of the subject, whereas its absence would be what enables him merely to rehearse his death (and so exorcise it) by having an object represent it. This lack is experienced as suffering, but it is also the breach that makes it possible to avoid completing the collection and thus definitively erasing reality. Let us therefore applaud La Bruyère's collector for never finding his last Callot, for if he had done so he would thereby have ceased to be the living and passionate man that he still was, after all. It might be added that madness begins once a collection is deemed complete and thus ceases to centre around its absent term.

This account of things is buttressed by another story told by Maurice Rheims. A bibliophile specializing in unique copies learns one day that a New York bookseller is offering a book that is identical to one of his prize possessions. He rushes to New York, acquires the book, summons a lawyer, has the offending second copy burnt before him and elicits an affidavit substantiating this act of destruction. Once he is back home, he inserts this legal document in his copy, now once again unique, and goes to bed happy.

Should we conclude that in this case the *series* has been abolished? Not at all. It only seems so, because the collector's original copy was in fact invested with the value of all virtual copies, and by destroying the rival copy the book collector was merely reinstituting the perfection of a compromised symbol. Whether denied, forgotten, destroyed, or merely virtual, the series is still present. The serial nature of the most mundane of everyday objects, as of the most transcendent of rarities, is what nourishes the relationship of ownership and the possibility of passionate play: without seriality no such play would be conceivable, hence no possession—and hence, too, properly speaking, no object. A truly unique, absolute object, an object such that it has no antecedents and is in no way dispersed in some series or other—such an object is unthinkable. It has no more existence than a pure sound. Just as harmonic series bring sounds up to their perceived quality, so paradigmatic series, whatever their degree of complexity, bring objects up to their symbolic quality—carrying them, in the same movement, into the sphere of the human relationship of mastery and play.

Objects and Habits: Wrist-Watches

Every object oscillates between a practical specificity, a function which is in a sense its manifest discourse, and absorption by a series or collection where it becomes one term in a latent, repetitive discourse—the most basic and tenacious of discourses. This discursive system of objects is analogous to the system of habits.[8]

Habits imply discontinuity and repetition—not continuity, as common usage suggests. By breaking up time, our "habitual" patterns dispel the anxiety-provoking aspect of the temporal continuum and of the absolute singularity of events. Similarly, it is thanks to their discontinuous integration into series that we put objects at our sole disposition, that we own them. This is the discourse of subjectivity itself, and objects are a privileged register of that discourse. Between the world's irreversible evolution and ourselves, objects interpose a discontinuous, classifiable, reversible screen which can be reconstituted at will, a segment of the world which belongs to us, responding to our hands and minds and delivering us from anxiety. Objects do not merely help us to master the world by virtue of their integration into instrumental series, they also help us, *by virtue of their integration into mental series*, to master time, rendering it discontinuous and classifying it, after the fashion of habits, and subjecting it to the same associational constraints as those which govern the arrangement of things in space.

There is no better illustration of this discontinuous and "habitual" function than the wrist-watch.[9] The watch epitomizes the duality of the way we experience objects. On the one hand, it tells us the actual time; and chronometric precision is *par excellence* the dimension of practical constraints, of society as external to us, and of death. As well as subjecting us to an irreducible temporality, however, the watch as an object helps us to appropriate time: just as the automobile "eats up" miles, so the watch-object eats up time.[10] By making time into a substance that can be divided up, it turns it into an object to be consumed. A perilous dimension of praxis is thus transformed into a domesticated quantity. Beyond just knowing the time, "possessing" the time in and through an object that is one's own, having the time continuously recorded before one's eyes, has become a crutch, a necessary reassurance, for civilized man. The time is no longer in the home, no longer the clock's beating heart, but its registration on the wrist continues to ensure the same organic satisfaction as the regular throbbing of an internal organ. Thanks to my watch, time presents itself simultaneously as the very dimension of my objectification and as a simple household necessity. As a matter of fact, any object might be used to demonstrate how even the dimension of objective constraint is incorporated by everyday experience; the watch, however, is the best example, by virtue of its explicit relationship to time.

Objects and Time: A Controlled Cycle

The problem of time is a fundamental aspect of collecting. As Maurice Rheims says: "A phenomenon that often goes hand in hand with the passion for collecting is the loss of any sense of the present time."[11] But is this really just a matter of an escape into nostalgia? Certainly, someone who identifies with Louis XVI down to the feet of his armchairs, or develops a true passion for sixteenth-century snuffboxes, is marking himself off from the present by means of a historical reference, yet this reference takes second place to his direct experience of collecting's systematic aspect. The deep-rooted power of collected objects stems neither from their uniqueness nor from their historical distinctiveness. It is not because of such considerations that the temporality of collecting is not real time but, rather, *because the organization of the collection itself replaces time*. And no doubt this is the collection's fundamental function: the resolving of real time into a systematic dimension. Taste, particularity, status, the discourse of society—any of these may cause the collection to open onto a broader relationship (though this will never go beyond a group of insiders); in all cases, however, the collection must remain, literally, a "pastime." Indeed, it abolishes time. More precisely, by reducing time to a fixed set of terms navigable in either direction, the collection represents the continual recommencement of a controlled cycle whereby man, at any moment and with complete confidence, starting with any term and sure of returning to it, is able to set his game of life and death in motion.

It is in this sense that the environment of private objects and their possession (collection being the most extreme instance) is a dimension of our life which, though imaginary, is absolutely essential. Just as essential as dreams. It has been said that if dreams could be experimentally suppressed, serious mental disturbances would quickly ensue. It is certainly true that were it possible to deprive people of the regressive escape offered by the game of possession, if they were prevented from giving voice to their controlled, self-addressed discourse, from using objects to recite themselves, as it were, outside time, then mental disorder would surely follow immediately, just as in the case of dream deprivation. We cannot live in absolute singularity, in the irreversibility signaled by the moment of birth, and it is precisely this irreversible movement from birth towards death that objects help us to cope with.

Of course the balance thus achieved is a neurotic one; of course this bulwark against anxiety is regressive, for time is objectively irreversible, after all, and even the objects whose function it is to protect us from it are perforce themselves carried off by it; and of course the defense mechanism that imposes discontinuity by means of objects is forever being contested, for the world and human beings are in reality *continuous*. But can we really speak here in terms of normality or anomaly? Taking refuge in a closed synchronicity may certainly be deemed denial of reality and flight if one considers that the object is the recipient of a cathexis that "ought" to have been invested in human relationships. But this is the price we pay for the vast regulating power of these mechanisms, which today, with the disappearance of the old religious and ideological authorities, are becoming the consolation of consolations, the everyday mythology absorbing all the *angst* that attends time, that attends death.

It should be clear that we are not here promoting any spontaneous mythology according to which man somehow extends his life or survives his death by means of the objects he possesses. The refuge-seeking procedure I have been describing depends not on an immortality, an eternity or a survival founded on the object *qua* reflection (something which man has basically never believed in) but, rather, on a more complex action which "recycles" birth and death into *a system of objects*. What man gets from objects is not a guarantee of life after death but *the possibility, from the present moment onwards, of continually experiencing the unfolding of his existence in a controlled, cyclical mode, symbolically transcending a real existence the irreversibility of whose progression he is powerless to affect.*

We are not far from the ball which the child (in Freud's account) causes to disappear and reappear in order to experience the absence and presence of its mother alternately (*Fort! Da! Fort! Da!*)—in order to counter her anxiety-provoking absence with this infinite cycle of disappearance and reappearance of the object. The symbolic implications of play within the series are not hard to discern here, and we may sum them up by saying that the object is *the thing with which we construct our mourning*: the object represents our own death, but that death is transcended (symbolically) by virtue of the fact that we *possess* the object; the fact that by introjecting it into a work of mourning—by integrating it into a series in which its absence and its re-emergence elsewhere "work" at replaying themselves continually, recurrently—we succeed in dispelling the anxiety associated with absence and with the reality of death. Objects allow us to apply the work of mourning to ourselves right now, in everyday life, and this in turn allows us to live—to live regressively, no doubt, but at least to live. A person who collects is dead, but he literally survives himself through his collection, which (even while he lives) duplicates him infinitely, beyond death, *by integrating death itself into the series, into the cycle*. Once again the parallel with dreams applies here. If any object's function—practical, cultural or social—means that it is the mediation of *a wish*, it is also, as one term among others in the systematic game that we have been describing, the voice *of desire*. Desire is, in fact, the motor of the repetition or substitution of oneself, along the infinite chain of signifiers, through or beyond death. And if the function of dreams is to ensure the continuity of sleep, that of objects, thanks to very much the same sort of compromise, is to ensure the continuity of life.[12]

The Sequestered Object: Jealousy

At the terminal point of its regressive movement, the passion for objects ends up as pure jealousy. The joy of possession in its most profound form now derives from the value that objects can have for others and from the fact of depriving them thereof. This jealous complex, though it is characteristic of the collector at his most fanatical, presides also, proportionately speaking, over the simplest proprietary reflex. A powerful anal-sadistic impulse, it produces the urge to sequester beauty so as to be the only one to enjoy it: a kind of sexually perverse behaviour widely present in a diffuse form in the relationship to objects.

What does the sequestered object represent? (Its objective value is secondary, of course—its attraction lies in the very fact of its confinement.) If you do not lend your car, your fountain pen or your wife to anyone, that is because these objects, according to the logic of jealousy, are narcissistic equivalents of the ego: to lose them, or for them to be damaged, means castration. The phallus, to put it in a nutshell, is not something one loans out. What the jealous owner sequesters and cleaves to is his own libido, in the shape of an object, which he is striving to exorcise by means of a system of confinement—the same system, in fact, by virtue of which collecting dispels anxiety about death. He castrates himself out of anguish about his own sexuality; or, more exactly, "he uses a symbolic castration—sequestration—pre-emptively, as a way of countering anxiety about *real* castration."[13] This desperate strategy is the basis of the horrible gratification that jealousy affords. For one is always jealous of oneself. It is oneself that one locks up and guards so closely. And it is from oneself that one obtains gratification.

Obviously, this jealous pleasure occurs in a context of absolute disillusionment, because systematic regression can never completely eradicate consciousness of the real world or of the futility of such behaviour. The same goes for collecting, whose sway is fragile at best, for the sway of the real world lies ever just behind it, and is continually threatening it. Yet this disillusionment is itself part of the system—indeed, is as responsible as satisfaction for setting the system in motion: disillusionment never refers to the world but, rather, to an ulterior term; disillusionment and satisfaction occupy sequential positions in the cycle. The neurotic activation of the system is thus attributable to this constitutive disillusionment. In such cases the series tends to run its course at a faster and faster pace, chasing its tail as differences wear out and the substitution mechanism speeds up. The system may even enter a destructive phase, implying the self-destruction of the subject. Maurice Rheims evokes the ritualized "execution" of collections—a kind of suicide based on the impossibility of ever circumscribing death. It is not rare in the context of the system of jealousy for the subject eventually to destroy the sequestered object or being out of a feeling that he can never completely rid himself of the adversity of the world, and of his own sexuality. This is the logical and illogical end of his passion.[14]

The Object Destructured: Perversion

The effectiveness of the system of possession is directly linked to its regressive character. And this regression in turn is linked to the very *modus operandi* of perversion. If perversion as it concerns objects is most clearly discernible in the crystallized form of fetishism, we are perfectly justified in noting how throughout the system, organized according to the same aims and functioning in the same ways, the possession of objects and the passion for them is, shall we say, *a tempered mode of sexual perversion*. Indeed, just as possession depends on the discontinuity of the series (real or virtual) and on the choice of a privileged term within it, so sexual perversion is founded on the inability to apprehend the other *qua* object of desire in his or her unique totality as a person, to grasp the other in any but a discontinuous way: the other is transformed into the paradigm of various eroticized parts of the body, a single one of which becomes the focus of objectification. A particular woman is no longer a woman but merely a sex, breasts, belly, thighs, voice and face—and preferably just one of them.[15] She thus becomes a constituent "object" in a series whose different terms are gazetted by desire, and whose real referent is by no means the loved person but, rather, the subject himself, collecting and eroticizing himself and turning the relationship of love into a discourse directed towards him alone.

The opening sequence in Jean-Luc Godard's film *Contempt* clearly illustrates this. The dialogue in this "nude" scene goes as follows.

"Do you love my feet?" the woman asks. (Note that throughout the scene she is inventorying herself in a mirror—this is not irrelevant, because in this way she attributes value to herself as she is seen, via her image, and thus, already, as spatially discontinuous.)

"Yes, I love them."

"Do you love my legs?"

"Yes."

"And my thighs?"

"Yes," he replies once more. "I love them."
(And so on, from foot to head, ending up with her hair.)
"So, you love me totally?"
"Yes, I love you totally."
"Me too, Paul," she says, summing up the situation.

It may be that the film's makers saw all this as the clarifying algebra of a demystified love. Be that as it may, such a grotesque reconstruction of desire is the height of inhumanity. Once broken down by body parts into a series, the woman as pure object is then reintegrated into the greater series of all woman-objects, where she is merely one term among others. The only activity possible within the logic of this system is the play of substitutions. This was what we recognized earlier as the motor of satisfaction in the collector.

In the love relationship the tendency to break the object down into discrete details in accordance with a perverse autoerotic system is slowed by the living unity of the other person.[16] When it comes to material objects, however, and especially to manufactured objects complex enough to lend themselves to mental dismantling, this tendency has free rein. With the automobile, for instance, it is possible to speak of "*my* brakes," "*my* tail fins," "*my* steering wheel;" or to say "*I* am braking," "*I* am turning" or "*I* am starting." In short, all the car's "organs" and functions may be brought separately into relation with the person of the owner in the possessive mode. We are dealing here not with a process of personalization at the social level but with a process of a projective kind. We are concerned not with *having* but with *being*. With the horse, despite the fact that this animal was a remarkable instrument of power and transcendence for man, this kind of confusion was never possible. The fact is that the horse is not made of pieces—and above all, that it is *sexed*. We can say "my horse" or "my wife," but that is as far as this kind of possessive denomination can go. That which has a sex resists fragmenting projection and hence also the mode of appropriation that we have identified as a perversion.[17] Faced by a living being, we may say "my" but we cannot say "I" as we do when we symbolically appropriate the functions and "organs" of a car. That type of regression is not available to us. The horse may be the recipient of powerful symbolic cathexes: we associate it with the wild sexuality of the rutting season, as with the wisdom of the centaur; its head is a terrifying phantasy linked to the image of the father, yet its calm embodies the protective strength of Cheiron the teacher. It is never cathected, however, in the simplistic, narcissistic, far more impoverished and infantile manner in which the ego is projected onto structural details of cars (in accordance with an almost delusional analogy with disassociated parts and functions of the human body). The existence of a dynamic symbolism of the horse may be attributed precisely to the fact that isolated identifications with distinct functions or organs of the horse are an impossibility; nor is there any prospect, therefore, of collapsing this relationship into an autoerotic "discourse" concerned with disconnected elements.

Fragmentation and regression of that kind presuppose a technique, but one which has become autonomous at the level of the part-object. A woman broken down into a syntagma of erogenous zones is classified exclusively by the functionality of pleasure, to which the response is an objectivizing and ritualizing erotic technique that masks the anxiety associated with the inter-personal relationship while at the same time serving as a genuine (gestural and effective) dose of reality at the very heart of perversion as a phantasy system. The fact is that every mental system needs a credibility factor of this sort—a foothold in the real, a technical rationale or justification. Thus the accelerator referred to in the words "I am accelerating," or the whole car implied when we say "my car," serves as the real, technical justification for a whole realm of narcissistic annexation *short* of reality. The same goes for erotic technique, when it is accepted for what it is; for at this level we are no longer in the genital sphere, which opens onto reality, onto pleasure, but, rather, in a regressive, anal sphere of sexual systematizing for which erotic gestures are merely the justification.

Clearly, then, "technical" is a very long way indeed from implying "objective." Technique does have this quality when it is socialized, when it is adopted by technology, and when it informs new structures. In the everyday realm, however, it constitutes a field that is always hospitable to regressive phantasies, because the possibility of a destructuring is ever imminent. Once assembled and mounted, the components of a technical object imply a certain coherence. But such a structure is always vulnerable to the human mind: held together from without by its function, it is purely formal for the psyche. The hierarchy of its elements can be dismantled at any time, and those elements made interchangeable within a paradigmatic system which the subject uses for his self-recitation. The object is discontinuous already—and certainly easy for thought to disassemble. Moreover, the task is all the easier now that the object—especially the technical object—is no longer lent unity by a set of human gestures and by human energy. Another reason why the car, in contrast to the horse, is such a perfect object for the purposes of narcissistic manipulation is that mastery over the horse is muscular and active, and calls for a gestural system designed to maintain balance, whereas mastery over a car is simplified, functional and abstract.

From Serial Motivation to Real Motivation

Hitherto our discussion has paid no heed whatsoever to the actual nature of the objects that are collected: we have concentrated on the systematic aspects of collecting and ignored the thematic. It is obvious, however, that collecting masterpieces is not exactly the same thing as collecting cigar bands. First of all, a distinction must be drawn between the concept of collection (Latin *colligere*, to choose and gather together) and the concept of accumulation. At the simplest level, matter of one kind or another is accumulated: old papers are piled up, or quantities of food are stored. This activity falls somewhere between oral introjection and anal retention. At a somewhat higher level lies the serial accumulation of identical objects. As for collecting proper, it has a door open onto culture, being concerned with differentiated objects which often have exchange value, which may also be "objects" of preservation, trade, social ritual, exhibition—perhaps even generators of profit. Such objects are accompanied by projects. And though they remain interrelated, their interplay involves the social world outside, and embraces human relationships.

However powerful external motivations may be, collections can never escape from their internal systematization; at best they may represent a compromise between internal and external factors, and even when a collection transforms itself into a discourse addressed to others, it continues to be first and foremost a discourse addressed to oneself. Serial motivation is discernible everywhere. Research shows that buyers of books published in series (such as *10/18* or *Que sais-je?*[18]), once they are caught up in collecting, will even acquire titles of no interest to them: the distinctiveness of the book relative to the series itself thus suffices to create a purely formal interest which replaces any real one. The motive of purchase is nothing but this contingent association. A comparable kind of behaviour is that of people who cannot read comfortably unless they are surrounded by all their books; in such cases the specificity of what is being read tends to evaporate. Even farther down the same path, the book itself may count less than the moment when it is put back in its proper place on the shelf. Conversely, once a collector's enthusiasm for a series wanes it is very difficult to revive, and now he may not even buy volumes of genuine interest to him. This is as much evidence as we need to draw a clear distinction between serial motivation and real motivation. The two are mutually exclusive and can coexist only on the basis of compromise, with a notable tendency, founded on inertia, for serial motivation to carry the day over the dialectical motivation of interest.[19]

Mere collecting, however, may sometimes create real interest. The person who sets out to buy every title in the *Que sais-je?* series may end up confining his collection to a single subject, such as music or sociology. Once a certain quantitative threshold is reached, sheer accumulation may occasionally give way to a measure of discrimination. There is no hard-and-fast rule here. Artistic masterpieces *may* be collected with the same regressive fanaticism as cheese labels; on the other hand, children who collect stamps are continually swapping them with their friends. No iron-clad connection exists, therefore, between a collection's thematic complexity and its real openness to the outside world. At best such complexity may give us a clue, may be grounds for a presumption of openness.

A collection can emancipate itself from unalloyed accumulation not only by virtue of its cultural complexity but also by virtue of what is missing from it, by virtue of its incompleteness. A lack here is always a specific demand, an appeal for such and such an absent object. And this demand, in the shape of research, passion, or messages to other people,[20] suffices to shatter that fatal enchantment of the collector which plunges him into a state of pure fascination. A recent television programme on collecting made the point well: every collector who presented his collection to the viewing audience would mention the very special "object" that he did not have, and invite everyone to find it for him. So, even though objects may on occasion lead into the realm of social discourse, it must be acknowledged that *it is usually not an object's presence but far more often its absence that clears the way for social intercourse*.

A Discourse Addressed to Oneself

It remains characteristic of the collection that sooner or later a radical change will occur capable of wrenching it out of its regressive system and orientating it towards a project or task (whether status-related, cultural or commercial is of no consequence, just so long as an object eventually brings one human being face to face with another—at which point the object has become a message). All the same, no matter how open a collection is, it will always harbour an irreducible element of non-relationship to the world. Because he feels alienated and abolished by a social discourse whose rules escape him, the collector strives to reconstitute a discourse that is transparent to him, a discourse whose signifiers he controls and whose referent *par excellence* is himself. In this he is doomed to failure: he cannot see that he is simply transforming an open-ended objective discontinuity into a closed subjective one, where even the language he uses has lost any general validity. This kind of totalization by means of objects always bears the stamp of solitude. It fails to communicate with the outside, and communication is missing within it. In point of fact, moreover, we cannot avoid the question whether objects can indeed ever come to constitute any other language than this: can man ever use objects to set up a language that is more than a discourse addressed to himself?

The collector is never an utterly hopeless fanatic, precisely because he collects objects that in some way always prevent him from regressing into the ultimate abstraction of a delusional state, but at the same time the discourse he thus creates can never—for the very same reason—get beyond a certain poverty and infantilism. Collecting is always a limited, repetitive process, and the very material objects with which it is concerned are too concrete and too discontinuous ever to be articulated as a true dialectical structure.[21] So if non-collectors are indeed "nothing but morons," collectors, for their part, invariably have something impoverished and inhuman about them.

Notes

[1] *La vie étrange des objets* (Paris: Plon, 1959), p. 28. [*Translator's note:* There is an English translation by David Pryce-Jones: *Art on the Market* (London: Weidenfeld & Nicolson, 1961). I have not used it here.]

[2] Ibid., p. 33.

[3] M. Fauron, president of the cigar-band collectors' association, in *Liens* (review of the Club français du Livre), May 1964.

⁴ Rheims, *La vie étrange des objets*, p. 50.

⁵ It also creates disillusion, of course, itself bound up with the tautological character of the system.

⁶ The *series* is practically always a kind of game that makes it possible to select any one term and invest it with the privileged status of a *model*. A child is throwing bottle-tops: which one will go the farthest? It is no coincidence if the same one always comes out ahead: this is his favourite. The model he thus constructs, the hierarchy he sets up, is in fact himself—for he does not identify himself with one bottle-top but, rather, with the fact that one bottle-top always wins. And he is just as present in each of the other tops, unmarked terms in the antagonism between winner and losers: throwing the bottle-tops one by one is playing at constituting oneself as a series in order then to constitute oneself as a model. Here, in a nutshell, is the psychology of the collector, and a collector who collects only privileged or "unique" objects is simply making sure that he himself is the object that always wins.

⁷ Any term in the series may become the final term: any Callot can be the one to "round out Callot."

⁸ Moreover, any object immediately becomes the foundation of a network of habits, the focus of a set of behavioural routines. Conversely, there is probably no habit that does not centre on an object. In everyday existence the two are inextricably bound up with each other.

⁹ The watch is also indicative (as is the disappearance of clocks) of the irresistible tendency of modern objects towards miniaturization and individualization. It is also the oldest, the smallest, the closest to us, and the most valuable of personal machines—an intimate and highly cathected mechanical talisman which becomes the object of everyday complicity, fascination (especially for children), and jealousy.

¹⁰ Exactness about time parallels speed in space: time has to be gobbled up as completely as possible.

¹¹ *La vie étrange des objets*, p. 42.

¹² A story told by Tristan Bernard provides an amusing illustration of the fact that collecting is a way of playing with death (that is, a passion), and in consequence stronger, symbolically, than death itself. There was once a man who collected children: legitimate, illegitimate, children of a first or a second marriage, foundlings, by-blows, and so on. One day he gave a house party at which his entire "collection" were present: a cynical friend of his remarked, however, "There is one kind of child you do not have." "What type?" the host wanted to know. "A posthumous child," came the answer. Whereupon this passionate collector first got his wife pregnant and promptly thereafter committed suicide.

The same system is to be found, minus the narrative trappings, in games of chance. This is the reason for their fascination, which is even more intense than that of collecting. Such games imply a pure transcendence of death: subjectivity cathects the pure series with an imaginary mastery, quite certain that whatever the ups and downs of the play, no one has the power to reintroduce into it the *real* conditions of life and death.

¹³ Of course this also goes for pets, and by extension for the "object" in the sexual relationship, whose manipulation in jealousy is of a similar kind.

¹⁴ We must not confuse disillusionment, an internal motor of the regressive system of the series, with the lack we spoke of above, which on the contrary tends to foster emergence from the system. Disillusionment causes the subject to tighten his retrogressive embrace of the series; lack causes him to evolve (relatively speaking) in the direction of the outside world.

¹⁵ The regressive tendency, ever more specialized and impersonal, may converge on the hair or the feet, or, ultimately, crystallize—at the opposite pole to any living being—on a garter or a brassiere; we thus come back to the material object, whose possession may be described as the perfect way of eliminating the presence of the other.

¹⁶ This explains why the passionate feelings are transferred to the fetish, whose function is a radical simplification of the living sexual object which makes this object equivalent to the penis and cathects it accordingly.

¹⁷ By the same token possessive identification operates in the case of living beings only to the extent that such beings may be perceived as asexual: "Does our head hurt?", we may say to a baby. When we are confronted by a sexed being, however, this kind of confusional identification is halted by castration anxiety.

[18] [*Translator's note:* These are well-known series of pocket books in uniform format. *Que sais-je?* is a series of short monographs on a vast array of topics.]

[19] This distinction between serial satisfaction and pleasure proper is an essential one. True pleasure is a sort of pleasure-in-pleasure whereby mere satisfaction is transcended as such, and grounds itself in a relationship. In serial satisfaction, by contrast, this second-level pleasure, this qualitative dimension of pleasure, disappears, is missing or unfulfilled. Satisfaction must depend on linear succession alone: an unattainable totality is extended by means of projection and compensated for by means of repetition. People stop reading the books they buy, then proceed to buy more and more. Similarly the repetition of the sexual act, or a multiplicity of sexual partners, may serve indefinitely as an ersatz form of love as exploration. Pleasure in pleasure is gone, only satisfaction remains—and the two are mutually exclusive.

[20] Even in this case, however, the collector tends to call upon other people solely as observers of his collection, integrating them as third parties only in an already constituted subject–object relationship.

[21] As distinct from science or memory, for example—which also involve collecting, but the collecting of facts or knowledge.

23

THE POWER OF REVERSIBILITY THAT EXISTS IN THE FATAL
INTERVIEW WITH
D. GUILLEMOT AND D. SOUTIF

Jean Baudrillard

DG/DS   Are you a philosopher, a sociologist, a writer, a poet, none of these or all at the same time?

I am neither a philosopher nor a sociologist. I haven't followed the appropriate academic path nor worked in the right institutions. I am in sociology at university, but I don't recognize myself in sociology or in philosophizing philosophy. Theorist? I agree. Metaphysician? Perhaps. Moralist? I don't know. My work has never been academic, nor is it getting more literary. It's evolving, it's getting less theoretical, without feeling the need to furnish proof or rely on references.

DG/DS   In Fatal Strategies *you talk about cancerous society and of a catastrophe that is lying in wait for us. Are we there or moving that way?*

It would be stupid to prophesy an apocalypse in the literal sense of the term. My idea is that the catastrophe has already happened, it's here already.

From *Baudrillard Live: Selected Interviews* (1993). Edited by Mike Gane. New York: Routledge, pp. 43–49.

What interests me is precisely beyond the catastrophe, what I would call its hypertelia. Catastrophe is acceleration, precipitation, excess, but not necessarily annihilation. Once I used to analyse things in critical terms, of revolution; now I do it in terms of mutation.

I am not a prophet of doom. I say that in our world there is a logic that is catastrophic in the literal sense, but not in the romantic or sentimental sense of the term. The "cancerous society" is a metaphor. One has the right to push writing and hypotheses to the very end, to points where, perhaps at the limit, they no longer have any meaning, but that is where they are going. In the literal sense it is true that there is a cancerous form, a metastatic form of the creeping proliferation of things, but I don't want to offer cancer as a concept. I am talking about overgrowth (*excroissance*) instead of growth (*croissance*), and that form can just as easily invade theory as the social fabric or the economy and production. It is obvious in the production of information and communication, in material goods and sexual contacts: this is overproduction that doesn't any more know what it's for but for the moment finds a sort of logic in its own proliferation.

DG/DS   Could not technology make it possible to restore a sense of order? As far as information is concerned, is there not some way that techniques would make it possible to control this process of proliferation?

Information nevertheless thrives as a force for progress, for balance and enrichment, but I don't think it would be possible to master it. There are perhaps phases in the history of technology. For technology as a whole, we could say what McLuhan says about the mass media: the medium becomes the message. Technology itself becomes the message; it doesn't push things forward or transform the world, it becomes the world. And this substitution of one thing for another might be considered perilous, because it is no longer a question of restoring balance or order.

With information technology, for example, there is an effect of the realization of the world. The world, which from the dawn of time has been myth, fantasy, fable, becomes realized through technology. This materialism seems to me to be a catastrophe in the etymological sense of the term. It is a sort of death, where everything takes on the garb of reality. You can imagine a point where all the thoughts waiting to be thought will be immediately realizable by means of a computer. I am not condemning technology, it's fascinating, it can produce marvellous special effects. But with this faculty of giving reality to the world, then the possible, the imaginary, the illusory all disappear. Now, the illusory is perhaps vital. A world without any illusory effects will be completely obscene, material, exact, perfect.

DG/DS   And where does writing stand now, that old technology that has wrought many changes in its time and that you still use? Doesn't it function in the mode of proliferation?

Yes, and nobody quite knows how to hold it back. It seems that we have crossed a certain boundary, and that a certain self-regulation that used to

come into play, even biologically, in relation to the species, no longer operates. There is now a possibility of limitless proliferation in a world that has
lost all sense of perspective, where sight, distance and judgement have been
lost. And judgement is no longer needed in a world that is simply there, immanent, realized.

At the limit the effect of something written is nil today. I can choose not
to go on writing because I am not caught up in a coercive culture that compels a writer to write, and an intellectual to think. I began to write when I
wanted to, and I will stop if it ceases to be worthwhile. I need a challenge
myself, there's got to be something at stake. If that is taken away, then I will
stop writing. I'm not mad. At a given moment, however, you cause things to
exist, not by producing them in the material sense of the term, but by defying
them, by confronting them. Then at that moment it's magic. And it's not only
writing that functions like that. I don't know if we have a relationship with
other people in terms of desire, but we certainly have one in terms of defiance. We don't exist unless we are subject to a degree of defiance. We need
to be desired, caressed, but we also need to be challenged and thus seduced.
There is a game, which has nothing to do with the forced realization of the
world, a game in which things demand to be solicited, diverted, seduced.
You've got to be able to make them appear as well as disappear; to play the
whole game. Writing is nothing but that, and theory as well. It is knowing
how to conjure up concepts, effects, and knowing how to resolve them. Culture is not just a simple question of producing ideas or differences. It's also a
question of knowing how to cast a spell.

We thoroughly understand the rules of production, but not the rules of
this particular game. I think we should compare them. On the one hand banality, and on the other hand, this rule of the game whose effects may perhaps be mastered but which belongs to a more secret order: the fated.

It is nevertheless quite possible that we might not today be able to distinguish between fatality and banality. What interests me, therefore, is not
fatality in the sense of *fatum*, timeless and transhistorical, but the modern
variety of fatality, closely linked with the banal. Banality is the fatality of our
modern world.

DG/DS   Could you tell us where you stand with regard to psychoanalysis?

Psychoanalysis has become useless, a burden. It satisfies a sort of dizziness for
explanations, for self-obsession and for reproducing itself. The word was one
of the fundamental tools of analysis, then everything began to spin round, and
here too there was a delirium of conceptual production, which got more and
more sophisticated. Curiously, it has ceased to have any effect. I am not talking
about psychoanalysis in its early days. But I do criticize the present-day variety
because everything that's at stake must go beyond it and cause it to shatter.

DG/DS   In Fatal Strategies *we don't know what geographical space you allude to, whether it's a planetary space or not.*

I don't talk about people in the sociological sense. The masses are not locatable in terms of population, they are not the sum of locatable individuals. It's the mass effect, the mass forms that I analyse, and which, somewhere, no longer produces any difference. This something which is there but which doesn't produce any difference is an extraordinary challenge to symbolic order of any kind, be it political, social or whatever.

My analysis, if you put it back into a realistic, geographical frame of reference, is not going to apply more or less well to such and such a model. It is a logical hypothesis of radicality, and it was inspired by the so-called developed countries, particularly the United States. But the Third World is also totally caught up in this explosion of effects, this loss of causality, this proliferation, as in demography for example. It is impossible that one part of the world's population should stick to relatively traditional, logical relationships of production or penury while another part enters another phase. The whole of our world has entered into the same phase; whether one is rich or poor does not perhaps play an important role.

DG/DS   You write that people don't seek collective happiness, but rather ecstasy and the spectacle. What do you mean by that?

I don't know what people are looking for. They have been taught to look for things like happiness, but deep down that doesn't interest them, any more than producing or being produced. What interests them is rather something that belongs to the realm of fascination, of games, but not in the frivolous sense. The world is a game. Rituals are regaining their importance, and what is a ritual if not a rule of the game, another type of relationship, not of forces, but of metamorphoses? People can sometimes cling passionately to extremely harsh and cruel logics but not for work, retirement, social security.

Ritual didn't exist in savage times only to disappear in our modern age and to be reborn as a revival of some archaic process. It has always been there, and it isn't only against reality that one struggles. That's the whole problem. If the world is reality, then effectively the logic is one of a transformation and a realization of the world, and that's all. But if the world is also illusion, appearance, then that is mastered in another way. There are different logics, different rules, and I believe that nobody has forgotten and nobody has renounced that game. Fashion, for instance, is a continuing collective passion, putting aside any perspective, and you can't say that it is archaic. All transformation of things into spectacle: it is this function of simulation which is perhaps what really makes them work, not their rational and economic mechanisms (*dispositif*).

If Soviet society really functioned in accordance with its system of values, its bureaucracy, its ideology, it would have crumbled a long time ago. This society exists and no doubt will exist for a long time because what works is the game of bureaucracy. Derision is internal to its functioning. It doesn't really run on its bureaucracy, because the people wouldn't survive in that case. Italy also functions on derision for the real state of things, which is a state of political and economic confusion. There is a collective complicity, an agreement that all should continue on a lower plane (*état second*). The real social bond is a pact which is the contrary of the social contract, a symbolic pact of allurement, complicity, derision. That is why socialism is not possible: it wants to bring everything back to the social contract and eliminate this sort of avoidance (*détournement*), this second game, this secret complicity, this pathology of social relationships where all people's imagination and passion is exercised in the double games of the maintenance of fiefdoms and territories.

The socialists are not the only ones to make mistakes. It is simply that they are the only ones who want to make reality transparent, and extirpate all the irrationalities, including all the signs and images which are vehicles for the effects of derision. If they managed to eliminate all that they would put an end to society's survival. But fortunately people work against the grain of any political system which, in appearance, represents the others and makes itself obeyed. In fact, the rule of the game is more secret than that: everything goes on in an ambience of profound derision, and somewhere the murder of that symbolic class is achieved. Everything that has conferred upon it power, status, prestige must be destroyed, killed.

DG/DS   This idea resurfaces in your eulogy of the sexual object.

The sexual object is not something that plays at being a subject of desire and at liberating itself but one that prefers to be pure object, no longer allowing itself to be judged, watched nor, basically, desired. Exhibition is the perfect form of obscenity. That is what gives it its power.

Nobody has won, nobody has lost. It is quite possible that women have resisted, survived, by the same effect of derision, of the seduction that I was just talking about. When you try to explain that to the feminists, they find it quite unacceptable. There have been dreadful misunderstandings. I've been accused of pushing women back into seduction. "Women have been stripped of everything; they're left with nothing but their power of seduction," complain the feminists. That is not at all what I meant. Seduction is a subversive power, it makes it possible to have mastery over that rather secret rule of the game, mastery not of power relations but another type of relationship. In that sense, nobody has won and nobody has lost. It would be too easy to say that men have won that age-old struggle. The feminists need the ancestral female woe in order to exist. They have defined themselves as movements in relation to what they claim from society. It is vital for them that their woe has always existed and will always exist. They have shown more detestation for me than they have for the machos. A macho is never anything else but a macho. All you have to do is fight against him. But somebody who comes along and tells you that you have much more sovereignty over men than you think, that throws your mechanism (*dispositif*) into confusion.

The feminists have rejected me definitively. It's a pity. The problematic is completely closed today, and curiously psychoanalysis has thrown no light on the matter. There have been a lot of psychoanalytical studies carried out by women, but it all crystallizes on relations with the mother. Psychoanalysis has put its entire conceptual edifice at the service of that but hasn't thrown any light on the question. In any case they do not want light.

DG/DS   Has sexual liberation failed? Indeed, did it ever happen?

Whether it has happened or not is a secondary question. You can only find that out from the statistics and they are all indecipherable. I would like to know just what people mean when they recount their behaviour. People are so naive about this. They think that if you ask people about their sexual behaviour they're going to tell you the truth. In fact, it's impossible to know what it is.

DG/DS   There's been talk about trying to liberate us from lots of things, but in the end it turned out not to be that which is interesting.

The effect of rupture is always interesting. The liberation of productive forces did get people to work. All the revolutions have been liberations in that sense. They shattered the old structures in order to capture people's potential energy with a definite aim in view. The hair-brained liberation that people dreamed about in 1968: in the sense that things would be free to become anything at all, to contain their own purpose, that is the aesthetic vision of liberation. But in reality all liberations have always led to servitude at another level.

DG/DS   You often allude to biology, you talk about cloning and the genetic code. But you seldom allude to neurophysiology, the biology of the brain, which the media are making a big noise about. What do you think about this upsurge of interest in the neuronal?

I think it's grotesque. I have nothing to do with such truths. It's going in the same direction as everything else, and it's a more subtle, more miniaturized terminal. It doesn't interest me. What I'm interested in is myth. With this proliferation in miniaturization, this pyramidalization of things which renders everything else useless, one can nevertheless ask oneself what a body is. If everything boils down to a definition, either by genetic code or by the brain, the body becomes useless. It's vertiginous! But at least we are still free to consider it an aberration. I am tempted to think this through right to the end; to see what is going to happen at the far limit of these aberrations and of the pathology of the modern world. Is this world irredeemably lost? I don't know. It is so functionalized that everything you might call game, illusion, even language itself, risks remaining caught up in it. However, let's not indulge in complacent catastrophism; things develop by themselves, perhaps, and to apply to them pseudo-moral ideas of humanist deontology—a discourse that has existed ever since there was science and technology—that won't change anything at all.

And then, there will always be a way of playing with the systems, data processing included. We have the impression that this computer network is all-powerful, and that virtually, in ten years' time, the world will be computer-run (*télématisé*). But it won't happen like that, because things don't operate only at the level of their realistic evolution. Take the exact sciences: the further they advance in hyper-detailed realism, the more the object of study disappears. The more they hunt the object of study into the inner recesses of its real existence, the more it eludes them. That is my only hope.

Analysis in demiurgic manipulative terms, with an ultra-power always on the horizon, we know that that is no longer exactly true and that there are some strange turns of events. Take the example of nuclear weapons. We know that it is the very proliferation of nuclear weapons that stops nuclear war from breaking out, even if nobody wants to admit it. It is fortunate that they have produced a hundred times too much! If ever they manage to find a little theatre well suited to nuclear war, it will start. We are protected by the proliferation, the ecstasy of destruction. We are stuck at a stage of phantasmagoric nuclear destruction that doesn't take place. This fatality, if it is ours, is not interesting. Fatality fascinates me, but not this functionalist, catastrophic fatality. There is another sort. I count on a reversible fatality, on the power of reversibility that exists in the fatal to defy and thwart this process. You can create as many social institutions as you want, there will always be this infra-resistance, this infra-distortion, which will ensure that, fortunately, the social will not function. That is what interests me, and I don't see why it shouldn't be the same where science and technology are concerned.

24

HISTORY, DISCOURSE AND DISCONTINUITY

Michel Foucault

Q: Doesn't a thought which introduces constraint of the system and discontinuity in the history of the mind remove all basis for a progressive political intervention? Does it not lead to the following dilemma:

—either the acceptance of the system,

—or the appeal to an uncontrolled event, to the irruption of exterior violence which alone is capable of upsetting the system?

MF: I have chosen the last of the questions put to me (not without regret for abandoning the others): 1) because at first glance it surprised me, and because I became quickly convinced that it concerned the very core of my work; 2) because it allowed me to offer at least a few of the answers which I would have liked to give for the others; 3) because it gave expression to questioning which no theoretical work today can eschew.

I must admit that you have characterized with extreme accuracy what I have undertaken to do, and that you have at the same time singled out the point of inevitable discord: "to introduce constraint of the system and discontinuity in the history of the mind." Yes, I recognize that this is an almost unjustifiable statement. With diabolical pertinency you have succeeded in giving a definition of my work to which I cannot avoid subscribing, but for which no one would, reasonably, ever wish to assume responsibility. I suddenly sense

From *Foucault Live (Interviews, 1961–1984)* (1989). Edited by Sylvère Lotringer; translated by Lysa Hochroth and John Johnston. Brooklyn, NY: Semiotext(e), pp. 33–50.

how bizarre my position is, how strange and hardly justifiable. And I now perceive how much this work, which was no doubt somewhat solitary, but always patient, with no other law but its own and sufficiently carried out, I thought, to be able to stand by itself, has deviated in relation to the best-established norms, how discordant it was.

However, two or three details in the very accurate definition which you propose bother me, preventing me from (perhaps allowing me to avoid) agreeing completely with it.

First of all you use the word *system* in the singular. Now, I am a pluralist. Here's what I mean. (You will allow me, I think, to speak not only of my last book, but also of those which preceded it; this is because together they form a cluster of research whose themes and chronological reference points are quite adjacent; also because each one constitutes a descriptive experiment which is opposed to and therefore relates to the other two by a certain number of traits.) I am a pluralist: the problem which I have set myself is that of the *individualization* of discourses. There exist for individualizing the discourses criteria which are known and reliable (or almost): the linguistic system to which they belong, the identity of the subject which has articulated them. But other criteria, which are not less familiar, are much more enigmatic. When one speaks of *psychiatry*, or of *medicine*, or of *grammar*, or of *biology*, or of *economics*, what is one speaking of? What are these curious entities which we believe we can recognize at first glance but whose limits we would be at a loss to define? Some of these units seem to go back to the dawn of human history (medicine as well as mathematics), whereas others have appeared recently (economics, psychiatry), and still others have perhaps disappeared (casuistry). To these units new terms are endlessly added and they are constantly modified by them (the strange units of sociology and psychology which since their appearance have not ceased to start afresh). There are units which are obstinately maintained after so many errors, neglect, so much innovation, so many metamorphoses and which sometimes undergo such radical mutations that one would have difficulty in considering them as identical to themselves (how can one affirm that economics remains the same, uninterrupted, from the physiocrats to Keynes?).

Perhaps there are discourses which can at each moment redefine their own individuality (for example, mathematics can reinterpret at each point in time the totality of its history); but in each of the cases that I have cited, the discourse cannot restore the totality of its history within the unity of a strict framework. There remain two traditional recourses. The historical-transcendental recourse: an attempt to find, beyond all historical manifestation and historical origin, a primary formation, the opening of an inexhaustible horizon, a plan which would move backward in time in relation to every event, and which would maintain throughout history the constantly unwinding plan of an unending unity. The empirical or psychological recourse: seeking out the founder, interpreting what he meant, detecting the implicit meanings which were lying silent and dormant in his discourse, following the thread or the destiny of these meanings, describing the traditions and the influences, fixing the moment of awakenings, of lapses, of awareness, of crises, of changes in the mind, the sensitivity or the interest of men. Now it seems to me that the first of these recourses is tautological, the second extrinsic and unessential. It is by marking out and by systematizing their very character that I would like to attempt to individualize the large units which scan simultaneously or successively the world of our discourses.

I have retained three groups of criteria:

1) The criteria of *formation*. What permits us to individualize a discourse such as political economy or general grammar, is not the unity of an object; it is not a formal structure; not is it a conceptual coherent architecture; it is not a fundamental philosophical choice; it is rather the existence of rules of formation for all its objects (however scattered they may be), for all its operations (which often can neither be superimposed nor linked together in succession), for all its concepts (which may very well be incompatible), for all its theoretical options (which are often mutually exclusive). There is an individualized discursive formation every time one can define a similar set of rules.

2) The criteria of *transformation* or of *threshold*. I shall say that natural history (or psycho-pathology) are units of discourse, if I can define the conditions which must have been brought together at a very precise moment of time, in order that its objects, its operations, its concepts and its theoretical options could be formed; if I can define what internal modifications it was capable of, finally if I can define from what threshold of transformation new rules have been brought into play.

3) The criteria of *correlation*. I will say that clinical medicine is an autonomous discursive formation if I can define the whole of the relations which define it and situate it among the other types of discourse (as biology, chemistry, political theory or the analysis of society) and in the nondiscursive context in which it functions (institutions, social relations, economic and political circumstances).

These criteria allow us to substitute differentiated analyses for the broad themes of general history (whether it concern "the progress of reason" or "the spirit of a century"). They allow us to describe, as *epistemic* of a period, not the sum of its knowledge, nor the general style of its research, but the deviation, the distances, the oppositions, the differences, the relations of its multiple scientific discourses: the *epistemic* is not *a sort of grand unifying theory*, it is a space of *dispersion*, it is an *open field of relationships and no doubt indefinitely describable*. They allow us furthermore to describe not broad history which would carry off all the sciences in a single swoop, but the types of history—that is to say, what was retained and transformed—which characterize the different discourses (the history of mathematics does not follow the same model as the history of biology, which does not follow the same model of psycho-pathology either): the *epistemic is not a slice of history* common to all the sciences: it is *a simultaneous play of specific remanences*. Finally they allow us to situate the different thresholds in their respective place: for nothing proves in advance (and nothing demonstrates after examination either) that their chronology is the same for all types of discourse; the threshold which one can describe for the analysis of language at the beginning of the nineteenth century has doubtless no counterpart in the history of mathematics; and, what is more paradoxical, the threshold of formation for political economy (noted by Ricardo) does not coincide with the constitution—by Marx—of an analysis of society and of history.[1] *The Epistemic is not a general stage of reason; it is a complex relationship of successive displacement in time.*

Nothing, you see, is more foreign to me than the quest for a constraining sovereign and unique form. I do not seek to detect, starting from various signs, the unitary spirit of an epoch, the general form of its conscience: something like a *Weltanschauung*. Nor have I described either the emergence and eclipse of a formal structure which might reign for a time over all the manifestations of thought: I have not written the history of a transcendental eclipse. Nor, finally, have I described thoughts or century-old sensitivities coming to life, stuttering, struggling and dying out like great phantoms—like souls playing out their shadow theater against the backdrop of history. I have studied, one after another, whole sets of discourses; I have characterized them; I have defined the play of rules, of transformations, of thresholds, of remanences. I have compounded them, I have described clusters of relationships. Wherever I have deemed it necessary I have allowed the *systems* to proliferate.

*   *   *   *   *

You say, a thought which "emphasizes discontinuity." This, indeed, is a notion whose importance today—amongst historians as with linguists—cannot be underestimated. But the use of the singular does not appear to me to be entirely suitable. Here again, I am a pluralist. My problem is to substitute the analysis of *different types of transformation* for the abstract general and wearisome form of "change" in which one so willingly thinks in terms of succession. This implies two things: setting aside the old forms of weak continuity through which one ordinarily attenuates the raw fact of change (tradition, influence, habits of thought, broad mental forms, constraints of the human mind), and stubbornly stressing instead the lively intensity of the difference: establishing meticulously the deviation. Next, discarding all the psychological explanations of change (the genius of the great inventors, crises of conscience, the appearance of a new form of mind); and defining with the greatest care the transformations which have—I don't say provoked—but constituted the change. Replacing, in short, the theme of becoming (general form, abstract element, primary cause and universal effect, a confused mixture of the identical and the new) by the analysis of the transformations in their specificity.

(1) *Within* a given discursive formation, detecting the changes which affect the objects, the operations, the concepts, the theoretical options. Thus, one can distinguish (I limit myself to the example of *general grammar*): the changes by deduction or implication (the theory of verb-copula implied the

distinction between a substantive root and a verbal inflexion); the changes by generalization (extension to the verb of the theory of word designation, and consequent disappearance of the verb-copula theory); the changes by limitation (the concept of attribute is specified by the notion of complement); the changes by passing to the complementary (from the project of constructing a universal and readily understood language is derived the search for the hidden secrets of the most primitive of languages); the changes by passing to the other term of an alternative (primacy of vowels or primacy of consonants in the constitution of roots); the changes through permutation of dependencies (one can establish the theory of the verb on the theory of the noun or inversely); the changes by exclusion or inclusion (the analysis of languages as systems of representative signs renders obsolete the search for their relationship which is reintroduced, on the other hand, by the quest of a primitive language).

These different types of change constitute in themselves altogether the whole of the characteristic *derivations* of a discursive formation.

(2) Detecting the changes which affect discursive formations *themselves*:

—displacement of boundaries which define the field of possible objects (the medical object at the beginning of the nineteenth century ceases to be taken in a surface of classification; it is marked out in the three dimensional space of the body);

—new position and new role of the speaking subject in the discourse (the subject in the discourse of the naturalists of the eighteenth century becomes exclusively a *looking* subject following a grid, and *noting* according to a code; it ceases to be listening, interpreting, deciphering);

—new functions of language with respect to objects (beginning with Tournefort the role of the discourse of the naturalist is not to penetrate into things, to capture from them the language which they secretly enclose, nor to bring it to light; but to extend a surface of transcription where the form, the number, the size and the disposition of elements can be translated in a univocal manner);

—new form of localization and of circulation of the discourse in society (the clinical discourse is not formulated in the same places, it does not have the same recording procedures, it is not diffused, it is not cumulative, it is not conserved nor is it contested in the same way as the medical discourse of the eighteenth century).

All these changes of a type superior to the preceding ones define the transformations which affect the discursive areas themselves: *mutations*.

(3) Finally, the third type of changes, those which affect simultaneously several discursive formations:

—reversal in the hierarchical order (the analysis of language had, during the classical period, a directing role which it has lost, in the first years of the nineteenth century, to the benefit of biology);

—change in the nature of the directing role (classical grammar, as a general theory of signs, guaranteed in other areas the transposition of an instrument of analysis; in the nineteenth century, biology assures the "metaphorical" importation of a number of concepts: organisms-organization; function-social function; life-life of words or of languages);

—functional displacements: the theory of the continuity of beings which, in the eighteenth century depended upon the philosophical discourse, is taken over in the nineteenth century by the scientific discourse.

All these transformations of a type superior to the two others characterize the changes peculiar to epistemic itself.

Redistributions

There you have a small number (about fifteen, perhaps) of different changes which one can assign to discourses. You see why I would prefer that one say that I have stressed not discontinuity, but *the discontinuities* (that is to say, the different transformations which it is possible to describe concerning two states of discourse). But the important thing for me, now, is not to establish an exhaustive typology of these transformations.

1) The important thing is to offer as the content of the wearisome and empty concept of "change" a play of specified modifications. The history of "ideas" or of "sciences" must not be the list of innovations, but the descriptive analysis of the different transformations that take place. [2]

2) What is important to me is not to confuse such an analysis with a psychological diagnosis. It is legitimate to ask oneself whether the person whose work bears such an ensemble of modifications had genius or what had been the experiences of his early infancy. But it is another thing to describe the field of possibilities, the form of operations, the types of transformations which characterize his discursive practice.

3) What is important to me is to show that there are not on the one hand inert discourses, already more than half dead, and then, on the other hand, an all-powerful subject which manipulates them, upsets them, renews them; but that the discoursing subjects belong to the discursive field—they have their place there (and possibilities of their displacements), their function (and possibilities of their functional mutation). The discourse is not the place where pure subjectivity irrupts; it is a space of positions and of differentiated functionings for the subjects.

4) What is important to me above all is to define amongst all these transformations the play of dependencies.

—*intradiscursive* dependencies (between the objects, the operations, the concepts of the same formation).

—*interdiscursive* dependencies (between different discursive formations, such as the correlations which I have started in *The Order of Things* between natural history, economics, grammar and the theory of representation).

—*extradiscursive* dependencies (between discursive transformations and others which have been produced elsewhere than in the discourse: such as the correlations studied in *Madness and Civilization* and in *The Birth of the*

Clinic between the medical discourse and a whole play of economic, political and social changes).

I would like to substitute this whole play of dependencies for the uniform, simple notion of assigning causality; and by eliminating the prerogative of the endlessly accompanying cause, bring out the bundle of polymorphous correlations.

As you see, there is absolutely no question of substituting a "discontinuous" category for the no less abstract and general one of the "continuous." I am attempting, on the contrary, to show that discontinuity is not a monotonous and unthinkable void between events, a void which one must hasten to fill (two perfectly symmetrical solutions) with the dismal plentitude of the cause or by the suppleness and agility of the mind; but that it is a play of specific transformations different from one another (each having its conditions, its rules, its level) and linked among themselves according to schemes of dependence. History is the descriptive analysis and the theory of these transformations.

* * * * *

A last point on which I hope to be able to be more brief. You use the expression: "history of the mind." In fact, I intended rather to write a history of discourse. You may ask: What's the difference? "You do not study the texts which you take as raw material according to their grammatical structure: you do not describe the semantic field which they cover: it is not language which is your object. And so? What do you seek if not to discover the thought which animates them and to reconstitute the representations of which they have given a durable translation, perhaps, but undoubtedly an unfaithful one? What do you seek if not to rediscover behind them the intention of the men who have formulated them, the meanings which, voluntarily or unbeknownst to them, they have deposited therein, this imperceptible supplement to the linguistic system which is something like the beginning of liberty or the history of the mind?"

Therein lies, perhaps, the essential point. You are right: what I am analyzing in the discourse is not the system of its language, nor, in a general way, the formal rules of its construction: for I do not care about knowing what renders it legitimate or gives it its intelligibility and allows it to serve in communication. The question which I ask is not that of codes but of events: the law of existence of the terms, that which has rendered them possible—they and no other in their place: the conditions of their particular emergence; their correlation with other previous or simultaneous events, discursive or not. This question, however, I try to answer without referring to the awareness, obscure or explicit, of the speaking subjects; without relating the facts or discourse to the will—perhaps involuntary—of their authors; without invoking that intention of saying which is always excessive in relation to what is said; without trying to seize hold of the inaudible when a word doesn't occur in the text.

So that what I am doing is neither a formalization nor an exegesis. But an *archaeology*: that is to say, as its name indicates only too obviously, the description of the *record*. By this word, I do not mean the mass of texts which have been collected at a given period, or chanced to have survived oblivion from this period. I mean all the rules which at a given period and for a definite society defined:

1) the limits and the forms of *expressibility*: what is it possible to speak of? What has been constituted as the field of discourse? What type of discursivity has been appropriated to such and such a domain (what has been designated as the subject; what has one wished to make a descriptive science of; to what has one given a literary formulation, etc.)?

2) the limits and the forms of *conservation*: what are the terms destined to disappear without any trace? Which ones are destined, on the other hand, to enter into the memory of men through ritualistic recitation, pedagogy and teaching, entertainment or holiday, publicity? Which ones are noted for being capable of re-use, and toward what ends? Which ones are put in circulation and in what groups? Which are those which are repressed and censured?

3) the limits and the forms of *memory* such as it appears in the different discursive formations: which are the terms which everyone recognizes as valid or questionable, or definitely invalid? Which ones have been abandoned as negligible and which ones have been excluded as foreign? What types of relationships are established between the system of present terms and the body of past terms?

4) the limits and the forms of *reactivation*: amongst the discourses of previous epochs or of foreign cultures, which are the ones that are retained, which are valued, which are imported, which one tries to reconstitute? And what does one do with them, what transformations does one impose upon them (commentary, exegesis, analysis), what system of appreciation does one apply to them, what role does one give them to play?

5) the limits and the forms of *appropriation*: what individuals, what groups, what classes have access to such a kind of discourse? In what way is the relationship between the discourse and whoever gives it, and whoever receives it institutionalized? In what way is the relationship of the discourse to its author shown and defined? How does the struggle for taking over the discourse take place between classes, nations, linguistic, cultural or ethnic collectivities?

It is against this background that the analyses which I have begun are set; it is towards it that they are directed. I am writing, therefore, not a history of the mind, according to the succession of its forms or according to the thickness of its deposited meanings. I do not question the discourses concerning what silently they mean, but on the fact and the conditions of their manifest appearance; not on the contents which they may conceal, but on the field where they coexist, remain and disappear. It is a question of an analysis of the discourses in their exterior dimensions. From whence arise three consequences:

1) Treat the past discourse not as a theme for a *commentary* which would revive it, but as a *monument*[3] to be described in its characteristic disposition.

2) Seek in the discourse not its laws of construction, as do the structural methods, but its conditions of existence.

3) Refer the discourse not to the thought, to the mind or to the subject which might have given rise to it, but to the practical field in which it is deployed.

*   *   *   *   *

Forgive me for being so lengthy, so laborious, just to propose three slight changes in your definition and to ask your agreement, so that we may speak about my work as an attempt to introduce "diversity *of the systems* and the play of discontinuities in the history of the *discourses*." Do not imagine that I want to distort the issue; or that I seek to avoid the point of your question by discussing its terms *ad infinitum*. But prior agreement was necessary. Now I have my back to the wall. I must answer.

Certainly not the question of whether *I* am a reactionary; nor whether my texts *are* (in themselves, intrinsically, through a certain number of well-coded signs). You ask me a much more serious question, the only one, I believe, which can legitimately be raised. You question me on the *relationships* between what I say and a certain political practice.

It seems to me that two answers can be offered to this question. One concerns the critical operations which my discourse carries out in its own domain (the history of ideas, of sciences, of thought, of knowledge . . .): was what it puts out of circulation indispensable to a progressive politics? The other concerns the field of analysis and the realm of objects which my discourse attempts to bring out: how can they be articulated in the exercise of a progressive politics?

I shall sum up as follows the critical operations which I have undertaken:

1) *To establish limits* where the history of thought, in its traditional form, gave itself a limitless space. In particular:

a) to challenge again the great interpretive postulate according to which the reign of the discourse would have no designated boundaries; mute things and silence itself would be able still to hear the deeply varied murmur of the meaning; in what men do not say they would continue to speak; a world of slumbering texts would await us in the blank pages of our history. In opposition to this theme I would like to substitute the notion that the discourses are limited practical domains which have their boundaries, their rules of formation, their conditions of existence: the historical base of the discourse is not a more profound discourse—at once identical and different;

b) to challenge again the theme of a sovereign subject which would come from the outside to animate the inertia of the linguistic codes, and which would deposit in the discourse the indelible trace of its liberty; to challenge again the theme of a subjectivity which would constitute the meanings and then would transcribe them into the discourse. In opposition to these themes I would like to substitute pin-pointing the origin of the roles and of the operations exercised by the different "discoursing" subjects.

c) to challenge again the theme of the indefinitely receding origin, and the idea that in the realm of thought, the role of history is to awaken what has been forgotten, to eliminate the occultations, to erase—or to obstruct again—the barriers. In opposition to this theme I would like to substitute the analysis of discursive systems, historically defined, to which one can affix thresholds, and assign conditions of birth and disappearance.

In a word, to establish these limits, to question again these three themes of the origin, the subject and the implicit meaning, is to undertake—a difficult task, very strong resistance indeed proves it—to liberate the discursive field from the historical-transcendental structure which the philosophy of the nineteenth century has imposed on it.

2) *To eliminate ill-considered oppositions.* Here are a few of them in their order of increasing importance: the opposition between the liveliness of innovations and the dead weight of tradition, the inertia of acquired knowledge or the old tracings of thought; the opposition between the average forms of knowledge (which would represent its everyday mediocrity) and its deviating forms (which would manifest the singularity or the solitude characteristic of genius); the opposition between periods of stability or of universal convergence and moments of effervescence when consciences enter into crisis, when sensibilities are metamorphosed, when all notions are revised, overturned, revivified, or for an indefinite time, fall into disuse. For all these dichotomies I would like to substitute the analysis of the field of simultaneous differences (which define at a given period the possible dispersal of knowledge) and of successive differences (which define the whole of the transformations, their hierarchy, their dependence, their level). Whereas one used to relate the history of tradition and of invention, of the old and the new, of the dead and the living, of the closed and the open, of the static and of the dynamic, I undertake to relate the history of ideas as the sum total of the specified and descriptive forms of the non-identity. And thus I would like to free it of the triple metaphor which has encumbered it for more than a century (the evolutionist, which imposes upon it the division between the regressive and the adaptive; the biological which separates the inert from the living; the dynamic which opposes movement and immobility).

3) *To lift the restriction* which has been directed at the discourse in its very existence (and therein lies, for me, the most important of the critical operations that I have undertaken). This restriction consists of several aspects:

a) never treating the discourse except as an unimportant element without its own consistency nor inherent laws (a pure translation surface for mute things; a simple place of expression for thought, imagination, knowledge, unconscious themes);

b) recognizing in the discourse only the patterns of a psychological and individualizing model (the work of an author, and—why not?—his juvenilia or his mature work), the patterns of a linguistic or rhetorical model (a genre, a style), the patterns of a semantic model (an idea, a theme);

c) admitting that all the operations are made before the discourse and outside of it (in the ideality of thought or in the serious realm of mute practices); that the discourse, consequently, is but a slight addition which adds an almost impalpable fringe to things and to the mind; a surplus which *goes without saying*, since it does nothing else except to say what has been said.

To this restriction, I would object that the discourse is not nothing or almost nothing. And what it is—what defines its own consistency, what allows one to make an historical analysis of it—is not what one "meant" to say (that obscure and heavy weight of intentions which supposedly weighs, in the shadow, with a much greater heaviness than the things said); it is not what has remained silent (those imposing things which do not speak, but which leave their traceable marks, their black profile against the light surface of what is said): the discourse is constituted by the difference between what one could say correctly at one period (according to the rules of grammar and those of logic) and what is actually said. The discursive field is, at a specific moment, the law of this difference. It thus defines a number of operations which do not belong to the order of linguistic construction or of formal deduction. It deploys a "neutral" domain in which speech and writing can cause the system of their opposition and the difference of their functioning to vary. It appears as a whole group of practical rules which do not consist simply in giving a visible and exterior body to the inner agility of thought, nor in offering to the solidity of things the reflecting surface which will duplicate them. At the bottom of this restriction which has weighed upon the discourse (to the advantage of the thought-language, history-truth, word-writing, words-things opposition), there was the refusal to recognize that in the discourse something is formed (according to well-definable rules); that this something exists, subsists, changes, disappears (according to rules equally definable); in short, that, side by side with all which a society can produce ("side by side": that is to say, in a relationship which can be assigned to all that), there is formation and transformation of "things said." It is the history of these "things said" that I have undertaken.

4) Finally, the last critical task (which sums up and embraces all the others): *freeing from their uncertain status* this ensemble of disciplines which one calls history of ideas, history of sciences, history of thought, history of knowledge, of concepts or of conscience. This certainly manifests itself in several ways:

—difficulties in limiting the domains: where does the history of sciences end, where does the history of opinions and beliefs begin? How are the history of concepts and the history of notions or themes to be separated? Where lies the boundary between the history of knowledge and that of the imagination?

—difficulty in defining the nature of the object: does one write the history of what has been known, acquired, forgotten, or the history of mental forms, or the history of their interference? Does one write the history of characteristic features which are held in common by men of one period or of one culture? Does one describe a collective spirit? Does one analyze the (teleological or genetic) history of reason?

—difficulty in assigning the relationship between these facts of thought or of knowledge and the other areas of historical analysis: must one treat them as signs of something else (of a social relationship, or a political situation, of an economic determination)? Or as their result? Or as their refraction through a consciousness? Or as the symbolic expression of their total form?

For so many uncertainties I would like to substitute the analysis of the discourse itself in its conditions of formation, in the series of its modifications, and in the play of its dependencies and of its modifications, and in the play of its dependencies and of its correlations. The discourse would thus appear in a describable relationship with the whole of other practices. Instead of having to deal with an economic, social, political history embracing a history of thought (which would be its expression and something like its duplicate), instead of having to deal with a history of ideas which would be referred (either through a play of signs and of expressions, or by relations of causality) to extrinsic conditions, one would be dealing with a history of discursive practices in the specific relationships which link them to the other practices. There is no question of composing a *global history*—which would regroup all its elements around one principle or one unique form—but rather of opening up the field of a *general history* in which one could describe the peculiarity of practices, the play of their relations, the form of their dependencies. And it is in the area of this general history that the historical analysis of discursive practices could be circumscribed as a discipline.

These, then, are more or less the critical operations that I have undertaken. Now allow me to call you to witness the question that I ask of those who might become alarmed: "Is a progressive politics linked (in its theoretical thinking) to the themes of meaning, of origin, of the constituent subject, in short, to all the themes which guarantee to history the inexhaustible presence of the Logos, the sovereignty of a pure subject, and the profound teleology of an original destination? Is a progressive politics bound to such a form of analysis—or with its being challenged? And is such a politics bound to all the dynamic, biological, evolutionary metaphors through which one masks the difficult problem of historical change—or, on the contrary, to their meticulous destruction? And further: is there some necessary relationship between a progressive politics and the refusal to recognize in the discourse anything else except a thin transparency which flickers for a moment at the limit of things and of thoughts, then disappears immediately? Can one believe that this politics has any interest in rehashing one more time the theme—I would have thought that the existence and the practice of the revolutionary discourse in Europe for more than 200 years might have been able to free us from it—that words are just air, an exterior whispering, a sound of wings which one hears with difficulty in the seriousness of history and the silence of thought? Finally must one think that a progressive politics is linked to the devaluation of discursive practices, so that a history of the mind, of conscience, of reason, of knowledge, of ideas or opinions might triumph in its certain ideality?"

It seems to me that I perceive, on the other hand—and quite clearly—the perilous ease which the politics you speak of would assume, if it gave itself the guarantee of a primitive foundation or of a transcendental teleology, if it persistently transformed time into metaphors through the images of life or the models of movement, if it renounced the difficult task of a general analysis of practices, of their relations, of their transformations, to take refuge in a global history of totalities, of expressive relationships, of symbolic values and of all those secret meanings in which thoughts and things are enveloped.

*   *   *   *   *

You have a right to say to me: "This is all very well: the critical operations which you are making are not as blameworthy as they might appear at first glance. But, after all, how can this work of a termite on the origin of philology, of economics, or of pathological anatomy concern politics, and be included among the problems which pertain to it today? There was a time when philosophers did not devote themselves with so great a zeal to the dust of archives . . . " To which I will answer, more or less: "There exists today a problem which is not without importance for political practice: the problem of the laws, of the conditions of exercise, of functioning, of the institutionalizing of scientific discourses. That's what I have undertaken to analyze historically—by choosing the discourses which have, not the strongest epistemological structure (mathematics or physics), but the densest and most complex field of positivity (medicine, economics, social sciences)."

Take a simple example: the formation of the clinical discourse which has characterized medicine from the beginning of the nineteenth century until the present, approximately. I have chosen it because we are dealing with a very definite, historical fact, and because one cannot refer its establishment back to some remote origin; because it would be very irresponsible to denounce it as a "pseudo-science"; and above all because it is easy to grasp "intuitively" the relationship between this scientific mutation and a number of precise political events: those which one groups—even on the European scale—under the title of the French Revolution. The problem is to give to this still vague relationship an analytical content.

First hypothesis: it is the conscience of men which has become modified (under the influence of economic, social, political changes); and their view of illness has, by this very fact, been altered: they have recognized its political consequences (uneasiness, discontent, revolts in populations whose health is deficient); they have perceived its economic implications (the desire of employers to have at their disposal a healthy work force; the wish of the bourgeoisie in power to transfer to the State the expenses of assistance); they have therein transposed their conception of society (a single medicine with a universal value, with two distinct fields of application: the hospital for the poor classes; the free and competitive practice for the rich); they have therein transcribed their new conception of the world: desacralization of the corpse, which has permitted autopsies; a greater importance accorded the living body as an instrument of work; the concern for health replacing the preoccupation with salvation. In all this, there are many things which are true; but, on the one hand, they do not account for the formation of a scientific discourse; and on the other hand, they could only have come into existence, and with the effects that one has been able to establish, to the extent that the medical discourse had received a new standard.

Second hypothesis: the fundamental notions of clinical medicine would be derived, by transposition, from a political practice or at least from the theoretical forms in which it is reflected. The ideas of organic solidarity, of functional cohesion, of tissulary communication, the abandonment of the principle of classification in favor of an analysis of the whole body corresponded to a political practice which revealed, beneath stratifications which were still feudal, social relationships of the functional and economic type. Or else, do not the refusal to see in sickness a large family of almost botanical species, and the effort to find the pathological juncture, its mechanism of development, its cause and, in the final analysis, its therapeutic, correspond to the project, in the ruling social class, of no longer controlling the world by theoretical knowledge alone, but by a mass of applicable knowledge, its decision to accept no longer as nature that which would be imposed upon her as a limit and as an evil? Such analyses do not appear to me to be pertinent either, because they avoid the essential problem: what should be, in the midst of the other discourses, and in a general way, of the other practices, the mode of existence and function of the medical discourse in order that such transpositions or such correspondences are produced?

That is why I would change the point of attack in relation to the traditional analyses. If indeed there is a link between political practice and the medical discourse, it is not, it seems to me, because this practice changed, initially, the conscience of men, the way they perceive things or conceive of the world, and then finally the form of their knowledge and its content, nor is it because this was reflected at first, in a more or less clear and systematic way, in concepts, notions or themes which have been subsequently imported into medicine. It is in a much more direct manner: political practice has transformed not the meaning or the form of the discourse, but the conditions of its emergence, insertion and functioning; it has transformed the mode of existence of the medical discourse. And this has come about through a number of operations described elsewhere and which I sum up here: new criteria to designate those who receive by law the right to hold a medical discourse; new division of the medical object through the application of another scale of observation which is superimposed on the first without erasing it (sickness observed statistically on the level of a population); new law of assistance which creates a hospital space for observation and surgery (space which is organized, furthermore, according to an economic principle, since the sick person benefiting from the care must compensate through the medical lesson which he gives; he pays for the right of being cared for by the obligation of being examined, and this goes up to, and includes, death); a new mode of registering, of preserving, of accumulating, of diffusing and of teaching the medical discourse (which must no longer express the experience of the physician but constitute, first of all, a document on illness); new functioning of the medical discourse in the system of administrative and political control of the population (society as society is considered and "treated" according to the categories of health and pathology.).

Now—and here's where the analysis becomes complex—these transformations in the conditions of existence and functioning of the discourse are neither "reflected" nor "translated" nor "expressed" in the concepts, the methods or the data of medicine: they modify its rules of formation. What is transformed by political practice is not the medical "objects" (political practice does not change, this is quite evident, the "morbid species" into "lesional infections"), but the system which offers to the medical discourse a possible object (whether it be a population surveyed and indexed, whether it be a total pathological evolution in an individual whose antecedents have been established and whose disturbances or their abatement are daily observed, whether it be an anatomical autopsied area); what is transformed by political practice is not the methods of analysis but the system of their formation (administrative recording of illnesses, of deaths, of their causes, of admissions and dismissals from hospital, setting up of archives, relations between medical personnel and patients in the hospital field); what has been transformed by political practice is not the concepts but their system of formation; the substitution of the concept of "tissue" for that of "solid" is obviously not the result of a political change; but what political practice has modified is the system of formation of the concepts: for the intermittent mutation of the effects of illness, and for the hypothetical designation of a functional cause, it has allowed the substitution of a tight, almost continual, anatomical graph supported in depth, and local points of reference of anomalies, of their field of dispersion and of their eventual routes of diffusion. The haste with which one ordinarily relates the contents of a scientific discourse to a political practice hides, in my mind, the level where the articulation can be described in precise terms.

It seems to me, that starting from such an analysis, one can understand:

1) how to describe a whole group of relations between a scientific discourse and a political practice, the details of which it is possible to follow and whose subordination one can grasp. Very direct relations since they no longer have to pass through the conscience of the speaking subjects nor through the efficacity of thought. Yet, indirect relations since the data of a scientific discourse can no longer be considered as the immediate expression of a social rapport or of an economic situation.

2) how to assign the proper role of political practice in relation to a scientific discourse. It does not have a thaumaturgic role of creation: it does not bring forth sciences out of nothing; it transforms the conditions of existence and the systems of functioning of the discourse. These changes are not

arbitrary nor "free": they operate in a realm which has its own configuration and which consequently does not offer limitless possibilities of modification. The political practice does not reduce to nothing the consistency of the discursive field in which it operates.

Nor does it have a universal, critical role. It is not in the name of a political practice that one can judge the scientific quality of a science (unless the latter claims to be, in one way or another, a theory of politics). But in the name of a political practice one can question the mode of existence and the functioning of a science.

3) how the relations between a political practice and a discursive field can be articulated in turn on relations of another order. Thus medicine, at the beginning of the nineteenth century, is at once linked to a political practice (on a mode which I analyzed in *The Birth of the Clinic*), and to a whole group of "interdiscursive" changes which were simultaneously produced in several disciplines (substitutions for an analysis of the order and of taxonomical characters, of an analysis of solidarities, of functionings, of successive series), which I have described in *The Order of Things*.

4) how phenomena which one is in the habit of placing in the foreground (influence, communication of models, transfer and metaphorization of concepts) find their historical condition of possibility in these first modifications: for example, the importation in the analysis of society, of biological concepts such as those of organism, of function of evolution, even of sickness, played, in the nineteenth century, the role which one recognizes (much more important, much more ideologically loaded than the "naturalist" comparisons of preceding periods) only in proportion to the regulation given to the medical discourse by political practice.

Through this very long example I am anxious to show you but one thing: how what I am attempting to bring out through my analysis—the *positivity* of discourses, their conditions of existence, the systems which regulate their emergence, their functioning and their transformations—can concern political practice; to show you what this practice can do with it: to convince you that by outlining this theory of the scientific discourse, by making it appear as an ensemble of regulated practices, being articulated in an analyzable fashion upon other practices, I am not just enjoying myself by making the game more complicated for certain spirited souls. I am trying to define in what way, to what extent, to what level the discourse, and particularly the scientific discourses, can be objects of a political practice, and in what system of dependency they can be in relation to it.

Allow me once more to call you to witness the question I ask: Isn't this politics well known which answers in terms of thought or conscience, in terms of pure ideality or psychological traits, when one speaks to it of a practice, of its conditions, of its rules, of its historical changes? Isn't this politics well known which, since the beginning of the nineteenth century, stubbornly persists in seeing in the immense domain of practice only the epiphany of a triumphant reason, or in deciphering in it only the historic-transcendental destination of the West? And more precisely: does the refusal to analyze the conditions of existence and the rules of the scientific discourses, in what they possess both specific and dependent, not condemn all politics to a perilous choice: either to place upon a mode which one can, indeed, call, if one wishes, "technocratic," the validity and efficacy of a scientific discourse, whatever may be the real conditions of its exercise and the whole of the practices upon which it is articulated (thus establishing the scientific discourse as a universal rule for all the other practices, without taking into account the fact that it is itself a regulated and conditioned practice); or else, to intervene directly in the discursive field as if it didn't have its own consistency, making of it the raw material of a psychological inquisition (judging what is said by the who says it), or practicing the symbolic valorization of the notions (by discerning in a science the concepts which are "reactionary" and those which are "progressive").

*   *   *   *   *

I should like to conclude by submitting several hypotheses to you:

—A progressive politics is one which recognizes the historical conditions and the specified rules of a practice, whereas other politics recognize only ideal necessities, univocal determinations, or the free play of individual initiatives.

—A progressive politics is one which defines in a practice the possibilities of transformations and the play of dependencies between these transformations, whereas other politics rely on the uniform abstraction of change or the thaumaturgical presence of genius.

—A progressive politics does not make of man or of conscience or of the subject in general the universal operator of all the transformations: it defines the levels and the different functions which the subjects can occupy in a domain which has its rules of formation.

—A progressive politics does not consider that the discourses are the result of mute processes or the expression of a silent conscience, but rather that—science, or literature or religious statements, or political discourses— they form a practice which is articulated upon the other practices.

—A progressive politics, with respect to the scientific discourse, does not find itself in a position of "perpetual demand" or of "sovereign criticism," but it must know the manner in which the diverse scientific discourses, in their positivity (that is to say, as practices linked to certain conditions, obedient to certain rules, and susceptible to certain transformation) are part of a system of correlations with other practices.

This is the point where what I have been trying to do for about ten years now encounters the question which you are asking me. I ought to say: that's the point where your question—which is so legitimate and pertinent— reaches the heart of my own undertaking. If I were to reformulate this undertaking—under the pressure of your questioning which has not ceased to occupy me for almost two months—here is, more or less, what I would say:

"To determine, in its diverse dimensions, what must have been in Europe, since the seventeenth century, the mode of existence of discourses and particularly of the scientific discourses (their rules of formation, with their conditions, their dependencies, their transformations), in order that the knowledge which is ours today could come to exist, and, in a more precise manner, that knowledge which has taken as its domain this curious object which is man."

I know, almost as much as any other person, how "thankless" such research can be—in the strict sense of the term—how irritating it is to approach the discourses not from the sweet, mute and intimate conscience which is expressed in them, but from an obscure ensemble of anonymous rules. I know how unpleasant it is to bring out the limits and the necessities of a practice, whereas one was in the habit of seeing unfold in a pure transparency the play of genius and liberty. I know how provoking it is to treat as a cluster of transformations this history of discourses which, until now, was animated by the reassuring metamorphoses of life and the intentional continuity of the past. Finally I know how unbearable it is to cut up, analyze, combine, recompose all these texts which have now returned to silence, without the transfigured face of the author being even discernible in it inasmuch as each person wants to put, thinks he is putting of "himself" in his own discourse, when he undertakes to speak: what! so many words piled up, so many marks made on so much paper and offered to innumerable eyes, such a great zeal to preserve them beyond the gesture which articulates them, such a profound reverence determined to preserve them and inscribe them in the memory of men—all this, so that nothing will remain of this poor hand which has traced them, of this anxiety which sought to appease itself in them, and of this completed life which has nothing left but them for survival? Discourse, in its deepest determination, would not be a "trace"? And its murmur would not be the place of unsubstantial immortality? Would one have to admit that the time of the discourse is not the time of the conscience carried to the dimensions of history, or the time of present history in the form of conscience? Would I have to suppose that, in my discourse, my survival is not at stake? And that, by speaking, I do not exorcise my death, but that I establish it; or rather that I abolish all inwardness in this outside which is so unconcerned with my life, and so neutral, that it does not distinguish between my life and my death?

I indeed understand all this and people's uneasiness. They undoubtedly have had enough difficulty in recognizing that their history, their economics, their social practices, the language which they speak, the mythology of their ancestors, even the fables which were told them in their childhood, obey rules which they are not aware of, they hardly wish to be dispossessed, in addition, of this discourse in which they wish to be able to say immediately, directly, what they are thinking, what they believe or imagine; they will prefer to deny that the discourse is a complex and differentiated practice obeying rules and analyzable transformations, rather than be deprived of this tender certainty, so consoling, of being able to change, if not the world, if not life, at least their "meaning" only through the freshness of a word which would come only from themselves and would remain indefinitely so very close to the source. So many things, in their language, have already escaped them; they do not want to lose, in addition, what they say, this little fragment of discourse—word or writing, it matters little—whose frail and uncertain existence is to extend their life further in time and space. They cannot bear—and one can understand them somewhat—being told: discourse is not life; its time is not yours; in it you will not reconcile yourself with death; it is quite possible that you have killed God under the weight of all that you have said; but don't think that you will make, from everything that you say, a man who will live longer than he. In each sentence that you pronounce—and very precisely in this one that you are busy writing at this moment, you have been answering a question so intently, for so many pages, through which you have felt personally concerned and who are going to sign this text with your name—in every sentence there reigns the nameless law, the white indifference: "What does it matter who is speaking; someone has said: what does it matter who is speaking."

Translated by Anthony M. Nazzaro

Notes

1. This fact, already pointed out by Oscar Lange, explains at once the limited and so perfectly circumscribed place which the concepts of Marx occupy in the epistemological field which extends from Petty to contemporary econometrics, and the founding character of these same concepts for a theory of history.
2. In which I follow the examples of the method given on several occasions by M. Canguilhem.
3. I borrow this word from M. Canguilhem. He describes, better than I have done myself, what I have wished to do.

25

THE HISTORY OF
SEXUALITY

Michel Foucault

For a long time, one of the characteristic privileges of sovereign power was the right to decide life and death. In a formal sense, it derived no doubt from the ancient *patria potestas* that granted the father of the Roman family the right to "dispose" of the life of his children and his slaves; just as he had given them life, so he could take it away. By the time the right of life and death was framed by the classical theoreticians, it was in a considerably diminished form. It was no longer considered that this power of the sovereign over his subjects could be exercised in an absolute and unconditional way, but only in cases where the sovereign's very existence was in jeopardy: a sort of right of rejoinder. If he were threatened by external enemies who sought to overthrow him or contest his rights, he could then legitimately wage war, and require his subjects to take part in the defense of the state; without "directly proposing their death," he was empowered to "expose their life": in this sense, he wielded an "indirect" power over them of life and death.[1] But if someone dared to rise up against him and transgress his laws, then he could exercise a direct power over the offender's life: as punishment, the latter would be put to death. Viewed in this way, the power of life and death was not an absolute privilege: it was conditioned by the defense of the sovereign, and his own survival. Must we follow Hobbes in seeing it as the transfer to the prince of the natural right possessed by every individual to defend his life even if this meant the death of others? Or should it be regarded as a specific right that was manifested with the formation of that new juridical being, the sovereign?[2] In any case, in its modern form—relative and limited—as in its ancient and absolute form, the right of life and death is a dissymmetrical one. The sovereign exercised his right of life only by exercising his right to kill, or by refraining from killing; he evidenced his power over life only through the death he was capable of requiring. The right which was formulated as the "power of life and death" was in reality the right to *take* life or *let* live. Its symbol, after all, was the sword. Perhaps this juridical form must be referred to a historical type of society in which power was exercised mainly as a means of deduction (*prélèvement*), a subtraction mechanism, a right to appropriate a portion of the wealth, a tax of products, goods and services, labor and blood, levied on the subjects. Power in this instance was essentially a right of seizure: of things, time, bodies, and ultimately life itself; it culminated in the privilege to seize hold of life in order to suppress it.

Since the classical age the West has undergone a very profound transformation of these mechanisms of power. "Deduction" has tended to be no longer the major form of power but merely one element among others, working to incite, reinforce, control, monitor, optimize, and organize the forces under it: a power bent on generating forces, making them grow, and ordering them, rather than one dedicated to impeding them, making them submit, or destroying them. There has been a parallel shift in the right of death, or at least a tendency to align itself with the exigencies of a life-administering power and to define itself accordingly. This death that was based on the right of the sovereign is now manifested as simply the reverse of the right of the social body to ensure, maintain, or develop its life. Yet wars were never as bloody as they have been since the nineteenth century, and all things being equal, never before did regimes visit such holocausts on their own populations. But this formidable power of death—and this is perhaps what accounts for part of its force and the cynicism with which it has so greatly expanded its limits—now presents itself as the counterpart of a power that exerts a positive influence on life, that endeavors to administer, optimize, and multiply it, subjecting it to precise controls and comprehensive regulations. Wars are no longer waged in the name of a sovereign who must be defended; they are waged on behalf of the existence of everyone; entire populations are mobilized for the purpose of wholesale slaughter in the name of life necessity: massacres have become vital. It is as managers of life and survival, of bodies and the race, that so many regimes have been able to wage so many wars, causing so many men to be killed. And through a turn that closes the circle, as the technology of wars has caused them to tend increasingly toward all-out destruction, the decision that initiates them and the one that terminates them are in fact increasingly informed by the naked question of survival. The atomic situation is now at the end point of this process: the power to expose a whole population to death is the underside of the power to guarantee an individual's continued existence. The principle underlying the tactics of battle—that one has to be capable of killing in order to go on living—has become the principle that defines the strategy of states. But the existence in question is no longer the juridical existence of sovereignty; at stake is the biological existence of a population. If genocide is indeed the dream of modern powers, this is not because of a recent return of the ancient right to kill; it is because power is situated and exercised at the level of life, the species, the race, and the large-scale phenomena of population.

On another level, I might have taken up the example of the death penalty. Together with war, it was for a long time the other form of the right of the sword; it constituted the reply of the sovereign to those who attacked his will, his law, or his person. Those who died on the scaffold became fewer and fewer, in contrast to those who died in wars. But it was for the same reasons that the latter became more numerous and the former more and more rare. As soon as power gave itself the function of administering life, its reason for being and the logic of its exercise—and not the awakening of humanitarian feelings—made it more and more difficult to apply the death penalty. How could power exercise its highest prerogatives by putting people to death, when its main role was to ensure, sustain, and multiply life, to put this life in order? For such a power, execution was at the same time a limit, a scandal, and a contradiction. Hence capital punishment could not be maintained except by invoking less the enormity of the crime itself than the monstrosity of the criminal, his incorrigibility, and the safeguard of society. One had the right to kill those who represented a kind of biological danger to others.

One might say that the ancient right to *take* life or *let* live was replaced by a power to *foster* life or *disallow* it to the point of death. This is perhaps what explains that disqualification of death which marks the recent wane of the rituals that accompanied it. That death is so carefully evaded is linked less to a new anxiety which makes death unbearable for our societies than to the fact that the procedures of power have not ceased to turn away from death. In the passage from this world to the other, death was the manner in which a terrestrial sovereignty was relieved by another, singularly more powerful sovereignty; the pageantry that surrounded it was in the category of political ceremony. Now it is over life, throughout its unfolding, that power establishes its dominion; death is power's limit, the moment that escapes it; death becomes the most secret aspect of existence, the most "private." It is not surprising that suicide—once a crime, since it was a way to usurp the power of death which the sovereign alone, whether the one here below or the Lord above, had the right to exercise—became, in the course of the nineteenth century, one of the first conducts to enter into the sphere of sociological analysis; it testified to the individual and private right to die, at the borders and in the interstices of power that was exercised over life. This determination to die, strange and yet so persistent and constant in its manifestations, and consequently so difficult to explain as being due to particular circumstances or individual accidents, was one of the first astonishments of a society in which political power had assigned itself the task of administering life.

In concrete terms, starting in the seventeenth century, this power over life evolved in two basic forms; these forms were not antithetical, however; they constituted rather two poles of development linked together by a whole intermediary cluster of relations. One of these poles—the first to be formed, it seems—centered on the body as a machine: its disciplining, the optimization of its capabilities, the extortion of its forces, the parallel increase of its usefulness and its docility, its integration into systems of efficient and economic controls, all this was ensured by the procedures of power that characterized the *disciplines*: an *anatomo-politics of the human body*. The second, formed somewhat later, focused on the species body, the body imbued with the mechanics of life and serving as the basis of the biological processes: propagation, births and mortality, the level of health, life expectancy and longevity, with all the conditions that can cause these to vary. Their supervision was effected through an entire series of interventions and *regulatory controls: a bio-politics of the population*. The disciplines of the body and the regulations of the population constituted the two poles around which the organization of power over life was deployed. The setting up, in the course of the classical age, of this great bipolar technology—anatomic and biological, individualizing and specifying, directed toward the performances of the body, with attention to the processes of life—characterized a power whose highest function was perhaps no longer to kill, but to invest life through and through.

The old power of death that symbolized sovereign power was now carefully supplanted by the administration of bodies and the calculated management of life. During the classical period, there was a rapid development of various disciplines—universities, secondary schools, barracks, workshops. there was also the emergence, in the field of political practices and economic observation, of the problems of birthrate, longevity, public health, housing, and migration. Hence there was an explosion of numerous and diverse techniques for achieving the subjugation of bodies and the control of populations, marking the beginning of an era of "biopower." The two directions taken by its development still appeared to be clearly separate in the eighteenth century. With regard to discipline, this development was embodied in institutions such as the army and the schools, and in reflections on tactics, apprenticeship, education, and the nature of societies, ranging from the strictly military analyses of Marshal de Saxe to the political reveries of Guibert or Servan. As for population controls, one notes the emergence of demography, the evaluation of the relationship between resources and inhabitants, the constructing of tables analyzing wealth and its circulation: the work of Quesnay, Moheau, and Süssmilch. The philosophy of the "Ideologists," as a theory of ideas, signs, and the individual genesis of sensations, but also a theory of the social composition of interests—Ideology being a doctrine of apprenticeship, but also a doctrine of contracts and the regulated formation of the social body—no doubt constituted the abstract discourse in which one sought to coordinate these two techniques of power in order to construct a general theory of it. In point of fact, however, they were not to be joined at the level of a speculative discourse, but in the form of concrete arrangements (*agencements concrets*) that would go to make up the great technology of power in the nineteenth century: the deployment of sexuality would be one of them, and one of the most important.

This bio-power was without question an indispensable element in the development of capitalism; the latter would not have been possible without the controlled insertion of bodies into the machinery of production and the adjustment of the phenomena of population to economic processes. But this was not all it required; it also needed the growth of both these factors, their reinforcement as well as their availability and docility; it had to have methods of power capable of optimizing forces, aptitudes, and life in general without at the same time making them more difficult to govern. If the development of the great instruments of the state, as *institutions* of power, ensured the maintenance of production relations, the rudiments of anatomo- and bio-politics, created in the eighteenth century as *techniques* of power present at every level of the social body and utilized by very diverse institutions (the family and the army, schools and the police, individual medicine and the administration of collective bodies), operated in the sphere of economic processes, their development, and the forces working to sustain them. They also acted as factors of segregation and social hierarchization, exerting their influence on the respective forces of both these movements, guaranteeing relations of domination and effects of hegemony. The adjustment of the accumulation of men to that of capital, the joining of the growth of human groups to the expansion of productive forces and the differential allocation of profit, were made possible in part by the exercise of bio-power in its many forms and modes of application. The investment of the body, its valorization, and the distributive management of its forces were at the time indispensable.

One knows how many times the question has been raised concerning the role of an ascetic morality in the first formation of capitalism; but what occurred in the eighteenth century in some Western countries, an event bound up with the development of capitalism, was a different phenomenon having perhaps a wider impact than the new morality; this was nothing less than the entry of life into history, that is, the entry of phenomena peculiar to the life of the human species into the order of knowledge and power, into the sphere of political techniques. It is not a question of claiming that this was the moment when the first contact between life and history was brought about. On the contrary, the pressure exerted by the biological on the historical had remained very strong for thousands of years; epidemics and famine were the two great dramatic forms of this relationship that was always dominated by the menace of death. But through a circular process, the economic—and primarily agricultural—development of the eighteenth century, and an increase in productivity and resources even more rapid than the demographic growth it encouraged, allowed a measure of relief from these profound threats: despite some renewed outbreaks, the period of great ravages from starvation and plague had come to a close before the French Revolution; death was ceasing to torment life so directly. But at the same time, the development of the different fields of knowledge concerned with life in general, the improvement of agricultural techniques, and the observations and measures relative to man's life and survival contributed to this relaxation: a relative control over life averted some of the imminent risks of death. In the space for movement thus conquered, and broadening and organizing that space, methods of power and knowledge assumed responsibility for the life processes and undertook to control and modify them. Western man was gradually learning what it meant to be a living species in a living world, to have a body, conditions of existence, probabilities of life, an individual and collective welfare, forces that could be modified, and a space in which they could be distributed in an optimal manner. For the first time in history, no doubt, biological existence was reflected in political existence; the fact of living was no longer an inaccessible substrate that only emerged from time to time, amid the randomness of death and its fatality; part of it passed into knowledge's field of control and power's sphere of intervention. Power would no longer be dealing simply with legal subjects over whom the ultimate dominion was death, but with living beings, and the mastery it would be able to exercise over them would have to be applied at the level of life itself; it was the taking charge of life, more than the threat of death, that gave power its access even to the body. If one can apply the term *bio-history* to the pressures through which the movements of life and the processes of history interfere with one another, one would have to speak of *bio-power* to designate what brought life and its mechanisms into the realm of explicit calculations and made knowledge-power an agent of transformation of human life. It is not that life has been totally integrated into techniques that govern and administer it; it constantly escapes them. Outside the Western world, famine exists, on a greater scale than ever; and the biological risks confronting the species are perhaps greater, and certainly more serious, than before the birth of microbiology. But what might be called a society's "threshold of modernity" has been reached when the life of the species is wagered on its own political strategies. For millennia, man remained what he was for Aristotle: a living animal with the additional capacity for a political existence; modern man is an animal whose politics places his existence as a living being in question.

This transformation had considerable consequences. It would serve no purpose here to dwell on the rupture that occurred then in the pattern of scientific discourse and on the manner in which the twofold problematic of life and man disrupted and redistributed the order of the classical episteme. If the question of man was raised—insofar as he was a specific living being, and specifically related to other living beings—the reason for this is to be sought in the new mode of relation between history and life: in this dual position of life that placed it at the same time outside history, in its biological environment, and inside human historicity, penetrated by the latter's techniques of knowledge and power. There is no need either to lay further stress on the proliferation of political technologies that ensued, investing the body, health, modes of subsistence and habitation, living conditions, the whole space of existence.

Another consequence of this development of bio-power was the growing importance assumed by the action of the norm, at the expense of the juridical system of the law. Law cannot help but be armed, and its arm, *par excellence*, is death; to those who transgress it, it replies, at least as a last resort, with that absolute menace. The law always refers to the sword. But a power whose task is to take charge of life needs continuous regulatory and corrective mechanisms. It is no longer a matter of bringing death into play in the field of sovereignty, but of distributing the living in the domain of value and utility. Such a power has to qualify, measure, appraise, and hierarchize, rather than display itself in its murderous splendor; it does not have to draw the line that separates the enemies of the sovereign from his obedient subjects; it effects distributions around the norm. I do not mean to say that the law fades into the background or that the institutions of justice tend to disappear, but rather that the law operates more and more as a norm, and that the judicial institution is increasingly incorporated into a continuum of apparatuses (medical, administrative, and so on) whose functions are for the most part regulatory. A normalizing society is the historical outcome of a technology of power centered on life. We have entered a phase of juridical regression in comparison with the pre-seventeenth-century societies we are acquainted with; we should not be deceived by all the Constitutions framed throughout the world since the French Revolution, the Codes written and revised, a whole continual and clamorous legislative activity: these were the forms that made an essentially normalizing power acceptable.

Moreover, against this power that was still new in the nineteenth century, the forces that resisted relied for support on the very thing it invested, that is, on life and man as a living being. Since the last century, the great struggles that have challenged the general system of power were not guided by the belief in a return to former rights, or by the age-old dream of a cycle of time or a Golden Age. One no longer aspired toward the coming of the emperor of the poor, or the kingdom of the latter days, or even the restoration of our imagined ancestral rights; what was demanded and what served as an objective was life, understood as the basic needs, man's concrete essence, the realization of his potential, a plenitude of the possible. Whether or not it was Utopia that was wanted is of little importance; what we have seen has been a very real process of struggle; life as a political object was in a sense taken at face value and turned back against the system that was bent on controlling it. It was life more than the law that became the issue of political struggles, even if the latter were formulated through affirmations concerning rights. The "right" to life, to one's body, to health, to happiness, to the satisfaction of needs, and beyond all the oppressions or "alienations," the "right" to rediscover what one is and all that one can be, this "right"—

which the classical juridical system was utterly incapable of comprehending—was the political response to all these new procedures of power which did not derive, either, from the traditional right of sovereignty.

This is the background that enables us to understand the importance assumed by sex as a political issue. It was at the pivot of the two axes along which developed the entire political technology of life. On the one hand it was tied to the disciplines of the body: the harnessing, intensification, and distribution of forces, the adjustment and economy of energies. On the other hand, it was applied to the regulation of populations, through all the far-reaching effects of its activity. It fitted in both categories at once, giving rise to infinitesimal surveillances, permanent controls, extremely meticulous orderings of space, indeterminate medical or psychological examinations, to an entire micro-power concerned with the body. But it gave rise as well to comprehensive measures, statistical assessments, and interventions aimed at the entire social body or at groups taken as a whole. Sex was a means of access both to the life of the body and the life of the species. It was employed as a standard for the disciplines and as a basis for regulations. This is why in the nineteenth century sexuality was sought out in the smallest details of individual existences; it was tracked down in behavior, pursued in dreams: it was suspected of underlying the least follies, it was traced back into the earliest years of childhood; it became the stamp of individuality—at the same time what enabled one to analyze the latter and what made it possible to master it. But one also sees it becoming the theme of political operations, economic interventions (through incitements to or curbs on procreation), and ideological campaigns for raising standards of morality and responsibility: it was put forward as the index of a society's strength, revealing of both its political energy and its biological vigor. Spread out from one pole to the other of this technology of sex was a whole series of different tactics that combined in varying proportions the objective of disciplining the body and that of regulating populations.

Whence the importance of the four great lines of attack along which the politics of sex advanced for two centuries. Each one was a way of combining disciplinary techniques with regulative methods. The first two rested on the requirements of regulation, on a whole thematic of the species, descent, and collective welfare, in order to obtain results at the level of discipline; the sexualization of children was accomplished in the form of a campaign for the health of the race (precocious sexuality was presented from the eighteenth century to the end of the nineteenth as an epidemic menace that risked compromising not only the future health of adults but the future of the entire society and species); the hysterization of women, which involved a thorough medicalization of their bodies and their sex, was carried out in the name of the responsibility they owed to the health of their children, the solidity of the family institution, and the safeguarding of society. It was the reverse relationship that applied in the case of birth controls and the psychiatrization of perversions: here the intervention was regulatory in nature, but it had to rely on the demand for individual disciplines and constraints (*dressages*). Broadly speaking, at the juncture of the "body" and the "population," sex became a crucial target of a power organized around the management of life rather than the menace of death.

The blood relation long remained an important element in the mechanisms of power, its manifestations, and its rituals. For a society in which the systems of alliance, the political form of the sovereign, the differentiation into orders and castes, and the value of descent lines were predominant; for a society in which famine, epidemics, and violence made death imminent, blood constituted one of the fundamental values. It owed its high value at the same time to its instrumental role (the ability to shed blood), to the way it functioned in the order of signs (to have a certain blood, to be of the same blood, to be prepared to risk one's blood), and also to its precariousness (easily spilled, subject to drying up, too readily mixed, capable of being quickly corrupted). A society of blood—I was tempted to say, of "sanguinity"—where power spoke *through* blood: the honor of war, the fear of famine, the triumph of death, the sovereign with his sword, executioners, and tortures; blood was *a reality with a symbolic function*. We, on the other hand, are in a society of "sex," or rather a society "with a sexuality": the mechanisms of power are addressed to the body, to life, to what causes it to proliferate, to what reinforces the species, its stamina, its ability to dominate, or its capacity for being used. Through the themes of health, progeny, race, the future of the species, the vitality of the social body, power spoke *of* sexuality and *to* sexuality; the latter was not a mark or a symbol, it was an object and a target. Moreover, its importance was due less to its rarity or its precariousness than to its insistence, its insidious presence, the fact that it was everywhere an object of excitement and fear at the same time. Power delineated it, aroused it, and employed it as the proliferating meaning that had always to be taken control of again lest it escape; it was *an effect with a meaning-value*. I do not mean to say that a substitution of sex for blood was by itself responsible for all the transformations that marked the threshold of our modernity. It is not the soul of two civilizations or the organizing principle of two cultural forms that I am attempting to express; I am looking for the reasons for which sexuality, far from being repressed in the society of that period, on the contrary was constantly aroused. The new procedures of power that were devised during the classical age and employed in the nineteenth century were what caused our societies to go from a *symbolics of blood to an analytics of sexuality*. Clearly, nothing was more on the side of the law, death, transgression, the symbolic, and sovereignty than blood; just as sexuality was on the side of the norm, knowledge, life, meaning, the disciplines, and regulations.

Sade and the first eugenists were contemporary with this transition from "sanguinity" to "sexuality." But whereas the first dreams of the perfecting of the species inclined the whole problem toward an extremely exacting administration of sex (the art of determining good marriages, of inducing the desired fertilities, of ensuring the health and longevity of children), and while the new concept of race tended to obliterate the aristocratic particularities of blood, retaining only the controllable effects of sex, Sade carried the exhaustive analysis of sex over into the mechanisms of the old power of sovereignty and endowed it with the ancient but fully maintained prestige of blood; the latter flowed through the whole dimension of pleasure—the blood of torture and absolute power, the blood of the caste which was respected in itself and which nonetheless was made to flow in the major rituals of parricide and incest, the blood of the people, which was shed unreservedly since the sort that flowed in its veins was not even deserving of a name. In Sade, sex is without any norm or intrinsic rule that might be formulated from its own nature; but it is subject to the unrestricted law of a power which itself knows no other law but its own; if by chance it is at times forced to accept the order of progressions carefully disciplined into successive days, this exercise carries it to a point where it is no longer anything but a unique and naked sovereignty: an unlimited right of all-powerful monstrosity.

While it is true that the analytics of sexuality and the symbolics of blood were grounded at first in two very distinct regimes of power, in actual fact the passage from one to the other did not come about (any more than did these powers themselves) without overlappings, interactions, and echoes. In different ways, the preoccupation with blood and the law has for nearly two centuries haunted the administration of sexuality. Two of these interferences are noteworthy, the one for its historical importance, the other for the problems it poses. Beginning in the second half of the nineteenth century, the thematics of blood was sometimes called on to tend its entire historical weight toward revitalizing the type of political power that was exercised through the devices of sexuality. Racism took shape at this point (racism in its modern, "biologizing," statist form): it was then that a whole politics of settlement (*peuplement*), family, marriage, education, social hierarchization, and property, accompanied by a long series of permanent interventions at the level of the body, conduct, health, and everyday life, received their color and their justification from the mythical concern with protecting the purity of the blood and ensuring the triumph of the race. Nazism was doubtless the most cunning and the most naïve (and the former because of the latter) combination of the fantasies of blood and the paroxysms of a disciplinary power. A eugenic ordering of society, with all that implied in the way of extension and intensification of micro-powers, in the guise of an unrestricted state control (*étatisation*), was accompanied by the oneiric exaltation of a superior blood; the latter implied both the systematic genocide of others and the risk of exposing oneself to a total sacrifice. It is an irony of history that the Hitlerite politics of sex remained an insignificant practice while the blood myth was transformed into the greatest blood bath in recent memory.

At the opposite extreme, starting from this same end of the nineteenth century, we can trace the theoretical effort to reinscribe the thematic of sexuality in the system of law, the symbolic order, and sovereignty. It is to the political credit of psychoanalysis—or at least, of what was most coherent in it—that it regarded with suspicion (and this from its inception, that is, from the moment it broke away from the neuropsychiatry of degenerescence) the irrevocably proliferating aspects which might be contained in these power mechanisms aimed at controlling and administering the everyday life of sexuality: whence the Freudian endeavor (out of reaction no doubt to the great surge of racism that was contemporary with it) to ground sexuality in the law—the law of alliance, tabooed consanguinity, and the Sovereign-Father, in short, to surround desire with all the trappings of the old order of power. It was owing to this that psychoanalysis was—in the main, with a few exceptions—in theoretical and practical opposition to fascism. But this position of psychoanalysis was tied to a specific historical conjuncture. And yet, to conceive the category of the sexual in terms of the law, death, blood, and sovereignty—whatever the references to Sade and Bataille, and however one might gauge their "subversive" influence—is in the last analysis a historical "retro-version." We must conceptualize the deployment of sexuality on the basis of the techniques of power that are contemporary with it.

People are going to say that I am dealing in a historicism which is more careless than radical; that I am evading the biologically established existence of sexual functions for the benefit of phenomena that are variable, perhaps, but fragile, secondary, and ultimately superficial; and that I speak of sexuality as if sex did not exist. And one would be entitled to object as follows: "You claim to analyze in detail the processes by which women's bodies, the lives of children, family relationships, and an entire network of social relations were sexualized. You wish to describe that great awakening of sexual concern since the eighteenth century and our growing eagerness to suspect the presence of sex in everything. Let us admit as much and suppose that the mechanisms of power were in fact used more to arouse and "excite" sexuality than to repress it. But here you remain quite near to the thing you no doubt believe you have gotten away from; at bottom, when you point out phenomena of diffusion, anchorage, and fixation of sexuality, you are trying to reveal what might be called the organization of "erotic zones" in the social body; it may well be the case that you have done nothing more than transpose to the level of diffuse processes mechanisms which psychoanalysis has identified with precision at the level of the individual. But you pass over the thing on the basis of which this sexualization was able to develop and which psychoanalysis does not fail to recognize—namely, sex. Before Freud, one sought to localize sexuality as closely as possible: in sex, in its reproductive functions, in its immediate anatomical localizations; one fell back upon a biological minimum: organ, instinct, and finality. You, on the other hand, are in a symmetrical and inverse position: for you, there remain only groundless effects, ramifications without roots, a sexuality without a sex. What is this if not castration once again?"

Here we need to distinguish between two questions. First, does the analysis of sexuality necessarily imply the elision of the body, anatomy, the biological, the functional? To this question, I think we can reply in the negative. In any case, the purpose of the present study is in fact to show how deployments of power are directly connected to the body—to bodies, functions, physiological processes, sensations, and pleasures; far from the body having to be effaced, what is needed is to make it visible through an analysis in which the biological and the historical are not consecutive to one another, as in the evolutionism of the first sociologists, but are bound together in an increasingly complex fashion in accordance with the development of the modern technologies of power that take life as their objective. Hence I do not envisage a "history of mentalities" that would take account of bodies only through the manner in which they have been perceived and given meaning and value; but a "history of bodies" and the manner in which what is most material and most vital in them has been invested.

Another question, distinct from the first one: this materiality that is referred to, is it not, then, that of sex, and is it not paradoxical to venture a history of sexuality at the level of bodies, without there being the least question of sex? After all, is the power that is exercised through sexuality not directed specifically at that element of reality which is "sex," sex in general? That sexuality is not, in relation to power, an exterior domain to which power is applied, that on the contrary it is a result and an instrument of power's designs, is all very well. But as for sex, is it not the "other" with respect to power, while being the center around which sexuality distributes its effects? Now, it is precisely this idea of sex *in itself* that we cannot accept without examination. Is "sex" really the anchorage point that supports the manifestations of sexuality, or is it not rather a complex idea that was formed inside the deployment of sexuality? In any case, one could show how this idea of sex took form in the different strategies of power and the definite role it played therein.

All along the great lines which the development of the deployment of sexuality has followed since the nineteenth century, one sees the elaboration of this idea that there exists something other than bodies, organs, somatic localizations, functions, anatomo-physiological systems, sensations, and pleasures; something else and something more, with intrinsic properties and laws of its own: "sex." Thus, in the process of hysterization of women, "sex" was defined in three ways: as that which belongs in common to men and women; as that which belongs, *par excellence*, to men, and hence is lacking in women; but at the same time, as that which by itself constitutes woman's body, ordering it wholly in terms of the functions of reproduction and keeping it in constant agitation through the effects of that very function. Hysteria was interpreted in this strategy as the movement of sex insofar as it was the "one" and the "other," whole and part, principle and lack. In the sexualization of childhood, there was formed the idea of a sex that was both present (from the evidence of anatomy) and absent (from the standpoint of physiology), present too if one considered its activity, and deficient if one referred to its reproductive finality; or again, actual in all its manifestations, but hidden in its eventual effects, whose pathological seriousness would only become apparent later. If the sex of the child was still present in the adult, it was in the form of a secret causality that tended to nullify the sex of the latter (it was one of the tenets of eighteenth- and nineteenth-century medicine that precocious sex would eventually result in sterility, impotence, frigidity, the inability to experience pleasure, or the deadening of the senses); by sexualizing childhood, the idea was established of a sex characterized essentially by the interplay of presence and absence, the visible and the hidden; masturbation and the effects imputed to it were thought to reveal in a privileged way this interplay of presence and absence, of the visible and the hidden.

In the psychiatrization of perversions, sex was related to biological functions and to an anatomo-physiological machinery that gave it its "meaning," that is, its finality; but it was also referred to an instinct which, through its peculiar development and according to the objects to which it could become attached, made it possible for perverse behavior patterns to arise and made their genesis intelligible. Thus "sex" was defined by the interlacing of function and instinct, finality and signification; moreover, this was the form in which it was manifested, more clearly than anywhere else, in the model perversion, in that "fetishism" which, from at least as early as 1877, served as the guiding thread for analyzing all the other deviations. In it one could clearly perceive the way in which the instinct became fastened to an object in accordance with an individual's historical adherence and biological inadequacy. Lastly, in the socialization of procreative behavior, "sex" was described as being caught between a law of reality (economic necessity being its most abrupt and immediate form) and an economy of pleasure which was always attempting to circumvent that law—when, that is, it did not ignore it altogether. The most notorious of "frauds," coitus interruptus, represented the point where the insistence of the real forced an end to pleasure and where the pleasure found a way to surface despite the economy dictated by the real. It is apparent that the deployment of sexuality, with its different strategies, was what established this notion of "sex"; and in the four major forms of hysteria, onanism, fetishism, and interrupted coition, it showed this sex to be governed by the interplay of whole and part, principle and lack, absence and presence, excess and deficiency, by the function of instinct, finality, and meaning, of reality and pleasure.

The theory thus generated performed a certain number of functions that made it indispensable. First, the notion of "sex" made it possible to group together, in an artificial unity, anatomical elements, biological functions, conducts, sensations, and pleasures, and it enabled one to make use of this fictitious unity as a causal principle, an omnipresent meaning, a secret to be discovered everywhere: sex was thus able to function as a unique signifier and as a universal signified. Further, by presenting itself in a unitary fashion, as anatomy and lack, as function and latency, as instinct and meaning, it was able to mark the line of contact between a knowledge of human sexuality and the biological sciences of reproduction; thus, without really borrowing anything from these sciences, excepting a few doubtful analogies, the knowledge of sexuality gained through proximity a guarantee of quasi-scientificity;

but by virtue of this same proximity, some of the contents of biology and physiology were able to serve as a principle of normality for human sexuality. Finally, the notion of sex brought about a fundamental reversal; it made it possible to invert the representation of the relationships of power to sexuality, causing the latter to appear, not in its essential and positive relation to power, but as being rooted in a specific and irreducible urgency which power tries as best it can to dominate; thus the idea of "sex" makes it possible to evade what gives "power" its power; it enables one to conceive power solely as law and taboo. Sex—that agency which appears to dominate us and that secret which seems to underlie all that we are, that point which enthralls us through the power it manifests and the meaning it conceals, and which we ask to reveal what we are and to free us from what defines us—is doubtless but an ideal point made necessary by the deployment of sexuality and its operation. We must not make the mistake of thinking that sex is an autonomous agency which secondarily produces manifold effects of sexuality over the entire length of its surface of contact with power. On the contrary, sex is the most speculative, most ideal, and most internal element in a deployment of sexuality organized by power in its grip on bodies and their materiality, their forces, energies, sensations, and pleasures.

It might be added that "sex" performs yet another function—that runs through and sustains the ones we have just examined. Its role in this instance is more practical than theoretical. It is through sex—in fact, an imaginary point determined by the deployment of sexuality—that each individual has to pass in order to have access to his own intelligibility (seeing that it is both the hidden aspect and the generative principle of meaning), to the whole of his body (since it is a real and threatened part of it, while symbolically constituting the whole), to his identity (since it joins the force of a drive to the singularity of a history). Through a reversal that doubtless had its surreptitious beginnings long ago—it was already making itself felt at the time of the Christian pastoral of the flesh—we have arrived at the point where we expect our intelligibility to come from what was for many centuries thought of as madness; the plenitude of our body from what was long considered its stigma and likened to a wound; our identity from what was perceived as an obscure and nameless urge. Hence the importance we ascribe to it, the reverential fear with which we surround it, the care we take to know it. Hence the fact that over the centuries it has become more important than our soul, more important almost than our life; and so it is that all the world's enigmas appear frivolous to us compared to this secret, minuscule in each of us, but of a density that makes it more serious than any other. The Faustian pact, whose temptation has been instilled in us by the deployment of sexuality, is now as follows: to exchange life in its entirety for sex itself, for the truth and the sovereignty of sex. Sex is worth dying for. It is in this (strictly historical) sense that sex is indeed imbued with the death instinct. When a long while ago the West discovered love, it bestowed on it a value high enough to make death acceptable; nowadays it is sex that claims this equivalence, the highest of all. And while the deployment of sexuality permits the techniques of power to invest life, the fictitious point of sex, itself marked by that deployment, exerts enough charm on everyone for them to accept hearing the grumble of death within it.

By creating the imaginary element that is "sex," the deployment of sexuality established one of its most essential internal operating principles: the desire for sex—the desire to have it, to have access to it, to discover it, to liberate it, to articulate it in discourse, to formulate it in truth. It constituted "sex" itself as something desirable. And it is this desirability of sex that attaches each one of us to the injunction to know it, to reveal its law and its power; it is this desirability that makes us think we are affirming the rights of our sex against all power, when in fact we are fastened to the deployment of sexuality that has lifted up from deep within us a sort of mirage in which we think we see ourselves reflected—the dark shimmer of sex.

"It is sex," said Kate in *The Plumed Serpent*. "How wonderful sex can be, when men keep it powerful and sacred, and it fills the world! like sunshine through and through one!"

So we must not refer a history of sexuality to the agency of sex; but rather show how "sex" is historically subordinate to sexuality. We must not place sex on the side of reality, and sexuality on that of confused ideas and illusions; sexuality is a very real historical formation; it is what gave rise to the notion of sex, as a speculative element necessary to its operation. We must not think that by saying yes to sex, one says no to power; on the contrary, one tracks along the course laid out by the general deployment of sexuality. It is the agency of sex that we must break away from, if we aim—through a tactical reversal of the various mechanisms of sexuality—to counter the grips of power with the claims of bodies, pleasures, and knowledges, in their multiplicity and their possibility of resistance. The rallying point for the counterattack against the deployment of sexuality ought not to be sex-desire, but bodies and pleasures.

"There has been so much action in the past," said D. H. Lawrence, "especially sexual action, a wearying repetition over and over, without a corresponding thought, a corresponding realization. Now our business is to realize sex. Today the full conscious realization of sex is even more important than the act itself."

Perhaps one day people will wonder at this. They will not be able to understand how a civilization so intent on developing enormous instruments of production and destruction found the time and the infinite patience to inquire so anxiously concerning the actual state of sex; people will smile perhaps when they recall that here were men—meaning ourselves—who believed that therein resided a truth every bit as precious as the one they had already demanded from the earth, the stars, and the pure forms of their thought; people will be surprised at the eagerness with which we went about pretending to rouse from its slumber a sexuality which everything—

our discourses, our customs, our institutions, our regulations, our knowl-edges—was busy producing in the light of day and broadcasting to noisy ac-companiment. And people will ask themselves why we were so bent on ending the rule of silence regarding what was the noisiest of our preoccupa-tions. In retrospect, this noise may appear to have been out of place, but how much stranger will seem our persistence in interpreting it as but the re-fusal to speak and the order to remain silent. People will wonder what could have made us so presumptuous; they will look for the reasons that might explain why we prided ourselves on being the first to grant sex the importance we say is its due and how we came to congratulate ourselves for finally—in the twentieth century—having broken free of a long period of harsh repression, a protracted Christian asceticism, greedily and fastidi-ously adapted to the imperatives of bourgeois economy. And what we now perceive as the chronicle of a censorship and the difficult struggle to re-move it will be seen rather as the centuries-long rise of a complex deploy-ment for compelling sex to speak, for fastening our attention and concern upon sex, for getting us to believe in the sovereignty of its law when in fact we were moved by the power mechanisms of sexuality.

People will be amused at the reproach of pansexualism that was once aimed at Freud and psychoanalysis. But the ones who will appear to have been blind will perhaps be not so much those who formulated the objection as those who discounted it out of hand, as if it merely expressed the fears of an outmoded prudishness. For the first, after all, were only taken unawares by a process which had begun long before and by which, unbeknown to them, they were already surrounded on all sides; what they had attributed solely to the genius of Freud had already gone through a long stage of prep-aration; they had gotten their dates wrong as to the establishment, in our so-ciety, of a general deployment of sexuality. But the others were mistaken concerning the nature of the process; they believed that Freud had at last, through a sudden reversal, restored to sex the rightful share which it had been denied for so long; they had not seen how the good genius of Freud had placed it at one of the critical points marked out for it since the eighteenth century by the strategies of knowledge and power, how wonderfully effective he was—worthy of the greatest spiritual fathers and directors of the classical period—in giving a new impetus to the secular injunction to study sex and transform it into discourse. We are often reminded of the countless proce-dures which Christianity once employed to make us detest the body; but let us ponder all the ruses that were employed for centuries to make us love sex, to make the knowledge of it desirable and everything said about it precious. Let us consider the stratagems by which we were induced to apply all our skills to discovering its secrets, by which we were attached to the obligation to draw out its truth, and made guilty for having failed to recognize it for so long. These devices are what ought to make us wonder today. Moreover, we need to consider the possibility that one day, perhaps, in a different econ-omy of bodies and pleasures, people will no longer quite understand how the ruses of sexuality, and the power that sustains its organization, were able to subject us to that austere monarchy of sex, so that we became dedicated to the endless task of forcing its secret, of exacting the truest of confessions from a shadow.

The irony of this deployment is in having us believe that our "liberation" is in the balance.

Notes

[1] Samuel von Pufendorf, *Le Droit de la nature* (French trans., 1734), p. 445.

[2] "Just as a composite body can have properties not found in any of the simple bodies of which the mixture consists, so a moral body, by virtue of the very union of persons of which it is composed, can have certain rights which none of the individuals could expressly claim and whose exercise is the proper function of leaders alone." Pufendorf, *Le Droit de la nature*, p. 452.

BIBLIOGRAPHY

Works about I. A. Richards

Abrams, M. H. "Belief and the Suspension of Disbelief." In *Literature and Belief*. Ed. M. H. Abrams. New York: Columbia University Press, 1958, pp. 1–30.

Aiken, Henry David. "A Pluralistic Analysis of Aesthetic Value." *Philosophical Review*, 59 (October 1950), 493–513.

Beale, Walter H. "Richard M. Weaver: Philosophical Rhetoric, Cultural Criticism, and the First Rhetorical Awakening." *College English*, 52 (October 1990), 626–40.

Belgion, Montgomery. "What is Criticism?" *Criterion*, 10 (October 1930), 118–39.

Bentley, Eric Russell. "An Examination of Modern Critics: 1: The Early I. A. Richards, an Autopsy." *Rocky Mountain Review*, 8 (1944), 29–36.

Berthoff, Ann E. *Forming, Thinking, Writing: The Composing Imagination*. Rochelle Park, NJ: Hayden, 1978.

Berthoff, Ann E. "From *Mencius on the Mind* to *Coleridge on Imagination*." *Rhetoric Society Quarterly*, 18 (Spring 1988), 163–66.

Berthoff, Ann E. "I. A. Richards." In *Traditions of Inquiry*. Ed. John Brereton. New York: Oxford University Press, 1985, pp. 50–80.

Berthoff, Ann E. "I. A. Richards and the Audit of Meaning." *New Literary History*, 14 (Autumn 1982), 63–79.

Berthoff, Ann E. *The Making of Meaning: Metaphors, Models, and Maxims for Writing Teachers*. Montclair, NJ: Boynton/Cook, 1981.

Berthoff, Ann E. "I. A. Richards and the Philosophy of Rhetoric." *Rhetoric Society Quarterly*, 10 (Fall 1980), 195–210.

Bethell, S. L. "Suggestions towards a Theory of Value." *Criterion*, 14 (January 1935), 239–50.

Bilsky, Manuel. "Discussion: I. A. Richards on Belief." *Philosophy and Phenomenological Research*, 12 (September 1951), 105–15.

Bilsky, Manuel. "I. A. Richards' Theory of Metaphor." *Modern Philology*, 50 (November 1952), 130–37.

Bilsky, Manuel. "I. A. Richards' Theory of Value." *Philosophy and Phenomenological Research*, 14 (June 1954), 536–45.

Bizzell, Patricia, and Bruce Herzberg. "Knowledge and Argument: An Example from English Studies." In *Argument in Transition: Proceedings of the Third Summer*

Conference on Argumentation. Ed. David Zarefsky, Malcolm O. Sillars, and Jack Rhodes. Annandale, VA: Speech Communication Association, 1983, pp. 127–34.

Black, Max. *Language and Philosophy: Studies in Method*. Ithaca: Cornell University Press, 1949.

Black, Max. "Some Objections to Ogden and Richards' Theory of Interpretation." *Journal of Philosophy*, 39 (May 21, 1942), 281–90.

Black, Max. "A Symposium on Emotive Meaning: Some Questions about Emotive Meaning." *Philosophical Review*, 57 (1948), 111–26.

Blackmur, R. P. *Language as Gesture: Essays in Poetry*. 1935; rpt. New York: Harcourt, Brace, 1952.

Blackmur, R. P. "San Giovanni in Venere: Allen Tate as Man of Letters." *Sewanee Review*, 67 (1959), 614–31.

Blankenship, Jane. "I. A. Richards' 'Context' Theorem." *Rhetoric Society Quarterly*, 18 (Spring 1988), 153–58.

Booth, T. Y. "I. A. Richards and the Composing Process." *College Composition and Communication*, 37 (December 1986), 453–65.

Booth, T. Y. "The Meaning of Language If Any." *Rhetoric Society Quarterly*, 10 (Fall 1980), 211–30.

Bredin, Hugh. "I. A. Richards and the Philosophy of Practical Criticism." *Philosophy and Literature*, 10 (April 1986), 26–36.

Brower, Reuben, Helen Vendler, and John Hollander, eds. *I. A. Richards: Essays in His Honor*. New York: Oxford University Press, 1973.

Browne, Stephen H. "I. A. Richards (1893–1979)." In *Twentieth-Century Rhetorics and Rhetoricians: Critical Studies and Sources*. Ed. Michael G. Moran and Michelle Ballif. Westport, CT: Greenwood, 2000, pp. 304–12.

Brown, Stuart C. "Richards, I. A. (1893–1979)." In *Encyclopedia of Rhetoric and Composition: Communication from Ancient Times to the Information Age*. Ed. Theresa Enos. New York: Garland, 1996, pp. 631–34.

Chisholm, Roderick M. "Intentionality and the Theory of Signs." *Philosophical Studies*, 3 (1952), 56–63.

Conley, Thomas M. *Rhetoric in the European Tradition*. New York: Longman, 1990.

Corts, Paul R. "I. A. Richards on Rhetoric and Criticism." *Southern Speech Journal*, 36 (Winter 1970), 115–26.

Crane, R. S. "I. A. Richards on the Art of Interpretation." *Ethics*, 59 (January 1949), 112–26.

Cruttwell, Patrick. "Second Thoughts: IV: I. A. Richards' *Practical Criticism*." *Essays in Criticism*, 8 (January 1958), 1–15.

Daiches, David. "The Principles of Literary Criticism: The Fifth of the 'Books that Changed Our Minds.'" *New Republic*, 98 (1939), 95–98.

Derrick, Thomas J. "I. A. Richards' Rhetorical Theories in the Classroom." *Rhetoric Society Quarterly*, 10 (Fall 1980), 240–53.

Douglass, David. "Issues in the Use of I. A. Richards' Tenor-Vehicle Model of Metaphor." *Western Journal of Communication*, 64 (Fall 2000), 405–24.

Eastman, Max. *The Literary Mind: Its Place in an Age of Science*. New York: Charles Scribner's Sons, 1931.

Eliot, T. S. *The Use of Poetry and the Use of Criticism: Studies in the Relation of Criticism to Poetry in England*. London: Faber and Faber, 1933.

Elton, William. *A Guide to the New Criticism*. Chicago: Modern Poetry Association, 1948.

Empson, William. *The Structure of Complex Words*. Norfolk, CT: New Directions, n.d.

Enholm, Donald K. "The Most Significant Passage for Rhetorical Theory in the Work of I. A. Richards." *Rhetoric Society Quarterly*, 18 (Spring 1988), 181–89.

Enholm, Donald K. "Rhetoric as an Instrument for Understanding and Improving Human Relations." *Southern Speech Communication Journal*, 41 (Spring 1976), 223–36.

Fisher, B. Aubrey. "I. A. Richards' Context of Language: An Overlooked Contribution to Rhetorico-Communication Theory." *Western Speech*, 35 (Spring 1971), 104–11.

Fisher, Walter R. "The Importance of Style in Systems of Rhetoric." *Southern Speech Journal*, 27 (Spring 1962), 173–82.

Fogarty, Daniel. *Roots for a New Rhetoric*. New York: Bureau of Publications, Teachers College, Columbia University, 1959.

Foss, Karen A. "Celluloid Rhetoric: The Use of Documentary Film to Teach Rhetorical Theory." *Communication Education*, 32 (January 1983), 51–61.

Foss, Sonja K. "Rhetoric and the Visual Image: A Resource Unit." *Communication Education*, 31 (January 1982), 55–66.

Foster, Richard. *The New Romantics: A Reappraisal of the New Criticism*. Bloomington: Indiana University Press, 1962.

Gabin, Rosalind J. "The Most Significant Passage from Rhetoric in the Work of I. A. Richards." *Rhetoric Society Quarterly*, 18 (Spring 1988), 167–71.

Garko, Michael G., and Kenneth N. Cissna. "An Axiological Reinterpretation of I. A. Richards' Theory of Communication and Its Application to the Study of Compliance-Gaining." *Southern Speech Communication Journal*, 53 (Winter 1988), 121–39.

Gentry, George. "Reference and Relation." *Journal of Philosophy*, 40 (May 13, 1943), 253–61.

Glicksberg, Charles I. "I. A. Richards and the Science of Criticism." *Sewanee Review*, 46 (October/December 1938), 520–33.

Graff, Gerald E. "The Later Richards and the New Criticism." *Criticism*, 9 (Summer 1967), 229–42.

Hamilton, G. Rostrevor. *Poetry and Contemplation: A New Preface to Poetics*. New York: Macmillan, 1937.

Harding, D. W. "Evaluations (I): I. A. Richards." *Scrutiny*, 1 (March 1933), 327–38.

Hardy, William G. *Language, Thought, and Experience: A Tapestry of the Dimensions of Meaning*. Baltimore: University Park Press, 1978.

Heath, Robert L. "Kenneth Burke's Poetics and the Influence of I. A. Richards: A Cornerstone for Dramatism." *Communication Studies*, 40 (Spring 1989), 54–65.

Hochmuth, Marie. "I. A. Richards and the 'New Rhetoric.'" *Quarterly Journal of Speech*, 44 (February 1958), 1–16.

Hotopf, W. H. N. *Language, Thought, and Comprehension: A Case Study of the Writings of I. A. Richards*. Bloomington: Indiana University Press, 1965.

Hyman, Stanley Edgar. *The Armed Vision: A Study in the Methods of Modern Literary Criticism*. New York: Alfred A. Knopf, 1948.

Isenberg, Arnold. "Critical Communication." *Philosophical Review*, 58 (1949), 330–44.

James, D. G. *Scepticism and Poetry: An Essay on the Poetic Imagination*. London: George Allen and Unwin, 1937.

Jensen, Keith. "I. A. Richards and His Models." *Southern Speech Communication Journal*, 37 (Spring 1972), 304–14.

Johannesen, Richard L. "Attitude of Speaker toward Audience: A Significant Concept for Contemporary Rhetorical Theory and Criticism." *Central States Speech Journal*, 25 (Summer 1974), 95–104.

Jordan, William J., and W. Clifton Adams. "I. A. Richards' Concept of Tenor-Vehicle Interaction." *Central States Speech Journal*, 27 (Summer 1976), 136–43.

Karnani, Chetan. *Criticism, Aesthetics and Psychology: A Study of the Writings of I. A. Richards*. New Delhi, Ind.: Arnold-Heinemann, 1977.

King, Andrew. "The Most Significant Passage in I. A. Richards for the Theory and Practice of Rhetoric." *Rhetoric Society Quarterly*, 18 (Spring 1988), 159–62.

Kneupper, Charles W. "The Referential-Emotive Distinction: A Significant Passage for Understanding I. A. Richards." *Rhetoric Society Quarterly*, 18 (Spring 1988), 173–79.

Knight, E. Helen. "Some Aesthetic Theories of Mr. Richards." *Mind*, 36 (1927), 69–76.

Kotler, Janet. "On Reading I. A. Richards—Again and Again." *Rhetoric Society Quarterly*, 10 (Fall 1980), 231–39.

Krieger, Murray. *The New Apologists for Poetry*. Minneapolis: University of Minnesota Press, 1956.

Law, Jules David. *The Rhetoric of Empiricism: Language and Perception from Locke to I. A. Richards*. Ithaca: Cornell University Press, 1993.

McCallum, Pamela. *Literature and Method: Towards a Critique of I. A. Richards, T. S. Eliot and F. R. Leavis*. New York: Gil and MacMillan, 1983.

McLuhan, H. M. "Poetic vs. Rhetorical Exegesis: The Case for Leavis against Richards and Empson." *Sewanee Review*, 52 (1944), 266–76.

Needham, John. *The Completest Mode: I. A. Richards and the Continuity of English Literary Criticism*. Edinburgh, Scot.: Edinburgh University Press, 1982.

Nichols, Marie Hochmuth. *Rhetoric and Criticism*. Baton Rouge: Louisiana State University Press, 1963.

Pollock, T. C. "A Critique of I. A. Richards' Theory of Language and Literature." In *A Theory of Meaning Analyzed*. Ed. M. Kendig. Lakeville, CT: Institute of General Semantics, 1942, pp. 1–25.

Pollock, Thomas Clark. *The Nature of Literature: Its Relation to Science, Language and Human Experience*. Princeton: Princeton University Press, 1942, pp. 145–61.

Pottle, Frederick A. *The Idiom of Poetry*. Ithaca: Cornell University Press, 1946.

Ragsdale, J. Donald. "Problems of Some Contemporary Notions of Style." *Southern Speech Journal*, 35 (Summer 1970), 332–41.

Ransom, John Crowe. *The New Criticism*. Norfolk, CT: New Directions, 1941.

Ransom, John Crowe. "A Psychologist Looks at Poetry." *Virginia Quarterly Review*, 11 (October 1935), 575–92.

Righter, William. *Logic and Criticism*. London: Routledge and Kegan Paul, 1963.

Rudolph, G. A. "The Aesthetic Field of I. A. Richards." *Journal of Aesthetics and Art Criticism*, 14 (March 1956), 348–58.

Russo, John Paul. "Belief and Sincerity in I. A. Richards." *Modern Language Quarterly*, 47 (June 1986), 154–91.

Russo, John Paul. *I. A. Richards: His Life and Work*. Baltimore: Johns Hopkins University Press, 1989.

Russo, John Paul. "I. A. Richards in Retrospect." *Critical Inquiry*, 8 (Summer 1982), 743–60.

Schiller, Jerome. "An Alternative to 'Aesthetic Disinterestedness.'" *Journal of Aesthetics and Art Criticism*, 22 (Spring 1964), 295–302.

Schiller, Jerome P. *I. A. Richards' Theory of Literature*. New Haven: Yale University Press, 1969.

Sesonske, Alexander. "Truth in Art." *Journal of Philosophy*, 53 (May 24, 1956), 345–53.

Sibley, Francis M. "How to Read I. A. Richards." *American Scholar*, 42 (Spring 1973), 318–28.

Sondel, Bess. "An Analysis of *The Meaning of Meaning*." In *The Humanity of Words*. By Bess Sondel. Cleveland: World, 1958, pp. 43–78.

Spaulding, John Gordon. "Elementalism: The Effect of an Implicit Postulate of Identity on I. A. Richards' Theory of Poetic Value." In *A Theory of Meaning Analyzed*. Ed. M. Kendig. Lakeville, CT: Institute of General Semantics, 1942, pp. 26–35.

Stevenson, Charles L. *Ethics and Language*. New Haven: Yale University Press, 1944.

Stolnitz, Jerome. *Aesthetics and Philosophy of Art Criticism: A Critical Introduction*. Boston: Houghton Mifflin, 1960.

Talmor, Sascha. "I. A. Richards Revisited." *Durham University Journal*, 80 (1988), 317–20.

Tate, Allen. *On the Limits of Poetry: Selected Essays: 1928–1948*. New York: Swallow/ William Morrow, 1948.

Twitchett, E. G. "A Vision of Judgment." *London Mercury*, 20 (October 1929), 598–605.

Vivas, Eliseo. "Four Notes on I. A. Richards' Aesthetic Theory." *Philosophical Review*, 44 (July 1935), 354–67.

Wagner, Geoffrey. "American Literary Criticism: The Continuing Heresy." *Southern Review* [Adelaide, Austral.], 2 (1968), 82–89.

Watson, George. "The Amiable Heretic: I. A. Richards 1893–1979." *Sewanee Review*, 104 (April/June 1996), 248–62.

Wolleck, René. "On Rereading I. A. Richards." *Southern Review*, 3 [new series] (Summer 1967), 533–54.

Wells, Susan. "Richards, Burke and the Relation between Rhetoric and Poetics." *Pre/Text*, 7 (Spring/Summer 1986), 59–75.

West, Alick. *Crisis and Criticism*. London: Lawrence and Wishart, 1937.

Wimsatt, William K., Jr., and Cleanth Brooks. *Literary Criticism: A Short History*. New York: Alfred A. Knopf, 1957.

Works about Ernesto Grassi

Anderson, Wayne C. "'Perpetual Affirmations, Unexplained': The Rhetoric of Reiteration in Coleridge, Carlyle, and Emerson." *Quarterly Journal of Speech*, 71 (February 1985), 37–51.

Baer, Eugen. "Introduction." In "Noetic Philosophizing: Rhetoric's Displacement of Metaphysics *Alcestis* and *Don Quixote*." By Ernesto Grassi and Emilio Hidalgo-Serna. Trans. Eugen Baer. *Philosophy and Rhetoric*, 30 (1997), 105–12.

Condit, Celeste Michelle. "Kenneth Burke and Linguistic Relativity: Reflections on the Scene of the Philosophy of Communication in the Twentieth Century." In *Kenneth Burke and Contemporary European Thought: Rhetoric in Transition*. Ed. Bernard L. Brock. Tuscaloosa: University of Alabama Press, 1995, pp. 207–62.

Golden, James L., Goodwin F. Berquist, and William E. Coleman. "Emerging European Perspectives on Rhetoric." In *The Rhetoric of Western Thought*. 4th ed. Ed. James L. Golden, Goodwin F. Berquist, and William E. Coleman. Dubuque, IA: Kendall/Hunt, 1989, pp. 428–46.

Golden, James L., Goodwin F. Berquist, and William E. Coleman. "Emerging European Perspectives on Rhetoric." In *Essays on the Rhetoric of the Western World*. Ed. Edward P. J. Corbett, James L. Golden, and Goodwin F. Berquist. Dubuque, IA: Kendall/Hunt, 1990, pp. 375–93.

Enos, Theresa, and Stuart C. Brown. "Ernesto Grassi." In *Professing the New Rhetorics: A Sourcebook*. Englewood Cliffs, NJ: Prentice Hall/Blair, 1994, pp. 90–104.

Farrell, Thomas B. "Rhetorical Resemblance: Paradoxes of a Practical Art." *Quarterly Journal of Speech*, 72 (February 1986), 1–19.

Fierz, Charles L. "Philosophical Implications of Ernesto Grassi: A New Foundation of Philosophy?" *Philosophy and Rhetoric*, 27 (1994), 104–20.

Foss, Karen A. "Ernesto Grassi." In *Twentieth-Century Rhetorics and Rhetoricians: Critical Studies and Sources*. Ed. Michael G. Moran and Michelle Balif. Westport, CT: Greenwood, 2000, pp. 185–89.

Foss, Karen A. "Grassi, Ernesto." *Encyclopedia of Rhetoric and Composition: Communication from Ancient Times to the Information Age*. Ed. Theresa Enos. New York: Garland, 1996, pp. 298–99.

"Grassi, Ernesto." *Who's Who in the World*. Chicago: Marquis Who's Who, 1976, p. 308.

Heim, Michael. "A Philosophy of Comparison: Heidegger and Lao Tzu." *Journal of Chinese Philosophy*, 11 (December 1984), 307–23.

Heim, Michael. "Grassi's Experiment: The Renaissance through Phenomenology." *Research in Phenomenology*, 18 (1988), 233–63.

Hidalgo-Serna, Emilio, and Massimo Marassi. *Studi in memoria di Ernesto Grassi*. Naples: La Città del Sole, 1996.

Krois, John Michael. "Comment on Professor Grassi's Paper." In *Vico and Contemporary Thought*. Ed. Giorgio Tagliacozzo, Michael Mooney, and Donald P. Verene. Atlantic Highlands, NJ: Humanities, 1976, pp. 185–87.

Marassi, Massimo. "Rhetoric and Historicity (An Introduction)." Trans. Kiaran O'Malley. *Philosophy and Rhetoric*, 21 (1988), 245–59.

McPhail, Mark Lawrence. "Coherence as Representative Anecdote in the Rhetorics of Kenneth Burke and Ernesto Grassi." In *Kenneth Burke and Contemporary European Thought: Rhetoric in Transition*. Ed. Bernard L. Brock. Tuscaloosa: University of Alabama Press, 1995, pp. 76–118.

Pietropaolo, Domenico. "Grassi, Vico, and the Defense of the Humanist Tradition." *New Vico Studies*, 10 (1992), 1–10.

Ratto, Franco. Rev. of *Studi in memoria di Ernesto Grassi*. Ed. Emilio Hidalgo-Serna and Massimo Marassi. *Forum Italicum*, 31 (Spring 1997), 236–47.

Tagliacozzo, Giorgio. "L'istante iniziale della carriera vichiana di Grassi." Trans. for Karen A. Foss by Luisella Corbellari. In *Studi in memoria di Ernesto Grassi*. Ed. Emilio Hidalgo-Serna and Massimo Marassi. Vol. 1. Naples: La Città del Sole, 1996, pp. 379–83.

Vattimo, Gianni. "Grassi tra Vico e Heidegger." Trans. for Karen A. Foss by Luisella Corbellari. *La Stampa* [Turin, Italy], December 27, 1991, p. 16.

Veit, Walter. "The Potency of Imagery—the Impotence of Rational Language: Ernesto Grassi's Contribution to Modern Epistemology." *Philosophy and Rhetoric*, 17 (1984), 221–39.

Vincenzo, Joseph. "Discovery of Italian Humanism: The Case of Ernesto Grassi." *Italian Culture*, 8 (1991), 163–85.

Verene, Donald Phillip. "Philosophy, Argument, and Narration." *Philosophy and Rhetoric*, 22 (1989), 141–44.

Verene, Donald Phillip. "Preface." In *Folly and Insanity in Renaissance Literature*. By Ernesto Grassi and Maristella Lorch. Binghamton, NY: Medieval & Renaissance Texts & Studies, 1986.

Verene, Donald Phillip. "Response to Grassi." *Philosophy and Rhetoric*, 19 (1986), 134–37.

Zagacki, Kenneth S. "Vaclav Havel and the Rhetoric of Folly." *Southern Communication Journal*, 62 (Fall 1996), 17–30.

Works about Chaïm Perelman and Lucie Olbrechts-Tyteca

Abbott, Don. "The Jurisprudential Analogy: Argumentation and the New Rhetoric." *Central States Speech Journal*, 25 (Spring 1974), 50–55.

Anderson, John R. "The Audience as a Concept in the Philosophic Rhetoric of Perelman, Johnstone, and Natanson." *Southern Speech Communication Journal*, 38 (Fall 1972), 39–50.

Apostal, Leo. "What Is the Force of an Argument?" *Review of International Philosophy*, 33 (1979), 99–109.

Arnold, Carroll C. "Perelman's New Rhetoric." *Quarterly Journal of Speech*, 56 (February 1970), 87–92.

Barker, Evelyn M. "A Neo-Aristotelian Approach to Dialectical Reasoning." *Review of International Philosophy*, 34 (1980), 482–89.

Bator, Paul G. "The 'Good Reasons Movement': A 'Confounding' of Dialectic and Rhetoric?" *Philosophy and Rhetoric*, 21 (1988), 38–47.

Betz, Joseph. "The Relationship between Love and Justice: A Survey of the Five Possible Positions." *Journal of Value Inquiry*, 4 (Fall 1970), 191–203.

Bitzer, Lloyd F., and Edwin Black, eds. *The Prospect of Rhetoric*. Englewood Cliffs, NJ: Prentice-Hall, 1971.

Bizzell, Patricia, and Bruce Herzberg. "Chaïm Perelman." In *The Rhetorical Tradition: Readings from Classical Times to the Present*. Ed. Patricia Bizzell and Bruce Herzberg. Boston: St. Martin's Press, 1990, pp. 1066–68.

Bodenheimer, Edgar. "Perelman's Contribution to Legal Methodology." *Northern Kentucky Law Review*, 12 (1985), 391–418.

Braet, Antoine. "The Classical Doctrine of *Status* and the Rhetorical Theory of Argumentation." *Philosophy and Rhetoric*, 20 (November 1987), 79–93.

Carr, Thomas M., Jr. "Some Consequences of *The New Rhetoric*: A Critical Study." *Argumentation*, 7 (November 1993), 475–79.

Carranza, Isolda E. "Winning the Battle in Private Discourse: Rhetorical-Logical Operations in Storytelling." *Discourse and Society*, 10 (1999), 509–41.

"Chaïm Perelman." *Who's Who in World Jewry: A Biographical Dictionary of Outstanding Jews*. Ed. J. J. Carmin Karpman. New York: Pittman, 1955, p. 681.

Corgan, Verna C. "Perelman's Universal Audience as a Critical Tool." *Journal of the American Forensic Association*, 23 (Winter 1987), 147–57.

Cox, J. Robert. "The Die Is Cast: Topical and Ontological Dimensions of the Locus of the Irreparable." *Quarterly Journal of Speech*, 68 (August 1982), 227–39.

Christie, George C. "The Universal Audience and Predictive Theories of Law." *Law and Philosophy*, 5 (December 1986), 343–50.

Crosswhite, James. "Being Unreasonable: Perelman and the Problem of Fallacies." *Argumentation*, 7 (November 1993), 385–402.

Crosswhite, James. "Is There an Audience for This Argument? Fallacies, Theories, and Relativisms." *Philosophy and Rhetoric*, 28 (1995), 134–45.

Crosswhite, James. "Universality in Rhetoric: Perelman's Universal Audience." *Philosophy and Rhetoric*, 22 (1989), 157–73.

Dearin, Ray D. "Chaïm Perelman (1912–1984)." In *Twentieth-Century Rhetorics and Rhetoricians: Critical Studies and Sources*. Ed. Michael G. Moran and Michelle Ballif. Westport, CT: Greenwood, 2000, pp. 289–303.

Dearin, Ray D. "Olbrechts-Tyteca, Lucie (1899–1988)." In *Encyclopedia of Rhetoric and Composition: Communication from Ancient Times to the Information Age*. Ed. Theresa Enos. New York: Garland, 1996, pp. 477–78.

Dearin, Ray D. "Perelman, Chaïm (1912–1984)." In *Encyclopedia of Rhetoric and Composition: Communication from Ancient Times to the Information Age*. Ed. Theresa Enos. New York: Garland, 1996, pp. 501–02.

Dearin, Ray D. "Perelman's Concept of 'Quasi-Logical' Argument: A Critical Elaboration." In *Advances in Argumentation Theory and Research*. Ed. J. Robert Cox and Charles Arthur Willard. Carbondale: Southern Illinois University Press, 1982, pp. 78–94.

Dearin, Ray D. "The Philosophical Basis of Chaïm Perelman's Theory of Rhetoric." *Quarterly Journal of Speech*, 55 (October 1969), 213–24.

Dearin, Ray D., ed. *The New Rhetoric of Chaïm Perelman: Statement and Response*. Lanham, MA: University Press of America, 1989.

Dearin, Ray D. "The Rhetorical Legacy of Chaïm Perelman: An Editorial Note." *Journal of the American Forensic Association*, 22 (Fall 1985), 63–64.

DePoe, Stephen P. "Arthur Schlesinger, Jr.'s 'Middle Way Out of Vietnam': The Limits of 'Technocratic Realism' as the Basis for Foreign Policy Dissent." *Western Journal of Speech Communication*, 52 (Spring 1988),147–66.

Dunlap, David Douglas. "The Conception of Audience in Perelman and Isocrates: Locating the Ideal in the Real." *Argumentation*, 7 (November 1993), 461–74.

Ede, Lisa S. "Rhetoric Versus Philosophy: The Role of the Universal Audience in Chaïm Perelman's *The New Rhetoric*." *Central States Speech Journal*, 32 (Summer 1981), 118–25.

Eemeren, Frans H. van, Rob Grootendorst, Francisca Snoeck Henkenmans, J. Anthony Blair, Ralph H. Johnson, Erik C. W. Krabbe, Christian Plantin, Douglas N. Walton, Charles A. Willard, John Woods, and David Zarefsky. *Fundamentals of Argumentation Theory*. Mahwah, NJ: Lawrence Erlbaum, 1996.

Eemeren, Frans H. van, and Rob Grootendorst. "Perelman and the Fallacies." *Philosophy and Rhetoric*, 28 (1995), 122–33.

Enos, Theresa, and Stuart C. Brown. "Chaïm Perelman, 1912–1984." In *Professing the New Rhetorics: A Sourcebook*. Ed. Theresa Enos and Stuart C. Brown. Englewood Cliffs, NJ: Prentice Hall, 1994, pp. 145–77.

Ewin, R. E. "On Justice and Injustice." *Mind*, 79 (April 1970), 200–16.

Fincher, Cameron. "What Is Rhetorical Reasoning?" *Research in Higher Education*, 35 (1994), 387–91.

Fisher, Walter R. *Human Communication as Narration: Toward a Philosophy of Reason, Value, and Action*. Columbia: University of South Carolina Press, 1987.

Frank, David A. "Dialectical Rapprochement in the New Rhetoric." *Argumentation and Advocacy*, 34 (Winter 1998), 111–26.

Frank, David A. "The New Rhetoric, Judaism, and Post-Enlightenment Thought: The Cultural Origins of Perelmanian Philosophy." *Quarterly Journal of Speech*, 83 (August 1997), 311–31.

Funk, David A. "Juridical Science Paradigms as Newer Rhetorics in 21st-Century Jurisprudence." *Northern Kentucky Law Review*, 12 (1985), 419–66.

Golden, James L., and Joseph J. Pilotta, eds. *Practical Reasoning in Human Affairs: Studies in Honor of Chaïm Perelman*. Dordrecht, Neth.: D. Reidel, 1986.

Golden, James L., Goodwin F. Berquist, and William E. Coleman. "Chaïm Perelman on Practical Reasoning." In *The Rhetoric of Western Thought*. 4th ed. Ed. James

L. Golden, Goodwin F. Berquist, and William E. Coleman. Dubuque, IA: Kendall/Hunt, 1989.

Goldstick, D. "Methodological Conservatism." *American Philosophy Quarterly*, 8 (April 1971), 186–91.

Goodnight, G. Thomas. "A New Rhetoric for a New Dialectic: Prolegomena to a Responsible Public Argument." *Argumentation*, 7 (1993), 329–43.

Goodwin, David. "The Dialectic of Second-Order Distinctions: The Structure of Arguments about Fallacies." *Informal Logic*, 14 (1992), 11–22.

Goodwin, David. "Distinction, Argumentation, and the Rhetorical Construction of the Real." *Argumentation and Advocacy*, 27 (Spring 1991), 141–58.

Goodwin, Jean. "Perelman, Adhering, and Conviction." *Philosophy and Rhetoric*, 28 (1995), 215–33.

Gràcio, Rui Alexandre Lalanda Martins. "Perelman's Rhetorical Foundation of Philosophy." *Argumentation*, 7 (November 1993), 439–49.

Gross, Alan. "Rhetoric as a Technique and a Mode of Truth: Reflections on Chaïm Perelman." *Philosophy and Rhetoric*, 33 (2000), 319–35.

Gross, Alan. "A Theory of the Rhetorical Audience: Reflections on Chaïm Perelman." *Quarterly Journal of Speech*, 85 (May 1999), 203–11.

Grosse, W. Jack. "Chaïm Perelman and *The New Rhetoric*." *Northern Kentucky Law Review*, 12 (1985), vii.

Haarscher, Guy, "Perelman and Haberman." *Law and Philosophy*, 5 (December 1986), 331–42.

Hasain, Marouf, Jr., Celeste Michelle Condit, and John Louis Lucaites. "The Rhetorical Boundaries of 'The Law': A Consideration of the Rhetorical Culture of Legal Practice and the Case of 'Separate but Equal' Doctrine." *Quarterly Journal of Speech*, 82 (November 1996), 323–42.

Hermann, Donald H. J. "Legal Reasoning as Argumentation." *Northern Kentucky Law Review*, 12 (1985), 467–510.

Hostetler, Michael J. "William Jennings Bryan as Demosthenes: The Scopes Trial and the Undelivered Oration, '*On Evolution*.'" *Western Journal of Communication*, 62 (Spring 1998), 165–80.

Jacobson, Arthur J. "Taking Responsibility: Law's Relation to Justice and D'Amato's Deconstructive Practice." *Northwestern University Law Review*, 90 (Summer 1996), 26–36.

Johnstone, Henry W., Jr. "Editor's Introduction." *Argumentation*, 7 (November 1993), 379–84.

Johnstone, Henry W., Jr. "New Outlooks on Controversy." *Review of Metaphysics*, 12 (September 1958), 57–67.

Johnstone, Henry W., Jr. "A New Theory of Philosophical Argumentation." *Philosophy and Phenomenological Research*, 15 (December 1954), 244–52.

Johnstone, Henry W., Jr. "Philosophical Argument and the Rhetorical Wedge." *Communication and Cognition*, 24 (1991), 77–92.

Johnstone, Henry W., Jr. "Some Reflections on Argumentation." In *La Théorie de l'argumentation: perspectives et applications*. Paris: Beatrice-Nauwelaerts, n.d., pp. 30–39.

Johnstone, Henry W., Jr. *Validity and Rhetoric in Philosophical Argument*. University Park, PA: Dialogue Press of Man & World, 1978.

Kamenka, Eugene, and Alice E. S. Tay. "The Traditions of Justice." *Law and Philosophy*, 5 (December 1986), 281–313.

Karon, Louise A. "Presence in *The New Rhetoric.*" *Philosophy and Rhetoric*, 9 (Spring 1976), 96–111.

Kienpointner, Manfred. "The Empirical Relevance of Perelman's New Rhetoric." *Argumentation*, 7 (November 1993), 419–37.

Kienpointner, Manfred. "Toward a Typology of Argumentative Schemes." In *Argumentation: Across the Lines of the Discipline*. Ed. Frans H. van Eemeren, Rob Grootendorst, J. Anthony Blair, and Charles A. Willard. Dordrecht, Neth.: Foris, 1987, pp. 275–87.

Kluback, William. "The Implications of Rhetorical Philosophy." *Law and Philosophy*, 5 (December 1986), 315–30.

Kluback, William. "The New Rhetoric as a Philosophical System." *Journal of the American Forensic Association*, 17 (Fall 1980), 73–79.

Kluback, William, and Mortimer Becke. "The Significance of Chaïm Perelman's Philosophy of Rhetoric." *Review of International Philosophy*, 33 (1979), 33–46.

Kneupper, Charles W. "The Tyranny of Logic and the Freedom of Argumentation." *Pre/Text*, 5 (Summer 1984), 113–21.

Langsdorf, Lenore. "Dialogue, Distanciation, and Engagement: Toward a Logic of Televisual Communication." *Informal Logic*, 10 (1988), 151–68.

Laughlin, Stanley K., and Daniel T. Hughes. "The Rational and the Reasonable: Dialectical or Parallel Systems." In *Practical Reasoning in Human Affairs: Studies in Honor of Chaïm Perelman*. Ed. James L. Golden and Joseph L. Pilotta. Dordrecht, Neth.: D. Reidel, 1986, 187–205.

Long, Richard. "The Role of Audience in Chaïm Perelman's New Rhetoric." *Journal of Advanced Composition*, 4 (1983), 107–17.

Loreau, Max. "Rhetoric as the Logic of Behavioral Science." Trans. Lloyd I. Watkins and Paul D. Brandes. *Quarterly Journal of Speech*, 50 (October 1964), 323–24.

McBride, William L. "Professor Perelman and Authority." *Northern Kentucky Law Review*, 12 (1985), 511–18.

Mader, Thomas F. "On Presence in Rhetoric." *College Composition and Communication*, 24 (December 1973), 375–82.

Mattis, Noéme Perelman. "Perelman and Olbrechts-Tyteca: A Personal Recollection." Unpublished statement read by Ray Dearin at the Speech Communication Association Convention, 1994.

Measell, James S. "Perelman on Analogy." *Argumentation and Advocacy*, 22 (Fall 1985), 65–71.

Meyer, Michel. "Forward—The Modernity of Rhetoric." In *From Metaphysics to Rhetoric*. Ed. Michel Meyer. Dordrecht, Neth.: Kluwer, 1989), 1–14.

Meyer, Michel. "The Perelman-Rawls Debate on Justice." *Review of International Philosophy*, 29 (1975), 316–31.

Mieczyslaw, Maneli. "The New Rhetoric and Dialectics." *Revue de Philosophie International*, 33 (1979), 216–38.

Mieczyslaw, Maneli. "Perelman's Achievement beyond Traditional Philosophy and Politics." *Law and Philosophy*, 5 (December 1986), 351–91.

Mieczyslaw, Maneli. *Perelman's New Rhetoric as Philosophy and Methodology for the Next Century*. Dordrecht, Neth.: Kluwer, 1994.

Myers, Frank. "Political Argumentation and the Composite Audience: A Case Study." *Quarterly Journal of Speech*, 85 (February 1999), 55–71.

Oliver, Robert T. "Philosophy and/or Persuasion." In *La Théorie de l'argumentation: perspectives et applications*. Paris: Beatrice-Nauwelaerts, n.d., pp. 571–80.

Olson, Kathryn M. "The Role of Dissociation in Redeeming Knowledge Claims: Nineteenth-Century Shakers' Epistemological Resistance to Decline." *Philosophy and Rhetoric*, 28 (1995), 45–68.

Parker, Douglas H. "Rhetoric, Ethics and Manipulation." *Philosophy and Rhetoric*, 5 (Spring 1972), 69–87.

Pattaro, Enrico. "Jurists, Judges and Valid Law." *Northern Kentucky Law Review*, 12 (1985), 519–36.

Raphael, David D. "Perelman on Justice." *Review of International Philosophy*, 33 (1979), 260–76.

Ray, John W. "Perelman's Universal Audience." *Quarterly Journal of Speech*, 64 (December 1978), 361–75.

Rosen, Stanley H. "Thought and Action." *Inquiry*, 2 (1959), 65–84.

Rotenstreich, Nathan. "Argumentation and Philosophical Clarification." *Philosophy and Rhetoric*, 5 (Winter 1972), 12–23.

Rotenstreich, Nathan. "On Constructing a Philosophical System." In *La Théorie de l'argumentation: perspectives et applications*. Paris: Beatrice-Nauwelaerts, n.d., pp. 179–94.

Schiappa, Edward. "Arguing about Definitions." *Argumentation*, 7 (November 1993), 403–17.

Schiappa, Edward. "Dissociation in the Arguments of Rhetorical Theory." *Argumentation and Advocacy*, 22 (Fall 1985), 72–82.

Scott, Robert L. "Chaïm Perelman: Persona and Accommodation in the New Rhetoric." *Pre/Text*, 5 (Summer 1984), 89–95.

Scult, Allen. "A Note on the Range and Utility of the Universal Audience." *Journal of the American Forensic Association*, 22 (Fall 1985), 83–87.

Scult, Allen. "Perelman's Universal Audience: One Perspective." *Central States Speech Journal*, 27 (Fall 1976), 176–80.

Secor, Marie J. "Perelman's Loci in Literary Argument." *Pre/Text*, 5 (Summer 1984), 97–110.

Secor, Marie J. "Recent Research in Argumentation Theory." *Technical Writing Teacher*, 14 (Fall 1987), 337–54.

Sillars, Malcolm O. "Audiences, Social Values, and the Analysis of Argument." *Speech Teacher*, 22 (November 1973), 291–303.

Sillars, Malcolm O., and Patricia Ganer. "Values and Beliefs: A Systematic Basis for Argumentation." In *Advances in Argumentation Theory and Research*. Ed. J. Robert Cox and Charles Arthur Willard. Carbondale: Southern Illinois University Press, pp. 184–201.

Simons, Herbert W. "Judging a Policy Proposal by the Company It Keeps: The Gore–Perot NAFTA Debate." *Quarterly Journal of Speech*, 82 (August 1996), 274–87.

Stone, Julius. "The Way of a Judge With a Principle—A Tribute to Professor Chaïm Perelman." *Northern Kentucky Law Review*, 12 (1985), 537–66.

Tammelo, Ilmar. "The Rule of Law and the Rule of Reason in International Legal Relations." In *La Théorie de l'argumentation: perspectives et applications*. Paris: Beatrice-Nauwelaerts, n.d., pp. 335–68.

Valauri, John T. "Confused Notions and Constitutional Theory." *Northern Kentucky Law Review*, 12 (1985), 567–93.

Vandamme, Fernand. "New Rhetorics and Non-Fregean Logics." *Communication and Cognition*, 24 (1991), 389–401.

Van Noorden, Sally. "Rhetorical Arguments in Aristotle and Perelman." *Review of International Philosophy*, 33 (1979), 178–87.

Waggenspach, Beth M. "Awakening Society to False Perceptions about Women." In *Rhetorical Studies in Honor of James L. Golden*. Ed. Lawrence W. Hugneberg. Dubuque, IA: Kendall/Hunt, 1986, pp. 163–78.

Walker, Gregg B., and Malcolm O. Sillars. "Where Is Argument?: Perelman's Theory of Values." In *Perspectives on Argument*. Ed. Robert Trapp and Janice Schuetz. Prospect Heights, IL: Waveland, 1990, pp. 134–50.

Wallace, Karl R. "'*Topoi*' and the Problem of Invention." *Quarterly Journal of Speech*, 58 (December 1972), 387–95.

Wangerin, Paul T. "A Multidisciplinary Analysis of the Structure of Persuasive Arguments." *Harvard Journal of Law and Public Policy*, 16 (1993), 195–239.

Warnick, Barbara. "Lucie Olbrechts-Tyteca's Contribution to *The New Rhetoric*." In *Listening to Their Voices: The Rhetorical Activities of Historical Women*. Ed. Molly Meijer Wertheimer. Columbia: University of South Carolina Press, 1997, pp. 69–85.

Warnick, Barbara. "[Review of] *Practical Reasoning in Human Affairs*." *Philosophy and Rhetoric*, 21 (1988), 158–62.

Warnick, Barbara, and Susan L. Kline. "*The New Rhetoric*'s Argument Schemes: A Rhetorical View of Practical Reasoning." *Argumentation and Advocacy*, 29 (Summer 1992), 1–15.

Wiethoff, William E. "Critical Perspectives on Perelman's Philosophy of Legal Argument." *Journal of the American Forensic Association*, 22 (Fall 1985), 88–95.

Wintgens, Luc J. "Rhetoric, Reasonableness and Ethics: An Essay on Perelman." *Argumentation*, 7 (November 1993), 451–60.

Wroblewski, Jerzy. "Semantic Basis of the Theory of Legal Interpretation." In *La Théorie de l'argumentation: perspectives et applications*. Paris: Beatrice-Nauwelaerts, n.d., pp. 397–416.

Zagacki, Kenneth. "Spatial and Temporal Images in the Biodiversity Dispute." *Quarterly Journal of Speech*, 85 (November 1999), 417–35.

Zaner, Richard M. "Rejoinder to Messrs. Johnstone and Perelman." *Philosophy and Rhetoric*, 1 (Summer 1968), 171–73.

Works about Stephen Toulmin

Abelson, Raxiel. "In Defense of Formal Logic." *Philosophy and Phenomenological Research*, 21 (March 1961), 333–46.

Adams, Elie Maynard. *Ethical Naturalism and the Modem World-View*. Chapel Hill: University of North Carolina, 1960.

Aiken, Henry David. "Moral Reasoning." *Ethics*, 64 (October 1953), 24–37.

Allen, Paul. *Proof of Moral Obligation in Twentieth-Century Philosophy*. New York: Lang, 1988.

Ambrester, Marcus L., and Glynis Holm Strause. *A Rhetoric of Interpersonal Communication*. Prospect Heights, IL: Waveland, 1984.

Anderson, Ray Lynn, and C. David Mortensen. "Logic and Marketplace Argumentation." *Quarterly Journal of Speech*, 53 (April 1967), 143–50.

Arnold, Carroll C. *Public Speaking as a Liberal Art*. Boston: Allyn and Bacon, 1964.

Arras, John D. "Getting Down to Cases: The Revival of Casuistry in Bioethics," *Journal of Medicine and Philosophy*, 16 (1991), 29–51.

Benoit, William Lyon. "An Empirical Investigation of Argumentative Strategies Employed in Supreme Court Opinions." In *Dimensions of Argument: Proceedings of the Second Summer Conference on Argumentation*. Ed. George Ziegelmueller and Jack Rhodes. Annandale, VA: Speech Communication Association, 1981, pp. 179–95.

Beresford, Eric B. "Can Phronesis Save the Life of Medical Ethics?" *Theoretical Medicine*, 17 (1996), 209–24.

Berleant, Arnold. "The Social Postulate of Theoretical Ethics." *Journal of Value Inquiry*, 4 (1970), 1–16.

Binkley, Luther J. *Contemporary Ethical Theories*. New York: Philosophical Libraries, 1961.

Blackwell, Richard J. "Toulmin's Model of an Evolutionary Epistemology." *Modern Scholasticism*, 51 (1973), 63.

Bove, Paul A. "The Rationality of Disciplines: The Abstract Understanding of Stephen Toulmin." In *After Foucault: Humanistic Knowledge, Postmodern Challenges*. Ed. Jonathan Arac. New Brunswick: Rutgers University Press, 1988, pp. 42–70.

Brockriede, Wayne. "The Contemporary Renaissance in the Study of Argument." In *Argument in Transition: Proceedings of the Third Summer Conference on Argumentation*. Ed. David Zarefsky, Malcolm O. Sillars, and Jack Rhodes. Annandale, VA: Speech Communication Association, 1983, pp. 17–26.

Brockriede, Wayne, and Douglas Ehninger. "Toulmin on Argument: An Interpretation and Application." *Quarterly Journal of Speech*, 46 (February 1960), 44–53.

Burleson, Brant R. "A Cognitive-Developmental Perspective on Social Reasoning Processes." *Western Journal of Speech Communication*, 45 (Spring 1981), 133–47.

Burleson, Brant R. "On the Analysis and Criticism of Arguments: Some Theoretical and Methodological Considerations." *Journal of the American Forensic Association*, 15 (Winter 1979), 137–47.

Burleson, Brant R. "On the Foundations of Rationality: Toulmin, Habermas, and the *a Priori* of Reason." *Journal of the American Forensic Association*, 16 (Fall 1979), 112–27.

Byker, Donald, and Loren J. Anderson. *Communication as Identification*. New York: Harper and Row, 1975.

Carleton, Lawrence Richard. "Problems, Methodology, and Outlaw Science." *Philosophy and the Social Sciences*, 12 (June 1982), 143–51.

Castaneda, H. N. "On a Proposed Revolution in Logic." *Philosophy of Science*, 27 (July 1960), 279–92.

Cohen, L. Jonathan. "Is the Progress of Science Evolutionary?" *British Journal for the Philosophy of Science*, 24 (1973), 41–61.

Connell, Jeanne. "Reconstructing a Modern Definition of Knowledge: A Comparison of Toulmin and Dewey." In *Philosophy of Education*. Ed. Neiman Alven. Urbana, IL: Philosophy of Education Society, 1995, pp. 222–34.

Cooley, J. C. "On Mr. Toulmin's Revolution in Logic." *Journal of Philosophy*, 56 (March 1959), 297–319.

Cowan, J. L. "The Uses of Argument: an Apology for Logic," *Mind*, 73 (1964), 27–45.

Cox, J. Robert. "Investigating Policy Argument as a Field." In *Dimensions of Argument: Proceedings of the Second Summer Conference on Argumentation*. Ed. George Ziegelmueller and Jack Rhodes. Annandale, VA: Speech Communication Association, 1981, pp. 126–42.

Crable, Richard E. *Argumentation as Communication: Reasoning with Receivers*. Columbus, OH: Merrill, 1976.

Cronkhite, Gary. *Persuasion: Speech and Behavioral Change.* Indianapolis: Bobbs-Merrill, 1969.

D'Angelo, Gary. "A Schema for the Utilization of Attitude Theory within the Toulmin Model of Argument." *Central States Speech Journal*, 22 (Summer 1971), 100–09.

Dellapenna, Joseph W., and Kathleen M. Farrell. "Modes of Judicial Discourse: The Search for Argument Fields." In *Argumentation: Analysis and Practices.* Ed. Frans H. van Eemeren, Rob Grootendorst, J. Anthony Blair, and Charles A. Willard. Dordrecht, Neth.: Foris, 1987, pp. 94–101.

Dingle, Herbert. "The Logical Status of Psycho-analysis." *Analysis*, 9 (1949), 63–66.

Donmoyer, Robert. "The Rescue from Relativism: Two Failed Attempts and an Alternative Strategy." *Educational Researcher*, 14 (December 1985), 13–20.

Dykstra, Vergil H. "The Place of Reason in Ethics." *Review of Metaphysics*, 8 (March 1955), 458–67.

Eemeren, Frans H. van. "A World of Difference: The Rich State of Argumentation Theory." *Informal Logic*, 17 (1995), 144–58.

Ehninger, Douglas, and Wayne Brockriede. *Decision by Debate.* New York: Dodd, Mead, 1963.

Engelhardt, H. Tristram, Jr. "Causal Accounts in Medicine: A Commentary on Stephen Toulmin." In *Changing Values in Medicine.* Ed. Eric J. Cassell. New York: University Press of America, 1979, pp. 73–81.

Fine, Arthur. "Creativity: Is Science Really a Special Case?: Response." *Comparative Literature Studies*, 17 (June 1980), 201–05.

Fine, Arthur I. "Explaining the Behavior of Entities." *Philosophical Review*, 75 (October 1966), 496–509.

Fisher, Alec. "[Review of] *Dialectics and the Macrostructure of Argument*, by James B. Freeman." *Informal Logic*, 14 (1992), 193–204.

Fisher, Frank. "Science and Critique in Political Discourse: Elements of a Postpositivistic Methodology." *New Political Science*, 9/10 (Summer/Fall 1982), 9–32.

Fisher, Walter R. "Good Reasons: Fields and Genre." In *Dimensions of Argument: Proceedings of the Second Summer Conference on Argumentation.* Ed. George Ziegelmueller and Jack Rhodes. Annandale, VA: Speech Communication Association, 1981, pp. 114–25.

Flew, Anthony. "Pycho-Analytic Explanation." *Analysis*, 10 (1949), 8–14.

Flynn, James R. "The Realm of the Moral." *American Philosophical Quarterly*, 13 (1976), 273–86.

Freeley, Austin J., and David L. Steinberg. *Argumentation and Debate: Critical Thinking for Reasoned Decision Making.* Belmont, CA: Wadsworth, 2000.

Freeman, James B. *Thinking Logically: Basic Concepts for Reasoning.* Englewood Cliffs, NJ: Prentice Hall, 1988.

Freeman, James B. *Dialectics and the Macrostructure of Argument.* New York: Foris, 1991.

Fuller, Steve. "Being There with Thomas Kuhn: A Parable for Postmodern Times." *History and Theory*, 31 (October 1992), 241–75.

Fulkerson, Richard. "Technical Logic, Comp-Logic, and the Teaching of Writing." *College Composition and Communication*, 39 (December 1988), 436–52.

Goodnight, G. Thomas. "The Personal, Technical, and Public Spheres of Argument: A Speculative Inquiry into the Art of Public Deliberation." *Journal of the American Forensic Association*, 28 (Spring 1982), 214–27.

Graham, Loren R. "The Multiple Connections between Science and Ethics." *Hastings Center Report*, 9 (June 1979), 35–40.

Gulley, Halbert E. *Discussion, Conference and Group Processes*. New York: Holt, Rinehart and Winston, 1960.

Hample, Dale. "The Functions of Argument." In *Dimensions of Argument: Proceedings of the Third Summer Conference on Argumentation*. Ed. David Zarefsky, Malcolm O. Sillars, and Jack Rhodes. Annandale, VA: Speech Communication Association, 1981, pp. 560–75.

Handler, Ernst W. "The Evolution of Economic Theories: A Formal Approach." *Erkenntnis*, 8 (July 1982), 65–96.

Hardie, W. F. R. "Mr. Toulmin on the Explanation of Human Conduct." *Analysis*, 11 (1950), 1–8.

Hayes, James T. "'Creation-Science' Is Not 'Science?' Argument Fields and Public Argument." In *Dimensions of Argument: Proceedings of the Third Summer Conference on Argumentation*. Ed. David Zarefsky, Malcolm O. Sillars, and Jack Rhodes. Annandale, VA: Speech Communication Association, 1981, pp. 416–22.

Hempel, C. G. "What Kind of Discipline Is Logic?" *Journal of Symbolic Logic*, 20 (March 1955), 541–45.

Houser, Lloyd. "The Classification of Science Literatures by their 'Hardness.'" *Library and Information Science Research*, 8 (October/December 1986), 357–72.

Jacobs, Struan. "Stephen Toulmin's Theory of Conceptual Evolution." In *Issues in Evolutionary Epistemology*. Ed. Kai Hahlweg and C. A. Hooker. Albany: State University of New York Press, 1989, pp. 510–23.

Kaeser, E. "Physical Laws, Physical Entities, and Ontology." *Dialectica*, 31 (1977), 273–99.

Kaplan, Jorton A. *Justice, Human Nature, and Political Obligation*. New York: Free, 1976.

Karbach, Joan. "Using Toulmin's Model of Argumentation." *Journal of Teaching Writing*, 6 (Spring 1987), 81–91.

Keenan, James F. "The Casuistry of John Major: Nominalist Professor of Paris (1506–1531)." *Annual of the Society of Christian Ethics* (1993), pp. 205–21.

Keene, Michael L. "Teaching Toulmin Logic." *Teaching English in the Two-Year College*, 5 (Spring 1979), 193–98.

Keough, Colleen M. "The Nature and Function of Argument in Organizational Bargaining Research." *Southern Speech Communication Journal*, 53 (Fall 1987), 1–17.

Kerner, George C. *The Revolution in Ethical Theory*. New York: Oxford University Press, 1966.

Klumpp, James F. "A Dramatistic Approach to Fields." In *Dimensions of Argument: Proceedings of the Second Summer Conference on Argumentation*. Ed. George Ziegelmueller and Jack Rhodes. Annandale, VA: Speech Communication Association, 1981, pp. 44–55.

Kneupper, Charles W. "On Argument and Diagrams." *Journal of the American Forensic Association*, 14 (Spring 1978), 181–86.

Kneupper, Charles. "Teaching Argument: An Introduction to the Toulmin Model." *College Composition and Communication*, 29 (October 1978), 237–41.

Kneupper, Charles W. "The Tyranny of Logic and the Freedom of Argumentation." *Pre/Text*, 5 (Summer 1984), 113–21.

Kordig, Carl R. "Evolutionary Epistemology Is Self-Referentially Inconsistent." *Philosophy and Phenomenological Research*, 42 (March 1982), 449–50.

Kordig, Carl R. "On Prescribing Description." *Synthese*, 18 (1968), 459–61.

Kuester, Harold H. "The Dependence of Stephen Toulmin's Epistemology on a Description/Prescription Dichotomy." *Philosophical Research Archives*, 11 (1985), 521–29.

Lawler, Ronald David. *Philosophical Analysis and Ethics*. Milwaukee: Bruce, 1968.

Lewis, Albert. "Stephen Toulmin: A Reappraisal." *Central States Speech Journal*, 23 (Spring 1972), 48–55.

McCann, Thomas M. "Student Argumentative Writing Knowledge and Ability at Three Grade Levels." *Research in the Teaching of English*, 23 (February 1989), 62–76.

McCroskey, James C. "Toulmin and the Basic Course." *Speech Teacher*, 14 (March 1965), 91–100.

Mcgrath, Patrick. *The Nature of Moral Judgement: A Study in Contemporary Moral Philosophy* (London: Sheed and Ward, 1967).

McKerrow, Ray E. "On Fields and Rational Enterprises." In *Dimensions of Argument: Proceedings of the Summer Conference on Argumentation*. Ed. Jack Rhodes and Sara Newell. Annandale, VA: Speech Communication Association, 1981, pp. 401–13.

Mehl, Peter J. "William James's Ethics and the New Casuistry." *International Journal of Applied Philosophy*, 11 (1996), 41–50.

Miller, Carolyn R. "Fields of Argument and Special Topoi." In *Dimensions of Argument: Proceedings of the Third Summer Conference on Argumentation*. Ed. David Zarefsky, Malcolm O. Sillars and Jack Rhodes. Annandale, VA: Speech Communication Association, 1981, pp. 147–59.

Miller, Gerald R., and Thomas R. Nilsen. *Perspectives on Argumentation*. Chicago: Scott, Foresman, 1966.

Mills, Glen E. *Reason in Controversy: On General Argumentation*. Boston: Allyn and Bacon, 1968.

Mitroff, Ian I. "On the Structure of Dialectical Reasoning in the Social and Policy Sciences." *Theory and Decision*, 14 (December 1982), 331–50.

Mitroff, Ian I., Harold Quinton, and Richard O. Mason. "Beyond Contradiction and Consistency: A Design for a Dialectical Policy System." *Theory and Decision*, 15 (June 1983), 107–20.

Nielsen, Kai. "Good Reasons in Ethics: An Examination of the Toulmin–Hare Controversy." *Theoria*, 24 (1958), 9–28.

Nielsen, Kai. "The Functions of Moral Discourse." *The Philosophical Quarterly*, 7 (1957), 236–48.

Ogden, Schubert Miles. *The Reality of God, and Other Essays*. New York: Harper and Row, 1966.

Palmer, L. M. "Stephen Toulmin: Variations on Vichian Themes." *Scientia*, 227 (1982), 89–104.

Perry, David L. "Cultural Relativism in Toulmin's Reason in Ethics." *Personalist*, 47 (Summer 1966), 328–39.

Peters, Richard. "Cause, Cure and Motive." *Analysis*, 10 (1950), 103–08.

Purtill, Richard L. "Toulmin on Ideals of Natural Order." *Synthese*, 22 (1971), 431–37.

Reinhard, John C. "The Role of Toulmin's Categories of Message Development in Persuasive Communication: Two Experimental Studies on Attitude Change." *Journal of the American Forensic Association*, 20 (Spring 1984), 206–23.

Rieke, Richard D., and Malcolm O. Sillars. *Argumentation and the Decision-Making Process*. New York: Longman, 1997.

Rowland, Robert. "Argument Fields." In *Dimensions of Argument: Proceedings of the Second Summer Conference on Argumentation*. Ed. George Ziegelmueller and Jack Rhodes. Annandale, VA: Speech Communication Association, 1981, pp. 456–79.

Rowland, Robert. "The Influence of Purpose on Fields of Argument." *Journal of the American Forensic Association*, 28 (Spring 1982), 228–46.

Rybacki, Karen C., and Donald J. Rybacki. *Advocacy and Opposition: An Introduction to Argumentation* (Boston: Allyn and Bacon, 2000).

Schmidt, David P. "Patterns of Argument in Business Ethics." *Journal of Business Ethics*, 5 (1986), 501–09.

Schmidt, Vivien. "The Historical Approach to Philosophy of Science: Toulmin in Perspective." *Metaphilosophy*, 19 (1988), 223–36.

Schon, Donald. "Ultimate Rules and the Rational Settlement of Ethical Conflicts." *Philosophy and Phenomenological Research*, 19 (September 1958), 53–64.

Schuetz, Janice. "The Genesis of Argumentative Forms and Fields." In *Dimensions of Argument: Proceedings of the Second Summer Conference on Argumentation*. Ed. George Ziegelmueller and Jack Rhodes. Annandale, VA: Speech Communication Association, 1981, pp. 279–94.

Schultz, Lucille M., and Chester H. Laine. "A Primary Trait Scoring Grid with Assessment and Instructional Uses." *Journal of Teaching Writing*, 5 (Spring 1986), 77–89.

Secor, Marie J. "Recent Research in Argumentation Theory." *Technical Writing Teacher*, 14 (Fall 1987), 337–54.

Seibert, Thomas M. "The Arguments of a Judge." In *Argumentation: Analysis and Practices*. Ed. Frans H. van Eemeren, Rob Grootendorst, J. Anthony Blair, and Charles A. Willard. Dordrecht, Neth.: Foris, 1987, pp. 119–22.

Shaida, S. A. "Nature of Ethical Statements." *Indian Philosophical Quarterly*, 3 (1976), 335–43.

Shafer, Charles B. "'Think Like a Lawyer': Valid Law School Admonition?" In *Dimensions of Argument: Proceedings of the Second Summer Conference on Argumentation*. Ed. George Ziegelmueller and Jack Rhodes. Annandale, VA: Speech Communication Association, 1981, pp. 242–78.

Shapere, Dudley. "Mathematical Ideals and Metaphysical Concepts." *Philosophical Review*, 69 (July 1960), 376–85.

Sherif, Carolyn W., Muzafer Sherif, and Roger E. Nebergall. *Attitude and Attitude Change: The Social Judgement-Involvement Approach*. Philadelphia: W. B. Saunders, 1965.

Siegel, H. "Truth, Problem Solving and the Rationality of Science." *Studies in History and Philosophy of Science*, 14 (June 1983), 89–112.

Sloman, A. "Rules of Inference, or Suppressed Premises?" *Mind*, 73 (1964), 84–96.

Sterba, James P. "Toulmin to Rawls." In *Ethics in the History of Western Philosophy*. Ed. Robert J. Cavalier. New York: St. Martin's, 1989, pp. 399–420.

Stone, Harold. "A Note on Vico Studies Today: Toulmin and the Development of Academic Disciplines." *New Vico Studies* (1983), pp. 69–76.

Stratman, James F. "Teaching Written Argument: The Significance of Toulmin's Layout for Sentence-Combining." *College English*, 44 (November 1982), 718–34.

Stygall, Gail. "Toulmin and the Ethics of Argument Fields: Teaching Writing and Argument." *Journal of Teaching Writing*, 6 (Spring 1987), 93–107.

James M. Tallmon. "How Jonsen Really Views Casuistry: A Note on the Abuse of Father Wildes." *Journal of Medicine and Philosophy*, 19 (1994), 103–13.

Trent, Jimmie D. "Toulmin's Model of an Argument: An Examination and Extension," *Quarterly Journal of Speech*, 54 (October 1968), 252–59.

Wadia, P. S. "Why Should I Be Moral?" *Australasian Journal of Philosophy*, 42 (1964), 216–26.

Wenzel, Joseph W. "On Fields of Argument as Propositional Systems." *Journal of the American Forensic Association*, 28 (Spring 1982), 204–13.

Westfall, R. S. "Toulmin and Human Understanding." *Journal of Modern History*, 47 (1975), 691–98.

Wildes, Kevin W. "The Priesthood of Bioethics and the Return of Casuistry." *Journal of Medicine and Philosophy*, 18 (1993), 33–50.

Willard, Charles Arthur. "Argument Fields." In *Advances in Argumentation Theory and Research*. Ed. J. Robert Cox and Charles Arthur Willard. Carbondale: Southern Illinois University, 1982, pp. 24–77.

Willard, Charles Arthur. *Argumentation and the Social Grounds of Knowledge*. Tuscaloosa: University of Alabama Press, 1983.

Willard, Charles Arthur. "Field Theory: A Cartesian Meditation." In *Dimensions of Argument: Proceedings of the Second Summer Conference on Argumentation*. Ed. George Ziegelmueller and Jack Rhodes. Annandale, VA: Speech Communication Association, 1981, pp. 21–43.

Willard, Charles Arthur. "Some Questions about Toulmin's View of Argument Fields." In *Proceedings of the Summer Conference on Argumentation*. Ed. Jack Rhodes and Sara Newell. Annandale, VA: Speech Communication Association, 1980, pp. 348–400.

Willard, Charles Arthur. "The Status of the Non-Discursiveness Thesis." *Journal of the American Forensic Association*, 17 (Spring 1981), 190–214.

Willard, Charles Arthur. *A Theory of Argumentation*. Tuscaloosa: University of Alabama Press, 1989.

Willard, Charles Arthur. "On the Utility of Descriptive Diagrams for the Analysis and Criticism of Arguments." *Communication Monographs*, 43 (November 1976), 308–19.

Wilson, F. "Explanation in Aristotle, Newton, and Toulmin [Part 1]." *Philosophy of Science*, 36 (September 1969), 291–310.

Wilson, F. "Explanation in Aristotle, Newton, and Toulmin [Part 2]." *Philosophy of Science*, 36 (December 1969), 400–28.

Windes, Russell R., and Arthur Hastings. *Argumentation and Advocacy*. New York: Random, 1965.

Zappel, Kristiane. "Argumentation and Literary Text: Towards an Operational Model." In *Argumentation: Analysis and Practices*. Ed. Frans H. van Eemeren, Rob Grootendorst, J. Anthony Blair, and Charles A. Willard. Dordrecht, Neth.: Foris, 1987, pp. 217–24.

Zarefsky, David. "Persistent Questions in the Theory of Argument Fields." *Journal of the American Forensic Association*, 28 (Spring 1982), 191–203.

Zarefsky, David. "'Reasonableness' in Public Argument: Fields as Institutions." In *Dimensions of Argument: Proceedings of the Second Summer Conference on Argumentation*. Ed. George Ziegelmueller and Jack Rhodes. Annandale, VA: Speech Communication Association, 1981, pp. 88–100.

Zeigler, Earle F. "Applied Ethics in Sport and Physical Education." *Philosophy in Context*, 13 (1983), 52–64.

Works about Richard Weaver

Ashin, Mark. "The Argument of Madison's 'Federalist,' No. 10." *College English*, 15 (October 1953), 37–45.

Auerbach, M. Morton. *The Conservative Illusion*. New York: Columbia University Press, 1959.

Baker, Virgil L., and Ralph T. Eubanks. *Speech in Personal and Public Affairs*. New York: David McKay, 1965.

Beale, Walter H. "Richard M. Weaver: Philosophical Rhetoric, Cultural Criticism, and the First Rhetorical Awakening." *College English*, 52 (October 1990), 626–40.

Bliese, John. "Richard M. Weaver and the Rhetoric of a Lost Cause." *Rhetoric Society Quarterly*, 19 (Fall 1989), 313–25.

Bliese, John. "Richard M. Weaver: Conservative Rhetorician." *Modern Age*, 21 (Fall 1977), 377–86.

Bliese, John. "Richard Weaver: Rhetoric and the Tyrannizing Image." *Modern Age*, 28 (Spring/Summer 1984), 208–14.

Bliese, John R. E. "The Conservative Rhetoric of Richard M. Weaver: Theory and Practice." *Southern Communication Journal*, 54 (Summer 1989), 401–21.

Bliese, John R. E. "Richard Weaver's Axiology of Argument." *Southern Speech Communication Journal*, 44 (Spring 1979), 275–88.

Bormann, Dennis R. "The 'Uncontested Term' Contested: An Analysis of Weaver on Burke." *Quarterly Journal of Speech*, 57 (October 1971), 298–305.

Bradford, M. E. "The Agrarianism of Richard Weaver: Beginnings and Completions." *Modern Age*, 14 (Summer/Fall 1970), 249–56.

Campbell, John Angus. "Edmund Burke: Argument from Circumstance in Reflections on the Revolution in France." *Studies in Burke and His Time*, 12 (Winter 1970–71), 1764–83.

Clark, Thomas D. "The Ideological Bases of Richard Weaver's Rhetorical Theory." In *In Search of Justice: The Indiana Tradition in Speech Communication*. Ed. Richard J. Jensen and John C. Hammerback. Amsterdam, Neth.: Rodopi, 1987, pp. 23–35.

Conley, Thomas M. *Rhetoric in the European Tradition*. New York: Longman, 1990.

Corder, Jim W. *Uses of Rhetoric*. Philadelphia: J. B. Lippincott, 1971.

Cushman, Donald P., and Gerard A. Hauser. "Weaver's Rhetorical Theory: Axiology and the Adjustment of Belief, Invention, and Judgment." *Quarterly Journal of Speech*, 59 (October 1973), 319–29.

Davidson, Donald. "Grammar and Rhetoric: The Teacher's Problem." *Quarterly Journal of Speech*, 39 (December 1953), 401–36.

Davidson, Donald. "The Vision of Richard Weaver: A Foreword." In *The Southern Tradition at Bay: A History of Postbellum Thought*. By Richard M. Weaver. Ed. George Core and M. E. Bradford. New Rochelle, NY: Arlington, 1968, pp. 13–25.

Davidson, Eugene. "Richard Malcolm Weaver—Conservative." *Modern Age*, 7 (Summer 1963), 226–30.

Diamonstein, Barbara D. "A Turn to the Right." *Saturday Review*, 49 (1966), 38–39.

Duffy, Bernard K. "The Platonic Functions of Epideictic Rhetoric." *Philosophy and Rhetoric*, 16 (1983), 79–93.

Duffy, Bernard K., and Martin Jacobi. *The Politics of Rhetoric: Richard M. Weaver and the Conservative Tradition*. Westport, CT: Greenwood, 1993.

Duffy, Bernard K., and Martin J. Jacobi. "Weaver, Richard M. (1910–1953)." In *Encyclopedia of Rhetoric and Composition: Communication from Ancient Times to the Information Age*. Ed. Theresa Enos. New York: Garland, 1996, pp. 757–60.

East, John P. "Richard M. Weaver: The Conservatism of Affirmation." *Modern Age*, 19 (Fall 1975), 338–54.

Ebbitt, Wilma R. "Two Tributes to Richard M. Weaver: Richard M. Weaver, Teacher of Rhetoric." *Georgia Review*, 17 (Winter 1963), 415–18.

Einhorn, Lois J. "The Argumentative Dimensions of Theorizing: Toward a Method for Analyzing Theories of Rhetoric." *Central States Speech Journal*, 36 (Winter 1985), 282–93.

Enholm, Donald K., David Curtis Skaggs, and W. Jeffrey Welsh. "Origins of the Southern Mind: The Parochial Sermons of Thomas Cradock of Maryland, 1744–1770." *Quarterly Journal of Speech*, 73 (May 1987), 200–18.

Eubanks, Ralph T. "Axiological Issues in Rhetorical Inquiry." *Southern Speech Communication Journal*, 44 (Fall 1978), 11–24.

Eubanks, Ralph T. "Nihilism and the Problem of a Worthy Rhetoric." *Southern Speech Journal*, 33 (Spring 1968), 187–99.

Eubanks, Ralph T. "Richard M. Weaver, Friend of Traditional Rhetoric." In *Language is Sermonic: Richard M. Weaver on the Nature of Rhetoric*. Ed. Richard L. Johannesen, Rennard Strickland, and Ralph T. Eubanks. Baton Rouge: Louisiana State University Press, 1970, pp. 3–6.

Eubanks, Ralph T. "Two Tributes to Richard M. Weaver: Richard M. Weaver: In Memoriam." *Georgia Review*, 17 (Winter 1963), 412–15.

Eubanks, Ralph T., and Virgil L. Baker. "Toward an Axiology of Rhetoric." *Quarterly Journal of Speech*, 48 (April 1962), 157–68.

Fisher, Walter R. "Advisory Rhetoric: Implications for Forensic Debate." *Western Speech*, 29 (Spring 1965), 114–19.

Floyd, James M., and W. Clifton Adams. "A Content-Analysis Test of Richard M. Weaver's Critical Methodology." *Southern Speech Communication Journal*, 41 (Summer 1976), 374–87.

Follette, Charles. "Deep Rhetoric: A Substantive Alternative to Consequentialism in Exploring the Ethics of Rhetoric 1." In *Dimensions of Argument: Proceedings of the Second Summer Conference on Argumentation*. Ed. George Ziegelmueller and Jack Rhodes. Annandale, VA: Speech Communication Association, 1981, pp. 989–1002.

Foss, Sonja K. "Abandonment of Genus: The Evolution of Political Rhetoric." *Central States Speech Journal*, 33 (Summer 1982), 367–78.

Foss, Sonja K. "Rhetoric and the Visual Image: A Resource Unit." *Communication Education*, 31 (January 1982), 55–66.

Gayner, Jeffery B. "The Critique of Modernity in the Work of Richard M. Weaver." *Intercollegiate Review*, 14 (Spring 1979), 97–104.

Geiger, George R. "We Note . . . the Consequences of Some Ideas." *Antioch Review*, 8 (June 1948), 251–54.

Golden, James L., Goodwin F. Berquist, and William E. Coleman. *The Rhetoric of Western Thought*. 7th ed. Dubuque, IA: Kendall/Hunt, 2000.

Hart, Jeffrey. "Dream Weaver." *National Review*, 48 (March 25, 1996), 60–61.

Hart, Roderick P. "The Functions of Human Communication in the Maintenance of Public Values." In *Handbook of Rhetorical and Communication Theory*. Ed. Carroll C. Arnold and John Waite Bowers. Boston: Allyn and Bacon, 1984, pp. 749–91.

Haskell, Robert E., and Gerard A. Hauser. "Rhetorical Structure: Truth and Method in Weaver's Epistemology." *Quarterly Journal of Speech*, 64 (October 1978), 233–45.

Hayakawa, S. I. *Symbol, Status, and Personality*. 1950; rpt. New York: Harcourt Brace and World, 1963.

"In Memoriam, Richard M. Weaver." *New Individualist Review*, 2 (Spring 1963), 2.

Irwin, Clark T., Jr. "Rhetoric Remembers: Richard Weaver on Memory and Culture." *Today's Speech*, 21 (Spring 1973), 21–26.

Jacobi, Martin J., and Bernard K. Duffy. "Richard M. Weaver (1911–1963)." In *Twentieth-Century Rhetorics and Rhetoricians: Critical Studies and Sources*. Ed. Michael G. Moran and Michelle Ballif. Westport, CT: Greenwood, 2000, pp. 343–52.

Johannesen, Richard L. "Attitude of Speaker toward Audience: A Significant Concept for Contemporary Rhetorical Theory and Criticism." *Central States Speech Journal*, 25 (Summer 1974), 95–104.

Johannesen, Richard L. "Conflicting Philosophies of Rhetoric/Communication: Richard M. Weaver versus S. I. Hayakawa." *Communication*, 7 (1983), 289–315.

Johannesen, Richard L. "Richard M. Weaver on Standards for Ethical Rhetoric." *Central States Speech Journal*, 29 (Summer 1978), 127–37.

Johannesen, Richard L. "Richard M. Weaver's Uses of Kenneth Burke." *Southern Speech Communication Journal*, 52 (Spring 1987), 312–30.

Johannesen, Richard L. "Richard Weaver's View of Rhetoric and Criticism." *Southern Speech Journal*, 32 (Winter 1966), 133–45.

Johannesen, Richard L. "Some Pedagogical Implications of Richard M. Weaver's Views on Rhetoric." *College Composition and Communication*, 29 (October 1978), 272–79.

Johannesen, Richard L., Rennard Strickland, and Ralph T. Eubanks. "Richard M. Weaver on the Nature of Rhetoric: An Interpretation." In *Language is Sermonic: Richard M. Weaver on the Nature of Rhetoric*. Ed. Richard L. Johannesen, Rennard Strickland, and Ralph T. Eubanks. Baton Rouge: Louisiana State University Press, 1970, pp. 7–30.

Kendall, Willmoore. "How to Read Richard Weaver: Philosopher of 'We the (Virtuous) People.'" *Intercollegiate Review*, 2 (September 1965), 77–86.

Kendall, Willmoore. *The Conservative Affirmation*. Chicago: Henry Regnery, 1963.

Kirk, Russell. *Beyond the Dreams of Avarice*. Chicago: Henry Regnery, 1956.

Kirk, Russell. "Richard Weaver, RIP." *National Review*, 14 (April 23, 1963), 308.

Kirschke, James. "The Ethical Approach: The Literary Philosophy of Richard M. Weaver." *Intercollegiate Review*, 14 (Spring 1979), 87–94.

Lora, Ronald. *Conservative Minds in America*. Chicago: Rand McNally, 1971.

Medhurst, Martin J. "The First Amendment vs. Human Rights: A Case Study in Community Sentiment and Argument from Definition." *Western Journal of Speech Communication*, 46 (Winter 1982), 1–19.

Medhurst, Martin J. "The Sword of Division: A Reply to Brummett and Warnick." *Western Journal of Speech Communication*, 46 (Fall 1982), 383–90.

Meyer, Frank S. "Richard M. Weaver: An Appreciation." *Modern Age*, 14 (Summer/Fall 1970), 243–48.

Middleton, David. "The *Summa Theologica* of Richard Weaver." *Sewanee Review*, 106 (July/September 1998), 517–25.

Milione, E. Victor. "The Uniqueness of Richard M. Weaver." *Intercollegiate Review*, 2 (September 1965), 67–86.

Montgomery, Marion. "Richard M. Weaver, 1948." *Modern Age*, 26 (Summer/Fall 1982), 252–55.

Montgomery, Marion. "Richard Weaver against the Establishment: An Essay Review." *Georgia Review*, 23 (Winter 1969), 433–59.

Nash, George H. *The Conservative Intellectual Movement in America Since 1945*. New York: Basic, 1976.

Natanson, Maurice. "The Limits of Rhetoric." *Quarterly Journal of Speech*, 41 (April 1955), 133–39.

Payne, Melinda A., Suzanne M. Ratchford, and Lillian N. Wolley. "Richard M. Weaver: A Bibliographic Essay." *Rhetoric Society Quarterly*, 19 (Fall 1989), 327–32.

Powell, James. "The Conservatism of Richard M. Weaver: The Foundations of Weaver's Traditionalism." *New Individualist Review*, 3 (1964), 3–6.

Regnery, Henry. *Memoirs of a Dissident Publisher*. New York: Harcourt Brace Jovanovich, 1979.

Rossiter, Clinton. *Conservatism in America*. New York: Alfred A. Knopf, 1956.

Schliessmann, Mike. "Free Speech and the Rights of Congress: Robert M. Lafollette and the Argument from Principle." In *Free Speech Yearbook 1978*. Falls Church, VA: Speech Communication Association, 1978, pp. 38–44.

Scotchie, Joseph. *Barbarians in the Saddle: An Intellectual Biography of Richard M. Weaver*. New Brunswick, NJ: Transaction, 1997.

Scotchie, Joseph, ed. *The Vision of Richard Weaver*. New Brunswick, NJ: Transaction, 1995.

Smith, William Raymond. *History as Argument: Three Patriotic Historians of the American Revolution*. The Hague, Neth.: Mouton, 1966.

Smith, William Raymond. *The Rhetoric of American Politics: A Study of Documents*. Westport, CT: Greenwood, 1969.

Sproule, J. Michael. "An Emerging Rationale for Revolution: Argument from Circumstance and Definition in Polemics against the Stamp Act, 1765–1766." *Today's Speech*, 23 (Spring 1975), 17–21.

Sproule, J. Michael. "Using Public Rhetoric to Assess Private Philosophy: Richard M. Weaver and Beyond." *Southern Speech Communication Journal*, 44 (Spring 1979), 289–308.

Szasz, Thomas. *The Myth of Psychotherapy: Mental Healing as Religion, Rhetoric, and Repression*. Garden City, NY: Anchor/Doubleday, 1978.

Thorne, Melvin J. *American Conservative Thought since World War II: The Core Ideas*. New York: Greenwood, 1990.

Vivas, Eliseo. "Introduction to *Life without Prejudice*." In *Life without Prejudice and Other Essays*. By Richard Weaver. Chicago: Henry Regnery, 1965, pp. vii–xvii.

Weisman, Eric R. "The Good Man Singing Well: Stevie Wonder as Noble Lover." *Critical Studies in Mass Communication*, 2 (June 1985), 136–51.

White, Bruce A. "Richard M. Weaver: Dialectic Rhetorician." *Modern Age*, 26 (Summer/Fall 1982), 256–59.

Winterowd, W. Ross. *Rhetoric: A Synthesis*. New York: Holt, Rinehart and Winston, 1968.

Winterowd, W. Ross. "Richard M. Weaver: Modern Poetry and the Limits of Conservative Criticism." *Western Speech*, 37 (Spring 1973), 129–38.

Wolfe, Gregory. *Right Mind: A Sourcebook of American Conservative Thought*. Chicago: Regnery, 1987.

Young, Fred Douglas. *Richard M. Weaver: 1910–1963: A Life of the Mind*. Columbia: University of Missouri Press, 1995.

Works about Kenneth Burke

Aaron, Daniel. *Writers on the Left*. 1961; rpt. New York: Avon, 1965.

Abbott, Don. "Marxist Influences on the Rhetorical Theory of Kenneth Burke." *Philosophy and Rhetoric*, 7 (Fall 1974), 217–33.

Abdulla, Adnan K. *Catharsis in Literature*. Bloomington: Indiana University Press, 1985.

Adams, Robert M. *Strains of Discord: Studies in Literary Openness*. Ithaca: Cornell University Press, 1958.

Aden, Roger C., Rita L. Rahoi, and Christina S. Beck. "'Dreams are Born on Places Like This': The Process of Interpretive Community Formation at the *Field of Dreams* Site." *Communication Quarterly*, 43 (Fall 1995), 368–80.

Aeschbacher, Jill. "Kenneth Burke, Samuel Beckett, and Form." *Today's Speech*, 21 (Summer 1973), 43–47.

Ambrester, Marcus L., and Glynis Holm Strause. *A Rhetoric of Interpersonal Communication*. Prospect Heights, IL: Waveland, 1984.

Ambrester, Roy. "Identification Within: Kenneth Burke's View of the Unconscious." *Philosophy and Rhetoric*, 7 (Fall 1974), 205–16.

"Announcement." *Dial*, 86 (January 1929), 90.

Appel, Edward C. "Burlesque Drama as a Rhetorical Genre: The Hudibrastic Ridicule of William F. Buckley, Jr." *Western Journal of Communication*, 60 (Summer 1996), 269–84.

Appel, Edward C. "Implications and Importance of the Negative in Burke's Dramatistic Philosophy of Language." *Communication Quarterly*, 41 (Winter 1993), 51–65.

Appel, Edward C. "The Perfected Drama of Reverend Jerry Falwell." *Communication Quarterly*, 35 (Winter 1987), 26–38.

Appel, Edward C. "The Rhetoric of Dr. Martin Luther King, Jr.: Comedy and Context in Tragic Collision." *Western Journal of Communication*, 61 (Fall 1997), 376–402.

Auden, W. H. "A Grammar of Assent." *New Republic*, 105 (July 14, 1941), 59.

Aune, James Arnt. "Burke's Palimpsest: Rereading *Permanence and Change*." *Communication Studies*, 42 (Fall 1991), 234–37.

Babcock, C. Merton. "A Dynamic Theory of Communications." *Journal of Communication*, 2 (May 1952), 64–68.

Baer, Donald M. "A Comment on Skinner as Boy and on Burke as S ▲." *Behaviorism*, 4 (Fall 1976), 273–77.

Baird, A. Craig. *Rhetoric: A Philosophical Inquiry*. New York: Ronald, 1965.

Baker, Lewis. "Little Kenny Has His Fits." *Pre/Text*, 6 (Fall/Winter 1985), 379–80.

Baker, Lewis. "Some Manuscript Collections Containing Kenneth Burke Materials." *Pre/Text*, 6 (Fall/Winter 1985), 307–11.

Baker, Scott. "Response to the Film, *Platoon*: An Analysis of the Vietnam Veteran as Journalist-Critic and 'Priest.'" *Southern Communication Journal*, 55 (Winter 1990), 123–43.

Baxter, Gerald D., and Pat M. Taylor. "Burke's Theory of Consubstantiality and Whitehead's Concept of Concrescence." *Communication Monographs*, 45 (June 1978), 173–80.

Bellairs, John, Philip Waldron, and Manfred Mackenzie. "Critical Exchange: Variations on a Vase." *Southern Review* [Adelaide, Austral.], 1 (1965), 58–73.

Bello, Richard. "A Burkeian Analysis of the 'Political Correctness' Confrontation in Higher Education." *Southern Communication Journal*, 61 (Spring 1996), 243–52.

Benne, Kenneth D. "Education for Tragedy: I." *Educational Theory*, 1 (November 1951), 199–210, 217.

Benne, Kenneth D. "Education for Tragedy: II." *Educational Theory*, 1 (December 1951), 274–83.

Bennett, William. "Kenneth Burke: A Philosophy in Defense of Un-reason." In *Philosophers on Rhetoric: Traditional and Emerging Views*. Ed. Donald G. Douglas. Skokie, IL: National Textbook, 1973, pp. 243–51.

Bennett, W. Lance. "Political Scenarios and the Nature of Politics." *Philosophy and Rhetoric*, 8 (Winter 1975), 23–42.

Benoit, William L. "Systems of Explanation: Aristotle and Burke on 'Cause.'" *Rhetoric Society Quarterly*, 13 (Winter 1983), 41–58.

Berlin, Isaiah. "An Exchange on Machiavelli: Isaiah Berlin Replies." *New York Review of Books*, 18 (April 6, 1972), 36–37.

Berthold, Carol A. "Kenneth Burke's Cluster-Agon Method: Its Development and an Application." *Central States Speech Journal*, 27 (Winter 1976), 302–09.

Bewley, Marius. *The Complex Fate: Hawthorne, Henry James and Some Other American Writers*. London: Chatto and Windus, 1968.

Bewley, Marius. "Kenneth Burke as Literary Critic." *Scrutiny*, 15 (December 1948), 254–77.

Biesecker, Barbara A. *Addressing Postmodernity: Kenneth Burke, Rhetoric, and a Theory of Social Change*. Tuscaloosa: University of Alabama Press, 1997.

Biesecker, Barbara. "Kenneth Burke's *Grammar of Motives*: Speculations on the Politics of Interpretation." In *Rhetoric and Ideology: Compositions and Criticisms of Power*. Ed. Charles W. Kneupper. Arlington, TX: Rhetoric Society of America, 1989, pp. 82–89.

Birdsell, David S. "Ronald Reagan on Lebanon and Grenada: Flexibility and Interpretation in the Application of Kenneth Burke's Pentad." *Quarterly Journal of Speech*, 73 (August 1987), 267–79.

Blackmur, R. P. *The Double Agent: Essays in Craft and Elucidation*. New York: Arrow, 1935.

Blackmur, R. P. *Language as Gesture: Essays in Poetry*. 1935; rpt. New York: Harcourt, Brace, 1952.

Blackmur, R. P. *The Lion and the Honeycomb: Essays in Solicitude and Critique*. 1935; rpt. New York: Harcourt, Brace, 1955.

Blankenship, Jane, and Barbara Sweeney. "The 'Energy' of Form." *Central States Speech Journal*, 31 (Fall 1980), 172–83.

Blankenship, Jane, Edwin Murphy, and Marie Rosenwasser. "Pivotal Terms in the Early Works of Kenneth Burke." *Philosophy and Rhetoric*, 7 (Winter 1974), 1–24.

Blankenship, Jane, Marlene G. Fine, and Leslie K. Davis. "The 1980 Republican Primary Debates: The Transformation of Actor to Scene." *Quarterly Journal of Speech*, 69 (February 1983), 25–36.

Blankenship, Jane, and Janette Kenner Muir. "On Imagining the Future: The Secular Search for 'Piety.'" *Communication Quarterly*, 35 (Winter 1987), 1–12.

Blau, Herbert. "Kenneth Burke: Tradition and the Individual Critic." *American Quarterly*, 6 (1954), 323–36.

Bloom, Harold. *The Breaking of the Vessels*. Chicago: University of Chicago Press, 1982.

Bloom, Harold. "A Tribute to Kenneth Burke." *Book World*, May 31, 1981, p. 4.

Booth, Wayne C. *Critical Understanding: The Powers and Limits of Pluralism*. Chicago: University of Chicago Press, 1979.

Booth, Wayne C. "Kenneth Burke's Way of Knowing." *Critical Inquiry*, 1 (September 1974), 1–22.

Bostdorff, Denise M. "Making Light of James Watt: A Burkean Approach to the Form and Attitude of Political Cartoons." *Quarterly Journal of Speech*, 73 (February 1987), 43–59.

Bostdorff, Denise M., and Phillip K. Tompkins. "Musical Form and Rhetorical Form: Kenneth Burke's *Dial* Reviews as Counterpart to *Counter-Statement*." *Pre/Text*, 6 (Fall/Winter 1985), 235–52.

Branaman, Ann. "Reconsidering Kenneth Burke: His Contributions to the Identity Controversy." *Sociological Quarterly*, 35 (August 1994), 443–55.

Brissett, Dennis, and Charles Edgley, eds. *Life as Theatre: A Dramaturgical Sourcebook*. Chicago: Aldine, 1975.

Brock, Bernard L. "Epistemology and Ontology in Kenneth Burke's Dramatism." *Communication Quarterly*, 33 (Spring 1985), 94–104.

Brock, Bernard L., ed. *Kenneth Burke and Contemporary European Thought: Rhetoric in Transition*. Tuscaloosa: University of Alabama Press, 1995.

Brock, Bernard. "Political Speaking: A Burkeian Approach." In *Critical Responses to Kenneth Burke: 1924–1966*. Ed. William H. Rueckert. Minneapolis: University of Minnesota Press, 1969, pp. 444–55.

Brock, Bernard L. "The Dramatistic Approach: Rhetorical Criticism: A Burkeian Approach Revisited." In *Methods of Rhetorical Criticism: A Twentieth-Century Perspective*. 3rd ed. Ed. Bernard L. Brock, Robert Scott, and James W. Chesebro. Detroit: Wayne State University Press, 1990, pp. 183–95.

Brock, Bernard L. "The Role of Paradox and Metaphor in Kenneth Burke's Dramatism." *Communication Quarterly*, 33 (Winter 1985), 18–22.

Brown, Janet. "Kenneth Burke and *The Mod Donna*: The Dramatistic Method Applied to Feminist Criticism." *Central States Speech Journal*, 29 (Summer 1978), 138–46.

Brown, Merle E. *Kenneth Burke*. University of Minnesota Pamphlets on American Writers, No. 75. Minneapolis: University of Minnesota Press, 1969.

Brummett, Barry. "Burkean Comedy and Tragedy, Illustrated in Reactions to the Arrest of John DeLorean." *Central States Speech Journal*, 35 (Winter 1984), 217–27.

Brummett, Barry. "Burkean Scapegoating, Mortification, and Transcendence in Presidential Campaign Rhetoric." *Central States Speech Journal*, 32 (Winter 1981), 254–64.

Brummett, Barry. "Burkean Transcendence and Ultimate Terms in Rhetoric by and about James Watt." *Central States Speech Journal*, 33 (Winter 1982), 547–56.

Brummett, Barry. "Burke's Representative Anecdote as a Method in Media Criticism." *Critical Studies in Mass Communication*, 1 (June 1984), 161–76.

Brummett, Barry. "Electric Literature as Equipment for Living: Haunted House Films." *Critical Studies in Mass Communication*, 2 (September 1985), 247–61.

Brummett, Barry. "Gastronomic Reference, Synecdoche, and Political Images." *Quarterly Journal of Speech*, 67 (May 1981), 138–45.

Brummett, Barry. "The Homology Hypothesis: Pornography on the VCR." *Critical Studies in Mass Communication*, 5 (September 1988), 202–16.

Brummett, Barry, ed. *Landmark Essays on Kenneth Burke*. Davis, CA: Hermagoras, 1993.

Brummett, Barry. "A Pentadic Analysis of Ideologies in Two Gay Rights Controversies." *Central States Speech Journal*, 30 (Fall 1979), 250–61.

Brummett, Barry. "Presidential Substance: The Address of August 15, 1973." *Western Speech Communication*, 39 (Fall 1975), 249–59.

Brummett, Barry. "The Representative Anecdote as a Burkean Method, Applied to Evangelical Rhetoric." *Southern Speech Communication Journal*, 50 (Fall 1984), 1–23.

Brummett, Barry. "Symbolic Form, Burkean Scapegoating, and Rhetorical Exigency in Alioto's Response to the 'Zebra' Murders." *Western Journal of Speech Communication*, 44 (Winter 1980), 64–73.

Buehler, Daniel O. "Permanence and Change in Theodore Roosevelt's Conservative Jeremiad." *Western Journal of Communication*, 62 (Fall 1998), 439–58.

Burgess, Parke G. "The Dialectic of Substance: Rhetoric vs Poetry." *Communication Quarterly*, 33 (Spring 1985), 105–12.

Burgess, Parke G. "The Forum: Murder Will Out—But as Rhetoric?" *Quarterly Journal of Speech*, 60 (April 1974), 225–31.

"Burke, Kenneth (Duva)." *New Encyclopaedia Britannica*. Vol. 2. Chicago: Encyclopaedia Britannica, 1986, 653.

Burkholder, Thomas R. "Kansas Populism, Woman Suffrage, and the Agrarian Myth: A Case Study in the Limits of Mythic Transcendence." *Communication Studies*, 40 (Winter 1989), 292–307.

Burks, Don. "KB at Home" (photographs). *Pre/Text*, 6 (Fall/Winter 1985), 293–95.

Burks, Don M. "Dramatic Irony, Collaboration, and Kenneth Burke's Theory of Form." *Pre/Text*, 6 (Fall/Winter 1985), 255–73.

Burks, Don M. "Kenneth Burke: The Agro-Bohemian 'Marxoid.'" *Communication Studies*, 42 (Fall 1991), 219–33.

Burks, Virginia. "Sculptured Bust of KB" (photographs). *Pre/Text*, 6 (Fall/Winter 1985), 296–303.

Bygrave, Stephen. *Kenneth Burke: Rhetoric and Ideology*. New York: Routledge, 1993.

Byker, Donald, and Loren J. Anderson. *Communication as Identification: An Introductory View*. New York: Harper and Row, 1975.

Cain, William E. *The Crisis in Criticism: Theory, Literature, and Reform in English Studies*. Baltimore: Johns Hopkins University Press, 1984.

Cali, Dennis D. "Chiara Lubich's 1977 Templeton Prize Acceptance Speech: Case Study in the Mystical Narrative." *Communication Studies*, 44 (Summer 1993), 132–43.

Campbell, Finley C. "Voices of Thunder, Voices of Rage: A Symbolic Analysis of a Selection from Malcolm X's Speech, 'Message to the Grass Roots.'" *Speech Teacher*, 19 (March 1970), 101–10.

Carlson, A. Cheree. "Defining Womanhood: Lucretia Coffin Mott and the Transformation of Femininity." *Western Journal of Communication*, 58 (Spring 1994), 85–97.

Carlson, A. Cheree. "Gandhi and the Comic Frame: 'Ad Bellum Purificandum.'" *Quarterly Journal of Speech*, 72 (November 1986), 446–55.

Carlson, A. Cheree. "Limitations on the Comic Frame: Some Witty American Women of the Nineteenth Century." *Quarterly Journal of Speech*, 74 (August 1988), 310–22.

Carlson, A. Cheree. "Narrative as the Philosopher's Stone: How Russell H. Conwell Changed Lead into Diamonds." *Western Journal of Speech Communication*, 53 (Fall 1989), 342–55.

Carlson, A. Cheree. "'You Know It When You See It': The Rhetorical Hierarchy of Race and Gender in *Rhinelander v. Rhinelander*." *Quarterly Journal of Speech*, 85 (May 1999), 111–28.

Carlson, A. Cheree, and John E. Hocking. "Strategies of Redemption at the Vietnam Veterans' Memorial." *Western Journal of Speech Communication*, 52 (Summer 1988), 203–15.

Carpenter, Ronald H. "A Stylistic Basis of Burkeian Identification." *Today's Speech*, 20 (Winter 1972), 19–24.

Carrier, James G. "Knowledge, Meaning, and Social Inequality in Kenneth Burke." *American Journal of Sociology*, 88 (July 1982), 43–61.

Carrier, James G. "Misrecognition and Knowledge." *Inquiry*, 22 (August 1979), 321–42.

Carter, C. Allen. Kenneth Burke and the Scapegoat Process. Norman: University of Oklahoma Press, 1996.

Carter, C. Allen. "Forum: Late Burke." *Quarterly Journal of Speech*, 86 (May 2000), 232–36.

Cathcart, Robert. *Post Communication: Critical Analysis and Evaluation*. Indianapolis: Bobbs-Merrill, 1966.

Chapel, Gage William. "Television Criticism: A Rhetorical Perspective." *Western Speech Communication*, 39 (Spring 1975), 81–91.

Charland, Maurice. "Constitutive Rhetoric: The Case of the *Peuple Québécois.*" *Quarterly Journal of Speech*, 73 (May 1987), 133–50.

Chase, Richard. "Rhetoric of Rhetoric." In *The New Partisan Reader, 1945–1953.* Ed. William Phillips and Philip Rahv. New York: Harcourt, Brace, 1953, pp. 590–93.

Cheney, George. "The Rhetoric of Identification and the Study of Organizational Communication." *Quarterly Journal of Speech*, 69 (May 1983), 143–58.

Cheney, George, and Phillip K. Tompkins. "Coming to Terms with Organizational Identification and Commitment." *Central States Speech Journal*, 38 (Spring 1987), 1–15.

Chesebro, James W. "Communication, Values, and Popular Television Series—A Seventeen-Year Assessment." *Communication Quarterly*, 39 (Summer 1991), 197–225.

Chesebro, James W. "A Construct for Assessing Ethics in Communication." *Central States Speech Journal*, 20 (Summer 1969), 104–14.

Chesebro, James W. "Epistemology and Ontology as Dialectical Modes in the Writings of Kenneth Burke." *Communication Quarterly*, 36 (Summer 1988), 175–91.

Chesebro, James W. "Extending the Burkeian System: A Response to Tompkins and Cheney." *Quarterly Journal of Speech*, 80 (February 1994), 83–90.

Chesebro, James W. "Extensions of the Burkeian System." *Quarterly Journal of Speech*, 78 (August 1992), 356–68.

Chesebro, James W., and Caroline D. Hamsher. "Rhetorical Criticism: A Message-Centered Approach." *Speech Teacher*, 22 (November 1973), 282–90.

Chesebro, James W., Davis A. Foulger, Jay E. Nachman, and Andrew Yannelli. "Popular Music as a Mode of Communication, 1955–1982." *Critical Studies in Mass Communication*, 2 (June 1985), 115–35.

Christiansen, Adrienne E., and Jeremy J. Hanson. "Comedy as Cure for Tragedy: Act Up and the Rhetoric of AIDS." *Quarterly Journal of Speech*, 82 (May 1996), 157–70.

Clark, Robert D. "Lessons from the Literary Critics." *Western Speech*, 21 (Spring 1957), 83–89.

Coe, Richard M. *Form and Substance: An Advanced Rhetoric.* New York: John Wiley, 1981.

Coe, Richard M. "It Takes Capital to Defeat Dracula: A New Rhetorical Essay." *College English*, 48 (March 1986), 231–42.

Coe, Richard M. "Richard M. Coe Responds." *College English*, 49 (February 1987), 222–23.

Collins, Catherine Ann, and Jeanne E. Clark. "Jim Wright's Resignation Speech: De-Legitimization or Redemption?" *Southern Communication Journal*, 58 (Fall 1992), 67–75.

Combs, James E. *Dimensions of Political Drama.* Santa Monica, CA: Goodyear, 1980.

Combs, James E., and Michael W. Mansfield. *Drama in Life: The Uses of Communication in Society.* New York: Hastings, 1976.

Comprone, Joseph. "Kenneth Burke and the Teaching of Writing." *College Composition and Communication*, 29 (December 1978), 336–40.

Comprone, Joseph J. "Burke's Dramatism as a Means of Using Literature to Teach Composition." *Rhetoric Society Quarterly*, 9 (Summer 1979), 142–55.

Condit, Celeste. "Framing Kenneth Burke: Sad Tragedy or Comic Dance?" *Quarterly Journal of Speech*, 80 (February 1994), 77–82.

Condit, Celeste Michelle. "Post-Burke: Transcending the Sub-Stance of Dramatism." *Quarterly Journal of Speech*, 78 (August 1992), 349–55.

Condit, Celeste Michelle, and J. Ann Selzer. "The Rhetoric of Objectivity in the Newspaper Coverage of a Murder Trial." *Critical Studies in Mass Communication*, 2 (September 1985), 197–216.

Conley, Thomas M. *Rhetoric in the European Tradition*. New York: Longman, 1990.

Conrad, Charles. "Agon and Rhetorical Form: The Essence of 'Old Feminist' Rhetoric." *Central States Speech Journal*, 32 (Spring 1981), 45–53.

Conrad, Charles. "Phases, Pentads, and Dramatistic Critical Process." *Central States Speech Journal*, 35 (Summer 1984), 94–104.

Conrad, Charles, and Elizabeth A. Macom. "Re-Visiting Kenneth Burke: Dramatism/Logology and the Problem of Agency." *Southern Communication Journal*, 61 (Fall 1995), 11–28.

Cooks, Leda, and David Descutner. "Different Paths from Powerlessness to Empowerment: A Dramatistic Analysis of Two Eating Disorder Therapies." *Western Journal of Communication*, 57 (Fall 1993), 494–514.

Corcoran, Farrell. "The Bear in the Back Yard: Myth, Ideology, and Victimage Ritual in Soviet Funerals." *Communication Monographs*, 50 (December 1983), 305–20.

Cowley, Malcolm. "A Critic's First Principle." *New Republic*, 129 (September 14, 1953), 16–17.

Cowley, Malcolm. *Exile's Return: A Literary Odyssey of the 1920's*. New York: Viking, 1951.

Cowley, Malcolm. "Prolegomena to Kenneth Burke." *New Republic*, 72 (June 5, 1950), 18–19.

Cox, James M. "Remembering Kenneth Burke." *Sewanee Review*, 102 (July/September 1994), 439–43.

Crable, Bryan. "Burke's Perspective on Perspectives: Grounding Dramatism in the Representative Anecdote." *Quarterly Journal of Speech*, 86 (August 2000), 318–33.

Crable, Richard E. "Ethical Codes, Accountability, and Argumentation." *Quarterly Journal of Speech*, 64 (February 1978), 23–32.

Crable, Richard E., and John J. Makay. "Kenneth Burke's Concept of Motives in Rhetorical Theory." *Today's Speech*, 20 (Winter 1972), 11–18.

Crable, Richard E., and Steven L. Vibbert. "Argumentative Stance and Political Faith Healing: 'The Dream Will Come True.'" *Quarterly Journal of Speech*, 69 (August 1983), 290–301.

Cragan, John F., and Donald C. Shields. *Symbolic Theories in Applied Communication Research: Bormann, Burke and Fisher*. Cresskill, NJ: Hampton, 1995.

Cranston, Maurice. *The Mask of Politics and Other Essays*. London: Allen Lane, 1973.

Crenshaw, Carrie. "The 'Protection' of 'Woman': A History of Legal Attitudes Toward Women's Workplace Freedom." *Quarterly Journal of Speech*, 81 (February 1995), 63–82.

"Critic, Poet Kenneth Burke, 84 Will Receive Literature Medal." *Denver Post*, April 20, 1981, p. 32.

Crocker, J. Christopher. "The Social Functions of Rhetorical Forms." In *The Social Use of Metaphor: Essays on the Anthropology of Rhetoric*. Ed. J. David Sapir and J. Christopher Crocker. Philadelphia: University of Pennsylvania Press, 1977, pp. 33–66.

Crowell, Laura. "Three Sheers for Kenneth Burke." *Quarterly Journal of Speech*, 63 (April 1977), 150–67.

Crusius, Timothy W. "A Case for Kenneth Burke's Dialectic and Rhetoric." *Philosophy and Rhetoric*, 19 (1986), 23–37.

Crusius, Timothy W. *Kenneth Burke and the Conversation After Philosophy*. Carbondale: Southern Illinois University Press, 1999.

Day, Dennis. "The Forum: Kenneth Burke and Identification—A Reply." *Quarterly Journal of Speech*, 47 (December 1961), 415–16.

Day, Dennis G. "Persuasion and the Concept of Identification." *Quarterly Journal of Speech*, 46 (October 1960), 270–73.

Demo, Anne Teresa. "The Guerrilla Girls' Comic Politics of Subversion." *Women's Studies in Communication*, 23 (Spring 2000), 133–56.

De Mott, Benjamin. "The Little Red Discount House." *Hudson Review*, 15 (Winter 1962–63), 551–64.

Desilet, Gregory. "Nietzsche Contra Burke: The Melodrama in Dramatism." *Quarterly Journal of Speech*, 75 (February 1989), 65–83.

Dickey, James. *Babel to Byzantium: Poets and Poetry Now*. New York: Farrar, Straus, and Giroux, 1968.

Donoghue, Denis. *Ferocious Alphabets*. New York: Columbia University Press, 1984.

Donoghue, Denis. "K. B.—In Memory." *Sewanee Review*, 102 (July/September 1994), 443–45.

Duerden, Richard Y. "Kenneth Burke's Systemless System: Using Pepper to Pigeonhole an Elusive Thinker." *Journal of Mind and Behavior*, 3 (Autumn 1982), 323–36.

Duffy, Bernard I. "Reality as Language: Kenneth Burke's Theory of Poetry." *Western Review*, 12 (Spring 1948), 132–45.

Duncan, Hugh D. *Communication and Social Order*. New York: Bedminster, 1962.

Duncan, Hugh D. "Introduction." In *Permanence and Change: An Anatomy of Purpose*. Indianapolis: Bobbs-Merrill, 1965, pp. xiii–xliv.

Duncan, Hugh D. "Literature as Equipment for Action: Burke's Dramatistic Conception." In *The Sociology of Art and Literature: A Reader*. Ed. Milton C. Albrecht, James H. Barnett, and Mason Griff. New York: Praeger, 1970, pp. 713–23.

Duncan, Hugh D. "Sociology of Art, Literature and Music: Social Contexts of Symbolic Experience." In *Modern Sociological Theory*. Ed. Howard Becker and Alvin Boskoff. New York: Holt, Rinehart and Winston, 1957, pp. 482–97.

Duncan, Hugh D. *Symbols and Social Theory*. New York: Oxford University Press, 1969.

Duncan, Hugh D. *Symbols in Society*. New York: Oxford University Press, 1968.

Duncan, Hugh Dalziel. *Language and Literature in Society*. Chicago: University of Chicago Press, 1953.

Duncan, Hugh Dalziel. "The Symbolic Act: Basic Propositions on the Relationship between Symbols and Society—Theory That How We Communicate Determines How We Relate as Human Beings." In *Communication: Theory and Research*. Ed. Lee Thayer. Springfield, IL: Charles C. Thomas, 1967, pp. 194–227.

Durham, Weldon. "Kenneth Burke's Concept of Substance." *Quarterly Journal of Speech*, 66 (December 1980), 351–64.

Edelman, Murray. *The Symbolic Uses of Politics*. Urbana: University of Illinois Press, 1964.

Edwards, Janis L. "The Very Model of a Modern Major (Media) Candidate: Colin Powell and the Rhetoric of Public Opinion." *Communication Quarterly*, 46 (Spring 1998), 163–76.

Elton, William. *A Guide to the New Criticism*. Chicago: Modern Poetry Association, n.d.

Engnell, Richard A. "Materiality, Symbolicity, and the Rhetoric of Order: 'Dialectical Biologism' as Motive in Burke." *Western Journal of Communication*, 62 (Winter 1998), 1–25.

Enholm, Donald K. "Rhetoric as an Instrument for Understanding and Improving Human Relations." *Southern Speech Communication Journal*, 41 (Spring 1976), 223–36.

Ericson, Jon M. "Evaluative and Formulative Functions in Speech Criticism." *Western Speech*, 32 (Summer 1968), 173–76.

Ewbank, Henry L. "The Constitution: Burkeian, Brandeisian and Borkian Perspectives." *Southern Communication Journal*, 61 (Spring 1996), 220–32.

Feehan, Michael. "Kenneth Burke's Contribution to a Theory of Language." *Semiotica*, 76 (1989), 245–66.

Feehan, Michael. "Kenneth Burke's Discovery of Dramatism." *Quarterly Journal of Speech*, 65 (December 1979), 405–11.

Feehan, Michael. "Oscillation as Assimilation: Burke's Latest Self-Revisions." *Pre/Text*, 6 (Fall/Winter 1985), 319–27.

Feehan, Michael. "The Role of 'Attitudes' in Dramatism." In *Visions of Rhetoric: History, Theory and Criticism*. Ed. Charles W. Kneupper. Arlington, TX: Rhetoric Society of America, 1987, pp. 68–76.

Feehan, Michael. "3 Days and 3 Terms with KB." *Pre/Text*, 6 (Fall/Winter 1985), 143–61.

Fergusson, Francis. *The Idea of a Theater*. New York: Doubleday Anchor, 1949.

Fiedelson, Charles, Jr. *Symbolism and American Literature*. Chicago: University of Chicago Press, 1953.

Fiordo, Richard. "Kenneth Burke's Semiotic." *Semiotica*, 23 (1978), 53–75.

Fisher, Jeanne Y. "A Burkean Analysis of the Rhetorical Dimensions of a Multiple Murder and Suicide." *Quarterly Journal of Speech*, 60 (April 1974), 175–89.

Fisher, Jeanne Y. "The Forum: Rhetoric as More than Just a Well Man Speaking: A Rejoinder." *Quarterly Journal of Speech*, 60 (April 1974), 231–34.

Fisher, Walter R. "The Importance of Style in Systems of Rhetoric." *Southern Speech Journal*, 27 (Spring 1962), 173–82.

Fisher, Walter R., and Wayne Brockriede. "Kenneth Burke's Realism." *Central States Speech Journal*, 35 (Spring 1984), 35–42.

Fogarty, Daniel. *Roots for a New Rhetoric*. New York: Bureau of Publications, Teachers College, Columbia University, 1959.

Ford, Newell F. "Kenneth Burke and Robert Penn Warren: Criticism by Obsessive Metaphor." *Journal of English and Germanic Philology*, 53 (1954), 172–77.

Foss, Karen A. "Celluloid Rhetoric: The Use of Documentary Film to Teach Rhetorical Theory." *Communication Education*, 32 (January 1983), 51–61.

Foss, Karen A. "John Lennon and the Advisory Function of Eulogies." *Central States Speech Journal*, 34 (Fall 1983), 187–94.

Foss, Karen A. "Singing the Rhythm Blues: An Argumentative Analysis of the Birth-Control Debate in the Catholic Church." *Western Journal of Speech Communication*, 47 (Winter 1983), 29–44.

Foss, Sonja K. "Constituted by Agency: The Discourse and Practice of Rhetorical Criticism." In *Speech Communication: Essays to Commemorate the 75th Anniversary of The Speech Communication Association*. Ed. Gerald M. Phillips and Julia T. Wood. Carbondale: Southern Illinois University Press, 1989, pp. 33–51.

Foss, Sonja K. "Feminism Confronts Catholicism: A Study of the Use of Perspective by Incongruity." *Women's Studies in Communication*, 3 (Summer 1979), 7–15.

Foss, Sonja K. "Retooling an Image: Chrysler Corporation's Rhetoric of Redemption." *Western Journal of Speech Communication*, 48 (Winter 1984), 75–91.

Foss, Sonja K. *Rhetorical Criticism: Exploration and Practice*, 2nd ed. Prospect Heights, IL: Waveland, 1996.

Foss, Sonja K. "Rhetoric and the Visual Image: A Resource Unit." *Communication Education*, 31 (January 1982), 55–66.

Foss, Sonja K., and Cindy L. Griffin. "A Feminist Perspective on Rhetorical Theory: Toward a Clarification of Boundaries." *Western Journal of Communication*, 56 (Fall 1992), 330–49.

Fraiberg, Louis. *Psychoanalysis and American Literary Criticism*. Detroit: Wayne State University Press, 1960.

Frank, Armin Paul. *Kenneth Burke*. New York: Twayne, 1969.

Frank, Armin Paul. "Notes on the Reception of Kenneth Burke in Europe." In *Critical Responses to Kenneth Burke: 1924–1966*. Ed. William H. Rueckert. Minneapolis: University of Minnesota Press, 1969, pp. 424–43.

Frank, Armin Paul, and Mechthild Frank. "The Writings of Kenneth Burke." In *Critical Responses to Kenneth Burke: 1924–1966*. Ed. William H. Rueckert. Minneapolis: University of Minnesota Press, 1969, pp. 495–512.

Fry, Virginia H. "A Juxtaposition of Two Abductions for Studying Communication and Culture." *American Journal of Semiotics*, 5 (1987), 81–93.

Gabin, Rosalind J. "Entitling Kenneth Burke." *Rhetoric Review*, 5 (January 1987), 196–210.

Gaines, Robert N. "Identification and Redemption in Lysias' *Against Eratosthenes*." *Central States Speech Journal*, 30 (Fall 1979), 199–210.

Gallo, Louis. "Kenneth Burke: The Word and the World." *North Dakota Quarterly*, 42 (Winter 1974), 33–45.

Garlitz, Robert E. "The Sacrificial Word in Kenneth Burke's Logology." *Recherches anglaises et américaines*, 12 (1979), 33–44.

Gaske, Paul C. "The Analysis of Demagogic Discourse: Huey Long's 'Every Man a King' Address." In *American Rhetoric from Roosevelt to Reagan: A Collection of Speeches and Critical Essays*. Ed. Halford Ross Ryan. Prospect Heights, IL: Waveland, 1983, pp. 49–67.

Geiger, Don. "A 'Dramatic' Approach to Interpretative Analysis." *Quarterly Journal of Speech*, 38 (April 1952), 189–94.

Geiger, Don. *The Sound, Sense, and Performance of Literature*. Chicago: Scott, Foresman, 1963.

Gibson, Chester. "Eugene Talmadge's Use of Identification During the 1934 Gubernatorial Campaign in Georgia." *Southern Speech Journal*, 35 (Summer 1970), 342–49.

Glicksberg, Charles I. *American Literary Criticism, 1900–1950*. New York: Hendricks, 1951.

Glicksberg, C. I. "Kenneth Burke: The Critic's Critic." *South Atlantic Quarterly*, 36 (1937), 74–84.

Goedkoop, Richard J. "Taking the Sword from the Temple: Walter Flowers and the Rhetoric of Form." *Pennsylvania Speech Communication Annual*, 38 (1982), 25–31.

Gomme, Andor. *Attitudes to Criticism*. Carbondale: Southern Illinois University Press, 1966.

Goodall, Jr., H. Lloyd, Gerald L. Wilson, and Christopher L. Waagen. "The Performance Appraisal Interview: An Interpretive Reassessment." *Quarterly Journal of Speech*, 72 (February 1986), 74–87.

Goodheart, Eugene. "Burke Revisited." *Sewanee Review*, 102 (July/September 1994), 424–38.

Gregg, Richard B. "Kenneth Burke's Prolegomena to the Study of the Rhetoric of Form." *Communication Quarterly*, 26 (Fall 1978), 3–13.

Greiff, Louis K. "Symbolic Action in Hardy's *The Woodlanders*: An Application of Burkian Theory." *Thomas Hardy Yearbook*, 14 (1987), 52–62.

Griffin, Charles J. G. "'Movement as Motive': Self-Definition and Social Advocacy in Social Movement Autobiographies." *Western Journal of Communication*, 64 (Spring 2000), 148–64.

Griffin, Leland M. "A Dramatistic Theory of the Rhetoric of Movements." In *Critical Responses to Kenneth Burke: 1924–1966*. Ed. William H. Rueckert. Minneapolis: University of Minnesota Press, 1969, pp. 456–78.

Griffin, Leland M. "The Rhetorical Structure of the 'New Left' Movement: Part I." *Quarterly Journal of Speech*, 50 (April 1964), 113–35.

Griffin, Leland M. "When Dreams Collide: Rhetorical Trajectories in the Assassination of President Kennedy." *Quarterly Journal of Speech*, 70 (May 1984), 111–31.

Gronbeck, Bruce E. "Dramaturgical Theory and Criticism: The State of the Art (or Science?)." *Western Journal of Speech Communication*, 44 (Fall 1980), 315–30.

Gronbeck, Bruce E. "John Morley and the Irish Question: Chart-Prayer-Dream." *Speech Monographs*, 40 (November 1973), 287–95.

Gusfield, Joseph. "The Literary Rhetoric of Science: Comedy and Pathos in Drinking Driver Research." *American Sociological Review*, 41 (1976), 16–34.

Gusfield, Joseph R. *The Culture of Public Problems: Drinking-Driving and the Symbolic Order*. Chicago: University of Chicago Press, 1981.

Gusfield, Joseph R. *Symbolic Crusade: Status Politics and the American Temperance Movement*. Urbana: University of Illinois Press, 1963.

Hagan, Michael R. "Kenneth Burke and Generative Criticism of Speeches." *Central States Speech Journal*, 22 (Winter 1971), 252–57.

Hagen, Peter L. "'Pure Persuasion' and Verbal Irony." *Southern Communication Journal*, 61 (Fall 1995), 46–58.

Hahn, Dan F., and Anne Morlando. "A Burkean Analysis of Lincoln's Second Inaugural Address." *Presidential Studies Quarterly*, 9 (Fall 1979), 376–79.

Hamlin, William J., and Harold J. Nichols. "The Interest Value of Rhetorical Strategies Derived from Kenneth Burke's Pentad." *Western Speech*, 37 (Spring 1973), 97–102.

Harrington, David V., Philip M. Keith, Charles W. Kneupper, Janice A. Tripp, and William F. Woods. "A Critical Survey of Resources for Teaching Rhetorical Invention." *College English*, 40 (February 1979), 641–61.

Harris, Wendell V. "The Critics Who Made Us: Kenneth Burke." *Sewanee Review*, 96 (Summer 1988), 452–63.

Hartman, Geoffrey H. *Criticism in the Wilderness: The Study of Literature Today*. New Haven: Yale University Press, 1980.

Hauser, Gerard A. "An Afternoon with Burke and Cowley." *Pre/Text*, 6 (Fall/Winter 1985), 177–80.

Hauser, Gerard A. *Introduction to Rhetorical Theory*. New York: Harper and Row, 1986.

Hawhee, Debra. "Burke and Nietzsche." *Quarterly Journal of Speech*, 85 (May 1999), 129–45.

Hawley, Andrew. "Art for Man's Sake: Christopher Caudwell as Communist Aesthetician. *College English*, 30 (October 1968), 1–19.

Hayakawa, S. I. "The Linguistic Approach to Poetry." *Poetry*, 60 (1942), 86–94.

Heath, Bob. "Kenneth Burke's Perspective on Perspectives." *Pre/Text*, 6 (Fall/Winter 1985), 275–89.

Heath, Robert L. "Dialectical Confrontation: A Strategy of Black Radicalism." *Central States Speech Journal*, 24 (Fall 1973), 168–77.

Heath, Robert L. "Kenneth Burke on Form." *Quarterly Journal of Speech*, 65 (December 1979), 392–404.

Heath, Robert L. "Kenneth Burke's Break with Formalism." *Quarterly Journal of Speech*, 70 (May 1984), 132–43.

Heath, Robert L. "Kenneth Burke's Poetics and the Influence of I. A. Richards: A Cornerstone for Dramatism." *Communication Studies*, 40 (Spring 1989), 54–65.

Heath, Robert L. *Realism and Relativism: A Perspective on Kenneth Burke*. Macon, GA: Mercer University Press, 1986.

Heinz, Bettina, and Ronald Lee. "Getting Down to the Meat: The Symbolic Construction of Meat Consumption." *Communication Studies*, 49 (Spring 1998), 86–99.

Heisey, D. Ray, and J. David Trebing. "A Comparison of the Rhetorical Visions and Strategies of the Shah's White Revolution and the Ayatollah's Islamic Revolution." *Communication Monographs*, 50 (June 1983), 158–74.

Henderson, Greig E. *Kenneth Burke: Literature and Language as Symbolic Action*. Athens: University of Georgia Press, 1988.

Hershey, Lewis B. "Burke's Aristotelianism: Burke and Aristotle on Form." *Rhetoric Society Quarterly*, 16 (Summer 1986), 181–85.

Hicks, Granville. "Counterblasts on 'Counter-Statement.'" *New Republic*, 69 (December 9, 1931), 101.

Hickson, Mark, III. "Kenneth Burke's Affirmation of 'No' and the Absence of the Present." *Etc.*, 33 (March 1976), 44–48.

Hoban, James L., Jr. "Rhetorical Rituals of Rebirth." *Quarterly Journal of Speech*, 66 (October 1980), 275–88.

Hoban, James L., Jr. "Solzhenitsyn on Detente: A Study of Perspective by Incongruity." *Southern Speech Communication Journal*, 42 (Winter 1977), 163–77.

Hochmuth, Marie. "Burkeian Criticism." *Western Speech*, 21 (Spring 1957), 89–95.

Hochmuth, Marie. "Kenneth Burke and the 'New Rhetoric.'" *Quarterly Journal of Speech*, 38 (April 1952), 133–44.

Hoffman, Frederick F. *Freudianism and the Literary Mind*. Baton Rouge: Louisiana State University Press, 1945.

Hoffman, Frederick J., Charles Allen, and Carolyn F. Ulrich. *The Little Magazine: A History and a Bibliography*. Princeton: Princeton University Press, 1946.

Holland, L. Virginia. *Counterpoint: Kenneth Burke and Aristotle's Theories of Rhetoric*. New York: Philosophical Library, 1959.

Holland, L. Virginia. "Kenneth Burke's Dramatistic Approach in Speech Criticism." *Quarterly Journal of Speech*, 41 (December 1955), 352–58.

Holland, L. Virginia. "Kenneth Burke's Theory of Communication." *Journal of Communication*, 10 (December 1960), 174–84.

Holland, Virginia. "Rhetorical Criticism: A Burkeian Method." *Quarterly Journal of Speech*, 39 (December 1953), 443–50.

Holman, C. Hugh. "The Defense of Art Criticism since 1930." In *The Development of American Literary Criticism*. Ed. Floyd Stoval. Chapel Hill: University of North Carolina Press, 1955, pp. 199–245.

Hopper, Stanley Romaine. "Mysticism as a Solution to the Poet's Dilemma: Notes and Commentary on a Lecture by Kenneth Burke." In *Spiritual Problems in Contemporary Literature: A Series of Addresses and Discussions*, ed. Stanley Romaine Hopper. New York: Harper, 1952, pp. 95–105.

Howell, Wilbur Samuel. "Colloquy: II. The Two-Party Line: A Reply to Kenneth Burke." *Quarterly Journal of Speech*, 62 (February 1976), 69–77.

Howell, Wilbur Samuel. "Peter Ramus, Thomas Sheridan, and Kenneth Burke: Three Mavericks in the History of Rhetoric." In *Retrospectives and Perspectives: A Symposium in Rhetoric*. Ed. Turner S. Kohler, William E. Tanner, and J. Dean Bishop. Denton: Texas Women's University Press, 1978, pp. 91–105.

Howell, Wilbur Samuel. *Poetics, Rhetoric, and Logic.* Ithaca: Cornell University Press, 1975.

Howell, Wilbur Samuel. "Rhetoric and Poetics: A Plea for the Recognition of the Two Literatures." In *The Classical Tradition: Literary and Historical Studies in Honor of Harry Caplan.* Ed. Luitpold Wallach. Ithaca: Cornell University Press, 1966, pp. 374–90.

Hubbard, Bryan. "Reassessing Truman, the Bomb, and Revisionism: The Burlesque Frame and Entelechy in the Decision to Use Atomic Weapons against Japan." *Western Journal of Communication,* 62 (Summer 1998), 348–85.

Hubler, Edward. "The Sunken Aesthete." *English Institute Essays,* 1950. Ed. Alan S. Downer. New York: Columbia University Press, 1951, pp. 32–56.

Huyink, Cynthia J. "A Dramatistic Analysis of *Sexual Politics* by Kate Millett." *Women's Studies in Communication,* 3 (Summer 1979), 1–6.

Hyman, Stanley Edgar. *The Armed Vision: A Study in the Methods of Modern Literary Criticism.* 1947; rpt. New York: Vintage, 1955.

Hyman, Stanley Edgar. *The Critic's Credentials.* Ed. Phoebe Pettingell. New York: Atheneum, 1978.

Irmscher, William F. *The Holt Guide to English: A Contemporary Handbook of Rhetoric, Language, and Literature.* 2nd ed. New York: Holt, Rinehart and Winston, 1976.

Irmscher, William F. "Kenneth Burke." In *Traditions of Inquiry.* Ed. John Brereton. New York: Oxford University Press, 1985, pp. 105–35.

Ivie, Robert L. "Presidential Motives for War." *Quarterly Journal of Speech,* 60 (October 1974), 337–45.

Ivie, Robert L. "Progressive Form and Mexican Culpability in Polk's Justification for War." *Central States Speech Journal,* 30 (Winter 1979), 311–20.

Ivie, Robert L., and Joe Ayres. "A Procedure for Investigating Verbal Form." *Southern Speech Communication Journal,* 43 (Winter 1978), 129–45.

Jameson, Frederic R. "Critical Response: Ideology and Symbolic Action." *Critical Inquiry,* 5 (1978), 417–22.

Jameson, Frederic R. "The Symbolic Inference: Or, Kenneth Burke and Ideological Analysis." *Critical Inquiry,* 4 (Spring 1978), 507–23.

Jarrell, Randall. "Changes of Attitude and Rhetoric in Auden's Poetry." *Southern Review,* 7 (1941–42), 326–49.

Jay, Gregory S. "Burke Re-Marx." *Pre/Text,* 6 (Fall/Winter 1985), 169–75.

Jay, Paul. "Kenneth Burke: A Man of Letters." *Pre/Text,* 6 (Fall/Winter 1985), 221–33.

Jennermann, Donald L. "Some Freudian Aspects of Burke's Aristotelian Poetics." *Recherches anglaises et américaines,* 12 (1979), 65–81.

Jensen, J. Vernon. "The Rhetorical Strategy of Thomas H. Huxley and Robert G. Ingersoll: Agnostics and Roadblock Removers." *Speech Monographs,* 32 (March 1965), 59–68.

Johannesen, Richard L. "Attitude of Speaker toward Audience: A Significant Concept for Contemporary Rhetorical Theory and Criticism." *Central States Speech Journal,* 25 (Summer 1974), 95–104.

Johannesen, Richard L. "Richard M. Weaver's Uses of Kenneth Burke." *Southern Speech Communication Journal,* 52 (Spring 1987), 312–30.

Joost, Nicholas. *Scofield Thayer and* The Dial. Carbondale: Southern Illinois University Press, 1964.

Josephson, Matthew. *Life among the Surrealists: A Memoir*. New York: Holt, Rinehart and Winston, 1962.

Kaelin, Eugene. *An Existentialist Aesthetic: The Theories of Sartre and Merleau-Ponty*. Madison: University of Wisconsin Press, 1962.

Kauffman, Charles. "Names and Weapons." *Communication Monographs*, 56 (September 1989), 271–85.

Keith, Philip M. "Burke for the Composition Class." *College Composition and Communication*, 28 (December 1977), 348–51.

Keith, Philip M. "Burkeian Invention: Two Contrasting Views: Burkeian Invention, from Pentad to Dialectic." *Rhetoric Society Quarterly*, 9 (Summer 1979), 137–41.

Kelley, Colleen E. "The 1984 Campaign Rhetoric of Representative George Hansen: A Pentadic Analysis." *Western Journal of Speech Communication*, 51 (Spring 1987), 204–17.

Kelley, Colleen E. "The Public Rhetoric of Mikhail Gorbachev and the Promise of Peace." *Western Journal of Speech Communication*, 52 (Fall 1988), 321–34.

Kenny, Robert Wade. "The Rhetoric of Kevorkian's Battle." *Quarterly Journal of Speech*, 86 (November 2000), 386–401.

Kimberling, C. Ronald. *Kenneth Burke's Dramatism and Popular Arts*. Bowling Green, OH: Bowling Green State University Popular Press, 1982.

King, Robert L. "Transforming Scandal into Tragedy: A Rhetoric of Political Apology." *Quarterly Journal of Speech*, 71 (August 1985), 289–301.

Kirk, John W. "The Forum: Kenneth Burke and Identification." *Quarterly Journal of Speech*, 47 (December 1961), 414–15.

Kirk, John W. "Kenneth Burke's Dramatistic Criticism Applied to the Theater. *Southern Speech Journal*, 33 (Spring 1968), 161–77.

Klope, David C. "Defusing a Foreign Policy Crisis: Myth and Victimage in Reagan's 1983 Lebanon/Grenada Address." *Western Journal of Speech Communication*, 50 (Fall 1986), 336–49.

Klumpp, James F. "'Dancing with Tears in My Eyes': Celebrating the Life and Work of Kenneth Burke." *Southern Communication Journal*, 61 (Fall 1995), 1–10.

Klumpp, James, and Jeffrey Lukehart. "The Pardoning of Richard Nixon: A Failure in Motivational Strategy." *Western Journal of Speech Communication*, 42 (Spring 1978), 116–23.

Kneupper, Charles. "Burkeian Invention: Two Contrasting Views: Dramatistic Invention: The Pentad as a Heuristic Procedure." *Rhetoric Society Quarterly*, 9 (Summer 1979), 130–36.

Kneupper, Charles W. "Dramatism and Argument." In *Dimensions of Argument: Proceedings of the Second Summer Conference on Argument*. Ed. George Ziegelmueller and Jack Rhodes. Annandale, VA: Speech Communication Association, October 15, 1981, pp. 894–904.

Knox, George. *Critical Moments: Kenneth Burke's Categories and Critiques*. Seattle: University of Washington Press, 1957.

Kreilkamp, Thomas. *The Corrosion of the Self: Society's Effects on People*. New York: New York University Press, 1976.

Kuseski, Brenda K. "Kenneth Burke's 'Five Dogs' and Mother Teresa's Love." *Quarterly Journal of Speech*, 74 (August 1988), 323–33.

Kuypers, Jim A. "From Science, Moral-Poetics: Dr. James Dobson's Response to the Fetal Tissue Research Initiative." *Quarterly Journal of Speech*, 86 (May 2000), 146–67.

Lake, Randall A. "Order and Disorder in Anti-Abortion Rhetoric: A Logological View." *Quarterly Journal of Speech*, 79 (November 1984), 425–43.

Lazer, Hank. "Thinking of Kenneth Burke." *Pre/Text*, 6 (Fall/Winter 1985), 132–41.

Lazier, Gil. "Burke, Behavior, and Oral Interpretation." *Southern Speech Journal*, 31 (Fall 1965), 10–14.

Lee, Ronald. "The New Populist Campaign for Economic Democracy: A Rhetorical Exploration." *Quarterly Journal of Speech*, 72 (August 1986), 274–89.

Leff, Michael C. "Redemptive Identification: Cicero's Catilinarian Orations." In *Explorations in Rhetorical Criticism*. Ed. G. P. Mohrmann, Charles J. Stewart, and Donovan J. Ochs. University Park: Pennsylvania State University Press, 1973, pp. 158–77.

Lemon, Lee T. *The Partial Critics*. New York: Oxford University Press, 1965.

Lentricchia, Frank. *Criticism and Social Change*. Chicago: University of Chicago Press, 1983.

Lessl, Thomas M. "Science and the Sacred Cosmos: The Ideological Rhetoric of Carl Sagan." *Quarterly Journal of Speech*, 71 (May 1985), 175–87.

Lewis, Clayton W. "Identifications and Divisions: Kenneth Burke and the Yale Critics." *Southern Review*, 22 (Winter 1986), 93–102.

Ling, David A. "A Pentadic Analysis of Senator Edward Kennedy's Address to the People of Massachusetts, July 25, 1969." *Central States Speech Journal*, 21 (Summer 1970), 81–86.

McConachie, Bruce A. "Towards a Postpositivist Theatre History." *Theatre Journal*, 37 (December 1985), 465–86.

McGill, V. J. "Comments on Burke's Propositions." *Science and Society*, 2 (Spring 1938), 253–56.

Mackey-Kallis, Susan, and Dan F. Hahn. "Questions of Public Will and Private Action: The Power of the Negative in the Reagans' 'Just Say No' Morality Campaign." *Communication Quarterly*, 39 (Winter 1991), 1–17.

Mackey-Kallis, Susan, and Dan Hahn. "Who's to Blame for America's Drug Problem?: The Search for Scapegoats in the 'War on Drugs.'" *Communication Quarterly*, 42 (Winter 1994), 1–20.

Mackin, Jr., James A. "A Trinitarian Logology." *Southern Communication Journal*, 60 (Spring 1995), 195–210.

Macksoud, S. John. "Kenneth Burke on Perspective and Rhetoric." *Western Speech*, 33 (Summer 1969), 167–74.

Macksoud, S. John, and Ross Altman. "Voices in Opposition: A Burkeian Rhetoric of *Saint Joan*." *Quarterly Journal of Speech*, 57 (April 1971), 140–46.

Mader, Thomas F. "Agitation over Aggiornamento: William Buckley vs. John XXIII." *Today's Speech*, 17 (November 1969), 4–15.

Maimon, Elaine P., Gerald L. Belcher, and Gail W. Hearn. *Writing in the Arts and Sciences*. Cambridge: Winthrop, 1981.

Mann, Charles W. "The KB Collection: The Penn State Library." *Pre/Text*, 6 (Fall/Winter 1985), 313–15.

Meadows, Paul. "The Semiotic of Kenneth Burke." *Philosophy and Phenomenological Research*, 18 (September 1957), 80–87.

Mechling, Elizabeth Walker, and Gale Auletta. "Beyond War: A Socio-Rhetorical Analysis of a New Class Revitalization Movement." *Western Journal of Speech Communication*, 59 (Fall 1986), 388–404.

Mechling, Elizabeth Walker, and Jay Mechling. "Sweet Talk: The Moral Rhetoric against Sugar." *Central States Speech Journal*, 34 (Spring 1983), 19–32.

Medhurst, Martin J. "McGovern at Wheaton: A Quest for Redemption." *Communication Quarterly*, 25 (Fall 1977), 32–39.

Meisenhelder, Thomas. "Law as Symbolic Action: Kenneth Burke's Sociology of Law." *Symbolic Interaction*, 4 (Spring 1981), 43–57.

Messner, Beth A., and Jacquelyn J. Buckrop. "Restoring Order: Interpreting Suicide through a Burkean Lens." *Communication Quarterly*, 48 (Winter 2000), 1–18.

Meyer, John. "Seeking Organizational Unity: Building Bridges in Response to Mystery." *Southern Communication Journal*, 61 (Spring 1996), 210–19.

Miller, Carolyn R. "Genre as Social Action." *Quarterly Journal of Speech*, 70 (May 1984), 151–67.

Moore, Marianne. *Predilections*. New York: Viking, 1955.

Moore, Mark P. "Life, Liberty, and the Handgun: The Function of Synecdoche in the Brady Bill Debate." *Communication Quarterly*, 42 (Fall 1994), 434–47.

Moore, Mark P. "'The Quayle Quagmire': Political Campaigns in the Poetic Form of Burlesque." *Western Journal of Communication*, 56 (Spring 1992), 108–24.

Moore, Mark P. "Rhetorical Subterfuge and 'The Principle of Perfection': Bob Packwood's Response to Sexual Misconduct Charges." *Western Journal of Communication*, 60 (Winter 1996), 1–20.

Moore, Mark P. "The Rhetoric of Ideology: Confronting a Critical Dilemma." *Southern Communication Journal*, 54 (Fall 1988), 74–92.

Morris, Barry Alan. "The Communal Constraints on Parody: The Symbolic Death of Joe Bob Briggs." *Quarterly Journal of Speech*, 73 (November 1987), 460–73.

Mouat, L. H. "An Approach to Rhetorical Criticism." In *The Rhetorical Idiom: Essays in Rhetoric, Oratory, Language, and Drama*. Ed. Donald C. Bryant. Ithaca: Cornell University Press, 1958, pp. 170–77.

Muller, Herbert J. *Science and Criticism: The Humanistic Tradition in Contemporary Thought*. New Haven: Yale University Press, 1943.

Mullican, James S. "A Burkean Approach to *Catch–22*." *College Literature*, 8 (Winter 1981), 42–52.

Munson, Gorham B. *Destinations: A Canvass of American Literature Since 1900*. New York: J. H. Sears, 1928.

Munson, Gorham B. "The Fledgling Years, 1916–1924." *Sewanee Review*, 40 (January/March 1932), 24–54.

Murphy, John M. "Comic Strategies and the American Covenant." *Communication Studies*, 40 (Winter 1989), 266–79.

Murphy, Marjorie N. "Silence, the Word, and Indian Rhetoric." *College Composition and Communication*, 21 (December 1970), 356–63.

Murray, Jeffrey W. "An Other Ethics for Kenneth Burke." *Communication Studies*, 49 (Spring 1998), 29–48.

Murray, Timothy C. "Kenneth Burke's Logology: A Mock Logomachy." In *Glyph 2: Johns Hopkins Textual Studies*. Ed. Samuel Weber and Henry Sussman. Baltimore: Johns Hopkins University Press, 1977, pp. 144–61.

Neild, Elizabeth. "Kenneth Burke and Roland Barthes: Literature, Language, and Society." *Recherches anglaises et américaines*, 12 (1979), 98–108.

Nelson, Jeffrey. "Using the Burkeian Pentad in the Education of the Basic Speech Student." *Communication Education*, 32 (January 1983), 63–68.

Nemerov, Howard. "The Agon of Will as Idea: A Note on the Terms of Kenneth Burke." *Furioso*, 2 (Spring 1947), 29–42.

Nemerov, Howard. "Everything, Preferably All at Once: Coming to Terms with Kenneth Burke." *Sewanee Review*, 79 (Spring 1971), 189–201.

Nemerov, Howard. "Four Poems: Gnomic Variations for Kenneth Burke." *Kenyon Review*, 5 [new series] (Summer 1983), 23–25.

Nichols, Marie Hochmuth. *Rhetoric and Criticism*. Baton Rouge: Louisiana State University Press, 1963.

Nimmo, Dan. *Political Communication and Public Opinion in America*. Santa Monica, CA: Goodyear, 1978.

Nimmo, Dan. *Subliminal Politics: Myths and Mythmakers in America*. Englewood Cliffs, NJ: Prentice-Hall, 1980.

Nimmo, Dan D. *Popular Images of Politics: A Taxonomy*. Englewood Cliffs, NJ: Prentice-Hall, 1974.

Nimmo, Dan, and James E. Combs. *Mediated Political Realities*. New York: Longman, 1983.

Norton, Janice. "Rhetorical Criticism as Ethical Action: Cherchez la Femme." *Southern Communication Journal*, 61 (Fall 1995), 29–45.

O'Connor, William Van. *An Age of Criticism: 1900–1950*. Chicago: Henry Regnery, 1952.

O'Keefe, Daniel J. "Burke's Dramatism and Action Theory." *Rhetoric Society Quarterly*, 8 (Winter 1978), 8–15.

O'Leary, Stephen D., and Mark H. Wright. "Psychoanalysis and Burkeian Rhetorical Criticism." *Southern Communication Journal*, 61 (Winter 1995), 104–21.

Osborn, Neal J. "Kenneth Burke's Desdemona: A Courtship of Clio?" *Hudson Review*, 19 (Summer 1966), 267–75.

Osborn, Neal J. "Toward the Quintessential Burke." *Hudson Review*, 21 (Summer 1968), 308–21.

Overington, Michael A. "Kenneth Burke and the Method of Dramatism." *Theory and Society*, 4 (1977), 131–56.

Overington, Michael A. "Kenneth Burke as a Social Theorist." *Sociological Inquiry*, 47 (1977), 133–41.

Pattison, Sheron Dailey. "Rhetoric and Audience Effect: Kenneth Burke on Form and Identification." In *Studies in Interpretation*. Ed. Esther M. Doyle and Virginia Hastings Floyd. Vol. 2. Amsterdam, Neth.: Rodopi, 1977, 183–98.

Paul, Sherman. "A Letter on Olson and Burke." *All Area*, 2 (1983), 64–65.

Payne, David. "Adaptation, Mortification, and Social Reform." *Southern Speech Communication Journal*, 51 (Spring 1986), 187–207.

Payne, David. "Political Vertigo in *Dead Poets Society*." *Southern Communication Journal*, 58 (Fall 1992), 13–21.

Payne, David. "*The Wizard of Oz*: Therapeutic Rhetoric in a Contemporary Media Ritual." *Quarterly Journal of Speech*, 75 (February 1989), 25–39.

Peterson, Tarla Rai. "The Meek Shall Inherit the Mountains: Dramatistic Criticism of Grand Teton National Park's Interpretive Program." *Central States Speech Journal*, 39 (Summer 1988), 121–33.

Peterson, Tarla Rai. "The Rhetorical Construction of Institutional Authority in a Senate Subcommittee Hearing on Wilderness Legislation." *Western Journal of Speech Communication*, 52 (Fall 1988), 259–76.

Peterson, Tarla Rai. "The Will to Conservation: A Burkeian Analysis of Dust Bowl Rhetoric and American Farming Motives." *Southern Speech Communication Journal*, 52 (Fall 1986), 1–21.

Pettigrew, Loyd S. "Psychoanalytic Theory: A Neglected Rhetorical Dimension." *Philosophy and Rhetoric*, 10 (Winter 1977), 46–59.

Poirier, Richard. "Frost, Winnicott, Burke." *Raritan*, 2 (Fall 1982), 114–27.

Pounds, Wayne. "The Context of No Context: A Burkean Critique of Rogerian Argument." *Rhetoric Society Quarterly*, 17 (Winter 1987), 45–59.

Powell, Kimberly A. "The Association of Southern Women for the Prevention of Lynching: Strategies of a Movement in the Comic Frame." *Communication Quarterly*, 43 (Winter 1995), 86–99.

Pritchard, John Paul. *Criticism in America*. Norman: University of Oklahoma Press, 1956.

Procter, David E. "The Rescue Mission: Assigning Guilt to a Chaotic Scene." *Western Journal of Speech Communication*, 51 (Summer 1987), 245–55.

Ragsdale, J. Donald. "Problems of Some Contemporary Notions of Style." *Southern Speech Journal*, 35 (Summer 1970), 332–41.

Ransom, John Crowe. "An Address to Kenneth Burke." *Kenyon Review*, 4 (1942), 218–37.

Rasmussen, Karen, and Sharon D. Downey. "Dialectical Disorientation in *Agnes of God*." *Western Journal of Speech Communication*, 53 (Winter 1989), 66–84.

Raymond, James C. *Writing (Is an Unnatural Act)*. New York: Harper and Row, 1980.

Rod, David K. "Kenneth Burke and Susanne K. Langer on Drama and Its Audience." *Quarterly Journal of Speech*, 72 (August 1986), 306–17.

Rod, David K. "Kenneth Burke's Concept of Entitlement." *Communication Monographs*, 49 (March 1982), 20–32.

Rodriguez, Linda. "The Latticework of Imagery." *Main Currents in Modern Thought*, 32 (September/October 1975), 24–28.

Romano, Carlin. "A Critic Who Has His Critics—Pro and Con." *Philadelphia Inquirer*, March 6, 1984, sec. D, p. 1.

Rosenfeld, Lawrence B. "Set Theory: Key to the Understanding of Kenneth Burke's Use of the Term 'Identification.'" *Western Speech*, 33 (Summer 1969), 175–83.

Rosteck, Thomas. "Irony, Argument, and Reportage in Television Documentary: *See It Now* versus Senator McCarthy." *Quarterly Journal of Speech*, 75 (August 1989), 277–98.

Rosteck, Thomas, and Michael Leff. "Piety, Propriety, and Perspective: An Interpretation and Application of Key Terms in Kenneth Burke's *Permanence and Change*." *Western Journal of Speech Communication*, 53 (Fall 1989), 27–41.

Rountree, Clarke. "Instantiating 'The Law' and its Dissents in *Korematsu v. United States*: A Dramatistic Analysis of Judicial Discourse." *Quarterly Journal of Speech*, 87 (February 2001), 1–24.

Rountree, J. Clarke, III. "Kenneth Burke: A Personal Retrospective." *Iowa Review*, 17 (Fall 1987), 15–23.

Rueckert, William H., ed. *Critical Responses to Kenneth Burke: 1924–1966*. Minneapolis: University of Minnesota Press, 1969.

Rueckert, William H. "Kenneth Burke and Structuralism." *Shenandoah*, 21 (Autumn 1969), 19–28.

Rueckert, William H. *Kenneth Burke and the Drama of Human Relations*. 1963; rpt. Berkeley: University of California Press, 1982.

Rueckert, William H. "Kenneth Burke's Encounters with Walt Whitman." *Walt Whitman Quarterly Review*, 6 (Fall 1988), 61–90.

Rushing, Janice Hocker. "Mythic Evolution of 'The New Frontier' in Mass Mediated Rhetoric." *Critical Studies in Mass Communication*, 3 (September 1986), 265–96.

Rushing, Janice Hocker. "Ronald Reagan's 'Star Wars' Address: Mythic Containment of Technical Reasoning." *Quarterly Journal of Speech*, 72 (November 1986), 415–33.

Rushing, Janice Hocker, and Thomas S. Frentz. "The Frankenstein Myth in Contemporary Cinema." *Critical Studies in Mass Communication*, 6 (March 1989), 61–80.

Rybacki, Karyn Charles, and Donald Jay Rybacki. "Competition in the Comic Frame: A Burkean Analysis of Vintage Sports Car Racing." *Southern Communication Journal*, 61 (Fall 1995), 76–90.

Sanbonmatsu, Akira. "Darrow and Rorke's Use of Burkeian Identification Strategies in *New York vs. Gitlow* (1920)." *Speech Monographs*, 38 (March 1971), 36–48.

Sapir, David, and J. Christopher Crocker, eds. *The Social Use of Metaphor: Essays on the Anthropology of Rhetoric*. Philadelphia: University of Pennsylvania Press, 1977.

Scheibel, Dean. "'If Your Roommate Dies, You Get a 4.0': Reclaiming Rumor with Burke and Organizational Culture." *Western Journal of Communication*, 63 (Spring 1999), 168–92.

Scheibel, Dean. "'Making Waves' with Burke: Surf Nazi Culture and the Rhetoric of Localism." *Western Journal of Communication*, 59 (Fall 1995), 253–69.

Schiappa, Edward, and Mary F. Keehner. "The 'Lost' Passages of *Permanence and Change*." *Communication Studies*, 42 (Fall 1991), 191–98.

Schlauch, Margaret. "A Reply to Kenneth Burke." *Science and Society*, 2 (Spring 1938), 250–53.

Schwartz, Joseph. "Kenneth Burke, Aristotle, and the Future of Rhetoric." *College Composition and Communication*, 17 (December 1966), 210–16.

Scodari, Christine. "Contemporary Film and the Representative Anecdote of 'Unmasking': Coping Strategies for a Narcissistic Society." *Central States Speech Journal*, 38 (Summer 1987), 111–21.

Scott, Robert L. "To Burke or Not to Burke: A Brief Note on the Pious Neo-Burkeians with a Glance at True Believerism Generally in the Quest for the Perfect Communicology." *Spectra* [Speech Communication Association], 11 (August 1975), 1–2.

Selzer, Jack. *Kenneth Burke in Greenwich Village: Conversing with the Moderns: 1915–1931*. Madison: University of Wisconsin Press, 1996.

Sharf, Barbara F. "A Rhetorical Analysis of Leadership Emergence in Small Groups." *Communication Monographs*, 45 (June 1978), 156–72.

Shaw, Leroy Robert. *The Playwright and Historical Change: Dramatic Strategies in Brecht, Hauptmann, Kaiser, and Wedekind*. Madison: University of Wisconsin Press, 1970.

Shoemaker, Francis, and Louis Forsdale, eds. *Communication in General Education*. Dubuque, IA: William C. Brown, 1960.

Shultz, Kara. "Every Implanted Child a Star (and Some Other Failures): Guilt and Shame in the Cochlear Implant Debates." *Quarterly Journal of Speech*, 86 (August 2000), 251–75.

Sillars, Malcolm O. "Rhetoric as Act." *Quarterly Journal of Speech*, 50 (October 1964), 277–84.

Simons, Herbert W., and Trevor Melia, eds. *The Legacy of Kenneth Burke*. Madison: University of Wisconsin Press, 1989.

Sivaramkrishna, M. "Epiphany and History: The Dialectic of Transcendence and *A Passage to India*." In *Approaches to E. M. Forster: A Centenary Volume*. Ed. Vasant A. Shahane. Atlantic Highlands, NJ: Humanities, 1981, pp. 148–61.

Slochower, Harry. *No Voice Is Wholly Lost: Writers and Thinkers in War and Peace*. New York: Creative Age, 1945.

Smith, Bernard. *Forces in American Criticism: A Study in the History of American Literary Thought*. New York: Harcourt, Brace, 1939.

Smith, Charles Daniel. "From the Discipline of Literary Criticism." *Today's Speech*, 3 (November 1955), 33–34.

Smith, Janice M. "Erik H. Erikson's Sex Role Theories: A Rhetoric of Hierarchical Mystification." *Today's Speech*, 21 (Spring 1973), 27–31.

Smith, Larry David. "The Nominating Convention as Purveyor of Political Medicine: An Anecdotal Analysis of the Democrats and Republicans of 1984." *Central States Speech Journal*, 38 (Fall/Winter 1987), 252–61.

Smith, Larry David, and James L. Golden. "Electronic Storytelling in Electoral Politics: An Anecdotal Analysis of Television Advertising in the Helms–Hunt Senate Race." *Southern Speech Communication Journal*, 53 (Spring 1988), 244–58.

Snyder, Lee. "Invitation to Transcendence: The *Book of Revelation*." *Quarterly Journal of Speech*, 86 (November 2000), 402–16.

Solomon, Martha. "Ideology as Rhetorical Constraint: The Anarchistic Agitation of 'Red Emma' Goldman." *Quarterly Journal of Speech*, 74 (May 1988), 184–200.

Solomon, Martha. "Redemptive Rhetoric: The Continuity Motif in the Rhetoric of Right to Life." *Central States Speech Journal*, 31 (Spring 1980), 52–62.

Solomon, Martha. "The Rhetoric of Dehumanization: An Analysis of Medical Reports of the Tuskegee Syphilis Project." *Western Journal of Speech Communication*, 49 (Fall 1985), 233–47.

Southwell, Samuel B. *Kenneth Burke and Martin Heidegger: With a Note against Deconstructionism*. Gainesville: University Presses of Florida, 1987.

Starosta, William J. "The United Nations: Agency for Semantic Consubstantiality." *Southern Speech Journal*, 36 (Spring 1971), 243–54.

States, Bert O. *Irony and Drama: A Poetics*. Ithaca: Cornell University Press, 1971.

States, Bert O. "Kenneth Burke and the Syllogism." *South Atlantic Quarterly*, 68 (Summer 1969), 386–98.

Stelzner, Hermann G. "'War Message,' December 8, 1941: An Approach to Language," *Speech Monographs*, 33 (November 1966), 419–37.

Stuart, Charlotte L. "The Constitution as 'Summational Anecdote.'" *Central States Speech Journal*, 25 (Summer 1974), 111–18.

Stuckey, Mary E., and Frederick J. Antczak. "The Battle of Issues and Images: Establishing Interpretive Dominance." *Communication Quarterly*, 42 (Spring 1994), 120–32.

Stull, Bradford T. *Religious Dialectics of Pain and Imagination*. Albany: State University of New York Press, 1994.

Sutton, Walter. *Modern American Criticism*. Englewood Cliffs, NJ: Prentice-Hall, 1963.

Swan, Susan Z. "Gothic Drama in Disney's *Beauty and the Beast*: Subverting Traditional Romance by Transcending the Animal-Human Paradox." *Critical Studies in Mass Communication*, 16 (September 1999), 350–69.

Tate, Allen. "Mr. Burke and the Historical Environment." *Southern Review*, 2 (1936–37), 363–72.

Tate, Allen. "A Note on Autotelism." *Kenyon Review*, 11 (Winter 1949), 13–16.

Terrill, Robert E. "Colonizing the Borderlands: Shifting Circumference in the Rhetoric of Malcolm X." *Quarterly Journal of Speech*, 86 (February 2000), 67–85.

Thomas, Douglas. "Burke, Nietzsche, Lacan: Three Perspectives on the Rhetoric of Order." *Quarterly Journal of Speech*, 79 (August 1993), 336–55.

Thompson, David W. "Interpretative Reading as Symbolic Action." *Quarterly Journal of Speech*, 42 (December 1956), 389–97.

Thorp, Willard. "American Writers on the Left." In *Socialism and American Life*. Vol. 1. Ed. Donald Drew Egbert and Stow Persons. Princeton: Princeton University Press, 1952, 601–20.

Tompkins, Philip K. "On Hegemony—'He Gave It No Name'—and Critical Structuralism in the Work of Kenneth Burke." *Quarterly Journal of Speech*, 71 (February 1985), 119–30.

Tompkins, Phillip K., and George Cheney. "On the Limits and Sub-Stance of Kenneth Burke and His Critics." *Quarterly Journal of Speech*, 79 (May 1993), 225–31.

Tompkins, Phillip K., Jeanne Y. Fisher, Dominic A. Infante, and Elaine L. Tompkins. "Kenneth Burke and the Inherent Characteristics of Formal Organizations: A Field Study." *Speech Monographs*, 42 (June 1975), 135–42.

Tonn, Mari Boor. "Donning Sackcloth and Ashes: *Webster v. Reproductive Health Services* and Moral Agony in Abortion Rights Rhetoric." *Communication Quarterly*, 44 (Summer 1996), 265–79.

Tonn, Mari Boor. "Elizabeth Gurley Flynn's *Sabotage*: 'Scene' as Both Controlling and Catalyzing 'Acts.'" *Southern Communication Journal*, 61 (Fall 1995), 59–75.

Tracy, David. "Mystics, Prophets, Rhetorics: Religion and Psychoanalysis." In *The Dial(s) of Psychoanalysis*. Ed. Françoise Meltzer. Chicago: University of Chicago Press, 1988, pp. 259–72.

Valesio, Paolo. *Novantiqua: Rhetorics as a Contemporary Theory*. Bloomington: Indiana University Press, 1980.

Vitanza, Victor J. "A Mal-Lingering Thought (Tragic-Comedic) About KB's Visit." *Pre/Text*, 6 (Fall/Winter 1985), 163–67.

Vitanza, Victor J. "Pre/face#8: *KB X 2*." *Pre/Text*, 6 (Fall/Winter 1985), 121–28.

Wadlington, Warwick. *The Confidence Game in American Literature*. Princeton: Princeton University Press, 1975.

Wagner, Geoffrey. "American Literary Criticism: The Continuing Heresy." *Southern Review* [Adelaide, Australia], 2 (1968), 82–89.

Walter, Otis M. "Toward an Analysis of Motivation." *Quarterly Journal of Speech*, 41 (October 1955), 271–78.

Wander, Philip C. "At the Ideological Front." *Communication Studies*, 42 (Fall 1991), 199–218.

Warnock, Tilly. "Anecdotes on Accessibility: KB in Wyoming." *Pre/Text*, 6 (Fall/Winter 1985), 203–17.

Warnock, Tilly. "Kenneth Burke (1897–1993)." In *Encyclopedia of Rhetoric and Composition: Communication from Ancient Times to the Information Age*. Ed. Theresa Enos. New York: Garland, 1996, pp. 90–92.

Warnock, Tilly. "Kenneth Duva Burke (1897–1993)." In *Twentieth-Century Rhetorics and Rhetoricians: Critical Studies and Sources*. Ed. Michael G. Moran and Michelle Ballif. Westport, CT: Greenwood, 2000, pp. 75–89.

Warnock, Tilly. "Reading Kenneth Burke: Ways In, Ways Out, Ways Roundabout." *College English*, 48 (January 1986), 62–75.

Warren, Austin. "Kenneth Burke: His Mind and Art." *Sewanee Review*, 41 (1933), 225–36, 344–64.

Warren, Austin. "The Sceptic's Progress." *American Review*, 6 (1936–37), 193–213.

Washburn, Richard Kirk. "Burke on Motives and Rhetoric." *Approach*, 9 (1953), 2–6.

Wasserstrom, William, ed. *A Dial Miscellany*. Syracuse, NY: Syracuse University Press, 1963.

Wasserstrom, William. "Marianne Moore, *The Dial*, and Kenneth Burke." *Western Humanities Review*, 17 (Summer 1963), 249–62.

Wasserstrom, William. *The Time of* The Dial. Syracuse, NY: Syracuse University Press, 1963.

Watson, Edward A. "Incongruity without Laughter: Kenneth Burke's Theory of the Grotesque." *University of Windsor Review*, 4 (Spring 1969), 28–36.

Watson, Karen Ann. "A Rhetorical and Sociolinguistic Model for the Analysis of Narrative." *American Anthropologist*, 75 (February 1973), 243–64.

Webster, Grant. *The Republic of Letters: A History of Postwar American Literary Opinion*. Baltimore: Johns Hopkins University Press, 1979.

Weier, Gary M. "Perspectivism and Form in Drama: A Burkean Analysis of *Julius Caesar*." *Communication Quarterly*, 44 (Spring 1996), 246–59.

Wellek, René. "Kenneth Burke and Literary Criticism." *Sewanee Review*, 79 (Spring 1971), 171–88.

Wellek, René. "The Main Trends of Twentieth-Century Criticism." *Yale Review*, 51 (Autumn 1961), 102–18.

Wells, Susan. "Richards, Burke and the Relation between Rhetoric and Poetics." *Pre/Text*, 7 (Spring/Summer 1986), 59–75.

Wess, Robert. *Kenneth Burke: Rhetoric, Subjectivity, Postmodernism*. New York: Cambridge University Press, 1996.

Wess, Robert. "Utopian Rhetoric in *The Man of Mode*." *Eighteenth Century: Theory and Interpretation*, 27 (Spring 1986), 141–61.

Westerfelhaus, Robert, and Diane Ciekawy. "Cleansing the Social Body: Witchcraft Accusation in an African Society as an Example of Multi-Hierarchical Victimage." *Communication Quarterly*, 46 (Summer 1998), 269–83.

White, Hayden, and Margaret Brose, eds. *Representing Kenneth Burke*. Baltimore: Johns Hopkins University Press, 1982.

Wilkie, Carol. "The Scapegoating of Bruno Richard Hauptmann: The Rhetorical Process in Prejudicial Publicity." *Central States Speech Journal*, 32 (Summer 1981), 100–10.

Wilkinson, Charles. "The Rhetorical Criticism of Movements: A Process Analysis of the Catonsville Nine Incident." *Journal of the Illinois Speech and Theatre Association*, 31 (1977), 23–36.

Williams, Dale E. "*2001: A Space Odyssey*: A Warning before Its Time." *Critical Studies in Mass Communication*, 1 (September 1984), 311–22.

Williams, William Carlos. "Kenneth Burke." *Dial*, 86 (January 1929), 6–8.

Winterowd, Ross. "Dear Peter Elbow." *Pre/Text*, 4 (Spring 1983), 95–101.

Winterowd, W. Ross. "Black Holes, Indeterminacy, and Paolo Freire." *Rhetoric Review*, 2 (September 1983), 28–35.

Winterowd, W. Ross. *The Contemporary Writer*. New York: Harcourt, Brace, Jovanovich, 1975.

Winterowd, W. Ross. "Kenneth Burke: An Annotated Glossary of His Terministic Screen and a 'Statistical' Survey of His Major Concepts." *Rhetoric Society Quarterly*, 15 (Summer/Fall 1985), 245–77.

Winterowd, W. Ross. *Rhetoric and Writing*. Boston: Allyn and Bacon, 1965.

Winterowd, W. Ross. *Rhetoric: A Synthesis*. New York: Holt, Rinehart and Winston, 1968.

Wise, Gene. *American Historical Explanations: A Strategy for Grounded Inquiry*. Minneapolis: University of Minnesota Press, 1980.

Woodward, Gary C. "Mystifications in the Rhetoric of Cultural Dominance and Colonial Control." *Central States Speech Journal*, 26 (Winter 1975), 298–303.

Wright, Mark H. "Burkeian and Freudian Theories of Identification." *Communication Quarterly*, 42 (Summer 1994), 301–10.

Wright, Mark H. "Identification and the Preconscious." *Communication Studies*, 44 (Summer 1993), 144–56.

Yagoda, Ben. "Kenneth Burke: The Greatest Literary Critic since Coleridge?" *Horizon*, 23 (June 1980), 66–69.

Yingling, Julie. "Women's Advocacy: Pragmatic Feminism in the YWCA." *Women's Studies in Communication*, 6 (Spring 1983), 1–11.

Young, Richard. "Invention: A Topographical Survey." In *Teaching Composition: 10 Bibliographical Essays*. Ed. Gary Tate. Fort Worth: Texas Christian University Press, 1976.

Zollschan, George K., and Michael A. Overington. "Reasons for Conduct and the Conduct of Reason: The Eightfold Route to Motivational Ascription." In *Social Change: Explorations, Diagnoses, and Conjectures*. Ed. George K. Zollschan and Walter Hirsch. New York: John Wiley, 1976, pp. 270–317.

Works about Jürgen Habermas

Abraham, David. "Persistent Facts and Compelling Norms: Liberal Capitalism, Democratic Socialism, and the Law." *Law & Society Review*, 28 (1994), 939–61.

Adamson, Walter L. "Beyond 'Reform or Revolution': Notes on Political Education in Gramsci, Habermas and Arendt." *Theory and Society*, 6 (November 1978), 429–60.

Afrasiabi, K. I. "Communicative Theory and Theology: A Reconsideration." *Harvard Theological Review*, 91 (January 1998), 75–887.

Agger, Ben. "Work and Authority in Marcuse and Habermas." *Human Studies*, 2 (July 1979), 191–208.

Ahlers, Rolf. "How Critical Is Critical Theory? Reflections on Jürgen Habermas." *Cultural Hermeneutics*, 3 (August 1975), 119–32.

Alexander, Jeffrey C. "The Parsons Revival in German Sociology." *Sociological Theory*, 2 (1984), 394–412.

Alexy, Robert. "Jürgen Habermas's Theory of Legal Discourse." *Cardozo Law Review*, 17 (March 1996), 1027–34.

Alford, C. Fred. "Is Jürgen Habermas's Reconstructive Science Really Science?" *Theory and Society*, 14 (May 1985), 321–40.

Alford, C. Fred. "Jürgen Habermas and the Dialectic of Enlightenment: What Is Theoretically Fruitful Knowledge?" *Social Research*, 52 (Spring 1985), 119–49.

Alford, C. Fred. *Science and the Revenge of Nature: Marcuse and Habermas*. Tampa: University of South Florida, 1985.

Allen, Robert van Roden. "Emancipation and Subjectivity: A Projected Kant-Habermas Confrontation." *Philosophy and Social Criticism*, 9 (Fall/Winter 1982), 283–301.

Alway, Joan. *Critical Theory and Political Possibilities: Conceptions of Emancipatory Politics in the Works of Horkheimer, Adorno, Marcuse, and Habermas*. Westport, CT: Greenwood, 1995.

Apel, Karl-Otto. "C. S. Peirce and the Post-Tarskian Problem of an Adequate Explication of the Meaning of Truth: Towards a Transcendental-Pragmatic Theory of Truth, Part II." *Transactions of the Charles S. Peirce Society*, 18 (Winter 1982), 3–17.

Apel, Karl-Otto. "Types of Social Science in the Light of Human Interests of Knowledge," *Social Research*, 44 (Autumn 1977), 425–70.

Arac, Jonathan. "The Function of Foucault at the Present Time." *Humanities in Society*, 3 (Winter 1980), 73–86.

Arato, Andrew, and Eike Gebhardt, eds. *The Essential Frankfurt School Reader*. New York: Continuum, 1982.

Árnason, Jóhann P. "Contemporary Approaches to Marx—Reconstruction and Deconstruction." *Thesis Eleven*, 9 (July 1984), 52–72.

Árnason, Jóhann P. "Universal Pragmatics and Historical Materialism." *Acta Sociologica*, 25 (1982), 219–33.

Ashenden, Samantha, and David Owen, eds. *Foucault contra Habermas*. Thousand Oaks, CA: Sage, 1999.

Aune, James A. "The Contribution of Habermas to Rhetorical Validity." *Journal of the American Forensic Association*, 16 (Fall 1979), 104–11.

Badillo, Robert Peter. *The Emancipative Theory of Jürgen Habermas and Metaphysics*. Washington, DC: Council for Research in Values and Philosophy, 1991.

Balbus, Isaac D. "Habermas and Feminism: (Male) Communication and the Evolution of (Patriarchal) Society." *New Political Science*, 13 (Winter 1984), 27–47.

Bar-Hillel, Y. "On Habermas' Hermeneutic Philosophy of Language." *Synthese*, 26 (1973), 1–12.

Barnes, Barry. *Interests and the Growth of Knowledge*. Boston: Routledge and Kegan Paul, 1977.

Bauman, Zygmunt. *Hermeneutics and Social Science*. New York: Columbia University Press, 1978.

Bauman, Zygmunt. "Ideology and the *Weltanschauung* of the Intellectuals." *Canadian Journal of Political and Social Theory*, 7 (Winter/Spring 1983), 104–17.

Bauman, Zygmunt. *Towards a Critical Sociology: An Essay on Commonsense and Emancipation*. London: Routledge and Kegan Paul, 1976.

Baynes, Kenneth. "Communicative Ethics, the Public Sphere and Communication Media." *Critical Studies in Mass Communication*, 11 (December 1994), 315–26.

Baynes, Kenneth. *The Normative Grounds of Social Criticism: Kant, Rawls, and Habermas*. Albany: State University of New York Press, 1992.

Baynes, Kenneth. "Rational Reconstruction and Social Criticism: Habermas's Model of Interpretive Social Science." *Philosophical Forum*, 21 (Fall/Winter 1989–90), 122–45.

Baynes, Kenneth, James Bohman, and Thomas McCarthy, eds. *After Philosophy: End or Transformation?* Cambridge: MIT Press, 1987.

Beatty, Joseph. "'Communicative Competence' and the Skeptic." *Philosophy and Social Criticism*, 6 (1979), 269–87.

Belliotti, Raymond A. "Radical Politics and Nonfoundational Morality." *International Philosophical Quarterly*, 29 (March 1989), 33–51.

Benhabib, Seyla. "Epistemologies of Postmodernism: A Rejoinder to Jean-François Lyotard. *New German Critique*, 33 (Fall 1984), 103–26.

Benhabib, Seyla. "In the Shadow of Aristotle and Hegel: Communicative Ethics and Current Controversies in Practical Philosophy." *Philosophical Forum*, 21 (Fall/Winter 1989–90), 1–31.

Benhabib, Seyla. "The Methodological Illusions of Modern Political Theory: The Case of Rawls and Habermas." *Neue Hefte für Philosophie*, 21 (1982), 47–74.

Benhabib, Seyla. "The Utopian Dimension in Communicative Ethics." *New German Critique*, 35 (Spring/Summer 1985), 83–96.

Bennett, W. Lance. "Communication and Social Responsibility." *Quarterly Journal of Speech*, 71 (August 1985), 259–88.

Bernsen, Niels Ole. "Elementary Knowledge: Transcendental Pragmatics without Consensus Theory and Ideal Community of Communication." *Acta Sociologica*, 25 (1982), 235–47.

Bernstein, Richard J., ed. *Habermas and Modernity*. Cambridge: MIT Press, 1985.

Bernstein, Richard J. *The Restructuring of Social and Political Theory*. New York: Harcourt Brace Jovanovich, 1976.

Bernstein, Richard J. "The Retrieval of the Democratic Ethos." *Cardozo Law Review*, 17 (March 1996), 1127–46.

Best, Steven. *The Politics of Historical Vision: Marx, Foucault, Habermas*. New York: Guilford, 1995.

Best, Steven, and Douglas Kellner. *Postmodern Theory: Critical Interrogations*. New York: Guilford, 1991.

Birchall, B. C. "Radicalisation of the Critique of Knowledge: Epistemology Overcome or Reinstatement of an Error?" *Man and World*, 10 (1977), 367–81.

Bixenstine, Edwin. "The Fact-Value Antithesis in Behavioral Science." *Journal of Humanistic Psychology*, 16 (Spring 1976), 35–57.

Blakeley, Thomas. "Responses to 'Theory and Practice.'" *Cultural Hermeneutics*, 2 (February 1975), 353–54.

Blakeley, Thomas J. "Praxis and Labor in Jürgen Habermas." *Studies in Soviet Thought*, 20 (October 1979), 291–94.

Blanchette, Oliva. "Language, the Primordial Labor of History: A Critique of Critical Social Theory in Habermas." *Cultural Hermeneutics*, 1 (February 1974), 325–82.

Blaug, Ricardo. "Between Fear and Disappointment: Critical, Empirical and Political Uses of Habermas." *Political Studies*, 65 (March 1997), 100–17.

Bleicher, Josef. *Contemporary Hermeneutics: Hermeneutics as Method, Philosophy and Critique*. London: Routledge and Kegan Paul, 1980.

Bleifer, Craig B. "Looking at Pornography through Habermasian Lenses: Affirmative Action for Speech." *Review of Law and Social Change*, 22 (1996), 153–201.

Blyler, Nancy Roundy. "Habermas, Empowerment, and Professional Discourse." *Technical Communication Quarterly*, 3 (Spring 1994), 125–45.

Bocock, Robert. *Freud and Modern Society: An Outline and Analysis of Freud's Sociology*. New York: Holmes and Meier, 1978.

Bohman, James F. "Communication, Ideology, and Democratic Theory." *American Political Science Review*, 84 (March 1990), 93–109.

Bohman, James F. "Emancipation and Rhetoric: The Perlocutions and Illocutions of the Social Critic." *Philosophy and Rhetoric*, 21 (1988), 185–204.

Bologh, Roslyn Wallach. *Dialectical Phenomenology: Marx's Method*. London: Routledge and Kegan Paul, 1979.

Botstein, Leon. "German Terrorism from Afar." *Partisan Review*, 46 (1979), 188–204.

Bottomore, Tom. *The Frankfurt School*. New York: Tavistock, 1984.

Bowring, Finn. "A Lifeworld without a Subject: Habermas and the Pathologies of Modernity." *Telos*, 106 (Winter 1996), 77–104.

Boyne, Roy, and Scott Lash. "Communicative Rationality and Desire." *Telos*, 61 (Fall 1984), 152–58.

Brand, A. "Interests and the Growth of Knowledge—A Comparison of Weber, Popper and Habermas." *Netherlands' Journal of Sociology*, 13 (July 1977), 1–20.

Brand, A. "Truth and Habermas' Paradigm of a Critical Social Science." *Sociologische Gids*, 23 (September/October 1976), 285–95.

Brewster, Philip, and Carl Howard Buchner. "Language and Critique: Jürgen Habermas on Walter Benjamin." *New German Critique*, 17 (Spring 1979), 15–29.

Brown, Michael E. "Sociology as Critical Theory." In *Theoretical Perspectives in Sociology*. Ed. Scott G. McNall. New York: St. Martin's, 1979, pp. 251–75.

Browning, Don S., and Francis Schüssler Fiorenza. *Habermas, Modernity, and Public Theology*. New York: Crossroad, 1992.

Bubner, Rüdiger. "Summation." *Cultural Hermeneutics*, 2 (February 1975), 359–62.

Bubner, Rüdiger. "Theory and Practice in the Light of the Hermeneutic-Criticist Controversy." *Cultural Hermeneutics*, 2 (February 1975), 337–52.

Burleson, Brant R. "On the Foundations of Rationality: Toulmin, Habermas, and the *a Priori* of Reason." *Journal of the American Forensic Association*, 16 (Fall 1979), 112–27.

Burleson, Brant R., and Susan L. Kline. "Habermas' Theory of Communication: A Critical Explication." *Quarterly Journal of Speech*, 65 (December 1979), 412–28.

Calhoun, Craig, ed. *Habermas and the Public Sphere*. Cambridge: MIT Press, 1992.

Calhoun, Craig. "Social Theory and the Law: Systems Theory, Normative Justification, and Postmodernism." *Northwestern University Law Review*, 83 (Fall 1988/Winter 1989), 398–460.

Campbell, John Angus. "A Rhetorical Interpretation of History." *Rhetorica*, 2 (Autumn 1984), 227–66.

Canovan, Margaret. "A Case of Distorted Communication: A Note on Habermas and Arendt." *Political Theory*, 11 (February 1983), 105–16.

Cerroni, Umberto. "The Problem of Democracy in Mass Society." Trans. Patrizia Heckle. *Praxis International*, 3 (April 1983), 34–53.

Chriss, James J. "Habermas, Goffman, and Communicative Action: Implications for Professional Practice." *American Sociological Review*, 60 (August 1995), 545–65.

Clement, Grace. "Is the Moral Point of View Monological or Dialogical? The Kantian Background of Habermas' Discourse Ethics." *Philosophy Today*, 33 (Summer 1989), 159–73.

Cohen, Jean. "Why More Political Theory?" *Telos*, 40 (Summer 1979), 70–94.

Cole, David. "Getting There: Reflections on Trashing from Feminist Jurisprudence and Critical Theory." *Harvard Women's Law Journal*, 8 (Spring 1985), 59–91.

Condit, Celeste Michelle. "Kenneth Burke and Linguistic Relativity: Reflections on the Scene of the Philosophy of Communication in the Twentieth Century." In *Kenneth Burke and Contemporary European Thought: Rhetoric in Transition*. Ed. Bernard L. Brock. Tuscaloosa: University of Alabama Press, 1995, pp. 207–62.

Connerton, Paul, ed. *Critical Sociology: Selected Readings*. New York: Penguin, 1976.

Connerton, Paul. *The Tragedy of Enlightenment: An Essay on the Frankfurt School*. Cambridge: Cambridge University Press, 1980.

Cook, Maeve. *Language and Reason: A Study of Habermas' Pragmatics*. Cambridge: MIT Press, 1994.

Cooren, François. "Toward Another Ideal Speech Situation: A Critique of Habermas' Reinterpretation of Speech Act Theory." *Quarterly Journal of Speech*, 86 (August 2000), 295–317.

Craib, Ian. *Modern Social Theory: From Parsons to Habermas*. New York: St. Martin's, 1984.

Culler, Jonathan. "Communicative Competence and Normative Force." *New German Critique*, 35 (Spring/Summer 1985), 133–44.

Cushman, Donald P., and David Dietrich. "A Critical Reconstruction of Jürgen Habermas' Holistic Approach to Rhetoric as Social Philosophy." *Journal of the American Forensic Association*, 16 (Fall 1979), 128–37.

Dallmayr, Fred R. *Beyond Dogma and Despair: Toward a Critical Phenomenology of Politics*. Notre Dame: University of Notre Dame Press, 1981.

Dallmayr, Fred R. "Critical Theory Criticized: Habermas's Knowledge and Human Interests and Its Aftermath." *Philosophy of the Social Sciences*, 2 (September 1972), 211–29.

Dallmayr, Fred R. "Reason and Emancipation: Notes on Habermas." *Man and World*, 5 (1972), 79–109.

Dallmayr, Fred R. *Twilight of Subjectivity: Contributions to a Post-Individualist Theory of Politics*. Amherst: University of Massachusetts Press, 1981.

Dan-Cohen, Meir. "Laws, Community, and Communication." *Duke Law Journal*, 1989 (December 1990), 1654–76.

Davey, Nicholas. "Habermas's Contribution to Hermeneutic Theory." *Journal of the British Society for Phenomenology*, 16 (May 1985), 109–31.

Davis, Charles. *Theology and Political Society: The Hulsean Lectures in the University of Cambridge, 1978*. New York: Cambridge University Press, 1980.

Deetz, Stanley. "Representation of Interests and the New Communication Technologies: Issues in Democracy and Policy." In *Communication and the Culture of Technology*. Ed. Martin J. Medhurst, Alberto Gonzalez, and Tarla Rai Peterson. Pullman: Washington State University Press, 1990.

Deflem, Mathieu. "The Boundaries of Abortion Law: Systems Theory from Parsons to Luhmann and Habermas." *Social Forces*, 76 (March 1998), 775–818.

Deflem, Mathieu. "Social Control and the Theory of Communicative Action." *International Journal of the Sociology of Law*, 22 (December 1994), 355–73.

d'Entrèves, Maurizio Passerin, and Seyla Benhabib, eds. *Habermas and the Unfinished Project of Modernity: Critical Essays on* The Philosophical Discourse of Modernity. Cambridge: MIT Press, 1997.

Depew, David J. "The Habermas–Gadamer Debate in Hegelian Perspective." *Philosophy and Social Criticism*, 8 (Winter 1981), 425–46.

Di Norcia, Vincent. "From Critical Theory to Critical Ecology." *Telos*, 22 (Winter 1974–75), 85–95.

Disco, Cornelis. "Critical Theory as Ideology of the New Class: Rereading Jürgen Habermas." *Theory and Society*, 8 (September 1979), 159–214.

Doxtader, Erik W. "The Entwinement of Argument and Rhetoric: A Dialectical Reading of Habermas' Theory of Communicative Action." *Argumentation and Advocacy*, 28 (Fall 1991), 51–63.

Dryzek, John S. "How Far Is It from Virginia and Rochester to Frankfurt? Public Choice as Critical Theory." *British Journal of Political Science*, 22 (July 1992), 397–417.

Dyzenhaus, David. "The Legitimacy of Legality." *University of Toronto Law Journal*, 46 (Winter 1996), 129–80

Ealy, Steven D. *Communication, Speech, and Politics*. Washington, DC: University Press of America, 1981.

Eastland, Lynette Seccombe. "Habermas, Emancipation, and Relationship Change: An Exploration of Recovery Processes as a Model for Social Transformation." *Applied Communication Research*, 22 (May 1994), 162–76.

Eder, Klaus. "Critique of Habermas's Contributions to the Sociology of Law." *Law and Society Review*, 22 (1988), 931–44.

Ewert, Gerry D. "Habermas and Education: A Comprehensive Overview of the Influence of Habermas in Educational Literature." *Review of Educational Research*, 61 (Fall 1991), 345–78.

Eyerman, Ron. "Social Movements and Social Theory." *Sociology*, 18 (February 1984), 73–82.

Eze, Emmanuel C. "*Out of Africa*: Communication Theory and Cultural Hegemony." *Telos*, 111 (Spring 1998), 139–61.

Factor, Regis A., and Stephen P. Turner. "The Critique of Positivist Social Science in Leo Strauss and Jürgen Habermas." *Sociological Analysis and Theory*, 7 (1977), 185–206.

Farganis, James. "A Preface to Critical Theory." *Theory and Society*, 2 (Winter 1975), 483–508.

Farrell, Thomas B. "Comic History Meets Tragic Memory: Burke and Habermas on the Drama of Human Relations." In *Kenneth Burke and Contemporary European Thought: Rhetoric in Transition*. Ed. Bernard L. Brock. Tuscaloosa: University of Alabama Press, 1995, pp. 34–75.

Farrell, Thomas B. "Habermas on Argumentation Theory: Some Emerging Topics." *Journal of the American Forensic Association*, 16 (Fall 1979), 77–82.

Farrell, Thomas B. "The Ideality of Meaning of Argument: A Revision of Habermas. In *Dimensions of Argument: Proceedings of the Second Summer Conference on Argumentation*. Ed. George Ziegelmueller and Jack Rhodes. Annandale, VA: Speech Communication Association, October 15, 1981, pp. 905–26.

Farrell, Thomas B. "Knowledge, Consensus, and Rhetorical Theory." *Quarterly Journal of Speech*, 62 (February 1976), 1–14.

Farrell, Thomas B., and James Aune. "Critical Theory and Communication: A Selective Literature Review." *Quarterly Journal of Speech*, 65 (February 1979), 93–120.

Faught, Jim. "Objective Reason and the Justification of Norms." *California Sociologist*, 4 (Winter 1981), 33–53.

Feldman, Stephen M. "The Persistence of Power and the Struggle for Dialogic Standards in Postmodern Constitutional Jurisprudence: Michelman, Habermas, and Civic Republicanism." *Georgetown Law Journal*, 81 (July 1993), 2243–90.

Feenberg, Andrew. *Lukács, Marx and the Sources of Critical Theory*. Totowa, NJ: Rowman Littlefield, 1981.

Ferrara, Allessandro. "A Critique of Habermas's *Diskursethik*." In *The Interpretation of Dialogue*. Ed. Tullio Maranhao. Chicago: University of Chicago Press, pp. 303–37.

Fields, A. Belden. "In Defense of Political Economy and Systemic Analysis: A Critique of Prevailing Theoretical Approaches to the New Social Movements." In *Marxism and the Interpretation of Culture*. Ed. Cary Nelson and Lawrence Grossberg. Urbana: University of Illinois Press, 1988, pp. 141–56.

Fischer, Frank. "Science and Critique in Political Discourse: Elements of a Postpositivistic Methodology." *New Political Science*, 9/10 (Summer/Fall 1982), 9–32.

Fisher, Walter R. "The Narrative Paradigm: An Elaboration." *Communication Monographs*, 52 (December 1985), 347–67.

Fitzgerald, Ross, ed. *Human Needs and Politics*. New York: Pergamon, 1977.

Flöistad, Guttorm. "Social Concepts of Action: Notes on Habermas's Proposal for a Social Theory of Knowledge." *Inquiry*, 13 (Summer 1970), 175–98.

Flood, Tony. "Jürgen Habermas's Critique of Marxism." *Science and Society*, 41 (Winter 1977–78), 448–64.

Flynn, Bernard Charles. "Reading Habermas Reading Freud." *Human Studies*, 8 (1985), 57–76.

Flyvvbjerg, Bent. "Habermas and Foucault: Thinkers for Civil Society?" *British Journal of Sociology*, 49 (June 1998), 210–33.

Forbath, William E. "Short-Circuit: A Critique of Habermas's Understanding of Law, Politics, and Economic Life." *Cardozo Law Review*, 17 (March 1996), 1441–56.

Forester, John. "A Critical Empirical Framework for the Analysis of Public Policy." *New Political Science*, 3 (Summer/Fall 1982), 33–61.

Forester, John, ed. *Critical Theory and Public Life*. Cambridge: MIT Press, 1985.

Forester, John. "Hannah Arendt and Critical Theory: A Critical Response." *Journal of Politics*, 43 (February 1981), 196–202.

Forester, John. "The Policy Analysis-Critical Theory Affair: Wildavsky and Habermas as Bedfellows?" *Journal of Public Policy*, 2 (May 1982), 145–64.

Foss, Karen A. "Habermas, Jürgen (b. 1929)." *Encyclopedia of Rhetoric and Composition: Communication from Ancient Times to the Information Age*. Ed. Theresa Enos. New York: Garland, 1996, pp. 309–11.

Foster, William P. "Administration and the Crisis in Legitimacy: A Review of Habermasian Thought." *Harvard Educational Review*, 50 (November 1980), 496–505.

Francesconi, Robert. "The Implications of Habermas's Theory of Legitimation for Rhetorical Criticism." *Communication Monographs*, 53 (March 1986), 16–35.

Frankel, Boris. "The State of the State: Marxist Theories after Leninism." *Theory and Society*, 7 (January/March 1979), 199–242.

Frankenberg, Günter. "Why Care?—The Trouble with Social Rights." *Cardozo Law Review*, 17 (March 1996), 1365–90.

Fraser, Nancy. *Unruly Practices: Power, Discourse, and Gender in Contemporary Social Theory*. Minneapolis: University of Minnesota Press, 1989.

Fraser, Nancy. "What's Critical about Critical Theory? The Case of Habermas and Gender." *New German Critique*, 35 (Spring/Summer 1985), 97–131.

Freiberg, J. W., ed. *Critical Sociology: European Perspectives*. New York: Irvington, 1979.

Frisby, David. "The Frankfurt School: Critical Theory and Positivism." In *Approaches to Sociology: An Introduction to Major Trends in British Sociology*. Ed. John Rex. London: Routledge and Kegan Paul, 1974, pp. 205–29.

Furth, Hans. "A Developmental Interpretation of Habermas's Concept of Communicative Action." *Human Development*, 27 (May/August 1984), 183–87.

Fusfield, William. "Communication without Constellation? Habermas's Argumentative Turn in (and Away from) Critical Theory." *Communication Theory*, 7 (November 1997), 301–20.

Gadamer, Hans-Georg. *Philosophical Hermeneutics*. Trans. and ed. David E. Linge. Berkeley: University of California Press, 1976.

Gadamer, Hans-Georg. "Responses to 'Theory and Practice.'" *Cultural Hermeneutics* (February 1975), 357.

Gall, Robert S. "Between Tradition and Critique." *Auslegung*, 8 (Winter 1981), 5–18.

Gay, William. "Justification of Legal Authority: Phenomenology vs. Critical Theory." *Journal of Social Philosophy*, 11 (May 1980), 1–8.

Geuss, Raymond. *The Idea of a Critical Theory: Habermas and the Frankfurt School*. New York: Cambridge University Press, 1981.

Giddens, Anthony. *Central Problems in Social Theory: Action, Structure and Contradiction in Social Analysis*. Berkeley: University of California Press, 1979.

Giddens, Anthony. *New Rules of Sociological Method: A Positive Critique of Interpretative Sociologies*. New York: Basic, 1976.

Giddens, Anthony. *Profiles and Critiques in Social Theory*. Berkeley: University of California Press, 1982.

Giddens, Anthony. "Reason without Revolution? Habermas's *Theorie Des Kommunikativen Handelns*." *Praxis International*, 2 (October 1982), 318–38.

Giddens, Anthony. *Studies in Social and Political Theory*. London: Hutchinson, 1977.

Golden, James L., Goodwin F. Berquist, and William E. Coleman. "Emerging European Perspectives on Rhetoric." In *The Rhetoric of Western Thought*. 4th ed. Ed. James L. Golden, Goodwin F. Berquist, and William E. Coleman. Dubuque, IA: Kendall/Hunt, 1989, pp. 428–46.

Gonzalez, Hernando. "Interactivity and Feedback in Third World Development Campaigns." *Critical Studies in Mass Communication*, 6 (September 1989), 295–314.

Goodrich, Peter. "Habermas and the Postal Rule." *Cardozo Law Review*, 17 (March 1996), 1457–76.

Görtzen, René, and Frederik Van Gelder. "Jürgen Habermas: The Complete Oeuvre. A Bibliography of Primary Literature, Translations and Reviews." *Human Studies*, 2 (October 1979), 285–300.

Gottlieb, Roger S. "The Contemporary Critical Theory of Jürgen Habermas." *Ethics*, 91 (January 1981), 280–95.

Gottlieb, Roger S. "Habermas and Critical-Reflective Emancipation." In *Rationality To-Day*. Ed. Theodore F. Geraets. Ottawa, Can.: University of Ottawa Press, 1979, pp. 434–40.

Gould, Mark. "Law and Philosophy: Some Consequences for the Law Deriving from the Sociological Reconstruction of Philosophical Theory." *Cardozo Law Review*, 17 (March 1996), 1239–1363.

Gouldner, Alvin W. *The Dialectic of Ideology and Technology: The Origins, Grammar and Future of Ideology*. New York: Seabury, 1976.

Gouldner, Alvin W. *The Future of Intellectuals and the Rise of the New Class: A Frame of Reference, Theses, Conjectures, Arguments, and an Historical Perspective on the Role of Intellectuals and Intelligentsia in the International Class Contest of the Modern Era*. New York: Seabury, 1979.

Griffin, Cindy L. "The Essentialist Roots of the Public Sphere: A Feminist Critique." *Western Journal of Communication*, 60 (Winter 1996), 21–39.

Gross, David. "On Critical Theory." *Humanities in Society*, 4 (Winter 1981), 89–100.

Grundmann, Reiner, and Christos Mantziaris. "Fundamental Intolerance or Civil Disobedience? Strange Loops in Liberal Theory." *Political Theory*, 19 (November 1991), 572–605.

Gunson, Darryl, and Chik Collins. "From the *I* to the *We*: Discourse Ethics, Identity, and the Pragmatics of Partnership in the West of Scotland." *Communication Theory*, 7 (November 1997), 277–300.

Günther, Klaus. "Communicative Freedom, Communicative Power, and Jurisgenesis." *Cardozo Law Review*, 17 (March 1996), 1035–58.

Guss, Donald L. "Enlightenment as Process: Milton and Habermas." *PMLA*, 106 (October 1991), 1156–69.

Gutting, Gary. "Continental Philosophy of Science." In *Current Research in Philosophy of Science*. Ed. Peter D. Asquith and Henry E. Kyburg, Jr. East Lansing, MI: Philosophy of Science Association, 1979.

Haarscher, Guy. "Perelman and Habermas." *Law and Philosophy*, 5 (December 1986), 331–42.

Haes, Julian. "The Problem of Cultural Relativism: Habermas and the Curriculum." *Sociological Review*, 28 (November 1980), 717–43.

Hall, J. A. "Gellner and Habermas on Epistemology and Politics or Need We Feel Disenchanted?" *Philosophy of the Social Sciences*, 12 (December 1982), 387–407.

Hall, John A. *Diagnoses of Our Time: Six Views on Our Social Condition*. London: Heinemann Educational, 1981.

Hamilton, Peter. *Knowledge and Social Structure: An Introduction to the Classical Argument in the Sociology of Knowledge*. Boston: Routledge and Kegan Paul, 1974.

Hartmann, Klaus. "Human Agency between Life-World and System: Habermas's Latest Version of Critical Theory." *Journal of the British Society for Phenomenology*, 16 (May 1985), 145–55.

Healy, Paul. "Between Habermas and Foucault: On the Limits and Possibilities of Critical and Emancipatory Reason." *South African Journal of Philosophy*, 16 (November 1997), 140–49.

Hearn, Francis. "Toward a Critical Theory of Play." *Telos*, 30 (Winter 1976–77), 145–60.

Heather, Gerald P., and Matthew Stolz. "Hannah Arendt and the Problem of Critical Theory." *Journal of Politics*, 41 (February 1979), 2–22.

Heather, Gerald P., and Matthew F. Stolz. "Reply to Professor Forester." *Journal of Politics*, 43 (February 1981), 203–07.

Hekman, Susan. "Some Notes on the Universal and Conventional in Social Theory: Wittgenstein and Habermas." *Social Science Journal*, 20 (April 1983), 1–15.

Held, David. "The Battle Over Critical Theory." *Sociology*, 12 (September 1978), 553–60.

Held, David. *Introduction to Critical Theory: Horkheimer to Habermas*. Berkeley: University of California Press, 1980.

Held, David, and Larry Simon. "Habermas' Theory of Crisis in Late Capitalism." *Radical Philosophers' Newsjournal*, 6 (1976), 1–19.

Held, David, and Lawrence Simon. "Toward Understanding Habermas." *New German Critique*, 7 (Winter 1976), 136–45.

Heller, Agnes. "The Discourse Ethics of Habermas: Critique and Appraisal." *Thesis Eleven*, 10/11 (November/March 1984–85), 5–17.

Heller, Agnes. "Marxist Ethics and the Future of Eastern Europe: An Interview with Agnes Heller." Trans. David J. Parent. *Telos*, 38 (Winter 1978–79), 153–74.

Hesse, Mary. "In Defence of Objectivity." *British Academy*, 58 (1972), 275–92.

Hesse, Mary. *Revolutions and Reconstructions in the Philosophy of Science*. Bloomington: Indiana University Press, 1980.

Hill, Melvyn Alan. "Jürgen Habermas: A Social Science of the Mind." *Philosophy of the Social Sciences*, 2 (September 1972), 247–59.

Hohendahl, Peter. "Critical Theory, Public Sphere and Culture: Jürgen Habermas and his Critics." Trans. Marc Silberman. *New German Critique*, 16 (Winter 1979), 89–118.

Hohendahl, Peter. "The Dialectic of Enlightenment Revisited: Habermas' Critique of the Frankfurt School." *New German Critique*, 35 (Spring/Summer 1985), 3–26.

Hohendahl, Peter. *The Institution of Criticism*. Ithaca: Cornell University Press, 1982, pp. 242–80.

Hohendahl, Peter. "Jürgen Habermas: 'The Public Sphere' (1964)." Trans. Patricia Russian. *New German Critique*, 3 (Fall 1974), 45–48.

Hollinger, Robert. "Practical Reason and Hermeneutics." *Philosophy and Rhetoric*, 18 (1985), 113–22.

Honneth, Axel. "Communication and Reconciliation: Habermas' Critique of Adorno." *Telos*, 39 (Spring 1979), 45–61.

Honneth, Axel. "Moral Consciousness and Class Domination: Some Problems in the Analysis of Hidden Morality." Trans. Mitchell G. Ash. *Praxis International*, 2 (April 1982), 12–25.

Honneth, Axel. "Work and Instrumental Action." Trans. Mitchell G. Ash. *New German Critique*, 26 (Spring 1982), 31–54.

Honneth, Axel. "Work and Instrumental Action: On the Normative Basis of Critical Theory." Trans. Mitchell G. Ash. *Thesis Eleven*, 516 (1982), 162–84.

Honneth, Axel, Thomas McCarthy, Claus Offe, and Albrecht Wellmer, eds *Cultural-Political Interventions in the Unfinished Project of Enlightenment*. Trans. Barbara Fultner. Cambridge: MIT Press, 1992.

Horster, Detlef. *Habermas: An Introduction*. Philadelphia: Pennbridge, 1992.

How, Alan R. "A Case of Creative Misreading: Habermas's Evaluation of Gadamer's Hermeneutics. *Journal of the British Society for Phenomenology*, 16 (May 1985), 132–44.

How, Alan R. "Dialogue as Productive Limitation in Social Theory: The Habermas–Gadamer Debate." *Journal of the British Society for Phenomenology*, 11 (May 1980), 131–43.

How, Alan. *The Habermas–Gadamer Debate and the Nature of the Social: Back to Bedrock*. Brookfield, VT: Avebury Ashgate, 1995.

Howard, Dick. "Law and Political Culture." *Cardozo Law Review*, 17 (March 1996), 1391–29.

Howard, Dick. *The Marxian Legacy*. 2nd ed. Minneapolis: University of Minnesota Press, 1988.

Howard, Dick. "Moral Development and Ego Identity: A Clarification." *Telos*, 27 (Spring 1976), 176–82.

Howard, Dick. "A Politics in Search of the Political." *Theory and Society*, 1 (Fall 1974), 271–306.

Hoy, David Couzens. *The Critical Circle: Literature, History, and Philosophical Hermeneutics*. Berkeley: University of California Press, 1978.

Hoy, David Couzens. "Interpreting the Law: Hermeneutical and Poststructuralist Perspectives." *Southern California Law Review*, 58 (January 1985), 136–76.

Hummel, Ralph P. *The Bureaucratic Experience*, 2nd ed. New York: St. Martin's, 1982.

Huspek, Michael. "Taking Aim on Habermas's Critical Theory: On the Road toward a Critical Hermeneutics." *Communication Monographs*, 58 (June 1991), 225–33.

Huspek, Michael. "Toward Normative Theories of Communication with Reference to the Frankfurt School: An Introduction." *Communication Theory*, 7 (November 1997), 265–76.

Huyssen, Andreas. "Mapping the Postmodern." *New German Critique*, 33 (Fall 1984), 5–52.

Inglis, Fred. "Good and Bad Habitus: Bourdieu, Habermas and the Condition of England." *Sociological Review*, 27 (May 1979), 353–69.

Ingram, David. *Habermas and the Dialectic of Reason*. New Haven: Yale University Press, 1987.

Ingram, David. "Habermas on Aesthetics and Rationality: Completing the Project of Enlightenment." *New German Critique*, 53 (Spring/Summer 1991), 67–103.

Ingram, David. "The Historical Genesis of the Gadamer/Habermas Controversy." *Auslegung*, 10 (Spring/Summer 1983), 86–151.

Ingram, David. "The Possibility of a Communication Ethic Reconsidered: Habermas, Gadamer, and Bourdieu on Discourse." *Man and World*, 15 (1982), 149–61.

Jacob, Margaret C. "The Mental Landscape of the Public Sphere: A European Perspective." *Eighteenth-Century Studies*, 28 (Fall 1994), 95–113.

Jacobson, Arthur J. "Law and Order." *Cardozo Law Review*, 17 (March 1996), 919–33.

Jacobson, David C. "Rationalization and Emancipation in Weber and Habermas." *Graduate Faculty Journal of Sociology*, 1 (Winter 1976), 18–31.

James, David. "From Marx to Incoherence: A Critique of Habermas." *Journal of Social Philosophy*, 12 (January 1981), 10–16.

Jansen, Sue Curry. "Power and Knowledge: Toward a New Critical Synthesis." *Journal of Communication*, 33 (Summer 1983), 342–54.

Jay, Martin. *The Dialectical Imagination: A History of the Frankfurt School and the Institute of Social Research, 1923–1950*. Boston: Little, Brown, 1973.

Jay, Martin. "Habermas and Modernism." *Praxis International*, 4 (April 1984), 1–15.

Jay, Martin. *Marxism and Totality: The Adventures of a Concept from Lukács to Habermas*. Berkeley: University of California Press, 1984.

Jay, Martin. "Should Intellectual History Take a Linguistic Turn? Reflections on the Habermas–Gadamer Debate." In *Modern European Intellectual History: Reappraisals and New Perspectives*. Ed. Dominick LaCapra and Steven L. Kaplan. Ithaca: Cornell University Press, 1982.

Johnson, Pauline. *Feminism as Radical Humanism*. Boulder, CO: Westview, 1994.

Kahn, Victoria. "Habermas, Machiavelli, and the Humanist Critique of Ideology." *PMLA*, 105 (May 1990), 464–76.

Keane, John. "Elements of a Radical Theory of Public Life: From Tönnies to Habermas and Beyond." *Canadian Journal of Political and Social Theory*, 6 (Fall 1982), 11–49.

Keane, John. "Notes: On Belaboring the Theory of Economic Crisis: A Reply to Laska." *New German Critique*, 4 (Winter 1975), 125–30.

Keane, John. "On Tools and Language: Habermas on Work and Interaction." *New German Critique*, 6 (Fall 1975), 82–100.

Keat, Russell. *The Politics of Social Theory: Habermas, Freud and the Critique of Positivism*. Chicago: University of Chicago Press, 1981.

Kellner, Douglas. "Critical Theory, Democracy and Human Rights." *New Political Science*, 1 (1979), 12–18.

Kelly, Michael, ed. *Critique and Power: Recasting the Foucault/Habermas Debate*. Cambridge: MIT Press, 1994.

Kelly, Michael. "The Dialectical/Dialogical Structure of Ethical Reflection." *Philosophy and Rhetoric*, 22 (1989), 174–93.

Kelly, Michael. "MacIntyre, Habermas, and Philosophical Ethics." *Philosophical Forum*, 21 (Fall/Winter 1989–90), 70–93.

Kemp, Ray, and Philip Cooke. "Repoliticising the 'Public Sphere': A Reconsideration of Habermas." *Social Praxis: International and Interdisciplinary Quarterly of Social Sciences*, 8 (1981), 125–42.

Kisiel, Theodore. "Habermas' Purge of Pure Theory: Critical Theory without Ontology?" *Human Studies*, 1 (April 1978), 167–83.

Kisiel, Theodore. "Ideology Critique and Phenomenology: The Current Debate in German Philosophy." *Philosophy Today*, 14 (1971), 151–60.

Kline, Susan L. "The Ideal Speech Situation: A Discussion of Its Presuppositions." In *Dimensions of Argument: Proceedings of the Second Summer Conference on Argumentation*. Ed. George Ziegelmueller and Jack Rhodes. Annandale, VA: Speech Communication Association, October 15, 1981, pp. 927–39.

Kline, Susan L. "Toward a Contemporary Linguistic Interpretation of the Concept of Stasis." *Journal of the American Forensic Association*, 16 (Fall 1979), 95–103.

Kortian, Garbis. *Metacritique: The Philosophical Argument of Jürgen Habermas*. Trans. John Raffan. New York: Cambridge University Press, 1980.

Krueger, Marlis. "Notes on a Materialistic Theory of Interaction." *Cornell Journal of Social Relations*, 11 (Spring 1976), 97–104.

LaCapra, Dominick. "Habermas and the Grounding of Critical Theory." *History and Theory*, 16 (1977), 237–64.

Langsdorf, Lenore. "Refusing Individuality: How Human Beings Are Made into Subjects." *Communication Theory*, 7 (November 1997), 321–42.

Lash, Scott. "Postmodernity and Desire." *Theory and Society*, 14 (January 1985), 1–33.

Laska, Peter. "Notes: A Note on Habermas and the Labor Theory of Value." *New German Critique*, 3 (Fall 1974), 154–62.

Lechte, John. "Jürgen Habermas." In *Fifty Key Contemporary Thinkers: From Structuralism to Postmodernity*. New York: Routledge, 1994, pp. 186–91.

Leeper, Roy V. "Moral Objectivity, Jürgen Habermas's Discourse Ethics, and Public Relations." *Public Relations Review*, 22 (Summer 1996), 133–50.

Leiss, William. *The Domination of Nature*. New York: George Braziller, 1972.

Leiss, William. "The Problem of Man and Nature in the Work of the Frankfurt School." *Philosophy of the Social Sciences*, 5 (1975), 163–72.

Lemert, Charles C. *Sociology and the Twilight of Man: Homocentrism and Discourse in Sociological Theory*. Carbondale: Southern Illinois University Press, 1979.

Lenhardt, Christian K. "Rise and Fall of Transcendental Anthropology." *Philosophy of the Social Sciences*, 2 (September 1972), 231–46.

Lenoble, Jacques. "Law and Undecidability: A New Vision of the Proceduralization of Law." *Cardozo Law Review*, 17 (March 1996), 935–1004.

Lepenies, Wolf. "Anthropology and Social Criticism: A View of the Controversy between Arnold Gehlen and Jürgen Habermas." *Human Context*, 3 (July 1971), 205–25.

Lesnoff, Michael. "Technique, Critique and Social Science." In *Philosophical Disputes in the Social Sciences*. Ed. S. C. Brown. Atlantic Highlands, NJ: Humanities, 1979, pp. 89–116.

Li, Kit-Man. *Western Civilization and Its Problems: A Dialogue between Weber, Elias, and Habermas*. Brookfield, VT: Ashgate, 1999.

Lobkowicz, Nicolaus. "Interest and Objectivity." *Philosophy of the Social Sciences*, 2 (September 1972), 193–210.

Luban, David. "On Habermas on Arendt on Power." *Philosophy and Social Criticism*, 6 (Spring 1979), 79–95.

Lucaites, John Louis. "Rhetoric and the Problem of Legitimacy." In *Dimensions of Argument: Proceedings of the Second Summer Conference on Argumentation*. Ed. George Ziegelmueller and Jack Rhodes. Annandale, VA: Speech Communication Association, October 15, 1981, pp. 799–811.

Luhmann, Niklas. "*Iquod Omnes Tangit*: Remarks on Jürgen Habermas's Legal Theory." *Cardozo Law Review*, 17 (March 1996), 883–99.

McCarthy, T. A. "A Theory of Communicative Competence." *Philosophy of the Social Sciences*, 3 (June 1973), 135–56.

McCarthy, Thomas. "Complexity and Democracy, or The Seducements of Systems Theory." *New German Critique*, 35 (Spring/Summer 1985), 27–53.

McCarthy, Thomas. *The Critical Theory of Jürgen Habermas*. Cambridge: MIT Press, 1978.

McCarthy, Thomas. *Ideals and Illusions: On Reconstruction and Deconstruction in Contemporary Critical Theory*. Cambridge: MIT Press, 1991.

McCarthy, Thomas. "Kantian Constructivism and Reconstructivism: Rawls and Habermas in Dialogue." *Ethics*, 105 (October 1994), 44–63.

McCarthy, Thomas. "Legitimacy and Diversity: Dialectical Reflections on Analytical Distinctions." *Cardozo Law Review*, 17 (March 1996), 1083–1125.

McCarthy, Thomas. "Rationality and Discourse." In *Rationality To-Day*. Ed. Theodore F. Geraets. Ottawa, Can.: University of Ottawa, 1979, pp. 441–47.

McCarthy, Thomas. "Rationality and Relativism in Habermas' Critical Theory." *Noûs*, 14 (March 1980), 75–76.

McCarthy, Thomas. "Reflections on Rationalization in the Theory of Communicative Action." *Praxis International*, 4 (July 1984), 177–91.

McCarthy, Thomas A. "Responses to 'Theory and Practice.'" *Cultural Hermeneutics*, 2 (1975), 157.

McCormick, John P. "Max Weber and Jürgen Habermas: The Sociology and Philosophy of Law during Crises of the State." *Yale Journal of Law and the Humanities*, 9 (Summer 1997), 297–44.

McCumber, John. "Critical Theory and Poetic Interaction." *Praxis International*, 5 (October 1985), 268–82.

McGuire, R. R. "Speech Acts, Communicative Competence and the Paradox of Authority." *Philosophy and Rhetoric*, 10 (Winter 1977), 30–45.

McGuire, Steven. "Moral Relativism and Habermas." *ALSA Forum*, 6 (1982), 23–31.

McIntosh, Donald. "Habermas on Freud." *Social Research*, 44 (Autumn 1977), 562–98.

McKerrow, Raymie E. "Critical Rhetoric: Theory and Praxis." *Communication Monographs*, 56 (June 1989), 91–111.

McNall, Scott G., ed. *Theoretical Perspectives in Sociology*. New York: St. Martin's, 1979.

Maddox, Randy L. "Hermeneutic Circle—Vicious or Victorious." *Philosophy Today*, 27 (Spring 1983), 66–76.

Madsen, Peter. "History and Consciousness: Cultural Studies between Reification and Hegemony." *Thesis Eleven*, 5/6 (1982), 204–14.

Mariante, Benjamin R. "The Frankfurt School and the Sociology of Religion: Religion a la Marx and Freud." *Humboldt Journal of Social Relations*, 9 (Fall/Winter 1981/82), 75–89.

Marković, Mihailo. The Idea of Critique in Social Theory. *Praxis International*, 3 (July 1983), 108–20.

Marx, Werner. Habermas' Philosophical Conception of History. *Cultural Hermeneutics*, 3 (July 1976), 335–47.

Matuštík, Martin J. *Postnational Identity: Critical Theory and Existential Philosophy in Habermas, Kierkegaard, and Havel*. New York: Guilford, 1993.

Maus, Ingeborg. "Liberties and Popular Sovereignty: On Jürgen Habermas's Reconstruction of the System of Rights." *Cardozo Law Review*, 17 (March 1996), 825–82.

Meehan, Johanna, ed. *Feminists Read Habermas: Gendering the Subject of Discourse*. New York: Routledge, 1995.

Mellos, Koula. "The Habermasian Perspective in the Critique of Technocratic Consciousness." *Revue de l'Universiti d'Ottawa*, 47 (October/December 1977), 427–51.

Mendelson, Jack. "The Habermas–Gadamer Debate." *New German Critique*, 18 (1979), 44–73.

Milić, Vojin. "Method of Critical Theory." *Praxis*, 7 (1971), 625–56.

Miller, James. "Some Implications of Nietzsche's Thought for Marxism." *Telos*, 37 (Fall 1978), 22–41.

Miller, Toby. *The Well-Tempered Self: Citizenship, Culture, and the Postmodern Subject*. Baltimore: Johns Hopkins University Press, 1993.

Misgeld, Dieter. "Between Philosophy and Science: The Critical Theory of the Frankfurt School of Social Research." *Laurentian University Review*, 4 (1972), 22–34.

Misgeld, Dieter. "Critical Hermeneutics versus Neoparsonianism?" *New German Critique*, 35 (Spring/Summer 1985), 55–82.

Misgeld, Dieter. "Discourse and Conversation: The Theory of Communicative Competence and Hermeneutics in the Light of the Debate between Habermas and Gadamer." *Cultural Hermeneutics*, 4 (December 1977), 321–44.

Misgeld, Dieter. "Habermas's Retreat from Hermeneutics: Systems Integration, Social Integration and the Crisis of Legitimation." *Canadian Journal of Political and Social Theory*, 5 (Winter/Spring 1981), 8–44.

Misgeld, Dieter. "Ultimate Self-Responsibility, Practical Reasoning, and Practical Action: Habermas, Husserl, and Ethnomethodology on Discourse and Action." *Human Studies*, 3 (July 1980), 255–78.

Mootz, Francis J. "The Ontological Basis of Legal Hermeneutics: A Proposed Model of Inquiry Based on the Work of Gadamer, Habermas, and Ricoeur." *Boston University Law Review*, 68 (May 1988), 523–617.

Motzkin, Gabriel. "Habermas's Ideal Paradigm of Law." *Cardozo Law Review*, 17 (March 1996), 1431–39.

Mueller, Claus. *The Politics of Communication: A Study in the Political Sociology of Language, Socialization, and Legitimation*. New York: Oxford University Press, 1973.

Murray, John Patrick. "Enlightenment Roots of Habermas' Critique of Marx." *Modern Schoolman*, 57 (November 1979), 1–24.

Natoli, Joseph, and Linda Hutcheon, eds. *A Postmodern Reader*. Albany: State University of New York Press, 1993.

Navasky, Victor. "Scoping Out Habermas." *Media Studies Journal*, 9 (Summer 1995), 117–24.

Newman, Jay. "Some Tensions in Spinoza's Ethical Theory." *Indian Philosophical Quarterly*, 7 (April 1980), 357–74.

Nichols, Christopher. "Science or Reflection: Habermas on Freud." *Philosophy of the Social Sciences*, 2 (September 1972), 261–70.

Nielsen, Kai. "Enlightenment and Amoralism." *Agora*, 4 (1979–80), 85–89.

Nielsen, Kai. "The Political Relevance of Habermas." *Radical Philosophers' Newsjournal*, 7 (1977), 1–11.

Nielsen, Kai. "Rationality as Emancipation and Enlightenment." *International Studies in Philosophy*, 10 (1978), 33–50.

Nielsen, Kai. "Rationality, Needs and Politics: Remarks on Rationality as Emancipation and Enlightenment." *Cultural Hermeneutics*, 4 (July 1977), 281–308.

Nielsen, Kai. "Technology as Ideology." In *Research in Philosophy and Technology: An Annual Compilation of Research*. Ed. Paul T. Durbin. Vol. 1. Greenwich, CT: Jai, 1978, pp. 131–47.

Nielsen, Kai. "True Needs, Rationality and Emancipation." In *Human Needs and Politics*. Ed. Ross Fitzgerald. Elmsford, NY: Pergamon, 1977, pp. 142–56.

Nordquist, Joan, comp. *Jürgen Habermas (II): A Bibliography*. Santa Cruz, CA: Reference and Research Services, 1991.

Norris, Christopher. *Uncritical Theory: Postmodernism, Intellectuals and the Gulf War*. Amherst: University of Massachusetts Press, 1992.

Northey, Rod. "Conflicting Principles of Canadian Environmental Reform: Trubeck and Habermas v. Law and Economics and the Law Reform Commission." *Dalhousie Law Journal*, 11 (March 1988), 639–62.

Nussbaum, Charles. "Habermas on Speech Acts: A Naturalistic Critique." *Philosophy Today*, 42 (Summer 1998), 126–45.

O'Neill, John, ed. *On Critical Theory*. New York: Seabury, 1976.

Outhwaite, William. *Habermas: A Critical Introduction*. Cambridge, UK: Polity, 1994.

Overend, Tronn. "Enquiry and Ideology: Habermas' Trichotomous Conception of Science." *Philosophy of the Social Sciences*, 8 (March 1978), 1–13.

Overend, Tronn. "Interests, Objectivity and 'The Positivist Dispute' in Social Theory." *Social Praxis: International and Interdisciplinary Quarterly of Social Sciences*, 6 (1979), 69–91.

Overend, Tronn. "The Socialization of Philosophy: Two Monistic Fallacies in Habermas' Critique of Knowledge." *Philosophical and Phenomenological Research*, 38 (1977), 119–24.

Overend, Tronn. "Social Realism and Social Idealism: Two Competing Orientations on the Relation between Theory, Praxis, and Objectivity." *Inquiry*, 21 (Autumn 1978), 271–311.

Palermo, James. "Pedagogy as a Critical Hermeneutic." *Cultural Hermeneutics*, 3 (August 1975), 137–46.

Parsons, Stephen D. "Explaining Technology and Society: The Problem of Nature in Habermas." *Philosophy of the Social Sciences*, 22 (June 1992), 218–30.

Patterson, Dennis M. "Hegel and Postmodernity." *Cardozo Law Review*, 10 (March/April 1989), 1665–72.

Peters, John Durham. "Distrust of Representation: Habermas on the Public Sphere." *Media, Culture and Society*, 15 (October 1993), 541–71.

Pettit, Philip. "Habermas on Truth and Justice." In *Marx and Marxisms*. Ed. G. H. R. Parkinson. New York: Cambridge University Press, 1982, pp. 207–28.

Petryszak, Nicholas. "The Frankfurt School's Theory of Manipulation." *Journal of Communication*, 27 (Summer 1977), 32–40.

Phillips, Kendall R. "The Spaces of Public Dissension: Reconsidering the Public Sphere." *Communication Monographs*, 63 (September 1996), 231–48.

Pietrykowski, Bruce. "Knowledge and Power in Adult Education: Beyond Freire and Habermas." *Adult Education Quarterly*, 46 (Winter 1996), 82–97.

Pilotta, Joseph J. "Pilotta on Habermas." *Quarterly Journal of Speech*, 67 (February 1981), 105–08.

Plaut, Martin. "The Problem of Positivism in the Work of Nicos Poulantzas." *Telos*, 36 (Summer 1978), 159–67.

Plaut, Raymond. "Jürgen Habermas and the Idea of Legitimation Crisis." *European Journal of Political Research*, 10 (1982), 341–52.

Plevin, Arlene. "Green Guilt: An Effective Rhetoric or Rhetoric in Transition?" *Technical Communication Quarterly*, 6 (Spring 1997), 125–39.

Posner, Roland. "Discourse as a Means to Enlightenment: On the Theories of Rational Communication of Habermas and Albert." In *Language in Focus: Foundations, Methods and Systems*. Ed. Asa Kasher. Boston: D. Reidel, 1976, pp. 641–60.

Poster, Mark. "Technology and Culture in Habermas and Baudrillard." *Contemporary Literature*, 22 (1981), 456–76.

Power, Michael K. "Habermas and the Counterfactual Imagination." *Cardozo Law Review*, 17 (March 1996), 1005–25.

Prado, Plinio Walder, Jr. "Argument and Aesthetics: Reflections on Communication and the Differend." *Philosophy Today*, 36 (Winter 1992), 351–66

Press, Andrea L., and Elizabeth R. Cole. "Reconciling Faith and Fact: Pro-Life Women Discuss Media, Science and the Abortion Debate." *Critical Studies in Mass Communication*, 12 (December 1995), 380–402.

Preuß, Ulrich K. "Communicative Power and the Concept of Law." *Cardozo Law Review*, 17 (March 1996), 1179–92.

Pryor, Bob. "Saving the Public Sphere through Rational Discourse." In *Dimensions of Argument: Proceedings of the Second Summer Conference on Argumentation*. Ed. George Ziegelmueller and Jack Rhodes. Annandale, VA: Speech Communication Association, October 15, 1981, pp. 848–64.

Pusey, Michael. *Jürgen Habermas*. London: Tavistock, 1987.

Radnitzky, Gerard. *Contemporary Schools of Metascience*. New York: Humanities, 1970.

Raffel, Stanley. *Habermas, Lyotard and the Concept of Justice*. London: Macmillan, 1992.

Rainey, R. Randall, and William Rehg. "The Marketplace of Ideas, the Public Interest, and Federal Regulation of the Electronic Media: Implications of Habermas' Theory of Democracy." *Southern California Law Review*, 69 (September 1996), 1923–87.

Ramsey, Ramsey Eric. "Communication and Eschatology: The Work of Waiting, an Ethics of Relief, and Areligious Religiosity." *Communication Theory*, 7 (November 1997), 343–61.

Rasmussen, David M. "Advanced Capitalism and Social Theory: Habermas on the Problem of Legitimation." *Cultural Hermeneutics*, 3 (July 1976), 349–66.

Rasmussen, David M. "Jurisprudence and Validity." *Cardozo Law Review*, 17 (March 1996), 1059–82.

Raulet, Gerard. "The Agony of Marxism and the Victory of the Left." *Telos*, 55 (Spring 1983), 163–78.

Ray, L. J. "Habermas, Legitimation, and the State." *Journal for the Theory of Social Behavior*, 8 (July 1978), 149–63.

Rehg, William. "Against Subordination: Morality, Discourse, and Decision in the Legal Theory of Jürgen Habermas." *Cardozo Law Review*, 17 (March 1996), 1147–62.

Reid, Herbert G., and Ernest J. Yanarella. "Critical Political Theory and Moral Development: On Kohlberg, Hampden-Turner, and Habermas." *Theory and Society*, 4 (Winter 1977), 505–41.

Ricoeur, Paul. "Ethics and Culture: Habermas and Gadamer in Dialogue." *Philosophy Today*, 17 (1973), 153–65.

Ricoeur, Paul. *Hermeneutics and Human Sciences: Essays on Language, Action and Interpretation*. Trans. and ed. John B. Thompson. New York: Cambridge University Press, 1981.

Riedmüller, Barbara. "Crisis as Crisis of Legitimation: A Critique of J. Habermas's Concept of a Political Crisis Theory." *International Journal of Politics*, 7 (1977), 83–117.

Roberts, David, ed. *Reconstructing Theory: Gadamer, Habermas, Lubmann*. Victoria, Aust.: Melbourne University Press, 1995.

Roberts, Patricia. "Habermas, *Philosophes*, and Puritans: Rationality and Exclusion in the Dialectical Public Sphere." *Rhetoric Society Quarterly*, 26 (Winter 1996), 47–68.

Roberts, Patricia. "Habermas' Varieties of Communicative Action: Controversy without Combat." *Journal of Advanced Composition*, 11 (Fall 1991), 409–24.

Roblin, Ronald, ed. *The Aesthetics of the Critical Theorists: Studies on Benjamin, Adorno, Marcuse, and Habermas*. Lewiston, NY: Edwin Mellen, 1990.

Rockmore, Tom. "Habermas and the Reconstruction of Historical Materialism." *Journal of Value Inquiry*, 13 (Fall 1979), 195–206.

Rockmore, Tom. *Habermas on Historical Materialism*. Bloomington: Indiana University Press, 1989.

Rockmore, Tom. "Marxian Man." *Monist*, 61 (January 1978), 56–71.

Roderick, Rick. *Habermas and the Foundations of Critical Theory*. New York: St. Martin's, 1986.

Roderick, Rick. "Habermas on Rationality." *Man and World*, 18 (1985), 203–18.

Rodger, John J. "On the Degeneration of the Public Sphere." *Political Studies*, 33 (June 1985), 203–17.

Rorty, Richard. "Epistemological Behaviorism and the De-Transcendentalization of Analytic Philosophy." *Neue Hefte für Philosophie*, 14 (1978), 115–42.

Rosenfeld, Michel. "Can Rights, Democracy, and Justice be Reconciled through Discourse Theory? Reflections on Habermas's Proceduralist Paradigm of Law." *Cardozo Law Review*, 17 (March 1996), 791–824.

Rossvaer, Viggo. *Kant's Moral Philosophy: An Interpretation of the Categorical Imperative*. Oslo, Norw. Universiteforlag, 1979.

Rotenstreich, Nathan. "Conservatism and Traditionalism." *Praxis International*, 3 (January 1984), 412–22.

Roth, Mike. "With Marx against Marx? Histomat, and Histomat2: An Alternative to Jurgen Habermas' Theses towards the Reconstruction of Historical Materialism." Trans. Michael Eldred. *Thesis Eleven*, 3 (1982), 135–47.

Rule, James B. *Insight and Social Betterment: A Preface to Applied Social Science*. New York: Oxford University Press, 1978.

Rumberg, Dirk. "Literature on the German 'Historikerstreit.'" *Millennium: Journal of International Studies*, 17 (1988), 351–56.

Sabia, Daniel R., Jr., and Jerald Wallulis, eds. *Changing Social Science: Critical Theory and Other Critical Perspectives*. Albany: State University of New York Press, 1983.

Sajó, András. "Constitutional Adjudication in Light of Discourse Theory." *Cardozo Law Review*, 17 (March 1996), 1193–1229.

Schlink, Bernhard. "The Dynamics of Constitutional Adjudication." *Cardozo Law Review*, 17 (March 1996), 1231–38.

Schmidt, James. "Jürgen Habermas and the Difficulties of Enlightenment." *Social Research*, 49 (Spring 1982), 181–208.

Schmidt, James. "Offensive Critical Theory? Reply to Honneth." *Telos*, 39 (Spring 1979), 62–70.

Schmidt, James. "Praxis and Temporality: Karel Kosik's Political Theory." *Telos*, 33 (Fall 1977), 71–84.

Schrag, Calvin O. *Communicative Rhetoric and the Claims of Reason*. Evanston, IL: School of Speech, Northwestern University, 1989.

Schroyer, Trent. *The Critique of Domination: The Origins and Development of Critical Theory*. New York: George Braziller, 1973.

Schroyer, Trent. "Critique of the Instrumental Interest in Nature." *Social Research*, 50 (Spring 1983), 158–84.

Schroyer, Trent. "The Dialectical Foundations of Critical Theory: Jürgen Habermas' Metatheoretical Investigations." *Telos*, 12 (Summer 1972), 93–114.

Schroyer, Trent. "Marx and Habermas." *Continuum*, 8 (1970), 52–64.

Schroyer, Trent. "Methodological Grounds for a Reflexive Science." *Contemporary Crises*, 8 (January 1984), 19–32.

Schroyer, Trent. "The Re-politicization of the Relations of Production: An Interpretation of Jürgen Habermas' Analytic Theory of Late Capitalist Development." *New German Critique*, 5 (Spring 1975), 107–28.

Schwartz, Ronald David. "Habermas and the Politics of Discourse." *Canadian Journal of Political and Social Theory*, 5 (Winter/Spring 1981), 45–68.

Schweickart, Patrocinio. "'What Are We Doing, Really?'—Feminist Criticism and the Problem of Theory." *Canadian Journal of Political and Social Theory*, 9 (Winter 1985), 148–64.

Scott, John. "On the Classification and Synthesis of Sociological Knowledge." *Jewish Journal of Sociology*, 18 (December 1976), 155–64.

Scott, John P. "Critical Social Theory: An Introduction and Critique." *British Journal of Sociology*, 29 (March 1978), 1–21.

Sennat, Julius. *Habermas and Marxism: An Appraisal*. Beverly Hills, CA: Sage, 1979.

Sewart, John J. "Critical Theory and the Critique of Conservative Method." *American Sociologist*, 13 (February 1978), 15–22.

Shapiro, H. Svi. "Habermas, O'Connor, and Wolfe, and the Crisis of the Welfare-Capitalist State: Conservative Politics and the Roots of Educational Policy in the 1980s." *Educational Theory*, 33 (Summer/Fall 1983), 135–47.

Shapiro, Jeremy J. "The Dialectic of Theory and Practice in the Age of Technological Rationality: Herbert Marcuse and Jürgen Habermas." In *Unknown Dimension: European Marxism since Lenin*. Ed. Dick Howard and Karl E. Klare. New York: Basic, 1972, pp. 276–303.

Shapiro, Jeremy J. "From Marcuse to Habermas." *Continuum*, 8 (1970), 65–76.

Shapiro, Jeremy J. "Reply to Miller's Review of Habermas' Legitimation Crisis." *Telos*, 27 (Spring 1976), 170–76.

Siebert, Rudolf J. "Communication without Domination." In *Communication in the Church*. Ed. Gregory Baum and Andrew Greeley. New York: Seabury, 1978, pp. 81–94.

Siebert, Rudolf J. *The Critical Theory of Religion; The Frankfurt School: From Universal Pragmatic to Political Theology*. New York: Mouton, 1985.

Siebert, Rudolf J. *From Critical Theory of Society to Theology of Communicative Praxis*. Washington, DC: University Press of America, 1979.

Silvers, Stuart. "The Critical Theory of Science." *Zeitschrift für Allgemein Wissenschafts Theorie*, 4 (1973), 108–32.

Skjei, Erling. "A Comment on Performative, Subject, and Proposition in Habermas's Theory of Communication." *Inquiry*, 28 (March 1985), 87–122.

Sluga, Hans. *The Break. Habermas, Heidegger, and the Nazis*. Ed. Christopher Ocker. San Anselmo, CA: Center for Hermeneutical Studies, 1992.

Smart, Barry. *Sociology, Phenomenology and Marxian Analysis: A Critical Discussion of the Theory and Practice of a Science of Society*. London: Routledge and Kegan Paul, 1976.

Smith, A. Anthony. "Two Theories of Historical Materialism: G. A. Cohen and Jürgen Habermas." *Theory and Society*, 13 (July 1984), 513–40.

Smith, M. B. "Dialectical Social-Psychology: Comments on a Symposium." *Personality and Social Psychology Bulletin*, 3 (Fall 1977), 719–24.

Smith, Tony. *The Role of Ethics in Social Theory: Essays from a Habermasian Perspective*. Albany: State University of New York Press, 1991.

Smith, Tony. "The Scope of the Social Sciences in Weber and Habermas." *Philosophy and Social Criticism*, 8 (Spring 1981), 69–83.

Snedeker, George. "Western Marxism and the Problem of History. " *Psychology and Social Theory*, 4 (1984), 41–50.

Solum, Lawrence Byard. "Freedom of Communicative Action: A Theory of the First Amendment Freedom of Speech." *Northwestern University Law Review*, 83 (Fall 1988/Winter 1989), 54–135.

Sollner, Alfons. "Anxiety and Politics: Neo-Conservatism and Critical Theory." *Telos*, 60 (Summer 1984), 129–31.

Stockman, Norman. "Habermas, Marcuse and the *Aufhebung* of Science and Technology." *Philosophy of the Social Sciences*, 8 (March 1978), 15–35.

Sullivan, William M. "Communication and the Recovery of Meaning: An Interpretation of Habermas." *International Philosophical Quarterly*, 18 (March 1978), 69–86.

Sullivan, William M. "Two Options in Modern Social Theory: Habermas and Whitehead." *International Philosophical Quarterly*, 15 (March 1975), 83–98.

Sumner, Colin. "The Rule of Law and Civil Rights in Contemporary Marxist Theory." *Kapitalistate*, 9 (1981), 63–91.

Taylor, Laurie. "Freud." *New Society*, 42 (December 8, 1977), 515–18.

Teigas, Demetrius. *Knowledge and Hermeneutic Understanding: A Study of the Habermas-Gadamer Debate*. Cranbury, NJ: Associated University Presses, 1995.

Teubner, Gunther. "*De Collisione Discursuum*: Communicative Rationalities in Law, Morality, and Politics." *Cardozo Law Review*, 17 (March 1996), 901–18.

Teubner, Gunther. "Substantive and Reflexive Elements in Modern Law." *Law & Society Review*, 17 (1983), 239–85.

Therborn, Goran. "Jürgen Habermas: A New Eclecticism." *New Left Review*, 67 (May/June 1971), 69–83.

Thompson, John B. *Critical Hermeneutics: A Study in the Thought of Paul Ricoeur and Jürgen Habermas*. Cambridge: Cambridge University Press, 1981.

Thompson, John B. "Ideology and the Critique of Domination II." *Canadian Journal of Political and Social Theory*, 8 (Winter/Spring 1984), 179–96.

Thompson, John B., and David Held. *Habermas: Critical Debates*. Cambridge: MIT Press, 1982.

Torpey, J. "Ethics and Critical Theory: From Horkheimer to Habermas." *Telos*, 69 (Fall 1986), 68–84.

Tranöy, Kurt Erik. "The Foundations of Cognitive Activity: An Historical and Systematic Sketch." *Inquiry*, 19 (Summer 1976), 131–50.

Turner, Bryan S., ed. *Theories of Modernity and Postmodernity*. Newbury Park, CA: Sage, 1990.

Turski, George. "Some Considerations on Intersubjectivity and Language." *Gnosis*, 1 (Spring 1979), 29–44.

Tymieniecka, Anna-Teresa, and Calvin O. Schrag, eds. *Foundations of Morality, Human Rights, and the Human Sciences: Phenomenology in a Foundational Dialogue with the Human Sciences*. London: D. Reidel, 1983.

van den Berg, Axel. "Critical Theory: Is There Still Hope?" *American Journal of Sociology*, 86 (November 1980), 449–78.

Van Hooft, Stan. "Habermas' Communicative Ethics." *Social Praxis: International and Interdisciplinary Quarterly of Social Sciences*, 4 (1976–77), 147–75.

van Steenbergen, Bart, ed. *The Condition of Citizenship*. London: Sage, 1994.

Verene, Donald Phillip, ed. *Hegel's Social and Political Thought: The Philosophy of Objective Spirit*. [Atlantic Highlands], NJ: Humanities, 1980.

Wallulis, Jerald. *The Hermeneutics of Life History: Personal Achievement and History in Gadamer, Habermas, and Erikson*. Evanston, IL: Northwestern University Press, 1990.

Walsh, Thomas G. "Enlightenment, Counter-Enlightenment, and Beyond." *International Social Science Review*, 2 (Spring 1993), 60–71.

Ware, Robert X. "Habermas's Evolutions." *Canadian Journal of Philosophy*, 12 (September 1982), 591–620.

Weiner, Richard R. "Retrieving Civil Society in a Postmodern Epoch." *Social Science Journal*, 28 (1991), 307–23.

Wellmer, Albrecht. *Critical Theory of Society*. New York: Herder and Herder, 1971.

Wellmer, Albrecht. "Models of Freedom in the Modern World." *Philosophical Forum*, 21 (Fall/Winter 1989–90), 227–52.

Wellmer, Albrecht. "Reason, Utopia, and the Dialectic of Enlightenment." *Praxis International*, 3 (July 1983), 83–107.

Wenzel, Joseph W. "Habermas' Ideal Speech Situation: Some Critical Questions." In *Dimensions of Argument: Proceedings of the Second Summer Conference on Argumentation*. Ed. George Ziegelmueller and Jack Rhodes. Annandale, VA: Speech Communication Association, October 15, 1981, pp. 940–54.

Wenzel, Joseph W. "Jürgen Habermas and the Dialectical Perspective on Argumentation." *Journal of the American Forensic Association*, 16 (Fall 1979), 83–94.

White, Stephen K., ed. *The Cambridge Companion to Habermas*. New York: Cambridge University Press, 1995.

White, Stephen K. "Habermas' Communicative Ethics and the Development of Moral Consciousness." *Cultural Hermeneutics*, 2 (1984), 25–47.

White, Stephen K. "On the Normative Structure of Action: Gewirth and Habermas." *Review of Politics*, 44 (April 1982), 282–301.

White, Stephen K. "Reason and Authority in Habermas: A Critique of the Critics." *American Political Science Review*, 74 (December 1980), 1007–17.

White, Stephen K. *The Recent Work of Jürgen Habermas: Reason, Justice and Modernity*. New York: Cambridge University Press, 1988.

Whitebook, Joel. "The Problem of Nature in Habermas." *Telos*, 40 (Summer 1979), 41–69.

Wilbur, Ken. *A Sociable God: A Brief Introduction to a Transcendental Sociology*. San Francisco: McGraw-Hill, 1983.

Wilby, Peter. "Habermas and the Language of the Modern State." *New Society*, 47 (March 22, 1979), 667–69.

Wilson, H. T. "The Meaning and Significance of 'Empirical Method' for the Critical Theory of Society." *Canadian Journal of Political and Social Theory*, 3 (Fall 1979), 57–68.

Wilson, H. T. "The Poverty of Sociology: 'Society' as Concept and Object in Sociological Theory." *Philosophy of the Social Sciences*, 8 (June 1978), 187–204.

Wilson, H. T. "Response to Ray." *Philosophy of the Social Sciences*, 11 (March 1981), 45–48.

Winfield, Richard. "The Dilemma of Labor." *Telos*, 24 (Summer 1975), 115–28.

Winters, Lawrence E. "Habermas' Theory of Truth and Its Centrality in His Critical Project." *Graduate Faculty Philosophical Journal*, 3 (Fall/Winter 1973), 1–21.

Wisman, Jon D. "Toward a Humanist Reconstruction of Economic Science." *Journal of Economic Issues*, 13 (March 1979), 19–48.

Wolff, Janet. "Hermeneutics and the Critique of Ideology." *Sociological Review*, 23 (November 1975), 811–28.

Wood, Allen W. "Habermas' Defense of Rationalism." *New German Critique*, 35 (Spring/Summer 1985), 145–64.

Wuthnow, Robert, James Davison Hunter, Albert Bergesen, and Edith Kurzweil. *Cultural Analysis: The Work of Peter L. Berger, Mary Douglas, Michel Foucault, and Jürgen Habermas*. Boston: Routledge and Kegan Paul, 1984.

Young, Iris M. "Toward a Critical Theory of Justice." *Social Theory and Practice*, 7 (Fall 1981), 279–302.

Young, Robert E. *A Critical Theory of Education: Habermas and Our Children's Future*. New York: Harvester Wheatsheaf, 1989.

Zimmerman, Rolf. "Emancipation and Rationality: Foundational Problems in the Theories of Marx and Habermas" *Ratio*, 26 (December 1984), 143–65.

Works about bell hooks

Bartlett, Alison. "A Passionate Subject: Representations of Desire in Feminist Pedagogy." *Gender and Education*, 10 (March 1998), 85–92.

Bérubé, Michael. "Public Academy." *New Yorker*, 70 (January 9, 1995), 73–80.

Birmingham, Elizabeth. "Reframing the Ruins: Pruitt-Igoe, Structural Racism, and African American Rhetoric as a Space for Cultural Critique." *Western Journal of Communication*, 63 (Summer 1999), 291–309.

Brown, Larry, "Politics, Theory, and the Role of the Black Intellectual." *Critical Survey*, 9 (1997), 121–37.

Crenshaw, Carrie. "Resisting Whiteness' Rhetorical Silence." *Western Journal of Communication*, 61 (Summer 1997), 253–78.

Dash, Paul. "Thoughts on a Relevant Art Curriculum for the 21st Century." *Journal of Art and Design Education*, 18 (1999), 123–27.

Dieckmann, Lara E. "Hooks, Bell." In *Significant Contemporary American Feminists: A Biographical Sourcebook*. Westport, CT: Greenwood, 1999, pp. 125–32.

Edelstein, Marilyn. "Resisting Postmodernism; or, 'A Postmodernism of Resistance: Bell Hooks and the Theory Debates.'" In *Other Sisterhoods: Literary Theory and U. S. Women of Color*. Ed. Sandra Kumamoto Stanley. Urbana: University of Illinois Press, 1998, pp. 86–118.

Florence, Namulundah. *Bell Hooks' Engaged Pedagogy: A Transgressive Education for Critical Consciousness*. Westport, CT: Bergin and Garvey, 1998.

Fox, Tom. "Literacy and Activism: A Response to Bell Hooks." *Journal of Advanced Composition*, 14 (Fall 1994), 564–70.

Goldzwig, Steven R. "Multiculturalism, Rhetoric and the Twenty-first Century." *Southern Communication Journal*, 63 (Summer 1998), 273–90.

Grünell, Marianne, and Sawitri Saharson. "State of the Art: Bell Hooks and Nira Yuval-Davis on Race, Ethnicity, Class and Gender." *European Journal of Women's Studies*, 6 (1999), 203–18.

Hasseler, Terri A. "Socially Responsible Rage: 'Postcolonial' Feminism, Writing, and the Classroom." *Feminist Teacher*, 12 (1999), 213–22.

Henry, JoAnne F., and Carolyn Reyes. "Talking Back: A Conversation between Third World Diva Girls." *Journal of Women and Religion*, 12 (Winter 1993), 28–32.

"Hooks, Bell." In *Current Biography Yearbook*. Ed. Judith Graham. New York: H. W. Wilson, 1995, pp. 253–56.

"Hooks, Bell." In *World Authors*. Ed. Clifford Thompson. New York: H. W. Wilson, 1999, pp. 125–32.

Jones, Lisa. "Rebel without a Pause." *Village Voice*, 37 (October 13, 1992), literary supplement, 10.

Leatherman, Courtney. "A Name for Herself." *Chronicle of Higher Education*, 41 (May 19, 1995), A22–24.

Martin, Joan M. "The Notion of Difference for Emerging Womanist Ethics: The Writings of Audre Lorde and Bell Hooks." *Journal of Feminist Studies in Religion*, 9 (Fall 1993), 139–51.

Meyer, Karen. "Reflections on Being Female in School Science: Toward a Praxis of Teaching Science." *Journal of Research in Science Teaching*, 35 (1998), 463–71.

Middleton, Joyce Irene. "Bell Hooks on Literacy and Teaching: A Response." *Journal of Advanced Composition*, 14 (Fall 1994), 559–64.

Olson, Lester C. "On the Margins of Rhetoric: Audre Lorde Transforming Silence into Language and Action." *Quarterly Journal of Speech*, 83 (February 1997), 49–70.

Reed, Adolph. "What Are the Drums Saying, Booker?: The Current Crisis of the Black Intellectual." *Village Voice*, 40 (April 11, 1995), 31–36.

Shugart, Helene A. "Counterhegemonic Acts: Appropriation as a Feminist Rhetorical Strategy." *Quarterly Journal of Speech*, 83 (May 1997), 210–29.

Spayde, Jon, and Laura Shackleford. "100 Visionaries." *Utne Reader*, 67 (January/February 1995), 54–81.

Wander, Philip. "Marxism, Post-Colonialism, and Rhetorical Contextualization." *Quarterly Journal of Speech*, 82 (November 1996), 402–26.

Works about Jean Baudrillard

Adair, Gilbert. *The Postmodernist Always Rings Twice: Reflections on Culture in the 90s*. London: Fourth Estate, 1992.

Ballard, J. G. "In Response to Jean Baudrillard: A Response to the Invitation to Respond." *Science-Fiction Studies*, 18 (November 1991), 329.

Bauman, Zygmunt. *Intimations of Postmodernity*. New York: Routledge, 1992, pp. 149–55.

Best, Steven, and Douglas Kellner. *Postmodern Theory: Critical Interrogations*. New York: Guilford, 1991.

Bogard, William. "Closing Down the Social: Baudrillard's Challenge to Contemporary Sociology." *Sociological Theory*, 8 (Spring 1990), 1–15.

Bogard, William. "Sociology in the Absence of the Social: The Significance of Baudrillard for Contemporary Thought." *Philosophy and Social Criticism*, 13 (1987), 227–42.

Bogue, Ronald L. "Pasta, Barthes, and Baudrillard." *Bucknell Review*, 27 (1982), 125–39.

Boyne, Roy, and Ali Rattansi, eds. *Postmodernism and Society*. New York: St. Martin's, 1990.

Butler, Rex. *Jean Baudrillard: The Defence of the Real*. Thousand Oaks, CA: Sage, 1999.

Byerly, Carolyn M., and Catherine A. Warren. "At the Margins of Center: Organized Protest in the Newsroom." *Critical Studies in Mass Communication*, 13 (March 1996), 1–23.

Callens, Johan. "Diverting the Integrated Spectacle of War: Sam Shepard's *States of Shock*." *Text and Performance Quarterly*, 20 (July 2000), 290–306.

Carrier, David. "Baudrillard as Philosopher or, The End of Abstract Painting." *Arts Magazine*, 63 (September 1988), 52–60.

Chang, Briankle G. "Mass, Media, Mass Mediation: Jean Baudrillard's Implosive Critique of Modern Mass-Mediated Culture." *Current Perspectives in Social Theory*, 7 (1986), 157–81.

Chang, Briankle G. "World and/or Sign: Toward a Semiotic Phenomenology of the Modern Life-World." *Human Studies*, 10 (October 1987), 311–31.

Chapman, Rowena, and Jonathan Rutherford, eds. *Male Order: Unwrapping Masculinity*. London: Lawrence & Wishart, 1988.

Cheal, David. "Social Construction of Consumption." *International Sociology*, 5 (September 1990), 299–317.

Collins, James. "Postmodernism and Cultural Practice: Redefining the Parameters." *Screen*, 28 (Spring 1987), 11–24.

Csicsery-Ronay, Jr., Istvan. "The SF of Theory: Baudrillard and Haraway." *Science-Fiction Studies*, 18 (November 1991), 387–404.

D'Amico, Robert. "Desire and the Commodity Form." *Telos*, 35 (Spring 1978), 88–122.

Denzin, Norman K. *Blue Velvet*: Postmodern Contradictions." *Theory, Culture & Society*, 5 (1988), 461–73.

Denzin, Norman K. *Images of Postmodern Society: Social Theory and Contemporary Cinema*. Newbury Park, CA: Sage, 1991, pp. 29–52.

Denzin, Norman K. "On Semiotics and Symbolic Interactionism." *Symbolic Interaction*, 10 (Spring 1987), 1–19.

Denzin, Norman K. *"Paris, Texas* and Baudrillard on America." *Theory, Culture & Society*, 8 (1991), 121–33.

De Vos, Luk, ed. *Just the Other Day: Essays on the Suture of the Future*. Antwerp, Belg.: Uitgeverij EXA, 1985.

Faurschou, Gail. "Fashion and the Cultural Logic of Postmodernity." *Canadian Journal of Political and Social Theory*, 11 (1987), 68–82.

Featherstone, Mike. "Consumer Culture: An Introduction." *Theory, Culture & Society*, 1 (1983), 4–9.

Fekete, John, ed. *Life After Postmodernism: Essays on Value and Culture*. New York: St. Martin's, 1987.

Fekete, John, ed. *The Structural Allegory: Reconstructive Encounters with the New French Thought*. Minneapolis: University of Minnesota Press, 1984.

Frankovits, André, ed. *Seduced and Abandoned: The Baudrillard Scene*. New York: Semiotext(e), 1984.

Gablik, Suzi. "Dancing with Baudrillard." *Art in America*, 76 (June 1988), 27, 29.

Gallop, Jane. "French Theory and the Seduction of Feminism." In *Men in Feminism*. Ed. Alice Jardine and Paul Smith. New York: Methuen, 1987, pp. 111–15.

Gane, Mike. *Baudrillard: Critical and Fatal Theory*. New York: Routledge, 1991.

Gane, Mike. *Baudrillard's Bestiary: Baudrillard and Culture*. New York: Routledge, 1991.

Gane, Mike. "Ironies of Postmodernism: Fate of Baudrillard's Fatalism." *Economy and Society*, 19 (August 1990), 314–33.

Gane, Mike. "Radical Theory: Baudrillard and Vulnerability." *Theory, Culture & Society*, 12 (November 1995), 109–23.

Genosko, Gary. *Baudrillard and Signs: Signification Ablaze*. New York: Routledge, 1994.

Giradin, Jean-Claude. "Toward a Politics of Signs: Reading Baudrillard." *Telos*, 20 (Summer 1974), 127–37.

Goodnight, G. Thomas. "The Firm, the Park and the University: Fear and Trembling on the Postmodern Trail." *Quarterly Journal of Speech*, 81 (August 1995), 267–90.

Gottdiener, M. *Postmodern Semiotics: Material Culture and the Forms of Postmodern Life*. Cambridge, MA: Blackwell, 1995.

Griffin, David Ray, ed. *Sacred Interconnections: Postmodern Spirituality, Political Economy, and Art*. Albany: State University of New York Press, 1990.

Halley, Peter. "The Crisis in Geometry." *Arts Magazine*, 58 (Summer 1984), 111–15.

Harland, Richard. *Superstructuralism: The Philosophy of Structuralism and Post-Structuralism*. New York: Methuen, 1987.

Harms, John B., and David R. Dickens. "Postmodern Media Studies: Analysis or Symptom?" *Critical Studies in Mass Communication*, 13 (September 1996), 210–27.

Hayles, N. Katherine. "In Response to Jean Baudrillard: The Borders of Madness." *Science-Fiction Studies*, 18 (November 1991), 321–23.

Hebdige, Dick. "Banalarama, or Can Pop Save us All?" *New Statesman & Society*, 1 (December 9, 1988), 29–32.

Horrocks, Chris, and Zoran Jevtic. *Introducing Baudrillard*. Ed. Richard Appignanesi. New York: Totem, 1996.

Howe, Stephen. "Where Dreams Come True." *New Statesman & Society*, 1 (November 11, 1988), 39.

Hunter, Dianne, ed. *Seduction and Theory*. Urbana: University of Illinois Press, 1989.

Jones, John Paul III, Wolfgang Natter, and Theodore R. Schatzki, eds. *Postmodern Contentions: Epochs, Politics, Space*. New York: Guilford, 1993.

Kellner, Douglas, ed. *Baudrillard: A Critical Reader*. Cambridge, MA: Blackwell, 1994.

Kellner, Douglas. "Baudrillard, Semiurgy and Death." *Theory, Culture & Society*, 4 (1987), 125–46.

Kellner, Douglas. "Boundaries and Borderlines: Reflections on Jean Baudrillard and Critical Theory." *Current Perspectives in Social Theory*, 9 (1989), 5–22.

Kellner, Douglas. *Jean Baudrillard: From Marxism to Postmodernism and Beyond*. Stanford: Stanford University Press, 1989.

Kellner, Douglas. "Postmodernism as Social Theory: Some Challenges and Problems." *Theory, Culture & Society*, 5 (June 1988), 239–69.

Kraidy, Marwan M. "The Global, the Local, and the Hybrid: A Native Ethnography of Glocalization." *Critical Studies in Mass Communication*, 16 (December 1999), 456–76.

Kroker, Arthur. *The Possessed Individual: Technology and Postmodernity*. London: New World Perspectives, 1992.

Kroker, Arthur, and Marilouise Kroker, eds. *Ideology and Power in the Age of Lenin in Ruins*. New York: St. Martin's, 1991.

Kuftinec, Sonja. "[Walking through a] Ghost Town: Cultural Hauntologie in Mostar, Bosnia-Herzegovina or Mostar: A Performance Review." *Text and Performance Quarterly*, 18 (April 1998), 81–95.

Landon, Brooks. "In Response to Jean Baudrillard: Responding to the Killer B's." *Science-Fiction Studies*, 18 (November 1991), 326–27.

Lash, Scott. "Dead Symbols: An Introduction." *Theory, Culture & Society*, 12 (November 1995), 71–78.

Lechte, John. *Fifty Key Contemporary Thinkers from Structuralism to Postmodernity*. New York: Routledge, 1994.

Levin, Charles. "Baudrillard: Critical Theory and Psychoanalysis." *Canadian Journal of Political and Social Theory*, 8 (Spring 1984), 35–52.

Levin, Charles. "Carnal Knowledge of Aesthetic States: The Infantile Body, the Sign, and the Postmortemist Condition." *Canadian Journal of Political and Social Theory*, 11 (1987), 90–110.

Levin, Charles. *Jean Baudrillard: A Study in Cultural Metaphysics*. New York: Prentice Hall, 1996.

Linker, Kate. "From Imitation to the Copy to Just Effect: On Reading Jean Baudrillard." *ArtForum*, 22 (April 1984), 44–47.

Linker, Kate. "On Artificiality." *Flash Art*, 111 (March 1983), 33–35.

Love, Lisa L., and Nathaniel Kohn. "This, That, and the Other: Fraught Possibilities of the Souvenir." *Text and Performance Quarterly*, 21 (January 2001), 47–63.

Luke, Timothy. "Jean Baudrillard and the Political Economy of the Sign." *Art Papers*, 10 (January/February 1986), 22–25.

Luke, Timothy W. "Power and Politics in Hyperreality: The Critical Project of Jean Baudrillard." *Social Science Journal*, 28 (1991), 347–67.

Luke, Timothy W. "Regulating the Haven in a Heartless World: The State and Family under Advanced Capitalism." *New Political Science*, 7 (Fall 1981), 51–74.

MacDonald, Erik. "Max Headroom: CCCCatching the Wave." *Jump Cut*, 34 (March 1989), 5–11.

Mathy, Jean-Philippe. *Extrême Occident: French Intellectuals and America*. Chicago: University of Chicago Press, 1993.

McKerrow, Raymie E. "Space and Time in the Postmodern Polity." *Western Journal of Communication*, 63 (Summer 1999), 271–90.

Mitchell, Gordon R. "Placebo Defense: Operation Desert Mirage? The Rhetoric of Patriot Missile Accuracy in the 1991 Persian Gulf War." *Quarterly Journal of Speech*, 86 (May 2000), 121–45.

Morris, Meaghan. "Banality in Cultural Studies." *Discourse*, 10 (Spring/Summer 1978), 3–29.

Murray, Patrick, and Jeanne A. Schuler. "Post-Marxism in a French Context." *History of European Ideas*, 9 (1988), 321–34.

Naremore, James, and Patrick Brantlinger. *Modernity and Mass Culture*. Bloomington: Indiana University Press, 1991.

Nordquist, Joan, comp. *Jean Baudrillard: A Bibliography*. Santa Cruz, CA: Reference and Research Services, 1991.

Norris, Christopher. *Uncritical Theory: Postmodernism, Intellectuals, and the Gulf War*. Amherst: University of Massachusetts Press, 1992.

Pefanis, Julian. *Heterology and the Postmodern: Bataille, Baudrillard, and Lyotard*. Durham, NC: Duke University Press, 1991.

Phillips, Kendall R. "A Rhetoric of Controversy." *Western Journal of Communication*, 63 (Fall 1990), 488–510.

Piper, Alison. "Some Have Credit Cards and Others Have Giro Cheques: 'Individuals' and 'People' as Lifelong Learners in Late Modernity." *Discourse and Society*, 11 (October 2000), 515–42.

Porush, David. "In Response to Jean Baudrillard: The Architextuality of Transcendence." *Science-Fiction Studies*, 18 (November 1991), 323–25.

Poster, Mark. "Technology and Culture in Habermas and Baudrillard." *Contemporary Literature*, 22 (1981), 456–76.

Pyke, Steve. *Philosophers*. 2nd ed. London: Zelda Cheatle, 1995.

Roderick, Rick. "Beyond a Boundary: Baudrillard and New Critical Theory." *Current Perspectives in Social Theory*, 9 (1989), 3–4.

Rojek, Chris. "Baudrillard and Leisure." *Leisure Studies*, 9 (January 1990), 7–20.

Rojek, Chris, and Bryan S. Turner, eds. *Forget Baudrillard?* New York: Routledge, 1993.

Sandywell, Barry. "Forget Baudrillard?" *Theory, Culture & Society*, 12 (November 1995), 125–52.

Schwichtenberg, Cathy. "Madonna's Postmodern Feminism: Bringing the Margins to the Center." *Southern Communication Journal*, 57 (Winter 1992), 120–31.

Simons, Herbert W., and Michael Billig, eds. *After Postmodernism: Reconstructing Ideology Critique*. Thousand Oaks, CA: Sage, 1994.

Singer, Brian. "Baudrillard's Seduction." *Canadian Journal of Political and Social Theory*, 15 (1991), 139–51.

Sobchak, Vivian. "In Response to Jean Baudrillard: Baudrillard's Obscenity." *Science-Fiction Studies*, 18 (November 1991), 327–29.

Stearns, William, and William Chaloupka, eds. *Jean Baudrillard: The Disappearance of Art and Politics*. New York: St. Martin's, 1992.

Turner, Bryan S., ed. *Theories of Modernity and Postmodernity*. Newbury Park, CA: Sage, 1990.

Valente, Joseph. "Hall of Mirrors: Baudrillard on Marx." *Diacritics*, 15 (Summer 1985), 54–65.

Vine, Richard. "The 'Ecstasy' of Jean Baudrillard." *The New Criterion*, 7 (May 1989), 39–48.

Wernick, Andrew. "Sign and Commodity: Aspects of the Cultural Dynamic of Advanced Capitalism." *Canadian Journal of Political and Social Theory*, 15 (1991), 68–90.

Wilcox, Leonard. "Baudrillard, Delillo's *White Noise*, and the End of Heroic Narrative." *Contemporary Literature*, 32 (Fall 1991), 346–65.

Zurbrugg, Nicholas. "Baudrillard, Modernism, and Postmodernism." *Economy and Society*, 22 (November 1993), 482–500.

Zurbrugg, Nicholas. "Postmodernity, *Métaphore manquée*, and the Myth of the Trans-avant-garde." *Leonardo*, 21 (1988), 61–70.

Works about Michel Foucault

Albury, W. R., and D. R. Oldroyd. "From Renaissance Mineral Studies to Historical Geology, in the Light of Michel Foucault's *The Order of Things*." *British Journal for the History of Science*, 10 (November 1977), 187–215.

Allen, Robert van Roden. "Discourse and Sexuality: Toward the Texture of Eros." *Semiotext(e)*, 4 (1981), 249–58.

Almansi, Guido. "Foucault and Magritte." *History of European Ideas*, 3 (1982), 303–09.

Appignanesi, Lisa, ed. *Ideas from France: The Legacy of French Theory: ICA Documents*. London: Free Association, 1989.

Arac, Jonathan, ed. *After Foucault: Humanistic Knowledge, Postmodern Challenges*. New Brunswick: Rutgers University Press, 1988.

Arac, Jonathan. "Foucault and Central Europe: A Polemical Speculation." *Boundary 2*, 21 (Fall 1994), 197–210.

Arac, Jonathan. "The Function of Foucault at the Present Time." *Humanities in Society*, 3 (Winter 1980), 73–86.

Archambault, Paul J. "Michel Foucault's Last Discourse on Language." *Papers on Language and Literature*, 21 (Fall 1985), 433–42.

Armstrong, Timothy J., trans. and ed. *Michel Foucault: Philosopher*. New York: Harvester Wheatsheaf, 1992.

Aron, Harry. "Wittgenstein's Impact on Foucault." In *Wittgenstein and His Impact on Contemporary Thought*. Proceedings of the Second International Wittgenstein Symposium. Ed. Elisabeth Leinfellner, Werner Leinfellner, Hal Berghel, and Adolf Hiffiner. Vienna, Austria: Hölder, Pichler, Tempsky, 1978, pp. 58–60.

Aronowitz, Stanley. "History as Disruption." *Humanities in Society*, 2 (Spring 1979), 125–52.

Ashenden, Samantha, and David Owen, eds. *Foucault contra Habermas: Recasting the Dialogue between Genealogy and Critical Theory*. Thousand Oaks, CA: Sage, 1999.

Bahr, Ehrhard. "In Defense of Enlightenment: Foucault and Habermas." *German Studies Review*, 11 (1988), 97–109.

Balbus, Isaac D. "Disciplining Women: Michel Foucault and the Power of Feminist Discourse." *Praxis International*, 5 (January 4, 1986), 466–83.

Bannet, Eve Tavor. *Structuralism and the Logic of Dissent: Barthes, Derrida, Foucault, Lacan.* Urbana: University of Illinois Press, 1989.

Barker, James R., and George Cheney. "The Concept and the Practices of Discipline in Contemporary Organizational Life." *Communication Monographs,* 61 (March 1994), 19–43.

Barthes, Roland. *Critical Essays.* Trans. Richard Howard. Evanston, IL: Northwestern University Press, 1972.

Baudrillard, Jean. *Forget Foucault and Forget Baudrillard: An Interview with Sylvère Lotringer.* New York: Semiotext(e), 1987.

Baudrillard, Jean. "Forgetting Foucault." Trans. Nicole Dufresne. *Humanities in Society,* 3 (Winter 1980), 87–111.

Bennington, Geoff P. "Cogito Incognito: Foucault's 'My Body, This Paper, This Fire.'" *Oxford Literary Review,* 4 (Autumn 1979), 5–8.

Berlin, James. "Revisionary History: The Dialectical Method." *Pre/Text,* 8 (Spring/ Summer 1987), 47–61.

Bernauer, James. "Feature Review-Article: Foucault's Political Analysis." *IPQ: International Philosophical Quarterly,* 22 (March 1982), 87–95.

Bernauer, James W. "Michel Foucault's Ecstatic Thinking." *Philosophy and Social Criticism,* 12 (1987), 156–93.

Bernauer, James W. *Michel Foucault's Force of Flight: Toward an Ethics for Thought.* Atlantic Highlands, NJ: Humanities, 1990.

Bernauer, James, and David Rasmussen, eds. *The Final Foucault.* Cambridge: MIT Press, 1988.

Bersani, Leo. "The Subject of Power." *Diacritics,* 7 (September 1977), 2–21.

Biemel, Walter. "Philosophy and Art." *Man and World,* 12 (1979), 267–83.

Blair, Carole. "The Statement: Foundation of Foucault's Historical Criticism." *Western Journal of Speech Communication,* 51 (Fall 1987), 364–83.

Blair, Carole, and Martha Cooper. "The Humanist Turn in Foucault's Rhetoric of Inquiry." *Quarterly Journal of Speech,* 73 (May 1987), 151–71.

Blanchot, Maurice. "Michel Foucault as I Imagine Him." In *Foucault/Blanchot.* New York: Zone, 1987, pp. 61–109.

Bloland, Harland G. "Postmodernism and Higher Education." *Journal of Higher Education,* 66 (September/October 1995), 521–59.

Bouchard, Donald F. "For Life and Action: Foucault, Spectacle, Document." *Oxford Literary Review,* 4 (1980), 20–28.

Bourdieu, Pierre, and Jean-Claude Passeron. "Sociology and Philosophy in France Since 1945: Death and Resurrection of a Philosophy without Subject." *Social Research,* 34 (Spring 1967), 162–212.

Bóve, Paul A. "The End of Humanism: Michel Foucault and the Power of Disciplines." *Humanities in Society,* 3 (Winter 1980), 23–40.

Brodeur, Jean-Paul. "McDonell on Foucault: Supplementary Remarks." *Canadian Journal of Philosophy,* 7 (September 1977), 555–68.

Brown, B., and M. Cousins. "The Linguistic Fault: The Case of Foucault's Archaeology." *Economy and Society,* 9 (August 1980), 251–78.

Brown, P. L. "Epistemology and Method: Althusser, Foucault, Derrida." *Cultural Hermeneutics,* 3 (1975), 147–63.

Bruce, Douglas R. "Silence, Rhetoric, and Freedom: Explicating Foucault through Augustine." In *Visions of Rhetoric: History, Theory and Criticism.* Ed. Charles W. Kneupper. Arlington, TX: Rhetoric Society of America, 1987, pp. 157–68.

Burrell, Gibson. "Modernism, Post Modernism and Organizational Analysis 2: The Contribution of Michel Foucault." *Organization Studies*, 9 (1988), 221–35.

Butler, Judith. "Variations on Sex and Gender: Beauvoir, Wittig, and Foucault." *Praxis International*, 5 (January 4, 1986), 505–16.

Canguilhem, Georges. "Report from Mr. Canguilhem on the Manuscript Filed by Mr. Michel Foucault, Director of the Institut Français of Hamburg, in Order to Obtain Permission to Print His Principal Thesis for the Doctor of Letters." Trans. Ann Hobart. *Critical Inquiry*, 21 (Winter 1995), 277–98.

Caputo, John, and Mark Yount, eds. *Foucault and the Critique of Institutions*. University Park: Pennsylvania State University Press, 1993.

Carroll, David. *Paraesthetics: Foucault, Lyotard, Derrida*. New York: Methuen, 1987.

Carroll, David. "The Subject of Archeology or the Sovereignty of the Episteme." *MLN*, 93 (May 1978), 695–722.

Casey, Edward S. "The Place of Space in *The Birth of the Clinic*." *Journal of Medicine and Philosophy*, 12 (November 1987), 351–56.

Cavallari, Hector Mario. "*Savoir* and *Pouvoir*: Michel Foucault's Theory of Discursive Practice." *Humanities in Society*, 3 (Winter 1980), 55–72.

Chua, Beng-Huat. "The Structure of the Contemporary Sociological Problematic: A Foucaultian View." *American Sociologist*, 15 (May 1980), 82–93.

Clark, E. Culpepper, and Raymie E. McKerrow. "The Historiographical Dilemma in Myrdal's American Creed: Rhetoric's Role in Rescuing a Historical Moment." *Quarterly Journal of Speech*, 73 (August 1987), 303–16.

Clark, Michael. *Michel Foucault, an Annotated Bibliography: Tool Kit for a New Age*. New York: Garland, 1983.

Clauss, Sidonie. "John Wilkins' Essay toward a Real Character: Its Place in the Seventeenth-Century Episteme." *Journal of the History of Ideas*, 43 (October/ December 1982), 531–53.

Clifford, Michael R. "Crossing (out) the Boundary: Foucault and Derrida on Transgressing Transgression." *Philosophy Today*, 31 (Fall 1987), 223–33.

Cobley, Evelyn. "Toward History as Discontinuity: The Russian Formalists and Foucault." *Mosaic*, 20 (Spring 1987), 41–56.

"Cogito Incognito: Foucault's 'My Body, This Paper, This Fire.'" *Oxford Literary Review*, 4 (Autumn 1979), 5–8.

Colburn, Jr., Kenneth. "Desire and Discourse in Foucault: The Sign of the Fig Leaf in Michelangelo's *David*." *Human Studies*, 10 (1987), 61–79.

Cooper, Barry. *Michel Foucault: An Introduction to the Study of His Thought*. New York: Edwin Mellen, 1981.

Cooper, Martha. "Foucault, Michel (1926–1984)." In *Encyclopedia of Rhetoric and Composition: Communication from Ancient Times to the Information Age*. Ed. Theresa Enos. New York: Garland, 1996, pp. 272–74.

Cooper, Martha. "Reconceptualizing Ideology according to the Relationship between Rhetoric and Knowledge/Power." In *Rhetoric and Ideology: Compositions and Criticisms of Power*. Ed. Charles W. Kneupper. Arlington, TX: Rhetoric Society of America, 1989, pp. 30–41.

Cooper, Martha. "Rhetorical Criticism and Foucault's Philosophy of Discursive Events." *Central States Speech Journal*, 39 (Spring 1988), 1–17.

Cooper, Martha, and John J. Makay. "Knowledge, Power, and Freud's Clark Conference Lectures." *Quarterly Journal of Speech*, 74 (November 1988), 416–33.

Cousins, Mark, and Athar Hussain. *Michel Foucault*. London: Macmillan, 1984.

Cousins, Mark, and Athar Hussain. "The Question of Ideology—Althusser, Pecheux and Foucault." In *Power, Action and Belief: A New Sociology of Knowledge?* Ed. John Law. Boston: Routledge and Kegan Paul, 1986.

Cranston, Maurice. *The Mask of Politics and Other Essays.* London: Allen Lane, 1973.

Cranston, Maurice. "Michel Foucault." *Encounter,* 30 (June 1968), 34–42.

Cranston, Maurice. *Philosophy and Language.* Toronto: Canadian Broadcasting Corporation, 1969.

Culler, Jonathan. "The Linguistic Basis of Structuralism." In *Structuralism: An Introduction.* Ed. David Robey. Oxford: Clarendon, 1973, pp. 20–36.

Dallmayr, Fred R. *Polis and Praxis: Exercises in Contemporary Political Theory.* Cambridge: MIT Press, 1984.

Dallmayr, Fred R., and Gisela J. Hinkle. "Editors' Preface: Foucault *in memoriam* (1926–1984)." *Human Studies,* 10 (1987), 3–13.

D'Amico, Robert. "The Contours and Coupures of Structuralist Theory." *Telos,* 17 (Fall 1973), 70–97.

D'Amico, Robert. "Desire and the Commodity Form." *Telos,* 35 (Spring 1978), 88–122.

D'Amico, Robert. "Introduction to the Foucault-Deleuze Discussion." *Telos,* 16 (Summer 1973), 101–02.

D'Amico, Robert. "Text and Context: Derrida and Foucault on Descartes." In *The Structural Allegory: Reconstructive Encounters with the New French Thought.* Ed. John Fekete. Minneapolis: University of Minnesota Press, 1984, pp. 164–82.

Danaher, Geoff, Tony Schirato, and Jen Webb. *Understanding Foucault.* Thousand Oaks, CA: Sage, 2000.

Dean, Mitchell. *Critical and Effective Histories: Foucault's Methods and Historical Sociology.* New York: Routledge, 1994.

Defolter, Rolf S. "On the Methodological Foundation of the Abolitionist Approach to the Criminal Justice System: A Comparison of the Ideas of Hulsman, Mathiesen and Foucault." *Contemporary Crises,* 10 (1986), 39–62.

Deleuze, Gilles. *Foucault.* Trans. and ed. Séan Hand. Minneapolis: University of Minnesota Press, 1988.

Derrida, Jacques. *Writing and Difference.* Trans. Alan Bass. Chicago: University of Chicago Press, 1978.

Descombes, Vincent. *Modern French Philosophy.* Trans. L. Scott-Fox and J. M. Harding. New York: Cambridge University Press, 1980.

Dews, Peter. "The Nouvelle Philosophie and Foucault." *Economy and Society,* 8 (May 1979), 127–68.

Dews, Peter. "Power and Subjectivity in Foucault." *New Left Review,* 144 (March/April 1984), 72–95.

Diamond, Irene, and Lee Quinby, eds. *Feminism and Foucault: Reflections on Resistance.* Boston: Northeastern University Press, 1988.

Doerner, Klaus. *Madmen and the Bourgeoisie: A Social History of Insanity and Psychiatry.* Trans. Joachim Neugroschel and Jean Steinberg. Oxford: Basil Blackwell, 1981.

Donato, Eugenio. "Structuralism: The Aftermath." *Sub-Stance,* 7 (Fall 1973), 9–26.

Donzelot, Jacques. "The Poverty of Political Culture." Trans. Couze Venn. *Ideology and Consciousness,* 5 (Spring 1979), 73–86.

Doran, Nob. "Maintaining the Simulation Model in the Era of the 'Social': The 'Inquiry' System of Canadian Workers' Compensation, 1914–1984." *Canadian Review of Sociology and Anthropology,* 31 (1994), 446–69.

Dreyfus, Hubert L. "Foucault's Critique of Psychiatric Medicine." *Journal of Medicine and Philosophy*, 12 (November 1987), 311–33.

Dreyfus, Hubert L., and Paul Rabinow. *Michel Foucault: Beyond Structuralism and Hermeneutics*. Chicago: University of Chicago Press, 1982.

Eagleton, Terry. "Foucault, Michel." In *International Encyclopedia of Communications*. Ed. Erik Barnouw. Vol. 2. New York: Oxford University Press, 1989, pp. 201–02.

Emad, Parvis. "Foucault and Biemel on Representation: A Beginning Inquiry." *Man and World*, 12 (1979), 284–97.

Eribon, Didier. *Michel Foucault*. Trans. Betsy Wing. Cambridge: Harvard University Press, 1991.

Faubion, James D., ed. *Rethinking the Subject: An Anthology of Contemporary European Social Thought*. Boulder, CO: Westview, 1995.

Ferguson, Kathy E. *The Feminist Case against Bureaucracy*. Philadelphia: Temple University Press, 1984.

Fillingham, Lydia Alix. *Foucault for Beginners*. New York: Writers and Readers, 1993.

Fine, Bob. "The Birth of Bourgeois Punishment." *Crime and Social Justice*, 13 (Summer 1980), 19–26.

Fine, Bob. "Struggles against Discipline: The Theory and Politics of Michel Foucault." *Capital and Class*, 9 (1979), 75–96.

Flaherty, P. "(Con)textual Contest: Derrida and Foucault on Madness and the Cartesian Subject." *Philosophy of the Social Sciences*, 16 (1986), 157–75.

Flynn, Bernard Charles. "Foucault and the Body Politic." *Man and World*, 20 (1987), 65–84.

Flynn, Bernard Charles. "Michel Foucault and Comparative Civilizational Study." *Philosophy and Social Criticism*, 5 (July 1978), 146–58.

Flynn, Bernard Charles. "Michel Foucault and the Husserlian Problematic of a Transcendental Philosophy of History." *Philosophy Today*, 22 (Fall 1978), 224–38.

Flynn, Bernard. "Sexuality, Knowledge and Power in the Thought of Michel Foucault." *Philosophy and Social Criticism*, 8 (Fall 1981), 329–48.

Flynn, Thomas. "Foucault as Parrhesiast: His Last Course at the College de France (1984)." *Philosophy and Social Criticism*, 12 (1987), 213–29.

Foss, Sonja K., and Ann Gill. "Michel Foucault's Theory of Rhetoric as Epistemic." *Western Journal of Speech Communication*, 51 (Fall 1987), 384–401.

Frank, III, Arthur W. "The Politics of the New Positivity: A Review Essay of Michel Foucault's *Discipline and Punish*." *Human Studies*, 5 (January/March 1982), 61–67.

Frank, Luanne. "Michel Foucault (1926–1984)." In *Twentieth Century Rhetorics and Rhetoricians: Critical Studies and Sources*. Ed. Michael G. Moran and Michelle Ballif. Westport, CT: Greenwood, 2000, pp. 169–84.

Fraser, Nancy. "Foucault on Modern Power: Empirical Insights and Normative Confusions." *Praxis International*, 1 (October 1981), 272–87.

Fraser, Nancy. "Foucault's Body Language: A Post-Humanist Political Rhetoric?" *Salmagundi*, 61 (Fall 1983), 55–70.

Fraser, Nancy. "Michel Foucault: A 'Young Conservative'?" *Ethics*, 96 (October 1985), 165–84.

Fraser, Nancy. *Unruly Practices: Power, Discourse and Gender in Contemporary Social Theory*. Minneapolis: University of Minnesota Press, 1989.

Freundlieb, Dieter. "Rationalism v. Irrationalism? Habermas's Response to Foucault." *Inquiry*, 31 (June 1988), 171–92.

Friedrich, Otto, and Sandra Burton. "France's Philosopher of Power." *Time*, November 16, 1981, pp. 147–48.

Funt, David Paul. "The Structuralist Debate." *Hudson Review*, 22 (Winter 1969–70), 623–46.

Gandelman, Claude. "Foucault as Art Historian." *Hebrew University Studies in Literature and the Arts*, 13 (1985), 266–80.

Gane, Mike, ed. *Towards a Critique of Foucault*. New York: Routledge and Kegan Paul, 1986.

Gane, Mike, and Terry Johnson, eds. *Foucault's New Domains*. New York: Routledge, 1993.

Gaonkar, Dilip Parameshwar. "Foucault on Discourse: Methods and Temptations." *Journal of the American Forensic Association*, 18 (Spring 1982), 246–57.

Gemin, Joseph. "Manufacturing Codependency: Self-Help as Discursive Formation." *Critical Studies in Mass Communication*, 14 (September 1997), 249–66.

Giddens, Anthony. *Profiles and Critiques in Social Theory*. Berkeley: University of California Press, 1982.

Gilder, Eric. "The Process of Political Praxis: Efforts of the Gay Community to Transform the Social Signification of AIDS." *Communication Quarterly*, 37 (Winter 1989), 27–38.

Gillan, Garth. "Foucault's Philosophy." *Philosophy and Social Criticism*, 12 (1987), 145–55.

Gordon, Colin. "Birth of the Subject." *Radical Philosophy*, 17 (Summer 1977), 15–25.

Gordon, Colin. "Introduction to Pasquino and Procacci." *Ideology and Consciousness*, 4 (Autumn 1978), 37–39.

Gordon, Colin. "Question, Ethos, Event: Foucault on Kant and Enlightenment." *Economy and Society*, 15 (February 1986), 71–87.

Greene, Ronald Walter. "Another Materialist Rhetoric." *Critical Studies in Mass Communication*, 15 (March 1998), 21–41.

Griffioen, Sander. "Changes in the Climate of Thought." Trans. J. A. Peterson. *Philosophia Reformata*, 46 (1981), 103–18.

Grossberg, Lawrence. "Strategies of Marxist Cultural Interpretation." *Critical Studies in Mass Communication*, 1 (December 1984), 392–421.

Grumley, John E. *History and Totality: Radical Historicism from Hegel to Foucault*. New York: Routledge, 1989.

Guédon, Jean Claude. "Michel Foucault: The Knowledge of Power and the Power of Knowledge." *Bulletin of the History of Medicine*, 51 (1977), 245–77.

Gutting, Gary, ed. *The Cambridge Companion to Foucault*. New York: Cambridge University Press, 1994.

Gutting, Gary. "Continental Philosophy of Science." In *Current Research in Philosophy of Science*. Ed. Peter D. Asquith and Henry E. Kyburg, Jr. East Lansing, MI: Philosophy of Science Association, 1979, pp. 94–117.

Gutting, Gary. *Michel Foucault's Archaeology of Scientific Reason*. New York: Cambridge University Press, 1989.

Habermas, Jürgen. *The Philosophical Discourse of Modernity: Twelve Lectures*. Trans. Frederick Lawrence. Cambridge: MIT Press, 1987.

Hacking, Ian. "Michel Foucault's Immature Science." *Noûs*, 13 (March 1979), 39–51.

Hall, Stuart. "Signification, Representation, Ideology: Althusser and the Post-Structuralist Debates." *Critical Studies in Mass Communication*, 2 (June 1985), 91–114.

Harvard-Watts, John. "Michel Foucault." *Times Literary Supplement*, July 31, 1970, p. 855.

Hattiangadi, J. N. "Language Philosophy: Hacking: Foucault." *Dialogue*, 17 (1978), 513–28.

Hayman, Ronald. "Cartography of Discourse? On Foucault." *Encounter*, 47 (December 1976), 72–75.

Hengehold, Laura. "An Immodest Proposal: Foucault, Hysterization, and the 'Second Rape.'" *Hypatia*, 9 (Summer 1994), 88–107.

Hekman, Susan J., ed. *Feminist Interpretations of Michel Foucault*. University Park: Pennsylvania State University Press, 1996.

Henning, E. M. "Archaeology, Deconstruction, and Intellectual History." In *Modern European Intellectual History: Reappraisals and New Perspectives*. Ed. Dominick LaCapra and Steven L. Kaplan. Ithaca: Cornell University Press, 1982, pp. 153–96.

Hinkle, Gisela J. "Foucault's Power/Knowledge and American Sociological Theorizing." *Human Studies*, 10 (1987), 35–59.

Hodges, Jill, and Athar Hussain. "La police des families." *Ideology and Consciousness*, 5 (1979), 87–123.

Hooke, Alexander E. "The Order of Others: Is Foucault's Antihumanism against Human Action?" *Political Theory*, 15 (February 1987), 38–60.

Horowitz, Gad. "The Foucaultian Impasse: No Sex, No Self, No Revolution." *Political Theory*, 15 (February 1987), 61–80.

Horrocks, Chris, and Zoran Jevtic. *Foucault for Beginners*. Cambridge: Icon, 1997.

Hoy, David Couzens, ed. *Foucault: A Critical Reader*. New York: Basil Blackwell, 1986.

Hoy, David Couzens. "Power, Repression, Progress: Foucault, Lukes, and the Frankfurt School." *TriQuarterly*, 52 (Fall 1981), 43–63.

Hoy, David Couzens. "Taking History Seriously: Foucault, Gadamer, Habermas." *Union Seminary Quarterly Review*, 34 (Winter 1979), 85–95.

Huppert, George. "*Divinatio et Eruditio*: Thoughts on Foucault." *History and Theory*, 13 (1974), 191–207.

Hutton, Patrick H. "The History of Mentalities: The New Map of Cultural History." *History and Theory*, 20 (1981), 237–59.

Ijsseling, S. "Foucault with Heidegger." *Man and World*, 19 (1986), 413–24.

Ijsseling, Samuel. *Rhetoric and Philosophy in Conflict: An Historical Survey*. The Hague, Neth.: Martinus Nijhoff, 1976.

Jacoby, Russell. "The Jargon of the Discourse." *Humanities in Society*, 2 (Spring 1979), 149–52.

Jameson, Fredric. *The Prison-House of Language: A Critical Account of Structuralism and Russian Formalism*. Princeton: Princeton University Press, 1972.

Kaplan, Martha. "Panopticon in Poona: An Essay on Foucault and Colonialism." *Cultural Anthropology*, 10 (1995), 85–98.

Keenan, Tom. "The 'Paradox' of Knowledge and Power: Reading Foucault on a Bias." *Political Theory*, 15 (February 1987), 5–37.

Kelly, Michael, ed. *Critique and Power: Recasting the Foucault/Habermas Debate*. Cambridge: MIT Press, 1994.

Kendall, Gavia, and Gary Wickham. *Using Foucault's Methods*. Thousand Oaks, CA: Sage, 1999.

Krippendorff, Klaus. "Undoing Power." *Critical Studies in Mass Communication*, 12 (June 1995), 101–32.

Kroker, Arthur. "Modern Power in Reverse Image: The Paradigm Shift of Michel Foucault and Talcott Parsons. In *The Structural Allegory: Reconstructive Encounters with the New French Thought*. Ed. John Fekete. Minneapolis: University of Minnesota Press, 1984, pp. 74–103.

Kurzweil, Edith. *The Age of Structuralism: Lévi-Strauss to Foucault*. New York: Columbia University Press, 1980.

Kurzweil, Edith. "Michel Foucault: Ending the Era of Man." *Theory and Society*, 4 (1977), 395–420.

Kurzweil, Edith. "Michel Foucault's History of Sexuality as Interpreted by Feminists and Marxists." *Social Research*, 53 (Winter 1986), 647–63.

Kusch, Martin. *Foucault's Strata and Fields: An Investigation into Archaeological and Genealogical Science Studies*. Boston: Kluwer, 1991.

LaCapra, Dominick, and Steven L. Kaplan, eds. *Modern European Intellectual History*. Ithaca: Cornell University Press, 1982.

LaFountain, Marc J. "Foucault and Dr. Ruth." *Critical Studies in Mass Communication*, 6 (June 1989), 123–37.

Laing, R. D. "Sanity and 'Madness': The Invention of Madness." *New Statesman*, 71 (June 16, 1967), 843.

Lapointe, Francois H. "Michel Foucault: A Bibliographic Essay." *Journal of the British Society for Phenomenology*, 4 (May 1973), 195–97.

Lapointe, Francois H., and Claire Lapointe. "Bibliografia: Essay: Michel Foucault: A Bibliographic." *Dialogos*, 10 (April 1974), 153–57.

Lapointe, Francois H., and Claire Lapointe. "Bibliografia: Michel Foucault." *Dialogos*, 11 (November 1977), 245–54.

Lavers, Annette. "Man, Meaning and Subject: A Current Reappraisal." *Journal of the British Society for Phenomenology*, 1 (October 1970), 44–49.

Leary, David E. "Essay Review: Michel Foucault, an Historian of the Sciences Humaines." *Journal of the History of the Behavioral Sciences*, 12 (July 1976), 286–93.

Lechte, John. *Fifty Key Contemporary Thinkers: From Structuralism to Postmodernity*. New York: Routledge, 1994.

Lecourt, Dominique. *Marxism and Epistemology: Bachelard, Canguilhem and Foucault*. London: NLB, 1975.

Leland, Dorothy. "On Reading and Writing the World: Foucault's History of Thought." *Clio*, 4 (February 1975), 225–43.

Lemert, Charles C., and Garth Gillan. *Michel Foucault: Social Theory and Transgression*. New York: Columbia University Press, 1982.

Lemert, Charles, and Garth Gillan. "The New Alternative in Critical Sociology: Foucault's Discursive Analysis." *Cultural Hermeneutics*, 4 (December 1977), 309–20.

Lentricchia, Frank. *Ariel and the Police: Michel Foucault, William James, Wallace Stevens*. Madison: University of Wisconsin Press, 1988.

LeSage, Laurent. *The New French Criticism: An Introduction and a Sampler*. University Park: Pennsylvania State University Press, 1967.

Levy, Zeev. "The Structuralist Epistemology of Michel Foucault" [in Hebrew]. *Iyyun*, 25 (January/April 1974), 39–51; English summary, pp. 133–34.

Looser, Devoney. "Feminist Theory and Foucault: A Bibliographic Essay." *Style*, 26 (Winter 1992), 593–603.

Lowell, Edmunds. "Foucault and Theories." *Classical and Modern Literature*, 8 (1988), 79–91.

Maass, Peter, and David Brock. "The Power and Politics of Michel Foucault." *Inside* [magazine of the *Daily Californian*, University of California, Berkeley], 7 (April 22, 1983), pp. 7, 20–22.

McBride, Maggie. "A Foucauldian Analysis of Mathematical Discourse." *For the Learning of Mathematics*, 9 (February 1989), 40–46.

Macdonell, Diane. *Theories of Discourse: An Introduction*. Oxford: Basil Blackwell, 1986.

McDonell, Donald J. "On Foucault's Philosophical Method." *Canadian Journal of Philosophy*, 7 (September 1977), 537–53.

McKerrow, Raymie E. "Critical Rhetoric: Theory and Praxis." *Communication Monographs*, 56 (June 1989), 91–111.

McMullen, Roy. "Michel Foucault." *Horizon*, 11 (Autumn 1969), 36–39.

McNay, Lois. *Foucault: A Critical Introduction*. New York: Continuum, 1994.

McNay, Lois. *Foucault and Feminism: Power, Gender and the Self*. Boston: Northeastern University Press, 1992.

Macey, David. *The Lives of Michel Foucault: A Biography*. New York: Pantheon, 1993.

Mahon, Michael. *Foucault's Nietzschean Genealogy: Truth, Power, and the Subject*. Albany: State University of New York Press, 1992.

Major-Poetzl, Pamela. *Michel Foucault's Archaeology of Western Culture*. Chapel Hill: University of North Carolina Press, 1983.

Mall, James P. "Foucault as Literary Critic." In *French Literary Criticism*. Ed. Philip Crant. Columbia: University of South Carolina, 1977, pp. 197–204.

Martin, Luther H., Huck Gutman, and Patrick H. Hutton, eds. *Technologies of the Self: A Seminar with Michel Foucault*. Amherst: University of Massachusetts Press, 1988.

Maslan, Mark. "Foucault and Pragmatism." *Raritan*, 7 (Winter 1988), 94–114.

May, Todd. *Between Genealogy and Epistemology: Psychology, Politics, and Knowledge in the Thought of Michel Foucault*. University Park: Pennsylvania State University Press, 1993.

Megill, Allan. "Foucault, Structuralism, and the Ends of History." *Journal of Modern History*, 51 (September 1979), 451–503.

Megill, Allan. *Prophets of Extremity: Nietzsche, Heidegger, Foucault, Derrida*. Berkeley: University of California Press, 1985.

Megill, Allan. "The Reception of Foucault by Historians." *Journal of the History of Ideas*, 48 (June/March 1987), 117–41.

Merquior, J. G. *Foucault*. Berkeley: University of California Press, 1987.

"Michel Foucault." In *After Philosophy: End or Transformation?* Ed. Kenneth Baynes, James Bohman, and Thomas McCarthy. Cambridge: MIT Press, 1987, pp. 95–99.

Midelfort, H. C. Erik. "Madness and Civilization in Early Modern Europe: A Reappraisal of Michel Foucault." In *After the Reformation: Essays in Honor of J. H. Hexter*. Ed. Barbara C. Malament. n. p.: University of Pennsylvania Press, 1980, pp. 247–65.

Miel, Jan. "Ideas or Epistemes: Hazard versus Foucault." *Yale French Studies*, 49 (1973), 231–45.

Minson, Jeff. "Strategies for Socialists? Foucault's Conception of Power." *Economy and Society*, 9 (February 1980), 1–43.

Moore, Mary Candace. "Ethical Discourse and Foucault's Conception of Ethics." *Human Studies*, 10 (1987), 81–95.

Moss, Jeremy. *The Later Foucault: Politics and Philosophy*. Thousand Oaks, CA: Sage, 1998.

Nakayama, Thomas K., and Robert L. Krizek. "Whiteness: A Strategic Rhetoric." *Quarterly Journal of Speech*, 81 (August 1995), 291–309.

Nehamas, Alexander. "What an Author Is." *Journal of Philosophy*, 83 (November 1986), 685–91.

Noiriel, Gérard. "Foucault and History: The Lessons of a Disillusion." *Journal of Modern History*, 66 (September 1994), 547–68.

Norris, Christopher. *Uncritical Theory: Postmodernism, Intellectuals and the Gulf War*. Amherst: University of Massachusetts Press, 1992.

Nye, Robert A. "Crime in Modern Societies: Some Research Strategies for Historians." *Journal of Social History*, 11 (Summer 1978), 491–507.

O'Farrell, Clare. *Foucault: Historian or Philosopher?* New York: St. Martin's, 1989.

O'Hara, Daniel T. *Radical Parody: American Culture and Critical Agency after Foucault*. New York: Columbia University Press, 1992.

O'Neill, John." The Disciplinary Society: From Weber to Foucault." *British Journal of Sociology*, 37 (March 1986), 42–60.

Ostrander, Greg. "Foucault's Disappearing Body." *Canadian Journal of Political and Social Theory*, 11 (1987), 120–33.

Owen, David. *Maturity and Modernity: Nietzsche, Weber, Foucault and the Ambivalence of Reason*. New York: Routledge, 1994.

Pace, David. "Structuralism in History and the Social Sciences." *American Quarterly*, 30 (1978), 282–97.

Paden, Roger. "Foucault's Anti-Humanism." *Human Studies*, 10 (1987), 123–41.

Pasquino, Pasquale. "Michel Foucault (1926–84): *The Will to Knowledge*." Trans. Chloe Chard. *Economy and Society*, 15 (February 1986), 97–109.

Paternek, Margaret A. "Norms and Normalization: Michel Foucault's Overextended Panoptic Machine." *Human Studies*, 10 (1987), 97–121.

Payer, Pierre J. "Foucault on Penance and the Shaping of Sexuality." *Studies in Religion*, 14 (Summer 1985), 313–20.

Pettit, Philip. *The Concept of Structuralism: A Critical Analysis*. Berkeley: University of California Press, 1975.

"Philosopher and Author M. Foucault." *Chicago Tribune*, June 26, 1984, sec. 1, p. 12.

Philp, Mark. "Foucault on Power: A Problem in Radical Translation?" *Political Theory*, 11 (February 1983), 29–52.

Poster, Mark. "Foucault and History." *Social Research*, 49 (Spring 1982), 116–41.

Poster, Mark. *Foucault, Marxism and History: Mode of Production versus Mode of Information*. Cambridge: Polity, 1984.

Poster, Mark. "Foucault's True Discourses." *Humanities in Society*, 2 (Spring 1979), 153–66.

Poster, Mark. "Foucault, the Present and History." *Cultural Critique*, 8 (1988), 105–21.

Poster, Mark. "The Future according to Foucault: The Archaeology of Knowledge and Intellectual History." In *Modern European Intellectual History: Reappraisals and New Perspectives*. Ed. Dominick LaCapra and Steven L. Kaplan. Ithaca: Cornell University Press, 1982, pp. 137–52.

Pratt, Vernon. "Foucault and the History of Classification Theory." *Studies in History and Philosophy of Science*, 8 (1977), 163–71.

Quinby, Lee. *Freedom, Foucault, and the Subject of America*. Boston: Northeastern University Press, 1991.

Rabkin, Gerald. "Waiting for Foucault: New Theatre Theory." *Performing Art Journal*, 42 (1992), 90–101.

Racevskis, Karlis. "The Discourse of Michel Foucault: A Case of an Absent and Forgettable Subject." *Humanities in Society*, 3 (Winter 1980), 41–53.

Racevskis, Karlis. *Michel Foucault and the Subversion of Intellect*. Ithaca: Cornell University Press, 1983.

Radford, Gary P. "Positivism, Foucault, and the Fantasia of the Library: Conceptions of Knowledge and the Modern Library Experience." *Library Quarterly*, 62 (1992), 408–24.

Rajchman, John. "Ethics after Foucault." *Social Text*, 13/14 (Winter/Spring 1986), 165–83.

Rajchman, John. "Foucault's Art of Seeing." *October*, 44 (Spring 1988), 89–117.

Rajchman, John. *Michel Foucault: The Freedom of Philosophy*. New York: Columbia University Press, 1985.

Rajchman, John. "Nietzsche, Foucault and the Anarchism of Power." *Semiotext(e)*, 3 (1978), 96–107.

Rajchman, John. *Truth and Eros: Foucault, Lacan, and the Question of Ethics*. New York: Routledge, 1991.

Ramazanoglu, Caroline, ed. *Against Foucault: Explorations of Some Tensions between Foucault and Feminism*. New York: Routledge, 1993.

Ransom, John S. *Foucault's Discipline: The Politics of Subjectivity*. Durham, NC: Duke University Press, 1997.

Rawlinson, Mary C. "Foucault's Strategy: Knowledge, Power, and the Specificity of Truth." *Journal of Medicine and Philosophy*, 12 (November 1987), 371–95.

Ray, S. Alan. *The Modern Soul: Michel Foucault and the Theological Discourse of Gordon Kaufman and David Tracy*. Philadelphia: Fortress, 1987.

Remen, Kathryn. "The Theatre of Punishment: David Henry Hwang's *M. Butterfly* and Michel Foucault's *Discipline and Punish*." *Modern Drama*, 37 (1994), 391–400.

Riddel, Joseph N. "Re-Doubling the Commentary." *Contemporary Literature*, 20 (Spring 1979), 237–50.

Rodríguez, Ilia. "News Reporting and Colonial Discourse: The Representation of Puerto Ricans in U.S. Press Coverage of the Spanish-American War." *Howard Journal of Communications*, 9 (October/December 1998), 283–301.

Rolleston, James. "The Expressionist Moment: Heym, Trakl, and the Problem of the Modern." *Studies in Twentieth-Century Literature*, 1 (Fall 1976), 65–90.

Rorty, Richard. *Consequences of Pragmatism (Essays: 1972–1980)*. Minneapolis: University of Minnesota Press, 1982.

Rorty, Richard. "Method, Social Science, and Social Hope." *Canadian Journal of Philosophy*, 11 (December 1981), 569–88.

Rose, Gillian. *Dialectic of Nihilism: Post-Structuralism and Law*. Oxford: Basil Blackwell, 1984.

Ross, Stephen David. "Belonging to a Philosophic Discourse." *Philosophy and Rhetoric*, 19 (1986), 166–77.

Roth, Michael S. "Foucault's 'History of the Present.'" *History and Theory*, 20 (February 1981), 32–46.

Rothstein, Eric. "Foucault, Discursive History, and the Auto-Affection of God." *Modern Language Quarterly*, 55 (December 1994), 383–414.

Rousseau, G. S. "Whose Enlightenment? Not Man's: The Case of Michel Foucault." *Eighteenth-Century Studies*, 6 (Winter 1972–73), 238–56.

Said, Edward W. "Abecedarium culturae: Structuralism, Absence, Writing." *TriQuarterly*, 20 (Winter 1971), 33–71.

Said, Edward W. *Beginnings: Intention and Method*. New York: Basic, 1975.

Said, Edward W. "Linguistics and the Archeology of Mind." *IPQ: International Philosophical Quarterly*, 11 (March 1971), 104–34.

Said, Edward W. "Michel Foucault as an Intellectual Imagination." *Boundary*, 1 (1972), 1–27.

Said, Edward W. "Michel Foucault, 1926–1984." *Raritan*, 4 (Fall 1984), 1–11.

Said, Edward W. "The Problem of Textuality: Two Exemplary Positions." *Critical Inquiry*, 4 (Summer 1978), 673–714.

Said, Edward W. *The World, the Text, and the Critic*. Cambridge: Harvard University Press, 1983.

Sangren, P. Steven. "'Power against Ideology: A Critique of Foucaultian Usage." *Cultural Anthropology*, 10 (1995), 3–40.

Sawicki, Jana. "Heidegger and Foucault: Escaping Technological Nihilism." *Philosophy and Social Criticism*, 13 (1987), 155–73.

Schatzki, Theodore R. "Theory at Bay: Foucault, Lyotard, and Politics of the Local." In *Postmodern Contentions: Epochs, Politics, Space*. Eds. John Paul Jones III, Wolfgang Natter, and Theodore R. Schatzki. New York: Guilford, 1993, pp. 39–64.

Schneck, Stephen Frederick. "Michel Foucault on Power/Discourse, Theory and Practice." *Human Studies*, 10 (1987), 15–33.

Schor, Naomi. "Dreaming Dissymmetry: Barthes, Foucault, and Sexual Difference." In *Men in Feminism*. Ed. Alice Jardine and Paul Smith. New York: Methuen, 1987, pp. 98–110.

Scott, Charles E. "History and Truth." *Man and World*, 15 (1982), 55–66.

Stott, Charles E. "The Power of Medicine, The Power of Ethics." *Journal of Medicine and Philosophy*, 12 (November 1987), 335–50.

Sedgwick, Peter. "Mental Illness Is Illness." *Salmagundi*, 20 (Summer/Fall 1972), 196–224.

Sedgwick, Peter. *Psycho Politics*. New York: Harper and Row, 1982.

Seem, Mark D. "Liberation of Difference: Toward a Theory of Antiliterature." *New Literary History*, 5 (Autumn 1973), 119–33.

Shaffer, E. S. "The Archaeology of Michel Foucault." *Studies in History and Philosophy of Science*, 7 (1976), 269–75.

Shapiro, Michael J. *Language and Political Understanding: The Politics of Discursive Practices*. New Haven: Yale University Press, 1981.

Shapiro, Michael J. "The Rhetoric of Social Science: The Political Responsibilities of the Scholar." In *The Rhetoric of the Human Sciences: Language and Argument in Scholarship and Public Affairs*. Ed. John S. Nelson, Allan Megill, and Donald N. McCloskey. Madison: University of Wisconsin Press, 1987, p. 363–80.

Sharratt, Bernard. "Notes after Foucault." *New Blackfriars*, 53 (June 1972), 251–64.

Shepherdson, Charles. "A Loss for Words: Literature and Method in *The Order of Things*." *Literature and Psychology*, 40 (1994), 1–27.

Sheridan, Alan. *Michel Foucault: The Will to Truth*. New York: Tavistock, 1980.

Shiner, Larry. "Foucault, Phenomenology and the Question of Origins." *Philosophy Today*, 26 (1982), 312–21.

Shiner, Larry. "Reading Foucault: Anti-Method and the Genealogy of Power-Knowledge." *History and Theory*, 21 (November 3, 1982), 382–98.

Sholle, David J. "Critical Studies: From the Theory of Ideology to Power/Knowledge." *Critical Studies in Mass Communication*, 5 (March 1988), 16–41.

Shumway, David R. *Michel Foucault*. Boston: Twayne, 1989.

Silverman, Hugh J. "Jean-Paul Sartre versus Michel Foucault on Civilizational Study." *Philosophy and Social Criticism*, 5 (July 1978), 160–71.

Silverman, Hugh J. "Michel Foucault's Nineteenth-Century System of Thought and the Anthropological Sleep." *Seminar*, 3 (1979), 1–8.

Silverman, Hugh J., ed. *Piaget, Philosophy and the Human Sciences*. Atlantic Highlands, NJ: Humanities, 1980.

Sluga, Hans. "Foucault, the Author, and the Discourse." *Inquiry*, 28 (December 1985), 403–15.

Smart, Barry. "Discipline and Social Regulation: On Foucault's Genealogical Analysis." In *The Power to Punish: Contemporary Penalty and Social Analysis*. Ed. David Garland and Peter Young. Atlantic Highlands, NJ: Humanities, 1983, pp. 62–83.

Smart, Barry. *Foucault, Marxism and Critique*. Boston: Routledge and Kegan Paul, 1983.

Smart, Barry. "Foucault, Sociology, and the Problem of Human Agency." *Theory and Society*, 11 (1982), 121–41.

Smart, Barry. *Michel Foucault*. New York: Tavistock, 1985.

Snyder, Carol. "Analyzing Classifications: Foucault for Advanced Writers." *College Composition and Communication*, 35 (May 1984), 209–16.

Spicker, Stuart F. "An Introduction to the Medical Epistemology of Georges Canguilhem: Moving beyond Michel Foucault." *Journal of Medicine and Philosophy*, 12 (November 1987), 397–411.

Spitzack, Carole. "Confession and Signification: The Systematic Inscription of Body Consciousness." *Journal of Medicine and Philosophy*, 12 (November 1987), 357–69.

Sprinker, Michael. "The Use and Abuse of Foucault." *Humanities in Society*, 3 (Winter 1980), 1–21.

Steiner, George. "Steiner Responds to Foucault." *Diacritics*, 1 (Winter 1971), 59.

Stempel, Daniel. "Blake, Foucault, and the Classical Episteme." *PLMA*, 96 (May 1981), 388–407.

Stewart, David. "Why Foucault?" *Architecture and Urbanism*, 121 (October 1980), 100–06.

Stone, Lawrence. "An Exchange with Michel Foucault." *New York Review of Books*, 30 (March 31, 1983), 42–44.

Struever, Nancy S. "Vico, Foucault, and the Strategy of Intimate Investigation." In *New Vico Studies*. Ed. Giorgio Tagliacozzo and Donald Phillip Verene. Vol. 2. New York: Institute for Vico Studies, 1984, 41–57.

Tambling, Jeremy. "Prison-Bound: Dickens and Foucault." *Essays in Criticism*, 36 (January 1986), 11–31.

Tejera, V. "The Human Sciences in Dewey, Foucault and Buchler." *Southern Journal of Philosophy*, 18 (Summer 1980), 221–35.

Thiele, Leslie Paul. "Foucault's Triple Murder and the Modern Development of Power." *Canadian Journal of Political Science*, 19 (June 1986), 243–60.

Thomas, Calvin. "Baudrillard's Seduction of Foucault." In *Jean Baudrillard: The Disappearance of Art and Politics*. Ed. William Stearns and William Chaloupka. New York: St. Martin's, 1992, pp. 131–45.

Thomas, David. "Sociology and Common Sense." *Inquiry*, 21 (Spring 1978), 1–32.

Trethewey, Angela. "Resistance, Identity, and Empowerment: A Postmodern Feminist Analysis of Clients in a Human Service Organization." *Communication Monographs*, 64 (December 1997), 281–301.

Turner, Byran S. "The Government of the Body: Medical Regimens and the Rationalization of Diet." *British Journal of Sociology*, 33 (June 1982), 254–69.

Van Den Abbeele, Georges. "Sade, Foucault, and the Scene of Enlightenment Lucidity." *Stanford French Review*, 11 (Spring 1987), 7–16.

Veyne, Paul. "The Final Foucault and His Ethics." Trans. Catherine Porter and Arnold I. Davidson. *Critical Inquiry*, 20 (Autumn 1993), 1–9.

Visker, Rudi. *Michel Foucault: Genealogy as Critique*. Trans. Chris Turner. New York: Verso, 1995.

Wellbery, David E. "Theory of Events: Foucault and Literary Criticism." *Revue Internationale de Philosophie*, 162–63 (1987), 420–32.

Wendt, Ronald F. "Answers to the Gaze: A Genealogical Poaching of Resistances." *Quarterly Journal of Speech*, 82 (August 1996), 251–73.

White, Hayden. "Michel Foucault." In *Structuralism and Since: From Lévi-Strauss to Derrida*. Ed. John Sturrock. Oxford: Oxford University Press, 1979, pp. 81–115.

White, Hayden. "Power and the Word." *Canto*, 2 (Spring 1978), 164–72.

White, Hayden. *Topics of Discourse: Essays in Cultural Criticism*. Baltimore: Johns Hopkins University Press, 1978.

White, Hayden V. "Foucault Decoded: Notes from Underground." *History and Theory*, 12 (1973), 23–54.

White, Stephen K. "Foucault's Challenge to Critical Theory." *American Political Science Review*, 80 (June 1986), 419–32.

Williams, Karel. "Unproblematic Archaeology." *Economy and Society*, 3 (February 1974), 41–68.

Wuthnow, Robert, James Davison Hunter, Albert Bergesen, and Edith Kurzweil. *Cultural Analysis: The Works of Peter L. Berger, Mary Douglas, Michel Foucault, and Jürgen Habermas*. Boston: Routledge and Kegan Paul, 1984.